6-30

AN AMERICAN REFORMATION

A Documentary History

Other books by Sydney E. Ahlstrom

"The Middle Period (1840–80)" in THE HARVARD DIVINITY
SCHOOL, edited by George H. Williams, 1954.

"Theology in America: A Historical Survey" in THE SHAPING OF
AMERICAN RELIGION, vol. 1, edited by James Ward Smith
and A. Leland Jamison, 1961.

Ed. and Introduction, THEOLOGY IN AMERICA: THE MAJOR
PROTESTANT VOICES FROM PURITANISM TO
NEO-ORTHODOXY, 1967.

Ed. and Introduction, TRANSCENDENTALISM IN NEW ENGLAND,
by Octavius Brooks Frothingham, reprint ed., 1959.

A RELIGIOUS HISTORY OF THE AMERICAN PEOPLE, 1972.

AN AMERICAN
REFORMATION

of Unitarian Christianity

SYDNEY E. AHLSTROM
JONATHAN S. CAREY

 WESLEYAN UNIVERSITY PRESS
MIDDLETOWN, CONNECTICUT

The Dudleian lecture "Natural Religion," by Frederic Henry Hedge, is reprinted by permission of the Harvard University Archives.

Published by Wesleyan University Press, 110 Mt. Vernon Street, Middletown, Connecticut 06457.

Distributed by Harper & Row, Publishers, Keystone Industrial Park, Scranton, Pennsylvania 18512.

LIBRARY OF CONGRESS CATALOGING IN PUBLICATION DATA
Main entry under title:

An American reformation.

   "Other books by Sydney E. Ahlstrom": p.
   Bibliography: p.
   Includes index.
   1. Unitarianism—United States—Addresses, essays,
lectures.   I. Ahlstrom, Sydney E.   II. Carey, Jonathan S.,
1951–
BX9842.A45   1985   288'.73   84–20850
ISBN 0–8195–5080–9

Manufactured in the United States of America

First edition

To Nancy and Sarah

Contents

Editors' Preface   xi

Introduction   3

CHRISTIAN UNITARIANISM DEFINED   4

THE INTELLECTUAL BACKGROUND: RENAISSANCE
   HELLENISM TO SCOTTISH REALISM   6

THE AMERICAN SCENE   16

THE DOCTRINE OF THE LIBERAL FAITH   18

I ORIGINS AND FOUNDING   43

Natural Religion as Distinguished from
   Revealed (1759)   45
EBENEZER GAY

Seasonable Thoughts on the State of Religion in
   New-England (1743)   60
CHARLES CHAUNCY

A Statement of Reasons for Not Believing the
   Doctrines of Trinitarians (1819)   67
ANDREWS NORTON

A Letter to the Rev. Samuel C. Thacher (1815)   76
WILLIAM ELLERY CHANNING

Unitarian Christianity (1819)   90
WILLIAM ELLERY CHANNING

Likeness to God (1828)   118
WILLIAM ELLERY CHANNING

Antiquity and Revival of Unitarian Christianity (1831)   136
WILLIAM WARE

The King's Chapel Liturgy (1785)   151
KING'S CHAPEL

Annual Report of the Executive Committee of the
American Unitarian Association (1826)   164
AMERICAN UNITARIAN ASSOCIATION

II DOCTRINES AND THEOLOGY   175

Catechism for Children and Youth [The Worcester
Catechism] (1821)   177
MINISTERS OF THE WORCESTER ASSOCIATION

The Nature of Man (1820)   199
HENRY WARE

Reason and Revelation (1838)   210
ABIEL ABBOT LIVERMORE

The Incarnation (1854)   221
OLIVER STEARNS

Christ the Divine Word (1872)   231
EDMUND HAMILTON SEARS

The Holy Spirit (1844)   239
ANDREW PRESTON PEABODY

Baptism (ca. 1872)   251
LEONARD JARVIS LIVERMORE

On the Uses of the Communion (1841)   256
ORVILLE DEWEY

Regeneration (1853)   267
WILLIAM GREENLEAF ELIOT

The Apostle Paul (1854) and the Epistle of Paul
to the Romans (1854)   277
ABIEL ABBOT LIVERMORE

The Christian Church (1866)   292
JAMES FREEMAN CLARKE

The Day of Judgment (1861)   301
JAMES WALKER

Unitarian Hymns   311
JOHN QUINCY ADAMS, HENRY WARE, JR.,
EDMUND HAMILTON SEARS, FREDERIC
  HENRY HEDGE,
NATHANIEL L. FROTHINGHAM,
  JOHN PIERPONT,
ELIZA LEE CABOT FOLLEN, SARAH FLOWER ADAMS

III ETHICS AND MORAL THEOLOGY   321

Of the Nature and Principle of Evangelical
    Obedience (1755)   323
JONATHAN MAYHEW

The Comparative Moral Tendency of the Leading
    Doctrines of Calvinism and the Sentiments of
    Unitarians (1823)   332
JARED SPARKS

Two Selections on the Christian's Social
    Responsibility (1838)   340
JOSEPH TUCKERMAN

The Christian Theory of Life (1849)   350
WILLIAM ROUNSEVILLE ALGER

IV UNCERTAINTIES AND CONFLICT   357

Philosophical Difficulties in the "Unitarian
    Controversy" (1823)   359
HENRY WARE

Sober Thoughts on the State of the Times (1835)   362
HENRY WARE, JR.

The Suspense of Faith, A Discourse on the State of
    the Church (1859)   371
HENRY WHITNEY BELLOWS

V THE CHALLENGE OF EMERSON AND TRANSCENDENTALISM   399

Natural Religion (1851)   401
FREDERIC HENRY HEDGE

Antisupernaturalism in the Pulpit (1864)   419
FREDERIC HENRY HEDGE

The Personality of Deity (1838)   432
HENRY WARE, JR.

Unitarianism, Transcendentalism, and the Bible (1857)   441
GEORGE EDWARD ELLIS

A Discourse on the Latest Form of Infidelity (1839)   445
ANDREWS NORTON

Bibliographical Essay   463
Bibliography   469
Index   479

Editors' Preface

"I never did any thing with more satisfaction than by contributing a mite towards removing some of the shackles of the human mind." These were former President John Adams's observations on his gift of one hundred dollars to the Harvard Divinity School in 1815. The circular letter that produced this response had been prepared by John Thornton Kirkland, then president of Harvard. Both men were Unitarians who were responding to the need for a liberal seminary now that the forces of orthodoxy had settled their internal quarrels and founded a theological institution of their own at Andover, Massachusetts. Andover's founders had ambitious plans for a new kind of postgraduate school. If Harvard did not improve its own makeshift arrangements for ministerial training, the churches of northeastern New England that cherished a broad and liberal religious tradition would lack a comparably educated clergy.[1] Despite the impact of "Mr. Madison's War on the New England economy," sufficient funds were gathered to set the new divinity school on its course. During the succeeding half-century, it nurtured an unusually gifted clergy and became a major factor in the intellectual and literary renaissance whose core was Boston-Cambridge-Concord. This acknowledged American renaissance was, in effect, a flowering of Unitarian culture.

Almost all of the illustrious men and women who contributed to this quickening of art and learning in New England were raised in or converted to the serene and humane religious outlook that counted William Ellery Channing as its most eloquent and authoritative spokesman. Channing voiced one of the earliest American calls for a national literature. Among the greatest of those who responded was the son of the distinguished minister of Boston's First Church, William Emerson. And few indeed were the Transcendentalists in the train of Ralph Waldo Emerson who were not, like him, reared in Unitarian homes or educated in Unitarian institutions. Almost the entire group of America's classic historians were Unitarian raised or educated: William Hickling Prescott, John Lothrop Motley, Francis Parkman, John Gorham Palfrey, and, at farther remove, Henry Adams. Out of the same culture came that important

1. The founding dates of the earliest divinity schools in this country are: Andover (1808), Princeton (1812), Harvard (1815), Bangor (1816), Auburn (1818), General (1819), and Yale (1822).

quartet of early American students in Germany: George Bancroft, George Ticknor, Edward Everett, and Frederic Henry Hedge, each of whom made his distinct mark on American intellectual development. A kindred spirit, also important as a mediator of German thought, was James Freeman Clarke, the father of American concern for comparative religion. Popular figures in American literary history such as Nathaniel Hawthorne, Herman Melville, Horatio Alger (who began his career as a Unitarian minister), Henry Wadsworth Longfellow (whose brother was a minister), James Russell Lowell (who was the son of Charles Lowell, minister of the West Church in Boston for more than fifty years), the Reverend Edward Everett Hale, and Oliver Wendell Holmes all emerged from a Unitarian environment. So did painters and architects, reformers and utopian dreamers, and scholars and scientists who have escaped widespread public notice. The feminist movement in America gained early support from Unitarianism. Various institutions were made to flourish, and periodicals were founded and sustained. At no other time in our national history has a single system of nurture produced a cultural renaissance of equal variety and brilliance.

Some of the men and women who sprang from this background became rebellious critics of their heritage; in the Transcendental movement, for example, attacks on the tradition were a significant element, although many critics were, like Emerson, grateful for much of their heritage. Loyal or critical, they testify to the dynamic qualities of the outlook on life and the world that shaped the mind of New England's maritime province.

Geography, climate, the Puritan heritage, the Yankee spirit, patriotic optimism, the political economy of the United States, and world trade— these and many other factors conspired for a brief period to produce a uniquely rich spiritual and material ethos. The Unitarian churches and their supporting institutions, together with their lay and clerical leaders, defined the prevailing ideals and world-view; they related the contemporary state of affairs to past tradition and future hopes. After the passage of two or three generations, Unitarianism would lose this functional relationship to the social order—but that is a story for another book.

The purpose of this volume is to understand the religious point of view that formed the background or foundation for the New England renaissance. Theologically, it was an American Reformation—the distinctive transformation of Christianity and Calvinism in the eighteenth century through Arminianism and other Enlightenment influences into nineteenth-century liberal Christianity. This movement, which became especially strong among the Harvard-educated clergy of eastern Massachusetts, assumed its basic character by 1815 and despite attacks and criticism was maintained without major alteration as a fundamentally Christian synthesis. This American Reformation saw itself as an attempt to restore primitive Christianity. Boston became its center; Channing, its Luther.

This Unitarianism was more coherent, integrated, and rigorously reasoned than historians have admitted. The half-century before the Civil War was its greatest period. More than a century later, however, after the intellectual and moral upheavals of the 1960s created a radically transformed religious ethos, one can better appreciate the proud but often derided claim of Unitarians that a hundred years earlier they had given the Christian good news a more nearly universal range. The early motto *aletheia en Christo*—Truth in Christ—has long since been discarded. A new kind of pluralism, ranging over post-Emersonian Transcendentalists to humanists, atheists as well as theists, has arisen in the religious denomination that was once steadfastly rooted to the Christian "Faith once delivered to the saints."

The decline of Christian Unitarianism began with the division in the movement precipitated, created, or exaggerated by Emerson, Theodore Parker, and other Transcendentalists; but the two parties to this controversy have met with an unequal fate at the hands of posterity. The scholars of American intellectual history, in their eagerness to locate the source of Transcendentalism, have described the social setting of the new movement and the lives and ideas of its advocates, but they have tended to ignore the Unitarians who provided the cultural environment. On insufficient grounds, they have championed the attack on "the corpse-cold Unitarianism of Brattle Street" and left it to be what Emerson said it was: a "thin porridge" of "pale negations."

Unitarian writers have often been so eager to smooth over the controversial aspects of their history that they have failed to deal adequately with their conservative tradition. Some have presented the Liberal Faith in evolutionary categories, the new Unitarianism gradually releasing itself from the outmoded and unenlightened bonds of the old, which invested the Bible with authority and believed that Christ had a truly divine mission. Others have been generally uncritical and eulogistic of the founders, and their beliefs, praising them for their personal character, their reforming zeal, or their valor as religious pathbreakers. Only in the last several decades has scholarly activity begun to gain momentum, with the work of C. Conrad Wright, William R. Hutchison, Daniel Walker Howe, and Lawrence Buell.

The student of American thought still can refer to no adequate exposition of the liberal Christian theology advocated by Andrews Norton, William Ellery Channing, Henry Ware, James Walker, Francis Bowen, and many others. Perry Miller set the stage with his anthology on the

Puritans and provided part of the script with his volume on the Transcendentalists. This anthology is meant to fill in part of the intervening
period with many important yet difficult to obtain selections from the
leaders who wrote on many topics, from the person and work of Jesus
Christ, to baptism and communion, to the nature of the Church itself.

The Introduction which follows tries to place Unitarian writings of
the nineteenth century in a perspective that can, on the one hand, emphasize their distinctive features and, on the other, indicate their relation to the wider Christian tradition. It is thus to some extent a commentary on Channing's urgent question: "Who shall sunder me from
such men as Fénelon, and Pascal, and Borromeo, from Archbishop
Leighton, Jeremy Taylor, and John Howard?"
    To this end, the first section explores the origins and founding of Chris-
tian Unitarianism from the eighteenth century to the establishment of the
American Unitarian Association in 1825 and the publication of its first
annual report. The second section considers doctrines and theology, including Unitarian attitudes to the sacraments, theological anthropology,
and ecclesiology. The third section examines ethics and moral theology,
which present fundamental themes in Unitarianism. The fourth section
reviews developing uncertainties and conflict within the denomination. In
the concluding section, the challenge of Emerson and transcendentalism
is considered as Christian Unitarians confronted what they considered to
be "the latest form of infidelity" to their faith. The headnotes to individual sections are intended to complete the Introduction, providing further discussion of certain central issues and biographical accounts of the
movement's distinguished leaders.
    The Introduction is primarily an essay in the history of ideas. Neither
the logical and scriptural bases of Unitarian theology, for example, nor
the political, social, or economic contexts in which it arose are systematically evaluated. Purely narrative exposition of New England church history has been kept to a minimum.
    The problem of selecting writings was simplified by the fact that little
or nothing, except for certain works of Channing and a few polemical
pamphlets of the Transcendentalist controversy, is generally available
today. Three principles have guided our choice: to emphasize works representative of eighteenth- and nineteenth-century Christian Unitarian
thought, works of intrinsic merit, and those of larger historical significance because of authorship, subject matter, or circumstances of publication. Several event-making statements are included: Channing's first open
letter in the salvo that set in motion the Unitarian counterattack in 1815;
Channing's Baltimore Sermon, which became the movement's chief man-

ifesto; Henry Ware's extended reply to Leonard Woods; Andrews Norton's *Statement of Reasons;* the younger Ware's answer to Emerson's Divinity School Address; Henry W. Bellows's sensational but now almost forgotten summons to churchly revival; and Frederic Henry Hedge's critique of traditional natural theology.

The arrangement of the selections is for the most part thematic or topical rather than chronological, although the first section bears fairly early dates and the last two, considerably later dates. If these writings had been presented simply in the order in which they were written, the larger and more important purpose would be nullified. During the immensely important period with which we are concerned, the continuities or stable aspects of Unitarianism outweighed in significance the novelties and alterations. It was from this fairly set position that Unitarians first stood off orthodoxy on the right and, later, Transcendentalism on the left; a topical arrangement best conveys the structure of this outlook as well as its basic consistency and cohesiveness.

We have tried to keep footnotes to the bare minimum, limiting them chiefly to the identification of quoted material. The bibliographical essay will assist those who wish to pursue the subject further.

It has seemed more worthwhile to limit the number of selections than to abbreviate them unduly. The following selections are only slightly abridged unless specific notice to the contrary is given in the headnote to the selection. Because these writings date from an era that put a higher premium on rhetorical flourish than does our own, we have eliminated what seemed to be unnecessary elaboration, illustration, repetition, and demonstration—in each case indicating deletions in the usual manner. In no instance, we hope, has the structure or overall spirit of the work been sacrificed or altered. For those who wish the complete text, full bibliographical information is provided. Footnotes to anthologized materials are always those of the original author unless identified as being by the editors [Eds.]. Words within brackets are the editors'.

Just as Unitarianism is composed of institutions and personalities, so is this book. The authors would like to thank the librarians of the Harvard Divinity School, Yale University, and the Princeton Theological Seminary for their assistance. The Unitarian Universalist Association in Boston, Massachusetts, allowed access to its archives. The Reverend Dr. Virgil E. Murdock, of the Benevolent Fraternity of Unitarian Universalist Churches, kindly supplied a copy of the Tuckerman selection. The First and Second Church of Boston offered its magnificent tower as an office for the completion of the manuscript—the best ivory tower possible.

Professor Conrad Wright, of Harvard University, rendered invaluable assistance, with his formidable knowledge of American Unitarianism. The Reverend Dr. Walter D. Kring checked numerous references in the final manuscript. Mr. Eugene Navias, of the Unitarian Universalist Association, offered much help with hymnological research. The Reverend Dr. Rhys Williams, Miss Susan C. Twist, and Mr. John Owen Snyder provided assistance in many ways to see this book to completion. Overall, though, we express thanks to Nancy and Sarah, who provided much support. It goes without saying, yet it needs to be said, that the shortcomings and errors are our own.

S. E. A.
Yale University
J. S. C.
Oxford University

Professor Ahlstrom did not live to see the publication of this book. The first draft of the manuscript was his, begun in the 1950s, and then shelved until our collaboration beginning in 1977. His introduction remains from the original. Our manuscript was completed before his death.

The Reformation has been making a vigorous advance. The commotion has been extensive, the tossing has been fearful, the alarm and bustle of those exposed to the spray have been loud and earnest. At length the height of the swell seems to have passed. There are symptoms of greater quiet and repose. To change the figure, the heat of the battle is over; the great battle has been fought; and it is time to look about us, and see what is the result, where the world stands, and what use is to be made of the losses and the acquisitions of the contest.

—Henry Ware, Jr.
SOBER THOUGHTS ON THE
STATE OF THE TIMES (1835)

INTRODUCTION

❧ Introduction

On Sunday morning, September 9, 1832, Ralph Waldo Emerson, descendant of six generations of New England clergymen, delivered his farewell sermon to the congregation of Boston's Second Church.[1] The twenty-nine-year-old minister, who had served this church for three years, ostensibly left the Unitarian ministry because he had doubts about the sacrament of the Lord's Supper. Recent scholarship, however, has suggested a multitude of reasons why this young man, who would become well known in later years as the Sage of Concord, exchanged the ministerial for the literary life. Six years later, addressing the graduating class of the Harvard Divinity School, he revealed how far from the faith of his fathers he had come. "In this refulgent summer," Emerson began, "it has been a luxury to draw the breath of life." With evocative charm he then painted the beauties of the world and suggested the "sublime creed [that] the world is not the product of manifold power but of one will, of one mind." He later went on to decry the sins of the Church: its "noxious exaggeration about the *person* of Jesus" and its refusal to make preaching an "expression of the moral sentiment in application to the duties of life." It had spoken instead of revelation as something "long ago given and done, as if God were dead." Now its message could not be heard "through the sleep of indolence and over the din of routine." He bade the young seminarians to be newborn bards of the Holy Ghost, to "let the breath of new life be breathed . . . through the forms already existing." He looked to a time when miracle would be seen as "one with the blowing clover and the falling rain" and when duty would be seen as "one thing with Science, with Beauty, and with Joy."[2]

Historians would call this address a milestone in the development of the Liberal Faith; indeed, cautious Unitarians feared that they heard in these calmly spoken words the fulfillment of the prophecy attributed to Moses Stuart of Andover that Unitarianism was the halfway house to infidelity. They answered with firmness, calling the address an incoherent rhapsody. With their independence from Congregational orthodoxy barely

1. Octavius Brooks Frothingham, *Transcendentalism in New England*, sermon, pp. 363–380.
2. Joseph I. Blau, ed., *American Philosophic Addresses, 1700–1900*, pp. 588–604. Address delivered on July 15, 1838.

won, they again took to the field of controversy to meet the challenge of Transcendentalism.

In the winter of 1844, the liberal churches of Boston were crackling with controversy, and on December 26, First Church, established by such men as John Winthrop and John Cotton, was filled to overflowing for the traditional Thursday Lecture. The excess of people was unusual. Many great men in the past had taken their turn or specially honored the occasion, but with the passing years, the lectures had lost their appeal. "The sinners had ceased to expect awakening, and staid away. None came but saints, and these came not with jubilant feet."[3] On this forenoon, the Reverend Theodore Parker of West Roxbury was to speak. Having resisted previous attempts to exclude him from Unitarian ministerial fellowship, he now laid down the challenge anew with a sermon titled "The Revelation of Jesus to His Age and the Ages." It was a frank exposition of the historical Jesus of German scientific Biblical criticism from one of the first scholars of comparative religion, and Boston orthodoxy of nearly all shades regarded it as an affront and a scandal.

This time action was taken: the "great and Thursday Lecture" was quietly returned to the jurisdiction of the minister of the First Church, Dr. Nathaniel L. Frothingham, who was thereafter free to invite whom he would. Gradually it became clear that the Unitarian clergy with the manifest support of most of their parishioners had drawn a circle and left Theodore Parker out. This was the first major act of exclusion in American Unitarian history, and it demonstrated in a spectacular way the existence of what discerning observers had long been able to see: a definable Liberal Faith was emerging, a Unitarian Christianity.[4]

Christian Unitarianism Defined

Unitarians themselves were often chary of self-definition, but they were emphatically Christians, and most of them would have agreed with the Reverend Frederick A. Farley that theirs was an evangelical Christianity. Andrew Preston Peabody, a leading Unitarian for a generation, even thought that the Apostles' Creed was "simply Unitarian, while the Nicene Creed is expressly anti-Trinitarian, making Christ a derived and, thus, of

3. Octavius Brooks Frothingham, *Theodore Parker,* p. 214.
4. Unitarians often discussed whether they were better named "Christian Unitarian" or "Unitarian Christian." In 1819 Channing was probably right in choosing the latter. Since that time, however, various groups within the larger movement have designated themselves as being specifically "Humanist," "Theist," or "Christian."

necessity, a subordinate being."[5] But perhaps most illustrative of the confessional position of the Unitarians was the personal statement that the Reverend James Walker wrote when he came to his parish in Charlestown, Massachusetts in 1818. He went on to become a professor at and later president of Harvard University, but from this creed he did not depart.

I believe in God, the Creator and Preserver of all things, visible and invisible.

I believe in Jesus Christ, the Son of God, the Messiah of the Hebrew prophets, and the only appointed Saviour of mankind.

I believe in the sacred Scriptures, that they were dictated by inspiration, and form the only standard of faith and practice.

I believe in the divine institution of the visible Church, in the resurrection of the dead, man's future accountability, and life everlasting.[6]

More official, as well as more florid, was the statement made about thirty-five years later by the Executive Committee of the American Unitarian Association, when they sought to distinguish their views from the errors of Transcendentalism:

We desire, in a denominational capacity, to assert our profound belief in the Divine origin, the Divine authority, the Divine sanctions of the religion of Jesus Christ. This is the basis of our associated action. We desire openly to declare and record our belief as a denomination, so far as it can be officially represented by the American Unitarian Association, that God, moved by his own love, did raise up Jesus to aid in our redemption from sin, did by him pour a fresh flood of purifying life through the withered veins of humanity and along the corrupted channels of the world, and is, by his religion, for ever sweeping the nations with regenerating gales from heaven, and visiting the hearts of men with celestial solicitations. We receive the teachings of Christ, separated from all foreign admixtures and later accretions, as infallible truth from God.[7]

These pronouncements make clear that Unitarians considered themselves a part of the Christian tradition. But they do not reveal or explain Unitarianism's three most fundamental departures from orthodox theology: (1) a belief that man is by nature good, not totally depraved; (2)

---

5. Andrew Preston Peabody, "Early New England Unitarians," in Channing Hall Lectures, *Unitarianism: Its Origin and History,* p. 156.
6. *History of the Harvard Church in Charlestown, 1815–1879,* p. 169.
7. "Report of the Executive Committee," American Unitarian Association, *Twenty-Eighth Report of the American Unitarian Association (May 24, 1853),* Boston, pp. 22–23.

a revised and more human view of God's attributes, with an emphasis on His love that precluded such doctrines as predestination, eternal damnation of the unregenerate, and the vicarious sacrifice or satisfaction theory of the Atonement; and (3) a belief that the doctrine of the Trinity was an unscriptural tritheism that veiled the true mission of Christ and the nature of Christian worship. The last of these, which led to the coinage of the opprobrious name of Unitarian—when most of the liberals would have preferred the title of Catholic Christian or Liberal Christian—was by no means of primary importance. Rather, all of these doctrinal revisions were aspects of the need to counter the rise of religious rationalism and the optimistic view of man's destiny. It was in this spirit, not in the spirit of ancient Christological controversies, that Unitarians invested old words—whether of creed or Bible—with new and liberal meanings.

The Unitarians' gradually maturing religious philosophy was nevertheless deeply rooted in the past. The problems which stimulated their thought were ancient, and the pattern of solution to which they most persistently recurred had a venerable lineage. For them, history had portentous meanings. Through the Puritans, whom they admired almost excessively, they fell heir to the polity and theology of the Calvinistic Reformation. At the same time, they lived in an Age of Reason which had sprung from the Renaissance. They credited both the Reformers and the humanists with ending medieval thralldom, for they also felt in mental bondage and in need of responding to Christianity with an enlightened freedom of inquiry. Yet even in the Middle Ages they found individuals worthy of praise: prophets of the Christian life like St. Francis, rationalistic theologians like Abelard, and the great mystics who seemed to pursue their religious life almost in spite of the Church. The dual heritage of antiquity, moreover, they faced with the same catholicity of spirit. Classical authors formed the core of their educational curriculum, while the Bible stood at the center of their thought world.

The Intellectual Background: Renaissance Hellenism to Scottish Realism

The problem of creating a new philosophy of religion was faced squarely by Jewish scholars like Philo Judaeus, who, after studying in the philosophical schools of Greece, attempted a reformulation of the Old Testament faith. Simply stated, the problem was, and is, this: how does one who accepts the articles of prophetic religion on faith justify oneself as a rational being; how does one explain the meaning of faith philosophically? The prophetic religion in question was then, Judaism, and, later, Christianity. Fundamental Judeo-Christian doctrine involved a transcendent God, whose glory the firmament was telling, and man, who was created in His image. The Jews had created the myth of the Will of God—the great Thou who confronted every man. Their religion, when not obscured by ritualism and rabbinic law, was a dynamic encounter that demanded the impossible *imitatio Dei* from the creature. Virtue thus arose out of dependence on God and was as far beyond formulation as God was beyond human knowledge. Christ was the ultimate Suffering Servant who arose from the Chosen People to further reveal God's Will. St. Paul, the ideal type of the Christian apostle, testified of a trusting faith in Christ, who had fulfilled the time and saved man through the Grace of God. That this proved to be "foolishness to the Greeks" invites consideration of the intellectual tradition that Paul confronted when he preached at Athens (Acts 17:18).

It was from the Greeks that the Western rational tradition stems, for they were the first to invert the religious problem of man, bringing reasonable proof to the critical rather than demanding acceptance from the faithful. The position they took allowed of varied emphasis, however, and during the long reach of Classical civilization (600 B.C.–400 A.D.) this whole range of variation was exploited. The early naturalists approached the problem of the nature of things empirically, from the standpoint of human experience and observation of the world. Hippocrates, the Father of Medicine, typified this outlook. Plato followed Parmenides in shifting the emphasis to eternal ideas, which alone transcend the flux of time and history. It was thus he who made the world safe for philosophers and justified Alfred North Whitehead's famous remark that all of Western philosophy is a series of footnotes to Plato.[8] This speculative Platonic tradition developed in two directions: toward empiricism, in the moderate realism of Aristotle; and into a rational mysticism, in the works of later Neo-Platonists. With Plotinus (205–207 A.D.) the Platonic identification of intellect and the Divine became the foundation for defining a process of reflexive introspection whereby one confronted the immanent God in one's own soul. In this mystical view, Hellenic thought comes full circle and reveals its internal unity in yet another way: for here in the mystical confrontation of God is empirical knowledge. God, in a final and irrefutable way, is before the apprehending mind.

A less integrally related aspect of Classical thought was the latter-day moralism of Stoics and Epicureans. Coming after the decline of the great

8. Alfred North Whitehead, *Process and Reality*, pt. II, ch. 1, sec. 1, "The safest general characterization of the European philosophical tradition is that it consists of a series of footnotes to Plato."

speculative schools and during the age of empire that followed in the wake of Alexander the Great (d. 323 B.C.), these philosophers were tuned not so much to the eternal verities of metaphysics as to the girding of individuals in an alien and unstable world. Their philosophy was essentially materialistic, pessimistic, and ethical in emphasis, and was formulated to help people face the inexorable dictates of fate through its exhortations to duty, fortitude, or quiet withdrawal. Philosophy, for the Stoics especially, was ethics; the fundamental fact of the universe was the natural law that ruled it.

Much of Christian doctrinal history centers around the attempts to bring together the prophetic faith and various aspects of this seemingly antithetical Hellenic tradition. St. Paul, for the most part, resisted a Greek interpretation; the author of the Fourth Gospel yielded to some extent; and all of the early Christian Fathers wrestled with the problem. The violent debates about the nature of Christ in the fourth century—for Arius no less than for Athanasius—were rooted in Greek metaphysical conceptions. The same can be said for the great theological systems of Clement of Alexandria, St. Augustine, and St. Thomas Aquinas and the mystical theology of Meister Eckhardt and St. John of the Cross. "Oh Galilean, thou hast conquered!" cried Julian the Apostate, the Neo-Platonic emperor, on his deathbed (363 A.D.). But had he foreseen the course of Western Christian thought—especially the Neo-Platonic elements of it—he might well have silenced his despair.

The attempt to achieve a Judeo-Hellenic synthesis was thus pursued from the earliest times, on through the Middle Ages, along essentially the same lines. But it was the ferment of the Renaissance that most directly adumbrated the issue that Unitarians were to face.

The Renaissance, of course, was many things. Socially and economically the term connotes significant and widespread changes. Intellectually it was a period of quickening interest in the scientific study of man and nature, and of rediscovering the richness of a more pure Classical literary and philosophical tradition. Socially there came a secularization of power: the decline of the Church, the rise of commercial society, and the development of the nation-state, which increasingly operated according to its own autonomous principles of statecraft. Along with this came the secularization of thought: the increasing concern for science, technology, and the social sciences. This trend was marked as well by the tendency to regard even economics as an autonomous science. Later, business itself would be seen to be operating under its own laws. In terms of religious ideas, these new intellectual currents were given added importance by the appearance of lay philosophers, often under secular patronage, who dealt with a whole gamut of problems that had been the almost exclusive preserve of clerical thinkers. Reason and freedom were the keynotes of this gradual change, and especially as the Renaissance gave way to the Enlightenment, the Age of Reason, religious ideas were translated into these new modes of thinking. In the history of Christian thought, therefore, the great era of eighteenth-century rational theology must be understood as a continuing Hellenic revival, or, as Peter Gay has suggested, a revival of paganism.

The Reformation represents a different tradition, although it owed much to the Renaissance. It was, in fact, a revolt in the most profound sense. On the political level, the Reformers challenged the authority and corruptions of the Church; on the religious, they condemned medieval scholasticism no less than secular rationalism. Luther and Calvin were Judaic and prophetic in outlook, outraged as much by the rationalizations of Scripture that vitiated faith as by the ecclesiastical mechanics that exaggerated the merit of works. They deplored both the egocentricity of the rational mystic's introspective union with God and the denial of inherent sinfulness implicit in monistic theories of God's immanence. The Reformation was to a considerable degree a counter-Renaissance, and the thought of its great leaders cannot be subsumed under the categories of Classical philosophy insofar as counter-Renaissance implies the revival of occultism and cabalism, as well as theology.

The history of post-Reformation theology reveals either a gradual reassertion of medieval modes of thought or the gradual victory of Renaissance ideas. Lutheranism lapsed into a new scholastic orthodoxy, and important branches of the Calvinistic movement were compromised similarly. It is in this context that the appearance of the post-Reformation heroes of the Unitarian Reformation should be considered, for they are best understood as a subsidiary fruitage of the Renaissance. The inspiration of these liberals came from various quarters—medieval pantheistic mysticism as reinforced by the revival of Platonic studies; the new emphasis on practical, this-worldly moralism; and the naturalistic (and often nominalistic) outlook of scientific investigators. Regardless of how these attitudes were blended, they represented a Renaissance rather than a Reformation orientation for the new movement.

Out of Renaissance Italy, says Adolf Harnack, came a whole crowd of anti-Trinitarians.[9] Lelio Sozzini (Laelius Socinus, b. 1525), the Patriarch of Unitarianism, who fled from Siena to Geneva, was the son of a great humanistic professor of jurisprudence; his nephew, Faustus Sozzini (b. 1539), who organized Polish Unitarianism around the Raco-

9. A. Harnack, *History of Dogma,* vol. VII.

vian Catechism, came from the same Italian city and background. Bernardino Ochino (b. 1487), former general of the Franciscan Observants and later vicar-general of the Capuchins, left Italy and Catholicism for Switzerland, where he became a preacher to the Italian congregation at Zurich and a follower of Michael Servetus. Giorgio Biandrata, who fathered a similar liberal movement in Transylvania, and Giacomo Contio, who propagated Unitarian doctrines in England, were among the many others who indicate the close relationship between Italy and the demand for a more philosophical understanding of Christianity. Michael Servetus, who was martyred by John Calvin (1553), though not an Italian, was like Biandrata a physician; he framed Unitarian views of the Godhead in terms of Neo-Platonic philosophy with a heavy tincture of hermeticism. Similarly, northern Europeans who have won a place in Unitarian sympathies, Zwingli in Switzerland, the mild and reasonable Erasmus, or the humanistic apostles of the inner light, Hans Denck and Luther's coadjutor, Melancthon, show the profound contact made with the Hellenic spirit that the Renaissance championed.

Although anti-Trinitarianism came to be very widely diffused, as Earl Morse Wilbur's two-volume classic *History of Unitarianism* indicates, it was naturally the English movement that was most significant for American thought. Despite the congenial political views, the active interest in science, and the deep love for creedal freedom that feature this English movement, its reasoning ultimately carried it far beyond what most American Unitarians were willing to accept.

During the first century after the English Reformation, anti-Trinitarians were little more than a convenient object of orthodox scorn and oppression. But as the Calvinistic phase of the Reformation yielded gradually to, first, the humanistic tradition and, then, the Aristotelianism of the judicious Richard Hooker and the Platonism of Cambridge, various types of latitudinarian thought began to make headway not only in the establishment but also in the Nonconformist churches. John Milton and Algernon Sidney were only two of the most prominent of the many who moved toward Arian views of the Trinity. Isaac Newton, John Locke, and Samuel Clarke (who was once described by Voltaire as the only Englishman who could think) were also claimed for the Unitarian tradition. Such liberal views flourished in many contexts, but they were particularly pronounced in the Presbyterian congregations, which in the period after the Toleration Act (1689) were ordinarily more free than other denominations from strict confessional ties.

John Biddle (1615–62) was perhaps the first open advocate of a frankly Unitarian theology, but the organization of a distinct movement was the work of a small group of closely related and similar-minded men in the eighteenth century. Joseph Priestley (1733–1804), the important scientist, was the leading intellectual spirit of the group. His great co-worker in these projects and the founder of the first explicitly Unitarian church in England (Essex Street Chapel, 1774) was Theophilus Lindsey, a liberal Anglican who left the Church after the failure of the Feathers Petition for moderation of the Thirty-nine Articles of Religion. The third member of the founding trio was Thomas Belsham (1750–1829), Priestley's successor at the new theological school at Hackney and Lindsey's successor at Essex Hall. All were outspoken polemists—to the point that Priestley was eventually driven out of England and migrated to Pennsylvania—and bitter critics of orthodoxy. In 1815 one of Belsham's works would become a major factor in the Unitarian controversy in New England.

The doctrines these three promulgated were by and large uncongenial to most American liberals. The system they evolved was dogmatic, crabbed, and narrow; indeed, it was a liberal scholasticism. English Unitarians called themselves Socinians, but actually their proclamation of the simple humanity of Jesus was far removed from the views of Socinus. Their outlook was essentially naturalistic, although they maintained that the Bible was inspired and quoted from it endlessly, holding even to certain supernatural aspects of its message. Philosophically they were necessitarian followers of Anthony Collins and David Hartley, who were so successful in defending these doctrines, moreover, that for a half-century they were virtually one with English Unitarianism.

Yet it is not the thin red line of anti-Trinitarianism heroes and martyrs that constitutes the tradition most appealing and significant for American Unitarians. The New England liberals were a geographically removed phase of the two centuries of rational Christianity that dominated the thought of English churchmen, both Anglican and Nonconformist, after the English Reformation had given way to a more modern spirit. The appeal to the old heresiarch, Arius of Alexandria, was chiefly sentimental. The Racovian Catechism of Faustus Socinus was basically alien and unacceptable. Even the names Arian and Socinian, used to identify various departures from traditional theology, had only a vague and inaccurate relation to the original ideas.

The issues at stake in this long period of English theological controversy were clearly laid out by Lord Herbert of Cherbury, the father of Deism (1583–1648). His *De Veritate* (1624) is a milestone in the development of modern rationalism; it is the first major work of English secular philosophy, heavy with Platonic and Neo-Platonic overtones. Herbert's five common notions of religion remained fundamental to both

Deists and advocates of rational Christianity. According to Herbert, one must believe (1) in a Supreme Being; (2) in the need to worship him; (3) in the pursuit of a pious and virtuous life as the best form of worship; (4) in repentance; and (5) in rewards and punishments in the next world.

In the great Deistic Controversy that followed, English religious thought focused on the issues that Herbert delineated, and Christians were forced to disprove the Deist charge that Christianity at best did no more than indirectly voice the principles of natural religion. Until the middle of the eighteenth century, the arguments centered on the internal or speculative grounds for believing in the reasonableness of Christianity; during the next eighty years, an increasing accent was placed upon the external evidences of the truths of Biblical religion. The nature of the early phase of the controversy was in large part determined by the shift of emphasis signalized in the works of John Locke (1632–1704).

Locke shifted the basis of the argument from a priori or speculative grounds to more empirical (sensationalist) grounds by insisting that all knowledge stemmed from experience. But he himself set the pattern for the Christian opposition to Deism in *The Reasonableness of Christianity.* He insisted that revelation did tell man things above reason or beyond ordinary experience, but he denied that there was anything in it contrary to reason. He reduced the conditions of salvation taught by Scripture to two: faith and repentance, that is, belief that Jesus was the Messiah and the good life. This, he said, is reasonable; furthermore, it is attested by the miracles and countless evidences in nature and man. What Locke did thereby was to establish philosophically the position defended by John Tillotson, archbishop of Canterbury and the most famous preacher of his day. Tillotson argued that "natural religion is the foundation of all revealed religion, and revelation is designed simply to establish its duties."[10] Faith thus involved no other faculty than reason: it is "the persuasion of the mind concerning any thing."[11]

In the second phase of English rationalism, evidences became even more important in the arguments of Christian apologists, with both the sensationalist philosophy and the advances of science stimulating the new emphasis. The magnificent integration of immediate phenomena and the starry heavens accomplished by Isaac Newton's *Principia* (1687) was fundamental to this development, but lesser minds were challenged to fill in the details. The most important of these thinkers was William Paley (1743–1805).

10. John Tillotson, *Works,* vol. ii, p. 333.
11. *Ibid.,* vol. xi, p. 203.

His famous work on *The Evidences of Christianity* (1794) was said to be rivaled only by Euclid's geometry as a model of lucid presentation, and for over a century it was almost as widely studied. In this work, he marshaled the available arguments for the validity of the Gospel account of the life and miracles of Jesus. In another work, he performed the same task for the life and epistles of Paul. Paley epitomized the confident natural theology of his age. "I take my stand in human anatomy," he wrote.[12] However, he went on to elaborate other aspects of his detailed argument from design. He proved that God was the maker of the whole marvelous and orderly universe, and that this "Watchmaker God" was also the benevolent "Author of Christian revelation." Even the doctrine of future punishment was seen as a sanction of a good Lord, who used this device to lure selfish men into happiness.

Evidential arguments had been formulated in ancient Greece and used in the Middle Ages. Archbishop Richard Whately, in the Noetic School at Oxford, and many others gave them further popularity and elaboration. The Bridgewater Treatises (1833–36) marked the most extravagant development and the concluding phase of this approach. In these eight treatises, notable scientists were commissioned to write proofs of the power, wisdom, and goodness of God, as manifested in the Creation. Sir Charles Bell's *The Hand, Its Mechanism and Vital Endowments as Evincing Design* reveals to what length they went.

This immensely self-assured and optimistic movement did, nevertheless, face certain obstacles; preeminent among them was the common observation that there was much pain, venality, and brutality to account for in the world. Of the great apologists of the time, Bishop Joseph Butler (1692–1752) was among the few who squarely confronted "the disorders of the present state."[13] In his gloomy way he claimed no more than an analogical argument for the existence of God; he did not believe that all the evidences being adduced could be legitimately applied to the God of the Bible. Butler might not have gone so far as John Donne, an earlier dean of St. Paul's, who found all coherence gone in the universe, but he did see a problem, and his book *The Analogy of Religion, Natural and Revealed, To the Constitution and Course of Nature* became a classic and a standard schoolroom text.

The other great obstacle to orthodox defenders was philosophical. It came in the form of the devastating logic of David Hume (1711–76), a quiet and retiring Scotsman, who capsized the sensationalist ship which Christian rationalists, such as Bishop George Berkeley, had loaded with

12. William Gorham Paley, *Natural Theology*, p. 344.
13. Joseph Butler, *The Analogy of Religion*, ch. VII, pt. I, especially pp. 182–183.

such heavy apologetical cargo. Hume denied that the ideas of Locke had any sure reference to reality, including the reality of consciousness. He argued further that traditional conceptions of cause and effect were based on unwarranted assumptions and that with them fell the related arguments for God. The traditional basis for speculative ethics, metaphysics, or natural theology and the argument from miracles were similarly collapsed by this naturalistic line of reasoning. Hume was dismissed in many quarters, but among other Scotsmen an answer was formulated; a whole school of philosophers at Edinburgh, Glasgow, and Aberdeen reasserted the "common sense" of the situation.

What then was the answer to Hume? In one way these Scotsmen revived the conceptions of Herbert and the Cambridge Platonists, asserting that man is born with given intellectual powers which enable him to know reality itself, not representations of reality. In their theory of knowledge, however, they did not rest their case with a mere declaration or appeal to the common sense of the multitude, as has often been said. Reid, especially, examined the root propositions of the sensationalists and suggested an alternative formulation.

In ethical theory, the Scottish Realists held that human beings also possessed active or moral powers. Conscience was literally a faculty by which one discerns right from wrong. The implication that the principle of self-love solved ethical problems was violently opposed, as was any deterministic system that deprived a person of responsibility for actions. Considered as a whole, therefore, the system of the Scottish Realists, although deeply involved in the sensationalist tradition, represents a broader, more speculative, more classic spirit that not even the mediocrity of most of its expositors could hide. It was informed by a spirit more catholic than those of the opposing schools that followed in the train of Hume, Hartley, and Priestley.

The vogue of the Common Sense philosophy was tremendous during the eighteenth and nineteenth centuries. Dugald Stewart was lionized as the foremost philosopher of his day, and the Scottish system made a great impact in France. In America it became the veritable reigning philosophy in many centers of learning. A long line of presidents of Princeton fostered the system. At Harvard and among Unitarians, Scottish Realism became a standard formulation.

This then was the state of religious thought during the eighteenth century in Great Britain. With strict authority gone, fearing the tumult and wildness that came from individual scriptural analysis or the promptings of the inner spirit, and yielding above all to the dominant attitudes of the Enlightenment, the age resorted to common sense. In one way or another the whole vast controversial literature of the epoch (except for the dissonant notes of revivalistic movements) is concerned with the rational justification for assenting to Christian doctrines, and in the progress of these debates, the doctrines themselves were softened, rounded-off, and remolded so as to be more in accord with the intellectual tendencies of the times.

With this retrospect, the main inspirations for the founders of the Liberal Faith in New England have been reviewed. The important thing is not the uncertain tradition of anti-Trinitarian dissent that runs from Arius to Servetus to Belsham. The theology of the Trinity was only one of many liberal revisions of traditional dogma that the mood of rationalistic analysis produced. To penetrate this mood is the important thing, and this involves something much more basic than doctrinal exposition. In Boston, no less than in Edinburgh or London, the Renaissance and its logical and historical fulfillment, the Age of Reason, determined the major motives of the liberal outlook. New England Unitarians were not extremists, however, and they turned to this orthodox rationalism of Britain not only because it was available but also because it was free from the radical spirit that had brought violence and revolution to France. The questions Americans were asking, moreover, were answered most directly by Anglicans like Paley and Samuel Clarke, Presbyterians like Nathaniel Lardner, Independents like Philip Doddridge, moderate Arian Unitarians like Richard Price, and the Scottish school of philosophers.

Ambivalence or *compromise* is perhaps the key word for the point of view these men held in common. They stood between the Deists who contended for the all-sufficiency of natural religion and the old view, so capably reiterated by Henry Dodwell, that Christianity was not founded on argument. Probably none of them would have denied that faith could precede reason, yet they constantly endeavored to make the faith more credible. They moderated the offense, rationalized the paradox, and eliminated the mystery of the Evangel. It was with no intention of derogating the divinity of Christ that they spoke of the unity of the Godhead.

The cardinal idea was that man was good. "The Creator has not, indeed, implanted in the human mind anything that is, originally and in itself, evil. But, on the other hand, there is no part of our nature that does not become bad if not controlled and regulated by an enlightened conscience."[14] These ideas on man were a part of a larger philosophy of history, the essential doctrine of which was the idea of progress. Enlight-

14. Richard Whately, *Introductory Lessons on Morals*, p. 72.

enment and reason seemed to be opening up new vistas for the improvement of the human race. The Kingdom (or the Republic) of Heaven would be realized on this earth.

Against such an optimistic background the idea of God that Calvin delineated, and that Jonathan Edwards revived with such force, was regarded as barbaric and hateful. For this reason the English liberals not only moderated old dogmas of the depravity of man and his utter dependence on the Grace of God but also altered their idea of God. With more daring than medieval scholastics had shown and certainly more than the sixteenth-century Reformers, they assigned to God the attributes of love as seen and understood in people and then deduced that such a God would surely not be so vindictive as to promulgate the Gospel according to Calvin.

These revisions and others did undeniably undermine orthodox theology. Fundamentalists found it even more disturbing to have the liberals seeking and finding corroboration for their views in the Bible. Yet a salient fact remains: American Unitarianism was distinctive. It was a departure from these English views with a spirit and temper of its own. Rationalism and the prophetic tradition were blended in a special way that only the peculiar heritage of New England serves to explain. An American Reformation was in the making. The orthodox and liberals would be in constant debate over "The Faith Once Delivered to the Saints."[15] Who indeed represented the tradition? The polemical exchanges were fierce.

The American Scene

When Governor William Bradford recorded in his history of Plymouth Colony that "the Lords free people joyned them selves into a church estate,"[16] he could hardly have suspected that two centuries later the very church of his Pilgrims, by that time the prosperous congregation of the First Church in Plymouth, Massachusetts, would have become formally Unitarian. Yet by 1825, most of the oldest Congregational churches of eastern Massachusetts had left the ancient fold, and Boston had become (as it remains) the center of Unitarianism, while the movement's leaders continued to be New Englanders who were most usually educated at Harvard. Nor was this mere coincidence. Indeed, one of the most obvious facts is that the country's first organized denomination of liberal Christians emerged from a solid Puritan background. For this reason, no explanation of Unitarianism can avoid consideration of the nature of

15. Lyman Beecher, *Works,* vol. 2, *Sermons Delivered on Various Occasions,* pp. 243–300.
16. William Bradford, *The History of Plymouth Colony,* p. 6.

Puritan thought itself. On the other hand, the success of orthodoxy in defending certain old Congregational regions (notably Connecticut) lies in the broader context of New England history.

When the first Puritans came to New England, they carried with them Reformation history. The force of primitive Pauline Christianity, as proclaimed in the life and work of John Calvin, gave the chief vitality to their thinking and the greatest fervor to their piety. The heart of this legacy was dualism: the demonic and the divine, evil and good, the fallen human being and redeeming grace, the world and the transcendent God. It resisted any monistic synthesis that dissolved the tension, that made evil a phase of good, or that made humans themselves divine in a pantheistic sense. "That old Deluder, Satan," was profoundly respected. Sin was real. Regeneration, not mere right thinking, was tragically necessary.

But there was also in their theology a dynamic tension between reason and Scripture—and a great confidence that one would inevitably support the other. The covenant or federal theology that these fervent colonists brought to American shores was not the theology of Calvin but a complex and intricately systematized compromise, a compromise that avoided a strict interpretation of the doctrines of predestination and human depravity and that accommodated human freedom and the claims of reason.

The crux of the Puritan compromise lay in the Covenant of Grace, which was traced to Abraham's Old Testament encounter with the Lord. According to this doctrine, an admittedly omnipotent God agreed to bestow His grace on those who prepared themselves for the gift of grace, owned the covenant, and lived by faith in obedience to God's ordinances. It was thus a logical position driven between an extreme emphasis upon grace, on the one hand, and upon human capabilities, on the other, that is, between the errors of Antinomianism and of Arminianism. Since they considered both these errors to be terrible, moreover, they saw great need for "exactness in cutting the thread true." Cut it true they did! And if they made what can be called a legalistic concession to Arminians, who believed that man was free to accept or reject God's grace, they by no means sacrificed their sense of dependence on divine mercy. They knew that living by natural law (as though under the Covenant of Works) would never suffice. "We are Abraham's children," they believed: Christianity remained an adventure in obedience to God's revealed will.

If the Covenant of Grace was the heart of their theology, their dogmatics on reason had perhaps even greater historical consequences. In this regard, federal theologians had made an important departure from Reformation thinking by tempering their Calvinism with an essentially scholastic concept of rational thinking. Reason and revelation were the co-arbiters of the proper substance of belief. Against all anti-intellectual sectaries, knowledge was defended. "That God who is abstract wisdom, and delights that his rationall creatures should search after it, and that his Ministers should study to propagate it, will expect that you should be Foster-fathers of knowledge."[17] Nor was it merely a case of knowledge being good and ignorance, bad. Richard Baxter's almost definitive manifesto against all who deprecated reasoned analysis of Scripture asserted that aside from the obvious need to read and translate correctly, "We must use our best *Reason* . . . to discern the *Order* of sacred Verities . . . , discerning things more necessary from the less needful. . . . To gather just, and certain Inferences from Scripture Assertions; to apply general Rules to particular Cases, in matters of Doctrine, Worship, Discipline, and ordinary Practice."[18] Even this justification for the deduction of doctrine from the Word of God, however, does not fully reveal what Perry Miller has called the Puritans' "perverse tendency to make revelation natural and redemption rational."[19] They were at pains to demonstrate that revelation "teacheth nothing contrary to sense and reason."[20] Conversely, they went beyond the "scientific" concept of the uses of reason to the concept of reason itself as a source of truth. In this sense they were often of one mind with the school of Platonists at Cambridge. They avoided extremes like the mysticism of Plotinus; but they did not hesitate to assert that the soul was made for an end, and good, and therefore for a better than itself, therefore for God, therefore to enjoy union with him, and communion with those blessed excellencies of his.

The Doctrine of the Liberal Faith

The basic reasons for the emergence of liberal departure from Puritan theology were the same for colonial America as for England. Behind the process were the familiar forces of modernity: the development of commercial society, the expansion of scientific knowledge, and the maturation of Enlightenment optimism about nature, government, and the future. At the same time, the place of logic and reason in the Puritan synthesis was so important that the emergence of the Liberal Faith involved only an accentuation of a ground principle in the old theology. It could evolve almost imperceptibly.

Liberal Christianity was first formally institutionalized in the northern part of the eastern seaboard—from Newport, Rhode Island, to Bangor, Maine—where mercantile activity was quickening and city life becoming

17. Perry Miller, *The New England Mind,* p. 69.
18. *Ibid.,* p. 72.
19. *Ibid.,* p. 187.
20. *Ibid.,* p. 200.

more important. Boston, which was virtually the financial and cultural metropolis of the United States until 1850, grew from 18,000 in 1783 to 33,000 in 1810. By 1840 it had trebled to 93,383; the same trend characterized other centers. From the old families that profited from and controlled these developments came the civic, religious, and educational leaders; old Congregational churches as well as Harvard College reflected the change.

Harriet Beecher Stowe revealed this aspect of the new movement when she wrote in 1832 that "all the literary men of Massachusetts were Unitarian; all the trustees and professors of Harvard College were Unitarian; all the *élite* of wealth and fashion crowded Unitarian churches; the judges on the bench were Unitarian."[21] Octavius Brooks Frothingham, son of the First Church minister during the Parker uproar, made the same observations seventy years later: "Unitarianism was the religion of the educated, the refined, the scholarly, the wealthy, the leaders of society. Great merchants, politicians, statesmen, judges were apt to be members of Unitarian congregations."[22] Politically they were Federalist and later Whig. Alexander Hamilton, John Adams, and, later, Daniel Webster were their national heroes. In political economy they were conservative, and they welcomed the laissez-faire doctrines of Adam Smith. In social reform they were moderate, at first reluctant even to take up the antislavery cause. Their many philanthropies, however, revealed a wide awareness of social needs.

In the face of such influences not even the stern Puritan tradition could remain unbent, and slowly the ministers moderated their message. But the reasons why these men of affluence, learning, and influence preferred a liberal theology are not different from those which explain the whole intellectual drift of postmedieval history. The new intelligentsia turned from the prophetic to the rational ideas because they seemed useful, verifiable, and hence true. Education brought accentuated demands for religion free from paradox and mystery. People of means and accomplishments preferred a message assuring them of man's essential goodness. Leaders of a society that seemed to be moving onward to better things became convinced that there was also progress in religious ideas: they thought more pessimistic doctrines were dismal leftovers of a less fortunate age. After 1776 such attitudes were reinforced by the national experience whereby the thirteen colonies had struck off Old World fetters and embarked on an adventure of freedom and democracy. Indeed, when one considers the

21. Harriet Beecher Stowe, Letter to "My dear brother," in *The Autobiography of Lyman Beecher,* vol. II, ch. xiii, p. 82. Others have attributed these words to Lyman Beecher.
22. Octavius Brooks Frothingham, *Boston Unitarianism,* p. 193.

temptations to formulate a congenial theology, the miracle becomes the fact that the new theology retained as much as it did of the old.

The tendency to liberal theology that these social transitions encouraged was also facilitated by the Congregational polity of the churches from which Unitarianism for the most part came. "We covenant with the Lord and with one another," read the founding document of Salem's First Church, "and doe bynd our selves in ye presence of God, to walke together in all his waies, according as he is pleased to reveale himself unto us in his Blessed word of truth."[23] The congregation would decide whither the Lord would lead them, and they could "walke together" into Unitarianism without amending their covenant. Conservatives could lament the relaxation of old dogmas, but sanctions were lacking. In addition, proof of a demonstrable change was difficult to find, since the transition was gradual and as much a matter of temperament and mood as of doctrine. Devices for the enforcement of orthodoxy were developed, but only in Connecticut were people able to organize a consociation system that could effectively extirpate heresy from the Congregational churches.[24] In Massachusetts and other colonies (states) where the spirit of independence remained strong, there was no formal way of imposing confessional standards on the individual societies or ministers, and in 1705 the proposals of the Mathers for a more Presbyterian-type organization were defeated.

All through the eighteenth century, Harvard College, which might have developed into a stronghold of orthodoxy, became increasingly free from ecclesiastical regulation. Even controls on the training of young ministers were lacking. In 1792 the Boston Association of Ministers had asserted its right to certify candidates for the ministry in its realm, but by that time, from the orthodox point of view, much of the damage had already been done. When postgraduate instruction in divinity was finally regularized in 1811, it was done by Unitarians to offset the Andover Theological Institution. Before that date Harvard reflected rather than retarded the liberal trend. For three-quarters of a century after that date, the Har-

23. Joseph Henry Allen, "Historical Sketch of the Unitarian Movement," p. 171.

24. An example of this is the following case. A Yale graduate, the Reverend John Sherman (1772–1824), settled in Mansfield, Connecticut, in 1797. By 1805 he had become increasingly liberal. Although his preaching was still acceptable to the congregation, a deacon complained of his theology, and when the congregation did nothing about it, he appealed to the Ministerial Association, which suspended Sherman from preaching. He left Connecticut, although his congregation had invited him to remain as minister, and settled in New York. The consociation system was the reason for the paucity of Unitarian churches in Connecticut and its consequent removal from the Unitarian scene.

vard Divinity School faculty almost unanimously defended the classic Christian Unitarianism that is presented in this anthology.

Counteractive forces tempered American Unitarianism with the result that the prophetic motives of the Puritan legacy were never entirely abandoned. Of paramount importance in preserving a strong Biblical emphasis was the fact that the starting point of an American tradition in New England was Puritan. Unitarians could never dissociate the heroism and stern sense of rectitude which they admired from the enthusiastical tendencies which they suspected. The Gospel was thus woven so tightly into the fabric of New England thinking that no amount of modernism could disentangle it. When the people concerned belonged to the social class least likely to make revolutionary departures from tradition, such a force was especially strong.

The rural, frontier spirit constituted a second conservative constraint. New England was far removed from the closely integrated intellectual life of England and the Continent and in more immediate contact with the mysteries and uncertainties of country life. Rural people have traditionally been more conservative religiously, and in the context of the small New England town, the church and minister were in an excellent position to organize and foster this piety. Even a city like Boston constantly had its religious life revitalized by the influx of rural peoples and by the ordination of ministers whose views had been conditioned by youthful years in country parishes. On the national level, the western areas of the country exerted the same influence, and the sensational success of the revivalistic sects on the frontier spurred Presbyterians and Congregationalists into similar demonstrations of evangelical zeal.

A third powerful and continuing conservative influence on Unitarians was entrenched orthodoxy. To a large extent, its origins and source of strength were rural, and Connecticut was its stronghold, but its emissaries brought battle to the heartland of liberalism. During the eighteenth century, in particular, the New Light Divinity of Jonathan Edwards and his successors, combining a powerful reaffirmation and philosophical defense of traditional Calvinist doctrine with the use and approval of revivalism, reinvigorated the conservative churches and presented a challenge to "the broad and Catholick party." The theological tradition it fostered was, nevertheless, anomalous in its effects and significance to the rise of liberalism. The success of Edwards's attempt to create a philosophical faith tended ironically not only to strengthen rationalism but also to create a revulsion for Calvinism. Revivalistic excesses only heightened the revulsion. Longstanding divisions were deepened, and New England Congregationalism was torn asunder.

This American counterpart to the great European pietistic movement also came to influence Unitarian thought in another and more positive way. The Great Awakening produced a background in which feeling and the religious sense were paramount. This aspect of the New Divinity was attacked by many Old Calvinists who saw Samuel Hopkins and Andover Seminary to be almost as great a threat as the Unitarians.[25] Nor was the fear entirely unjustified, for conservative though Hopkinsians generally were, they tended toward a conception of piety that was alien to Calvin and susceptible to liberal interpretation. Hopkinsians, Unitarians, and Transcendentalists would probably all have agreed that mere assent to objective dogmatic formulae was overemphasized by old-line Calvinists. Channing *was* deeply influenced by Hopkins; and the latter's idea of piety became a permanent, traceable ingredient in Unitarian thought.

Thus both by challenge and by influence the spirit of the Puritans confronted the founders of the Liberal Faith. When the other conservative forces are considered as well, it becomes clearer why Unitarianism, like many another American intellectual movement, developed very differently from its counterpart in the more cosmopolitan culture of Europe.

The successive moderations of belief and practice, the early heralds of the Liberal Faith, and the long Unitarian Controversy are all familiar matters of history. Only a brief resumé is needed here. As early as 1662 the Half-Way Covenant had allowed children of Church members to become communicants without a special conversion experience, and in the Boston Platform of 1680 the rationalist principle was formally invoked. By the middle of the eighteenth century Congregational Church life, especially in the urban areas, had become formalized, comfortable, and routine. On the other hand, the Great Awakening, which once again emphasized the conversion experience, was viewed by the liberals with such revulsion that it strengthened their convictions. By 1800, therefore, the steady though quiet softening of doctrine that had accompanied these trends was clearly visible.

Guardians of orthodoxy had recognized an inclination to the abominable errors of Arius soon after 1700, and Cotton Mather was complaining in 1722 that too many men "after the manner of the Church-of-England men . . . do not preach much about the person of Christ."[26] Mather, however, was an alarmist, and even the deep concern over Arminianism revealed by Edwards twenty years later was to a large degree directed at transatlantic opponents. The industrious Dr. William B. Sprague, who compiled his *Annals of the American Pulpit* in nine vol-

25. See Ezra Stiles Ely, *A Contrast between Calvinism and Hopkinsianism.*
26. Joseph Henry Allen, "Historical Sketch of the Unitarian Movement," p. 176.

umes, was able to find forty-nine eighteenth-century Congregational ministers who entertained Unitarian views. But these early liberals are remembered less for specific tenets than for a gradual shift of emphasis, a more catholic spirit of toleration, and an opposition to enthusiastical religion. This was the familiar pattern of English moderate Christian rationalism.

Ebenezer Gay of Hingham, Massachusetts (d. 1787) has been frequently called the father of American Unitarianism, but it was Charles Chauncy (d. 1787), for sixty years pastor of First Church, who was the most distinguished of the early liberals. Although most famous as the opponent of Edwards and revivalism, he was the scholar of the movement and the first to publish a reasoned defense of belief in universal salvation. His contemporary, Jonathan Mayhew (d. 1766), who attributed his liberal and rational views to the influence of Dr. Gay, was the most outspoken polemicist. With his successor, Simeon Howard (d. 1804), he established a firm Unitarian tradition at West Church in Boston.

During these same years three eminent preachers in Salem were active in the vanguard: Thomas Barnard (d. 1836), John Prince (d. 1836), famed as an early scientist, and the most remarkable, William Bentley (d. 1819), the indefatigable diarist and linguist. In 1785 James Freeman (d. 1835), the lay reader of King's Chapel, converted the first Episcopal church in New England into the first avowedly Unitarian church in America. With his college classmate, Bentley, he had perhaps the most advanced views in the Boston area and was one of the very few who followed the English Unitarians.

Uncoordinated though the liberalism of these ministers was, the main lines of a school of thought are discernible in their pronouncements. It was fitting that Harvard College, from which every one of them was graduated, should become the focus of the inevitable doctrinal controversy. Whether the college caused or merely reflected the emergent liberalism, it was and would remain the center of the movement. The college had been noticeably moving away from the tradition of its founders ever since the election of President John Leverett in 1701. By 1800 David Tappan and Eliphalet Pearson were the only two effective defenders of orthodoxy on the faculty, and they were old and unequal to the task. The observation made in 1801 that "all the young men of talents in Harvard were Unitarian,"[27] was probably substantially true, and President Joseph Willard, though a nominal Trinitarian, was not by nature a man who would change things. Discontent smoldered until the deaths of Tappan (1803) and Willard (1804) sharpened the determination of conservatives to appoint safer successors. While Professor Pearson was

27. James W. Alexander, *Life of Archibald Alexander*, pp. 251–254.

acting president, the question of appointing an occupant to the Hollis Chair of Divinity, the oldest endowed chair in the country, became the first ground for open conflict. When the test of strength came in 1805, the conservatives lost, and Henry Ware, the well-known liberal pastor at Hingham, was elected by the pastors of the nearby churches to the professorship. Not even the stipulation in the endowment that the occupant of the chair be "sound and orthodox" proved a deterrent. Instead, it created new animosities, and the very conservative Reverend Jedidiah Morse (father of Samuel F. B. Morse) responded with his bitter pamphlet on the *True Reasons* which heightened the public awareness of the conflict. In 1806 the liberals scored another victory by electing Professor Webber rather than Pearson as president, and they followed this by the appointment of three other Unitarians to the staff. In 1810, with the election to the presidency of the Reverend John Thornton Kirkland, Harvard was virtually a Unitarian college. There was good reason for Belsham to rejoice in England that "the inquisitive and liberal spirit" was progressing unchecked in "the University of Cambridge."[28]

During the period of uneasiness after 1790 there had been several minor incidents, like Morse's diatribe against the threatening Bavarian Illuminati in 1798, and there were others that followed the Hollis Chair appointment. The organization of the new, confessional orthodox Park Street Church with the sound Edwardsean Edward Dorr Griffin as pastor (1809) and the stand of the Reverend John Codman of the Dorchester Church against exchanging pulpits with liberals (1812) revealed the growing intensity of the conflict. The conservatives usually took the initiative in these affairs, but the nascent Unitarian party did not remain silent. The attack on Hopkinsians, Andoverians, or New England Calvinists penned by the Reverend Horace Holley of the Hollis Street Church in Boston demonstrated their polemic spirit. "You are not only guilty of nonsense and impiety, but you render Christianity itself incredible and detestable; you are the fathers of future infidelity and atheism; and though you should come in the form of angels from heaven you must be denounced and resisted."[29] Despite the growing intensity of the dispute the outward forms of fellowship were maintained. In May 1808, for instance, Channing, Lowell, and Joseph Lathrop took part along with Morse at the ordination of the Reverend Joshua Huntington at the Third Church (Old South) of Boston—the only major church in the city not to go Unitarian during the ensuing controversy. Their spoken words nevertheless revealed the undercurrent of dissension.

Except for occasional verbal sorties, the Unitarian party had so far

28. Thomas Belsham, *Memoirs of the Late Reverend Theophilus Lindsey*, p. 273.
29. Quoted in James King Morse, *Jedidiah Morse*, pp. 140–141.

been indisposed to take the offensive, and in their preaching they avoided controversial topics. They were urbane and essentially pacific people who reveled in quiet harmony of mind and rejected the combative view. The editors of the *Monthly Anthology* revealed the same temperament: "They [the editors] are satisfied if they in any way contribute to the mild influence of our common Christianity, and to the elegant tranquility of literary life."[30] Ezra Stiles Gannett, remembering the Boston ministerial meetings of this period, emphasized the same aspects: "It was free, frank, cordial, and healthy to a most remarkable degree. Difference of age, of opinion, of taste, of situation, produced no estrangement nor coolness. Discussions in which we maintain opposite views caused no heart-burning or ungenerous criticism."[31]

Yet beneath the harmony of the spirit, which even their diversities and disagreements laid bare, there seems to have been a drift toward liberalism that their sermons did not always reveal. The gradual (perhaps unconscious) reading of new meanings into old words had progressed farther than they knew. This made it still more difficult for them to understand the zealotry of conservatives and led them to consider accusations of concealment or hypocrisy as malignant and indecent. When they finally were aroused, however, the inciting factor was not the accusation of heterodoxy, for such charges had been leveled for a generation; it was the threat of exclusion from the Congregational fellowship of New England.

Jedidiah Morse finally ended this uneasy quiesence, and the bludgeon he needed was the biography of Theophilus Lindsey written by that doughty warrior for English Unitarianism, Thomas Belsham. It was a polemical, dogmatic book that roamed over a wide range of controversies, vindicating Lindsey and lashing out at all forms of conservatism. Belsham's chapter 9, especially, on the "Progress and Present State of the Unitarian Churches in America," served Morse's purpose. Here was proof of infidelity. Nor was the change of King's Chapel to Unitarianism the only danger point, for Belsham testified that the new spirit was advancing throughout New England. Writing a terse preface and appending a statement of Belsham's creed, Morse published this chapter and certain letters from Americans that showed the spread of radicalism.[32] This was followed by a review in the conservative *Panoplist* by Jeremiah Evarts, a member of Old South Church. In the two documents Morse and Evarts did their best to confound the liberal enemy. They implied (though Dr.

30. M. A. DeWolfe Howe, ed., *Journal of the Proceedings of the Society which Conducts the Monthly Anthology and Boston Review*, p. 18.
31. William C. Gannett, *Ezra Stiles Gannett*, p. 99.
32. Morse's tract and related literature are bound in a separate volume, *Tracts on the Unitarian Controversy*.

Samuel Worcester, a contemporary, in a masterpiece of special pleading, later showed that they did not *say*) that the Boston liberals were Socinian humanitarians in the manner of Lindsey and Belsham. Furthermore, they spoke of the utter incompatibility of Unitarianism with the faith of the orthodox churches and urged that the orthodox separate in worship and communion from Unitarians.[33] The impact of Morse's pamphlet was immense, and five editions were sold out in as many months. The time for concealment was over; the veil had been torn away. The time for taking sides had come.

Channing's answer to Morse and Evarts and his later replies to new conservative attacks by Dr. Worcester opened a two-decade era of doctrinal controversy. Tracts, pamphlets, sermons, and books were published in profusion. Periodicals on both sides advanced the controversy. Writers, preachers, Biblical scholars, and dialecticians repeated the old arguments, formulated new ones, and coupled personal invective with both until finally, as new issues came to the fore, Unitarianism took a recognized place on the New England religious scene. Recognition, however, was not only an intellectual matter. After Channing's address at the ordination of Jared Sparks in Baltimore (May 1819), reconciliation was clearly out of the question. Circumstances demanded a departure from historic organization and associations.

As orthodox ministers gradually continued to exclude liberals from pulpit exchanges, the Unitarian societies began to gather under the liberal standard. Where a society was not united, the issue between factions was usually drawn by the need to elect a new minister, whereupon the minority withdrew whenever a compromise could not be reached. Even the parish of Jedidiah Morse was divided, when in 1817 the liberals withdrew to form Second (Harvard) Church in Charlestown. Yet neither the withdrawal of factions nor the formation of new societies (like Park Street Church) settled the problem of church property in the old churches. In 1820, therefore, it finally devolved upon the Supreme Court of Massachusetts to adjudicate the matter. In the historic case[34] of First Church in Dedham, Chief Justice Isaac Parker, himself a Unitarian, ruled that the property of an old town church (i.e., as differentiated from a separately incorporated society) could not be transferred by a majority of the church membership but only by a majority of the parish membership (i.e., the town voters). After 1820, because of this decision, an increasing number of the congregations became Unitarian.

33. *Ibid.*, p. 26.
34. George Edward Ellis, *A Half-Century of the Unitarian Controversy*, Appendix IV. The case is reported in Massachusetts Term Reports, XVI, pp. 488–522.

Having been excluded from the old fellowship, the Unitarians erected a new one. In the Boston area, where the movement centered, the old Association of Ministers became a virtual Unitarian agency. Dr. Channing, in the spring of 1820, augmented the opportunities for fellowship and association of the liberal ministers by instituting the Berry Street Conference, and during the years that followed it became an important agency for considering the needs and prospects of the Unitarian faith. Five years later, also at Channing's vestry, the American Unitarian Association was formed. The wisdom of forming this extraecclesiastical volunteer organization was widely questioned and long debated, but it became, nevertheless, the most important agency for the integration of Unitarian activities in the country until the formation of the National Conference forty years later (1865). By 1825, thus, Unitarianism was a denomination, with a basic organizational setup, ably edited journals of opinion, a spirited lay fellowship, and a strong sense of destiny. A decade later Dr. Henry Ware, Jr., could rightly declare, "We are a community by ourselves."[35]

Though it is difficult to judge the truth of Ware's further observation that the preceding quarter-century was the healthiest period in the moral life of Boston and its vicinity, there is little reason to doubt that during these years the Unitarians were possessed of their highest morale. Challenge brought reevaluation and affirmation, while out of the ferment arose a genuine Unitarian synthesis that was, in its theological aspects at least, well coordinated. The achievement of independence from orthodoxy, however, did not save them from further conflict. Moses Stuart represented the conservative school with the oft-attributed prophecy that Unitarianism was merely a halfway house on the road to infidelity (although William Wilberforce actually deserves credit for the statement). Despite vociferous denials of the accusation, winds of doctrine from England and Germany began to produce an effect in America that seemed to vindicate that ominous prophecy. Just when these new currents began to impinge on Unitarians is a moot question, but 1833 was in many ways a turning point. In that year the final disestablishment of the Congregational Church in Massachusetts was accomplished, and the greatest of all the Unitarian champions, Andrews Norton, signalizing the wide recognition of Transcendentalism as a more dangerous enemy than orthodoxy, turned his endeavors to combat on that front. The new liberal theology now required defense from an essentially philosophical attack that rendered the old scriptural weapons obsolete.

Ralph Waldo Emerson, who became the guiding spirit of this new

35. Joseph Henry Allen, "Historical Sketch of the Unitarian Movement," p. 200.

Transcendental interest, withdrew from the Unitarian ministry in 1832. Four years later he published his essay on "Nature," which sums up the rationale of the whole movement. Two years after this came his address to the Divinity School. Henry Ware, Jr., took up the challenge, and Andrews Norton wrote a burning *Discourse on the Latest Form of Infidelity.* From this point on, the controversy increased in intensity. The Reverend George Ripley of the Purchase Street Church in Boston published lengthy *Letters* defending the new Emersonian evangel, and in 1841 he abandoned the ministry and with his wife, Sophia, founded Brook Farm. In the same year Theodore Parker, at the settlement of the Reverend Charles C. Shackford in South Boston, delivered his radical sermon on "The Transient and the Permanent in Christianity," which along with Channing's address at Baltimore and Emerson's to the Divinity School must be reckoned as one of the most epoch-making pronouncements in Unitarian history.

Refusing to leave the denomination, Parker continued to widen the rift. He expanded the ideas presented in the Shackford settlement sermon in a Masonic Hall lecture series in 1841 and 1842, and published this as *A Discourse of Matters Pertaining to Religion.* He had already been barred from exchanging pulpits with many of the ministers, and in 1844 the wealthy and influential Reverend John T. Sargent, minister-at-large of the Benevolent Fraternity of Churches, was forced to resign because he offered his pulpit to the radical. Not even James Freeman Clarke had sufficient prestige to exchange with Parker without suffering an exodus of conservative members from his new and liberal Church of the Disciples. Finally, Parker's Thursday Lecture elicited exclusory action from the Boston Association of Ministers. When a group of Boston businessmen organized the Twenty-Eighth Congregational Society and called Parker to the city as its pastor, the cleavage between conservatives and radicals was aggravated even more.

During these years discourses, essays, books, and poems poured from industrious Transcendentalist pens. Orestes Brownson regaled a limited audience with the Boston *Quarterly Review* (1838–43). Margaret Fuller and Emerson published the *Dial* (1840–44). Ephemeral religious societies like Brownson's and socialistic communities like Brook Farm lent passing institutional form to the new ideas. Public meetings and innumerable lectures in the Lyceum courses gave a popular basis to the movement. The final result, however, was not formal or confined. Transcendentalism became, rather, an unorganized and indefinable impulse in a broad realm of American intellectual and social activities.

The Emersonian message was first of all a Hellenic revival. In this respect the frequent reference to the American renaissance is especially justified. But it was a selective revival inspired by German and British romanticism. It is also necessary to make a fundamental distinction between the poetic, literary, and contemplative approach to religion that Emerson best represents and the naturalistic aspects of Parker's preaching. Transcendentalism, in its major phases, was primarily and fundamentally a religious protest.

Emerson was a mystic and a pantheist and an idealist. Plotinus, whose *Enneads* he read with profound inspiration, is the prototype of this contemplative orientation to the Over-Soul. Though Emerson was not anti-Christian in the belligerent sense of many early Neo-Platonists, church and sacrament, no less than the Atonement of Christ, became irrelevant. The soul was a person's temple, there were sermons in stones, the universe was divine, salvation was the realization and fulfillment of the divine in humankind. What Emerson accomplished was, in religious terms, to eliminate almost completely the prophetic, Judaic element from the Christian heritage that had come down to him.

Theodore Parker represented another spirit, though he gave frequent voice to the Transcendentalist dicta that everyone was divine and endowed with an intuitive grasp of the basic truths of religion. His praise for Emerson was effusive and sincere. But he became above all a reformer, and the abolition of slavery occupied more and more of his time. Moreover, he was a scientific naturalist. Universal religion was the object of Parker's devotion, and the unfinished but major scholarly pursuit of his life was the history of religion. His interest in Biblical criticism was essentially destructionist. His translation and expansion of Wilhelm Martin Leberecht DeWette's (1780–1849) *Beitrage zur Einleitung in das Alte Testament* reveals his intentions. He used the orthodox exegesis of the New Testament only so he could pronounce it limited, parochial, and inadequate. At first deeply impressed by David Friedrich Strauss's *Das Leben Jesu,* but later more in sympathy with the historico-scientific attitude of Friedrich Christian Baur and the Tubingen school, he created a Jesus in completely humanistic terms, finding him frequently in error and morally imperfect. Parker's influence as a preacher and reformer was immense, but he became less of an inspiration to conservative Unitarians than to those who wished to consider the problems of religion in scientific or philosophic terms. He thus became the hero of a rising group of theists and humanists who gradually became dominant in Unitarianism.

The Transcendentalist impact on Unitarianism all but eliminated the conservative party from the denomination. "This outbreak, if I may call it so, of Mr. Parker," wrote Samuel Kirkland Lothrop, a minister in Boston, "disintegrated the clergy and the whole body of Unitarians, and dealt a blow from which Unitarianism has not, and probably as a religious denomination never will recover."[36] This extreme interpretation can be made, however, only if Transcendentalism is credited with liberating the other rationalistic and secular philosophic impulses that became predominant among Unitarians. It would perhaps be more accurate to say that "this outbreak" marks a turning point in the process by which Unitarianism was changed from a Christian denomination into a diversified and completely nonconfessional ethical and religious movement. It is not the purpose of this account to chronicle this aspect of the Transcendental influence but rather to indicate the more immediate effect of the new controversy on the ways of thinking of the defenders of Unitarian orthodoxy. These men resorted primarily to the resources implicit in the synthesis formed during the earlier controversy and consolidated during the relatively peaceful period between 1820 and 1835. Throughout the decades of the new controversy they remained essentially true to the fundamentals of Channing, Norton, and Ware. The ground on which they argued was, of course, changed drastically, and their defenses were erected now around different aspects of their belief. At some points they retreated to old orthodox positions, and at others they yielded to the Transcendental argument; but by and large, their tradition was enriched in many ways. Psychologically, they learned the meaning of Christian communion. The years of stress also brought them vast increases in philosophical acumen, greater knowledge of Christian history, and a more critical understanding of Biblical literature. In short, theirs was an American Reformation, Transcendentalism the renaissance for their initial ideas. Four aspects of the Unitarian response to Transcendentalism are of particular importance.

First, they discovered the importance of the simple affirmation of faith that had ever stood at the core of prophetic Christianity. This forced some men back almost into the strongholds of orthodoxy and even into alliance with the Presbyterian *Princeton Review!* One of the firmest and most authoritative statements on this issue was Frederic Henry Hedge's in his *Reason in Religion,* written while he was professor of ecclesiastical history at the Harvard Divinity School and minister in Brookline, Massachusetts. Although Hedge was a leading spirit of the Transcendental Club and sympathetic with much in German philosophical idealism, he drew a firm line:

I am far from maintaining that Christianity must stand or fall with the belief in miracles; but I do maintain that Christian churches, as organized bodies of believers, must stand or fall with the Christian Confession,—that is, the Con-

36. Thornton K. Lothrop, *Some Reminiscences of the Life of Samuel Kirkland Lothrop,* p. 202.

fession of Christ as divinely human Master and Head. . . . There must be a line somewhere . . . a line which defines it, and separates those who are in it from those who are without. The scope of the Liberal Church is large; but everything and everybody cannot be embraced in it.[37]

More and more they came to urge the cruciality of a supernatural Messianic interpretation of Christ and Christianity. In 1853 the American Unitarian Association affirmed this position with great emphasis, and the year following the Western Conference of Unitarians was even more explicit. In 1854 the Boston Association of Ministers made this a condition of certifying ministerial candidates, and in 1865 it was put into the preamble to the constitution of the new National Conference. Even such Radicals as the Reverend Cyrus A. Bartol of West Church, who opposed this preamble, insisted that the ultimate things were not "open to the roots like cases tried in court, whose decision may be adverse."[38] Events led the Unitarian conservatives, in other words, to affirm that Christianity involved a denial of absolute freedom.

Second, the Unitarians, in attacking romantic idealism, reinforced their own confidence in the premises of the Scottish Realists. Both Channing and Norton accepted their critique of British empiricism and found it an adequate refutation of the skeptical implications of that tradition which Hume laid bare. James Walker, as Alford professor, president of Harvard, and Lowell lecturer, was only one of the many who continued the same position; and in Professor Francis Bowen, the Common Sense philosophy found a champion who devoted his life to the cause. Working out his position along lines marked out by Bishop Butler, William Paley, and the Scottish school, Bowen, virtual tsar of Harvard philosophy for three decades, was the unalterable foe of intuitionalism, pantheism, and the emphasis on consciousness that distinguished all idealistic philosophies. He was also a critical expositor of German philosophy and the author of the first good American history of the movement. Walker and Bowen between themselves edited the works of Reid, Stewart, and Hamilton, and in countless essays and sermons they and many others propagated the Scottish system.

Third, among the more positive results of the Transcendental revolt was the qualified acceptance of certain views and interests that Theodore Parker had emphasized. In a practical way, Parker, with relentless fury, awakened Unitarian interest in the slavery question and other reforms. But he also had a great effect on their religious thinking, particularly in Biblical criticism and the history of religion. A school of Biblical criti-

37. Frederic H. Hedge, *Reason in Religion*, pp. 218–219.
38. *The Index*, No. 520, Dec. 11, 1879.

cism had begun with the work of Joseph Buckminster, Andrews Norton, John Gorham Palfrey, and George Noyes, but Parker must be credited with stimulating interest in the revolutionary historical and Biblical scholarship then being conducted in Germany. Although he ultimately led some men, including John Weiss and Francis E. Abbot, out of the Unitarian fellowship entirely, Parker was also the progenitor of a wide group of Neo-Christians who stayed in the Unitarian communion and considered themselves Christian but who denied the divine function of both Christ and the Bible.

Last and possibly the most important effect of Transcendentalism on Unitarianism was the impulse it gave to idealistic, intuitional philosophy and to the appreciation for the place of feeling and emotion in religion. The degree of acceptance given the new emphasis was varied. The venerable Converse Francis in the Divinity School at Harvard showed a qualified solicitude for it. Frederic Hedge, on the other hand, had championed German views ever since his five years in Germany as a student (1818–23), and he formulated his own Christian philosophy of religion largely on Transcendentalist grounds. A few Unitarians were led out of the Christian fold entirely, but in the years before the Civil War this was far from the rule. For most Unitarians, the Concord Philosophy (Emerson) merely joined with influences from abroad to modify the Common Sense philosophy. Particularly, they were led to state more boldly the Scottish doctrines about the innate moral and intellectual powers of man and to emphasize the psychological aspects of the Realist position. In these ways, Americans were making the same partial accommodations to Kantian conceptions that were being advocated in England and France by Sir William Hamilton and Victor Cousin. Both Walker and Bowen at Harvard were active in these efforts to adjust the old philosophy to the new criticisms. In the later period when the limitations of natural theology became more apparent, Unitarians repaired to Hamilton or Henry L. Mansel, who strove to put the ultimate religious problems beyond the reach of reason.

The whole question of influence is always tenuous and not susceptible to proof, but it is certain that no historian of American thought, either secular or religious, can neglect the important link between Transcendentalism and the almost unanimous academic acceptance of German idealism that prevailed toward the end of the nineteenth century. Long after the Civil War many Unitarians retained a position that was confessional even though the Scottish philosophy had been widely abandoned, but ultimately most liberal Christian philosophers, such as Charles C. Everett of the Harvard Divinity School or Josiah Royce in the philosophy department, deserted the traditional ground. The victory of idealism, of course, extended far beyond the Unitarian circle, but everywhere it tended to extinguish the evangelical component in liberal religious thought. It was the fear of precisely this development that motivated the traditional Unitarian resistance to the gospel of Emerson.

With this outline of the historical development of Unitarianism, we proceed to a discussion of the main Unitarian beliefs, which is opened by a consideration of the two premises most fundamental to their thinking: (1) that the Bible was the very Word of God, and (2) that it was a reasonable revelation requiring philosophic understanding.

"The Bible, the Bible, I say, the Bible only, is the religion of Protestants"[39] ran the oft-quoted declaration by William Chillingworth, who, though a nominal Anglican, was counted among the early English Socinians. His statement would stand for the American Unitarians, for they were by continual profession and demonstration Bible Christians: in the Holy Scriptures was the revealed Word of God and the true guide to salvation. Unitarianism, then, was a way of interpreting the Bible. It was a liberal exegesis of Scripture molded by a rational point of view.

Because Unitarians were, as a group, exceptionally learned in the humanistic arts, the classics, and the history of thought, as well as profoundly aware of their English and colonial traditions, they were deeply convinced that their interpretation of the Bible should be founded in a coherent philosophy of religion. Unlike the Baptists or Methodists or even the liberal Universalists, Unitarians were directly concerned with the development of rationalism, and their exegesis of Scripture must be interpreted in this context and with constant reference to the tension between these Hellenic philosophical ideas and the Judeo-Christian faith. Piety and morality, religion and philosophy were joined. How the full range of the Classical philosophic spectrum—from scientific empiricism to Neo-Platonic mysticism—came to bear on them has been discussed, as has their tendency to view the problems of theology from the Common Sense Realist point of view. This intellectual orientation had great theological consequences.

The place of Scottish Realism in the history of philosophy is by no means easily determined, but certain general relationships must be observed if its role in American thought is to be adequately understood. First among these is the fact that both the Scots and the German idealists as embodied in Kant were stimulated by the skepticism of David Hume and the mechanistic materialism of many Enlightenment philosophers. Their resolutions of the problems raised by these thinkers revealed much

39. William Chillingworth, *The Works of William Chillingworth, M.A.,* ch. VI, paragraph 56, p. 354.

in common. Both attacked the representational perception that had been established since Locke. Both sought that which underlies our experience and showed a similar interest in the detailed analysis of consciousness and the advance of psychological speculation. The differences are equally important. The Scots were traditional, derivative, and assertive, whereas Kant was critical, reconstructive, and immensely more original. Most of the Scots (Reid being a partial exception) emphasized underlying assumptions, whereas Kant's conditioning factor was his insistence that all human knowledge was phenomenal. In one sense, therefore, Kant's critique was a grave for Reid no less than for Locke.

A second and perhaps more profound observation, however, is that the Scots recurred to philosophical motives that lay far behind Kant. They continued the Classical enthusiasm of Shaftesbury, building on the speculative tradition of Greece. They accepted the Realist faith of Plato and Aristotle that God created minds that could perceive the essence of things. Like Herbert they appealed to Platonic ideas that the principles of virtue cannot be learned or taught, because they are innate. As emphasized by the greatest of the French Common Sense Realists, Théodore Jouffroy, their ethic was based on the Aristotelian idea of universal order, the relation of each individual to this cosmic rationale, and the identification of the Good with the fulfillment of one's essential nature. The main principles of Classical natural theology, like the argument from design, were refurbished and used. For this reason it is not surprising that Victor Cousin, who like Sir William Hamilton took many Kantian ideas into his own eclectic philosophy, edited the works of the Neo-Platonist Proclus and translated the works of Plato, or that echoes of the Cambridge Platonists can be heard in American Unitarian sermons.

These considerations help explain why Channing could blend the religious pietism of Hopkins with the Platonic idea of love and combine both with the ethics of the Scottish Realists. The philosophical basis of traditional Unitarian thought was never widely separated from that of the Transcendentalists, and Channing is a representative of this blending. Both are part of the revolt against empiricism. The crucial differences were two: (1) Unitarians insisted on the necessity of the Christian confession, whereas thoroughgoing Transcendentalists did not, and (2) the Unitarians' classical love of order, duty, and rectitude excluded romantic individualism and irrationalism. Because of these two factors, it is important to consider here the amazing adaptability of Scottish Realism to liberal Christian theology.

By denying the existence of the Cartesian and Lockean ideas that had been interposed between reality and the mind, the Scottish philosophy precluded both the nihilism of Hume and the solipsism of Fichte. It asserted that the active and moral powers of man provided the basis for ethical theory just as the intellectual powers enabled man to understand the world and interpret the Word. Scottish Realists could emphasize the human affections and moral powers and sound like Transcendentalists. On the other hand, emphasizing the intellectual powers, they could berate intuitionalists and pantheists in the name of science. Such dualism avoided the errors of both materialism and pantheism. Separation of God from man preserved the Christian idea of God's transcendence and made revelation necessary; yet it reestablished both the evidential and the deductive arguments basic to natural theology. Considering these advantages, it is hardly surprising that Scottish philosophy was so vigorously defended and ubiquitously used.

Natural theology was the foundation of Unitarian thought. It was constructed from a wide range of metaphysical arguments and empirical evidences, most of which had been developed in Classical times, Christianized in the Middle Ages, and elaborated by Deists and Christian rationalists in the eighteenth century. They followed the general lines laid down by Butler and Paley as modified by the critique of Hume and the reconstruction of the Scots. These reasonings proved the existence of a benevolent God who sustained physical and moral order in the universe. Immortality was made a necessary corollary to the state of affairs thus demonstrated. These truths were corroborated and enlarged upon by the Bible, the veracity of which was attested no less by its basic reasonableness than by the miracles. Christian doctrine, in turn, was interpreted so as to harmonize with the canons of natural theology and philosophy.

The name Unitarian does not indicate the correct doctrinal emphasis. The dogma that gave this name to the Liberal Faith was not the fundamental one to the new departure. Optimistic views about the human condition and prospects provided the most immediate point of departure from orthodoxy. The first great issue for the Unitarians was the problem of human destiny, though their conclusions on the subject were expressed in the context of their doctrines on God's benevolence. This new estimate of humankind conditioned the departure from Calvinism, and it merits discussion before their ideas of the doctrines of God, the Trinity, and related matters.

Historically, these views stem from the Renaissance. Classical thought provided the rational concept of a person's dignity, and Christianity provided the dynamic sense of destiny. The idea of progress took the place of the idea of Providence. Science, the new learning, expanding commerce, and growing prosperity increased the fervor with which the faith was held. One can discern during the post-Renaissance centuries a rising tide of optimism, a glowing sense of progress, and a lively hope that posterity would see a better world wherein reason reigned, justice according to natural law prevailed, and superstition and terror languished. With such hopes, the doctrine that a God of love should have created a depraved humanity became increasingly incongruous. The incongruity was, therefore, dissolved completely in the thought of the English Deists. That these ideas should inform the liberal Christian view of human nature was inevitable.

The American Unitarians, however, were not prepared to accept the Deist view. Their optimism in such matters was heavily qualified, as the immense popularity of the melancholy Butler reveals. The Reverend George E. Ellis of the Harvard Divinity School, summing up *A Half-Century of the Unitarian Controversy* in 1857, made these limits clear, and he spoke for his contemporaries as well:

Unitarians do not affirm that human beings are born *holy;* nor that the original elements of human nature are free from germs which grow and develop, if unrestrained, into sin. . . . Unitarians do not deny that all men are actually sinners, needing the renewing grace and the forgiveness of God, depending upon the Gospel of Christ as a remedial and redeeming religion, and having no hope other than that which Christ offers. Unitarians do not deny the great mystery which invests sin and evil, nor profess to have any marked advantage over Orthodoxy in looking back of that mystery or in dealing with it.[40]

What Unitarians found repulsive was the doctrine that man through the fault of Adam was totally depraved and incapable even of turning to accept the grace of God. "Now it is the height of absurdity," wrote Andrew Preston Peabody, "to maintain, that an almighty being can create what he hates and abhors, or that an infinitely good and holy being can create what is essentially evil and vile. It is intrinsically necessary, that whatever God creates should be good, very good, perfect in its kind and for its purpose."[41] Sin was man's doing, argued the Unitarians. The doctrine of irresistible, predestined grace was as reprehensible as physical determinism or necessitarianism. Christ through his Atonement reconciled human beings to God, and now they are morally obligated to repent and ask for God's saving Grace. "Yet Unitarianism recognizes the deep and the unsounded perplexities of this subject. No serious person can ever think or speak otherwise than with a profound and oppressive solemnity and dread about sin, the perversion and debasement of morals, the source of unmeasured woe, the defying attitude of human beings toward God."[42]

40. George Edward Ellis, *A Half-Century of the Unitarian Controversy*, p. 55.
41. Andrew Preston Peabody, *Lectures on Christian Doctrine*, p. 125.
42. George Edward Ellis, *A Half-Century of the Unitarian Controversy*, p. 87.

People were free, and it was the duty of the Church to confront them with the Gospel.

The nature of God was revealed in the Bible, the Old Testament proclaiming His omnipotence and justice, and the New Testament, His mercy. Thus the divine benevolence that the world evidenced was demonstrated by Him who so loved the world that he sent His son to redeem it. The cruel, vindictive God of Calvin and Edwards seemed unthinkable in this light, and Channing's first pronouncement of the Unitarian Controversy needed no reformulation or modification in the years that followed:

We consider the errours which relate to Christ's person as of little or no importance compared with the errour of those who teach, that God brings us into life wholly depraved and wholly helpless, that he leaves multitudes without that aid which is indispensably necessary to their repentance, and then plunges them into everlasting burnings and unspeakable torture, for not repenting.[43]

That God is love was the basic tenet of Unitarianism, and by love they meant human love. They thought in terms of an understandable human category which the doctrines of total depravity and predestination violated. The human heart and moral faculties proclaimed the absurdity of a God of love creating persons to be lost in sin. "We worship," wrote Channing, "that God, whom Jesus in his last moments worshipped, when he said, 'Father, into thy hands I commend my spirit.' . . . This worship we are persuaded, is the spring of purity, joy and hope, and we trust that it will prove to us a source of unfailing consolation amidst the trials, reproaches and rude assaults of the world."[44]

The problem of God, however, immediately involved the Trinity, the mystery of God the Father, Son, and Holy Spirit being one-in-three. On this matter, Unitarians were agreed on only one thing: that there is no distinction of persons in God. Over and over again they repeated that there is but one God, not three. Yet generally theirs was but a moderate revision of traditional doctrine. "Some suppose that Trinitarianism consists in believing in the Father, the Son, and the Holy Spirit. But we all believe in these," wrote Channing, "we all believe that the *Father* sent the *Son*, and gives to those that ask, the *Holy Spirit*. We are all Trinitarians, if this belief is Trinitarianism."[45] *Unitarian* was for the Americans a generic term. It included a wide variety of dissents, most of them

43. William E. Channing, *A Letter to the Rev. Samuel C. Thacher on the Aspersions Contained in a Late Number of the Panoplist*, p. 14.
44. William E. Channing, *Remarks on the Rev. Dr. Worcester's Letter to Mr. Channing*, p. 27.
45. *Ibid.*, p. 38.

being based on the writings of a broad range of nominally orthodox British writers. Channing affirmed explicitly the doctrine of Christ's pre-existence and asserted it to be the view of the majority of his brethren, although he admitted to disagreements. There was no argument, however, among traditional Unitarians as to the divinity of Jesus.

In the statement now given [wrote William Greenleaf Eliot, Jr., in 1852], I have expressed my whole belief concerning Christ. In the words of Peter, I say, "He is the Christ, the Son of the Living God." . . . We adopt it, word for word, as the confession of faith in this church, and are willing to receive no other. It constitutes us Unitarians. . . . You will . . . find, among nominal Unitarians, some who have almost no faith at all; who hold to Jesus only as they might hold to Socrates. I pass no sentence upon them . . . but I do say, that they are not to be taken as the exponents of the Unitarian faith.[46]

Perhaps nothing reveals the central position of Christ in Unitarianism so well as their constant emphasis on the Atonement. Channing made the substance of their belief clear at the outset of the controversy. "Jesus Christ, by his sufferings and intercession obtains forgiveness for sinful men, or . . . on account, or in consequence of what Christ has done and suffered, the punishment of sin is averted from the penitent, and blessings, forfeited by sin, are bestowed."[47] Channing, like many others, was a professed agnostic as to how this was accomplished. It was a problem that Scriptures seemed not to elucidate. Yet it can be safely said that in general Unitarians discarded the idea of the vicarious sacrifice and with it the satisfaction theory of the Atonement. Their reasons for doing so are almost made explicit in Peabody's bare description of that doctrine.

God has affixed to every sin . . . the penalty of eternal torments. God's justice forbids him to forgive man's iniquity, unless this penalty be in some way satisfied. Christ interposed, and took upon himself the weight of agony and torment, which those who are forgiven would otherwise have borne, and, because he thus suffered in their stead, they go clear.[48]

Unitarians formulated a doctrine more reasonably related to their concept of a loving God. They granted that the life and death of Christ achieved a reconciliation, but they insisted that it was essentially to reconcile guilty humanity to a Father of unchangeable love; for without the Cross, God's love would not have had its utmost manifestation. Dr. Gannett indicated how far such a view came from eliminating the doctrine's importance: "The fact is the essence of the gospel, and only they

46. William Greenleaf Eliot, *Our Lord Jesus Christ,* p. 41.
47. William E. Channing, *Remarks on the Rev. Dr. Worcester's Second Letter to Mr. Channing,* p. 14.
48. Andrew Preston Peabody, *Lectures on Christian Doctrine,* 2nd ed., p. 168.

who, in the apostle's phrase 'have received the atonement,' can have any personal knowledge of Christ as Saviour."[49] Nor, in 1857, was Gannett any more willing than Channing had been to rationalize the doctrine.

We need not understand in order to be saved. I repeat it,—I would to Heaven it could be repeated, with the voice as of many waters, that should drown the confusion of foolish, scandalous strife!—the mystery that lies behind the cross is not a subject for faith to lay hold of. That is God's secret counsel, which we should be careful lest we ignorantly, and therefore profanely, discuss.[50]

The Unitarian conception of piety was formed against the background of these central doctrines. Regeneration remained theoretically as important as ever, and correlatively so did worship. Unitarians felt the need for the purifying vision of God, the source of love; human defiance of God must be overcome. William H. Channing's little volume *The Perfect Life* is their finest statement of this aspect of religious aspiration. It reveals both the Biblical and rational aspects of their heritage. In considering the relation of religion to rational power, he echoes the vision of Plato's *Phaedrus:* "For it [religion] alone reveals to us the connection of the Intellect with God, its derivation from His Wisdom, its nearness to His Reason, its capacity of everlasting reception of His Light of Truth. Separated from God, I can regard my intellect only as a power, which is to endure a brief span, and which can advance but little beyond its present bounds."[51] This is the key to a rich tradition of mystic spirituality that inspires the sermons and devotions of such men as Francis William Pitt Greenwood and Ephraim Peabody.

Yet in Channing, as in many other Unitarians in whose religious writing runs this mystic strain, there was a fear of contemplative quietism. Morality and praise for the doers of the Word remained preeminent. Asseverations of the need for practical Christianity are legion. Their practical injunctions were not distinctive, however, and it is rather to their ethical theory that one must refer to see the spirit of their views. The idea that people were essentially selfish, they abhorred, and they underlined all the strictures of the Scottish Realists against the proponents of this view (Hobbes, Hume, Paley, Mandeville, and many others were refuted on this count). "Self-development," wrote Francis Bowen, is the primary goal of man, not "mere enjoyment" or "gratification of desire." Man was favored by a moral faculty, a conscience, "by the possession of which even more than the gift of reason, man is raised above all the other orders of created being. . . . Conscience is the inlet of a new set

49. William C. Gannett, "Mysteries," in *Ezra Stiles Gannett,* p. 436.
50. *Ibid.*
51. William H. Channing, *The Works of William E. Channing, D.D.,* p. 118.

of ideas. . . . The object of the intellect is truth; that of conscience is duty."[52] More explicitly, it was through love—love of others and love of God, for they tended away from Edwards' and Hopkins' distinction between the two—that the good life was achieved. In this manner their moral theory joined hands with their estimation of human goodness.

As to the content of their ethic, Unitarians agreed that the injunctions of Jesus were perfect, a supreme moral commitment. There was nothing greater than his exultation of the gentle virtues. Other ethical systems (such as those of Cicero or Zeno) or the ethics of other religions were compared and found wanting. Even James Freeman Clarke, after his extensive studies of comparative religion, recurred to the view that Christianity was a pleroma, or fullness of knowledge that "includes everything, [and] excludes nothing but limitation and deficiency."[53] It was also argued that no other system created such perfection as Jesus, since Socrates was on occasion coarse; Cicero, vain; and Cato the Elder, cruel. But Unitarians did not stop with this comparative weighing of ethical principles and results. They urged that the real importance of the Christian ethic was that it went beyond the Old Testament and unified sin.

Sin, as a definite quality, apart from sins, and possible even where there are no conspicuous sins, is an exclusively Christian idea; and it is of infinite moral importance. Sin is hydra-headed, yet has but one heart. . . . Its heart is autonomy, self-will, the ignoring of the divine will and law, the living without God in the world.[54]

The observation, of course, is not original; nor was it considered to be. Either as uttered in 1884 as lectures to Harvard ethics classes or in 1804 in the early controversy, it was the same. The important thing is that traditional Unitarianism never evaluated the Christian ethic solely in terms of the comparative value of its principles. Repentance and regeneration remained fundamental. "Without Christ we can do nothing," declared the Reverend F. W. P. Greenwood, the great preacher of King's Chapel, "nothing in the concerns and ways of our highest moral life."[55]

The hope for a moral life, therefore, rested on faith in the love of God. Humankind's estrangement from the ideal of the good could be ended only by the reconciliation with God made possible by the life and message of Christ, the one mediator. His sacrificial death had not satisfied God but had made virtue and salvation possible for humanity: this

52. Francis Bowen, *Metaphysics and Ethics,* pp. 275 and 296.
53. James F. Clarke, *Ten Great Religions,* p. 493.
54. Andrew Preston Peabody, *Moral Philosophy, a Series of Lectures,* pp. 202–203.
55. F. W. P. Greenwood, *Sermons of Consolation,* p. 146.

was the mysterious meaning of the Cross. Its efficacy was "Man-ward."[56]
The Cross, moreover, was the symbol of the ultimate rule of God's justice
and the assurance of eternal reward.

Such then was the Unitarianism of the liberals who severed their con-
nections with New England orthodoxy and took their separate stand on
the American religious scene. These views informed that influential
group of men who controlled the movement down to the Civil War and
after. Along the lines of this religious and philosophical synthesis, the
missionary activity of the new denomination was carried forward. From
the unproclaimed Unitarianism of such pioneers as Charles Chauncy to
the liberal theology of such later leaders as Henry W. Bellows, Frederic
H. Hedge, and James Freeman Clarke, the core of evangelical Christian
doctrine was retained, though to varying degrees.

As Americans, first in the colonies, later in a young, expanding nation,
most of them felt the impact of material progress, secularization, and
education. They were confronted, therefore, by what can nearly always
be resolved philosophically into the demands of rationalism. Yet they remained New Englanders to whom Puritanism was a very real heritage,
and although many orthodox dogmas were sacrificed, the party that resisted Emerson and Parker never bowed abjectly to Hellenic or modern
demands.

The result was a numerically small, geographically limited, but nevertheless strikingly homogeneous and influential group. A half-century
incloses its period of greatest power and efflorescence; but by the time
these traditional Unitarians were outnumbered in their National Conference, they had made an intellectual contribution to the nation's heritage
that went far beyond the boundaries of religion.

56. George Edward Ellis, *A Half-Century of the Unitarian Controversy*, pp.
191ff.

1 ORIGINS AND FOUNDING

🕮 Natural Religion as Distinguished from Revealed

EBENEZER GAY (1696–1787)

*E*benezer Gay, the father of American Unitarianism, was born in Dedham, Massachusetts, in August 1696. After graduating from Harvard College in 1714, he studied theology for several years. In 1717 he was ordained and installed in the Hingham church, sixteen miles outside of Boston. For over sixty-eight years he served this church. His influence on New England theology was substantial, because of both his renowned learning and his longevity. In his lifetime he witnessed the shift from Puritanism to emerging liberalism.

Gay had little sympathy with the work of the Great Awakening, sharing this sentiment with his close friends Chauncy and Mayhew, the first a colleague, the second a former student. By 1740 his increasing liberalism was evident, especially in his preaching, which was popular in the Boston area. In politics, however, Gay remained a Tory, praying for the king of England and his family at a time when his congregation was staunchly in favor of American independence.

But it is as a theologian that Gay is remembered: to read him is to grasp a mind capable of balancing Newton and Calvin while standing on a firm foundation of Scripture and Locke. His astuteness can be seen in his Dudleian Lecture, delivered at Harvard in 1759.

The lectures had been established eight years earlier in the will of Chief Justice Paul Dudley. Two of the defined topics were natural and revealed religion. Both Arminians and Calvinists had been invited to speak in the past; Gay, however, represented an intellect well versed in both systems and yet not explicitly identifiable with either, although his views about the Trinity had begun to shift during the Great Awakening. In his lecture, therefore, Gay stated that the gospel of Christ has provided a light to lighten the modern deistical Gentiles. The Christian of the mid-eighteenth century had to approach the Bible with an awareness of philosophy as well as theology, reason as well as revelation. This lecture

The sources of all documents are listed in the Bibliography alphabetically by author. Sources ascribed to institutions are listed alphabetically by institution and by the first primary word of the document's title.

signaled academic support for the full-fledged Unitarianism which would emerge in the early nineteenth century.

ROM. ii. 14, 15. *For when the Gentiles, which have not the Law, do by Nature the Things contained in the Law; these having not the Law, are a Law unto themselves: Which shew the Work of the Law written in their Hearts, their Conscience also bearing witness, and their thoughts the mean while accusing, or else excusing one another.*

The Belief of GOD's Existence is most essentially fundamental to all Religion, and having been at the first of the *Dudleian* Lectures established; the moral Obligation which it induceth upon the Nature of Man, may be the Subject of our present Inquiry.

A Devout *Hermit* being asked, How he could profit in Knowledge, living in a Desart, without Men and Books? answered, 'I have one Book which I am always studying, and turning over Day and Night: The Heavens, the Earth and the Waters, are the Leaves of which it consists.' The Characters of the Deity are plainly legible in the whole Creation around us: And if we open the Volume of our own Nature, and look within, we find there a Law written;—a Rule of virtuous Practice prescribed.

Religion and Law (divine) are Words of promiscuous Use; denoting in the general Signification thereof, *An Obligation lying upon Men to do those Things which the Perfections of God, relative unto them, do require of them.* In this Definition (whether exact and full, or not,) I mean to imply all Things incumbent on such reasonable Creatures as Men are, toward all Beings with which they are concerned, GOD, the Supreme, one another, and themselves; and which are incumbent on them, by vertue of the Perfections of God, in the Relation there is betwixt Him and them: other Obligation which can be supposed to any of the same Things, not being of the religious Kind. And in the doing those Things to which Religion is the Obligation, are included, besides the actual Performance, the Principles, Motives and Ends thereof; all that is necessary to render any Acts of Men, whether internal or external, such as the Perfections of the Deity require.

Religion is divided into natural and revealed:—*Revealed* Religion, is that which God hath made known to Men by the immediate Inspiration of his Spirit, the Declarations of his Mouth, and Instructions of his Prophets: *Natural,* that which bare Reason discovers and dictates: As 'tis delineated by the masterly Hand of St. *Paul,* the Apostle of the Gentiles, in the Words of holy Scripture now read—Which I take as a proper and advantageous Introduction to my intended Discourse on this Head, *Viz.*

That Religion is, in some measure, discoverable by the Light, and practicable to the Strength, of Nature; and is so far fitly called *Natural* by Divines and learned Men. The Religion which is possible to be discover'd by the Light, and practis'd by the Power of Nature, consists in rend'ring all those inward and outward Acts of Respect, Worship and Obedience unto God, which are suitable to the Excellence of his all-perfect Nature, and our Relation to Him, who is our Creator, Preserver, Benefactor, Lord, and Judge;—And in yielding to our Fellow-Men that Regard, Help and Comfort, which their partaking of the same Nature, and living in Society with us, give them a Claim to;—And in managing our Souls and Bodies, in their respective Actions and Enjoyments, in a way agreable to our *Make,* and conducive to our Ease and Happiness: And doing all from a Sense of the Deity, imposing the Obligation, and approving the Discharge of it. For 'tis a Regard to Him in every moral Duty that consecrates it, and makes it truly an Act of Religion. These Things, indeed, are contained in the Revelation of God, which affords the chief Assistance to our knowing and doing of them; and yet they belong to the Religion of Nature, so far as Nature supplies any Light and Strength to the Discovery and Practice of them.

I. That Religion is in some measure, discoverable by the Light of Nature. The Obligation lying on us to do those Things which the Perfections of God, as related to us, require, is discernable in the Light of natural Reason. This Faculty of the human Soul, exercised in the Contemplation of the universal Frame of Nature, or of any Parts thereof; and in the Observation of the general Course of Providence, or of particular Events therein, may convince Men of the Existence and Attributes of God, the alwise, powerful and good Maker, Upholder, and Governor of all Things. It may be questioned whether the reasoning Faculty, as it is in the Bulk of Mankind, be so acute and strong, as from the necessary eternal Existence of the Deity (which is as evident and incontestible, as that any Thing is) to prove all other Perfections do belong to God in an infinite Degree. If it be not easy to the Apprehension, that the Idea of necessary Self-existence includes every Perfection, and every Degree thereof, which can possibly be, or which implies not a Contradiction; yet it is plain to the lowest Capacity of those who, with a little Attention, survey the Works of God, that He is a Being of such Perfection: And that, since He is their Maker, Owner, and Benefactor, to whom they are indebted for all that they are, and have, and on whom they depend for all they need, or can enjoy; they are bound to yield unto Him, in the Temper of their Minds, and Manner of their Behaviour, toward Him, and his Creatures they are concerned with, all that Regard which Religion founded in the Nature of God, and in the Nature of Man, and the Relation there is between them implies. They may perceive their Obligation to reverence, adore, and worship a Being of such Perfection and Glory, as God is—to invoke the Almighty—pray unto Him, who is able to perform all Things for them; to give Thanks to Him, from whom they receive all Blessings; to aim and endeavour to please their Lord and Master, to whom they are accountable for their Actions, and who is just to punish their Offences, and bountiful to reward their Services.—They may discern the Wisdom and Goodness of their Maker, in designing and fitting them for a social Life in this World, and thence the sacred Engagements they are under to mutual Benevolence, commutative Justice, and all such Demeanour in their various Stations and Relations, as tends to promote the common Welfare, and the Good of Individuals.—Their Souls may know right well, how wonderfully God hath made them with Powers and Faculties superior to any bodily Endowments; which should not therefore be subjected to the Sway of bruitish Appetites and blind Passions. Reason may know it's [sic] divine Right to govern, to maintain it's [sic] Empire in the Soul, regulating the Passions and Affections; directing them to proper Objects, and stinting them to just Measures. Nature affords considerable Light for the Discovery, and Arguments for the Proof, of such Parts of Religion. . . . The Law of Nature is given by the God of Nature, who is Lord of all. He enacted it by creating and establishing a World of Beings in such Order, as he hath done. He publishes it to rational Creatures (as is necessary to it's binding them) in making them capable to learn from his Works, what is good, and what is required of them. Natural Conscience is his Voice, telling them their Duty. This (in part) is the *work of the Law in their Hearts.*—'Tis the Engravement of it there, answerable to the Writing of it on Tables, in order to it's being made known: And so Men are *a Law unto themselves,* are supply'd with a Rule of Actions within their own Breasts. The Righteousness which is of Nature (to adopt the Language of Inspiration) speaketh on some such wise, as doth that which is of Faith: *Say not in thine Heart who shall ascend into Heaven; or who shall descend into the Deep,* to bring us the Knowledge of our Duty? *The Word is nigh thee, even in thy Heart,* shewing thee what thou oughtest to do: *Conscience also bearing witness,* testifying for or against Men; according as they obey or disobey the Word of Reason, which is the Word of God: And so *their Thoughts*—the general Notions of Good and Evil in them, make them either to accuse themselves as Transgressors of a known Law, or else excuse them, as not having culpably done any Thing against it. In the due Exercise of their natural Faculties, Men are capable of attaining some Knowledge of God's Will, and their Duty, manifested in his Works, as if it were written in legible Characters on the Tables of their Hearts. And 'tis on this Account, that any Part of Religion is called Natural; and stands distinguished, in *Theology,* from that which is revealed.

II. That Religion is, in some Measure, practicable to the Strength of Nature. There is doing, as well as knowing, by Nature, the Things contained in the Law of it. Knowing them is but in order to the doing them: And the Capacity to know them would be in vain, (which nothing in Nature is) if there was no Ability to do them. Whoever observes the divine Workmanship in human Nature, and takes a Survey of the Powers and Faculties with which it is endowed, must needs see that it was designed and framed for the Practice of Virtue: That Man is not merely so much lumpish Matter, or a *mechanical* Engine, that moves only by the Direction of an impelling Force; but that he hath a Principle of Action within himself, and is an Agent in the strict and proper Sense of the Word. The special Endowment of his Nature, which constitutes him such, is the Power of Self-determination, or Freedom of Choice; his being possessed of which is as self-evident, as the Explanation of the Manner of it's operating, is difficult: He feels himself free to act one Way, or another: And as he is capable of distinguishing between different Actions, of the moral Kind; so is he likewise of chusing which he will do, and which leave undone. Further to qualify our Nature for virtuous or religious Practice (which necessarily must be of Choice) the Author of it hath annexed a secret Joy or Complacence of Mind to such Practice, and as sensible a Pain or Displicence to the contrary. And this inward Judgment which every one passes on his own Actions, is enforced with another Principle, which belongs more or less to our common Nature, viz. a Regard to the Judgment that is passed upon our Conduct by other Beings; especially Beings whose Favour or Displeasure is of any Importance to us: There is a secret Satisfaction of Soul, which ariseth from their Approbation; and as exquisite a Sense of Pain and Uneasiness from their Censure.—The Spirit of Man being thus formed within him, it is (according to the original Design and wise Contrivance of our Maker) naturally disposed toward Religion: It hath an Inclination thereto implanted in it, which under the Direction of right Reason, is an inward Spring of Motion and Action, when Reason alone would not give sufficient Quickness and Vigour in pursuing it's Dictates.

There may be something in the intelligent moral World analogous to Attraction in the material System—something that inclines and draws Men toward God, the Centre of their Perfection, and consummate Object of their Happiness; and which, if it's Energy were not obstructed, would as certainly procure such Regularity in the States and Actions of all intelligent Beings in the spiritual World, as that of Attraction doth in the Positions and Motions of all the Bodies in the material World.—"Created intelligent Beings (says Dr. *Cheyne*) are Images of the SUPREME IN-FINITE, as he calleth God. In Him there is an infinite Desire and Ardor of possessing and enjoying Himself, and his own infinite Perfections, in order to render Him happy; He himself is the sole Object of his own, and of the Felicity of all his Creatures. There must therefore be an Image of this his infinite Desire after Happiness in all his intelligent Creatures—a Desire after Happiness in a Re-union with Him. An intelligent Being, coming out of the Hands of infinite Perfection, with an Aversion, or even Indifferency, to be reunited with it's Author, the Source of it's utmost Felicity, is such a Shock, and Deformity in the beautiful Analogy of Things, such a Breach and Gap in the harmonious Uniformity, observable in all the Works of the Almighty, and that in the noblest and highest Part of his Works, as is not consistent with finite Wisdom and Perfection, much less with the supremely infinite Wisdom of the ALLPER-FECT.—This Principle was most certainly implanted in the Creation of intelligent Beings, in the very Fund and Substance of their Natures, thô there remains but few Footsteps and Instances of it's Being or Effects.—It wonderfully analogises with that of Attraction in the material World: As to the SUPREME INFINITE, it may very properly be called, his *Attraction* of them; and as to them, their *Central Tendency,* or Gravitation (so to speak) toward Him." This Tendency in human Nature, which that penetrating Enquirer into both the constituent Parts of it, accurately observes, is an Inclination to Religion—to many Offices and Acts of it, by which Men return and re-unite to the Author of their Beings; who hath so made all Nations of them, that they should seek the Lord, if haply they might *feel after him, and find him.* There is in the common Nature, which all partake of, a Propension to Acts, not only of human Kindness, but also of divine Worship; which excites to the Performance of them, when proper Occasions of doing them occur, without previous, express Deliberation and Determination concerning them: And to forbear them is a painful Restraint upon Nature; and to do the contrary, is thwarting it's Inclination, and wresting it from it's Bent.—There is observable in Man a *natural Proclivity* (as *Origen* termeth it) towards his Maker; to acknowledge God; especially on Occasions of Need or Distress to have recourse unto Him. And from hence ariseth so universal a Consent of Mankind in paying some Homage to the Deity, which is not always directed to the true, because so many blindly follow natural Inclination, without consulting Reason, which should be it's Guide. There is such a Disposition in human Nature as makes Religion agreable to it; so that Divines of great Name have affirm'd it to be essential thereto, and that which raises it above the Brutal; and Philosophers, from what is innate to Man, have defined him a *Creature capable of Religion.*—Whoever attends to this inward Furniture of our Nature for Religion, may easily perceive it to be God's Workmanship, primarily created unto good Works, that Men might walk in them. His Formation of them qualifys them, in a measure, for religious Practice; as for Regeneration, or Renovation of them doth more to. And his fitting them by Nature therefor, is a Work of his, to which the Work of Sanctification, in his furnishing them with Grace to evangelical Obedience, beareth Analogy. The former is the Work of the Law written in their Hearts, that they may do, as well as know, what it enjoins: The latter is the Impression of the Gospel upon them, that, thro' Christ's strengthening them, they may do what it requires. . . .

How far the Duties of Religion are possible to be performed by the Strength of Nature, in a lapsed State; and to what Measure of divine Approbation and Acceptance, Reason, unenlightened by Revelation, may not be able to determine.—The Law of Nature is purely a Law of Works, and requires perfect Obedience, which the Transgressors of it, as all Men are, cannot yield to it: And whether that which is wanting in their Obedience, may be supplied by Repentance and Humility in them, and by Mercy and Pardon in God, cannot be certainly known without a Revelation of his Will, on which it wholly depends. The Goodness of God, in the general Course of his Providence, toward sinful Mankind, sheweth Him to be placable, and leadeth them to Repentance; but doth not assure them of Pardon upon it, much less of the Reward of eternal Life, for imperfect, tho' it should be sincere, Obedience. If Reason doth not see and pronounce it inconsistent with the Perfections of God to pardon Sinners, on the sole Condition of their Repentance; yet it cannot infer from them, that he will:—All that it can say, is in the Words of a Heathen King, *Who can tell if the Lord will turn from his Anger, that we perish not?* Such Inducement they may have to repent, and turn from their evil Ways:—And it may farther encourage them to better Obedience, by suggesting the Consideration which may be had by a merciful God of the Frailty of their Nature, and the gracious Allowances He may possibly make them, whose Strength, so weak'ned as it is, cannot reach the Heighth of their Duty. In the Prescription of Duty, 'tis not unreasonable, that what may be required, even in Rigour, should be precisely determined, thô in Execution of Justice, or Dispensation of Recompence, Consideration may be had of our Weakness; whereby both the Authority of our Governor may be preserved, and his Clemency glorified. Men's Thoughts or Consciences accusing them for the Violation of the Law of Nature, implies a Fear which is not groundless, that they shall be brought into

Judgment: And their Thoughts excusing and approving of them for do-ing, in some Measure, what the Law requires, implies a Hope, which may not be altogether vain, that they shall be accepted. Thô it should be, as one saith, "That all the moral Virtues are so many Cyphers—unavailing Nothings, unless the Deity be placed as the principal Figure at the Head of them;" yet if practised out of any Sense of Duty to God, and with a View to pleasing Him, as it is possible they may be, and have been, shall we say, they are meerly splendid Vices in his Eyes; and that the most humble Prayers of natural Men are Blasphemies in his Ears? May there not be such a conscientious doing *by Nature the Things contained in the Law* of it, as, thrô the Riches of divine Bounty and Goodness, shall in some low Measure, compar'd with doing the same by Grace, be acceptable and rewardable? May not a *God of Knowledge, by whom Actions are weighed,* discern some Good in those done by the Strength of Nature, and approve the honest, thô weak, Efforts thereof, to serve him; and thereupon, besides outward Favours (of which He is liberal to all both good and bad Men) grant the Succours of his Grace, enabling them to do the same, and other Things to better Acceptance, and to the obtaining a greater Reward, even that which the Christian Revelation proposes; and is thereby differenced and distinguished from natural Religion?

And, now, if what hath been so imperfectly spoken, be according to the Truth in Nature, and not inconsistent with the Christian Verity, the proper Use and Improvement of it is, *To form a just Estimate of Natural Religion;* and guard against the dangerous Extremes in our Regards to it—Not to have a debasing, nor a too exalted Notion of it.

I. We should not depreciate and cry down Natural Religion, on Pre-tence of advancing the Honour of Revealed—as if they were two oppo-site Religions, and could no more stand together in the same Temple than Dagon and the Ark of God. Whatever Distinction we observe be-tween them, there is no Contrariety in the one to the other: They subsist harmoniously together, and mutually strengthen and confirm each other. Revealed Religion is an *Additional* to Natural; built, not on the Ruins, but on the strong and everlasting Foundations of it. Nothing therefore can be vainer and more preposterous, than the Attempt to raise the Credit of the one, upon the Discredit of the other; as if to allow any Virtue, or any Praise, in natural Religion, would be derogatory to the Honour of revealed: And to represent the former as insignificant to the grand Pur-pose of Religion, and chief End of Man; the glorifying and enjoying God:—As availing nothing towards Man's Recovery from a sinful State, and his Attainment unto Holiness and Happiness—As if his knowing and doing *by Nature the Things contained in the Law* of it, could be no more acceptable to his Maker, nor profitable to himself, than his Ignorance and Neglect of them: And whatever Improvement and Progress he made in natural Religion, he was not a Step nearer the Kingdom of God; nor a fairer Candidate for Heaven than a *Heathen-Man, or a Publican.* The Law of Nature, like that of *Moses,* may be serviceable unto Men, *as a School-Master to bring them to Christ,* for higher Instruction; especially where the Means of such are afforded; and so usher them into a State of Grace. Notwithstanding the Insufficiency of natural Religion to their Salvation, yet it may, in some Measure, prepare them to be Partakers of the Benefit, without any Diminution of the Glory of the Gospel, which is the Grant of it, or Detraction from the Merits of our blessed Redeemer, who is the Author of it. It is only by Grace that sinful Men can be saved; yet by making some good Use of their rational Powers (weakened as they be) in the Study and Practice of natural Religion, they may be in a better Preparation of Mind to comply with the Offers and Operations of divine Grace, than if they wholly give up themselves to the Conduct of sensual Appetites & Passions. Whether those Offers & Operations of divine Grace are designed for, and ever vouchsafed to such as are not favoured with Revelation; and it be possible for them to obtain Mercy, in the Day when God by Jesus Christ shall judge the Things which they have done, *according to the Gospel;* is a Point which Revelation only can determine; and is not my Province to discuss.

In the Preference we give to revealed Religion, we should not for the sake of any particular Truth we apprehend to be deliver'd in it, hastily renounce a Principle of natural Religion, seeming contrary thereto. Both should be carefully examined, before either be rejected: Else we may err, after the manner which the *Sadduces* did, *Not knowing the Scriptures, nor the Power of God.* It must be owing to our Ignorance, or Misapprehension of Things hard to be understood in the Book of Nature, and the Holy Bible, that we cannot reconcile them. No Doctrine, or Scheme of Religion, should be advanced, or received as scriptural and divine, which is plainly and absolutely inconsistent with the Perfections of God, and the Possibility of Things. Absurdities and Contradictions (from which few human Schemes are entirely free) are not to be obtruded upon our Faith. No Pretence of Revelation can be sufficient for the Admission of them. The manifest Absurdity of any Doctrine, is a stronger Argument that it is not of God, than any other Evidence can be that it is. "A Revelation must be agreable to the Nature of God, and Possibility of Things." We are not rashly to determine concerning one that it is not so, because we don't easily and clearly see it to be so: Nor plead that any may be so, which contradicts all our natural Ideas of the Attributes of God. To say, in Defence of any religious Tenets, reduced to Absurdity, that the Perfections of God, his Holiness, Justice, Goodness, are quite different Things in Him, from what, in an infintely lower Degree, they are in Men, is to overthrow all Religion both natural and revealed; and make our Faith, as well as Reason vain.—For, if we have no right Notions of the Deity, (as 'tis certain, upon this Supposition, we have none,) as we worship, so we believe, we know not what, or why. We don't know what Respects are due from us to the Perfections of God; or that any are required of us by Him. For, as well as any other moral Perfections, Truth may be quite different in God, from what it is in Men; and so there may be nothing of that which we conceive of as such, in his Assertions and Promises.—He may declare one Thing, and mean another; promise one Thing, and do another:—God may be True and Faithful, and yet deceive us; as well as Holy and Just, and do that which is not Right. Revelation gives us the same (tho' clearer) Ideas of the Attributes of God, which we have from Nature and Reason: And if it taught any Thing contrary thereto, it would unsay what it saith, and destroy it's own Credibility. To set the Gifts of God at variance, is to frustrate the good Design and deprive ourselves of the Benefit of them. Vehemently to decry Reason, as useless, or as a blind Guide, leading Men into Error and Hell; and to run down natural Religion as mere *Paganism,* derogates from the Credit of revealed, subverts our Faith in it, and dissolves our Obligation to practice it.

2. We should not magnify and extol natural Religion, to the Disparagement of Revealed. We cannot say, that the Light and Strength of Nature, how great soever, in it's original State of Rectitude, had no Assistance from Revelation, toward the first Man's actual Knowledge and Performance of his Duty to his Maker. At the first opening of his Eyes and Understanding, he might not by one intuitive View, have a clear and full Discernment of the Perfections of God stamped on his Works, and the moral Obligations engraved in his Heart.—God made Himself and his Will known to *Adam* in some other Way beside that of his Creation. There was some *other* Voice of the Lord, beside that of universal Nature's declaring his Being and Pleasure to him; and by which more might be spoken for his Instruction, than we have an Account of in the Mosaick History. And perhaps such Manifestation as God more immediately made of Himself to Man, put his Reason in Exercise for all the Discoveries it was capable of making afterwards from the Works of Creation. Had Man, with all his natural Endowments in their perfect Order and Strength, been placed in this World, and no Notice given him of it's Maker, might he not have stood wondring some Time at the amazing Fabrick, before he would have thence, by Deductions of Reason, argued an invisible Being, of eternal Power, Wisdom and Goodness, to be the Author of it and him; to whom he was therefore obliged to pay all Regards suitable to

such glorious Excellencies? Would he so soon and easily have made those Discoveries, which are necessary to the Perfection of natural Religion, understood and practic'd by him in Paradise, till he eat of *the Tree of Knowledge of Good and Evil?* If his being Created after the Image of God imports more, than his Formation with a sufficient Capacity in his Nature for, and entire Disposition to, even the actual Possession and Use of all that Knowledge, Righteousness and true Holiness, of which the Religion of Nature, consists; yet his falling into Sin, and effacing the divine Image in his Soul, greatly alter'd the Case, with respect to him, and his Posterity, and made Revelation a necessary Supplement of super-natural Light and Strength, for the Discovery and Performance of acceptable and available Religion. And such a Revelation, in it's first Degree and early Dawn of it, was graciously vouchsafed to Man, upon his Fall into a State of Darkness and Weakness, Sin and Misery.—Which Revelation continued, and gradually encreased, to the Church of God in all past Ages of it from the Beginning, hath done more to preserve and propagate that little even of natural Religion, which there hath been among Mankind, than all the boasted Improvements of Nature's dimmed Light, and enfeebled Powers have done. The first Parents of Mankind, no doubt, instructed their Children in the Principles and Duties of Religion, not only those which concern'd them as sinful Creatures, and are founded in the new and encouraging Relations God stands in to us, which the Gospel, published in Paradise, reveals, but also in those which are comprehended in the Law of their Creation: Otherwise they might not soon enough, if ever, have arriv'd to a competent Knowledge of them. It might have been long, e're Reason, uncultivated by Education, would by searching, have found out God—so much as that He is. Perhaps of it's own natural Motion, now become so dull and stupid, it would not have enquired after Him, or have proceeded far in the Discovery of Him. To a traditionary Revelation, how imperfect and obscure soever, amongst most Nations that have dwelt on the Face of the Earth, might be owing the Knowledge they had of God, and divine Things:—At least the Hint thus given them of such Things, might awake their rational Powers to any Exercise about them, which otherwise might have lain dormant in their benighted Minds.

Reason, as well as Revelation, teacheth us, that human Nature, in it's original Constitution, and as it came out of the Hands of a good Creator, must be Perfect in it's Kind, and that it since, by our Abuse of it, is wofully impaired. It might not approach quite so near the Angelical, yea, Divine Nature in it's integral State, as some imagine; nor might it by the Sin of the *Protoplast* fall quite so low, as others affirm; and become a strange heterogeneous Compound of two other Natures, retaining nothing of Humanity in it. The superior Excellency and Strength of innocent *Adam's* Soul, might not be so much above the common Standard, since, as the *Talmudists* describe his bodily Stature—so Tall, that, standing on the Earth, he could touch the Heavens with his Hand; yet it doubtless had every way the Advantage for the free and sublime Exercises of a rational Soul. Some appear to have an extravagantly high Opinion, and others a too debasing Notion of human Nature, even in it's lapsed Estate: There are still in it, as received by Derivation from apostate Parents, "some *legible Characters, Out-lines,* and *Lineaments* of it's Beauty; some *magnificent Ruins,* which shew what it had been, enough to demonstrate the original Impression of the divine Image and Law." It is, however disorder'd and debilitated, a rational Nature, capable of religious Knowledge and Practice. But can we guess, how much thereof it would attain to, in the short Time of this Life, if it were left altogether uncultivated in Individuals; and Mankind had run wild, like the Beasts of the Field? How much more would the Generality of 'em know, than what they know as *natural brute Beasts?* and in those Things have corrupted themselves: The higher Powers of their Nature not exerting themselves for the first Years of their Lives, and so the more subjected to the Sway of the inferior, might be of little Use toward the Discovery and Performance of the Things of Religion: Any innate Inclination to them might be smothered in the Crowd of worldly Lusts; the Attention of the Mind diverted from them, and all the Essays to do them, be hindered by the Amusements of sensual Pleasure, the Encroachments of secular Business, the Prevalence of bad Customs and Examples. The Capacities with which they are made, the Principles with which they are endowed, in order to their knowing of, and acting agreable to, moral Obligations, might be suppressed, and kept down by violent Appetites and Passions, and lie buried under earthly Affections. Men might have been absolutely without God in the World;—without any Sense of the Deity upon their Minds; without all Thought of any other Things than such as were just before them. Their Knowledge and Care might not have extended beyond the Sphere of Sense: Their Prudence might have appear'd only in Matters of a civil Life, and a temporary Concern; and possibly there wou'd have been no Religion in the World, but that which consisted merely in, as Atheists say, all was introduced by, *State-Policy.*

Thus much, I think, may be probably inferred from the History of all Ages of the World, in which the Nations which have not enjoyed the Revelation which God from Time to Time granted to his Church, have had so little of Natural Religion among them, mixed and spoiled with the grossest Errors, Superstitions, and Abominations. The Glimmerings of

Nature's Light, and small Remains of it's Strength, not being duly improved, were, in a manner, lost from among them, and they *sat in Darkness, and the Region of the Shadow of Death:* Thô what might be known of God, was manifest to them in his Works; and they had moreover some obscure Traditions, which gave Rise to their heathenish Worship, and according to which they ordered the Rites of it. While we are amaz'd at the Stupidity which they labour'd under in their reasonable Faculties, it sheweth us what is to be expected from savage, undisciplined Nature. We do not argue therefrom the Incapacity of human Reason, under all the Disadvantages of our lapsed State, to know and do better; but the Inefficacy of it, in fact, to the Purposes of Religion, when unassisted by Revelation.—And were it not for this, we may guess what a deplorable State of Ignorance and Wickedness, increasing from one Age to another, all Mankind would have been in at this Day. What hath polished Nature and refined Reason to boast of, in Matters of Religion, among the wisest and most learned of the Heathens? Did they *by Wisdom know God, and glorify Him as God.* Did *Athens,* that Eye of the World, see the *invisible Things of Him,* made visible enough in his Works to the Eye of human Understanding, *even his eternal Power and God-head?* The Altar erected there to the UNKNOWN GOD, was a Monument of their Ignorance of the true. If they worshipped Him at all, they *did it ignorantly, and were in all Things too superstitious.* Was the State of natural Religion better at *Rome,* when Learning flourished there, than that of the Christian is, now Popery prevails? They, *who professed themselves wise, became Fools;* as great, as if *they had said, There is no God,* in *changing the Glory of the incorruptible God, into an Image made like corruptible Man, and to Birds, and four-footed Beasts, and creeping Things;* and, *serving the Creature, more than the Creator;* and approving and doing those Things that are contrary, not only to the Religion, but even the Inclination of Nature.— Under much Doubt and Uncertainty have the ablest Writers of them left the first Principles of Natural Religion. It is enough (saith one) to raise the Pity of a Christian, when he reads *Cicero's* Discourse of the *Nature of the Gods,* to find the Disputants fighting in the dark, puzzling themselves, and one another, confounding Truth and Error; and at last drawing off almost on equal Terms without Victory's declaring on either Side.—Not to mention the Deficiencies and Errors in any Scheme of Natural Religion, which the learned Heathen ever presented the World with; I may say, that the Christian Revelation contains one far more entire and satisfying. The Principles and Duties of it are therein stated, explained, and enforced, in a Way far above whatever they were before. And 'tis not without Reason supposed, that they would not have been propounded so clearly and fully as they be, in the most celebrated Writings of Morality among the Heathen, had there been none of divine Inspiration among the People of God.

The Gospel of Christ hath to be sure been *a Light to lighten the* modern deistical *Gentiles:* For the juster Notions they have of the divine Attributes, and moral Duties than the ancient, they are greatly indebted to that Revelation which they decry. Not to say any Thing of those heavenly Truths and important Duties, which are taught only in the Bible; 'tis there we learn the Religion of Nature in it's greatest Purity; which, if there were nothing more to be said in it's Commendation might be enough to raise our Esteem of it. And the Grace of God appears in assisting Reason by Revelation in those Discoveries, which it possibly could, but never did, nor would make, without such Help.—And the same is true, with respect to the Performances of Duty: *In thy Light we see Light.* It is in the Light of Revelation, added to that of Nature, that Things are so plain and easy to our discerning, as that we are ready to think bare Reason must discover them to all Mankind, and that we, un-enlightned by the Gospel, should have known as much of the Principles and Duties of Natural Religion. But, if we are thence insensible of, and unthankful for, *the tender Mercy of our God,* whereby *the Day-spring from on High hath visited us,* we are stupidly inconsiderate; and need not (as we are apt) to smile at the odd Philosophy of the simple *Rustick,* who thought the World had little Benefit by the Light of the Sun, "Because it shin'd in the Day-time." By Means of Revelation we have the right Use of Reason, in Matters of Religion: And, by the due Exercise of Reason, so excited and directed, we have the inestimable Benefit of Revelation. Both are *good Gifts,—*Rays from *the Father of Lights,* to *enlighten every Man that cometh into the World.*—The Mind hath great Satisfaction in observing the harmonious Agrement between them, and the Objects of religious Knowledge and Faith appear the more beautiful and amiable in this double Light: And the better we understand and practise the Religion of Nature, the wiser and better Christians shall we be. . . .

It concerns us all to make Proficiency in Religion, answerable to our Capacities therefore, and the Means and Helps afforded us thereto—That having the Foundations of it well laid in our Minds, by convincing Reasons, and authentic Testimonies of Scripture, we go on to Perfection: Which that we may do;—Let us, as the Discourse now had, admonishes us, have a due Respect both to natural and revealed Religion: And not suffer our Zeal to swell so high, and move in so strong a Current towards the one, as shall prove a Drain from, and lower the Regard, which we owe to the other—Let us faithfully improve all the Light and Strength which natural Reason and divine Revelation supply, toward our knowing

and doing *whatsoever Things are true—honest—just—pure—lovely—and of good Report—in which there is any Virtue, and any Praise;* and so make continual Advance in Religion, 'till we come unto *a perfect Man,* in the reintegrated State of Nature—*unto the Measure of the Stature of the Fulness of CHRIST.*
AMEN

Seasonable Thoughts on the State of Religion in New-England

CHARLES CHAUNCY (1705–1787)

The great-grandson and namesake of the second president of Harvard College, Charles Chauncy became one of the leading liberal voices in eighteenth-century New England thought. He received his degree from Harvard in 1721 and then spent several years studying theology. He was called to be the co-minister of the First Church in Boston in 1727. This pulpit allowed him to exert a strong influence on the spiritual and ecclesiastical life of Boston and all New England itself, and Chauncy used his position effectively as a spokesman for rational supernaturalism.

During Chauncy's ministry, the Great Awakening occurred in New England. Chauncy attempted some temperate evangelical efforts, yet soon he began to warn his congregation against the enthusiasm sweeping the land, stressing that any faith must be balanced with the government of sound reason. In the beginning he stood almost alone in denouncing the revival.

In 1742 Chauncy published his *Enthusiasm Described and Caution'd Against*, his first published blast against the "religious Phrenzy" of the time. Shortly thereafter, he published an anonymous *Letter from a Gentleman in Boston, to Mr. George Wishart, One of the Ministers in Edinburgh, Concerning the State of Religion in New-England*. Here he suggested that the Great Awakening was more an expression of emotional enthusiasm than a rational inquiry into Christianity. These two publications brought the First Church minister into the public eye as the acknowledged leader against the abuses of revivalism.

His greatest contribution came in 1743. In March of that year, Jonathan Edwards, the undisputed champion of evangelical theology in New England, published a book supporting the Great Awakening, *Some Thoughts Concerning the Present Revival of Religion in New-England*. He argued that the abuses of the revival were not enough to discredit its honest efforts to promote the work of God in America. Chauncy disagreed and soon responded with *Seasonable Thoughts on the State of Religion in New-England*. The work was based on his own lengthy travels throughout New England, on his conversations with ministerial associates, and on his reading of many pamphlets and newspapers.

Whereas Edwards believed that religion was primarily a concern of the heart, Chauncy emphasized the head, to such an extent that Perry Miller considered his book a classic of hard-headed, dogmatic rationalism. And in his pedantic and Calvinistic manner, Chauncy revealed increasing Arminian leanings. Edwards may have possessed the keener, tighter mind, but Chauncy had greater ability to state his objections to the general work of the Great Awakening, to its arguments against Congregational polity, and to existing orthodoxy in general.

The following excerpt from Part II of *Seasonable Thoughts* reveals Chauncy's incipient Christian Unitarianism, which almost forty years later would be developed more fully in his *The Mystery Hid from Ages and Generations, Made Manifest by the Gospel-Revelation: or, The Salvation of all Men the Grand Thing Aimed in the Scheme of God.*

Representing the Obligations which lie upon the Pastors of these Churches in particular, and upon all in general, to use their Endeavours to suppress the Disorders prevailing in the Land; with the great Danger of their Neglect in so important a Matter.

Were the bad Things, accompanying the present religious Commotion, no other than a few accidental Imprudences, it would not be worth while to expend much Pains to guard People against them: Neither would it look like Friendship to the Cause of CHRIST, if any were "abundant in insisting on, and setting forth such Blemishes;" especially, if it were so done as to "manifest that they chose rather, and were more forward, to take Notice of what is amiss, than what is good and glorious." But the Case is widely different, when the Disorders, which may justly be complained of, are generally prevalent, and such as tend to the Destruction of Peace, with Truth and Loneliness. And as this is the real State of Things in the Land, at this Day, (if any Credit is due to the foregoing Pages) 'tis certainly Time, high Time, to appear openly and boldly for GOD, and lay ourselves out to the utmost, in all proper Ways, to give Check, if possible, to the Irregularities, which have so mingled themselves with Religion, as to "eclipse the Glory of it, and beget Jealousies and ill Thoughts in the Minds of many, about the whole of it."

The Obligations to this are solemn and weighty: And they are binding upon the Pastors of these Churches in particular, and upon all in general.

We, who have been made Overseers of the Flocks in this Land, are peculiarly oblig'd to use our Endeavours, in all suitable Ways, within our proper Sphere, to suppress these Disorders.

Faithfulness to Christ requires this of us. We are his Servants by office: And our business, as such, properly lies, in doing all we can to promote the Interest of his Kingdom. This is what we have been called to, and set apart for: And the Vows of GOD are upon us; and so be unto us, if we are unfaithful! And is this a Charge we shall be able wholly to escape the Guilt of, if we can behold the Rife of Error, in Opposition to the Truth as it is in JESUS; and the general Spread of Disorders, in various Kinds, in Contradiction to the plain Precepts of the Gospel; and yet sit still, and hold our Peace? Who will stand up for Christ, if we don't? Who are called hereto, if not his authorised Officers? This Matter belongeth to us. 'Tis the proper Business of our Station; and we shall neglect our Duty, and be faithless to the Charge committed to us, if we are meer Lookers on, and insert not ourselves in the Cause of Truth and Virtue, which is the Cause of CHRIST.

'Tis true, we shall do well to cease from Strife about Words to no profit: And as for foolish and unlearned Questions, they ought to be avoided, lest they increase to more Ungodliness. But when the Order of the Gospel is openly broke in upon; the Faith once delivered to the Saints grosly misinterpreted, to the subverting of Souls; and many evil Practices, in Consequence hereof, are generally gone into: I say, when this is the Case, where is our Fidelity to our Master and Lord, if we stand by unconcerned? Or, what is as bad, if we hold our Hands together, and do nothing? Are we not set for the Defence of the Gospel? And though as Servants of the Lord, we must not strive, but be gentle to all Men; yet, ought we not in Meekness to instruct those that oppose themselves, if peradventure GOD will give them Repentance, to the acknowledging of the Truth? And is not this the instituted Way of recovering such out of the Snare of the Devil, who have been taken captive at his Will? Has not the Bible made it an essential Ingredient in the Character of Gospel Ministers, that they be able by found Doctrine, both to exhort and convince Cain-sayers? And what will signify such an Ability, if, when there are many unruly and vain Talkers, and Deceivers, who subvert whole Houses, teaching Things which they ought not, we make no Use of it to stop their Mouths? Is it not the Command of GOD, that they be rebuked sharply, that they may be found in the Faith; not giving Heed to the Commandments of Men, that turn from the Truth? And can we satisfy our Consciences, while we live in the Neglect of so plain a Duty? An't we very Cowards in the Cause of Christ? Don't we discover a Want of Faithfulness towards him, who has put us into the Ministry?

We may preach often, and profess a great Affection for the Work of GOD, and have it perpetually in our Mouths; but if, at such a Day as this, when Error in Doctrine, and Practice, covers the Face of the Land, we are silent about the Matter, or mention it only after such a Manner, as to make it evident we are not in earnest in what we say, how can we be any other than culpably defective in our Duty to Christ? 'Tis for the Honour of his Name, and the Interest of his Kingdom, that we cry aloud and spare not. The Errors of the Times are not speculative Niceties, nor Matters of doubtful Disputation, but evident Breaches upon the Law of Faith, or the Rule of Duty, and in Instances of high Importance. The Gospel severely testifies against them, and Faithfulness to the Redeemer should put his Ministers upon doing so likewise.

But Faithfulness to our People as well as Christ obliges to this. The Oversight of them has been committed to our Charge; and we have solemnly engag'd before GOD, and the LORD JESUS CHRIST, *who shall judge the quick, and the Dead, at his Appearing, and his Kingdom,* not only to preach the Word to them, being instant in Season, and out of Season; but to reprove, rebuke, exhort, with all long-suffering and doctrine. And how shall we be able to fulfill this Engagement, if, when the Time is come, that they will not endure sound Doctrine, but after their own Lusts heap to themselves Teachers, having itching Ears, and turn away their Ears from the Truth, and are turned unto Fables: I say, how shall we approve ourselves faithful, if we are now wanting in our Care to warn them of their Danger, and put them under the Guard of heedful Caution? When can we more seasonably, or pertinently, apply to our People for their Direction, Admonition and Rebuke, than at a Time when they are either led into Error and Delusion, or are in Hazard of being so? We are set as Watchmen to our Churches; and whose Business is it to espy Danger, and give Warning, if not our's? Or, if, when we see Danger, we neglect to give Warning, where is our Faithfulness? We are called Shepherds; and shall we behave as such, if, when the Wolf comes to devour the Flock, we don't watch in all Things that we may be their Defence? Or, if they should wander out of the Path of Truth and Holiness, we don't use our Endeavours to reduce and bring them back?

'Tis one special Part of the Duty which we, who are Ministers, owe our People, to guard them, as much as may be, against the bad Influence of all Error, whether in Principle or Practice. And if Error should prevail, and begin generally to appear in its bad Effects, we should now be upon the Watch more than ever. Now is the Time, when we are particularly called to stand up for the good old Way, and bear faithful Testimony against every Thing, that may tend to cast a Blemish on true primitive Christianity. 'Tis the proper Work of the Day: And if we are silent, I see not but we are sinfully so. Says the excellent Calvin, whose Words are as well worthy of Regard in this, as in other Articles, "When any pernicious Sect begins to arise, but chiefly when it grows, 'tis the Duty of those whom GOD hath appointed to build up his Church, to oppose it strongly, and appear against it, before it gets Strength to corrupt and destroy all. And certainly, when there are Pastors of the Churches, they ought not only to dispense choice good Food to the Flock of Christ, but they must also watch against Wolves and Thieves, that if they will come in to the Flock, they may set them far away by their loud Outcries and Vociferations." And Luther speaks much in the same Strain, "Ministers ought not only to build up, but to defend. In a Time of Peace, their Duty is to teach; in a Time of War, to fight with and resist Satan, and eroneous Men." And 'tis, as he elsewhere expresses it, "A womanish Thing to sit in a Corner, and lie hid in some Hole; but worthy a Man to please the Cause of God and Truth." And so bad a thought had he of ministerial Silence in the Cause of Christ, that, in a Letter to Staupitius, he expresses himself in those very strong Words, "Let me be found any Thing, a proud Man, and guilty of all Wickedness, so I be not convicted of wicked Silence, whilst the Lord suffers."

We may think it enough, if we preach good Doctrine, and are laborious therein; "but, at such a Day as this, if we don't shew to our People a hearty Disaffection to the abounding Disorders in the Land, but seem rather doubtful and suspicious of their evil Tendency, we shall probably be the Occasion of Hurt instead of Good." People will take Advantage from what they observe in us, and be likely to make an ill Use of it: Nor would it be any Wonder, if, through the Subtility of Satan, they should be led into Error. "We, who are in the sacred Office, had Need to take Heed what we do, and how we behave at this Time. A less Thing in a Minister will encourage Disorders than in other Men. If we are silent, or say but little, in our publick Prayers and Preachings, about the bad Spirit appearing in so many evil Effects, or seem carefully to avoid speaking of it in Conversation, it will, and justly may, be interpreted by our People, that we, who are their Guides, and to whom they are to have their Eye for Spiritual Instruction, have no ill Opinion of it; and this will tend to produce the fame Sentiments in them, and what may be expected, as the Consequence, but the Increase of Confusion?" And may it not be feared, that the Extravagancies, which are now so general, are very much owing to the want of ministerial Faithfulness in terrifying against them, in Time? Are there none of the Pastors of these Churches, who, instead of condemning the Things that were evidently hurtful to the Cause of Christ, have pleaded on their Behalf? Or, at lest, palliated and excused them? Nay, have none daubed and flattered, beyond all Measure, the known Promoters of the worst Things prevailing in the Land? And is it any other than might be expected, when this has been their Conduct, that the People should be thrown into such a State of Disorder? Had we, who are interupted with the Care of Souls, been generally careful, in the Beginning of these Times, to point out the Things that were amiss; and had we, upon their first Appearance, used our faithful Endeavours to discourage their Growth, we should have been, I doubt not, a quite different Face of Things: And if we would now give Check to the Evils, which have gain'd Strength by being let too much alone, it must be by coming out boldly, and speaking plainly. And is it not Time to do so? There are few of our Churches, but Disorders are to be seen in them: And as to some of them, are they not broke to Pieces with Strife and Schism? Were ever poor Churches in a State of more doleful Confusion? And shall we still remain silent? Faithfulness to our People calls upon us to stir up our selves, no longer standing by as idle Spectators, not yet baiting betwixt two.

And this is what we are further obliged to, from the Example of those holy Men of GOD, who have gone before us in a bold and open Testimony against the like evil Things in their Day, which appear in our's. Soon after the Settlement of this Country, there was (as we have already seen) the Rife of a Spirit very like to that which now prevails: And it occasioned like Disturbance to the Churches. And what was the Method, our Fathers, in the Ministry, took for the Preservation of Religion, in a Time of such Disorders? Were they afraid to speak freely against them? Were they dispos'd to make a meer nothing of them? Did they strengthen the hands of those who tormented them, by sacrificing undue Honour to them? So far from it, that they did, in all the Ways they could devise, lay themselves out to put a stop to the Growth of them. They pray'd and preach'd against the Errors of their Day; they privately convers'd with the Opinionists, using their best Endeavours to enlighten and convince them; they consulted with one another, and with their Churches; and at length, there was a general Assembly of all the Churches in the Province, by their Elders and Delegates, who not only declared to the World their disapprobation of these Errors, but laboured to show the People that they were Errors, by the Light of Holy Scripture.

And when the same Spirit, which now troubles us, appear'd in England the last Century, what was the Behaviour of those who were esteemed the most pious, and eminently faithful Ministers of Christ? Why, they lifted up their Voice like a Trumpet, testifying against the Enthusiasm which was crumbling the Church into numberless Sects, and threatening to over-run the Nation. Many now approv'd themselves Champions for the Church, and Cause of GOD; and their Names, on this Account, have been handed down to Posterity with Honour. There has not appear'd among us any Error in Principle, any wildness in Imagination, any

Indecency in Language, any Irregularity in Practice, but we might have learn'd how to testify against it, from what they, in Faithfulness to Christ, and the Souls of People, have left in their Writings.

And the same Method was taken by the first Reformers, when Enthusiasm and Error began to lift up their Heads in Germany, and threaten to carry all before them. They did not consult how they might please Men, but appeared openly for GOD, and were resolv'd, at all Hazards, to plead for his Cause against the Distraction of the Times. Luther had no less, than fix public Disputations, at Wittingburg, against the Antinomians. I suppose the Persons he disputed with were Stork and Muncer, and those other pretended Prophets, who boasted of angelic Revelations, and immediate Converse with GOD; for these were the Men, who scattered the Seeds of false Doctrine in Wittingburg, and were hearkened unto by Reason of their great spiritual Pretences. . . .

But we, who are CHRIST'S Ministers, are still further obliged to discourage the Rise and Growth of Disorders in the Church, from the great Danger of a Neglect to so important a Matter.

There will be Danger in Respect of ourselves. For we have the Charge of Souls; and very awful is the Charge. 'Tis not altogether unlike that, *Keep this Man: If by any Means he be Missing, then shall thy Life be for his Life* (I Kings 20.39). Not that the Blood of any will be required at our Hands, if we have been faithful to warn them of the Error of the Wicked, that they may turn from it: In this case, if they turn not from their Way, but die in their Iniquity, we have deliverd our Souls. But if through Cowardice, or a Man-pleasing Disposition, they are let alone to be drawn into Error and Delusion, how can we answer for our Conduct? Shall we behave like faithful Ministers of JESUS CHRIST, if, at a Time when Disorders are become general, we take little or no Notice of them? Is there no Danger in such a Neglect? Should those of our Charge, by Means of our Silence, entertain a favourable Opinion of very ill Things, and go into the Practice of them, should not we, in a Sense, be chargeable with their Sin? 'Tis true, if, from an upright Heart we have endeavour'd to do our Duty, according to our best Light, we may hope for the Mercy of our Judge, though we should have fallen into Mistakes. But we had Need take Heed to ourselves that we be found faithful. . . .

A Statement of Reasons for Not Believing the Doctrines of Trinitarians

ANDREWS NORTON (1786–1853)

Andrews Norton was referred to more than once as the pope of Unitarianism. Octavius Brooks Frothingham accused him of thinking he had originated the Liberal Faith. Both remarks were justified. Norton was a firm-minded man not given to gentle concessions or wordy evasions; his extraordinary polemical vigor profoundly affected the new movement even though his views in the Transcendentalist controversy were generally farther to the right than those of his ministerial brethren. His influence on the Harvard Divinity School during its formative years cannot be overrated. He named the issues, chose the ground for argumentation, and developed the lines of attack and defense that became standard during the early phase of the Unitarian movement. With Channing the only possible exception, Norton was the most influential intellectual force in organized Unitarianism before the Civil War.

Norton maintained a long and active relationship with Harvard, where he received his A.B. in 1804 and an A.M. in 1807. After postgraduate theological studies he spent a year as a tutor at Bowdoin, afterward returning in that capacity to Harvard in 1811. His next venture was the *General Repository and Review,* but that journal failed after two years for want of an audience inclined to such heavy theological fare. From 1813 to 1819 he was librarian and Dexter Lecturer in Biblical Criticism and from 1819 to his retirement in 1830, professor supported by the same foundation. During the last two decades of his life he conducted his campaign for Unitarianism from the library of his spacious home near the university.

Norton's numerous writings document each stage of the Unitarian controversy, but since Biblical studies were his primary interest, he perhaps would have regarded his *Evidences of the Genuineness of the Gospels* and its complementary *Translation of the Gospels* as his major works. His attack on Transcendentalism, *The Latest Form of Infidelity,* has been more frequently remembered, however. In 1840 he arranged to republish for his Boston audience various attacks on the Transcendental philosophy first published in the Calvin-dyed *Princeton Review,* an action often misunderstood as a sign of desperation and even of betrayal.

This interpretation is an error, because Norton's reliance on the Scottish school in matters philosophical naturally allied him with many Calvinistic metaphysicians, as did his profound distaste for the pantheistic tendencies of German philosophy.

The *Statement of Reasons* presented here encompasses in its publication history Norton's crusade against religious error. It was first published in the *Christian Disciple* (1819) as a reply to Moses Stuart's *Letters*, which had in turn been provoked by Channing's Baltimore Sermon, given earlier that year. Before the end of 1819 Norton republished the article as a sixty-four-page booklet. After his retirement he began to prepare an enlarged edition of the *Statement*, which was brought out in 1833 as a volume of more than three hundred pages. This edition signalizes Norton's increasing concern for Transcendentalism as a threat. In the preface he calls attention to the alarming spread of infidelity, laying much blame at the door of orthodoxy for its retention of outmoded and unacceptable dogmatics. In 1856 Ezra Abbot, one of Norton's chief protégés in Biblical criticism, later to become Bussey Professor of New Testament Interpretation and Criticism at the Harvard Divinity School, edited a third and slightly amended edition of the work, which has been reprinted many times since by the American Unitarian Association.

The selection that follows is an abridgement of Norton's first separately published version of 1819.

The proper modern doctrine of the Trinity, as it is stated in the creeds of latter times, is, that there are three persons in the Divinity, who equally possess all divine attributes; and this doctrine is at the same time connected with an explicit statement that there is but one God. Now we do not believe this doctrine, because taken in connexion with that of the unity of God, it is a doctrine essentially incredible; one, which no man who has compared the two doctrines together with just conceptions of both, ever did, or ever could believe. Three persons, each equally possessing divine attributes, are three Gods. A person is a being. No one who has any correct notion of the meaning of words will deny this. And the being who possesses divine attributes must be God or a God. The doctrine of the Trinity, then, affirms that there are three Gods. It is affirmed at the same time, that there is but one God. But nobody can believe that there are three Gods, and that there is but one God.

This statement is as plain and obvious as any which can be made. But it certainly is not the less forcible, because it is perfectly plain and obvious. Some Trinitarians have indeed remonstrated against our charging those who hold the doctrine with the "ABSURDITIES consequent upon the language of their creed." We do not answer to this, that if men will talk absurdity, and insist that they are teaching truths of infinite importance, it is unreasonable for them to expect to be understood as meaning something entirely different from what their words express. The true answer is, that these complaints are wholly unfounded, and that the proper doctrine of the Trinity, as it has existed in latter times, is that which is expressed by the language which we have used, taken in its obvious acceptation. There is no reasonable pretence for saying, that *the great body of Trinitarians,* when they have used the word, *person,* have not meant to express proper personality. He who asserts the contrary, asserts a mere extravagance. He closes his eyes upon an obvious fact, and then affirms what he may fancy ought to have been, instead of what there is no doubt really has been. But on this subject we have something more to say, and we shall proceed in a moment to remark particularly, not only upon this, but upon the other evasions which have been resorted to, in order to escape the force of the statement which we have urged.

We wish, however, first to observe, that the ancient doctrine of the Trinity, as it existed before the council of Nice (A.D. 325) was VERY DIFFERENT from the modern, and has this great advantage over the latter, that when viewed in connexion with the unity of God, it is not *essentially* incredible. The orthodox doctrine, previous to the period just mentioned, taught that the Father alone was the Supreme God; and that the Son and Spirit were distinct beings, deriving their existence from him, and far inferior; each of whom, however, or at least the former, might, in a certain sense, be called God. The subject has been so thoroughly examined, that the correctness of this statement will not, we think, be questioned at the present day by any respectable writer. The theological student, who wishes to see in a small compass the authorities on which it is founded, may consult one or more of the works mentioned in the note below. We have stated that form of the doctrine which approached nearest to modern orthodoxy. But the subject of the personality and divinity of the Holy Spirit, it may be particularly observed, was in a very unsettled state before the council of Constantinople, A.D. 383. Gregory Nazianzen, in his eulogy of Athanasius, has the following passage respecting that great father of Trinitarian orthodoxy. "For when all others who held our doctrine were divided into three classes, the faith of many being unsound respecting the Son, that of still more concerning the Holy Spirit (on which subject to be least impious was thought to be piety) and a small number being sound in both respects; he first and alone, or with a very few, dared to confess in writing, clearly and explicitly, the true doctrine of the one Godhead and nature of the three persons. Thus that truth, a knowledge of which, as far as regards the Son, had been vouch-safed to many of the fathers before, he was finally inspired to maintain in respect to the Holy Spirit."

So much for the original doctrine of the Trinity. We shall now pro-ceed to state the different forms, which the modern doctrine has been made to assume, and in which its language has been explained, by those who have attempted to conceal or remove the direct opposition between this and the doctrine of the unity of God.

I. Many Trinitarian writers have maintained a modification of the doctrine, *in some respects similar* to what we have just stated to be its most ancient form. They considered the Father as the "fountain of the divinity," who alone is supreme, and whose existence is underived, and have regarded the Son and Spirit as deriving their existence from him and subordinate to him; but, at the same time, as equally with the Fa-ther possessing all divine attributes. . . . With regard to this account of the doctrine, it is an obvious remark, that the existence of the Son, and Spirit, is either *necessary,* or it is *not.* If their existence be necessary, we have then three beings *necessarily existing,* each possessing divine attributes, and consequently we have three Gods. If it be not necessary, but depen-dent on the will of the Father, then we say that the distance is infinite between underived and independent existence, and derived and depen-dent; between the supremacy of God, the Father, and the subordination of beings who exist only through his will. In the latter view of the doctrine, therefore, we clearly have but one God; but at the same time the mod-ern doctrine of the Trinity disappears. The form of statement too, just mentioned, must be abandoned; for it can hardly be pretended that these derived and dependent beings possess an equality in divine attributes, or are equal in nature to the Father. Beings, whose existence is dependent on the will of another, cannot be equal in power to the being on whom they are dependent. The doctrine, therefore, however disguised by the mode of statement which we are considering, must, in fact, resolve itself into an assertion of three Gods; or must, on the other hand, amount to nothing more than a form of Unitarianism. In the latter case, however objectionable and unfounded we may think it, it is not to our present purpose to argue against it; and in the former case, it is pressed with all the difficulties which bear upon the doctrine as commonly stated, and at the same time with new difficulties, which affect this particular form of statement. That the Son and the Spirit should exist necessarily, as well as the Father, and possess equally with the Father all divine attributes, and yet be subordinate and inferior to the Father; or in other words, that there should be two beings or persons, each of whom is properly and in the highest sense God, and yet that these two beings or persons should be subordinate and inferior to another being or person, who is God, is as incredible a proposition as the doctrine can involve.

II. Others again, who have chosen to call themselves Trinitarians, profess to understand by the word, *person,* something very different from what it commonly expresses; and regard it as denoting neither any *proper personality,* nor any *real distinction* in the divine nature. They use the word in a sense equivalent to that which the Latin word *persona* commonly signifies in classic writers; or which we usually express by the word, *character.* According to them, the Deity considered as existing in three different persons, is the Deity considered as sustaining three different characters. Thus some of them regard the three persons as denoting *the three relations* which he bears to men, as their Creator, (the Father,) their Redeemer, (the Son,) and their sanctifier, (the Holy Spirit.) Others found the distinction maintained in the doctrine on three attributes of God, as his goodness, wisdom, and power. Those who explain the Trinity in this manner are called *modal* or *nominal* Trinitarians. Their doctrine, as every one must perceive, is nothing more than simple Unitarianism disguised, if it may be said to be disguised, by a very improper use of language. Yet this doctrine, or rather a heterogeneous mixture of opinions in which this doctrine has predominated, has been, at times, considerably prevalent, and has almost come in competition with the proper doctrine.

III. But there are others, who maintain with those last mentioned, that in the terms employed in stating the doctrine of the Trinity, the word, *person,* is not to be taken in its usual acceptation; but who differ from them in maintaining that these terms ought to be understood as affirming a real threefold distinction in the Godhead. . . . When they speak particularly of the Father, the Son, or the Spirit, they speak of them unequivocally as persons in the proper sense of the word. They attribute to them *personal* attributes. They speak of each as sustaining *personal* relations peculiar to himself, and performing *personal* actions, perfectly distinct from those of either of the others. It was the Son who was SANCTIFIED, and SENT into the world; and the Father by whom he was sanctified and sent. It was the Son who became incarnate, and not the Father. It was the Son who made atonement for the sins of men, and the Father by whom the atonement was received. The Son was in the bosom of the Father, but the Father was not in the bosom of the Son. The Son was the Logos who was with God, but it would sound harsh to say, that the Father was with God. The Son was the first born of every creature, the image of the Invisible God, and did not desire to retain his equality with [likeness to] God. There is no one who would not be shocked at the thought of applying this language to the Father. Again, it was the Holy Spirit who was sent as the Comforter to our Lord's apostles, after his ascension, and not the Father nor the Son. All this, those who maintain the doctrine of three distinctions, but not of three persons, in the divine nature, must and do say and allow; and therefore they do in fact maintain, with other Trinitarians, that there are three divine persons, in the proper sense of the word, distinguished from each other. Their mode of statement has been adopted merely with a view of avoiding those obvious objections which overwhelm the doctrine as commonly expressed; and without any regard to its consistency with their real opinions, or with indisputable and acknowledged truths. The God and Father of our Lord Jesus Christ is an intelligent being, a person. There may seem something like irreverence in the very statement of this truth; but in reasoning respecting the doctrine of the Trinity, we are obliged to state even such truths as this. The Son of God is an intelligent being, a person. And no Christian, one would think, who reflects a moment upon his own belief, can doubt that these two persons are perfectly distinct from each other. Neither of them, therefore, is a mere distinction of the divine nature; or the same intelligent being regarded under different distinctions. Let us consider for a moment what sort of meaning would be forced upon the language of scripture, if, where the Father, and the Son of God are mentioned, you were to substitute the terms, "the first distinction in the Trinity," and "the second distinction in the Trinity," or, "God considered in the first distinction of his nature," and "God considered in the second distinction of his nature." We will not produce any examples, because it would appear to us very much like turning the scriptures into burlesque.

If you prove that the person, who is called the son of God, possesses divine attributes, you prove that there is another divine person beside the Father. In order to complete the Trinity, you must proceed to prove, *first,* THE PERSONALITY, and then the divinity, of the Holy Spirit. This is the only way in which the doctrine can be established. No one can pretend that there is any passage in the scriptures, in which it is expressly taught, that there is a threefold distinction of any sort in the divine nature. He who proves the doctrine of the Trinity from the scriptures, must do it by showing that there are three persons, the Father, the Son, and the Holy Spirit, who are respectively mentioned in the scriptures, as each possessing divine attributes. There is no other medium of proof. There is no other way in which the doctrine can be established. Of course it is the very method of proof to which, in common with other Trinitarians, those resort, who maintain that form of stating the doctrine which we are considering. It follows from this, that their real opinions must be in fact the same with those of other Trinitarians. Indeed to express our own view of the subject, the whole statement appears to us to be little more than a mere oversight, a mistake, into which some have fallen in their haste to escape from the objections which they have perceived might be urged against the common form of the doctrine.

The remarks, which we have made, appear to us plain, and such as may be easily understood by every reader. We have doubted, therefore, whether to add another, the force of which may not be at once perceived, except by those who are a little familiar with metaphysical studies. But as it seems to us to show decisively, that the statement which we are considering is untenable by any proper Trinitarian, we have thought, on the whole, that it might be worth while to subjoin it. In regard to the personality of the divine nature, the only question is, whether there are three persons, or whether there is but one person. Those with whom we are arguing, deny that there are three persons. Consequently they must maintain that there is but one person. They affirm, however, that there is a threefold distinction in the divine nature; that is, in the nature of this one person. But of the nature of any being, we can know nothing but by the attributes or properties of that being. We conceive that this is, at the present day, a fundamental and undisputed principle in metaphysics. Abstract all the attributes or properties of any being, and nothing remains of which you can form even an imagination. These are all which is cognizable by the human mind. When you say, therefore, that there is a threefold distinction in the nature of any being, the only meaning which the words will admit (in relation to the present subject) is, that the attributes or properties of this being may be divided into three distinct classes, which may be considered separately from each other. All, therefore, which is affirmed by the statement of those whom we are opposing is, that the attributes of that ONE PERSON who is God, may be divided into three distinct classes; or in other words, that God may be viewed in three different aspects in relation to his attributes. But this is nothing more than a *modal* or *nominal* Trinity. . . .

IV. But a very considerable proportion of Trinitarians, and some of them among the most eminent, have not shrunk from understanding the doctrine as affirming the existence of *three equal divine minds,* and consequently, to all common apprehension, of three Gods; and, at the same time, decidedly rejecting the doctrine of the unity of God, in that sense which is at once the popular and philosophical sense of the term. All the unity for which they contend, is only such as may result from these three divinities being inseparably conjoined, and having a mutual consciousness, or a mutual in-being; which last mode of existence is again expressed in the language of technical theology by the terms *perichoresis* or *circumincession.* . . .

With the doctrine of the Trinity, is connected that of the HYPO-STATIC UNION (as it is called,) or *the doctrine of the union of the divine and human natures in Christ, in such a manner that these two natures constitute but one person.* But this doctrine may be almost said to have preeminence in incredibility to that of the Trinity itself. The latter can be no object of belief when regarded in common with that of the Divine Unity; for, from these two doctrines, propositions result which directly contradict each other. But the former, without reference to any other doctrine, does in itself, as it seems to us, involve propositions as clearly self-contradictory as any which it is in the power of language to express. It teaches that Christ is both God and man. The proposition is very plain and intelligible. The words, *God* and *man,* are among those which are in most common use, and whose meaning is best defined and understood. . . . And we perceive that these ideas are perfectly incompatible with each other. Our idea of God is of an infinite being; our idea of man is of a finite being; and we perceive that the same being cannot be both infinite and finite. . . . We can conceive of nothing more unmeaning, *so far as it is intended to convey any proposition which the mind is capable of receiving,* than such language as we sometimes find used, in which Christ is declared to be at once the Creator of the universe, and a man of sorrows; God omniscient and omnipotent, and a feeble man of imperfect knowledge. Yet it is pretended, that this sort of language may be justified from the scriptures. . . .

We do not then believe the doctrine of the Trinity, nor that of the union of two natures in Christ, because they are doctrines, which, when fairly understood, it is impossible from the nature of the human mind we should believe. They involve, as it seems to us, manifest contradictions, and no man can believe what he perceives to be a contradiction. . . .

. . . In what we have already said we have not been bringing arguments to disprove the doctrines; we have merely been showing that they are intrinsically incapable of any proof whatever; for a contradiction cannot be proved; that they are of such a character, that it is impossible to bring any arguments in their support, and unnecessary to adduce any arguments against them. . . . If Christ and his apostles communicated a revelation from God, they could make no part of it, for a revelation from God cannot teach absurdities.

But here we have no intention to rest. If we were to do so, we suppose that, notwithstanding what we have said, the old unfounded complaint would be repeated once more, that we oppose reason to revelation; for there are those, who seem unable to comprehend the possibility that the doctrines of their sect may make no part of the Christian revelation. What pretence then, we ask, is there for asserting that the doctrines, of which we are speaking, are taught in the scriptures? Certainly they are no where *directly* taught. It cannot even be pretended that they are. . . .

Before concluding, we wish to say a word or two respecting our general views of religion; those views, the great characteristics of which Mr. Channing has so ably and eloquently explained and defended in the Sermon, which has given occasion to Professor Stuart's Letters. We are charged with depriving Christianity of all its value; of rejecting every thing but its name. Christianity, WE BELIEVE, has taught the Unity of God, and revealed him as the Father of his creatures. It has made known his infinite perfections, his providence, and his moral government. It has directed us to look up to Him as the Being, on whom we and all things are entirely dependent, and to look up to Him with perfect confidence and love. It has made known to us that we are to live forever; it has brought life and immortality to light. Man was a creature of this earth, and it has raised him to a far nobler rank, and taught him to regard himself as an immortal being, and the child of God. It has opened to the sinner the path of penitence and hope. It has afforded to virtue the highest possible sanctions. It gives to sorrow its best and often its only consolation. It has presented us in the life of our great Master with an example of that moral perfection, which is to be the constant object of our exertions. It has established the truths, which it teaches, upon evidence the most satisfactory. It is a most glorious display of the benevolence of God, and of his care for his creatures of this earth. . . .

A Letter to the Rev. Samuel C. Thacher

WILLIAM ELLERY CHANNING
(1780–1842)

Emerson, Bryant, Longfellow, Lowell, and Holmes all acknowledged
their debt to Channing. Indeed, on the base of the statue in Boston's Public Garden erected in his memory appear the words, "He breathed into
theology a humane spirit." Such is the way Dr. Channing influenced not
only his own but subsequent generations. His preaching placed him as
the unquestioned champion of what came to be known in Boston as
Channing Unitarianism.

Born in Newport, Rhode Island, the son of a lawyer, Channing grew
up under the preaching of Samuel Hopkins. Yet what probably had a
more determinative effect on his life was the fact that his father had gone
to conservative Princeton. Channing no doubt would have attended
Princeton if his father had lived; when he died, however, the boy was
sent off to Harvard, and its pronounced liberalism was to have a lasting
effect. Upon graduation in 1798 Channing became a private tutor in
Richmond, Virginia. At the age of twenty-three he was called to the Federal Street Church in Boston, and from 1803 to his death in 1842 this
pulpit became the most popular in Boston due to Channing's remarkable
eloquence.

In 1815, however, Channing became involved in a controversy with
Jedidiah Morse over the appointment of Henry Ware as Hollis Professor,
and more than homiletics was needed. Morse had written an article in the
Panoplist which warned readers about the insidious spread of Unitarianism. Without question, it was time for sides to form.

Channing proved the natural choice as a respondent. Instead of addressing the *Panoplist* author and his charges directly, Channing's answer took the form of an open letter to his friend and former student,
Samuel C. Thacher, with whom he had published a catechism in 1813.
Thacher was a brilliant scholar; when Kirkland was called to be president of Harvard, he had succeeded him at the New South Church. That
Channing should direct his letter to him was a wise move, his opponent
being formidable and yet a friend.

The following excerpt from that letter demonstrates how the liberals
perceived themselves and how they sought to be understood. It also reveals their arguments to be still in the embryonic stage in some ways.

Through three exchanges between Channing and Thacher, who insisted that the orthodox could not have fellowship with the Unitarians, the liberals became more articulate in their position. Four years later Channing's Baltimore Sermon would have an even more dramatic effect— American Unitarianism would be acknowledged on its own terms. The letter to Samuel Thacher, however, first reveals the tension within the Standing Order membership over the question of Christian fellowship between liberals and orthodox.

MY FRIEND AND BROTHER,

I have recollected with much satisfaction the conversation, which we held the other morning, on the subject of the late *Review* in the *Panoplist* for *June,* of a pamphlet, called "American Unitarianism." I was not surprised, but I was highly gratified, by the spirit with which you spoke of that injurious publication. Grief rather than indignation marked your countenance, and you mourned, that men, who bear the sacred and pacifick name of Christian, could prove so insensible to the obligations of their profession. Our conversation turned, as you recollect, on the *falsehood* of that Review; on its *motives;* and on the *duties* which are imposed on those ministers, whose good name and whose influence it was designed to destroy.

After leaving you, my thoughts still dwelt on the subject; and, painful as is the task, I have thought it my duty to exhibit to the publick the topicks which we discussed, as well as to add some reflections suggested by private meditation.

I bring to the subject a feeling, which I cannot well express in words, but which you can easily understand. It is a feeling, as if I were degrading myself by noticing the false and injurious charges contained in this review. I feel as if I were admitting, that we need vindication, that our reputations want support, that our characters and lives do not speak for themselves. My selfrespect too is wounded, by coming into contact with assailants, who not only deny us the name of Christians, but withhold from us the treatment of gentlemen. These feelings, united with my love of peace, would induce me to pass over the Review in silence, if it were limited to the sphere within which we are personally known. In this sphere, I trust, its bitterness, coarseness, and misrepresentations will work their own cure; and that no other defence is required, but the tenour of our ministry and lives. But the work, in which this article is published, is industriously spread through the country, and through all classes of society. The aspersions which it contains are also diffused, as widely as pos-

sible, by conversation and even by newspapers. We owe then to ourselves, and what is more important to the cause of christian truth and
charity, some remarks on the representations and spirit of the Review.
You can easily conceive, how difficult it is to read again and again such
a publication without catching some portion of an unchristian spirit. I
do indeed feel myself breathing an atmosphere to which I am not ac-
cutomed. But my earnest desire is to remember whose disciple I am, and
to temper displeasure with meekness and forgiveness.

The Panoplist Review, though extended over so many pages, may be
compressed into a very narrow space. It asserts, 1. That the ministers of
this town and its vicinity, and the great body of liberal christians are
Unitarians in Mr. Belsham's sense of the word: that is, they believe that
Jesus Christ is a mere man, who when on earth was liable to errour and
sin; to whom we owe no gratitude for benefits which we are now receiving; and for whose future interposition we have no reason to hope.

2. The Review asserts, that these ministers and liberal christians are
guilty of hypocritical concealment of their sentiments, and behave in a
base, cowardly and hypocritical manner.

3. Christians are called to come out and separate themselves from
these ministers and the liberal body of christians, and to withhold from
them christian communion.

I will consider these three heads in their order, and may then notice
some other topics introduced into the Review.

The *first* assertion to be considered is, that the ministers of this town
and vicinity, and the great body of liberal christians are Unitarians, in
Mr. Belsham's sense of that word; and I wish every reader to look back
and distinctly impress this sense on his memory. I am sensible that almost every liberal christian, who reads these pages, will regard this charge
with a mixture of surprise and indignation, and will almost doubt the
correctness of my statement of the Review. . . . The word *Unitarianism,*
as denoting this opposition to Trinitarianism, undoubtedly expresses the
character of a considerable part of the ministers of this town and its vicinity, and the commonwealth. But we both of us know, that their Unitarianism is of a very different kind from that of Mr. Belsham. We both
agreed in our late conference, that a majority of our brethren believe,
that Jesus Christ is more than man, that he existed before the world, that
he literally came from heaven to save our race, that he sustains other
offices than those of a teacher and witness to the truth, and that he still
acts for our benefit, and is our intercessor with the Father. This we agreed
to be the prevalent sentiment of our brethren. There is another class of
liberal christians, who, whilst they reject the distinction of three persons
in God, are yet unable to pass a definitive judgment on the various sys-

tems, which prevail, as to the nature and rank of Jesus Christ. They are met by difficulties on every side, and generally rest in the conclusion, that *He,* whom God has appointed to be our Saviour, must be precisely adapted to his work, and that acceptable faith consists in regarding and following him as our Lord, Teacher, and Saviour; without deciding on his nature or rank in the universe. There is another class, who believe the simple humanity of Jesus Christ; but these form a small proportion of the great body of Unitarians in this part of our country; and I very much doubt, whether of these, one individual can be found, who could conscientiously subscribe to Mr. Belsham's creed as given in the Review. The conduct of the Reviewers, in collecting all the opinions of that gentleman, not only on the Trinity, but on every other theological subject, in giving to the *whole* collection the name of *Unitarianism,* and in exhibiting this to the world as the creed of liberal christians in this region, is perhaps as criminal an instance of unfairness, as is to be found in the records of theological controversy. The fact is, that the great body of liberal christians would shrink from some of these opinions with as much aversion as from some of the gloomy doctrines of Calvin. You, my friend, well know, that Mr. Belsham is not acknowledged as a leader by any Unitarians in our country. I have heard from those, who are thought to approach him most nearly in opinion, complaints of the extravagance of some of his positions, as unjust and prejudicial to the cause which he has undertaken to defend.

I trust, that the statement which has now been made, will not be considered as casting the least reproach on those amongst us, who believe in the simple humanity of Jesus Christ. Whilst I differ from them in opinion, I have certainly no disposition to deny them the name and privileges of christians. There are gentlemen of this class, whom I have the happiness to know, in whom I discover the evidences of a scrupulous uprightness, and a genuine piety; and there are others, whose characters, as portrayed by their biographers, appear to me striking examples of the best influences of christianity. . . .

I repeat it, these remarks are not offered for the purpose of throwing any reproach on any class of Christians, but simply to repel a statement which is untrue, and which is intended to rank us under a denomination, which the people of this country have been industriously taught to abhor. It is this intention of rendering us odious, which constitutes the criminality of the charge, and which exposes its author to severe indignation. A man, who is governed by christian principles, will slowly and reluctantly become "the accuser of his brethren." He will inquire long and impartially before he attempts to fasten a bad name, (the most injurious method of assailing reputation) on an individual, and especially on a large class of the community. What severity of reproof then is merited by the author of this Review, who has laboured to attach, not only to professors, but to ministers of religion, a name and character which he hoped would awaken popular alarm, and endanger their influence, although a large majority of the accused have no participation in the pretended crime. That he intended to deceive, I am unwilling to assert; but the most charitable construction which his conduct will admit is, that his passions and party spirit have criminally blinded him, and hurried him into an act, which could have been authorized only by the strongest evidence, and the most impartial inquiry. The time may come, when he will view this transaction with other eyes; when the rage of party will have subsided; when the obligation of a fair and equitable temper will appear at least as solemn as the obligation of building up a sect; when misrepresentation, intended to injure, and originating, if not in malignity, yet in precipitancy and passion, will be felt to be a crime of no common aggravation. That this time may soon come, and may bring with it not only remorse, but sincere repentance, I know to be your wish, and I trust it is my own.

II. I now come to the *second* charge of the Review: That the ministers of Boston and the vicinity, and the most considerable members of the liberal party "operate in secret; entrust only the initiated with their measures; are guilty of hypocritical concealment of their sentiments; behave in a base and hypocritical manner, compared with which Mr. Belsham's conduct, rotten as he is in doctrine to the very core, is purity itself." Such is the *decent* language scattered through this Review. This charge is infinitely more serious than the first. To believe with Mr. Belsham is no crime. But artifice, plotting, hypocrisy *are* crimes; and if we practise them, we deserve to be driven not only from the ministry, not only from the church, but from the society of the decent and respectable. Our own hearts, I trust, tell us at once how gross are these aspersions, and our acquaintance with our brethren authorizes us to speak in their vindication with the same confidence as in our own.

It is not to be wondered at, that those, who have charged us with holding sentiments which we reject, should proceed to charge us with hypocritically concealing our sentiments. Most of us have often contradicted Mr. Belsham's opinions: and they who insist that these opinions are ours, will be forced to maintain that we practise deceit. They start with a falsehood, and their conclusion cannot therefore be true. . . .

With respect to yourself, my friend, I presume no one will charge you with hypocritical concealment. Your situation offers you no temptation; and no one who has heard you preach, can ever have suspected you of a leaning towards Trinitarianism. As to myself, I have ever been inclined to cherish the most exalted views of Jesus Christ, which are consistent with the supremacy of the Father; and I have felt it my duty to depart from Mr. Belsham, in perhaps every sentiment which is peculiar to him on this subject. I have always been pleased with some of the sentiments of Dr. Watts on the intimate and peculiar union between the Father and the Son. But I have always abstained most scrupulously from every expression which could be construed into an acknowledgment of the Trinity. My worship and sentiments have been Unitarian in the proper sense of that word. In conversation with my people, who have requested my opinion upon the subject, especially with those who consider themselves Trinitarians, I have spoken with directness and simplicity. Some of those who differ from me most widely, have received from me the most explicit assurances of my disbelief of the doctrine of the Trinity, and of my views in relation to the Saviour. As to my brethren in general, never have I imagined for a moment, from their preaching or conversation, that they had the least desire to be considered as Trinitarians; nor have I ever heard from them any views of God or of Jesus Christ, but Unitarian in the proper meaning of that word.

It is indeed true, as Mr. Wells says, that we seldom or never introduce the Trinitarian controversy into our pulpits. We are accustomed to speak of the Father as the only living and true God, and of Jesus Christ as his son, as a distinct being from him, as dependent on him, subordinate to him, and deriving all from him. This phraseology pervades all our prayers, and all our preaching. We seldom or never, however, refer to any different sentiments, embraced by other christians, on the nature of God or of Jesus Christ. We preach precisely as if no such doctrine as the Trinity had ever been known. We do not attempt to refute it, any more than to refute the systems of the Sabellians, the Eutychians, or the Nestorians, or of the other sects who have debated these questions with such hot and unprofitable zeal. But, in following this course, we are not conscious of having contracted, in the least degree, the guilt of insincerity. We have aimed at making no false impression. We have only followed a general system, which we are persuaded to be best for our people and for the cause of christianity; the system of excluding controversy as much as possible from our pulpits. In compliance with this system, I have never assailed Trinitarianism; nor have I ever said one word against Methodism, Quakerism, Episcopalianism, or the denomination of Baptists; and I may add Popery, if I except a few occasional remarks on the intolerance of that system. The name of these sects, with that single exception, has never passed my lips in preaching, through my whole ministry, which has continued above twelve years. We all of us think it best to preach the truth, or what we esteem to be the truth, and to say very little about errour, unless it be errour of a strictly practical nature. A striking proof of our sentiments and habits on this subject may be derived from the manner in which you and myself have treated Calvinism. We consider the errours which relate to Christ's person as of little or no importance compared with the errour of those who teach, that God brings us into life wholly depraved and wholly helpless, that he leaves multitudes without that aid which is indispensably necessary to their repentance, and then plunges them into everlasting burnings and unspeakable torture, for not repenting. This we consider as one of the most injurious errours which ever darkened the christian world; and none will pretend that we have any thing to fear from exposing this errour to our people. On the contrary, we could hardly select a more popular topick;—and yet our hearers will bear witness how seldom we introduce this topick into our preaching. The name of Calvinist has never, I presume, been uttered by us in the pulpit. Our method is, to state what we conceive to be more honourable, and ennobling, and encouraging views of God's character and government, and to leave these to have their effect, without holding up other christians to censure or contempt. We could, if we were to make strenuous efforts, render the name of Calvinist as much a word of reproach in our societies, as that of Unitarian is in some parts of our country. But we esteem it a solemn duty to disarm instead of exciting the bad passions of our people. We wish to promote among them a spirit of universal charity. We wish to make them condemn their own bad practices, rather than the erroneous speculations of their neighbour. We love them too sincerely to imbue them with the spirit of controversy.

In thus avoiding controversy, we have thought that we deserved, not reproach, but some degree of praise for our self denial. Every preacher knows how much easier it is to write a controversial than a practical discourse; how much easier it is to interest an audience by attacking an opposite party, than by stating to them the duties and motives of the gospel. We often feel, that our mode of preaching exposes us to the danger of being trite and dull; and I presume we have often been tempted to gratify the love of disputation which lurks in every society. But so deeply are we convinced, that the great end of preaching is to promote a spirit of love, a sober, righteous and godly life, and that every doctrine is to be urged simply and exclusively for this end, that we have sacrificed our ease, and have chosen to be less striking preachers, rather than to enter the lists of controversy. . . . —To conclude, we have never entered into discussions of the doctrine of the Trinity, because we are not governed by a proselyting temper. I will venture to assert, that there is not on earth a body of men who possess less of the spirit of proselytism, than the ministers of this town and vicinity. Accustomed as we are to see genuine piety in all classes of christians, in Trinitarians and Unitarians, in Calvinists and Arminians, in Episcopalians, Methodists, Baptists, and Congregationalists, and delighting in this character wherever it appears, we are little anxious to bring men over to our peculiar opinions. I could smile at the idea of a *Unitarian plot,* were not this fiction intended to answer so unworthy an end. . . . Our great and constant object has been to promote the spirit of Christ, and we have been persuaded, that in this way we should most effectually promote the interests of christian truth.

These remarks will shew, how entirely unfounded are the charges, which are adduced against us, of insincerity and base hypocrisy. And are we not authorized, my brother, to repel these charges with some degree of warmth? Are we not called to speak in the language of indignant and insulted virtue, as well as of pity and sorrow, in relation to the man, who is propagating these unmerited reproaches? We are christians by profession, and ministers of the Gospel, governed, as we humbly hope, by the principles of Jesus Christ. We honour his name; we remember his dying love with gratitude; and I hope we are ready to meet the loss of all things in his service; and yet we are represented to our people as unprincipled men, wearing a mask, and practising the basest arts. And we are thus loaded with invective and abuse, that we may be robbed of that influence, which, if we know ourselves, we wish to exert for the honour of God, and the salvation of mankind; that we may be robbed of the confidence and affection of our societies, and may be forsaken by them as unworthy the christian name. Need I ask, whether this be a light injury or an ordinary crime? . . .

III. I now come to the third head of the Review, which I propose to consider. The Reviewer, having charged us with holding the opinions of Mr. Belsham, and hypocritically concealing them, solemnly calls on christians who differ from us in sentiment, "to come out and be separate from us, and to withhold communion with us;" and a paragraph of the bitterest contempt and insult is directed against those ministers who, whilst they disagree on the controverted points of theology, are yet disposed to love and treat us as brethren. This language does not astonish me, when I recollect the cry of heresy which has been so loudly raised against this part of the country. But I believe that this is the first instance, in which christians have been deliberately called to deny us the christian name and privileges. As such let it be remembered; and let the consequences of it lie on its authors.

Why is it that our brethren are thus instigated to cut us off, as far as they have power, from the body and church of Christ? Let every christian weigh well the answer. It is not because we refuse to acknowledge Jesus Christ as our Lord and Master; it is not because we neglect to study his word; it is not, because our lives are wanting in the spirit and virtues of his gospel. It is, because after serious investigations, we cannot find in the Scriptures, and cannot adopt as instructions of our Master, certain doctrines, which have divided the church for ages, which have perplexed the best and wisest men, and which are very differently conceived even by those who profess to receive them. It is, in particular, because we cannot adopt the language of our brethren, in relation to a doctrine, which we cannot understand, and which is expressed in words not only unauthorized by the Scripture, but as we believe, in words employed without meaning, (unless they mean that there are three Gods,) by those who insist upon them. This is our crime, that we cannot think and speak with our brethren on subjects the most difficult and perplexing, on which the human mind was ever engaged. For this we are pursued with the cry of heresy, and are to have no rest until virtually excommunicated by our brethren. . . .

Most earnestly do I hope that christians will weigh well the nature and guilt of schism, the consequences of separation, and the spirit of their religion, before they adopt the measure recommended in this Review. For myself, the universe would not tempt me to bear a part in this work of dividing Christ's church, and of denouncing his followers. If there be an act which, above all others, is a transgression of the christian law, it is this. What is the language of our Master? "A *new* commandment I give unto you, that ye *love one another. By this shall all men know, that ye are my disciples,* if ye have *love one to another.*" "Bear ye one another's burdens," says St. Paul, "and so fulfil *the law of Christ.*" But what says this Review? "Cast out your brethren, and treat them as heathens." I know it will be said, that christians are not called upon to reject real christians, but hereticks and false pretenders to the name. But heresy, we have seen, is not a false opinion, but a sectarian spirit; and as to false pretences, we desire those who know us, to put their hands on their hearts, and to say, whether they can for a moment believe that we hypocritically profess to follow the instructions of Jesus Christ? Does charity discover nothing in our language and lives to justify the hope that we are united to Jesus Christ by love for his character, and by participation of his spirit? Most earnestly would I advise those persons who are inclined to follow the instigations of this Review, to think seriously before they act; to remember, that Jesus Christ has solemnly forbidden uncharitable judgment, that he regards the injuries which are done to his followers, through a censorious spirit, as done to himself, and that christians cannot more surely forsake their Lord, the Prince of peace, than by following an inciter to denunciation and division. . . .

Before I leave this question of separation, let me just observe, that by this Review, not only we and our brethren are cut off from the body of Christ; but the most venerable men who have left us, and who, when living, were esteemed ornaments of the church, such men as the late President Willard, Dr. Howard, Dr. Eckley, Dr. Eliot, and Dr. Barnard, are declared unworthy of the communion of the church on earth, and of course unfit for the fellowship of saints in heaven. It would be easy to show, that the same dreadful sentence is past on some of the most exemplary men in civil life, to whom this commonwealth is indebted for the stability of its civil and religious institutions. These all having lived, as they thought, in the faith of Christ, and having died with a hope in his precious promises, are now cut off from his church, and denied his name. What christian does not shudder at this awful temerity in a frail and erring fellow-being, who thus presumes to sit in judgment on men, who in purity and sincerity and devotion to God, were certainly not inferiour to himself? I stop here, for I wish not to indulge in language of severity; and this subject, if any, may be left to speak for itself to the heart of the christian.

Having thus considered the three principal heads in the Review, I now proceed, as I proposed, to offer a few words of friendly admonition, as to the temper and conduct which become our brethren and ourselves, under the injuries which we receive. The first suggestion you have undoubtedly anticipated. It is, that we remember the great duty which belongs to us as christians, of regarding our enemies with good will, if possible with a degree of approbation, at least with displeasure tempered with compassion. We profess to accord with that apostle, who has taught us that charity is greater than faith and hope, more excellent than the tongue of angels and the understanding of all mysteries. Let us prove our sincerity by our deeds. Let us cheerfully avail ourselves of every circumstance, which will justify the belief, that the cruel and bitter remarks of our adversaries proceed not from a wanton and unblushing contempt of truth, but from deep rooted prejudices, false views of religion, unsuspected biasses to censoriousness, and a disordered imagination; and whilst we lament that they do not partake more largely of the best influences of the gospel, let us be inclined to hope that their profession of the gospel is sincere, and that their departure from its spirit is unknown to themselves. As to the great mass of those christians, who view us with so much jealousy, we must remember, that they know us only by report, that they believe as they are taught by men to whom they ascribe an eminent sanctity, and that they are liable to be carried away on this, as on every other subject, by loud assertion, and by addresses to their fears. Accustomed as they are to hear us branded with names and epithets, to which they have attached no definite ideas, but which seem to them to express every thing depraved, can we wonder that they shrink from us with a kind of terrour? Towards this great class of our opposers, we certainly owe nothing but kindness; and we should esteem it an unspeakable happiness, that we can look with so much pleasure and hope on those by whom we are dreaded and shunned; that we are not obliged by our system to regard *our* adversaries as the enemies of God, and the objects of his wrath. On this point, above all others, I would be urgent. Our danger is, that reproach will hurry us into language or conduct unbecoming the spirit of our master. Let us remember that our opposers cannot ultimately injure us, unless we permit them to awaken bad passions, and to impair our virtues. Let us remember what is due from us to our religion. The more that our age is uncharitable, the more that the glory of the gospel is obscured by its being exhibited as a source of censoriousness and contention, the more we owe it to our Lord to wipe off this reproach from his truth, to shew the loveliness of his religion, to show its power in changing the heart into the image of divine forbearance and forgiveness. Is the gospel at this moment receiving deep wounds in the house of its friends? Let us guard with new jealousy its interests and honour.

The second suggestion I would offer, is this. Whilst we disapprove and lament the unchristian spirit of some of our opposers, and the efforts which are used to make us odious, let us yet acknowledge that there is kindness in that Providence, which permits this trial to befall us. We esteem it indeed a hardship to be numbered by our brethren among the enemies of that Saviour whom we love. But let us remember, that we as well as others need affliction: and it is my persuasion and hope that God intends by this dispensation to purify our characters and extend our usefulness. The singular prosperity which we have enjoyed, has undoubtedly exposed us to peculiar temptations. Perhaps in no part of the world is the condition of ministers more favoured than ours. Whilst we receive nothing of a superstitious homage or a blind submission, we find ourselves respected by all classes of society, and, may I not say, distinguished by the eminent, the enlightened and the good? We are received with a kind of domestick affection into the families of our parishioners. Our sufferings call forth their sympathy, and in sickness we enjoy every aid which tenderness and liberality can bestow. Our ministrations are attended with a seriousness, which, however due to the truth which we deliver, we often feel to be poorly deserved, by the imperfect manner in which it is dispensed. In our societies there are no divisions, no jealousies, no parties to disturb us. Whilst for these singular blessings, we should give thanks to the Author of all good, we should remember, that human virtue is often unable to sustain uninterrupted prosperity; that a condition so favoured tends to awaken pride and self-indulgence; and that

God, who knows us better than we know ourselves, may see that we need reproach and opposition to make us better men and better ministers. I can certainly say for myself, that the spirit of denunciation in our country, has led me to a more serious and habitual study of the scriptures, and to a deeper feeling of my responsibility, than I should have attained in a more peaceful condition. Let us then resign ourselves to God, who in infinite wisdom sees fit to expose us to the scourge of evil tongues. Let this trial awaken us to new watchfulness, devotion, and fidelity; and we may trust that it will be overruled to the extension of our usefulness, and to the promotion of pure and undefiled religion.

A third, and a very important suggestion is this: Let us hold fast our uprightness. I have said, that the opposition to which we are exposed has its advantages; but whilst it preserves us from the temptation of prosperity, it brings some temptation of its own, which we cannot too steadfastly resist. It will try our integrity. That our churches are to be generally shaken by the assault which is made upon them, I am far from believing. But some may suffer. It is not impossible, that the efforts which are now employed to direct against us the uncharitableness and mistaken zeal of the country, and to spread disaffection through the most uninstructed and the most easily excited classes of society, may produce some effect. We know the fluctuations of the human mind. We know that the sincerest christians are often unduly influenced by timidity, and may be brought to suspect a minister, when he is decried as a heretick, who is leading souls to hell. It requires more strength of nerves and more independence of mind than all good people possess, to withstand this incessant clamour. A storm then may be gathering over some of us, and the sufferers may be tempted to bend to it. But God forbid, my friend, that any of us should give support to the aspersions cast on our uprightness, by ever suppressing our convictions, or speaking a language foreign to our hearts. Through good report and through evil report, let us with simplicity and sincerity declare what we believe to be the will of God and the way to Heaven, and thus secure to ourselves that peace of conscience which is infinitely better than the smiles of the world. Let us never forget, that the most honoured condition on earth is that of being sufferers for the sake of righteousness, for adherence to what we deem the cause of God and holiness, and let us welcome suffering, if it shall be appointed us, as bringing us nearer to our persecuted Lord, and his injured apostles. My brother, we profess to count man's judgment as a light thing, to esteem this world and all which it offers to be vanity. We profess to look up to a heavenly inheritance, and to hope that we shall one day mingle with angels and just men made perfect. And with these sublime hopes, shall we tremble before frail and fallible fellow creatures, be depressed by difficulties, or shrink from the expression of what we deem important and useful truth? God forbid.

I have time to add but one more suggestion. Let us beware lest opposition and reproach lead any of us into a sectarian attachment to our peculiar opinions. This is a danger to which persons of ardent and irritable temper are peculiarly exposed. Too many of us are apt to cling to a system in proportion as it is assailed, to consider ourselves pledged to doctrines which we have openly exposed, to rally round them as if our own honour and interest were at stake, and to assert them with more and more positiveness, as if we were incapable of errour. This is the infirmity of our frail nature; and whilst we condemn it in others, let us not allow it in ourselves. Let us be what we profess to be, patient inquirers after truth, open to conviction, willing to listen to objections, willing to renounce errour, willing to believe that we as well as others may have been warped in our opinions, by education and situation, and that others may have acquired important truths which, through weakness or prejudice, we may have overlooked. . . .

I have thus, my brother, considered the charges, by which we and our brethren have been assailed, and have endeavoured to recommend the temper with which we should meet reproach and insult. I intended to offer a few remarks on some other topicks introduced into the Review: but this letter is already extended far beyond the limits which I originally prescribed. I cannot, however, pass over in silence the charges against Harvard University, that venerable institution, which so many excellent men in this commonwealth are accustomed to regard with filial affection and honour, and to which we are all so much indebted for the light of knowledge, and for whatever capacities of usefulness to society we may possess. The statement of the Reviewer, that the propagation of Unitarianism in that University is the object of regular and well concerted exertion, is altogether false. I am persuaded that such a plan never entered the thoughts of those to whom the department of theological instruction is entrusted. The books in which the classes are taught, were selected for the very purpose of avoiding, as far as possible, the controversies of theologians, and the communication of any peculiarities of opinion to the students. They are, "Grotius on the Truth of the Christian Religion," "Paley's Evidences," "Butler's Analogy," and "Griesbach's New Testament." . . .

I now commit this humble effort to promote the peace and union of the church, and the cause of truth and free inquiry, to the blessing of Almighty God. That in writing it, I have escaped every unchristian feeling, I dare not hope; and for every departure from the spirit of his gospel, I implore his forgiveness. If I have fallen into errour, I beseech him to discover it to my own mind, and to prevent its influence on the minds of others. It is an unspeakable consolation that we and our labours are in his hand, and that the cause of the gospel is his peculiar care. That he may honour us as the instruments of extending the knowledge and the spirit of the gospel, is the earnest prayer of your friend and brother in Christ.

❦ Unitarian Christianity

WILLIAM ELLERY CHANNING
(1780–1842)

Channing's sermon at the ordination of Jared Sparks (May 5, 1819, in Baltimore) has been justly regarded as the chief manifesto of American Unitarianism. A magisterial statement of both the formal and material principles of the new movement, it became a kind of declaration of independence from the Standing Order of Massachusetts.

The New England Unitarians regarded the event as an important stage for the spread of liberal principles. John Kirkland, president of Harvard College; John Gorham Palfrey, later dean of the Divinity School; and Henry Ware, Sr., Hollis Professor of Divinity, accompanied Channing to Baltimore for the ceremony in the newly constructed Unitarian church, which was called by several local ministers a Synagogue of Satan.

Geographically and theologically, Baltimore provided a significant pivot for dissemination of Unitarianism. As Channing wrote to a ministerial colleague in Maine: "[Sparks] wishes the presence of some gentlemen who are remote from Boston, to prove to our Southern brethren that our peculiarities are not confined to this town."[1]

Liberal trends in Christianity had been identified with Boston for at least a decade as the liberal and conservative elements of the Standing Order emerged. The Baltimore Sermon, however, brought the Unitarian message outside its native Congregationalism in Massachusetts and into a different religious climate, where neither Congregationalism nor Unitarianism was familiar, Presbyterianism being the dominant Protestant influence in the area. Channing was the logical choice for preacher. His well-known eloquence and his ability to be forthright in expression were equally important as he presented the Unitarian case concerning reason, revelation, and Scripture to an audience of northerners and southerners.

Many church historians in the twentieth century believe that the history of Christianity is the history of the interpretation of the Bible. Guided by this thesis the modern reader can perceive the impact of Channing's ninety-minute sermon calling for a reformation in the American churches. Indeed, one can see a number of parallels with the movement Luther began with his ninety-five theses. For both Luther and Channing set forth

1. Archives, First Unitarian Church of Baltimore, Maryland, 15 May 1815.

their ideas clearly, called for action, and found substantial response from orthodox and liberals alike.

Orthodox champions perceived the Baltimore Sermon's importance immediately and rushed to the attack. Two professors at Andover Seminary, Moses Stuart and Leonard Woods, responded in detail. At the same time, the number of liberal adherents increased after the publication of the sermon. As rejoinder followed rejoinder, orthodox against liberal, the Unitarian Controversy developed into a major event in American intellectual and theological history. The Baltimore Sermon by no means reveals every dimension of Channing's thought, but it does expound the essentials of liberal Christianity as most Christian Unitarians understood it in the antebellum era.

I THES. V. 21: *Prove all things; hold fast that which is good.*

The peculiar circumstances of this occasion not only justify, but seem to demand a departure from the course generally followed by preachers at the introduction of a brother into the sacred office. It is usual to speak of the nature, design, duties, and advantages of the Christian ministry; and on these topics I should now be happy to insist, did I not remember that a minister is to be given this day to a religious society, whose peculiarities of opinion have drawn upon them much remark, and may I not add, much reproach. Many good minds, many sincere Christians, I am aware, are apprehensive that the solemnities of this day are to give a degree of influence to principles which they deem false and injurious. The fears and anxieties of such men I respect; and, believing that they are grounded in part on mistake, I have thought it my duty to lay before you, as clearly as I can, some of the distinguishing opinions of that class of Christians in our country, who are known to sympathize with this religious society. I must ask your patience, for such a subject is not to be despatched in a narrow compass. I must also ask you to remember, that it is impossible to exhibit, in a single discourse, our views of every doctrine of Revelation, much less the differences of opinion which are known to subsist among ourselves. I shall confine myself to topics, on which our sentiments have been misrepresented, or which distinguish us most widely from others. May I not hope to be heard with candor? God deliver us all from prejudice and unkindness, and fill us with the love of truth and virtue.

There are two natural divisions under which my thoughts will be arranged. I shall endeavour to unfold, 1st, The principles which we adopt in interpreting the Scriptures. And 2dly, Some of the doctrines, which the Scriptures, so interpreted, seem to us clearly to express.

I. We regard the Scriptures as the records of God's successive revelations to mankind, and particularly of the last and most perfect revelation of his will by Jesus Christ. Whatever doctrines seem to us to be clearly taught in the Scriptures, we receive without reserve or exception. We do not, however, attach equal importance to all the books in this collection. Our religion, we believe, lies chiefly in the New Testament. The dispensation of Moses, compared with that of Jesus, we consider as adapted to the childhood of the human race, a preparation for a nobler system, and chiefly useful now as serving to confirm and illustrate the Christian Scriptures. Jesus Christ is the only master of Christians, and whatever he taught, either during his personal ministry, or by his inspired Apostles, we regard as of divine authority, and profess to make the rule of our lives.

This authority, which we give to the Scriptures, is a reason, we conceive, for studying them with peculiar care, and for inquiring anxiously into the principles of interpretation, by which their true meaning may be ascertained. The principles adopted by the class of Christians in whose name I speak, need to be explained, because they are often misunderstood. We are particularly accused of making an unwarrantable use of reason in the interpretation of Scripture. We are said to exalt reason above revelation, to prefer our own wisdom to God's. Loose and undefined charges of this kind are circulated so freely, that we think it due to ourselves, and to the cause of truth, to express our views with some particularity.

Our leading principle in interpreting Scripture is this, that the Bible is a book written for men, in the language of men, and that its meaning is to be sought in the same manner as that of other books. We believe that God, when he speaks to the human race, conforms, if we may so say, to the established rules of speaking and writing. How else would the Scriptures avail us more, than if communicated in an unknown tongue?

Now all books, and all conversation, require in the reader or hearer the constant exercise of reason; or their true import is only to be obtained by continual comparison and inference. Human language, you well know, admits various interpretations; and every word and every sentence must be modified and explained according to the subject which is discussed, according to the purposes, feelings, circumstances, and principles of the writer, and according to the genius and idioms of the language which he uses. These are acknowledged principles in the interpretation of human writings; and a man, whose words we should explain without reference to these principles, would reproach us justly with a criminal want of candor, and an intention of obscuring or distorting his meaning.

Were the Bible written in a language and style of its own, did it consist of words, which admit but a single sense, and of sentences wholly detached from each other, there would be no place for the principles now laid down. We could not reason about it, as about other writings. But such a book would be of little worth; and perhaps, of all books, the Scriptures correspond least to this description. The Word of God bears the stamp of the same hand, which we see in his works. It has infinite connexions and dependences. Every proposition is linked with others, and is to be compared with others; that its full and precise import may be understood. Nothing stands alone. The New Testament is built on the Old. The Christian dispensation is a continuation of the Jewish, the completion of a vast scheme of providence, requiring great extent of view in the reader. Still more, the Bible treats of subjects on which we receive ideas from other sources besides itself; such subjects as the nature, passions, relations, and duties of man; and it expects us to restrain and modify its language by the known truths, which observation and experience furnish on these topics.

We profess not to know a book, which demands a more frequent exercise of reason than the Bible. In addition to the remarks now made on its infinite connexions, we may observe, that its style nowhere affects the precision of science, or the accuracy of definition. Its language is singularly glowing, bold, and figurative, demanding more frequent departures from the literal sense, than that of our own age and country, and consequently demanding more continual exercise of judgment.—We find, too, that the different portions of this book, instead of being confined to general truths, refer perpetually to the times when they were written, to states of society, to modes of thinking, to controversies in the church, to feelings and usages which have passed away, and without the knowledge of which we are constantly in danger of extending to all times, and places, what was of temporary and local application.—We find, too, that some of these books are strongly marked by the genius and character of their respective writers, that the Holy Spirit did not so guide the Apostles as to suspend the peculiarities of their minds, and that a knowledge of their feelings, and of the influences under which they were placed, is one of the preparations for understanding their writings. With these views of the Bible, we feel it our bounden duty to exercise our reason upon it perpetually, to compare, to infer, to look beyond the letter to the spirit, to seek in the nature of the subject, and the aim of the writer, his true meaning; and, in general, to make use of what is known, for explaining what is difficult, and for discovering new truths.

Need I descend to particulars, to prove that the Scriptures demand the exercise of reason? Take, for example, the style in which they generally speak of God, and observe how habitually they apply to him human passions and organs. Recollect the declarations of Christ, that he came not to send peace, but a sword; that unless we eat his flesh, and drink his blood, we have no life in us; that we must hate father and mother, and pluck out the right eye; and a vast number of passages equally bold and unlimited. Recollect the unqualified manner in which it is said of Christians, that they possess all things, know all things, and can do all things. Recollect the verbal contradiction between Paul and James, and the apparent clashing of some parts of Paul's writings with the general doctrines and end of Christianity. I might extend the enumeration indefinitely; and who does not see, that we must limit all these passages by the known attributes of God, of Jesus Christ, and of human nature, and by the circumstances under which they were written, so as to give the language a quite different import from what it would require, had it been applied to different beings, or used in different connexions.

Enough has been said to show, in what sense we make use of reason in interpreting Scripture. From a variety of possible interpretations, we select that which accords with the nature of the subject and the state of the writer, with the connexion of the passage, with the general strain of Scripture, with the known character and will of God, and with the obvious and acknowledged laws of nature. In other words, we believe that God never contradicts, in one part of Scripture, what he teaches in another; and never contradicts, in revelation, what he teaches in his works and providence. And we therefore distrust every interpretation, which, after deliberate attention, seems repugnant to any established truth. We reason about the Bible precisely as civilians do about the constitution under which we live; who, you know, are accustomed to limit one provision of that venerable instrument by others, and to fix the precise import of its parts, by inquiring into its general spirit, into the intentions of its authors, and into the prevalent feelings, impressions, and circumstances of the time when it was framed. Without these principles of interpretation, we frankly acknowledge, that we cannot defend the divine authority of the Scriptures. Deny us this latitude, and we must abandon this book to its enemies.

We do not announce these principles as original, or peculiar to ourselves. All Christians occasionally adopt them, not excepting those who most vehemently decry them, when they happen to menace some favorite article of their creed. All Christians are compelled to use them in their controversies with infidels. All sects employ them in their warfare with one another. All willingly avail themselves of reason, when it can be pressed into the service of their own party, and only complain of it, when its weapons wound themselves. None reason more frequently than those from whom we differ. It is astonishing what a fabric they rear from a few slight hints about the fall of our first parents; and how ingeniously they extract, from detached passages, mysterious doctrines about the divine nature. We do not blame them for reasoning so abundantly, but for violating the fundamental rules of reasoning, for sacrificing the plain to the obscure, and the general strain of Scripture to a scanty number of insulated texts.

We object strongly to the contemptuous manner in which human reason is often spoken of by our adversaries, because it leads, we believe, to universal skepticism. If reason be so dreadfully darkened by the fall, that its most decisive judgments on religion are unworthy of trust, then Christianity, and even natural theology, must be abandoned; for the existence and veracity of God, and the divine original of Christianity, are conclusions of reason, and must stand or fall with it. If revelation be at war with this faculty, it subverts itself, for the great question of its truth is left by God to be decided at the bar of reason. It is worthy of remark, how nearly the bigot and the skeptic approach. Both would annihilate our confidence in our faculties, and both throw doubt and confusion over every truth. We honor revelation too highly to make it the antagonist of reason, or to believe that it calls us to renounce our highest powers.

We indeed grant, that the use of reason in religion is accompanied with danger. But we ask any honest man to look back on the history of the church, and say, whether the renunciation of it be not still more dangerous. Besides, it is a plain fact, that men reason as erroneously on all subjects, as on religion. Who does not know the wild and groundless theories, which have been framed in physical and political science? But who ever supposed, that we must cease to exercise reason on nature and society, because men have erred for ages in explaining them? We grant, that the passions continually, and sometimes fatally, disturb the rational faculty in its inquiries into revelation. The ambitious contrive to find doctrines in the Bible, which favor their love of dominion. The timid and dejected discover there a gloomy system, and the mystical and fanatical, a visionary theology. The vicious can find examples or assertions on which to build the hope of a late repentance, or of acceptance on easy terms. The falsely refined contrive to light on doctrines which have not been soiled by vulgar handling. But the passions do not distract the reason in religious, any more than in other inquiries, which excite strong and general interest; and this faculty, of consequence, is not to be renounced in religion, unless we are prepared to discard it universally. The true inference from the almost endless errors, which have darkened theology, is, not that we are to neglect and disparage our powers, but to exert them more patiently, circumspectly, uprightly. The worst errors, after all, having sprung up in that church, which proscribes reason, and demands from its members implicit faith. The most pernicious doctrines have been the growth of the darkest times, when the general credulity encouraged bad men and enthusiasts to broach their dreams and inventions, and to stifle the faint remonstrances of reason, by the menaces of everlasting perdition. Say what we may, God has given us a rational nature, and will call us to account for it. We may let it sleep, but we do so at our peril. Revelation is addressed to us as rational beings. We may wish, in our sloth, that God had given us a system, demanding no labor of comparing, limiting, and inferring. But such a system would be at variance with the whole character of our present existence; and it is the part of wisdom to take revelation as it is given to us, and to interpret it by the help of the faculties, which it everywhere supposes, and on which it is founded.

To the views now given, an objection is commonly urged from the character of God. We are told, that God being infinitely wiser than men, his discoveries will surpass human reason. In a revelation from such a teacher, we ought to expect propositions, which we cannot reconcile with one another, and which may seem to contradict established truths; and it becomes us not to question or explain them away, but to believe, and adore, and to submit our weak and carnal reason to the Divine Word. To this objection, we have two short answers. We say, first, that it is impossible that a teacher of infinite wisdom should expose those, whom he would teach, to infinite error. But if once we admit, that propositions, which in their literal sense appear plainly repugnant to one another, or to any known truth, are still to be literally understood and received, what possible limit can we set to the belief of contradictions? What shelter have we from the wildest fanaticism, which can always quote passages, that, in their literal and obvious sense, give support to its extravagances? How can the Protestant escape from transubstantiation, a doctrine most clearly taught us, if the submission of reason, now contended for, be a duty? How can we even hold fast the truth of revelation, for if one apparent contradiction may be true, so may another, and the proposition, that Christianity is false, though involving inconsistency, may still be a verity?

We answer again, that, if God be infinitely wise, he cannot sport with the understandings of his creatures. A wise teacher discovers his wisdom in adapting himself to the capacities of his pupils, not in perplexing them with what is unintelligible, not in distressing them with apparent contradictions, not in filling them with a skeptical distrust of their own powers. An infinitely wise teacher, who knows the precise extent of our minds, and the best method of enlightening them, will surpass all other instructors in bringing down truth to our apprehension, and in showing its loveliness and harmony. We ought, indeed, to expect occasional obscurity in such a book as the Bible, which was written for past and future ages, as well as for the present. But God's wisdom is a pledge, that whatever is necessary for *us,* and necessary for salvation, is revealed too plainly to be mistaken, and too consistently to be questioned, by a sound and upright mind. It is not the mark of wisdom, to use an unintelligible phraseology, to communicate what is above our capacities, to confuse and unsettle the intellect by appearances of contradiction. We honor our Heavenly Teacher too much to ascribe to him such a revelation. A revelation is a gift of light. It cannot thicken our darkness, and multiply our perplexities.

II. Having thus stated the principles according to which we interpret Scripture, I now proceed to the second great head of this discourse, which is, to state some of the views which we derive from that sacred book, particularly those which distinguish us from other Christians.

1. In the first place, we believe in the doctrine of God's UNITY, or that there is one God, and one only. To this truth we give infinite importance, and we feel ourselves bound to take heed, lest any man spoil us of it by vain philosophy. The proposition, that there is one God, seems to us exceedingly plain. We understand by it, that there is one being, one mind, one person, one intelligent agent, and one only, to whom underived and infinite perfection and dominion belong. We conceive, that these words could have conveyed no other meaning to the simple and uncultivated people who were set apart to be the depositaries of this great truth, and who were utterly incapable of understanding those hairbreadth distinctions between being and person, which the sagacity of later ages has discovered. We find no intimation, that this language was to be taken in an unusual sense, or that God's unity was a quite different thing from the oneness of other intelligent beings.

We object to the doctrine of the Trinity, that, whilst acknowledging in words, it subverts in effect, the unity of God. According to this doctrine, there are three infinite and equal persons, possessing supreme divinity, called the Father, Son, and Holy Ghost. Each of these persons, as described by theologians, has his own particular consciousness, will, and perceptions. They love each other, converse with each other, and delight in each other's society. They perform different parts in man's redemption, each having his appropriate office, and neither doing the work of the other. The Son is mediator and not the Father. The Father sends the Son, and is not himself sent; nor is he conscious, like the Son, of taking flesh. Here, then, we have three intelligent agents, possessed of different consciousnesses, different wills, and different perceptions, performing different acts, and sustaining different relations; and if these things do not imply and constitute three minds or beings, we are utterly at a loss to know how three minds or beings are to be formed. It is difference of properties, and acts, and consciousness, which leads us to the belief of different intelligent beings, and, if this mark fails us, our whole knowledge falls; we have no proof, that all the agents and persons in the universe are not one and the same mind. When we attempt to conceive of three Gods, we can do nothing more than represent to ourselves three agents, distinguished from each other by similar marks and peculiarities to those which separate the persons of the Trinity; and when common Christians hear these persons spoken of as conversing with each other, loving each other, and performing different acts, how can they help regarding them as different beings, different minds?

We do, then, with all earnestness, though without reproaching our brethren, protest against the irrational and unscriptural doctrine of the Trinity. "To us," as to the Apostle and the primitive Christians, "there is one God, even the Father." With Jesus, we worship the Father, as the only living and true God. We are astonished, that any man can read the New Testament, and avoid the conviction, that the Father alone is God. We hear our Saviour continually appropriating this character to the Father. We find the Father continually distinguished from Jesus by this title. "God sent his Son." "God anointed Jesus." Now, how singular and inexplicable is this phraseology, which fills the New Testament, if this title belong equally to Jesus, and if a principal object of this book is to reveal him as God, as partaking equally with the Father in supreme divinity! We challenge our opponents to adduce one passage in the New Testament, where the word God means three persons, where it is not limited to one person, and where, unless turned from its usual sense by the connexion, it does not mean the Father. Can stronger proof be given, that the doctrine of three persons in the Godhead is not a fundamental doctrine of Christianity?

This doctrine, were it true, must, from its difficulty, singularity, and importance, have been laid down with great clearness, guarded with great care, and stated with all possible precision. But where does this statement appear? From the many passages which treat of God, we ask for one, one only, in which we are told, that he is threefold being, or that he is three persons, or that he is Father, Son, and Holy Ghost. On the contrary, in the New Testament, where, at least, we might expect many express assertions of this nature, God is declared to be one, without the least attempt to prevent the acceptation of the words in their common sense; and he is always spoken of and addressed in the singular number, that is, in language which was universally understood to intend a single person, and to which no other idea could have been attached, without an express admonition. So entirely do the Scriptures abstain from stating the Trinity, that when our opponents would insert it into their creeds and doxologies, they are compelled to leave the Bible, and to invent forms of words altogether unsanctioned by Scriptural phraseology. That a doctrine so strange, so liable to misapprehension, so fundamental as this is said to be, and requiring such careful exposition, should be left so undefined and unprotected, to be made out by inference, and to be hunted through distant and detached parts of Scripture, this is a difficulty, which, we think, no ingenuity can explain.

We have another difficulty. Christianity, it must be remembered, was planted and grew up amidst sharp-sighted enemies, who overlooked no objectionable part of the system, and who must have fastened with great earnestness on a doctrine involving such apparent contradictions as the Trinity. We cannot conceive an opinion, against which the Jews, who prided themselves on an adherence to God's unity, would have raised an equal clamor. Now, how happens it, that in the apostolic writings, which relate so much to objections against Christianity, and to the controversies which grew out of this religion, not one word is said, implying that objections were brought against the Gospel from the doctrine of the Trinity, not one word is uttered in its defence and explanation, not a word to rescue it from reproach and mistake? This argument has almost the force of demonstration. We are persuaded, that had three divine persons been announced by the first preachers of Christianity, all equal, and all infinite, one of whom was the very Jesus who had lately died on a cross, this peculiarity of Christianity would have almost absorbed every other, and the great labor of the Apostles would have been to repel the continual assaults, which it would have awakened. But the fact is, that not a whisper of objection to Christianity, on that account, reaches our ears from the apostolic age. In the Epistles we see not a trace of controversy called forth by the Trinity.

We have further objections to this doctrine, drawn from its practical influence. We regard it as unfavorable to devotion, by dividing and distracting the mind in its communion with God. It is a great excellence of the doctrine of God's unity, that it offers to us ONE OBJECT of supreme homage, adoration, and love, One Infinite Father, one Being of beings, one original and fountain, to whom we may refer all good, in whom all our powers and affections may be concentrated, and whose lovely and venerable nature may pervade all our thoughts. True piety, when directed to an undivided Deity, has a chasteness, a singleness, most favorable to religious awe and love. Now, the Trinity sets before us three distinct objects of supreme adoration; three infinite persons, having equal claims on our hearts; three divine agents, performing different offices, and to be acknowledged and worshipped in different relations. And is it possible, we ask, that the weak and limited mind of man can attach itself to these with the same power and joy, as to One Infinite Father, the only First Cause, in whom all the blessings of nature and redemption meet as their centre and source? Must not devotion be distracted by the equal and rival claims of three equal persons, and must not the worship of the conscientious, consistent Christian, be disturbed by an apprehension, lest he withhold from one or another of these, his due proportion of homage?

We also think, that the doctrine of the Trinity injures devotion, not only by joining to the Father other objects of worship, but by taking from the Father the supreme affection, which is his due, and transferring it to the Son. This is a most important view. That Jesus Christ, if exalted into the infinite Divinity, should be more interesting than the Father, is precisely what might be expected from history, and from the principles of human nature. Men want an object of worship like themselves, and the great secret of idolatry lies in this propensity. A God, clothed in our form, and feeling our wants and sorrows, speaks to our weak nature more strongly, than a Father in heaven, a pure spirit, invisible and unapproachable, save by the reflecting and purified mind.—We think, too, that the peculiar offices ascribed to Jesus by the popular theology, make him the most attractive person in the Godhead. The Father is the depositary of the justice, the vindicator of the rights, the avenger of the laws of the Divinity. On the other hand, the Son, the brightness of the divine mercy, stands between the incensed Deity and guilty humanity, exposes his meek head to the storms, and his compassionate breast to the sword of the divine justice, bears our whole load of punishment, and purchases with his blood every blessing which descends from heaven. Need we state the effect of these representations, especially on common minds, for whom Christianity was chiefly designed, and whom it seeks to bring to the Father as the loveliest being? We do believe, that the worship of a bleeding, suffering God, tends strongly to absorb the mind, and to draw it from other objects, just as the human tenderness of the Virgin Mary has given her so conspicuous a place in the devotions of the Church of Rome. We believe, too, that this worship, though attractive, is not most fitted to spiritualize the mind, that it awakens human transport, rather than that deep veneration of the moral perfections of God, which is the essence of piety.

2. Having thus given our views of the unity of God, I proceed in the second place to observe, that we believe in the unity of Jesus Christ. We believe that Jesus is one mind, one soul, one being, as truly one as we are, and equally distinct from the one God. We complain of the doctrine of

the Trinity, that, not satisfied with making God three beings, it makes Jesus Christ two beings, and thus introduces infinite confusion into our conceptions of his character. This corruption of Christianity, alike repugnant to common sense and to the general strain of Scripture, is a remarkable proof of the power of a false philosophy in disfiguring the simple truth of Jesus.

According to this doctrine, Jesus Christ, instead of being one mind, one conscious intelligent principle, whom we can understand, consists of two souls, two minds; the one divine, the other human; the one weak, the other almighty; the one ignorant, the other omniscient. Now we maintain, that this is to make Christ two beings. To denominate him one person, one being, and yet to suppose him made up of two minds, infinitely different from each other, is to abuse and confound language, and to throw darkness over all our conceptions of intelligent natures. According to the common doctrine, each of these two minds in Christ has its own consciousness, its own will, its own perceptions. They have, in fact, no common properties. The divine mind feels none of the wants and sorrows of the human, and the human is infinitely removed from the perfection and happiness of the divine. Can you conceive of two beings in the universe more distinct? We have always thought that one person was constituted and distinguished by one consciousness. The doctrine, that one and the same person should have two consciousnesses, two wills, two souls, infinitely different from each other, this we think an enormous tax on human credulity.

We say, that if a doctrine, so strange, so difficult, so remote from all the previous conceptions of men, be indeed a part and an essential part of revelation, it must be taught with great distinctness, and we ask our brethren to point to some plain, direct passage, where Christ is said to be composed of two minds infinitely different, yet constituting one person. We find none. Other Christians, indeed, tell us, that this doctrine is necessary to the harmony of the Scriptures, that some texts ascribe to Jesus Christ human, and others divine properties, and that to reconcile these, we must suppose two minds, to which these properties may be referred. In other words, for the purpose of reconciling certain difficult passages, which a just criticism can in a great degree, if not wholly, explain, we must invent an hypothesis vastly more difficult, and involving gross absurdity. We are to find our way out of a labyrinth, by a clue which conducts us into mazes infinitely more inextricable.

Surely, if Jesus Christ felt that he consisted of two minds, and that this was a leading feature of his religion, his phraseology respecting himself would have been colored by this peculiarity. The universal language of men is framed upon the idea, that one person is one person, is one mind, and one soul; and when the multitude heard this language from the lips of Jesus, they must have taken it in its usual sense, and must have referred to a single soul all which he spoke, unless expressly instructed to interpret it differently. But where do we find this instruction? Where do you meet, in the New Testament, the phraseology which abounds in Trinitarian books, and which necessarily grows from the doctrine of two natures in Jesus? Where does this divine teacher say, "This I speak as God, and this as man; this is true only of my human mind, this only of my divine"? Where do we find in the Epistles a trace of this strange phraseology? Nowhere. It was not needed in that day. It was demanded by the errors of a later age.

We believe, then, that Christ is one mind, one being, and, I add, a being distinct from the one God. That Christ is not the one God, not the same being with the Father, is a necessary inference from our former head, in which we saw that the doctrine of three persons in God is a fiction. But on so important a subject, I would add a few remarks. We wish, that those from whom we differ, would weigh one striking fact. Jesus, in his preaching, continually spoke of God. The word was always in his mouth. We ask, does he, by this word, ever mean himself? We say, never. On the contrary, he most plainly distinguishes between God and himself, and so do his disciples. How this is to be reconciled with the idea, that the manifestation of Christ, as God, was a primary object of Christianity, our adversaries must determine.

If we examine the passages in which Jesus is distinguished from God, we shall see, that they not only speak of him as another being, but seem to labor to express his inferiority. He is continually spoken of as the Son of God, sent of God, receiving all his powers from God, working miracles because God was with him, judging justly because God taught him, having claims on our belief, because he was anointed and sealed by God, and as able of himself to do nothing. The New Testament is filled with this language. Now we ask, what impression this language was fitted and intended to make? Could any, who heard it, have imagined that Jesus was the very God to whom he was so industriously declared to be inferior; the very Being by whom he was sent, and from whom he professed to have received his message and power? Let it here be remembered, that the human birth, and bodily form, and humble circumstances, and mortal sufferings of Jesus, must all have prepared men to interpret, in the most unqualified manner, the language in which his inferiority to God was declared. Why, then, was this language used so continually, and without limitation, if Jesus were the Supreme Deity, and if this truth were an essential part of his religion? I repeat it, the human condition and sufferings of Christ tended strongly to exclude from men's minds the idea of his proper Godhead; and, of course, we should expect to find in the New Testament perpetual care and effort to counteract this tendency, to hold him forth as the same being with his Father, if this doctrine were, as is pretended, the soul and centre of his religion. We should expect to find the phraseology of Scripture cast into the mould of this doctrine, to hear familiarly of God the Son, of our Lord God Jesus, and to be told, that to us there is one God, even Jesus. But, instead of this, the inferiority of Christ pervades the New Testament. It is not only implied in the general phraseology, but repeatedly and decidedly expressed, and unaccompanied with any admonition to prevent its application to his whole nature. Could it, then, have been the great design of the sacred writers to exhibit Jesus as the Supreme God?

I am aware that these remarks will be met by two or three texts, in which Christ is called God, and by a class of passages, not very numerous, in which divine properties are said to be ascribed to him. To these we offer one plain answer. We say, that it is one of the most established and obvious principles of criticism, that language is to be explained according to the known properties of the subject to which it is applied. Every man knows, that the same words convey very different ideas, when used in relation to different beings. Thus, Solomon *built* the temple in a different manner from the architect whom he employed; and God *repents* differently from man. Now we maintain, that the known properties and circumstances of Christ, his birth, sufferings, and death, his constant habit of speaking of God as a distinct being from himself, his praying to God, his ascribing to God all his power and offices, these acknowledged properties of Christ, we say, oblige us to interpret the comparatively few passages which are thought to make him the Supreme God, in a manner consistent with his distinct and inferior nature. It is our duty to explain such texts by the rule which we apply to other texts, in which human beings are called gods, and are said to be partakers of the divine nature, to know and possess all things, and to be filled with all God's fulness. These latter passages we do not hesitate to modify, and restrain, and turn from the most obvious sense, because this sense is opposed to the known properties of the beings to whom they relate; and we maintain, that we adhere to the same principle, and use no greater latitude, in explaining, as we do, the passages which are thought to support the Godhead of Christ.

Trinitarians profess to derive some important advantages from their mode of viewing Christ. It furnishes them, they tell us, with an infinite atonement, for it shows them an infinite being suffering for their sins. The confidence with which this fallacy is repeated astonishes us. When pressed with the question, whether they really believe, that the infinite and unchangeable God suffered and died on the cross, they acknowledge that this is not true, but that Christ's human mind alone sustained the pains of death. How have we, then, an infinite sufferer? This language seems to us an imposition on common minds, and very derogatory to God's justice, as if this attribute could be satisfied by a sophism and a fiction.

We are also told, that Christ is a more interesting object, that his love and mercy are more felt, when he is viewed as the Supreme God, who left his glory to take humanity and to suffer for men. That Trinitarians are strongly moved by this representation, we do not mean to deny; but we think their emotions altogether founded on a misapprehension of their own doctrines. They talk of the second person of the Trinity's leaving his glory and his Father's bosom, to visit and save the world. But this second person, being the unchangeable and infinite God, was evidently incapable of parting with the least degree of his perfection and felicity. At the moment of his taking flesh, he was as intimately present with his Father as before, and equally with his Father filled heaven, and earth, and immensity. This Trinitarians acknowledge; and still they profess to be touched and overwhelmed by the amazing humiliation of this immutable being! But not only does their doctrine, when fully explained, reduce Christ's humiliation to a fiction, it almost wholly destroys the impressions with which his cross ought to be viewed. According to their doctrine, Christ was comparatively no sufferer at all. It is true, his human mind suffered; but this, they tell us, was an infinitely small part of Jesus, bearing no more proportion to his whole nature, than a single hair of our heads to the whole body, or than a drop to the ocean. The divine mind of Christ, that which was most properly himself, was infinitely happy, at the very moment of the suffering of his humanity. Whilst hanging on the cross, he was the happiest being in the universe, as happy as the infinite Father; so that his pains, compared with his felicity, were nothing. This Trinitarians do, and must, acknowledge. It follows necessarily from the immutableness of the divine nature, which they ascribe to Christ; so that their system, justly viewed, robs his death of interest, weakens our sympathy with his sufferings, and is, of all others, most unfavorable to a love of Christ, founded on a sense of his sacrifices for mankind. We esteem our own views to be vastly more affecting. It is our belief, that Christ's humiliation was real and entire, that the whole Saviour, and not a part of him, suffered, that his crucifixion was a scene of deep and unmixed agony. As we stand round his cross, our minds are not distracted, nor our sensibility weakened, by contemplating him as composed of incongruous and infinitely differing minds, and as having a balance of infinite felicity. We recognise in the dying Jesus but one mind. This, we think, renders his sufferings, and his patience and love in bearing them, incomparably more impressive and affecting than the system we oppose.

3. Having thus given our belief on two great points, namely, that there is one God, and that Jesus Christ is a being distinct from, and inferior to, God, I now proceed to another point, on which we lay still greater stress. We believe in the *moral perfection of God*. We consider no part of theology so important as that which treats of God's moral character; and we value our views of Christianity chiefly as they assert his amiable and venerable attributes.

It may be said, that, in regard to this subject, all Christians agree, that all ascribe to the Supreme Being infinite justice, goodness, and holiness. We reply, that it is very possible to speak of God magnificently, and to think of him meanly; to apply to his person high-sounding epithets, and to his government, principles which make him odious. The Heathens called Jupiter the greatest and the best; but his history was black with cruelty and lust. We cannot judge of men's real ideas of God by their general language, for in all ages they have hoped to soothe the Deity by adulation. We must inquire into their particular views of his purposes, of the principles of his administration, and of his disposition towards his creatures.

We conceive that Christians have generally leaned towards a very injurious view of the Supreme Being. They have too often felt, as if he were raised, by his greatness and sovereignty, above the principles of morality, above those eternal laws of equity and rectitude, to which all other beings are subjected. We believe, that in no being is the sense of right so strong, so omnipotent, as in God. We believe that his almighty power is entirely submitted to his perceptions of rectitude; and this is the ground of our piety. It is not because he is our Creator merely, but because he created us for good and holy purposes; it is not because his will is irresistible, but because his will is the perfection of virtue, that we pay him allegiance. We cannot bow before a being, however great and powerful, who governs tyrannically. We respect nothing but excellence, whether on earth or in heaven. We venerate not the loftiness of God's throne, but the equity and goodness in which it is established.

We believe that God is infinitely good, kind, benevolent, in the proper sense of these words; good in disposition, as well as in act; good, not to a few, but to all; good to every individual, as well as to the general system.

We believe, too, that God is just; but we never forget, that his justice is the justice of a good being, dwelling in the same mind, and acting in harmony, with perfect benevolence. By this attribute, we understand

God's infinite regard to virtue or moral worth, expressed in a moral government; that is, in giving excellent and equitable laws, and in conferring such rewards, and inflicting such punishments, as are best fitted to secure their observance. God's justice has for its end the highest virtue of the creation, and it punishes for this end alone, and thus it coincides with benevolence; for virtue and happiness, though not the same, are inseparably conjoined.

God's justice thus viewed, appears to us to be in perfect harmony with his mercy. According to the prevalent systems of theology, these attributes are so discordant and jarring, that to reconcile them is the hardest task, and the most wonderful achievement, of infinite wisdom. To us they seem to be intimate friends, always at peace, breathing the same spirit, and seeking the same end. By God's mercy, we understand not a blind instinctive compassion, which forgives without reflection, and without regard to the interests of virtue. This, we acknowledge, would be incompatible with justice, and also with enlightened benevolence. God's mercy, as we understand it, desires strongly the happiness of the guilty, but only through their penitence. It has a regard to character as truly as his justice. It defers punishment, and suffers long, that the sinner may return to his duty, but leaves the impenitent and unyielding, to the fearful retribution threatened in God's Word.

To give our views of God in one word, we believe in his Parental character. We ascribe to him, not only the name, but the dispositions and principles of a father. We believe that he has a father's concern for his creatures, a father's desire for their improvement, a father's equity in proportioning his commands to their powers, a father's joy in their progress, a father's readiness to receive the penitent, and a father's justice for the incorrigible. We look upon this world as a place of education, in which he is training men by prosperity and adversity, by aids and obstructions, by conflicts of reason and passion, by motives to duty and temptations to sin, by a various discipline suited to free and moral beings, for union with himself, and for a sublime and ever-growing virtue in heaven.

Now, we object to the systems of religion, which prevail among us, that they are adverse, in a greater or less degree, to these purifying, comforting, and honorable views of God; that they take from us our Father in heaven, and substitute for him a being, whom we cannot love if we would, and whom we ought not to love if we could. We object, particularly on this ground, to that system, which arrogates to itself the name of Orthodoxy, and which is now industriously propagated through our country. This system indeed takes various shapes, but in all it casts dishonor on the Creator. According to its old and genuine form, it teaches, that

God brings us into life wholly depraved, so that under the innocent features of our childhood is hidden a nature averse to all good and propense to all evil, a nature which exposes us to God's displeasure and wrath, even before we have acquired power to understand our duties, or to reflect upon our actions. According to a more modern exposition, it teaches, that we came from the hands of our Maker with such a constitution, and are placed under such influences and circumstances, as to render certain and infallible the total depravity of every human being, from the first moment of his moral agency; and it also teaches, that the offence of the child, who brings into life this ceaseless tendency to unmingled crime, exposes him to the sentence of everlasting damnation. Now, according to the plainest principles of morality, we maintain, that a natural constitution of the mind, unfailingly disposing it to evil and to evil alone, would absolve it from guilt; that to give existence under this condition would argue unspeakable cruelty; and that to punish the sin of this unhappily constituted child with endless ruin, would be a wrong unparalleled by the most merciless despotism.

This system also teaches, that God selects from this corrupt mass a number to be saved, and plucks them, by a special influence, from the common ruin; that the rest of mankind, though left without that special grace which their conversion requires, are commanded to repent, under penalty of aggravated woe; and that forgiveness is promised them, on terms which their very constitution infallibly disposes them to reject, and in rejecting which they awfully enhance the punishments of hell. These proffers of forgiveness and exhortations of amendment, to beings born under a blighting curse, fill our minds with a horror which we want words to express.

That this religious system does not produce all the effects on character, which might be anticipated, we most joyfully admit. It is often, very often, counteracted by nature, conscience, common sense, by the general strain of Scripture, by the mild example and precepts of Christ, and by the many positive declarations of God's universal kindness and perfect equity. But still we think that we see its unhappy influence. It tends to discourage the timid, to give excuses to the bad, to feed the vanity of the fanatical, and to offer shelter to the bad feelings of the malignant. By shocking, as it does, the fundamental principles of morality, and by exhibiting a severe and partial Deity, it tends strongly to pervert the moral faculty, to form a gloomy, forbidding, and servile religion, and to lead men to substitute censoriousness, bitterness, and persecution, for a tender and impartial charity. We think, too, that this system, which begins with degrading human nature, may be expected to end in pride; for pride grows out of a consciousness of high distinctions, however obtained, and no distinction is so great as that which is made between the elected and abandoned of God.

The false and dishonorable views of God, which have now been stated, we feel ourselves bound to resist unceasingly. Other errors we can pass over with comparative indifference. But we ask our opponents to leave to us a GOD, worthy of our love and trust, in whom our moral sentiments may delight, in whom our weaknesses and sorrows may find refuge. We cling to the Divine perfections. We meet them everywhere in creation, we read them in the Scriptures, we see a lovely image of them in Jesus Christ; and gratitude, love, and veneration call on us to assert them. Reproached, as we often are, by men, it is our consolation and happiness, that one of our chief offences is the zeal with which we vindicate the dishonored goodness and rectitude of God.

4. Having thus spoken of the unity of God; of the unity of Jesus, and his inferiority to God; and of the perfections of the Divine character; I now proceed to give our views of the mediation of Christ, and of the purposes of his mission. With regard to the great object which Jesus came to accomplish, there seems to be no possibility of mistake. We believe, that he was sent by the Father to effect a moral, or spiritual deliverance of mankind; that is, to rescue men from sin and its consequences, and to bring them to a state of everlasting purity and happiness. We believe, too, that he accomplishes this sublime purpose by a variety of methods; by his instructions respecting God's unity, parental character, and moral government, which are admirably fitted to reclaim the world from idolatry and impiety, to the knowledge, love, and obedience of the Creator; by his promises of pardon to the penitent, and of divine assistance to those who labor for progress in moral excellence; by the light which he has thrown on the path of duty; by his own spotless example, in which the loveliness and sublimity of virtue shine forth to warm and quicken, as well as guide us to perfection; by his threatenings against incorrigible guilt; by his glorious discoveries of immortality; by his sufferings and death; by that signal event, the resurrection, which powerfully bore witness to his divine mission, and brought down to men's senses a future life; by his continual intercession, which obtains for us spiritual aid and blessings; and by the power with which he is invested of raising the dead, judging the world, and conferring the everlasting rewards promised to the faithful.

We have no desire to conceal the fact, that a difference of opinion exists among us, in regard to an interesting part of Christ's mediation; I mean, in regard to the precise influence of his death on our forgiveness. Many suppose, that this event contributes to our pardon, as it was a principal means of confirming his religion, and of giving it a power over the mind; in other words, that it procures forgiveness by leading to that repentance and virtue, which is the great and only condition on which forgiveness is bestowed. Many of us are dissatisfied with this explanation, and think that the Scriptures ascribe the remission of sins to Christ's death, with an emphasis so peculiar, that we ought to consider this event as having a special influence in removing punishment, though the Scriptures may not reveal the way in which it contributes to this end.

Whilst, however, we differ in explaining the connexion between Christ's death and human forgiveness, a connexion which we all gratefully acknowledge, we agree in rejecting many sentiments which prevail in regard to his mediation. The idea, which is conveyed to common minds by the popular system, that Christ's death has an influence in making God placable, or merciful, in awakening his kindness towards men, we reject with strong disapprobation. We are happy to find, that this very dishonorable notion is disowned by intelligent Christians of that class from which we differ. We recollect, however, that, not long ago, it was common to hear of Christ, as having died to appease God's wrath, and to pay the debt of sinners to his inflexible justice; and we have a strong persuasion, that the language of popular religious books, and the common mode of stating the doctrine of Christ's mediation, still communicate very degrading views of God's character. They give to multitudes the impression, that the death of Jesus produces a change in the mind of God towards man, and that in this its efficacy chiefly consists. No error seems to us more pernicious. We can endure no shade over the pure goodness of God. We earnestly maintain, that Jesus, instead of calling forth, in any way or degree, the mercy of the Father, was sent by that mercy, to be our Saviour; that he is nothing to the human race, but what he is by God's appointment; that he communicates nothing but what God empowers him to bestow; that our Father in heaven is originally, essentially, and eternally placable, and disposed to forgive; and that his unborrowed, underived, and unchangeable love is the only fountain of what flows to us through his Son. We conceive, that Jesus is dishonored, not glorified, by ascribing to him an influence, which clouds the splendor of Divine benevolence.

We farther agree in rejecting, as unscriptural and absurd, the explanation given by the popular system, of the manner in which Christ's death procures forgiveness for men. This system used to teach as its fundamental principle, that man, having sinned against an infinite Being, has contracted infinite guilt, and is consequently exposed to an infinite penalty. We believe, however, that this reasoning, if reasoning it may be called, which overlooks the obvious maxim, that the guilt of a being must be proportioned to his nature and powers, has fallen into disuse. Still the system teaches, that sin, of whatever degree, exposes to endless punishment, and that the whole human race, being infallibly involved by their nature in sin, owe this awful penalty to the justice of their Creator. It teaches, that this penalty cannot be remitted, in consistency with the honor of the divine law, unless a substitute be found to endure it or to suffer an equivalent. It also teaches, that, from the nature of the case, no substitute is adequate to this work, save the infinite God himself; and accordingly, God, in his second person, took on him human nature, that he might pay to his own justice the debt of punishment incurred by men, and might thus reconcile forgiveness with the claims and threatenings of his law. Such is the prevalent system. Now, to us, this doctrine seems to carry on its front strong marks of absurdity; and we maintain that Christianity ought not to be encumbered with it, unless it be laid down in the New Testament fully and expressly. We ask our adversaries, then, to point to some plain passages where it is taught. We ask for one text, in which we are told, that God took human nature that he might make an infinite satisfaction to his own justice; for one text, which tells us, that human guilt requires an infinite substitute; that Christ's sufferings owe their efficacy to their being borne by an infinite being; or that his divine nature gives infinite value to the sufferings of the human. Not *one word* of this description can we find in the Scriptures; not a text, which even hints at these strange doctrines. They are altogether, we believe, the fictions of theologians. Christianity is in no degree responsible for them. We are astonished at their prevalence. What can be plainer, than that God cannot, in any sense, be a sufferer, or bear a penalty in the room of his creatures? How dishonorable to him is the supposition, that his justice is now so severe, as to exact infinite punishment for the sins of frail and feeble men, and now so easy and yielding, as to accept the limited pains of Christ's human soul, as a full equivalent for the endless woes due from the world? How plain is it also, according to this doctrine, that God, instead of being plenteous in forgiveness, never forgives; for it seems absurd to speak of men as forgiven, when their whole punishment, or an equivalent to it, is borne by a substitute? A scheme more fitted to obscure the brightness of Christianity and the mercy of God, or less suited to give comfort to a guilty and troubled mind, could not, we think, be easily framed.

We believe, too, that this system is unfavorable to the character. It naturally leads men to think, that Christ came to change God's mind rather than their own; that the highest object of his mission was to avert punishment, rather than to communicate holiness; and that a large part of religion consists in disparaging good works and human virtue, for the purpose of magnifying the value of Christ's vicarious sufferings. In this way, a sense of the infinite importance and indispensable necessity of personal improvement is weakened, and high-sounding praises of Christ's cross seem often to be substituted for obedience to his precepts. For ourselves, we have not so learned Jesus. Whilst we gratefully acknowledge, that he came to rescue us from punishment, we believe, that he was sent on a still nobler errand, namely, to deliver us from sin itself, and to form us to a sublime and heavenly virtue. We regard him as a Saviour, chiefly as he is in the light, physician, and guide of the dark, diseased, and wandering mind. No influence in the universe seems to us so glorious, as that over the character; and no redemption so worthy of thankfulness, as the restoration of the soul to purity. Without this, pardon, were it possible, would be of little value. Why pluck the sinner from hell, if a hell be left to burn in his own breast? Why raise him to heaven, if he remain a stranger to its sanctity and love? With these impressions, we are accustomed to value the Gospel chiefly as it abounds in effectual aids, motives, excitements to a generous and divine virtue. In this virtue, as in a common centre, we see all its doctrines, precepts, promises meet; and we believe, that faith in this religion is of no worth, and contributes nothing to salvation, any farther than as it uses these doctrines, precepts, promises, and the whole life, character, sufferings, and triumphs of Jesus, as the means of purifying the mind, of changing it into the likeness of his celestial excellence.

5. Having thus stated our views of the highest object of Christ's mission, that it is the recovery of men to virtue, or holiness, I shall now, in the last place, give our views of the nature of Christian virtue, or true holiness. We believe that all virtue has its foundation in the moral nature of man, that is, in conscience, or his sense of duty, and in the power of forming his temper and life according to conscience. We believe that these moral faculties are the grounds of responsibility, and the highest distinctions of human nature, and that no act is praiseworthy, any farther than it springs from their exertion. We believe, that no dispositions infused into us without our own moral activity, are of the nature of virtue, and therefore, we reject the doctrine of irresistible divine influence on the human mind, moulding it into goodness, as marble is hewn into a statue. Such goodness, if this word may be used, would not be the object of moral approbation, any more than the instinctive affections of inferior animals, or the constitutional amiableness of human beings.

By these remarks, we do not mean to deny the importance of God's aid or Spirit; but by his Spirit, we mean a moral, illuminating, and persuasive influence, not physical, not compulsory, not involving a necessity of virtue. We object, strongly, to the idea of many Christians respecting man's impotence and God's irresistible agency on the heart, believing that they subvert our responsibility and the laws of our moral nature, that they make men machines, that they cast on God the blame of all evil deeds, that they discourage good minds, and inflate the fanatical with wild conceits of immediate and sensible inspiration.

Among the virtues, we give the first place to the love of God. We believe, that this principle is the true end and happiness of our being, that we were made for union with our Creator, that his infinite perfection is the only sufficient object and true resting-place for the insatiable desires and unlimited capacities of the human mind, and that, without him, our noblest sentiments, admiration, veneration, hope, and love, would wither and decay. We believe, too, that the love of God is not only essential to happiness, but to the strength and perfection of all the virtues; that conscience, without the sanction of God's authority and retributive justice, would be a weak director; that benevolence, unless nourished by communion with his goodness, and encouraged by his smile, could not thrive amidst the selfishness and thanklessness of the world; and that self-government, without a sense of the divine inspection, would hardly extend beyond an outward and partial purity. God, as he is essentially goodness, holiness, justice, and virtue, so he is the life, motive, and sustainer of virtue in the human soul.

But, whilst we earnestly inculcate the love of God, we believe that great care is necessary to distinguish it from counterfeits. We think that much which is called piety is worthless. Many have fallen into the error, that there can be no excess in feelings which have God for their object; and, distrusting as coldness that self-possession, without which virtue and devotion lose all their dignity, they have abandoned themselves to extravagances, which have brought contempt on piety. Most certainly, if the love of God be that which often bears its name, the less we have of it the better. If religion be the shipwreck of understanding, we cannot keep too far from it. On this subject, we always speak plainly. We cannot sacrifice our reason to the reputation of zeal. We owe it to truth and religion to maintain, that fanaticism, partial insanity, sudden impressions, and ungovernable transports, are any thing rather than piety.

We conceive, that the true love of God is a moral sentiment, founded on a clear perception, and consisting in a high esteem and veneration, of his moral perfections. Thus, it perfectly coincides, and is in fact the same thing, with the love of virtue, rectitude, and goodness. You will easily judge, then, what we esteem the surest and only decisive signs of piety. We lay no stress on strong excitements. We esteem him, and him only a pious man, who practically conforms to God's moral perfections and government; who shows his delight in God's benevolence, by loving and serving his neighbour; his delight in God's justice, by being resolutely upright; his sense of God's purity, by regulating his thoughts, imagination, and desires; and whose conversation, business, and domestic life are swayed by a regard to God's presence and authority. In all things else men may deceive themselves. Disordered nerves may give them strange sights, and sounds, and impressions. Texts of Scripture may come to them as from Heaven. Their whole souls may be moved, and their confidence in God's favor be undoubting. But in all this there is no religion. The question is, Do they love God's commands, in which his character is fully expressed, and give up to these their habits and passions? Without this, ecstasy is a mockery. One surrender of desire to God's will, is worth a thousand transports. We do not judge of the bent of men's minds by their raptures, any more than we judge of the natural direction of a tree during a storm. We rather suspect loud profession, for we have observed, that deep feeling is generally noiseless, and least seeks display.

We would not, by these remarks, be understood as wishing to exclude from religion warmth, and even transport. We honor, and highly value, true religious sensibility. We believe, that Christianity is intended to act powerfully on our whole nature, on the heart as well as the understanding and the conscience. We conceive of heaven as a state where the love of God will be exalted into an unbounded fervor and joy; and we desire, in our pilgrimage here, to drink into the spirit of that better world. But we think, that religious warmth is only to be valued, when it springs naturally from an improved character, when it comes unforced, when it is the recompense of obedience, when it is the warmth of a mind which understands God by being like him, and when, instead of disordering, it exalts the understanding, invigorates conscience, gives a pleasure to common duties, and is seen to exist in connexion with cheerfulness, judiciousness, and a reasonable frame of mind. When we observe a fervor, called religious, in men whose general character expresses little refinement and elevation, and whose piety seems at war with reason, we pay it little respect. We honor religion too much to give its sacred name to a feverish, forced, fluctuating zeal, which has little power over the life.

Another important branch of virtue, we believe to be love to Christ. The greatness of the work of Jesus, the spirit with which he executed it, and the sufferings which he bore for our salvation, we feel to be strong claims on our gratitude and veneration. We see in nature no beauty to be compared with the loveliness of his character, nor do we find on earth a benefactor to whom we owe an equal debt. We read his history with delight, and learn from it the perfection of our nature. We are particularly touched by his death, which was endured for our redemption, and by that strength of charity which triumphed over his pains. His resurrection is the foundation of our hope of immortality. His intercession gives us boldness to draw nigh to the throne of grace, and we look up to heaven with new desire, when we think, that, if we follow him here, we shall there see his benignant countenance, and enjoy his friendship for ever.

I need not express to you our views on the subject of the benevolent virtues. We attach such importance to these, that we are sometimes reproached with exalting them above piety. We regard the spirit of love, charity, meekness, forgiveness, liberality, and beneficence, as the badge and distinction of Christians, as the brightest image we can bear of God, as the best proof of piety. On this subject, I need not, and cannot enlarge; but there is one branch of benevolence which I ought not to pass over in silence, because we think that we conceive of it more highly and justly than many of our brethren. I refer to the duty of candor, charitable judgment, especially towards those who differ in religious opinion. We think, that in nothing have Christians so widely departed from their religion, as in this particular. We read with astonishment and horror, the history of the church; and sometimes when we look back on the fires of persecution, and on the zeal of Christians, in building up walls of separation, and in giving up one another to perdition, we feel as if we were reading the records of an infernal, rather than a heavenly kingdom. An enemy to every religion, if asked to describe a Christian, would, with some show of reason, depict him as an idolater of his own distinguishing opinions, covered with badges of party, shutting his eyes on the virtues, and his ears on the arguments, of his opponents, arrogating all excellence to his own sect and all saving power to his own creed, sheltering under the name of pious zeal the love of domination, the conceit of infallibility, and the spirit of intolerance, and trampling on men's rights under the pretence of saving their souls.

We can hardly conceive of a plainer obligation on beings of our frail and fallible nature, who are instructed in the duty of candid judgment, than to abstain from condemning men of apparent conscientiousness and sincerity, who are chargeable with no crime but that of differing from us in the interpretation of the Scriptures, and differing, too, on topics of great and acknowledged obscurity. We are astonished at the hardihood of those, who, with Christ's warnings sounding in their ears, take on them the responsibility of making creeds for his church, and cast out professors of virtuous lives for imagined errors, for the guilt of thinking for themselves. We know that zeal for truth is the cover for this usurpation of Christ's prerogative; but we think that zeal for truth, as it is called, is very suspicious, except in men, whose capacities and advantages, whose patient deliberation, and whose improvements in humility, mildness, and candor, give them a right to hope that their views are more just than those of their neighbours. Much of what passes for a zeal for truth, we look upon with little respect, for it often appears to thrive most luxuriantly where other virtues shoot up thinly and feebly; and we have no gratitude for those reformers, who would force upon us a doctrine which has not sweetened their own tempers, or made them better men than their neighbours.

We are accustomed to think much of the difficulties attending religious inquiries; difficulties springing from the slow development of our minds, from the power of early impressions, from the state of society, from human authority, from the general neglect of the reasoning powers, from the want of just principles of criticism and of important helps in interpreting Scripture, and from various other causes. We find, that on no subject have men, and even good men, ingrafted so many strange conceits, wild theories, and fictions of fancy, as on religion; and remembering, as we do, that we ourselves are sharers of the common frailty, we dare not assume infallibility in the treatment of our fellow-Christians, or encourage in common Christians, who have little time for investigation, the habit of denouncing and condemning other denominations, perhaps more enlightened and virtuous than their own. Charity, forbearance, a delight in the virtues of different sects, a backwardness to censure and condemn, these are virtues, which, however poorly practised by us, we admire and recommend; and we would rather join ourselves to the church in which they abound, than to any other communion, however elated with the belief of its own orthodoxy, however strict in guarding its creed, however burning with zeal against imagined error.

I have thus given the distinguishing views of those Christians in whose names I have spoken. We have embraced this system, not hastily or lightly, but after much deliberation; and we hold it fast, not merely because we believe it to be true, but because we regard it as purifying truth, as a doctrine according to godliness, as able to "work mightily" and to "bring forth fruit" in them who believe. That we wish to spread it, we have no desire to conceal; but we think, that we wish its diffusion, because we regard it as more friendly to practical piety and pure morals than the opposite doctrines, because it gives clearer and nobler views of duty, and stronger motives to its performance, because it recommends religion at once to the understanding and the heart, because it asserts the lovely and venerable attributes of God, because it tends to restore the benevolent spirit of Jesus to his divided and afflicted church, and because it cuts off every hope of God's favor, except that which springs from practical conformity to the life and precepts of Christ. We see nothing in our views to give offence, save their purity, and it is their purity, which makes us seek and hope their extension through the world.

My friend and brother;—You are this day to take upon you important duties; to be clothed with an office, which the Son of God did not disdain; to devote yourself to that religion, which the most hallowed lips have preached, and the most precious blood sealed. We trust that you will bring to this work a willing mind, a firm purpose, a martyr's spirit, a readiness to toil and suffer for the truth, a devotion of your best powers to the interests of piety and virtue. I have spoken of the doctrines which you will probably preach; but I do not mean, that you are to give yourself to controversy. You will remember, that good practice is the end of preaching, and will labor to make your people holy livers, rather than skilful disputants. Be careful, lest the desire of defending what you deem truth, and of repelling reproach and misrepresentation, turn you aside from your great business, which is to fix in men's minds a living conviction of the obligation, sublimity, and happiness of Christian virtue. The best way to vindicate your sentiments, is to show, in your preaching and life, their intimate connexion with Christian morals, with a high and delicate sense of duty, with candor towards your opposers, with inflexible integrity, and with an habitual reverence for God. If any light can pierce and scatter the clouds of prejudice, it is that of a pure example. My brother, may your life preach more loudly than your lips. Be to this people a pattern of all good works, and may your instructions derive authority from a well-grounded belief in your hearers, that you speak from the heart, that you preach from experience, that the truth which you dispense has wrought powerfully in your own heart, that God, and Jesus, and heaven, are not merely words on your lips, but most affecting realities to your mind, and springs of hope and consolation, and strength, in all your trials. Thus laboring, may you reap abundantly, and have a testimony of your faithfulness, not only in your own conscience, but in the esteem, love, virtues, and improvements of your people.

To all who hear me, I would say, with the Apostle, Prove all things, hold fast that which is good. Do not, brethren, shrink from the duty of searching God's Word for yourselves, through fear of human censure and denunciation. Do not think, that you may innocently follow the opinions which prevail around you, without investigation, on the ground, that Christianity is now so purified from errors, as to need no laborious research. There is much reason to believe, that Christianity is at this moment dishonored by gross and cherished corruptions. If you remember the darkness which hung over the Gospel for ages; if you consider the impure union, which still subsists in almost every Christian country, between the church and state, and which enlists men's selfishness and ambition on the side of established error; if you recollect in what degree the spirit of intolerance has checked free inquiry, not only before, but since the Reformation; you will see that Christianity cannot have freed itself from all the human inventions, which disfigured it under the Papal tyranny. No. Much stubble is yet to be burned; much rubbish to be removed; many gaudy decorations, which a false taste has hung around Christianity, must be swept away; and the earth-born fogs, which have long shrouded it, must be scattered, before this divine fabric will rise before us in its native and awful majesty, in its harmonious proportions, in its mild and celestial splendors. This glorious reformation in the church, we hope, under God's blessing, from the progress of the human intellect, from the moral progress of society, from the consequent decline of prejudice and bigotry, and, though last not least, from the subversion of human authority in matters of religion, from the fall of those hierarchies, and other human institutions, by which the minds of individuals are oppressed under the weight of numbers, and a Papal dominion is perpetuated in the Protestant church. Our earnest prayer to God is, that he will overturn, and overturn, and overturn the strong-holds of spiritual usurpation, until HE shall come, whose right it is to rule the minds of men; that the conspiracy of ages against the liberty of Christians may be brought to an end; that the servile assent, so long yielded to human creeds, may give place to honest and devout inquiry into the Scriptures; and that Christianity, thus purified from error, may put forth its almighty energy, and prove itself, by its ennobling influence on the mind, to be indeed "the power of God unto salvation."

❧ Likeness to God

WILLIAM ELLERY CHANNING
(1740–1842)

"We are all as an unclean thing, and all our righteousnesses are as filthy rags, and we all do fade as a leaf." Thus proclaimed the prophet Isaiah (64:6); so preached most of the New England clergy. John Calvin, of course, was considered the greatest spokesman of the doctrine of original sin, which meant, as many a child learned in the early primers in America, "Through Adam's Fall / We sin all." In our depravity we can but turn to God in Christ and hope for salvation. Much of the Great Awakening was concerned with the immensity of our sins and the grace of God, which came by faith alone.

Channing Unitarianism, however, stressed moral perfectibility. By the development of our potential, which can be known most efficaciously in Christ, we can approach God. We can even dare to presume a likeness to God—in faith as well as works. This Unitarian doctrine of self-fulfillment found theological expression in Irenaean theology.

The orthodox were horrified to say the least by the presumptuousness of this doctrine. Channing's sermon elaborates this critical aspect of Unitarianism. Indeed, his position represents classic "perfectibilitarianism." The following sermon, delivered in 1828 at the ordination of F. A. Farley, offers the clearest expression of how nineteenth-century liberals would have interpreted the statement by Irenaeus that God became man that man might become God. In this case, the mediatorial relationship of Jesus Christ is decidedly different: each person is responsible ultimately for the likeness of God and hence must not rely on faith in Christ alone in order to know God. Channing's sermon presents the classic Unitarian statement which blended traditional Christian theology with the Renaissance belief in the dignity of man.

EPHESIANS V. I: *Be ye therefore followers of God, as dear children.*

To promote true religion is the purpose of the Christian ministry. For this it was ordained. On the present occasion, therefore, when a new teacher is to be given to the church, a discourse on the character of true religion will not be inappropriate. I do not mean, that I shall attempt, in the limits to which I am now confined, to set before you all its properties, signs, and operations; for in so doing I should burden your memories with divisions and vague generalities, as uninteresting as they would be unprofitable. My purpose is, to select one view of the subject, which seems to me of primary dignity and importance; and I select this, because it is greatly neglected, and because I attribute to this neglect much of the inefficacy, and many of the corruptions, of religion.

The text calls us to follow or imitate God, to seek accordance with or likeness to him; and to do this, not fearfully and faintly, but with the spirit and hope of beloved children. The doctrine which I propose to illustrate, is derived immediately from these words, and is incorporated with the whole New Testament. I affirm, and would maintain, that true religion consists in proposing, as our great end, a growing likeness to the Supreme Being. Its noblest influence consists in making us more and more partakers of the Divinity. For this it is to be preached. Religious instruction should aim chiefly to turn men's aspirations and efforts to that perfection of the soul, which constitutes it a bright image of God. Such is the topic now to be discussed; and I implore Him, whose glory I seek, to aid me in unfolding and enforcing it with simplicity and clearness, with a calm and pure zeal, and with unfeigned charity.

I begin with observing, what all indeed will understand, that the likeness to God, of which I propose to speak, belongs to man's higher or spiritual nature. It has its foundation in the original and essential capacities of the mind. In proportion as these are unfolded by right and vigorous exertion, it is extended and brightened. In proportion as these lie dormant, it is obscured. In proportion as they are perverted and overpowered by the appetites and passions, it is blotted out. In truth, moral evil, if unresisted and habitual, may so blight and lay waste these capacities, that the image of God in man may seem to be wholly destroyed.

The importance of this assimilation to our Creator, is a topic which needs no labored discussion. All men, of whatever name, or sect, or opinion, will meet me on this ground. All, I presume, will allow, that no good in the compass of the universe, or within the gift of omnipotence, can be compared to a resemblance of God, or to a participation of his attributes. I fear no contradiction here. Likeness to God is the supreme gift. He can communicate nothing so precious, glorious, blessed, as himself. To hold intellectual and moral affinity with the Supreme Being, to partake his spirit, to be his children by derivations of kindred excellence, to bear a growing conformity to the perfection which we adore, this is a felicity which obscures and annihilates all other good.

It is only in proportion to this likeness, that we can enjoy either God or the universe. That God can be known and enjoyed only through sympathy or kindred attributes, is a doctrine which even Gentile philosophy discerned. That the pure in heart can alone see and commune with the pure Divinity, was the sublime instruction of ancient sages as well as of inspired prophets. It is indeed the lesson of daily experience. To understand a great and good being, we must have the seeds of the same excellence. How quickly, by what an instinct, do accordant minds recognise one another! No attraction is so powerful as that which subsists between the truly wise and good; whilst the brightest excellence is lost on those who have nothing congenial in their own breasts. God becomes a real being to us, in proportion as his own nature is unfolded within us. To a man who is growing in the likeness of God, faith begins even here to change into vision. He carries within himself a proof of a Deity, which can only be understood by experience. He more than believes, he feels the Divine presence; and gradually rises to an intercourse with his Maker, to which it is not irreverent to apply the name of friendship and intimacy. The Apostle John intended to express this truth, when he tells us, that he, in whom a principle of divine charity or benevolence has become a habit and life, "dwells in God and God in him."

It is plain, too, that likeness to God is the true and only preparation for the enjoyment of the universe. In proportion as we approach and resemble the mind of God, we are brought into harmony with the creation; for, in that proportion, we possess the principles from which the universe sprung; we carry within ourselves the perfections, of which its beauty, magnificence, order, benevolent adaptations, and boundless purposes, are the results and manifestations. God unfolds himself in his works to a kindred mind. It is possible, that the brevity of these hints may expose to the charge of mysticism, what seems to me the calmest and clearest truth. I think, however, that every reflecting man will feel, that likeness to God must be a principle of sympathy or accordance with his creation; for the creation is a birth and shining forth of the Divine Mind, a work through which his spirit breathes. In proportion as we receive this spirit, we possess within ourselves the explanation of what we see. We discern more and more of God in every thing, from the frail flower to the everlasting stars. Even in evil, that dark cloud which hangs over the creation, we discern rays of light and hope, and gradually come to see, in suffering and temptation, proofs and instruments of the sublimest purposes of Wisdom and Love.

I have offered these very imperfect views, that I may show the great importance of the doctrine which I am solicitous to enforce. I would teach, that likeness to God is a good so unutterably surpassing all other good, that whoever admits it as attainable, must acknowledge it to be the chief aim of life. I would show, that the highest and happiest office of religion is, to bring the mind into growing accordance with God; and that by the tendency of religious systems to this end, their truth and worth are to be chiefly tried.

I am aware that it may be said, that the Scriptures, in speaking of man as made in the image of God, and in calling us to imitate him, use bold and figurative language. It may be said, that there is danger from too literal an interpretation; that God is an unapproachable being; that I am not warranted in ascribing to man a like nature to the Divine; that we and all things illustrate the Creator by contrast, not by resemblance; that religion manifests itself chiefly in convictions and acknowledgments of utter worthlessness; and that to talk of the greatness and divinity of the human soul, is to inflate that pride through which Satan fell, and through which man involves himself in that fallen spirit's ruin.

I answer, that, to me, Scripture and reason hold a different language. In Christianity particularly, I meet perpetual testimonies to the divinity of human nature. This whole religion expresses an infinite concern of God for the human soul, and teaches that he deems no methods too expensive for its recovery and exaltation. Christianity, with one voice, calls me to turn my regards and care to the spirit within me, as of more worth than the whole outward world. It calls us to "be perfect as our Father in heaven is perfect;" and everywhere, in the sublimity of its precepts, it implies and recognises the sublime capacities of the being to whom they are addressed. It assures us that human virtue is "in the sight of God of great price," and speaks of the return of a human being to virtue as an event which increases the joy of heaven. In the New Testament, Jesus Christ, the Son of God, the brightness of his glory, the express and unsullied image of the Divinity, is seen mingling with men as a friend and brother, offering himself as their example, and promising to his true followers a share in all his splendors and joys. In the New Testament, God is said to communicate his own spirit, and all his fulness to the human soul. In the New Testament man is exhorted to aspire after "honor, glory, and immortality"; and Heaven, a word expressing the nearest approach to God, and a divine happiness, is everywhere proposed as the end of his being. In truth, the very essence of Christian faith is, that we trust in God's mercy, as revealed in Jesus Christ, for a state of celestial purity, in which we shall grow for ever in the likeness, and knowledge, and enjoyment of the Infinite Father. Lofty views of the nature of man are bound up and interwoven with the whole Christian system. Say not, that these are at war with humility; for who was ever humbler than Jesus, and yet who ever possessed such a consciousness of greatness and divinity? Say not that man's business is to think of his sin, and not of his dignity; for great sin implies a great capacity; it is the abuse of a noble nature; and no man can be deeply and rationally contrite, but he who feels, that in wrong-doing he has resisted a divine voice, and warred against a divine principle, in his own soul.—I need not, I trust, pursue the argument from revelation. There is an argument from nature and reason, which seems to me so convincing, and is at the same time so fitted to explain what I mean by man's possession of a like nature to God, that I shall pass at once to its exposition.

That man has a kindred nature with God, and may bear most important and ennobling relations to him, seems to me to be established by a striking proof. This proof you will understand, by considering, for a moment, how we obtain our ideas of God. Whence come the conceptions which we include under that august name? Whence do we derive our knowledge of the attributes and perfections which constitute the Supreme Being? I answer, we derive them from our own souls. The divine attributes are first developed in ourselves, and thence transferred to our Creator. The idea of God, sublime and awful as it is, is the idea of our own spiritual nature, purified and enlarged to infinity. In ourselves are the elements of the Divinity. God, then, does not sustain a figurative resemblance to man. It is the resemblance of a parent to a child, the likeness of a kindred nature.

We call God a Mind. He has revealed himself as a Spirit. But what do we know of mind, but through the unfolding of this principle in our own breasts? That unbounded spiritual energy which we call God, is conceived by us only through consciousness, through the knowledge of ourselves.— We ascribe thought or intelligence to the Deity, as one of his most glorious attributes. And what means this language? These terms we have framed to express operations or faculties of our own souls. The Infinite Light would be for ever hidden from us, did not kindred rays dawn and brighten within us. God is another name for human intelligence raised above all error and imperfection, and extended to all possible truth.

The same is true of God's goodness. How do we understand this, but by the principle of love implanted in the human breast? Whence is it, that this divine attribute is so faintly comprehended, but from the feeble development of it in the multitude of men? Who can understand the strength, purity, fulness, and extent of divine philanthropy, but he in whom selfishness has been swallowed up in love?

The same is true of all the moral perfections of the Deity. These are comprehended by us, only through our own moral nature. It is conscience within us, which, by its approving and condemning voice, interprets to us God's love of virtue and hatred of sin; and without conscience, these glorious conceptions would never have opened on the mind. It is the lawgiver in our own breasts, which gives us the idea of divine authority, and binds us to obey it. The soul, by its sense of right, or its perception of moral distinctions, is clothed with sovereignty over itself, and through this alone, it understands and recognises the Sovereign of the Universe. Men, as by a natural inspiration, have agreed to speak of conscience as the voice of God, as the Divinity within us. This principle, reverently obeyed, makes us more and more partakers of the moral perfection of the Supreme Being, of that very excellence, which constitutes the rightfulness of his sceptre, and enthrones him over the universe. Without this inward law, we should be as incapable of receiving a law from Heaven, as the brute. Without this, the thunders of Sinai might startle the outward ear, but would have no meaning, no authority to the mind. I have expressed here a great truth. Nothing teaches so encouragingly our relation and resemblance to God; for the glory of the Supreme Being is eminently moral. We blind ourselves to his chief splendor, if we think only or mainly of his power, and overlook those attributes of rectitude and goodness, to which he subjects his omnipotence, and which are the foundations and very substance of his universal and immutable Law. And are these attributes revealed to us through the principles and convictions of our own souls? Do we understand through sympathy God's perception of the right, the good, the holy, the just? Then with what propriety is it said, that in his own image he made man!

I am aware, that it may be objected to these views, that we receive our idea of God from the universe, from his works, and not so exclusively from our own souls. The universe, I know, is full of God. The heavens and earth declare his glory. In other words, the effects and signs of power, wisdom, and goodness, are apparent through the whole creation. But apparent to what? Not to the outward eye; not to the acutest organs of sense; but to a kindred mind, which interprets the universe by itself. It is only through that energy of thought, by which we adapt various and complicated means to distant ends, and give harmony and a common bearing to multiplied exertions, that we understand the creative intelligence which has established the order, dependencies, and harmony of nature. We see God around us, because he dwells within us. It is by a kindred wisdom, that we discern his wisdom in his works. The brute, with an eye as piercing as ours, looks on the universe; and the page, which to us is radiant with characters of greatness and goodness, is to him a blank. In truth, the beauty and glory of God's works, are revealed to the mind by a light beaming from itself. We discern the impress of God's attributes in the universe, by accordance of nature, and enjoy them through sympathy.—I hardly need observe, that these remarks in relation to the universe apply with equal, if not greater force, to revelation.

I shall now be met by another objection, which to many may seem strong. It will be said, that these various attributes of which I have spoken, exist in God in Infinite Perfection, and that this destroys all affinity between the human and the Divine mind. To this I have two replies. In the first place, an attribute, by becoming perfect, does not part with its essence. Love, wisdom, power, and purity do not change their nature by enlargement. If they did, we should lose the Supreme Being through his very infinity. Our ideas of him would fade away into mere sounds. For example, if wisdom in God, because unbounded, have no affinity with that attribute in man, why apply to him that term? It must signify nothing. Let me ask what we mean, when we say that we discern the marks of intelligence in the universe? We mean, that we meet there the proofs of a mind like our own. We certainly discern proofs of no other; so that to deny this doctrine would be to deny the evidences of a God, and utterly to subvert the foundations of religious belief. What man can examine the structure of a plant or an animal, and see the adaptation of its parts to each other and to common ends, and not feel, that it is the work of an intelligence akin to his own, and that he traces these marks of design by the same spiritual energy in which they had their origin?

But I would offer another answer to this objection, that God's infinity places him beyond the resemblance and approach of man. I affirm, and trust that I do not speak too strongly, that there are traces of infinity in the human mind; and that, in this very respect, it bears a likeness to God. The very conception of infinity, is the mark of a nature to which no limit can be prescribed. This thought, indeed, comes to us, not so much from abroad, as from our own souls. We ascribe this attribute to God, because we possess capacities and wants, which only an unbounded being can fill, and because we are conscious of a tendency in spiritual faculties to unlimited expansion. We believe in the Divine infinity, through something congenial with it in our own breasts. I hope I speak clearly, and if not, I would ask those to whom I am obscure, to pause before they condemn. To me it seems, that the soul, in all its higher actions, in original thought, in the creations of genius, in the soarings of imagination, in its love of beauty and grandeur, in its aspirations after a pure and unknown joy, and especially in disinterestedness, in the spirit of self-sacrifice, and in enlightened devotion, has a character of infinity. There is often a depth in human love, which may be strictly called unfathomable. There is sometimes a lofty strength in moral principle, which all the power of the outward universe cannot overcome. There seems a might within, which can more than balance all might without. There is, too, a piety, which swells into a transport too vast for utterance, and into an immeasurable joy. I am speaking, indeed, of what is uncommon, but still of realities. We see, however, the tendency of the soul to the infinite, in more familiar and ordinary forms. Take, for example, the delight which we find in the vast scenes of nature, in prospects which spread around us without limits, in the immensity of the heavens and the ocean, and especially in the rush and roar of mighty winds, waves, and torrents, when, amidst our deep awe, a power within seems to respond to the omnipotence around us. The same principle is seen in the delight ministered to us by works of fiction or of imaginative art, in which our own nature is set before us in more than human beauty and power. In truth, the soul is always bursting its limits. It thirsts continually for wider knowledge. It rushes forward to untried happiness. It has deep wants, which nothing limited can appease. Its true element and end is an unbounded good. Thus, God's infinity has its image in the soul; and through the soul, much more than through the universe, we arrive at this conception of the Deity.

In these remarks I have spoken strongly. But I have no fear of expressing too strongly the connexion between the Divine and the human mind. My only fear is, that I shall dishonour the great subject. The danger to which we are most exposed, is that of severing the Creator from his creatures. The propensity of human sovereigns to cut off communication between themselves and their subjects, and to disclaim a common nature with their inferiors, has led the multitude of men, who think of God chiefly under the character of a king, to conceive of him as a being who places his glory in multiplying distinctions between himself and all other beings. The truth is, that the union between the Creator and the creature surpasses all other bonds in strength and intimacy. He penetrates all things, and delights to irradiate all with his glory. Nature, in all its lowest and inanimate forms, is pervaded by his power; and, when quickened by the mysterious property of life, how wonderfully does it show forth the perfections of its Author! How much of God may be seen in the structure of a single leaf, which, though so frail as to tremble in every wind, yet holds connexions and living communications with the earth, the air, the clouds, and the distant sun, and, through these sympathies with the universe, is itself a revelation of an omnipotent mind! God delights to diffuse himself everywhere. Through his energy, unconscious matter clothes itself with proportions, powers, and beauties, which reflect his wisdom and love. How much more must he delight to frame conscious and happy recipients of his perfections, in whom his wisdom and love may substantially dwell, with whom he may form spiritual ties, and to whom he may be an everlasting spring of moral energy and happiness! How far the Supreme Being may communicate his attributes to his intelligent offspring, I stop not to inquire. But that his almighty goodness will impart to them powers and glories, of which the material uni-

verse is but a faint emblem, I cannot doubt. That the soul, if true to itself
and its Maker, will be filled with God, and will manifest him, more than
the sun, I cannot doubt. Who can doubt it, that believes and understands
the doctrine of human immortality?

The views which I have given in this discourse, respecting man's participation of the Divine nature, seem to me to receive strong confirmation, from the title or relation most frequently applied to God in the New
Testament; and I have reserved this as the last corroboration of this doctrine, because, to my own mind, it is singularly affecting. In the New
Testament God is made known to us as a Father; and a brighter feature
of that book cannot be named. Our worship is to be directed to him as
our Father. Our whole religion is to take its character from this view
of the Divinity. In this he is to rise always to our minds. And what is it
to be a Father? It is to communicate one's own nature, to give life to
kindred beings; and the highest function of a Father is to educate the
mind of the child, and to impart to it what is noblest and happiest in his
own mind. God is our Father, not merely because he created us, or because he gives us enjoyment; for he created the flower and the insect, yet
we call him not their Father. This bond is a spiritual one. This name belongs to God, because he frames spirits like himself, and delights to give
them what is most glorious and blessed in his own nature. Accordingly,
Christianity is said, with special propriety, to reveal God as the Father,
because it reveals him as sending his Son to cleanse the mind from every
stain, and to replenish it for ever with the spirit and moral attributes of
its Author. Separate from God this idea of his creating and training up
beings after his own likeness, and you rob him of the paternal character.
This relation vanishes, and with it vanishes the glory of the Gospel, and
the dearest hopes of the human soul.

The greatest use which I would make of the principles laid down in
this discourse, is to derive from them just and clear views of the nature
of religion. What, then, is religion? I answer; it is not the adoration of
a God with whom we have no common properties; of a distinct, foreign,
separate being; but of an all-communicating Parent. It recognises and
adores God, as a being whom we know through our own souls, who has
made man in his own image, who is the perfection of our own spiritual
nature, who has sympathies with us as kindred beings, who is near us,
not in place only like this all-surrounding atmosphere, but by spiritual
influence and love, who looks on us with parental interest, and whose
great design it is to communicate to us for ever, and in freer and fuller
streams, his own power, goodness, and joy. The conviction of this near
and ennobling relation of God to the soul, and of his great purposes
towards it, belongs to the very essence of true religion; and true religion

manifests itself chiefly and most conspicuously in desires, hopes, and efforts corresponding to this truth. It desires and seeks supremely the assimilation of the mind to God, or the perpetual unfolding and enlargement of those powers and virtues by which it is constituted his glorious image. The mind, in proportion as it is enlightened and penetrated by true religion, thirsts and labors for a godlike elevation. What else, indeed, can it seek, if this good be placed within its reach? If I am capable of receiving and reflecting the intellectual and moral glory of my Creator, what else in comparison shall I desire? Shall I deem a property in the outward universe as the highest good, when I may become partaker of the very mind from which it springs, of the prompting love, the disposing wisdom, the quickening power, through which its order, beauty, and beneficent influences subsist? True religion is known by these high aspirations, hopes, and efforts. And this is the religion which most truly honors God. To honor him, is not to tremble before him as an unapproachable sovereign, not to utter barren praise which leaves us as it found us. It is to become what we praise. It is to approach God as an inexhaustible Fountain of light, power, and purity. It is to feel the quickening and transforming energy of his perfections. It is to thirst for the growth and invigoration of the divine principle within us. It is to seek the very spirit of God. It is to trust in, to bless, to thank him for that rich grace, mercy, love, which was revealed and proffered by Jesus Christ, and which proposes as its great end the perfection of the human soul.

I regard this view of religion as infinitely important. It does more than all things to make our connexion with our Creator ennobling and happy; and, in proportion as we want it, there is danger that the thought of God may itself become the instrument of our degradation. That religion has been so dispensed as to depress the human mind, I need not tell you; and it is a truth which ought to be known, that the greatness of the Deity, when separated in our thoughts from his parental character, especially tends to crush human energy and hope. To a frail, dependent creature, an omnipotent Creator easily becomes a terror, and his worship easily degenerates into servility, flattery, self-contempt, and selfish calculation. Religion only ennobles us, in as far as it reveals to us the tender and intimate connexion of God with his creatures, and teaches us to see in the very greatness which might give alarm, the source of great and glorious communications to the human soul. You cannot, my hearers, think too highly of the majesty of God. But let not this majesty sever him from you. Remember, that his greatness is the infinity of attributes which yourselves possess. Adore his infinite wisdom; but remember that this wisdom rejoices to diffuse itself, and let an exhilarating hope spring up, at the thought of the immeasurable intelligence which such a Father must communicate to his children. In like manner adore his power. Let the boundless creation fill you with awe and admiration of the energy which sustains it. But remember that God has a nobler work than the outward creation, even the spirit within yourselves; and that it is his purpose to replenish this with his own energy, and to crown it with growing power and triumphs over the material universe. Above all, adore his unutterable goodness. But remember, that this attribute is particularly proposed to you as your model; that God calls you, both by nature and revelation, to a fellowship in his philanthropy; that he has placed you in social relations, for the very end of rendering you ministers and representatives of his benevolence; that he even summons you to espouse and to advance the sublimest purpose of his goodness, the redemption of the human race, by extending the knowledge and power of Christian truth. It is through such views, that religion raises up the soul, and binds man by ennobling bonds to his Maker.

To complete my views of this topic, I beg to add an important caution. I have said that the great work of religion is, to conform ourselves to God, or to unfold the divine likeness within us. Let none infer from this language, that I place religion in unnatural effort, in straining after excitements which do not belong to the present state, or in any thing separate from the clear and simple duties of life. I exhort you to no extravagance. I reverence human nature too much to do it violence. I see too much divinity in its ordinary operations, to urge on it a forced and vehement virtue. To grow in the likeness of God, we need not cease to be men. This likeness does not consist in extraordinary or miraculous gifts, in supernatural additions to the soul, or in any thing foreign to our original constitution; but in our essential faculties, unfolded by vigorous and conscientious exertion in the ordinary circumstances assigned by God. To resemble our Creator, we need not fly from society, and entrance ourselves in lonely contemplation and prayer. Such processes might give a feverish strength to one class of emotions, but would result in disproportion, distortion, and sickliness of mind. Our proper work is to approach God by the free and natural unfolding of our highest powers, of understanding, conscience, love, and the moral will.

Shall I be told that, by such language, I ascribe to nature the effects which can only be wrought in the soul by the Holy Spirit? I anticipate this objection, and wish to meet it by a simple exposition of my views. I would on no account disparage the gracious aids and influences which God imparts to the human soul. The promise of the Holy Spirit is among the most precious in the Sacred Volume. Worlds could not tempt me to part with the doctrine of God's intimate connexion with the mind, and of his free and full communications to it. But these views are in no respect at variance with what I have taught, of the method by which we are to grow in the likeness of God. Scripture and experience concur in teaching, that, by the Holy Spirit, we are to understand a divine assistance adapted to our moral freedom, and accordant with the fundamental truth, that virtue is the mind's own work. By the Holy Spirit, I understand an aid, which must be gained and made effectual by our own activity; an aid, which no more interferes with our faculties, than the assistance which we receive from our fellow-beings; an aid, which silently mingles and conspires with all other helps and means of goodness; an aid, by which we unfold our natural powers in a natural order, and by which we are strengthened to understand and apply the resources derived from our munificent Creator. This aid we cannot prize too much, or pray for too earnestly. But wherein, let me ask, does it war with the doctrine, that God is to be approached by the exercise and unfolding of our highest powers and affections, in the ordinary circumstances of human life?

I repeat it, to resemble our Maker we need not quarrel with our nature or our lot. Our present state, made up, as it is, of aids and trials, is worthy of God, and may be used throughout to assimilate us to him. For example, our domestic ties, the relations of neighbourhood and country, the daily interchanges of thoughts and feelings, the daily occasions of kindness, the daily claims of want and suffering, these and the other circumstances of our social state, form the best sphere and school for that benevolence, which is God's brightest attribute; and we should make a sad exchange, by substituting for these natural aids, any self-invented artificial means of sanctity. Christianity, our great guide to God, never leads us away from the path of nature, and never wars with the unsophisticated dictates of conscience. We approach our Creator by every right exertion of the powers he gives us. Whenever we invigorate the understanding by honestly and resolutely seeking truth, and by withstanding whatever might warp the judgment; whenever we invigorate the conscience by following it in opposition to the passions; whenever we receive a blessing gratefully, bear a trial patiently, or encounter peril or scorn with moral courage; whenever we perform a disinterested deed; whenever we lift up the heart in true adoration to God; whenever we war against a habit or desire which is strengthening itself against our higher principles; whenever we think, speak, or act, with moral energy, and resolute devotion to duty, be the occasion ever so humble, obscure, familiar; then the divinity is growing within us, and we are ascending towards our Author. True religion thus blends itself with common life. We are thus to draw nigh to God, without forsaking men. We are thus, without parting with our human nature, to clothe ourselves with the divine.

My views on the great subject of this discourse have now been given.

I shall close with a brief consideration of a few objections, in the course of which I shall offer some views of the Christian ministry, which this occasion and the state of the world, seem to me to demand.—I anticipate from some an objection to this discourse, drawn as they will say from experience. I may be told, that, I have talked of the godlike capacities of human nature, and have spoken of man as a divinity; and where, it will be asked, are the warrants of this high estimate of our race? I may be told that I dream, and that I have peopled the world with the creatures of my lonely imagination. What! Is it only in dreams, that beauty and loveliness have beamed on me from the human countenance, that I have heard tones of kindness, which have thrilled through my heart, that I have found sympathy in suffering, and a sacred joy in friendship? Are all the great and good men of past ages only dreams? Are such names as Moses, Socrates, Paul, Alfred, Milton, only the fictions of my disturbed slumbers? Are the great deeds of history, the discoveries of philosophy, the creations of genius, only visions? O! no. I do not dream when I speak of the divine capacities of human nature. It is a real page in which I read of patriots and martyrs, of Fenelon and Howard, of Hampden and Washington. And tell me not that these were prodigies, miracles, immeasurably separated from their race; for the very reverence, which has treasured up and hallowed their memories, the very sentiments of admiration and love with which their names are now heard, show that the principles of their greatness are diffused through all your breasts. The germs of sublime virtue are scattered liberally on our earth. How often have I seen in the obscurity of domestic life, a strength of love, of endurance, of pious trust, of virtuous resolution, which in a public sphere would have attracted public homage. I cannot but pity the man, who recognises nothing godlike in his own nature. I see the marks of God in the heavens and the earth, but how much more in a liberal intellect, in magnanimity, in unconquerable rectitude, in a philanthropy which forgives every wrong, and which never despairs of the cause of Christ and human virtue. I do and I must reverence human nature. Neither the sneers of a worldly skepticism, nor the groans of a gloomy theology, disturb my faith in its godlike powers and tendencies. I know how it is despised, how it has been oppressed, how civil and religious establishments have for ages conspired to crush it. I know its history. I shut my eyes on none of its weaknesses and crimes. I understand the proofs, by which despotism demonstrates, that man is a wild beast, in want of a master, and only safe in chains. But, injured, trampled on, and scorned as our nature is, I still turn to it with intense sympathy and strong hope. The signatures of its origin and its end are impressed too deeply to be ever wholly effaced. I bless it for its kind affections, for its strong and tender love. I honor it for its struggles against oppression, for its growth and progress under the weight of so many chains and prejudices, for its achievements in science and art, and still more for its examples of heroic and saintly virtue. These are marks of a divine origin and the pledges of a celestial inheritance; and I thank God that my own lot is bound up with that of the human race.

But another objection starts up. It may be said, "Allow these views to be true; are they fitted for the pulpit? fitted to act on common minds? They may be prized by men of cultivated intellect and taste; but can the multitude understand them? Will the multitude feel them? On whom has a minister to act? On men immersed in business, and buried in the flesh; on men, whose whole power of thought has been spent on pleasure or gain; on men chained by habit and wedded to sin. Sooner may adamant be riven by a child's touch, than the human heart be pierced by refined and elevated sentiment. Gross instruments will alone act on gross minds. Men sleep, and nothing but thunder, nothing but flashes from the everlasting fire of hell, will thoroughly wake them."

I have all along felt that such objections would be made to the views I have urged. But they do not move me. I answer, that I think these views singularly adapted to the pulpit, and I think them full of power. The objection is that they are refined. But I see God accomplishing his noblest purposes by what may be called refined means. All the great agents of nature, attraction, heat, and the principle of life, are refined, spiritual, invisible, acting gently, silently, imperceptibly; and yet brute matter feels their power, and is transformed by them into surpassing beauty. The electric fluid, unseen, unfelt, and everywhere diffused, is infinitely more efficient, and ministers to infinitely nobler productions, than when it breaks forth in thunder. Much less can I believe, that in the moral world, noise, menace, and violent appeals to gross passions, to fear and selfishness, are God's chosen means of calling forth spiritual life, beauty, and greatness. It is seldom that human nature throws off all susceptibility of grateful and generous impressions, all sympathy with superior virtue; and here are springs and principles to which a generous teaching, if simple, sincere, and fresh from the soul, may confidently appeal.

It is said, men cannot understand the views which seem to me so precious. This objection I am anxious to repel, for the common intellect has been grievously kept down and wronged through the belief of its incapacity. The pulpit would do more good, were not the mass of men looked upon and treated as children. Happily for the race, the time is passing away, in which intellect was thought the monopoly of a few, and the majority were given over to hopeless ignorance. Science is leaving her solitudes to enlighten the multitude. How much more may religious teachers take courage to speak to men on subjects, which are nearer to them than the properties and laws of matter, I mean their own souls. The multitude, you say, want capacity to receive great truths relating to their spiritual nature. But what, let me ask you, is the Christian religion? A spiritual system, intended to turn men's minds upon themselves, to frame them to watchfulness over thought, imagination, and passion, to establish them in an intimacy with their own souls. What are all the Christian virtues, which men are exhorted to love and seek? I answer, pure and high motions or determinations of the mind. That refinement of thought, which, I am told, transcends the common intellect, belongs to the very essence of Christianity. In confirmation of these views, the human mind seems to me to be turning itself more and more inward, and to be growing more alive to its own worth, and its capacities of progress. The spirit of education shows this, and so does the spirit of freedom. There is a spreading conviction that man was made for a higher purpose than to be a beast of burden, or a creature of sense. The divinity is stirring within the human breast, and demanding a culture and a liberty worthy of the child of God. Let religious teaching correspond to this advancement of the mind. Let it rise above the technical, obscure, and frigid theology which has come down to us from times of ignorance, superstition, and slavery. Let it penetrate the human soul, and reveal it to itself. No preaching, I believe, is so intelligible, as that which is true to human nature, and helps men to read their own spirits.

But the objection which I have stated not only represents men as incapable of understanding, but still more of being moved, quickened, sanctified, and saved, by such views as I have given. If by this objection nothing more is meant, than that these views are not alone or of themselves sufficient, I shall not dispute it; for true and glorious as they are, they do not constitute the whole truth, and I do not expect great moral effects from narrow and partial views of our nature. I have spoken of the godlike capacities of the soul. But other and very different elements enter into the human being. Man has animal propensities as well as intellectual and moral powers. He has a body as well as mind. He has passions to war with reason, and self-love with conscience. He is a free being, and a tempted being, and thus constituted he may and does sin, and often sins grievously. To such a being, religion, or virtue, is a conflict, requiring great spiritual effort, put forth in habitual watchfulness and prayer; and all the motives are needed, by which force and constancy may be communicated to the will. I exhort not the preacher, to talk perpetually of man as "made but a little lower than the angels." I would not narrow him to any class of topics. Let him adapt himself to our whole and various nature. Let him summon to his aid all the powers of this world, and the world to come. Let him bring to bear on the conscience and the heart, God's milder and more awful attributes, the promises and threatenings of the divine word, the lessons of history, the warnings of experience. Let the wages of sin here and hereafter be taught clearly and earnestly. But amidst the various motives to spiritual effort, which belong to the minister, none are more quickening than those drawn from the soul itself, and from God's desire and purpose to exalt it, by every aid consistent with its freedom. These views I conceive are to mix with all others, and without them all others fail to promote a generous virtue. Is it said, that the minister's proper work is, to preach Christ, and not the dignity of human nature? I answer, that Christ's greatness is manifested in the greatness of the nature which he was sent to redeem; and that his chief glory consists in this, that he came to restore God's image where it was obscured or effaced, and to give an everlasting impulse and life to what is divine within us. Is it said, that the malignity of sin is to be the minister's great theme? I answer, that this malignity can only be understood and felt, when sin is viewed as the ruin of God's noblest work, as darkening a light brighter than the sun, as carrying discord, bondage, disease, and death into a mind framed for perpetual progress towards its Author. Is it said, that terror is the chief instrument of saving the soul? I answer, that if by terror, be meant a rational and moral fear, a conviction and dread of the unutterable evil incurred by a mind which wrongs, betrays, and destroys itself, then I am the last to deny its importance. But a fear like this, which regards the debasement of the soul as the greatest of evils, is plainly founded upon and proportioned to our conceptions of the greatness of our nature. The more common terror, excited by vivid images of torture and bodily pain, is a very questionable means of virtue. When strongly awakened, it generally injures the character, breaks men into cowards and slaves, brings the intellect to cringe before human authority, makes man abject before his Maker, and, by a natural reaction of the mind, often terminates in a presumptuous confidence, altogether distinct from virtuous self-respect, and singularly hostile to the unassuming, charitable spirit of Christianity. The preacher should rather strive to fortify the soul against physical pains, than to bow it to their mastery, teaching it to dread nothing in comparison with sin, and to dread sin as the ruin of a noble nature.

Men, I repeat it, are to be quickened and raised by appeals to their highest principles. Even the convicts of a prison may be touched by kindness, generosity, and especially by a tone, look, and address, expressing hope and respect for their nature. I know, that the doctrine of ages has been, that terror, restraint, and bondage are the chief safeguards of human virtue and peace. But we have begun to learn, that affection, confidence, respect, and freedom are mightier as well as nobler agents. Men can be wrought upon by generous influences. I would that this truth were better understood by religious teachers. From the pulpit, generous influences too seldom proceed. In the church, men too seldom hear a voice to quicken and exalt them. Religion, speaking through her public organs, seems often to forget her natural tone of elevation. The character of God, the principles of his government, his relations to the human family, the purposes for which he brought us into being, the nature which he has given us, and the condition in which he has placed us, these and the like topics, though the sublimest which can enter the mind, are not unfrequently so set forth as to narrow and degrade the hearers, disheartening and oppressing with gloom the timid and sensitive, and infecting coarser minds with the unhallowed spirit of intolerance, presumption, and exclusive pretension to the favor of God. I know, and rejoice to know, that preaching in its worst forms does good; for so bright and piercing is the light of Christianity, that it penetrates in a measure the thickest clouds in which men contrive to involve it. But that evil mixes with the good, I also know; and I should be unfaithful to my deep convictions, did I not say, that human nature requires for its elevation, more generous treatment from the teachers of religion.

I conclude with saying, let the minister cherish a reverence for his own nature. Let him never despise it even in its most forbidding forms. Let him delight in its beautiful and lofty manifestations. Let him hold fast as one of the great qualifications for his office, a faith in the greatness of the human soul, that faith, which looks beneath the perishing body, beneath the sweat of the laborer, beneath the rags and ignorance of the poor, beneath the vices of the sensual and selfish, and discerns in the depths of the soul a divine principle, a ray of the Infinite Light, which may yet break forth and "shine as the sun" in the kingdom of God. Let him strive to awaken in men a consciousness of the heavenly treasure within them, a consciousness of possessing what is of more worth than the outward universe. Let hope give life to all his labors. Let him speak to men, as to beings liberally gifted, and made for God. Let him always look round on a congregation with the encouraging trust, that he has hearers prepared to respond to the simple, unaffected utterance of great truths, and to the noblest workings of his own mind. Let him feel deeply for those, in whom the divine nature is overwhelmed by the passions. Let him sympathize tenderly with those, in whom it begins to struggle, to mourn for sin, to thirst for a new life. Let him guide and animate to higher and diviner virtue, those in whom it has gained strength. Let him strive to infuse courage, enterprise, devout trust, and an inflexible will, into men's labors for their own perfection. In one word, let him cherish an unfaltering and growing faith in God as the Father and quickener of the human mind, and in Christ as its triumphant and immortal friend. That by such preaching he is to work miracles, I do not say. That he will rival in sudden and outward effects what is wrought by the preachers of a low and terrifying theology, I do not expect or desire. That all will be made better, I am far from believing. His office is, to act on free beings, who, after all, must determine themselves; who have power to withstand all foreign agency; who are to be saved, not by mere preaching, but by their own prayers and toil. Still I believe that such a minister will be a benefactor beyond all praise to the human soul. I believe, and know, that, on those who will admit his influence, he will work deeply, powerfully, gloriously. His function is the sublimest under heaven; and his reward will be, a growing power of spreading truth, virtue, moral strength, love, and happiness, without limit and without end.

❧ Antiquity and Revival
of Unitarian Christianity

WILLIAM WARE (1797–1852)

The history of Christian Unitarianism has from its earliest American phases been the occasion for much confusion and many serious misconceptions. Not least among the causes for this state of affairs was the constant use of doctrinal names such as "Arminian," "Arian," and "Socinian," which, properly speaking, had little or no application to the movements so designated. This naming of various aspects of eighteenth-century religious thought after old and historically unique heresies gave rise to what Conrad Wright has correctly called a major fallacy of Unitarian interpretation. Once committed to this fallacy, both the liberals and their critics tended to see the history of modern Unitarianism as the ever-widening influence of Polish and Transylvanian anti-Trinitarianism, that movement then being traced backward to fourth-century Arianism and forward through the Dutch Remonstrance and the explicit English tradition of Socinian and Arian advocacy.

This channelized view prevented many from seeing the Liberal Faith in its own proper social and intellectual setting as an integrated Christian response to the pressures of eighteenth-century life and learning. Orthodox criticism consequently was often narrow in its analysis and in its proscription of specific heretical manifestations. The early American Unitarians were in large degree prisoners of precisely the same misconceptions. Before the appearance of Wright's excellent work *The Beginnings of Unitarianism in America,* Unitarian historiography had done very little to amend the situation.

The account of Unitarian origins and history republished here is typical of the traditional view. It reveals, among other things, how such an interpretation led Unitarians to identify their own views with a historical tradition for whose radical excesses they had in fact very little sympathy and how it tended to sever them from the larger movements of rational theology to which they properly belonged.

In seeking an essay on the "Antiquity and Revival of Unitarian Christianity" for its tract series, the American Unitarian Association did well to turn to William Ware, the erudite and versatile son of Henry Ware, the Hollis Professor of Divinity at Harvard. William Ware was born in

1797 when his father was still minister in Hingham, Massachusetts. He was graduated from Harvard in 1816, whereupon he began his theological studies, serving at the same time as a schoolteacher or as an assistant to Andrews Norton in the college library. In 1821 he was ordained as the first minister of the First Unitarian Society (All Souls Church) of New York City, the pulpit which Henry Bellows later occupied. He served this church until 1836. During this time he gained a reputation as a Classical scholar and popular writer. Beginning in 1836 he contributed to the *Knickerbocker Magazine* and in 1838 published *Zenobia; or, the Fall of Palmyra.* This work was followed by others on similar themes, *Aurelian* (first published as *Probus*), and *Julian.* After leaving New York he became proprietor and editor of the influential Unitarian *Christian Examiner.* From 1838 to his death he occupied himself variously as minister, writer, traveler, and lecturer. After years of intermittent illness he died in Boston just before he was scheduled to commence a lecture series on *The Works and Genius of Washington Allston.* The two-volume *American Unitarian Biography,* which he had edited in his declining years, indicates his continuing historical interests.

We hear it often urged, among other objections to the doctrines of Unitarian Christianity, that they are new, that they are now for the first time presented to the world; whereas if they are true and constitute a genuine part of the gospel, it is incredible that they should not early have been discovered to be there, and traces should not be found of them all along through the history of the church. We believe this to be the demonstrable fact; we believe them to have been the earliest of all the forms of Christianity which obtained a general currency and belief, and that from the time they were in a manner extinguished by the violent measures employed against them, they at intervals reappeared and were avowed by free and courageous minds, till at the present day they have spread themselves everywhere, where religious liberty is enjoyed.

Let us then look at the origin and trace the progress of Unitarian Christianity.

It cannot be supposed that we believe its origin to be less ancient than that of Christianity itself. It cannot be supposed that we should hold up any views of gospel truth to the world, which we did not conscientiously believe to have been preached by the founder of the religion and his immediate disciples. Unitarian Christianity we are confident is the Christianity of the Gospels, of the Acts, of the Epistles. It is the religion of the New Testament—the only religion of the New Testament. It is because we think thus, that we yield it our faith, and fervently pray that the time may soon come, as we believe it eventually will, when it shall be the faith of the world.

We believe the foundations of Unitarian Christianity were laid by Jesus Christ himself, when in those emphatic words, 'Hear, O Israel, the Lord our God is one Lord,' he re-announced the distinguishing tenet of the old religion as the corner stone of the new; when he said, 'there is none other good but one, that is God;' when he said, 'my Father is greater than I;' when he said, 'this is eternal life, to know Thee, the only true God, and Jesus Christ whom Thou hast sent;' when he said, 'of that day and hour knoweth no man, neither the Son, but the Father only;' when he said, 'I can of mine own self do nothing,' 'my doctrine is not mine, but his that sent me.' In these and a multitude of similar expressions and declarations do we trace the origin of Unitarian Christianity, to the highest antiquity, to the words of our Lord himself. We think the gospels, when judged by the same rules, and read in the same impartial spirit as other books, are plain books on this subject, and would never suggest to a mind which approached them wholly unprejudiced such a doctrine as that of the Trinity or the deity of Jesus Christ. Their general tenor and prevailing language, as well as express declarations, seem to give assurance that the tenets which we now draw from them, and no others, were the tenets of their writers.

Unless Unitarianism is the religion of the New Testament, unless it was the faith of its historians, it does not seem possible to explain the otherwise most extraordinary fact, that one of them, viz. Luke, should have written a whole gospel, in which it was his object to give a history of Jesus Christ and an account of his religion, and yet make no mention of such a doctrine as that of the Trinity—a doctrine, which, if true, was the most important doctrine of Christianity. And let it be observed, that the advocates of the doctrine themselves do not profess to draw one single text from this gospel, which so much as *implies* that Luke had ever heard of or intended to teach it. All this appears to us wholly inexplicable, if the doctrine be true. Had it been true—had Luke known of it, he must have regarded it as the most extraordinary doctrine of revelation; and it would have filled a conspicuous place in his history. It would at least have been named, have been explained, and we may even suppose defended; for it was such an infringement of the Jewish tenet of God's essential unity, as would need to be most fully and incontrovertibly established to be a new revelation from God, before it would be possible it should be believed. Yet we discover nothing of all this. But Luke has written his gospel evidently in utter ignorance of it; and here we find the origin of Unitarian Christianity. The same remarks, with slight modifications, are true also of the other Evangelists.

We pass then to the history of the Acts. In this book also, as well as in all the language of Jesus Christ himself, do we find the faith of Unitarian Christianity, and that alone. This book is the only account we have of the propagation of Christ's religion, from the time of the ascension of its founder down to the imprisonment of Paul at Rome—a period of about thirty years. Now if the doctrine of the Trinity had lain at the foundation of Christianity, as it must if it had been promulgated by Christ, can we suppose that in such a history this doctrine would never be so much as named, or its existence implied? Not only that, but a faith its very opposite repeatedly recorded as the faith which the Apostles preached?—Yet, this is all so. Read over from beginning to end the book of Acts, keeping in mind the supposed fact, that the doctrine of the Trinity is a fundamental truth of the gospel, and find if you can any evidence to support it. Believe that Luke, the author of this book, knew of this doctrine, regarded it, as in that case he must have done, as the grand essential of the religion, and then explain if you can the amazing fact that he passes it over in silence; that the Apostles, when in their preaching they were giving a representation of the great truths of the religion, pass it over in silence; that the Jews, in raising objections to the religion, pass over this most obnoxious doctrine, as it would have been to them, in silence. As you read and ponder this book, containing the only history we have of the state of Christianity for those thirty years, you will say to yourself,—the only explanation, the only possible one of all this is, that this doctrine is not a doctrine of Christianity; and you will feel that we are justified in referring to this book, as a history of the origin and early progress of Unitarian Christianity.

We believe then, on evidence afforded by the sacred books themselves, as we think, that these books contain the first accounts of the rise and early progress of Unitarian Christianity. Down to the close of the apostolic age, we see no proof from the opposite side to shake our firm, unhesitating belief, that to that time the whole body of the christian Church was Unitarian.

The book of Acts closes with Paul's imprisonment at Rome, in the year 64. There now follows a period, of which no distinct and minute history has come down to us. But Eusebius (who wrote in the fourth century) informs us that the history of the Acts was taken up and continued by a Jewish writer of the name of Hegesippus, whose works were early lost. His history came down to the middle of the second century. A few extracts have been found in the early Fathers, and one of them, as preserved by Eusebius, contains a list of those sects, which in the time of Hegesippus were deemed heretical. Among these (he enumerates eleven) is not one which held Unitarian sentiments. In all those which he names we notice a departure from these sentiments. The irresistible inference from this is, that in the middle of the second century Unitarian sentiments were not deemed heretical. We know from other sources, that at that time, and long before, there was a considerable body of Jewish Christians called Ebionites who held the doctrine of the simple humanity of Jesus Christ; yet they are not mentioned by Hegesippus. He regarded their opinions therefore as orthodox.

The next historical fact which is to be noticed is the very remarkable one, that, on the admission of the early Fathers, no doctrine approaching the deification of Jesus was broached, or known in the Church till the year 68—the year in which John wrote his Gospel. They are agreed in the opinion that till then none of the apostles or followers of our Lord had unfolded such a mystery. This fact is so important, however, that we give a few quotations from the Fathers of the third and fourth centuries, to which we ask the very careful attention of the reader.

Origen in the third century says, 'John alone introduced the knowledge of the eternity of Christ to the minds of the Fathers.'

Eusebius in the fourth century says, 'John began the doctrine of the divinity of Christ, that being reserved for him as the most worthy.'

Chrysostom in the same century says, 'The three first Evangelists treated of the fleshly dispensation and silently of his miracles indicated his dignity . . . John, therefore, the son of thunder, being the last advanced to the doctrine of the Logos.'—Again; he introduces John as holding a soliloquy with himself and saying, 'Why do I delay? Why have I longer patience? Why do I not bring forth the mystery hid from ages? . . . Why do I not write what Matthew, Mark and Luke, through a wise and praiseworthy fear, passed in silence according to the orders that were given them? . . . But I, leaving all things which have come to pass from time, and in time, will speak of that which was without time and uncreated, about the Logos of God.'

Jerome says, 'John the apostle wrote his gospel last of all, at the entreaty of the bishops of Asia, against Corinthus and other heretics, and especially the doctrine of the Ebionites then gaining ground, who said that Christ had no being before he was born of Mary; whence he was compelled to declare his divine origin.'

Theophylact writes, 'Therefore John began with the divinity of Christ, for whereas others had made no mention of his existence before the ages, he taught that doctrine, lest the Logos of God should have been thought to be a mere man, without any divinity.' And again—'John wrote lest men should never think highly concerning Christ, and imagines he had no being before he was born of Mary.'

These are remarkable admissions. They prove that these eminent Fathers of the third and fourth centuries believed that the deity of Christ was first taught not till the year 68, by the apostle John. If it was their opinion that all the apostles had themselves been enlightened in the knowledge of this mystery on the day of Pentecost, yet it was at the same time their belief that it had never been preached or divulged in any way by them, but that John was the first who published it. The others prepared the way. It was therefore by consequence their belief that the whole Church during that period was strictly Unitarian; that all who had been converted to Christianity by Christ and the Apostles during a ministry of nearly forty years were converts to Unitarian Christianity. They confess that the deity of Christ was then unknown.

By reference to language used by the same Fathers, the further fact may, in the next place, be established, that in *their* time, that is, in the third and fourth centuries, the body of the people were still Unitarians.

Origen, in the third century says—'There *are* those, who partake of the Logos which was from the beginning; but there are others, who know nothing but Jesus and him crucified, and think they have everything of the Logos when they acknowledge Christ according to the flesh; such is the multitude of those who believe.' Is not this remarkable? He affirms that the multitude of those who were Christians in his time received Jesus only according to the flesh, i.e. believed only in the fact that he was an inspired prophet and of course denied his deity. How did they come by their faith? How but by the teaching of Christ and the apostles. They did not learn it from the Fathers of this century (the third,) who had become Orthodox by the study of Plato; they could not have invented it themselves, for the common people are not given to speculation on philosophical and theological subjects; from whom then did they receive it, but by tradition from the Apostles? And we may say, that if the *great body* of Christians were Unitarian in the middle of the third century, it is a sufficient proof, that it was the original faith,—that *all* were so in the first century. For it does not admit of supposition, that having been taught by Christ and his apostles in the doctrine of his deity they should so soon have forsaken it. It is an axiom laid down, which cannot be disputed, which all history goes to confirm, that great bodies of the common people do not suddenly change their opinions. Especially was it unlikely that the body of the common people should so soon take up with an opinion, which degraded Christ from being God to the nature and condition of merely an inspired prophet. To have added to his dignity would be natural and likely, but not to take from it. . . .

It is here to be noticed as a well established fact, in regard to the opinions of all the Orthodox Fathers of the Church, before the council of Nice (in the year 325) that in their notions of the Trinity they differed very widely from those who now hold it, or who lived after that council. They universally ascribed a supremacy to the Father; their Trinity was not one of equal persons; there was still so much of the early doctrine concerning the nature of Christ prevailing in the community, and modifying their own sentiments, that they all maintained that the Son and the Spirit were both, in some sense, inferior to the Father. Orthodoxy at that time was what would now pass for little more than a form of Unitarianism. This fact speaks volumes as to the gradual formation of this doctrine; and therefore that it was not an original revelation.

Before the council of Nice, and chiefly in the early part of the fourth century, and the latter part of the third, there flourished several distinguished men, who embraced what would be termed heretical opinions on this great question. Of these were Theodotus of Byzantium—Praxeas the Montanist—Artemon—Noetas—Sabellius—and Paul bishop of Samosata. The last of these had numerous followers, called after him Paulians or Paulianists. His opinions, as described by Mosheim, were, 'that the Son and Holy Ghost exist in God in the same manner as the faculties of reason and activity do in man; that Christ was born a mere man, but that the reason and wisdom of the Father descended into him, and by him wrought miracles upon earth, and instructed the nations; and finally that on account of this union of the divine word (or reason) with the man Jesus, Christ might, though improperly, be called God.'

We are now arrived at the beginning of the fourth century, where we come in contact with the rise of *Arianism*.

This is another important fact in ecclesiastical history, to show the antiquity of Unitarian opinions. The Arianism of the fourth century is a long and important chapter in the history of the christian Church, and the evidence therefore, which it bears to the antiquity and former diffusion of Unitarianism, is proportionally ample and luminous. It is in general but little understood or remembered, how very near Unitarianism was being perpetuated as the orthodoxy of Christianity, in the fourth century—how long and tremblingly the balance hung, before it at last, more from accidental causes than any others, (humanly judging,) settled slowly on the side of Athanasianism. But let us look for a moment at the facts. Arius was a presbyter of Alexandria in lower Egypt. Having convinced himself of the prevailing errors among the learned, in relation to the Trinity and the person of Jesus Christ, he did not scruple publicly to avow his difference of opinion, and to offer to the world the arguments by which it was sustained. The consequence was, that his opinions among the inquiring and learned were very widely and cordially embraced—so much so as to alarm the bishop of Alexandria for the safety of the orthodox faith; and as the best means to crush the evil, the heretical presbyter was deposed from his office and banished the country. His opinions still grew, however, and caused so extensive a division in the Church, and so much bitter controversy, that the Emperor Constantine summoned a council of bishops at Nice for the determining of this question. The history of the doings of this council is very imperfect. . . .

By whatever majority the doctrine of the Trinity was carried, that majority itself was a divided and distracted body, being composed (in what proportions we do not learn,) of Tritheists and Sabellians; and Sabellians are Unitarians under another name. . . . The most violent measures, it is well known, were resorted to by Constantine, to intimidate the Arian members of the council. When we are told, that 'those who should resist the divine judgment of the synod' were threatened with immediate exile, 'the writings of Arius condemned to the flames, and capital punishment denounced against those in whose possession they should be found,' we are not permitted to regard the decision of this council, as giving any fair representation whatever of the state of opinion at the time it was held. Had the Emperor chanced to have been then an Arian, as he was a few years later, and had used the same means to carry his end, who can say that a Unitarian creed, instead of the Nicene and Athanasian, would not now grace the pages of the prayer books.

The doctrine of the Trinity was however voted to be true by this assembly, and became, as we may say, the established religion of the empire. But no sooner was this done, than new zeal seemed to actuate the Arians. The party still flourished and increased, and even the Emperor Constantine was at last converted by their arguments or their persuasions. Arius was recalled from banishment, loaded with favors, and, at the command of the Emperor, readmitted to the communion of the Church by the bishop of Constantinople. Unitarianism was now the religion of the state. It remained so under Constantius, Emperor of the East; and when the West also fell into his power, Arianism revived and triumphed there also. And so it continued alternately rising and falling, during a period of nearly half a century, till it expired beneath the rigorous methods adopted for its extinction by the Emperor Gratian, and Theodosius the Great. . . .

From this brief sketch of the history and fate of the opinions of Arius, who held one form of Unitarianism, a form still existing in the Church, we see the antiquity of these views, how great was their early popularity, how wide their diffusion, and how probable it was at one time—at more than one—that they might become the orthodoxy of the Church. We may say, for example, that had the life of Constantine been prolonged a few years, had he not suddenly died, just at the time Arius was risen again into credit, had not Arius himself—who is supposed to have been poisoned by his enemies—also died about the same time, it is highly probable his opinions would, through the favor they enjoyed at the court of the great Constantine, have attained a spread and a power, that would have insured them the same perpetuity, which a change of circumstances and new events conferred upon the rival faith. But let it not be forgotten, that during a period of nearly fifty years, under the successive reigns of Constantine, Constantius and Valens, Unitarianism was the established religion of the Roman Empire.

I pass over the long and dreary interval of the dark ages, during which, so entirely was opinion at the mercy of power, and so savage and summary were the methods of dealing with it and silencing it, that whatever opposed the reigning and established faith of the Catholic Church quietly sunk into oblivion. A general darkness and corruption prevailed and shed a deep gloom over the christian world. The universal ignorance in which mankind were buried prevented inquiry or discussion; fear restrained those who might think freely from uttering their opinion; superstition stood ready with her chains, her rack and her fagots, to silence forever the tongue that should dare to assail the integrity of the Catholic faith. No wonder that religion lay during that dismal night helpless and afraid. Even learning perished; for it was a crime for the philosopher to think out his problems, if they seemed in any way to clash with the faith or philosophy of the Church. We need not inquire what the fate of him would have been, who, with whatever sincerity he had arrived at his conclusions, should have dared to question the truth of the doctrine of the Trinity. That we hear little of Arianism during these centuries cannot surprise us.

We come now, then, to the era of the Reformation. Unitarianism revived with learning and religious freedom. It revived in the labors, the inquiries, and the religious zeal of two learned Italians, Lelius and Faustus Socinus. The first of these, in company with others of the same stamp, fired with the spirit of religious freedom which the efforts of Luther and his coadjutors had kindled throughout Europe, engaged in the discussion of theological questions with the priests and philosophers of the state of Venice. They did not, with Luther and others, stop at the more glaring abuses and corruptions of Popery. Enlightened probably by the writings of the famous Servetus, they felt that the doctrine of the Trinity was as little a part of true Scripture as that of transubstantiation; that the reasoning which was fatal to the latter was fatal also to the former. They did not scruple therefore to attack it in open public debate. But this was a freedom that could not be tolerated. It was producing effects upon the popular mind, that struck fear into the rulers of the Church. Immediate resort was had to those certain remedies of this kind of evil, the use of which the age justified, and the persons who had engaged in these discussions were, some banished, some cast into the dungeons of the inquisition, and two of them, Julius Trevisanus and Francis de Ruego put to death in Venice.—Lelius Socinus, among others, fled, and settled first in Switzerland. He afterwards visited Poland, where the sentiments which he avowed were already extensively received, and enjoyed a considerable share of public favor. The establishment of Unitarianism in this empire had taken place in consequence of the emigration thither, in 1546, of a Dutchman of the name of Spiritus, and otherwise called Adam Pastor. He made many converts by preaching and conversation, and the opinions rapidly spread. The success of these proscribed sentiments in this kingdom is to be ascribed to the circumstance, that it was the only one where religious liberty was enjoyed. In other kingdoms, even those in which the cause of the reformation prevailed, several edicts existed against all such as should go farther than the leading reformers went; especially against such as should deny the doctrine of the Trinity. In Poland it was better; and hence this country became the resort of those, whose heresy had banished them from the other parts of Europe. Hither, as has been said, came, in 1551, Lelius Socinus, and hither some years after, in 1579, came Faustus, his nephew.

A large community of Unitarians now grew up, with numerous churches and a flourishing institution at Racow for general and religious education. This Academy, or University, boasted the first scholars of Europe among its professors, and at one time counted more than a thousand students drawn from all parts of the civilized world. 'The Unitarian system,' says a biographer of Faustus Socinus, 'received from his labors and pen a method, consistency and connexion it wanted before. Many persons of rank and opulence became converts to it. It was for some years favored with the protection of the great, and assisted by the liberality of the rich.' Under the broad wing of religious liberty all was happy and prosperous; and Poland might justly feel proud, that it was within her borders that Christianity, after so general a corruption, first returned to nearly its original purity. . . .

But this season of prosperity and peace soon had its termination. The great success of Unitarianism was viewed with jealousy on all sides, and its ruin was decreed. Popery and bigotry were waiting for the hour of revenge and triumph, and it came. Catholics and Calvinistic Protestants here were of one heart and mind; they united to crush a common enemy. The first act of open hostility toward the Unitarians was directed against an opulent merchant of the name of Tyscovicious. He was cited to answer to some false and frivolous charges, and on being required to swear in the name of the triune God, refused. Proceedings were instituted, which ended in his condemnation. He was sentenced to have his tongue pierced for his alleged blasphemy; to have his hands and feet cut off; then to be beheaded, and last of all to have his body burned at the stake. This sentence was, at the instigation of the Jesuits, executed in all its horrible circumstances at Warsaw. As the war was now begun, and the Jesuits, with the Calvinists and Lutherans, felt their power over the common people, an occasion was not long wanting, which in their minds warranted a renewal of similar measures. On some act of disrespect committed by the students of the Academy at Racow towards the Catholic religion, the populace were excited by the arts of the priests against the whole body of the Unitarians. The country was roused, and by petition, threat, and popular tumult the government was compelled to act. Decrees were passed and issued (after some opposition) at Warsaw, depriving the Unitarians of their rights as citizens, closing their churches, their schools and institutions, and printing offices. The pastors and professors were banished. Subsequent edicts, still more severe, forbade the profession of Unitarianism on pain of death, and every Unitarian was required to quit the kingdom within three years. They fled in every direction; but took refuge chiefly in Holland and Transylvania. In the latter kingdom they enjoyed a quiet and safe asylum. Its prince was of their faith, and the greater portion of its inhabitants. Here this form of Christianity has continued to flourish to the present day; more than 40,000 of the citizens of that state openly professing it. Thus, after an existence of nearly a hundred years, great part of the time in a condition of much prosperity, enjoying the protection of the laws of a free country, Unitarianism was at last suppressed in Poland, by the same means which have so often proved, for a season at least, fatal to truth. Religious persecution, on the part of both Catholics and Protestants, accomplished its ruin.

While these things were transacting in Poland, about the middle of the 16th century, Michael Servetus, who since his twentieth year had been an unwearied advocate of the Unitarian faith, was engaged successively in Germany, France and Switzerland, in writing and disputing against the same doctrine, for assailing which Socinus had suffered banishment from his native land. The fate of Servetus was however far more cruel. It was his misfortune to have for his opponent the celebrated Calvin. Servetus persisting in spite of his remonstrances to maintain and defend his notions touching the Trinity, Calvin, having arrested him on his way through Geneva to Naples, procured his accusation, before the authorities of the city, of heretical and damnable errors. He was found guilty; and not choosing to recant, was thrown into prison. After a protracted trial a decree of death was obtained against him—death in its most cruel form—burning alive. And thus this learned and pious man, this accomplished scholar and friend of religion, for the high crime of having and expressing his own sincere opinions, was tortured to death at the stake. The character of Calvin has never recovered from the deep and ineffaceable stain of malignant cruelty, which this act has forever fastened upon it. Persecution for opinion, and to any extent, was allowed, it is true, by the spirit of the age. It was on all sides thought right and religious to torture or destroy the man, who did not or would not believe as those in power believed. But in this instance, there was a thirst of blood manifested in the movements of the Genevan reformer, that compel the belief that he was one who gave a spirit to the age rather than received one from it. How little was Christianity understood at the era of the Reformation! Why are men willing to suppose, that the reformers saw *all truth,* when they were so ignorant of the *spirit* of the Gospel?

About the same time, in England, Unitarianism was professed, notwithstanding the almost certain penalties of torture and death which awaited it, by a lady of family and character of the name of Joan Bocher, or as she is sometimes called, Joan of Kent. She too paid for her sincerity and ardor the forfeit of her life. The warrant for her death was signed with tears in his eyes—driven to it by the furious zeal of the bishops—by the young and gentle Edward VI.; and she was delivered over to the flames. At the same time, 1549, a Dutchman of the name of Van Paris, daring to believe his own belief concerning the person of Christ, and avowing his heretical opinion, was also burned alive.—In the reign of Elizabeth the same infernal principles held their sway, and she made herself infamous, as for other atrocious acts, so for burning alive several Unitarian Anabaptists, Hollanders, who had taken refuge in England from persecution at home.—James, also, signalized his reign by deeds alike savage. Two Englishmen, Leggat and Wightman, and a Spaniard were in his reign convicted of the high crime of denying the Trinity and holding Unitarian sentiments, and under a warrant signed by the King's hand, in doing which, it is said, he manifested great pleasure, they too were burned alive at the stake.

These, it is believed, were the last who have suffered death for their Unitarian opinions. The character of the times softened by degrees, and burning alive for this heresy was no longer tolerated. But the laws still inflicted death. An act passed by the Long Parliament, in 1643, places the denial of the doctrine of the Trinity upon the ground of felony, punishable with death. The courts and juries, however, were content with the lighter punishments of fine, banishment, and imprisonment. These were still the weapons, by which men were intimidated in the work of religious inquiry, and withheld from avowing publicly their belief. Some few, however, still had courage to brave the censures and power of the world. Among these was a Mr Biddle, of London, a man of eminent piety, who casting off all fear, but that of displeasing God by a cowardly suppression of a faith he believed to be the faith of Christ, printed, published and circulated his opinions concerning the person of Christ, and the unity of God, and was for this crime, after long and bitter persecution, thrown into prison, where he languished and died. About this time flourished Milton and Locke, both of whom are known by their writings to have been Unitarians. To these honorable names may be added, in the succeeding century, those of Nathaniel Lardner, and Sir Isaac Newton. Watts also is now known, by writings which he left, to have died an Antitrinitarian, and to have expressed regret that he had been the means, through his very popular hymns written in his younger days, of giving so wide a circulation to doctrines, which he was compelled on more mature deliberation and inquiry to reject. Had not the copyright been sold, and become too profitable to be surrendered, he would have recalled and suppressed the book.

Of the present condition of Unitarianism abroad, it is enough to say in few words, that it exists in every part of the British empire, and boasts a clergy as learned and as pious, as any other denomination. In Transylvania, it still retains its ancient sway. In this country, its success has been great—greater than could have been looked for, when the nature of the opposition it has had to encounter is taken into view. Every passion has been inflamed against it, every prejudice enlisted, every superstitious feeling appealed to; yet it has gone on, and though it has undoubtedly been greatly hindered and oppressed by these measures, it still has gone on and prospered. In almost every state it has its churches—in every little community its intelligent advocates and friends.

And now if the question be asked, which will naturally arise, why, if these opinions are true, and have the antiquity which is claimed for them they have not prevailed faster and farther, it may be answered;—that the history now given of them furnishes a satisfactory reply, in that spirit of deadly hate and hostility with which men have waged war against them. Trinitarianism was established, as we have seen, in the fourth century. That barbarous age allowed freely every penalty, even that of death in its most frightful forms, to be visited upon those who departed from the orthodox faith. The same principles have been acted upon almost ever since. What were the consequences? Those which were unavoidable in the nature of things. Men did not *dare,* after the faith of Athanasius was thus established and in power, to think for themselves, or if they dared to think, did not dare to speak. And during the dark ages, with here and there a solitary exception, the light of Unitarian Christianity accordingly went out. It was a dead and forgotten thing. But when courage was once more the Christian's birthright, through the noble efforts of Luther and the reformers, immediately there sprung up those, in the general cry of liberty, who spoke in behalf of the truth and beauty of Unitarian Christianity—who pleaded for the reformation, that it might not pause at the threshold, but press on and hold its seat in the inner temple and at the very altar of truth. But for this the world was not ready. And even the reformers themselves, some of whom suffered death at the hands of the Roman priesthood, and all of whom knew that if they fell into their power it would also be *their* certain fate, were weak enough, inconsistent enough, cruel enough, to visit the same punishment upon those, who in their opinion were guilty of the unpardonable sin of rejecting more than they did—of rejecting the doctrine of the Trinity. Yes, it was at the instigation of a Protestant reformer, that Servetus met his fate. And when sectarians of every other name among Protestants were tolerated, yet because the Trinity was denied, the full phial of civil and religious rage was poured out upon the unhappy Unitarians of Poland. Under such treatment, who would dare to declare himself a believer in the divine unity? Who that knew his estate, his good name, his liberty, or his life must answer for it, would dare to say, though he believed it with his whole heart, that there is but one God, even the Father? Some few indeed did it, and paid for their sincerity and noble courage with their lives. But in the nature of things, many could not be expected to do it. . . .

We have, in the foregoing pages, presented some of the grounds, upon which rest the claims of Unitarian Christianity to a high antiquity. Could it be traced back no farther than the time of Arius and Sabellius, still it could not with propriety be denominated a new opinion. Whether it be true, is another question, and to be determined by inquiries of an entirely different character. It is a sad error to suppose a doctrine true because it is old. The truth of Unitarianism can be ascertained only by an appeal to the fountain of all true religion, the words of Jesus Christ as recorded by the Evangelists. We believe Unitarian Christianity to be the only true Christianity, and for that reason, the oldest. And we are not more confident, that it is the oldest, and the truest, than that it will ere long triumph over all the various forms of error, which now prevail in the Church. It has now, we trust, in the providence of God, come forth from obscurity for the last time, never to disappear again, till it shall expire with the Gospel itself. As it began its career under the ministry of Christ and his Apostles, it will never close it, till the religion which they taught shall have answered all the designs contemplated by its almighty Author. May the time soon come, in this happy land, when Christians will dare to think and believe for themselves on this great subject. May the time come, when man shall no more dare to overawe, by threats or other means, his neighbor's mind in the formation or expression of his religious opinions, than he will to oppress or abridge his civil and political freedom. Then,—when Christians shall look at the subject with free and unbiassed minds, acting without fear of man or bodies of men, and it shall be esteemed honorable, and not reproachful, for a man to form his own opinions,—then may we look with certainty to the universal spread of the great truths, which we now labor to extend—then will the fabric of corrupt Christianity crumble and fall, as a thing that cannot stand in the light of free inquiry, enlightened reason, and sound scriptural interpretation.

❧ The King's Chapel Liturgy

King's Chapel has the distinction of being Unitarian in theology, Episcopal in worship, and Congregational in polity. Founded as the first Episcopal church in America in 1686, less than a hundred years later it became the first avowed Unitarian church in this country. Its development was therefore unique in the ecclesiastical history of New England; yet its importance in Christian Unitarianism is unquestioned.

In 1782 James Freeman (1759–1835) was invited to serve as lay reader in the church for six months. Freeman, a 1777 graduate of Harvard, soon expressed his doubts about the Trinity and its role in the prayer book. As he wrote to his father, "They allow me to make several alterations in the service, which liberty I frequently use. We can scarcely be called of the Church of England, for we disclaim the authority of that country in ecclesiastical as well as civil matters."[1] In 1785, still engaged by the wardens to lead services, he presented his objections; this led to a thorough revision of the service after the suggestions of Theophilus Lindsey and Samuel Clarke in England. It was accepted by a vestry vote of twenty to seven. The regular morning and evening services were abridged, the Nicene Creed omitted, and the Apostle's Creed retained, with the exception of the clauses "He descended into Hell" and "The Holy Catholic Church." In place of the Trinitarian doxology they substituted the Biblical "To the King eternal, immortal, invisible" (I Tim. 1:17). References to the second and third persons of the Trinity were modified.

The next year Freeman sought ordination into the Episcopal Church. The bishops in both Connecticut and New York refused him because of his beliefs. After much discussion, the congregation of King's Chapel ordained him, using the arguments of the Reverend William Hazlitt, father of the famous essayist and a friend of Freeman, as a basis for the decision.

King's Chapel became known as the Socinian Stone Chapel, and only the Reverend William Bentley of Salem staunchly defended Freeman and his congregation. The Preface which follows demonstrates how Freeman sought to make the prayer book a format for all Christians, arguing not just from Scripture but also from the Thirty-nine Articles (which were

1. Henry W. Foote, *James Freeman and King's Chapel, 1782–1787,* letter to his father, 24 December 1782, p. 7.

actually eliminated in his revised service) his proposals as to how a Christian society should worship God.

The history of Christian Unitarianism in America must acknowledge the early role of King's Chapel, although its pulpit never commanded the same attention and its ministers rarely participated in the major struggles involving the other Boston churches in the early days of the Unitarian Controversy. Indeed, its greatest contribution to the movement, in addition to being the first Unitarian church, was the preaching of F. W. P. Greenwood, long famous for the rhetorical beauty of his sermons though not for their theological brilliance.

The Preface is followed here by the section on Morning Prayer.

Preface to the First Edition. MDCCLXXXV

Many truly great and learned men, of the Church of England, as well divines as laymen, have earnestly wished to see their Liturgy reformed; but hitherto all attempts to reform it have proved ineffectual. The late happy revolution here hath forever separated all the Episcopal Societies in the United States of America, from the Church of England, of which the King of that country is the supreme head, and to whom all Archbishops, Bishops, Priests, and Deacons of that Church are obliged to take an oath of allegiance and supremacy, at the time of their consecration or ordination. Being torn from that King and Church, the Society for whose use this Liturgy is published, think themselves at liberty, and well justified even by the declarations of the Church of England, in making such alterations, as "the exigency of the times and occasions hath rendered expedient," and in expunging every thing which gave, or might be suspected to give, offence to tender consciences; guiding themselves however by "the holy scriptures, which," they heartily agree with the Church of England, "contain all things necessary to salvation," and that "whatsoever is not read therein, nor can be proved thereby, is not to be required of any man, that it should be believed as an article of faith, or be thought requisite or necessary to salvation." In the thirty-fourth of the Articles of the Church of England, it is declared, That "it is not necessary that traditions and ceremonies be in all places one, or utterly like; for at all times they have been diverse, and may be changed according to the diversity of countries, times, and men's manners, so that nothing be ordained against God's word." And by the twentieth of those Articles it is declared, That "the Church hath power to decree rites and ceremonies, and authority in controversies of faith." What is there meant by the word Church, will appear from the nineteenth of those Articles, which declares, "The visible

Church of Christ is a Congregation of faithful men, in which the pure word of God is preached, and the sacraments be duly ministered, according to CHRIST'S ordinance, in all those things that of necessity are requisite to the same. As the Church of Hierusalem, Alexandria, and Antioch have erred, so also the Church of Rome hath erred, not only in living, and manner of ceremonies, but also in matters of faith." At the Reformation, when the Book of Common Prayer of the Church of England was compiled, the Committee appointed to execute that business were obliged to proceed very tenderly and with great delicacy, for fear of offending the whole body of the people, just torn from the idolatrous Church of Rome; and many things were then retained, which have, in later times, given great offence to many, truly pious, Christians.

The Liturgy, contained in this volume, is such, as no Christian, it is supposed, can take offence at, or find his conscience wounded in repeating. The Trinitarian, the Unitarian, the Calvinist, the Arminian will read nothing in it which can give him any reasonable umbrage. GOD is the sole object of worship in these prayers; and as no man can come to GOD, but by the one Mediator, JESUS CHRIST, every petition is here offered in his name, in obedience to his positive command.* The Gloria Patri, made and introduced into the Liturgy of the Church of Rome by the decree of Pope Damasus, towards the latter part of the fourth century, and adopted into the Book of Common Prayer, is not in this Liturgy. Instead of that doxology, doxologies from the pure word of GOD are introduced. It is not our wish to make proselytes to any particular system or opinions of any particular sect of Christians.

Our earnest desire is to live in brotherly love and peace with all men, and especially with those who call themselves the disciples of JESUS CHRIST.

In compiling this Liturgy great assistance hath been derived from the judicious corrections of the Reverend Mr. Lindsey, who hath reformed the Book of Common Prayer according to the Plan of the truly pious and justly celebrated Doctor Samuel Clarke. Several of Mr. Lindsey's amendments are adopted entire. The alterations which are taken from him, and the others which are made, excepting the prayers for Congress and the General Court, are none of them novelties; for they have been proposed and justified by some of the first divines of the Church of England.

A few passages in the Psalter, which are liable to be misconstrued or misapplied, are printed in Italics, and are designed to be omitted in repeating the Psalms.

* In the original preface a large number of Biblical texts were quoted in support of this position. (Eds.)

Morning Prayer

At the beginning of Morning Prayer, the Minister shall read one or more of the following Sentences of Scripture; and then he shall read the Exhortation.

When the wicked man turneth away from his wickedness which he hath committed, and doeth that which is lawful and right, he shall save his soul alive. *Ezek.* xviii. 27.

I acknowledge my transgressions; and my sin is ever before me. *Psal.* li. 3.

Hide thy face from my sins; and blot out all mine iniquities. *Psal.* li. 9.

The sacrifices of God are a broken spirit; a broken and a contrite heart, O God, thou wilt not despise. *Psal.* li. 17.

Rend your heart, and not your garments, and turn unto the Lord your God; for he is gracious and merciful, slow to anger, and of great kindness, and repenteth him of the evil. *Joel,* ii. 13.

To the Lord our God belong mercies and forgivenesses, though we have rebelled against him; neither have we obeyed the voice of the Lord our God, to walk in his laws which he set before us. *Dan.* ix. 9, 10.

O Lord, correct me, but with judgment; not in thine anger, lest thou bring me to nothing. *Jer.* x. 24.

Repent ye; for the kingdom of heaven is at hand. *St. Matt.* iii. 2.

I will arise, and go to my Father, and will say unto him, Father, I have sinned against heaven, and before thee, and am no more worthy to be called thy son. *St. Luke,* xv. 18, 19.

Enter not into judgment with thy servant, O Lord; for in thy sight shall no man living be justified. *Psal.* cxliii. 2.

If we say that we have no sin, we deceive ourselves, and the truth is not in us; but if we confess our sins, God is faithful and just to forgive us our sins, and to cleanse us from all unrighteousness. 1 *John,* i. 8, 9.

The hour cometh, and now is, when the true worshippers shall worship the Father in spirit and in truth; for the Father seeketh such to worship him. God is a spirit, and they who worship him, must worship him in spirit and in truth. *St. John,* iv. 23, 24.

EXHORTATION.

Dearly beloved brethren, the Scripture moveth us in sundry places to acknowledge and confess our manifold sins and wickedness, and that we should not dissemble nor cloak them before the face of Almighty God our heavenly Father; but confess them with an humble, lowly, penitent, and obedient heart; to the end that we may obtain forgiveness of the same, by his infinite goodness and mercy. And although we ought, at all times, humbly to acknowledge our sins before God; yet ought we chiefly so to do, when we assemble and meet together, to render thanks for the great benefits that we have received at his hands, to set forth his most worthy praise, to hear his most holy word, and to ask those things which are requisite and necessary, as well for the body as the soul. Wherefore I pray and beseech you, as many as are here present, to accompany me, with a pure heart and humble voice, unto the throne of the heavenly grace, saying with me—

A general Confession to be said by the Minister and People.
Almighty and most merciful Father, We have erred and strayed from thy ways like lost sheep. We have followed too much the devices and desires of our own hearts. We have offended against thy holy laws. We have left undone those things which we ought to have done; And we have done those things which we ought not to have done. But thou, O Lord, have mercy upon us miserable offenders. Spare thou those, O God, who confess their faults. Restore thou those who are penitent, according to thy promises declared unto mankind in Christ Jesus our Lord. And grant, O most merciful Father, That we may hereafter live a godly, righteous, and sober life; To the glory of thy holy name.

The People shall answer here, and at the end of every Prayer, Amen.

Then shall the Minister say this Prayer.
O Lord, we beseech thee, mercifully hear our prayers, and spare all those who confess their sins unto thee; that they whose consciences by sin are accused, by thy merciful pardon may be absolved, through Christ our Lord. *Amen.*

Then the Minister shall say the Lord's Prayer; the People repeating it with him both here and wheresoever else it is used in Divine Service.
Our Father, who art in heaven, Hallowed be thy name. Thy kingdom come; Thy will be done on earth, as it is in heaven. Give us this day our daily bread. And forgive us our trespasses, As we forgive those who trespass against us. And lead us not into temptation, But deliver us from evil. For thine is the kingdom, and the power, and the glory, For ever and ever. *Amen.*

Then likewise he shall say,
O Lord, open thou our lips;
　　Answ. And our mouth shall show forth thy praise.

Here, all standing up, the Minister shall say,

    Min. Now unto the King eternal, immortal, invisible, the only wise God;

    Answ. Be honour and glory, through Jesus Christ for ever and ever. 1 *Tim.* i. 17; *Rom.* xvi. 27. *Amen.*

    Min. Praise ye the Lord.

    Answ. The Lord's name be praised.

Then shall be sung, or else said by the Minister and People, alternately, the following Anthem; except on the days for which other Anthems are appointed; which are Christmas Day, Good Friday, Easter, and Whitsunday.

VENITE, EXULTEMUS DOMINO.

O come, let us sing unto the Lord; let us heartily rejoice in the strength of our salvation.

    Let us come before his presence with thanksgiving; and show ourselves glad in him with psalms.

    For the Lord is a great God; and a great king above all gods.

    In his hand are all the corners of the earth; and the strength of the hills is his also.

    The sea is his, and he made it; and his hands prepared the dry land.

    O come, let us worship, and fall down, and kneel before the Lord our Maker.

    For he is the Lord our God; and we are the people of his pasture, and the sheep of his hand.

    O worship the Lord in the beauty of holiness; let the whole earth stand in awe of him.

    For he cometh, for he cometh to judge the earth; and with righteousness to judge the world, and the people with his truth.

Then shall be said, by the Minister and People, alternately, the Psalms for the Day. And at the close of the Psalms shall be repeated the following Doxology.

Now unto the King eternal, immortal, invisible, the only wise God;

    Be honour and glory, through Jesus Christ, for ever and ever. *Amen.*

Then may follow an Anthem, or a Voluntary on the Organ. After which the Minister shall read the FIRST LESSON, *taken out of the Old Testament; and at the end of it he shall say,* Here endeth the First Lesson.

Then shall be sung, or else said by the Minister and People, alternately, the following Hymn.

TE DEUM LAUDAMUS.

We praise thee, O God; we acknowledge thee to be the Lord.
All the earth doth worship thee, the Father everlasting.
To thee all angels cry aloud, the heavens and all the powers therein.
To thee cherubim and seraphim continually do cry,
Holy, holy, holy, Lord God of Sabaoth.
Heaven and earth are full of the majesty of thy glory.
The glorious company of the apostles, praise thee.
The goodly fellowship of the prophets, praise thee.
The noble army of martyrs, praise thee.
The holy church throughout all the world, doth acknowledge thee,
The Father of an infinite majesty;
Thine honorable, true, and only Son;
Also the Holy Ghost, the Comforter.
Thou art the King of glory, O Lord;
And Jesus Christ is thy well beloved Son.
When thou gavest him to deliver man, it pleased thee that he should be born of a virgin.
When he had overcome the sharpness of death, he did open the kingdom of heaven to all believers.
He sitteth at the right hand of God, in the glory of the Father.
We believe, that he shall come to be our judge.
We therefore pray thee, help thy servants, whom thou hast redeemed through his most precious blood.
Make them to be numbered with thy saints, in glory everlasting.
O Lord, save thy people, and bless thine heritage.
Govern them, and lift them up for ever.
Day by day we magnify thee;
And we worship thy name, ever, world without end.
Vouchsafe, O Lord, to keep us this day without sin.
O Lord, have mercy upon us; have mercy upon us.
O Lord, let thy mercy lighten upon us, as our trust is in thee.
O Lord, in thee have we trusted; let us never be confounded.

Or this Psalm.

EXALTABO TE, DEUS. PSALM CXLV.

I will magnify thee, O God, my King; and I will praise thy name for ever and ever.

Every day will I give thanks unto thee, and praise thy name for ever and ever.

Great is the Lord and marvellous, worthy to be praised; there is no end of his greatness.

One generation shall praise thy works unto another, and declare thy power.

The memorial of thine abundant kindness shall be shown; and men shall sing of thy righteousness.

The Lord is gracious and merciful, long suffering, and of great goodness.

The Lord is loving unto every man, and his mercy is over all his works.

All thy works praise thee, O Lord, and thy saints give thanks unto thee.

They show the glory of thy kingdom, and talk of thy power;

That thy power, thy glory, and mightiness of thy kingdom might be known unto men.

Thy kingdom is an everlasting kingdom, and thy dominion endureth throughout all ages.

The Lord upholdeth all such as fall, and lifteth up all those who are down.

The eyes of all wait upon thee, O Lord, and thou givest them their meat in due season.

Thou openest thine hand, and fillest all things living with plenteousness.

The Lord is righteous in all his ways, and holy in all his works.

The Lord is nigh unto all those who call upon him; yea, all such as call upon him faithfully.

He will fulfil the desire of those who fear him; he also will hear their cry, and will help them.

The Lord preserveth all those who love him; but scattereth abroad all the ungodly.

My mouth shall speak the praise of the Lord, and let all flesh give thanks unto his holy name for ever and ever. *Amen.*

Then shall the Minister read the SECOND LESSON *taken out of the New Testament; and at the end of it he shall say,* Here endeth the Second Lesson. *Then shall be sung, or else repeated by the Minister and People, alternately, the following Hymn.*

BENEDICTUS. ST. LUKE, I. 68.

Blessed be the Lord God of Israel; for he hath visited and redeemed his people.

And hath raised up a mighty salvation for us, in the house of his servant David;

As he spake by the mouth of his holy prophets, who have been since the world began;

That we should be saved from our enemies, and from the hand of all who hate us.

Or this Psalm.

JUBILATE DEO. PSALM C.

O be joyful in the Lord, all ye lands; serve the Lord with gladness, and come before his presence with a song.

Be ye sure that the Lord he is God; it is he who hath made us, and not we ourselves; we are his people, and the sheep of his pasture.

O go your way into his gates with thanksgiving, and into his courts with praise; be thankful unto him, and speak good of his name.

For the Lord is gracious, his mercy is everlasting, and his truth endureth from generation to generation.

Then shall be said these Prayers following, the Minister first saying,
Min. The Lord be with you;
Answ. And with thy spirit.
Min. Let us pray.
O Lord, show thy mercy upon us;
Answ. And grant us thy salvation.
Min. O God, make clean our hearts within us;
Answ. And take not thy Holy Spirit from us.

Then shall be said the COLLECT FOR THE DAY; *and then the service shall proceed as followeth.*

THE COLLECT FOR PEACE.

O God, who art the author of peace, and lover of concord, in knowledge of whom standeth our eternal life, whose service is perfect freedom; defend us thy humble servants in all assaults of our enemies, that we surely trusting in thy defence, may not fear the power of any adversaries, through Jesus Christ our Lord. *Amen.*

THE COLLECT FOR GRACE.

O Lord our heavenly Father, almighty and everlasting God, who hast safely brought us to the beginning of this day; defend us in the same with thy mighty power; and grant that this day we fall into no sin, neither run into any kind of danger; but that all our doings may be ordered by thy governance, to do always that which is righteous in thy sight, through Jesus Christ our Lord. *Amen.*

THE LITANY, OR GENERAL SUPPLICATION.

O God, our heavenly Father, have mercy upon us miserable sinners.

O God, our heavenly Father, have mercy upon us miserable sinners.

O God, who by thy Son hast redeemed the world, have mercy upon us miserable sinners.

O God, who by thy Son hast redeemed the world, have mercy upon us miserable sinners.

O God, who by thy Holy Spirit dost govern, direct, and sanctify the hearts of thy faithful servants, have mercy upon us miserable sinners.

O God, who by thy Holy Spirit dost govern, direct, and sanctify the hearts of thy faithful servants, have mercy upon us miserable sinners.

Remember not, Lord, our offences, neither take thou vengeance of our sins; spare us, good Lord, spare thy people whom thou hast redeemed by the most precious blood of thy Son, and be not angry with us forever.

Spare us, good Lord.

From all evil and mischief; from sin; from the assaults of temptation, from thy wrath, and from everlasting destruction,

Good Lord, deliver us.

From all blindness of heart; from pride, vain-glory, and hypocrisy; from envy, hatred, and malice, and all uncharitableness; from all inordinate and sinful affections, and from all the deceitful allurements of this transitory world,

Good Lord, deliver us.

From lightning, and tempest; from plague, pestilence, and famine; from battle, and murder, and from death unprepared for,

Good Lord, deliver us.

From all sedition, privy conspiracy, and rebellion; from all false doctrine, heresy, and schism; from hardness of heart, and contempt of thy word and commandment,

Good Lord, deliver us.

In all time of our tribulation; in all time of our prosperity, in the hour of death, and in the day of judgment,

Good Lord, deliver us.

We sinners do beseech thee to hear us, O Lord God, and that it may please thee to rule and govern thy holy church universal in the right way; and to illuminate all ministers of the gospel with true knowledge, and understanding of thy word; and that both by their preaching and living they may set it forth, and show it accordingly;

We beseech thee to hear us, good Lord.

That it may please thee to endue the President of these United States, the Governor of this Commonwealth, the Judges and Magistrates, and all others in authority, with wisdom and understanding; giving them grace to execute justice and to maintain truth;

We beseech thee to hear us, good Lord.

That it may please thee to bless all colleges and seminaries of learning; all instructers of youth, and all means of true knowledge, virtue, and piety;

We beseech thee to hear us, good Lord.

That it may please thee to bless and keep all thy people; to give to all nations, unity, peace, and concord; and to give us a heart to love and fear thee, and diligently to live after thy commandments;

We beseech thee to hear us, good Lord.

That it may please thee to give to all thy people increase of grace, to hear meekly thy word, and to receive it with pure affection, and to bring forth the fruits of the Spirit;

We beseech thee to hear us, good Lord.

That it may please thee to bring into the way of truth all such as have erred, and are deceived; to strengthen such as do stand; to comfort and help the weak hearted; to raise up those who fall; and finally to give us victory over all temptations;

We beseech thee to hear us, good Lord.

That it may please thee to succour, help, and comfort all who are in danger, necessity, and tribulation; to preserve all who travel by land or by water, all sick persons and young children; to show thy pity upon all prisoners and captives; to defend, and provide for, the fatherless children and widows, and all who are desolate and oppressed;

We beseech thee to hear us, good Lord.

That it may please thee to have mercy upon all men;

We beseech thee to hear us, good Lord.

That it may please thee to forgive our enemies, persecutors, and slanderers, and to turn their hearts;

We beseech thee to hear us, good Lord.

That it may please thee to give and preserve to our use the kindly fruits of the earth, so that in due time we may enjoy them;

We beseech thee to hear us, good Lord.

That it may please thee to give us true repentance, to forgive us all our sins, negligences, and ignorances, and to endue us with the grace of thy holy Spirit, to amend our lives according to thy holy word;

We beseech thee to hear us, good Lord.

O Lord, grant us thy peace.

Lord, have mercy upon us.
O Lord, deal not with us after our sins;
Neither reward us after our iniquities.

We humbly beseech thee, O Father, mercifully to look upon our infirmities; and for the glory of thy name, turn from us all those evils which we most justly have deserved; and grant that in all our troubles we may put our whole trust and confidence in thy mercy, and evermore serve thee in holiness and pureness of living, to thy honour and glory, through our only Mediator and Advocate, Jesus Christ our Lord. *Amen.*

The three Prayers following are to be said in the Morning, at those times when the Litany is not said.

A PRAYER FOR RULERS.

O Lord, our heavenly Father, high and mighty, King of kings, Lord of lords, who dost from thy throne behold all the dwellers upon the earth; most heartily we beseech thee with thy favour to behold the President, Vice President, and Congress of the United States, and so replenish them with the grace of thy holy Spirit, that they may always incline to thy will, and walk in thy way. Endue them plenteously with heavenly gifts, that in all their deliberations they may be enabled to promote the national prosperity, and to secure the peace, liberty, and safety of the United States throughout all generations. This we humbly ask in the name of Jesus Christ our Lord. *Amen.*

A PRAYER FOR THE CLERGY AND PEOPLE.

Almighty and everlasting God, who art the author of every good and perfect gift; send down upon all ministers of the gospel, and upon all congregations committed to their charge, the needful spirit of thy grace; and, that they may truly please thee, pour upon them the continual dew of thy blessing. Grant this, O heavenly Father, for thine infinite mercy's sake in Jesus Christ our Lord. *Amen.*

A PRAYER FOR ALL CONDITIONS OF MEN.

O God, the Creator and Preserver of all mankind, we humbly beseech thee for all sorts and conditions of men, that thou wouldest be pleased to make thy ways known unto them, thy saving health unto all nations. More especially we pray for the good estate of thy holy church; that it may be so guided and governed by thy good Spirit, that all who profess and call themselves Christians, may be led into the way of truth, and hold the faith in unity of spirit, in the bond of peace, and in righteousness of life. Finally, we commend to thy fatherly goodness, all those who are any ways afflicted or distressed in mind, body, or estate; that it may please thee to comfort and relieve them according to their several necessities; giving them patience under their sufferings, and a happy issue out of all their afflictions; and this we humbly ask as disciples of Jesus Christ our Lord. *Amen.*

If any desire the Prayers of the Congregation, the Notes are to be read here, by the Minister, and to be followed by the appropriate Prayers or Thanksgivings.

A GENERAL THANKSGIVING.

Almighty God, Father of all mercies, we thine unworthy servants do give thee most humble and hearty thanks for all thy goodness and loving kindness to us and to all men. We bless thee for our creation, preservation, and all the blessings of this life; but above all, for thine inestimable love in the redemption of the world by our Lord Jesus Christ; for the means of grace, and for the hope of glory. And we beseech thee, give us that due sense of all thy mercies, that our hearts may be unfeignedly thankful, and that we may show forth thy praise, not only with our lips, but in our lives, by giving up ourselves to thy service, and by walking before thee in holiness and righteousness all our days, through Jesus Christ our Lord; in whose name we ascribe unto thee all honour and glory, world without end. *Amen.*

A CONCLUDING PRAYER.

Almighty God, who hast given us grace at this time with one accord to make our common supplications unto thee, and hast promised by thy beloved Son, that where two or three are gathered together in his name, thou wilt grant their requests; fulfil now, O Lord, the desires and petitions of thy servants, as may be most expedient for them, granting us in this world knowledge of thy truth, and in the world to come life everlasting. *Amen.*

The grace of our Lord Jesus Christ, and the love of God, and the fellowship of the Holy Ghost, be with us all evermore. *Amen.*

END OF MORNING PRAYER.

❧ The Founding of the
American Unitarian Association

FIRST ANNUAL REPORT OF THE
EXECUTIVE COMMITTEE

The Standing Order was the traditional title for Congregational churches in eighteenth-century New England. It referred to the integration of church and state in the period. Citizens were taxed for the upkeep of the church, both building and minister, in their town. With the tensions between the orthodox and liberals that emerged in the nineteenth century, the old Standing Order lost its power; in fact, by 1833 the title no longer had any legal bearing in Massachusetts.

As more and more churches became Unitarian in the second decade, many of the younger ministers out of Harvard felt the need for an organizational base. The older ministers who had been a part of the Standing Order did not feel the same need, and hence debates about the creation of an association began.

Thirty or forty "gentlemen" had begun an Anonymous Association, which met in various homes and discussed religion, morals, and politics. In 1824 a letter was sent to its members with a proposal to establish an annual meeting to promote the union, sympathy, and cooperation in the cause of Christian truth and Christian charity. Ostensibly the desire was to publish tracts and other religious materials; but many of the gentlemen expressed concern that their religion was meant to be "practical"; others wanted an organization for the publication of theological doctrine.

In late January 1825 a small meeting was held in Channing's vestry at the Federal Street Church with the intention of founding an organization to promote Unitarianism. Even then reactions were mixed; Channing and Norton were cool to the proposal, but most of the younger men, including Ware and Bancroft, were strong defenders. Finally, on May 26, 1825, this group instituted the American Unitarian Association; its constitution stated: "The objects of this Association shall be to diffuse the knowledge and promote the interests of pure Christianity throughout our country."

Channing was offered the presidency, but refused. Aaron Bancroft from the Worcester church then became the first leader.

This *First Annual Report of the Executive Committee* offers an interesting look at the dissemination of Unitarianism, reflecting the way the

Boston leaders perceived themselves in relation to the rest of the country. Forty years later, the founding of a National Conference was deemed necessary, and six hundred would attend. In the early days, however, Unitarianism was still the "Boston Religion," as this document reveals.

The Executive Committee of the American Unitarian Association in offering their first annual report, cannot but express their gratification at the circumstances under which it is presented. They behold in the numbers and character of those who compose this meeting, not only a proof of interest in the Association, but evidence of its stability, and the promise of its future usefulness. In reviewing the past year, the Committee find much to encourage, and nothing to dishearten them; and this anniversary is welcomed by them with feelings of satisfaction, which a few months since they did not dare to anticipate. This Association was organized under some disadvantages. Its plan was suggested by a few gentlemen on the evening preceding the last election, at too late an hour to secure the advice and cooperation of many of those whose judgment would be useful in forming, and whose influence would be important in strengthening such a society. The time for a more general and effective concert seemed, however, to have arrived; and the presence of many Unitarians from distant towns, who annually assemble in this city, showed the necessity of an immediate effort for the accomplishment of this object. It would have been impossible to ascertain in a few hours the sentiments of the great body of Unitarian Christians, in relation to the measures, which they should adopt for the diffusion of pure religion. The friends of more united efforts than had hitherto been employed, trusted to their own convictions of duty, and to their belief that an occasion only was needed to call forth zeal and energy among us. From the circumstances, to which allusion has been made, the meeting at which the project of this Association was discussed, and its constitution adopted, was necessarily small. Notice could only be given at the close of the Berry Street Conference on Wednesday morning, that such a meeting would be held in the afternoon. At that meeting, it was unanimously voted, that it is expedient to form a society to be called the American Unitarian Association. At an adjourned meeting, held the next morning, a constitution, reported by a committee appointed for the purpose, was accepted, and the officers required by the constitution were elected. This brief statement will explain the fact, that the existence of this society was unknown to most Unitarians in this city and commonwealth, until some weeks after its organization; and will also show under what doubtful prospects of support it was commenced. The expectations of its early friends have not been disappointed, and the Committee hope, in the sketch, which they shall now give of their labours and success, to satisfy all inquiries respecting the utility of this institution, or the favour which has been bestowed upon it. . . . A correspondence was opened with Unitarians in various parts of our country; an agent was employed to visit some portions of New England, and copies of the Constitution and of a Circular, explaining the origin and purposes of the Association, were distributed. The result of these measures was favourable; the health of the agent allowed him to effect less than he wished, but he obtained many subscriptions, and was in every place received with kindness. Letters were addressed to the gentlemen who had been elected Vice Presidents, who acknowledged the appointment, and declared their approbation of the decisive step which Unitarian Christians had here taken. By a vote passed at the time of the organization of the Society, the Executive Committee were authorized to complete the number of Vice Presidents, but they have felt an unwillingness to make the choice, and the places of six officers have therefore remained vacant. A second Circular explanatory of the views of the Committee was printed in the course of the last winter, and has been useful in bringing the community to a better acquaintance with the course which it was intended to pursue, and the means by which assistance might be rendered. The Committee have been gratified by the sympathy expressed for them in the prosecution of their duties by Unitarians near and at a distance. They have been favoured with letters from Maine, New Hampshire, Vermont, Connecticut, Rhode Island, from all sections of this state, from the city of New York, and from the western part of the state of New York, from Philadelphia, Harrisburg, Northumberland, Pittsburgh, and Meadville in Pennsylvania, from Maryland, from the District of Columbia, from South Carolina, from Kentucky, and from Indiana. In all these letters the same interest is exhibited in the efforts which the Association promises to make for the diffusion of pure Christianity. Many of them have contained interesting accounts of the state of religion in different places, and especially correspondents have furnished the Committee with ample details respecting the history and condition of Unitarians in Pennsylvania. If similar accounts could be obtained from all the states of the Union, they would embody an amount of knowledge, that is now much wanted. And the Committee avail themselves of this opportunity to remind Unitarians, that they will render a service to the cause of truth by communicating facts connected with the progress and present state of Unitarian Christianity. The existence of a body of christians in the Western States, who have for years been Unitarians, have encountered persecution on account of their faith, and have lived in ignorance of others east of the mountains, who maintained many

similar views of christian doctrine, has attracted the attention of the Committee. Measures have been taken to ascertain more correctly the situation
and character of this fraternity, who have adopted various names significant of their attachment to freedom of inquiry, and to a purer gospel than
that embraced by other sects, and who, though they have refused to assume the title, openly avow themselves Unitarians. With two ministers
of this body a correspondence has been continued for some time. The
Committee have watched with peculiar interest the growth of the Christian Connexion, which is daily becoming more numerous and respectable.
From members of that body, they have received expressions of fraternal
regard; and although there should not be a more intimate union between
these disciples and ourselves, than now exists, yet we rejoice that they
have the same great work at heart, and we doubt not will prosecute it
perseveringly and successfully. The need of a more exact knowledge than
can be obtained from books, or even from correspondence, induced the
Committee to employ an agent, whose sole business it should be, by actual observation, to make himself familiar with the religious condition
of the Middle and Western States. This gentleman is now on a tour
through Pennsylvania, Ohio, Kentucky, Indiana and Illinois. He will probably spend some months in the journey, and has been directed to collect
and transmit to the Committee whatever facts in the ecclesiastical history
of those states he may obtain, as well as the result of his inquiries and observation concerning the present feelings and condition of the people.
The Committee do not possess such information as would enable them
to give an estimate of the number of Unitarian congregations in our country. Of New England it would be difficult to speak with certainty. There
are in almost every town Unitarians, in many towns of Massachusetts
they constitute the majority, in many more they have respectable, though
not large churches, but in far the greater number of parishes in New
England they are still blended with other sects, and either from a distrust
of their own strength, or from a reluctance to disturb the quiet of a religious society, or from local reasons, they make small exertions to secure
such an administration of the gospel, as may accord with their convictions
of truth. The number of these silent Unitarians is increasing, and at the
same time, more are manifesting a determination to assert their rights as
citizens and as christians. The Committee conceive that they have sufficient evidence of the increase of Unitarians in New England, especially
in Maine, in some parts of New Hampshire, and in the valley of the Connecticut in Massachusetts. They say this gladly, but not boastingly. The
progress of correct opinions has been more rapid than their supporters
could have expected for them. They are introducing themselves into
every village, and have given peace and joy to many who are yet un-

known to the company of their brethren. Before another anniversary, the Committee trust that they from whom the annual report shall proceed, will be able to present an exact statement of the number of Unitarian churches and ministers in the northern section of our Union. They do not attempt it now, because they have not the means of making it complete. In the Middle States also, Unitarianism is constantly acquiring new adherents. The erection of a second church in New York, the increased prosperity of the society in Philadelphia, and the commencement of a building for Unitarian worship in Harrisburg, the seat of government of Pennsylvania, are auspicious circumstances. From the Southern and Western divisions of our land, it is presumed that future correspondence and the communications of agents will furnish intelligence equally gratifying. We are assured that the society in Charleston, S.C. continues to prosper, that there are several churches in North Carolina, and that Unitarians are numerous in the states, which lie west of the Alleghany mountains.

The assistance which has been extended to the Association may not equal the expectations awakened by so general a sentiment of approbation as the Committee feel confident they may announce. The Treasurer's Report exhibits the amount received, and the Committee beg leave to state that the subscription is, they believe, larger than has ever before been collected in the same space of time by any Unitarian Society, and that these sums have not been drawn from this city, but, on the contrary, have been chiefly obtained in other places. The Committee have, also, found it difficult to prepare a system of cooperation, which should apply to all Unitarian societies, and have been more anxious during the first year of the Association, to give the public a thorough acquaintance with its designs, and to secure the patronage of a few in every place, on whom they might rely for future support, than to fill the treasury with money contributed by persons imperfectly acquainted with our purposes. Neither have they been able to make large appropriations, from a want of information concerning the manner in which the funds could best be expended. They have been engaged chiefly in exciting an interest in behalf of the Association, and in laying a foundation for future efforts. A few facts will show that they have not been unsuccessful. In Worcester county an Auxiliary Association has been formed, but no returns have yet been received from its officers. The formation of county associations does not, however, appear to the Committee to promise great good, and if the scheme which will be laid before this meeting, should be accepted, it will supersede the necessity of such associations. At New York and Philadelphia auxiliary associations have been formed. In Boston meetings were called by persons friendly to the Association, at which its objects were discussed, and votes of approbation and assistance were unanimously passed. These meetings were attended by gentlemen from all the Unitarian societies in this city, and from some of the neighbouring towns, and the spirit exhibited was such as offered the most cheering prospects to the friends of this institution. At the last of these meetings a committee was appointed to address a circular to the standing committees of the several parishes, inviting their cooperation in advancing the interests of the Association in their several societies. From this circular we beg leave to extract the following remarks:—

"The American Unitarian Association has been established from a persuasion, that the time has arrived, when it is necessary for those who profess the simple Unity of God, to adopt measures differing, in some respects, from those which they have heretofore pursued. By this we do not mean, that Unitarians should lay aside those means of support and defence upon which they have heretofore relied; or divest themselves of that charity, which they have always cherished towards those, who differ from them in sentiment. By a difference of measures we mean, that the circumstances of the times require a more systematic union, and 'a concentration of labours, by which interest may be awakened, confidence inspired, and efficiency produced.' The want of union among Christians of our denomination, is felt to be a great evil by those, who have directed their attention to this subject. Living in an age of unusual religious excitement, surrounded by numerous sects, all of which are zealously employed in disseminating their peculiar tenets, we should be wanting in duty to ourselves, and be doing injustice to the doctrines we profess, if we should allow them to fail in exercising their due influence, for the want of a corresponding zeal and interest. Our exertions have not been apparent, because insulated; and the contributions of many of our friends have been thrown into the treasuries of other denominations of Christians, from the want of some proper objects among ourselves, upon which they could be bestowed. We feel confident, that there are among us men of zeal and energy, who are both willing and able to exert themselves in the cause of religion; and that others, who are now indifferent to the subject, might by sympathy and encouragement be excited to similar exertions. All that is required, is, that they be brought together, and be made acquainted with each others' views and feelings; that they be allowed to unite their labours in one common field, and for one common end, and thereby warm each others' hearts and strengthen each others' hands. To produce this concert among Unitarians is one of the objects of the American Unitarian Association."

Sufficient time has not elapsed since the distribution of this Circular for any measures which might be adopted in consequence. The committees of the several churches have not since acted upon the subject, and the directors of this Association have thought it proper to defer any attempt at a general subscription in this city and vicinity, till their decision shall be made known. It is probable that auxiliary associations will be formed, as is recommended in that Circular, and that the Unitarians of Boston will generally become members of the Association. . . .

Having thus spoken of the means employed to extend the knowledge and influence of the Association, and to secure for it friends and resources, your Committee will state what has been done towards accomplishing the particular objects of this Society. The publication of tracts received their earliest attention, and arrangements were made for furnishing a succession of such as should contain an exposition and defence of Unitarian Christianity. Some difficulty has been experienced in obtaining tracts, which should at once be unexceptionable in doctrine and in spirit, and be suited to the peculiar wants of the community. Four tracts have been published by the Committee. One of these was written for the Association; the substance of another was taken from an old Unitarian writer; the copy-right of a third was purchased of the author, who had printed one edition; and the fourth was a reprint of a sermon delivered some years since in England. These have all been well received, of which the best proof was seen in the speedy call for a second edition of each of the three first. Of "The Faith once Delivered to the Saints," 5000 also have been printed, only 1200 of which are unsold; of "Sewall's Sermon on Human Depravity," an edition of 2000 was soon exhausted, and another has just been issued; of "Hutton's Sermon on the Attribute of Omniscience," 2000 copies were published, 1800 of which have been taken from the depository. Of these four tracts 17,000 copies have therefore been published by the Association. The Executive Committee have also obtained the copy right of the valuable tract entitled the "Unitarian's Answer," and of that which has been so deservedly popular, entitled, "Objections to Unitarian Christianity Considered." As soon as former editions are sold, these will be printed in a style similar to that of the other tracts of the Association. The Committee have been disappointed in their expectations of receiving original tracts for publication, and they have met with little success in their search after those, which they might reprint. It has been difficult to find such as were both short and comprehensive, suited for popular reading, and at the same time adapted to enlightened minds. It was the intention of the Committee to publish two tracts in every month, and this they still hope may be done. They believe that when the greatness of the demand is known, and the advantages which this Association offers for introducing any work into circulation, Unitarian writers will be induced to give us the fruits of their study. They can take no course more certain of diffusing their opinions throughout the country, none more sure of influencing the public mind. The Committee take pleasure in announcing, that a friend has committed to them an original tract, which will be immediately put to press, and that another has been promised them by a distinguished clergyman. They are desirous to publish practical tracts. Those which have been printed necessarily bear a doctrinal character; but the Committee have endeavoured to obtain others which should enforce the duties of piety and morality. They believe that it should be a primary object with this Association, to promote a spirit of devotion, and to inculcate the observance of christian duties among Unitarians; and they therefore hope, that a series of tracts, explaining the spirit and obligations of religion, will receive as great a share of attention, as those which illustrate and defend the principles of our faith. A system, which should bring their tracts into immediate and general use, was early made a topic of discussion by the Committee. The plan first adopted has been proved to be perplexing and insufficient for the purpose. Another has been substituted, which, it is hoped, will meet the wishes of every member of the Association. A general depository is established in this city, at which the tracts of the Association will always be found. They are printed in a uniform manner, in a handsome style, yet at a very low price, and bear double numbers on the pages, that they may be bound in volumes. A copy of each tract will be sent to every subscriber, through his minister or the agent in his town; and in the shire-towns, county depositories have been, or will be established, at which the publications of the Association may be obtained at the same price, as at the general agency. To agents, and to auxiliary associations, it is proposed to sell the tracts at a large discount. We believe that this method will be found both simple and effectual. The Committee will only add on this point, that the demand has greatly exceeded their anticipations, and has shown the importance of this branch of the Society's operations. . . .

The next duty which the Executive Committee considered incumbent on them, was the support of missionaries. They have been prevented from making such appropriations as they desired for this object, by the difficulty of finding persons, who could be employed in such service. They have made an appropriation of $100 to the Rev. James Kay, a valuable minister, who resides in Northumberland, Penn.; and who preaches at stated times in several neighbouring towns, and has spent a few sabbaths in Harrisburg. Your Committee believe him to be a worthy man, and one peculiarly fitted to increase the friends of Unitarian Christianity in that part of the country. He is expected to preach whenever he shall find a favourable opportunity. The Committee are persuaded that missionaries might be very usefully employed in the Western counties of Massachusetts, in New Hampshire, and perhaps in Vermont and Maine, who should not be confined to a particular spot, but be allowed to preach

wherever a Unitarian congregation may be gathered, and who might receive a part of their support from such congregations. The expediency of
employing a missionary in each of the cities of Boston and New York,
who should devote himself to the instruction of the poor, has been discussed in the Committee. The object has seemed to them very important,
and though no plan for the support of such missionaries, who, it seems to
the Committee, should draw their support from other sources than the
funds of this Association, has yet been matured, they hope it will not be
overlooked, but will receive attention in the ensuing year. It has been
already mentioned in this Report, that an agent is now engaged in making inquiries, which may facilitate the operations of the Association in
the Western States. We have reason to expect from him such intelligence,
as will justify liberal appropriations for the support of preachers in that
part of our country. The Committee have also felt themselves authorised
to comply with a request from a Unitarian society in Harrisburg, Penn.
for aid in the erection of a building for public worship. They have trans-
mitted $100 for this object. The central situation of Harrisburg, its im-
portance as the place at which the legislature of the state assemble, and
the exertions of the Unitarians, who belong to this society, together with
the success, which has attended their exertions, appeared to the Committee, to offer sufficiently strong reasons to warrant such an appropriation,
though they believe that the funds of the Association can generally be
better employed in some other manner.

The Committee have thus presented a full account of their proceedings
during the past year. They have chosen to enter into these details, rather
than to occupy the time of the meeting by a defence of the principles on
which the Association was established, or a theoretical exposition of the
good effects which might reasonably be anticipated from this Society.
Facts are more useful than speculations, and an explicit statement of the
measures, which have been devised or executed by those to whom the
affairs of the Association were intrusted, will better exhibit its character
and designs, than ingenious, or even sound reasoning on its probable utility. Neither did it seem to the Committee to be their office to advocate,
in this Report, the principles on which this Society was formed. They
prefer that these principles should be examined and defended in the course
of a free discussion. They cannot but indulge the hope, that the exposition
that has now been given, will remove any doubts which may have been
felt concerning the expediency of union with the Association. While the
Committee congratulate the officers and members on the degree of favour,
which has been shown to it, they mean not to deny that objections have
been started, and that some have been reluctant to add their names to the
list of its supporters. They have laboured to show the futility of these

objections, and to dissipate the fears expressed by good men, and decided Unitarians, that the new Society might be a source of evil rather than of good, of division rather than of harmony. They have strenuously opposed the opinion, that the object of its founders was to build up a party, to organize an opposition, to perpetuate pride and bigotry. Had they believed that such was its purpose, or such would be its effect, they would have withdrawn themselves from any connexion with so hateful a thing. They thought otherwise, and experience has proved that they did not judge wrongly. They have witnessed an increased zeal for pure and undefiled religion, the religion not of this man nor that party, but of Jesus Christ, our Master and Redeemer, brought into action, if it were not inspired, by the influence of this Association. They have heard words of congratulation, but none of bitterness; and they devoutly believe, that this Society is meant in the providence of God to be instrumental in diffusing the truths and the spirit of that gospel, for which his Son was sent, for which he toiled and suffered, and to establish which he poured out his blood. In the words of the Circular, which they have already quoted, "they care not for adding to the number of those, who merely call themselves Unitarians; but their object is to increase the number of those, who are Christians from examination and conviction; the number of consistent believers, whose lives comport with their principles; the number of those, who feel the influence and power of the precepts of Jesus Christ." In this cause, the cause of man's highest interest, the cause of universal love, they believe this Association is willing to employ all its energies and resources; and commending it to the favour of our Father in heaven, for whose glory they humbly trust it was established, they feel a confidence, which much disappointment alone can destroy, that it will be a blessing to future generations. It will, they hope, scatter the seeds of spiritual knowledge, which shall spring up in usefulness on earth, and shall yield a harvest of everlasting glory.

The Executive Committee beg leave to close their Report with two suggestions concerning the means of increasing the extent and efficiency of this Association.

It is essential that a general cooperation should be produced, and for this end, they propose the formation of an auxiliary association in every Unitarian congregation. They would press this on the attention of every person present at this meeting: and would express their strong persuasion, that this will be the most simple, permanent, and effectual method of accomplishing the purposes of the Association.

The Committee also advise that measures be taken to effect a union of the existing Unitarian Societies, viz. The Society for the Promotion of Christian Knowledge, Piety and Charity, The Evangelical Missionary Society, and The Publishing Fund, with the American Unitarian Association. Such a union will prevent any interference of one Society with another, and any impression which may be received, that they are hostile or unfriendly to one another. It will also render the operations of these societies more useful, will prevent an unnecessary waste of labour, and will make the information acquired by one, common to all. After these remarks, and with the desire of giving a practical direction to the discussions of the evening, the Committee offer the following resolutions for consideration:—

1. That the proposal to form a union with other Societies having similar objects, receives the approbation and concurrence of this Association.

2. That it is considered highly desirable that, as far as practicable, Auxiliaries be formed to the Association in every Unitarian congregation.

3. That this Association views with high gratification the prospect, which is opened of a more extended mutual acquaintance and cooperation among Unitarian christians throughout the world.

All which is respectfully submitted. . . .

II DOCTRINES AND THEOLOGY

❧ Catechism for Children and Youth

MINISTERS OF THE
WORCESTER ASSOCIATION

Since the earliest days of Christianity, religious instruction has been necessary. The word *catechism* literally means "instruction that comes by hearing"; however, Christians have produced elaborate instructional guides on the way of faith, ranging from the one composed by Cyril of Jerusalem in 350, to Martin Luther's during the Reformation and those of the Puritans in New England. Seventeenth-century Christians adopted the *Westminster Catechisms,* using the *Larger* to guide ministers in their teaching of the Reformed faith, the *Shorter* for teaching children. This latter catechism contains the famous beginning, "What is the chief end of man? Man's chief end is to glorify God, and to enjoy Him forever."

By the end of the eighteenth century the Calvinist influence in religious instruction began to wane. But in 1813 Channing and Thacher could agree that the principles of Christianity needed to be made explicit in teaching, and they published their *Elements of Religion and Morality in the Form of a Catechism.*

However, several years after the Baltimore Sermon, Channing wrote, "A catechism is a skeleton, a dead letter, a petrification. Wanting life, it can give none. A cold abstraction, it cannot but make religion repulsive to pupils whose age demands that truth should be embodied, set before their eyes, bound up with real life."[1] As the Unitarian Controversy developed in the pulpits, the idea of the Sunday School was effected, and how the young were to be instructed became an issue.

The Old Worcester Association of Massachusetts had published an earlier catechism, but in the latter part of the eighteenth century a confrontation between the orthodox and liberal camps brought about an end to this group. In 1815 several young Harvard Divinity School graduates revived the association, and six years later Aaron Bancroft, later the first president of the American Unitarian Association, Joseph Allen, and Nathaniel Thayer published the new Worcester Catechism, reprinted here.

The Worcester Catechism became a popular document in Unitarian churches. The first section contains much of the 1813 catechism published by Channing and Thacher; the following two sections reveal the type of Biblical material taught to Unitarian children. Rather than stress-

1. William E. Channing, "The Sunday-School," in *Works,* vol. 4, p. 364.

ing Biblical verse, the catechism seeks to convey the narrative quality of the Scriptures. For anyone acquainted with the more traditional documents of religious instruction, the style of the Worcester Catechism is unique. The modern reader will sense the Christian Unitarian mind in these pages. The reliance on the Bible is still present; the use of the Ten Commandments, the nature of Jesus Christ, and the sense of the sacraments are all treated.

Channing may have grown disillusioned with the traditional mode of catechetical instruction, but Christian life demands knowledge of the Bible as well as of doctrine. The challenge of this task becomes particularly clear when the reader considers a comment made by Ralph Waldo Emerson in his essay "Circles": "We can never see Christianity from the catechism:—from the pastures, from a boat in the pond, from amidst the songs of wood-birds we possibly may."[2] For the Christian Unitarian the church and Sunday School room were important, no mere scene in nature was satisfactory.

Question 1. When you look up to the sky, what do you see?
Answer. I see the sun, the moon, and the stars.
Q. 2. When you walk abroad into the fields, what do you see?
A. 1. I see trees, and grass, and flowers.
2. I see rocks, and hills, and brooks.
3. I see birds, and beasts, and many other living creatures.
Q. 3. Can you tell me who made all these things?
A. God made them and everything that is.
Q. 4. If God made them, and everything that is, then he made you?
A. Yes—God made me and all mankind.
Q. 5. What does God give you?
A. 1. He gives me life, and health, and strength.
2. He gives me power to see and hear, to speak and move.
3. He gives me power to think, and remember, and learn, and know when I do wrong.
4. He gives me my kind parents, my teachers, my friends, and my home.
5. He gives me my food, and clothes, and quiet sleep.
6. He gives me the air which I breathe, and the pleasant light which shines around me.
7. God gives me everything that I have.

2. Ralph Waldo Emerson, "Circles," in *Selections*, p. 201.

Q. 6. If God made you, and gives you all these good things, is he not a Father to you?

A. Yes; my father and my mother are my earthly parents; but God is my heavenly Father, and the Father of all mankind.

Q. 7. What did God make you and all mankind for?

A. He made us all that we might be good and happy.

Q. 8. What is it to be good?

A. To be good, is always to feel and act as I ought.

Q. 9. How ought you to feel and act towards God?

A. 1. I must often think of God as my Father in heaven.

2. I must love him better than I love any other being, and endeavor to please and obey him.

3. I must fear nothing so much as to offend him.

4. I must never speak of him in a careless manner, or take his name in vain.

5. I must pray to him for what I need, especially in the morning and at night.

6. I must thank him for what I receive, though it may not be all that I wish.

7. I must bear patiently the sickness and pain which he brings upon me, and try to be better for it.

Q. 10. What is your duty to your parents and instructors?

A. I must love and obey them, be ever ready to oblige them, and be thankful to them for all their tender care of me.

Q. 11. How should you treat those who are older than yourself?

A. I must treat them with respect, especially the aged and venerable.

Q. 12. What is your duty to your brothers and sisters?

A. I must love them, and always be affectionate and obliging to them.

Q. 13. How should you treat your young companions?

A. If they are good, I must love them too, and be happy to have their friendship.

Q. 14. But what if they are wicked?

A. If they are wicked I must avoid them, and not keep company with any who are fond of mischief, lest I should be like them.

Q. 15. What is your duty to those who have injured you?

A. I must not be angry, nor try to injure them, but be willing to forgive them; and if I have injured any, I must be sorry for it, and must ask their forgiveness.

Q. 16. What is your duty to the poor and unfortunate?

A. I must pity them, and show them kindness, and do all I can to make them happy.

Q. 17. What are the duties you owe to all around you?

A. 1. I must speak the truth always, keep my promises even upon the most trifling occasions, and never try to deceive by my looks, words, or actions.

2. I must be honest, and must take nothing which belongs to others.

3. I must not be cruel, and must not willingly give pain to anything which has life.

4. I must try to do all the good I can, and to make all around me happy.

Q. 18. What are your duties to yourself?

A. 1. I must be active and industrious.

2. I must be ready and happy to learn.

3. I must be contented and cheerful, even when I cannot have what I want.

4. I must not be fretful, wilful, or passionate.

5. I must not be proud or vain of anything which I have, but be modest and humble.

6. I must learn to give up and avoid everything which will do me hurt; I must be governed by reason and conscience, and not by my wishes.

Q. 19. Does God know whether you are good or not?

A. Yes; he knows all that I think, and speak, and do; and though I may deceive those around me, I can never deceive God.

Q. 20. Does God always see you?

A. 1. He sees me at all times, all the night, and all the day.

2. He sees me when I am alone, when no other person sees me.

Q. 21. What will God do for you if you are good?

A. If I am good, God will love me and delight to make me happy.

Q. 22. How shall you be happy *in this life,* if you are good?

A. 1. I shall have peace in my own mind.

2. I shall not be ashamed or afraid to have my actions known.

3. My parents and friends will love me, and will look on me with pleasure and hope.

Q. 23. What will God do if you are not good?

A. If I am not good, God will be displeased, and will punish me.

Q. 24. Why will God punish you if you are not good?

A. He will punish me to make me become good; for, if I am not good, I cannot be happy.

Q. 25. What must you expect *in this life,* if you do wrong?

A. 1. I shall feel pain, and fear, and shame, at thinking I have done wrong.

2. If I do not repent, I shall grow worse as I grow older.

3. My parents and friends will be displeased with me, and will look on me with sorrow.

Q. 26. What is it to sin against God?

A. To sin against God is, to do anything which I know to be wrong.

Q. 27. Why is this to sin against God?

A. Because God forbids me to do what I know to be wrong.

Q. 28. How should you feel and act when you have sinned?

A. 1. I should be sorry for the sin, and, as far as I can, I should repair it, and resolve and strive to do so no more.

2. I should humbly confess my sins to God, and should pray to him, through Jesus Christ, to forgive me and assist me in doing better.

Q. 29. Who is Jesus Christ?

A. He is the well-beloved Son of God, whom his Father sent into the world to be the Saviour of all who believe and obey him.

Q. 30. From what does Jesus Christ save us?

A. He saves us from error and sin, from death and misery.

Q. 31. What did Jesus Christ suffer for us?

A. 1. He was so poor that he had not where to lay his head.

2. He lived a life of hardship, travelling from place to place, that he might instruct men and do them good.

3. He was constantly opposed and persecuted by the Jews, who would not hearken to him.

4. At last, after a life of toil and suffering, he was betrayed by Judas, denied by Peter, and for a time deserted by all his friends.

5. False witnesses testified against him; he was reviled, and mocked, and scourged, and at last put to death with cruel tortures.

Q. 32. Was Jesus Christ willing to suffer all this?

A. Yes—he bore it patiently and cheerfully, being willing to die *the just for the unjust, that he might bring us to God.*

Q. 33. Is Jesus Christ dead now?

A. No; early on the first day of the week, which is now called the *Lord's day,* God brought him to life again; and after forty days took him up into heaven, where he still lives, and continually performs kind offices for us.

Q. 34. What do you learn by the resurrection of Christ from the dead, and his ascension into heaven?

A. I learn that all good persons, after death, will go to heaven, to live with God and Christ for ever.

Q. 35. After you die, shall you then live again?

A. Yes; God will bring me to life, and I shall never die again.

Q. 36. Shall you be happy or miserable, when you live again?

A. If I repent of my sins, and believe and obey the gospel, and strive to be good here, I shall be happy; but if I am wicked, I shall be miserable.

Q. 37. How shall you be happy in another world if you are good in this life?

A. 1. I shall have no sickness, nor sorrow, nor pain; but shall have rest and joy for ever.

2. I shall be like the angels in heaven, and shall have the friendship and love of all good beings.

3. I shall enjoy the presence and favor of God, and shall be always learning to love and serve him better.

Q. 38. How shall you be miserable in another world if you are wicked here?

A. I shall not be received into the light and joy of heaven, but shall be left to the fearful punishment which my sins deserve.

Q. 39. Where do we learn what we know concerning these things?

A. In the Bible, principally from the instructions of Jesus Christ.

Q. 40. What instructions did Jesus Christ give respecting the nature and worship of God?

A. "God is a spirit: and they that worship him, must worship him in spirit and in truth."

Q. 41. What assurance did Jesus give to encourage persons to pray?

A. "If ye then, being evil, know how to give good gifts to your children, how much more shall your Father which is in heaven, give good things to them that ask him."

Q. 42. What did Jesus teach us as the first and great commandment?

A. "Thou shalt love the Lord thy God with all thy heart, and with all thy soul, and with all thy mind."

Q. 43. What is the second?

A. "Thou shalt love thy neighbor as thyself."

Q. 44. What rule did Jesus give us to regulate our conduct towards others?

A. "Therefore all things whatsoever ye would that men should do to you, do ye even so to them."

Q. 45. What new commandment did Jesus give his disciples?

A. That they should love one another as he loved them.

Q. 46. What instructions did he give us for the treatment of our enemies?

A. "Love your enemies, bless them that curse you, do good to them that hate you, and pray for them that despitefully use you and persecute you."

Q. 47. What did he say of little children?

A. "Jesus took them up in his arms, put his hands upon them, and blessed them, and said, Suffer little children, and forbid them not, to come unto me, for of such is the kingdom of heaven."

Q. 48. What did he teach respecting Divine Providence?

A. He taught that God's care extends not only to man, but to the beasts and birds, and even to the herbs and flowers.

Q. 49. What were his instructions respecting the general resurrection?

A. "The hour is coming, in which all that are in their graves shall hear the voice of the Son of God and shall come forth; they that have done good, to the resurrection of life; and they that have done evil, unto the resurrection of condemnation."

Q. 50. Should you not love Jesus Christ for giving you these good instructions, and for all that he did and suffered for you?

A. Yes; I must love him, and be thankful to him, and endeavor to be like him; and when I am old enough, it will be my duty to remember and honor him by partaking of the Lord's Supper.

Q. 51. What else must you do to become good and happy in this life and in the life to come?

A. 1. I must read the Bible attentively and seriously, and such other good books as my parents and instructors wish me to read.

2. I must make a good use of the Lord's day. I must habitually attend public worship, be serious and attentive at church, and I must receive with cheerfulness and gratitude the instructions of my parents at home.

3. I must often think that God sees me.

4. I must recollect at night what I have done and thought and felt through the day, that I may make my future life better than the past.

5. Above all, I must pray to God, without whose blessing I can do nothing, for his assistance and direction.

PART II. *Questions on the Old Testament.*

INTRODUCTION.

Q. 1. What is the Bible?

A. It is a collection of sacred writings, sometimes called the Holy Scriptures, the Inspired Volume, or the Word of God.

Q. 2. Into what parts is it divided?

A. Into the Old and New Testaments.

Q. 3. When and by whom was the Bible written?

A. At different times and by different persons, who were appointed or particularly qualified by God for the purpose.

Q. 4. What languages was the Bible written in?

A. The Old Testament was written in the Hebrew language, and the New Testament in the Greek language.

Q. 5. When and by whom was the translation of the Bible made which is now in general use?

A. It was made, about two hundred years ago, by a number of learned men in England, and by the direction of king James the First.

Q. 6. Was the Bible originally divided into chapters and verses?

A. It was not: the division of the Bible into chapters was made only about six hundred years since; and the division into verses, not till two or three hundred years afterwards.

Q. 7. What is the name of the first book in the Bible?

A. Genesis, which contains an account of the creation of the world, and the earliest history of the human race.

Q. 8. At what period does this history commence?

A. Four thousand and four years before Jesus Christ was born, or nearly six thousand years ago.

Q. 9. In how many days did God create the heavens and the earth?

A. In six days.

Q. 10. What is said of the seventh day?

A. God rested on the seventh day, and made it holy.

Q. 11. What was the seventh day called?

A. The Sabbath, or the day of rest.

Q. 12. Who were our first parents?

A. Adam and Eve.

Q. 13. Where did God place them?

A. In a delightful place, called the Garden of Eden.

Q. 14. Why did God cast them out of the Garden of Eden?

A. Because they disobeyed him in eating the forbidden fruit.

Q. 15. Who were Cain and Abel?

A. Sons of Adam and Eve; Cain cultivated the ground; and Abel tended flocks.

Q. 16. What wicked act was Cain guilty of?

A. He became angry with his brother; and at a time when they were together in the field, he killed him.

Q. 17. Who was Enoch?

A. Enoch was a good man, who pleased God and was taken up to heaven without dying.

Q. 18. Why did God cover the earth with a great flood?

A. Because the inhabitants had become very wicked.

Q. 19. Who were saved alive in the ark?

A. Noah and his family, consisting of eight persons.

Q. 20. What was the ark?

A. A large vessel of wood made to float on the waters.

Q. 21. Why were Noah and his family preserved?

A. Because he was a good man, and sought to please God.

Q. 22. To what age did men live, before the flood?

A. To a much greater age than they live now; Methuselah, who was the oldest man, lived nine hundred and sixty-nine years.

Q. 23. Did they live so long after the flood?

A. No: they died much younger.

Q. 24. In what manner, and on what account, were Sodom and Gomorrah destroyed?

A. They were destroyed by fire and brimstone from heaven, on account of the great wickedness of the people who lived there.

Q. 25. What three distinguished Patriarchs do we read of in the book of Genesis?

A. Abraham, Isaac, and Jacob.

Q. 26. By what other name was Jacob sometimes called?

A. Israel, and his descendents *Israelites,* or *children of Israel.*

Q. 27. About what time did these patriarchs live?

A. About two thousand years after the creation, and two thousand before Jesus Christ.

Q. 28. How many sons had Jacob or Israel?

A. He had twelve sons, who were called the twelve patriarchs, or fathers of the twelve tribes of Israel.

Q. 29. Who was Joseph?

A. He was one of the twelve sons of Jacob, whom his brothers hated, because their father was partial to him.

Q. 30. What became of Joseph?

A. He was sold by his brothers to some merchants, who carried him into Egypt.

Q. 31. What became of him there?

A. He was very much beloved on account of his good behaviour, and became a great and happy man.

Q. 32. Did he ever see his father and brothers again?

A. Yes; when he was governor of Egypt, there was a great famine in all the land, and Joseph gave corn to his father and brothers, and they all came to Egypt and lived there.

Q. 33. How many persons went to Egypt with Jacob?

A. All his family, consisting of seventy persons.

Q. 34. How were the Israelites treated by the Egyptians?

A. With great kindness at first; but, after they had become numerous, the Egyptians were cruel to them, and made them slaves.

Q. 35. By whom were they delivered?

A. By Moses, a man whom God appointed for that purpose. God opened a way for them through the Red Sea, and the Egyptians, in attempting to overtake them, were drowned.

Q. 36. What was the number of the Israelites when they left Egypt?

A. Six hundred thousand men, besides women and children.

Q. 37. To what country did they intend to go?

A. To the land of Canaan, where their fathers had lived before they removed to Egypt.

Q. 38. How long did they wander about in the wilderness before they reached the land of Canaan?

A. Forty years, till nearly all those had perished, who were of age when they left Egypt.

Q. 39. How were they supported during this time?

A. God gave them food from heaven, which was called *manna.*

Q. 40. What instructions did God give them when they were at Mount Sinai?

A. He gave them the Ten Commandments and many other good laws, which they were required to observe.

Q. 41. What is the first commandment?

A. "Thou shalt have no other gods but me."

Q. 42. What is the second commandment?

A. "Thou shalt not make unto thee any graven image, or any likeness of anything that is in heaven above, or that is in the earth beneath, or that is in the water under the earth. Thou shalt not bow down thyself to them nor serve them; for I, the Lord thy God, am a jealous God, visiting the iniquity of the fathers upon the children unto the third and fourth generation of them that hate me, and showing mercy unto thousands of them that love me, and keep my commandments."

Q. 43. What is the third commandment?

A. "Thou shalt not take the name of the Lord thy God in vain, for the Lord will not hold him guiltless that taketh his name in vain."

Q. 44. What is the fourth commandment?

A. "Remember the Sabbath day, to keep it holy. Six days shalt thou labor and do all thy work, but the seventh is the Sabbath of the Lord thy God: in it thou shalt not do any work, thou, nor thy son, nor thy daughter, thy man-servant, nor thy maid-servant, nor thy cattle, nor thy stranger that is within thy gates; for in six days the Lord made heaven and earth, the sea, and all that in them is, and rested the seventh day; wherefore the Lord blessed the seventh day and hallowed it."

Q. 45. What is the fifth commandment?

A. "Honor thy father and thy mother, that thy days may be long upon the land which the Lord thy God giveth thee."

Q. 46. What is the sixth commandment?

A. "Thou shalt not kill."

Q. 47. What is the seventh commandment?

A. "Thou shalt not commit adultery."

Q. 48. What is the eighth commandment?

A. "Thou shalt not steal."

Q. 49. What is the ninth commandment?

A. "Thou shalt not bear false witness against thy neighbor."

Q. 50. What is the tenth commandment?

A. "Thou shalt not covet thy neighbor's house, thou shalt not covet thy neighbor's wife, nor his man-servant, nor his maid-servant, nor his ox, nor his ass, nor anything that is thy neighbor's."

Q. 51. Did Moses write any part of the Bible?

A. He wrote the five first books, called the *Pentateuch*.

Q. 52. What are the names of these books?

A. Genesis, Exodus, Leviticus, Numbers, and Deuteronomy.

Q. 53. Who was the leader of the Hebrews or Israelites, after Moses?

A. Joshua, who went with them to Canaan.

Q. 54. What was the country of Canaan afterwards called?

A. It was called Judea; it is now called *Palestine* and the *Holy Land*.

Q. 55. In what part of the world is it?

A. In Turkey, in Western Asia, on the Eastern shore of the Mediterranean sea.

Q. 56. By whom were the Israelites governed after they entered the land of Canaan?

A. By a succession of magistrates, who were called Judges.

Q. 57. Into how many tribes were the Israelites divided?

A. Into twelve tribes, after the twelve sons of Israel.

Q. 58. Who was the first king of the Hebrew nation?

A. Saul, a jealous and passionate man, who came to a miserable end.

Q. 59. Who succeeded him?

A. David, who is called *a man after God's own heart*. He was a good man, and wrote many pious hymns, which are called the *Psalms of David*.

Q. 60. Was David always good?

A. No: he was guilty of some great sins, and offended God; and made himself wretched.

Q. 61. Did he become good afterwards?

A. Yes; he repented of his sins, and humbled himself before God, and God forgave him.

Q. 62. What king succeeded David?

A. Solomon, his son, who was celebrated for his wisdom and riches.

Q. 63. What is related of king Solomon?

A. It was Solomon who built the temple, which was a splendid and beautiful church in the city of Jerusalem.

Q. 64. At what period was the temple built?

A. About three thousand years after the creation of the world, and about one thousand years before Jesus Christ was born.

Q. 65. Did Solomon write any part of the Bible?

A. He wrote the books of Proverbs and Ecclesiastes, and Canticles or Solomon's Song.

Q. 66. What was the character of Solomon?

A. He was a wise and just prince, and a great lover of peace; but too much devoted to sensual pleasures, which brought great evils upon him and his family.

Q. 67. Who succeeded Solomon in the kingdom?

A. His son Rehoboam; he was a proud and foolish prince, which caused ten tribes to revolt, and to choose another king.

Q. 68. Did the ten tribes ever return?

A. No: from this time, there were two separate kingdoms: one was called the *kingdom of Israel,* consisting of the ten tribes who refused to obey Rehoboam; and the other was called the *kingdom of Judah,* consisting of the two remaining tribes, those of Judah and Benjamin.

Q. 69. What was the general character of these two kingdoms?

A. In the kingdom of Israel, idolatry and wickedness greatly prevailed; in the kingdom of Judah, many of the kings who succeeded Rehoboam were distinguished for their piety, and there was much more regard for religion among the people.

Q. 70. What at last became of the kingdom of Israel?

A. It was destroyed by the Assyrians, and the ten tribes were carried into captivity, whence they returned no more.

Q. 71. Who were the Assyrians?

A. A great and strong nation, whose chief city was Nineveh.

Q. 72. What became of the kingdom of Judah?

A. It was invaded by the forces of Nebuchadnezzar, king of Babylon; the city of Jerusalem was taken and destroyed, and all the principal inhabitants of the city were carried captive to Babylon.

Q. 73. When did this happen?

A. About six hundred years before Christ, and one hundred and twenty after the destruction of the kingdom of Israel.

Q. 74. When and by whom were the Jews restored to their country?

A. They were restored by Cyrus the Persian, after a captivity of seventy years.

Q. 75. Who was the last of the Jewish prophets?

A. Malachi, who lived about four hundred years before the Christian era.

Q. 76. By whom is it supposed that the books of the Old Testament were first collected together into one volume?

A. By Ezra, after the return of the Jews from the Babylonish captivity.

Q. 77. What was the condition of the Jews, from this period till the time of Christ?

A. They were in a state of subjection to different foreign nations; and at length became tributary to the Romans.

Q. 78. Who reigned in Judea at the time Jesus was born?

A. A cruel tyrant, who was called Herod the Great, and who died a short time after the birth of Jesus Christ.

Q. 79. Who was the emperor of Rome at this time?

A. Augustus Caesar.

Q. 80. What was the condition of the Roman empire at this period?

A. Universal peace prevailed throughout the Roman empire, when Jesus, the Prince of Peace, was born.

Q. 81. What three great national feasts or festivals did God command the Jews to observe, which are mentioned in the New Testament?

A. The Feast of the Passover, the Feast of Pentecost, and the Feast of Tabernacles.

Q. 82. What was the design of the Feast of the Passover?

A. It was designed to commemorate the deliverance of the Israelites from the bondage of Egypt, and especially their preservation on that memorable night when the angel of God destroyed all the first born of the Egyptians, but *passed over,* that is, spared the Israelites.

Q. 83. At what time in the year was the Passover kept?

A. At the latter end of March.

Q. 84. What was the design of the Feast of Pentecost?

A. It was designed as a memorial of the giving of the law from Mount Sinai.

Q. 85. At what time in the year was it celebrated?

A. On the fiftieth day after the Passover, or about the middle of May, which, in Judea, is the time of harvest. Hence it is also called the Feast of Harvest.

Q. 86. What was the last great festival of the Jews?

A. The Feast of Tabernacles, which was so called in commemoration of the tabernacles or moveable tents in which they dwelt in their journeyings through the wilderness.

Q. 87. At what time in the year was this festival kept?

A. Six months after the Passover, or in the latter part of September.

PART III. *Questions on the New Testament.*

Q. 1. What is the second part of the Bible called?

A. It is called the New Testament.

Q. 2. By whom was the New Testament written?

A. It was written by the Apostles of Jesus Christ, or by men who were their companions, and who wrote under their inspection.

Q. 3. Which books of the New Testament are commonly called Gospels?

A. The four first, written by the evangelists, Matthew, Mark, Luke, and John.

Q. 4. What do the four Gospels contain?

A. The four Gospels contain, each, many important instructions of Jesus Christ, a brief history of his life, and an account of his sufferings, death, resurrection, and ascension into heaven.

Q. 5. Why are these books called Gospels?

A. Because they contain *good tidings* of God's love and mercy to men in providing for them a Saviour; Gospel signifies *good news*.

Q. 6. What opportunity had the writers of knowing the truth of what they related?

A. Two of them were the constant companions of Jesus; and the other two wrote from the testimony of persons who had been eyewitnesses and ministers of the word.

Q. 7. Who was Matthew?

A. Matthew was one of the twelve apostles, who had formerly been a publican, or a collector of taxes, but who accepted the invitation of Jesus to follow him.

Q. 8. Who was Mark?

A. Mark was *not* one of the apostles, but a Christian converted, as it is supposed, after our Lord's death, by the apostle Peter, who calls him *his son Marcus*.

Q. 9. Who was Luke?

A. Luke was *not* an apostle, but a learned Christian, the friend and companion of the apostle Paul, who calls him *the beloved physician*. It was he who wrote the Acts of the Apostles.

Q. 10. Who was John?

A. John was one of the twelve Apostles, a constant companion of our Lord, and is frequently mentioned as *the disciple whom Jesus loved*.

Q. 11. At what period did Jesus Christ come into the world?

A. Jesus Christ was born about four thousand years after the creation of the world; and it is from the time of his birth that our years are reckoned.

Q. 12. Who are the reputed parents of Jesus?

A. Joseph and Mary; but his birth is represented as being miraculous.

Q. 13. To what city did they belong?

A. They belonged to the city of Nazareth.

Q. 14. Where was Jesus born?

A. He was born at Bethlehem, whither his parents had gone to be taxed, or registered in obedience to the decree of Augustus, the Roman emperor.

Q. 15. What was the song of the angels on occasion of the birth of Jesus?

A. "They praised God, saying, Glory to God in the highest, on earth peace, good will toward men."

Q. 16. Who was king in Judea at the time Jesus was born?

A. Herod, commonly called Herod the Great, a cruel prince, who, that he might destroy Jesus, ordered all the children in Bethlehem and the neighbouring towns, under the age of two years, to be slain.

Q. 17. In what manner was the life of Jesus preserved?

A. His parents, by Divine direction, carried him to Egypt, where they remained till the death of Herod.

Q. 18. What is related of Jesus when he was twelve years old?

A. He went up to Jerusalem with his parents to keep the Feast of the Passover, and was found by them conversing with the learned Jews in the temple.

Q. 19. What is said of Jesus after his return to Nazareth?

A. He was subject to his parents, and grew in wisdom, and in stature, and in favour with God and man.

Q. 20. Who was John the Baptist?

A. John the Baptist was a person whom God sent as the precursor, or forerunner, of Jesus to prepare for his coming.

Q. 21. Why was he called the Baptist, *i.e.* the Baptizer?

A. Because he *baptized* his disciples; and also to distinguish him from the *evangelist* John.

Q. 22. What did John testify concerning Jesus?

A. That he was *the Christ,* that is, the Messiah whom the Jews expected, and *the Son of God.*

Q. 23. What became of John the Baptist?

A. He was beheaded in prison by Herod, one of the sons of Herod the Great, at the request of his niece, and to gratify his wife Herodias.

Q. 24. By whom was Jesus baptized?

A. He was baptized by John the Baptist.

Q. 25. What took place at the baptism?

A. "The Spirit of God descended as a dove and rested on him, and a

*voice came from heaven, saying, This is my beloved Son, in whom I am
well pleased."*

Q. 26. How old was Jesus at the time of his baptism?

A. He was about thirty years of age.

Q. 27. What happened to him soon after his baptism and before he
entered on his public ministry?

A. He was forty days in the wilderness, where he endured and over-
came several temptations.

Q. 28. Who were the companions of Jesus in his public ministry?

A. He chose twelve persons to attend him in his ministry, who were
commonly called *the Twelve Apostles.*

Q. 29. How long did our Saviour's ministry last?

A. It is commonly supposed that it lasted somewhat more than three
years; but many think that it lasted only one year and a few months.

Q. 30. What evidence did Jesus give of his being sent from God?

A. Besides much other convincing evidence, he wrought many miracles, such as no person could have wrought, unless God were with him.

Q. 31. Will you mention some of the most remarkable of our Lord's
miracles?

A. He converted water into wine at Cana, a city in Galilee.

2. Twice he fed many thousand persons with a few loaves and fishes.

3. He walked on the waves, and stilled the raging of the tempest.

4. He gave sight to the blind and hearing to the deaf; he made the
dumb to speak, and the lame to walk, and healed all kinds of diseases, by
his word.

5. He raised several persons from the dead, and one, namely, Lazarus,
out of the grave, after he had been dead four days.

Q. 32. What effect had the miracles of Jesus on the Jews?

A. Some were convinced by them that Jesus was their promised Messiah; but others accused him of being in fellowship with evil spirits, by
whose assistance he was enabled to perform these mighty works.

Q. 33. What was the principal cause of the opposition which Jesus
met with from the Jews?

A. He was not such a Messiah as they expected; and they were disappointed and angry, when they found that he refused to be their temporal
king.

Q. 34. How did the Jews manifest their displeasure at the conduct of
Jesus?

A. By watching for opportunities to take his life.

Q. 35. Where did Jesus spend the principal part of his ministry?

A. In Galilee, a country situated north of Jerusalem, and at a considerable distance from it.

Q. 36. Did not Jesus occasionally visit Jerusalem?

A. He did; especially at the celebration of the three great national festivals or feasts.

Q. 37. When did he make his last visit to Jerusalem?

A. At the Feast of the Passover.

Q. 38. Where did Jesus and the twelve apostles keep this passover?

A. In a large upper chamber, which had been selected for that purpose, probably on account of its retired situation.

Q. 39. What expressive act did Jesus perform while they were at table?

A. He washed his disciples' feet to teach them brotherly kindness and humility.

Q. 40. What ordinance did Jesus institute after they had eaten the passover?

A. He instituted the ordinance of the Lord's Supper, which was designed for his disciples in every age, and which consists in eating bread and drinking wine in remembrance of him.

Q. 41. What is the nature and use of the Lord's Supper?

A. By eating bread and drinking wine in remembrance of Christ, we keep alive the memory of his death and resurrection; we acknowledge ourselves to be Christians; we cherish a grateful sense of the blessings of the gospel of Christ; and strengthen our resolution to live as becomes his disciples.

Q. 42. To what place did Jesus and the disciples retire after supper was ended?

A. To a place called the Garden of Gethsemane at the foot of the Mount of Olives, where he was found by the men who had been sent to apprehend him.

Q. 43. Which of the disciples betrayed his Master?

A. Judas Iscariot betrayed Jesus for thirty pieces of silver.

Q. 44. What became of Judas Iscariot?

A. When he saw that Jesus was condemned, he became sensible of his guilt, and in remorse and despair he destroyed himself.

Q. 45. Which of the disciples denied his Master?

A. Peter denied him thrice; but immediately repented and wept bitterly for his offence.

Q. 46. What became of Peter after this?

A. He spent his life in preaching the gospel, and at length suffered martyrdom, as Jesus had forewarned him.

Q. 47. Whither was Jesus conveyed from the Garden of Gethsemane?

A. He was led first to the palace of Caiaphas, the high priest, and thence to Pilate, the Roman governor.

Q. 48. What did Pilate do with Jesus?

A. When he found that the Jews insisted on his death, he delivered him up to them to be crucified, although he himself was satisfied of his innocence.

Q. 49. Where was Jesus crucified?

A. At a place called Golgotha, just without the walls of the city.

Q. 50. Was he crucified immediately after his condemnation, or did he suffer other injuries before his death?

A. He was mocked, he was spit upon, he was crowned with thorns, he was scourged and wickedly abused, before they nailed him to the cross.

Q. 51. In what company was Jesus crucified?

A. He was crucified between two criminals, one on the right hand and the other on the left.

Q. 52. What prayer did he make, while he was hanging on the cross, in behalf of those who had brought him to this cruel death?

A. *"Father, forgive them, for they know not what they do."*

Q. 53. What were the last words spoken by Jesus before he expired?

A. *"Father, into thy hands I commend my spirit."*

Q. 54. What miracles attended his death?

A. The sun was darkened at noon for three hours together; there was an earthquake, which opened many graves; and the veil of the temple was rent in two pieces.

Q. 55. How was Jesus buried?

A. Joseph of Arimathea, a rich man, and one of his disciples, buried him in his own new tomb, and Pilate and the Jews set a guard of soldiers about it.

Q. 56. When did he rise from the dead?

A. Early on the first day of the week, which is therefore called the *Lord's day,* and which has ever since been kept holy by Christians, instead of the seventh day or the Jewish Sabbath.

Q. 57. How long had Jesus remained in the tomb?

A. From Friday, the day on which he was crucified, till the Lord's day, that is, *a part of three* days.

Q. 58. By whom was he seen after his resurrection?

A. He was seen many times by the Apostles and by other persons; and, on one occasion, he was seen by more than five hundred brethren at the same time.

Q. 59. How long did he remain on the earth after his resurrection?

A. About forty days, after which he was taken up into heaven, while the apostles were conversing with him.

Q. 60. What commission did Jesus give to his apostles, just before his ascension?

A. "Go ye into all the world and preach the gospel to every creature, baptizing them in the name of the Father, and of the Son, and of the Holy Spirit; teaching them to observe all things whatsoever I have commanded you."

Q. 61. What is meant by the ordinance of baptism?

A. The application of water in baptism represents the purity of heart and life required of all who become the disciples of Christ; and is the ordinance by which individuals are received into his church.

———

Q. 62. What does the book, called "The Acts of the Apostles," contain?

A. It contains a brief history of the first preaching of the Gospel, and particularly of the conversion, travels, and labours of the Apostle Paul.

Q. 63. What happened on the day of Pentecost, that is, about ten days after the ascension of Jesus?

A. The Apostles were then endowed with power from on high, by which they were enabled to preach the gospel in a great number of languages and to perform miracles.

Q. 64. What was the doctrine which the Apostles preached?

A. They preached that Jesus, who was crucified, was the Messiah, *i.e.* the Christ, the Son of God, and the Saviour of men; and that sinners who repent and believe in his name, should be saved.*

Q. 65. What success had their preaching?

A. Three thousand were converted and baptized in one day, and five thousand in another.

Q. 66. What effect had this on the chief men among the Jews?

A. They were indignant at the success of the apostles, and put two of them, Peter and John, in prison.

Q. 67. Who first suffered martyrdom?

A. The first Christian martyr was Stephen: the Jews stoned him to death.

Q. 68. What followed the death of Stephen?

A. A great persecution was raised against the Christians, in which a young man, by the name of Saul, was distinguished for his violence.

Q. 69. Who was Saul?

A. Saul was a learned and zealous Pharisee, a native of Tarsus, and a great enemy of the Christians. After his conversion he was called Paul.

Q. 70. In what manner was Saul converted?

A. As he was on his way to Damascus, to persecute the Christians, Je-

———

* This reply, which is given in the words of Dr. Watts, is such, it is hoped, as will meet the views of all who may make use of this book.

sus Christ appeared to him in a bright and overpowering light, and addressed him in these words,—*Saul, Saul, why persecutest thou me?*

Q. 71. What effect had this miracle on Saul?

A. From this time he became a zealous and successful preacher of the gospel, and was the author of thirteen Epistles, written to different churches or individuals, all of which are contained in the New Testament.

Q. 72. Who was the first Gentile, or heathen, converted to Christianity?

A. Cornelius, a Roman Centurion at Cesarea, a person distinguished for his piety and benevolence.

Q. 73. How was the conversion of the heathens regarded by the Jewish Christians at Jerusalem?

A. They were at first very unwilling to acknowledge them as their brethren.

Q. 74. Why was Paul called *the Apostle of the Gentiles,* and Peter *the Apostle of the Circumcision?*

A. They were so called, because Paul preached the gospel principally to the Gentiles or heathens; but Peter to the Jews, who are called *the Circumcision.*

Q. 75. Where were the disciples of Jesus first called Christians?

A. At Antioch.

Q. 76. What dissension arose among the Christians of Antioch?

A. Some of them taught that the heathen converts must be circumcised and conform to the laws of Moses, before they could be admitted into the Christian church; but Paul and Barnabas taught that it was not necessary.

Q. 77. What method did they adopt to decide this controversy?

A. Paul and Barnabas, with some others, were sent to Jerusalem to ask advice of the Apostles on the subject.

Q. 78. What was the decision of the Apostles?

A. They decided that gentile Christians were not required to observe the ritual laws of Moses.*

Q. 79. In what places did Paul preach the gospel?

A. He travelled over a great part of Asia Minor and through many countries of Europe three several times, and established Churches in a great number of cities and villages.

Q. 80. In what places did he remain for the longest period?

A. In Corinth and Ephesus; in the former of which he remained a year and six months, and in the latter nearly three years.

* This controversy respecting the obligation of the Mosaic law furnishes a key to the explanation of many difficulties in the Epistles of St. Paul.

Q. 81. What happened to Paul at Jerusalem, after he had completed his third Apostolical journey?

A. The Jews excited a tumult against him, on the ground that he had admitted a heathen convert into their temple, in contempt of their laws.

Q. 82. In what manner was he delivered out of their hands?

A. Lysias, a Roman officer, took Paul and conveyed him into the Castle, or Fort of Antonia.

Q. 83. Before whom was he carried to be examined?

A. He was carried before the council, that is, the Jewish Sanhedrim, after which he was brought back to the Castle.

Q. 84. Why was he, soon after this, removed from Jerusalem to Cesarea?

A. He was removed by the command of Lysias, to protect him from the malice of the Jews, who sought his life; and he was conveyed to Cesarea, that he might have his trial under Felix, the Roman governor, who resided in that city.

Q. 85. How long did Paul remain in Cesarea?

A. He was detained as a prisoner by Felix two years, till Felix was recalled, and Festus, a new governor, was put in his place.

Q. 86. To what place was Paul conveyed from Cesarea?

A. He was conveyed to Rome in company with Luke and many other prisoners.

Q. 87. What happened to them on their voyage?

A. They suffered shipwreck, and at length were driven into a harbour in the island of Melita or Malta.

Q. 88. How long did they remain at this island?

A. They remained there three months, after which they sailed to Rome.

Q. 89. How long did Paul remain a prisoner at Rome, and how did he employ his time there?

A. He was confined there two years, during which period he instructed all who came to him, in the Christian religion, and laid the foundation of a large and flourishing church.

Q. 90. Is it known what became of Paul after this?

A. The historical part of the New Testament extends no farther than to this period; but it is generally supposed, that he afterwards returned to Jerusalem, and again to Rome, where he suffered martyrdom during the persecution of Nero.

Q. 91. What is known concerning the Apostle John?

A. After many labors in the ministry, he was banished to the Isle of Patmos, where Jesus Christ appeared to him in visions, and gave him those instructions which are contained in the Apocalypse, i.e. the book of the Revelation.

Q. 92. What became of the other Apostles?

A. Ancient histories give us some uncertain accounts of their travels and their sufferings; but very little is known concerning them.

Q. 93. How did God punish the Jews for rejecting the Messiah and for their other crimes?

A. Forty years after the death of Jesus Christ, Jerusalem was taken and destroyed by the Romans; their beautiful temple was consumed by fire; a vast number of the Jews perished; and those who escaped death, were reduced to slavery, and dispersed throughout the world; and their descendants remain to this day in a state of dispersion, yet a distinct people.

Q. 94. How long did the persecutions of the Christians last?

A. They lasted about three hundred years, till Constantine the Great, the Roman emperor, embraced Christianity. But since that period different sects of Christians have often persecuted one another.

Q. 95. At what period was the Mahometan religion established?

A. About six hundred years after the birth of Jesus Christ, by the impostor Mahomet.

Q. 96. At what period did the Protestant Reformation commence?

A. About three hundred years ago, in Germany. It was begun by Martin Luther.

Q. 97. What are the two leading principles of Protestantism?

A. The sufficiency of the scriptures, and the right of private judgment. *The Bible, the Bible only, is the religion of the Protestants.*

❧ The Nature of Man

HENRY WARE (1764–1845)

In the constellation of American religious leaders, Henry Ware is one of the best known stars of the second magnitude. When, after long debate and by a one-vote margin, he was appointed to the Hollis professorship of divinity at Harvard in 1805 and when the orthodox party rose unsuccessfully to resist confirmation of his appointment to the Board of Overseers, he became a major figure in the ecclesiastical conflicts of his time. His life and thought have not yet received the intensive study they deserve, but nobody can justly challenge his immense contribution to the liberal cause. He gave thirty-five years of devoted service to Christian education at Harvard, being twice appointed acting president, preaching to students, giving postgraduate theological instruction both before and after the organization of the Divinity School, and, in the course of his long tenure, undertaking to teach at some time or other virtually every religious course (except Semetics) offered in the curriculum.

Henry Ware was born on a farm in Sherburne, Massachusetts, in 1764. His father died fifteen years later, but family sacrifices made possible his graduation from Harvard in 1785. After brief theological studies under the Reverend Timothy Hilliard of the First Parish in Cambridge, he was ordained to the ministry at the First Church in Hingham in 1787. Although a small salary and a growing family forced him into many non-pastoral duties, he earned a reputation that led to his appointment as the successor of David Tappan in the Hollis Chair.

His adversities, including constant overwork, were many. His first wife—the mother of ten children—died a few weeks after they had moved to Cambridge. His second wife died only eight days after their wedding in 1807. (To his third wife, however, nine children were born!) In later life a cataract on one eye became an increasing handicap, and an operation merely led to complications that hastened his death. After his retirement in 1840 he published *An Inquiry into the Foundation, Evidences and Truths of Religion,* but the exertions involved in this revision of his old academic lectures broke his health permanently.

Ware's greatest hour came during the years after Channing's 1819 Baltimore Sermon, and his most enduring claim to remembrance is the three volumes of controversial writings directed against Trinitarian orthodoxy, in general, and Professor Leonard Woods of Andover, in particular.

Channing's sermon had produced two critical blasts from Andover. One, on Biblical matters, by Moses Stuart was answered by Andrews Norton with his *Statement of Reasons.* A second, on more theological and philosophical subjects, came from Leonard Woods in the form of *Letters to Unitarians Occasioned by the Sermon of the Reverend William E. Channing at the Ordination of the Rev. J. Sparks.* Because of Channing's disinclination for open controversy, it became Ware's task to answer, which he did with *Letters Addressed to Trinitarians and Calvinists, Occasioned by Dr. Woods' Letters to Unitarians.* The "Wood'n Ware Controversy" wore on with Woods's inditing *A Reply to Ware's Letters to Trinitarians and Calvinists;* Ware's *Answer to Dr. Woods' Reply, in a Second Series of Letters Addressed to Trinitarians and Calvinists;* Woods's *Remarks on Ware's Answer;* and finally Ware's *A Postscript to the Second Series of Letters Addressed to Trinitarians and Calvinists, in Reply to the Remarks of Dr. Woods on those Letters.*

The general estimate of this long-drawn-out debate has been that Ware got the better of his opponent. There was orthodox criticism of Woods's argument even at the time. Strict Edwardsians were disgruntled to see him yield many old positions without a struggle. Nathaniel W. Taylor and his colleagues at Yale, on the other hand, thought the Andover professor had set the orthodox cause back fifty years with his wooden defense of old, and to them untenable, positions. It may have been this later criticism that led Woods to turn away from Harvard and begin a siege of Yale with another series of *Letters.*

Whether Ware "won" or not is hardly the most important issue. More significant is the fact that his three contributions to the controversy constitute a classic statement of Unitarian anthropology. The entire series will reward careful reading, though only the central statement of the first series of Ware's letters is reproduced in the following selection. That his account of human nature is optimistic certainly no one would deny. One may doubt, however, that it is romantic, as has been suggested. Ware's attitude toward romanticism is perhaps best suggested by his observation that of all the men who had studied in Germany, Edward Everett was the only man who had not been injured by it. A clue to the bent of his mind is found in the readings reported to have been his favorites during his declining years: the Bible, of course, and then the sermons of William Sherlock (1641?–1702) and William Paley (1743–1805), and the King's Chapel Liturgy. The selection that follows further elucidates the point.

. . . As the question, "what is the natural character of man," lies at the very foundation of the controversy between Unitarians on the one hand, and Trinitarians and Calvinists on the other, it will prepare us for a fair discussion of it, to examine in the first place, what is the precise difference of opinion between them on the subject.

Heretofore, those who claimed the title of Orthodox, and professed to follow the doctrine of Calvin, were satisfied with the language used by the Westminster divines in the Catechism and Confession of Faith, in which the doctrines of that reformer are expressed with remarkable precision and distinctness. In them the doctrine, which respects the natural state of man since the fall, and in consequence of that event, has two parts. They represent the first sin of our first parent, as *imputed* to all his posterity, who are said *to have sinned in him, and to have fallen with him;* and they teach the entire corruption of man's nature, *that he is utterly indisposed, and made opposite to all that is spiritually good, and wholly inclined to all evil,—under the displeasure and curse of God, and liable to all punishments in this world and that which is to come.*

It seems that the first part of this account, though it was formerly reckoned on of the principal tests of Orthodoxy, more zealously maintained than any other, is now given up. It is wholly omitted in the Creed adopted by the Theological Institution in Andover. It is expressly given up by Dr. Woods. . . . This change in the opinions of the Orthodox, and advance toward what we believe to be right views, we are glad to witness; and have no doubt that the same correct mode of thinking and reasoning, which has led to it, will lead also to the rejection of the other part of the doctrine, which has heretofore been considered as inseparably connected with it. We think that further reflection will convince them, that they are inseparably connected—that if the imputation of Adam's guilt is a solecism, and inconsistent with the moral character of God, it is equally so, that, in consequence of it, all his posterity should come into being with a nature so totally corrupt and inclined to sin, as to be incapable of any good. . . .

The doctrine respecting the natural condition of man, which I shall now state, and endeavour to maintain in opposition to this, may be expressed in the following manner.

Man is by nature, by which is to be understood, as he is born into the world, as he comes from the hands of the Creator, innocent and pure; free from all moral corruption, as well as destitute of all positive holiness; and, until he has, by the exercise of his faculties, actually formed a character either good or bad, an object of the divine complacency and favour. The complacency and favour of the Creator are expressed in all

202 DOCTRINES AND THEOLOGY

the kind provisions that are made by the constitution of things for his improvement and happiness. He is by nature no more inclined or disposed to vice than to virtue, and is equally capable in the ordinary use of his faculties, and with the common assistance afforded him, of either. He derives from his ancestors a frail and mortal nature; is made with appetites, which fit him for the condition of being in which God has placed him; but in order for them to answer all the purposes intended, they are so strong, as to be very liable to abuse by excess. He has passions implanted in him, which are of great importance in the conduct of life, but which are equally capable of impelling him into a wrong or a right course. He has natural affections, all of them originally good, but liable by a wrong direction to be the occasion of error and sin. He has reason and conscience to direct the conduct of life, and enable him to choose aright, which reason may yet be neglected, or perverted, and conscience misguided. The whole of these together make up what constitutes his trial and probation. They make him an accountable being, a proper subject to be treated, according as he shall make a right or wrong choice, being equally capable of either, and as free to the one as to the other.

That this, and not the scheme of innate moral depravity, is the truth, I shall endeavour now to show by arguments, drawn

    1. From observation and experience, and

    2. From the Scriptures.

It is my purpose, previous to entering on this discussion, to observe, what the Orthodox will not hesitate to admit, that judging beforehand, the scheme of total moral depravity, or of any original bias to evil rather than good, is something different from what we should expect, and involves great difficulty in reconciling it with the moral perfections of God. This, as I have before observed, is implied by Dr. Woods himself. I admit, with him, that this is not a sufficient reason for rejecting it in opposition to the evidence of fact, and of scripture, and for the reason which he gives, viz. that we are finite, and cannot so comprehend the purposes and conduct of an infinite being, as to be certain, that what seems to us inconsistent with his moral character, is so in reality. But *it is* a good reason for yielding our assent with caution, not till we have examined with care, and not without very satisfactory evidence. It is a reason for suspending our assent, and re-examining, so as to be entirely satisfied as to the fact. I have another remark also to make. The doctrine, it is confessed, is repulsive. The mind naturally revolts at it. It *seems* at first, to all men, universally, to be inconsistent with the divine perfection. But the first impression is made upon us by the nature which God has given us; and I think we would be slow to believe that a nature, thus given to all, is intended to mislead and actually does mislead all, on so important a question. . . .

I proceed now to the inquiry, what observation and experience teach us, as to the fact of human depravity. And here we must not forget, that the question is, not whether there is a great deal of wickedness in the world, but what is the source of that wickedness; not whether mankind are very corrupt, but how they become so; whether it is a character born with them, or acquired; whether it is what God made them, or what they have made themselves. All that is said of the prevalence of wickedness in the world may be true, and yet none of it the effect of an original taint, which men brought into the world with them; none of it making a part of their original nature. . . . All may be but the effect of neglect to restrain appetites, in themselves useful and good, to control and give a proper direction to passions designed to be useful and capable of the very best effects, and in general a failure to exercise properly in temptations and trials, the powers of direction and resistance, which were in themselves sufficient.

But, although this reply may be made, were the representation usually given of the human character, and of the prevalence of wickedness, correct in its fullest extent; I am satisfied that I am not called upon by truth to make that concession. I insist, that the account usually given of human wickedness is exaggerated. It is a partial account, and such as gives a very wrong impression. Men are not the mere brutes and fiends, which it would make them. There is much of good as well as of evil in the human character, and in the conduct of man. Indeed I hesitate not to say, that as much as there is of wickedness and vice, there is far more of virtue and goodness; as much as there is of ill-will, unkindness, injustice, and inhumanity, there is incomparably more of kindness, good disposition, pity, and charity. I insist, that if we take a fair and full view, we shall find that wickedness, far from being the prevailing part of the human character, makes but an inconsiderable part of it. That in by far the largest part of human beings, the just, and kind, and benevolent dispositions prevail beyond measure over the opposite; and that even in the worst men good feelings and principles are predominant, and they probably perform in the course of their lives many more good than bad actions; as the greatest liar does, by the constitution of his nature, doubtless speak many truths to every lie he utters. One great source of misapprehension is, that virtues and good qualities are silent, secret, noiseless; vices are bold, public, noisy, seen by all, felt by all, noted by all. . . .

What I assert upon this point, and think to be very obvious and capable of being made out to entire satisfaction is, that observation and experience are altogether favourable to the view I have stated of the human character and condition, and that without revelation there is nothing that would lead a reflecting man to the thought of an innate moral depravity. . . .

Our most correct ideas of human nature will be drawn from the characteristics of infancy, and the earliest indications of disposition, tendency, and character in the infant mind; and if the nature of man be corrupt, inclined to evil, and evil only, it will appear there with its unequivocal marks. But do we find it there, and is it the common, untaught sentiment of mankind, that it exists there? Far from it. Innocence, and simplicity, and purity are the characteristics of early life. Truth is natural; falsehood is artificial. Veracity, kindness, good-will flow from the natural feeling. Duplicity, and all the cold, and selfish, and calculating manners of society are the fruit of education, and intercourse with the world. We have marks enough of a feeble, helpless nature, calling for sympathy, assistance, support, kindness; but we see no proofs of depravity, of malignity, of inclination to evil in preference to good. How early does the infant discover affection, attachment, gratitude to those from whom it receives kindness! How universally is it an object of interest to those about it! Would it be so, if it manifested such tokens, as the Orthodox doctrine of depravity supposes, of an inclination, disposition, and tendency, wholly directed to evil, and if it appeared to possess nothing good, and no tendency to good? Instead of this, must it not naturally be the object of aversion and disgust, and especially so to pious and virtuous persons, who can only love and approve those, whom God loves and approves; and who therefore can see in little children, only objects of the divine displeasure and wrath, beings wholly averse to God and all that is good, and who deserve, not sympathy and affection, but all punishments of this world and the world to come?

It is often said, that children are naturally inclined to falsehood and deception, and that they early lie and deceive, rather than speak the truth. But this charge needs proof; and I apprehend it will be found, that evidence is abundantly against it, and in favour of the natural veracity of children. It will rarely be found, that children disregard the truth, till by example, or bad education, or peculiar circumstances of temptation, they have learned to overcome and counteract the tendency of nature. . . .

It is alleged also, that children are naturally cruel, and in proof of it, the pleasure they seem to take in torturing insects and small animals is sometimes mentioned. But the pleasure, which the convulsions and throes of a tortured insect or animal give to a child, arises from another source than cruelty, or the desire of giving pain. It is wholly to be attributed to the love of excitement, and the pleasure it takes in rapid and violent motion; and is wholly unconnected with the idea of suffering in the creature, with whose convulsions it is delighted. The same pleasure would be derived from the power of producing the same convulsive motions, and the same appearance in any inanimate substance. In proof of this, let a clear idea of the suffering of the insect be communicated to the child, and it will no longer take pleasure in its convulsions. A sentiment of compassion will be raised. It will be as eager to rescue it from its suffering, as before it was to inflict that suffering. . . . The same account is to be given of what is often called a mischievous disposition in children. It is not the love of mischief, but an exuberant love of activity. The mischief or inconvenience which they occasion to others is no part of the motive, but simply the love of action and strong excitement; and it may be accompanied with the kindest feelings, the most sincere desire of giving pleasure to others, and as sincere an unwillingness to give pain or to cause uneasiness or displeasure.

Indeed I know not a single mark of early depravity, common to children in general, which may not, as these are, be fairly traced to causes, which imply no degree of depravity, and no fault of character; or of disposition. Individuals there may be, who give very early tokens of great perversity of mind, and corruption of heart. But these are exceptions from the general character of human nature, and, as such, have no place in the present argument; and if they had any, would be decisive, not in favour of the Orthodox doctrine, but against it; as the *exception,* in its nature, proves the *opposite rule.* If great depravity is the exception, exemption from depravity must be the rule.

No man I am persuaded, was ever led by personal observation and experience to the thought of an original depravity of human nature, according to which, by the bias of nature, all, without exception, who come into the world, are from their birth inclined wholly to evil, and averse to good.

And as little, I am persuaded, would any one be led to such an opinion by the general current of scripture. I am led to think so by a general view of the commands, precepts, exhortations, promises, and threatenings of religion, and by the whole history of the divine dispensations to men; and also by attending to a great number of particulars, each of which, separately, seems to me to imply, that mankind come into the world innocent and pure, the objects of the complacency of the Creator, and no more inclined, by the nature God has given them, to sin, than to virtue; no more disposed to hate and disobey, than to love and obey their Maker. I shall instance only in one, but that alone, in my opinion, is decisive of the question. I refer to the manner in which little children are, on two occasions, spoken of by our Saviour, and on one by the Apostle Paul. (Matt. xix. 14.) "Suffer little children to come unto me—for of such is the kingdom of Heaven." . . . And could he, on another occasion, say, (Matt. xviii. 3,) "Unless ye be converted, and become as little children, ye cannot enter into the kingdom of God?" And again, (Mark 14. Luke xviii, 16,) "Whosoever shall not receive the kingdom of God as a little child, he shall not enter therein?"

Could the Apostle Paul recommend to the Corinthians (1 Cor. xiv. 20,) "Be not children in understanding, but in malice be ye children, but in understanding be men;" that is, in understanding, in the power of distinguishing right and wrong, and perceiving the truth, show yourselves to be men; but in your dispositions, in your moral characters, manifest the gentleness, and mildness, and purity of children? . . .

But there are, as I said, a few texts, from which the doctrine I am considering is inferred. . . . It is not pretended, I believe, by any of the defenders of the native, hereditary depravity of the human race, that the doctrine is, any where in scripture, expressly asserted. It is not a matter of direct assertion, but of inference. It is considered as implied in several passages. . . .

The first text adduced, as implying innate total depravity, is Gen. vi. 5. A few remarks will show how little it is to the purpose, and how far from supporting what is made to rest upon it. For, in the first place, it relates not to mankind universally, but to the degenerate race of men of that age, so remarkably and universally corrupt, beyond all that had gone before, or have followed since, as to call for the most signal tokens of the vengeance of heaven. In the second place, were it said of all men in every age, instead of being confined, as it is, to the inhabitants of the earth at that particular time, it would still be nothing to the purpose, for which it is brought. There is no assertion of native derived depravity, none of a corrupt nature, no intimation of hereditary guilt, no reference to innate aversion to good and inclination to evil. It is the mere assertion of a state of great corruption and wickedness, which no one denies. . . .

Universal expressions, like those in the texts in question, are so far from being always used in their strict literal sense, that they are *usually relative,* to be understood and interpreted in relation to the subject and occasion. Thus when it is said, (1 Tim. ii. 4,) "God will have all men to be saved and come to the knowledge of the truth," it relates to the question, whether any class or nations of men are excluded from the favour and good will of God, and therefore ought to be excluded from a share in the benevolent regards and prayers of Christians; so that *all men* means, not every individual, but all ranks, descriptions, and conditions of men. In the unlimited sense of the words it is not true. . . .

The same remark occurs with equal force in respect to the passage so much relied on in the xiv. Psalm. Not only is there no intimation of an inbred, innate, hereditary depravity, but only of great and general corruption of manners; but though a verbal universality is expressed, the very Psalm itself takes care to teach us with what qualifications it is to be understood. . . . The same is the case with each of the other Psalms, quoted by Paul in his Epistle to the Romans.

But it is of little comparative importance, whether the authors of the Psalms, or the Apostles in quoting them, meant to be understood as expressing a general truth in popular language, or as expressing themselves with literal philosophical exactness. Understand them in the most unlimited, unqualified sense, of which their words are capable, they express only what no one will deny, that all men are sinners. The question will still be open, as before, how this universality of sin and great corruption of manners are to be accounted for. Whether, as the advocates of Orthodoxy contend, men come into the world with a corrupt nature, prone only to wickedness, and utterly incapable of any good thought or action, till renewed by an influence of the holy spirit, which they can do nothing to procure; or as Unitarians believe, this corrupt nature is not what they received from God, but what they have made for themselves. That they were not made sinners, but became so by yielding to temptations, which it was in their power to resist, by obeying the impulse of the passions, and the calls of appetite, in opposition to the direction of reason and the notices of conscience; by subjecting themselves to the dominion of the inferior part of their nature, instead of putting themselves under the guidance of their superior faculties. . . .

It is unnecessary to multiply remarks on the next text brought to prove human depravity. (Jer. xvii. 9) "The heart is deceitful above all things, and desperately wicked." . . . The total irrelevancy of the text to the purpose for which it is brought, appears beset by considering the subject matter, about which it is introduced. The prophet is stating the safety of trusting in God, and the insecurity of trusting in men. The reason is, that men are deceitful, and not to be depended on. . . .

From the New Testament, the first passage selected, as implying the doctrine under consideration, is the answer of Christ to Nicodemus, (John iii. 3) "Except a man be born again, he cannot see the kingdom of God." . . .

A single consideration convinces me, that the inference is without foundation, and that the universal necessity of regeneration may consist with original innocency, and exemption from any prevailing tendency, as we are born into the world, to vice rather than virtue. . . .

The passage, (Rom. v. 12) "Wherefore, as by one man sin entered into the world, and death by sin, and so death passed upon all men, for that all have sinned," is of another kind, and to be shown to have no relation to the subject by other considerations. . . . It is a single phrase taken away from its connection, and what is more, out of the middle of an argument. . . . Understood literally, the only assertion it contains with certainty is that of a fact, which none will deny, the universality of sin, that *all* have sinned. . . . But there is another consideration, which ought to prevent this text from being considered of any weight on the subject. The whole passage in which it stands is one of the most intricate and difficult in the New Testament. The phrase, on which so much is made to depend, admits equally well of several different translations, each of which will give it a different meaning; and its connexion with the passage in which it stands is not such, as to help us, to any degree of certainty, in determining by which version its true sense is expressed. . . .

Ephesians ii. 3. "And were by nature children of wrath, even as others." . . . The whole of this refers to the same thing; not to the personal condition of individuals as such, but to that of the whole body of Christians, as quickened and raised from the moral and spiritual death of their original Jewish and heathen state; as delivered from the state of wrath, in which they had lived from their birth; and by the rich mercy of God and the faith of the Gospel, made to sit together in heavenly places, that is to enjoy all the privileges and hopes of Christians.

It has no reference therefore to the state in which persons are born into the world in all ages. Those now born into the world in Christian lands are not in the same sense that these Ephesians were, *children of wrath by nature,* but as these same Ephesians were after their conversion to Christianity, *saved by the grace of God, quickened, raised from the dead, made nigh by the blood of Christ, fellow-citizens with the saints, of the household of God.* . . .

We are called upon by the advocates for the doctrine of depravity to show, that it is inconsistent with the moral perfection of God; that it is not taught in the scriptures; and that all the wickedness in the world may be accounted for without admitting the doctrine.

With respect to the first, I might satisfy myself with saying, that it belongs to those, who maintain the doctrine, to prove its consistency with the moral perfection of God. But I have no wish to avail myself of the right, which every one has, who is called upon to prove a negative, of throwing back the burden of proof. It is one of those cases in which the negative is susceptible of satisfactory proof. . . .

Whatever the nature of man be, it is such, as he received at the hand of his Maker. Whatever tendency and proneness to evil there may be in him, as he is born into the world, it is no greater than his maker gave him. We assert then that no guilt, no fault can be attributed to him by his Maker for such proneness. If God be a just being, he cannot be displeased with him for being what he made him. If he be a good being, he cannot punish him for it. . . .

Now however consistent with justice may be the infliction of vindictive punishment, where it is in the power of the subject of it to be different from what he is, and to act otherwise than he does; it is contended that it cannot be so, where the guilt to be punished is inbred, a part of man's original nature, such as he came from the Creator's hands; where, in fact, the sinner is as his Maker sent him into the world, not as he has made himself by his own act, by the abuse, or neglect, or perversion of his power, and his faculties and affections.

That the doctrine is not contained in the scriptures I have endeavoured to show, by showing the insufficiency of the several [proof] texts from the Old and New Testament. . . .

When the extent and prevalence of wickedness in the world are urged as indicating an original inherent corruption, and we are called upon to account for it in a satisfactory manner, without admitting the Orthodox doctrine of depravity; I shall think it sufficient to refer you to the account which I have given of our moral constitution, and the state of trial in which we are placed. . . .

❧ Reason and Revelation

ABIEL ABBOT LIVERMORE (1811–1892)

No Christian movement has ever been able to ignore the issue of reason and revelation, nor has any expressly Christian theology ever escaped the claims of both. One may say indeed that the manner in which the balance is struck is one of the most determinative factors in every doctrinal system. Channing put the matter succinctly for his own time: "The great question is not, whether the trinity, or vicarious punishment, or innate sin, be true. There is a broader question which now divides us, and it is this,—*how far is* REASON *to be used in explaining* REVELATION? The Liberal Christian not only differs from his Orthodox brother on particular points, but differs in his mode of explaining that Book which they both acknowledge to be the umpire."[1] No intellectually alert Unitarian, with his views on natural theology and the Bible being what they were, could fail to make public his thoughts on this subject at some time or other; therefore, an abundant literature arose around the issue.

The essay by Abiel Abbot Livermore is eminently representative of the Unitarian view. It shows the Lockean cast of mind that generally characterized the movement until more idealistic modes of thought began to make inroads on the older rationalism. In many other spheres of thought these Unitarians followed the Scottish philosophers, but on the question of reason and revelation there can be little doubt that Locke's *The Reasonableness of Christianity* provided the cornerstone of their thinking.

Livermore was born in Wilton, New Hampshire, and schooled at Chelmsford and Exeter academies before going to Harvard, from which he was graduated in 1833. Three years later he completed his divinity studies there and settled in Keene, New Hampshire. There he served until 1850, when he accepted a call to the Unitarian Society in Cincinnati. Two years later he became one of the founders of the Western Conference of Unitarian Churches. Upon his appointment as editor of the *Christian Inquirer,* however, he moved to New York and organized Hope Unitarian Church in Yonkers. He also served as a nonresident professor at the new Meadville Theological School, then located in Allegheny, Pennsylvania, though later it was moved to Chicago. In 1863 Livermore

1. William E. Channing, "Address at the Formation of the Berry-Street Conference," *The Life of William Ellery Channing, D.D.,* ed. William Henry Channing, p. 218.

became president of that institution. In this capacity, and as a professor in a wide range of subjects, he served until 1890. Thus, for over half a century of enormous activity Livermore participated in almost every phase of Unitarian work.

The essay "Reason and Revelation" was especially important because it was circulated widely as a tract of the American Unitarian Association in addition to being included in Livermore's own widely read *Discourses.*

The present [discourse] will be devoted to the vindication and enforcement of the great truth, often overlooked and often misunderstood, that reason is to be used in religion as in other departments of life, and that man's ultimate reliance, for faith and practice, is upon his own mind, aided by God's word.

Man is gifted with a faculty or capacity, variously called in common parlance, reason, mind, common sense, understanding,—that searches, apprehends, and judges concerning all that falls within its cognizance. By this power, in proportion as it is swayed by hopes and fears, passion and conscience, as it is developed by education, or cramped by ignorance, he is able to discriminate between truth and error upon all subjects whatsoever. By this he generalizes principles from facts, and predicts facts from principles. Into this crucible he throws arts, sciences, philosophies, religions, and the dross and the gold are divided. Upon this foundation he relies for opinions, belief and practice. It is his sun and centre, his point of departure, and his point of arrival. For by it he determines the meaning even of Scripture itself, decides therefore what to believe, what do, whom worship, and which of the numerous and increasing theories of Christianity he shall adopt as his own.

This capacity is a divine principle in the human soul, as well as Revelation a divine communication. Both are the offspring of the Deity. This faculty is divine, as it is the direct handiwork of the Creator, not an inheritance from Adam, for "there is a spirit in man: and the inspiration of the Almighty giveth them understanding." From moment to moment, he impregnates it with his celestial fire, gives it its constant supply, and speaks through it with his venerable authority, which none shall gainsay with impunity. It is divine, so it lifts man above all other creatures of the earth, gives him a citizenship and a fellowship with the spiritual intelligences of higher worlds, and distantly assimilates the finite child to the infinite Father, enabling us to "be followers of God, as dear children."

Still man may pervert it. What does he not pervert? It is not infallible, like Revelation; but it is the instrument which God has given us to ascertain the import of even Revelation. He who renounces it, abandons one of the highest prerogatives of his being. He who brings against it "a railing accusation," does nothing less than slander the most illustrious specimen of the divine workmanship in the world. He who leaves it undeveloped, or allows it to languish and decay, commits a deadlier suicide than taking the bodily life. He who loses it and becomes insane, is justly deemed the most unfortunate of his kind, as absolved even from moral accountability, dead to the power of improvement. . . .

This faculty, in conjunction with conscience and the moral affections, composes man's religious nature and enables him to receive a revelation. Thus he has a foundation to stand upon. He can understand and apply to his wants the gracious communications of his Maker, and thereby "lay hold on eternal life."

Since, then, man was endowed with reason, it was to be expected that if God made a revelation of his will, it would address itself to, and harmonize with, that capacity in the recipient. Since we were created with religious natures and wants, it would have been a signal and perplexing departure from the customary modes of our heavenly Father's administration, if the religion he had commissioned to exercise our natures, and satisfy our wants, had warred against them.

What was to be expected has been fulfilled. The truths of the gospel possess the same congeniality with the human soul, as bread with the stomach, and light with the eye. There is no discrepancy between the workmanship of God in the soul, and the ways of God in the Bible; but the nicest concord, at once beautiful and convincing. The Almighty does not contradict himself. Reason and Revelation are twin agents, co-workers in the cause of the soul. The mind and truth, the soul and its Saviour, have a reciprocal fitness, each for each. Revelation is the teacher, Reason the pupil. Revelation assists, perfects, does not supplant or dethrone Reason. Without Revelation, Reason were in a cold, pale twilight; with it, man is surrounded with the pure light and warm flush of day. Without Reason, Revelation were of no more significance to man than to the ox, or the dove; with it, the saving truth is received, loved, and followed. How many works have been powerfully and successfully written to elucidate the internal evidence of Revelation, a large part of which consists of the facts of this exquisite harmony between the soul's capacities and needs, and the truths and promises of the Gospel.

But in dwelling thus upon the alliance between Revelation and Reason, it is not the least implied that man does not receive through the Scriptures, original, vital communications from his Maker. They teach many things above Reason, but not one syllable against it. What the wisest sages had speculated about the painful uncertainty, Jesus taught with the assurance of consciousness. The human heart, the divine counsels, and the secrets of eternity, were unveiled in his discourse, and stood forth as breathing realities. Old truths sprang into new life and power. What Reason in her best champions had only felt after, never fully found, still less proved, and efficiently spread amongst men, was now clothed with gigantic might and celestial beauty, and went forth "conquering and to conquer." He gave us a heavenly Father, and opened a heavenly hereafter before us,—thus giving the soul, in its dark and discouraging struggle with evil, all needed and possible guidance, strength, warning and consolation. All is plain and simple, yet how glorious!

"I hope," said the distinguished philosopher and Christian, John Locke, "it is no derogation to the Christian religion to say, that the fundamentals of it, that is, all that is necessary to be believed in by all men, is easy to be understood by all men. This I thought myself authorized to say, by the easy and very intelligible articles insisted on by our Saviour and his Apostles; which contain nothing but what could be understood by the bulk of mankind." Men like Locke, Milton, and Newton, the mightiest spirits God ever kindled on earth, have testified to the reasonableness of Christianity. Locke wrote a book to show it. Revelation has come from their searching investigations, like thrice refined gold from the furnace, bright and undiminished. Its evidences, its doctrines, its promises, its services, are all seen to be founded in nature and common sense, as well as guaranteed by the explicit will of the Most High. They have consequently remained fixed and firm against the assaults of acute infidels, as the steady earth beneath the gusty winds that sweep over its surface. They commend themselves to the good understandings of all, and testify that religion is eminently "a reasonable service."

But here a distinction is needed, that is often neglected. Because Revelation does not conflict with Reason, though it soars above Reason, it is far from being asserted that it does not contend against human nature and character, under some of their aspects. It harmonizes with the higher, but it clashes with the lower nature. This is our battle, spirit against flesh, and flesh against spirit; in taking sides with the spirit, Revelation therefore fights against the dominion of the flesh. Indeed, in that identical conflict consists its virtue, its use, just as medicine makes an enemy of disease, but not of the human constitution. Religion struggles, as for life, against the passions and appetites in their excesses. Yet this contest is often mistaken for a discordance between Reason and Revelation, whereas it is a notable instance of their agreement. For when Reason was too weak of her single strength to cope with the lusts of the flesh, Revelation descended as a kind friend to restore the reins to the rightful possessor. The strict Scripture doctrines may strive against worldliness and selfishness, they may prick men's hearts with pungent expositions of truth, earnest enforcements of duty; Heaven be thanked that they do, but they are all justified by Reason. They are never wanting in the most perfect rationality. For example, the truths that God is One, is a Spirit, is to be worshipped in spirit and truth,—are hard truths for a sensual world to feel and obey, but they stand good to Reason. The command to love our enemies is probably the hardest in the Bible to comply with, honestly and heartily, but not because it is irrational; it is seen, when all the circumstances of the case are considered, to be reasonable, sensible; but because it puts the curb on some of the strongest feelings of the human heart. It is at the antipodes of folly or absurdity, but it enjoins self-restraint, forbearance, forgiveness,—therefore the natural, that is, the sensual, selfish man, receives it not, loves it not. So, universally. In one word, Revelation may conflict with man's evil dispositions, and check his wrong tendencies; it is a noble proof of its divinity and its efficacy, that it does—that it makes alliance with Reason and conscience against their formidable assailants, but with Reason and conscience it no more wars than with the Supreme Intelligence from which it sprung. Its language is ever that of "truth and soberness," its spirit a "spirit of power, and of love, and of a sound mind."

Since, therefore, Reason capacitates man for Revelation, and harmonizes with it, we are not surprised, but prepared, to find that Revelation itself enjoins with deep emphasis the exercise of Reason. Perpetually it appeals to the rational principles in man. It invites and urges him to test the disclosures it makes by the light of his God-given spirit, "the elder scripture." Unlike some of its friends, so far from denying Reason and frowning upon free investigation, it commands the vigorous action of the mind upon its truths as a duty. Its precepts are, to "Search the Scriptures; not to believe every spirit, but to try the spirits whether they be of God; to prove all things, and hold fast that which is good; to understand the Scriptures; to judge what is right; to be men and not children in understanding; to be ready always to give an answer to every man that asketh you a reason of the hope that is in you, with meekness and fear." Indeed, what is the aim and sum of Revelation, but God reasoning with and instructing his erring children, making known to them truths above and beyond what their unaided minds could have reached; setting before them motives loftier than this world could furnish, and leading their hopes and aspirations upward to a life of eternal bliss and glory.

In the next place, it may be remarked, that facts substantiate what has now been said of the connexion between Reason and Revelation, so far as the practice of all denominations of Christians extends. Not one exception can be found. All use reason, all appeal to it, all abide by it, or by what to them is Reason. Where is the sect that does not exercise the understanding upon the doctrines of Christianity and the duties of life? Is it said that the Roman Catholic rests his faith on tradition and the infallibility of his Church? Then tradition and the infallibility of his Church are his sufficient reasons for his faith. He keeps on good terms with his understanding. Is it asserted that the Mystic believes in emotions, feelings, divine promptings, which he can neither analyze nor understand? Then certain operations of his own mind are his ultimate grounds of faith, and to him entirely rational grounds. He has no quarrel with reason in his own soul, however mad he may seem to other men. Is it stated that some believe in doctrines which present a downright contradiction to Reason, as that there are three persons in the Godhead, and yet only one God? Still their faith is just as rational to them, as mine is to me, who believe that there is only one person in the Godhead. Their faith is placed on that which has to them the greatest evidence of its being true, and is accordingly the most reasonable to them. Is it said that they place their faith not on Reason, but on the Bible? In that case, the Bible is their Reason; at least, they have reasons for making the Bible their Reason. Thus all sects do, in fact, whatever may be said to the contrary, appeal to Reason, first or last, in one way or another. What are religious controversies, in which all sects have participated, but reasonings on this side and that, to develop the relative strength of each? What are the volumes of Evidences of Christianity, of which every denomination has contributed its useful portion, but a solemn appeal at the bar of Reason is vindication of the truths of the Bible? What are the Commentaries, but helps to make the Scriptures better understood, to take faith off of the ground of implicit trust, and plant it more on that of personal knowledge and conviction? What are Sunday schools, sermons, lectures, tracts, periodicals, but means to make more intelligent, as well as more pious Christians? Is it not most evident, from this review of the beliefs and operations of all Christian denominations, that they use Reason in religion as in other departments of life? These interrogations are so plain that none but affirmative answers can be given them. It will therefore be seen to be a mistake, or to be mere affectation, to say that Reason is not to be employed in matters of faith and practice, when in truth all use it habitually, and must use it more or less, or sink themselves to the level of the irrational brute. No man can, no man does, proceed one step in belief, in interpretation, in conduct, without the guidance of Reason.

Wherein then, it may occur to some minds, are Unitarians, or rational Christians, different in respect to this point from other sects, which would perhaps deem the epithet rational to be a stigma? They are said to be different; it is rumored all over the country that they are a denomination by themselves; Christendom looks upon them with suspicion. What is their dark offence? They reason, but so does the Roman Catholic. They use their understandings in religion, but so does the Trinitarian. They throw the lights of biblical criticism upon the Holy Scriptures, that they may the more nearly arrive at the true sense of the inspired volume, but so equally does the Episcopalian. What then is their crime? Wherein is the point of difference? Simply, so far as yet appears, the distinction consists in their arriving at different results by the exercise of Reason; not in their using Reason, and other sects not using it. They lay stress upon the tenet which all actually employ. They avow earnestly the principle which all adopt, if we may judge of their rules by their practice.

But here a new element appears. It is charged upon them that they make Reason their goddess, that they exalt her above Revelation. If this were so, then they would indeed be an unique sect. But is it so? Let us see whether, in matters of Faith and in the interpretation of the Scriptures, they do not take the same course which all take.

First, in regard to Faith. It may be laid down as an axiom, that belief always rests on evidence of some sort, and that where there is no evidence, is it quite impossible that there should be any belief; the nature of faith precludes it. The evidence may be small—may be unsatisfactory to the majority of men; but evidence of some kind, of some degree, is indispensable. If a doctrine is positively irrational, it may be a call with here and there a mind to put forth more faith to embrace it, but with most it would prevent all faith whatever. But even in this extreme case, the reason that is wanting in one direction is supplied in another, else faith were still an impossibility. Thus some Christians believe in doctrines which they acknowledge are irrational, because the creed, or church, or Bible, as they suppose, upholds them; and then the creed, or church, or Bible, is their reason and evidence, though all other reason and evidence be against them. The Unitarian exercises his reason in settling the foundations of his faith; thus doing as all others do, and must do. But the question arises, does he not set Reason above Revelation? So it has been reported every where. No, never. He finds no occasion for such a competition between the dictates of his mind and the doctrines of the Scriptures. What Revelation teaches, he believes in, because it is perfectly rational, as well as because Revelation teaches it. Is it inquired, whether he would believe in a doctrine that was entirely irrational, provided the Scriptures contained it? His reply is, that he is not reduced to this alternative of crucifying Reason, or renouncing Revelation. The supposition is impossible. The Bible never does teach anything but what is reasonable, and therefore nothing but what he can and does believe. It were a daring proposition to advance, that God has contradicted, in one mode of his communication of truth, what he teaches by another. It is just as absurd to ask, whether we would believe an irrational doctrine because Revelation taught it, as whether we would do a vicious act because Revelation enjoined it. The cases are parallel, but neither is for a moment supposable. The Bible violates neither reason nor conscience; it offers no irrational doctrine for us to believe,—it commands no vicious deed for us to do.

To the view now presented of the necessity of intelligibleness in what we believe, and of evidence as a basis for faith, it is objected, that we are surrounded by mysteries, understand little in reality, and believe in many things which we cannot explain. Two things are confounded in such an objection, which ought to be carefully distinguished. I may believe in that which is above Reason, but that is quite different from believing in that which is against Reason. I may believe in mysteries, or, in the popular sense of that word, in many incomprehensible things,—things above men's experience and knowledge. I believe, for example, in the existence of God, which I can neither comprehend nor explain. But observe, I believe in the fact that He exists, which fact is supported by most abundant proof; I do not believe in the mode of his existence; I am not assured how he fills all with his august presence, and I can only believe as far as I have evidence for my belief. So far as his existence is a fact, I believe in it; so far as it is a mystery, I cannot believe in it, because I have no grounds for belief. I believe in the revolutions of worlds around worlds, through all the boundless heavens above and below, but I cannot understand nor elucidate the nature and essence of those centripetal and centrifugal forces that bind those stupendous masses in the exactest harmony as they fly on their swift courses. I believe in the fact for which there is good evidence, not in the mystery, the how, for which there is none. The secrets of attraction and gravitation cannot be classed amongst matters of faith, because there is no proof what those secrets are. The facts are all that can come within the bounds of credence. Nobody else, any more than the Unitarian, believes in irrational doctrines, that is, doctrines irrational to the believer. It cannot be done. The doctrines must move over from the ground of no reason to the ground of reason, before they can be believed. Evidence of many kinds there is, but evidence of some kind there must be, or belief is dead. The most absurd things in the world have been believed, not as they were absurd, but as they had some basis of reason, however narrow or shallow. To speak of Faith without reason, would be to say that there were rivers without fountains, and effects without causes. In exercising his Reason in matters of Faith, the Unitarian does no more than, nor differently from, all other Christian believers.

Next, turn to the interpretation of the Scriptures: Unitarians are accused of setting their reason up as a standard above the Bible. But they do no such thing. They but do what all do. If they err, then all err, in using their minds to understand the word of God. The Bible is our standard. What it teaches respecting truth and duty, we receive, we believe in, with implicit love and trust. But the grand, dividing question, is, what *does* it teach? It is not the same thing, the same sense, to all. The Bible is nothing more nor less than the meaning of the Bible, and that meaning varies with every mind. It teaches one set of doctrines to the Baptist, another to the Quaker, another to the Methodist. "Men labor," as Cecil acutely remarked, "to make the Bible *their* Bible." In fact every sect has its own Bible, inasmuch as each has its own sense of the book. The Scriptures, then, are the standard, but it is a different standard to different men. Religious controversy is the struggle which each denomination makes to render the Bible *their* Bible. Reformation in the Christian Church is but the constant bringing of man's sense of sacred Writ nearer to its absolute sense, the one God who gave it; the advancement of the imperfect human idea up to the glorious clear significance of the divine mind.

Nor is this difficulty of arriving at the absolute truth of the sacred volume, escaped by the instrumentality of creeds. For if not at first, which is generally the case, yet afterwards, the creed, like the Bible, conveys different senses to different minds, and so what was designed for an explanation, soon needs itself to be explained. Hence arise ambiguities and discussions; the sectarian banner becomes itself the signal of war; and old churches and assemblies fall to pieces to be re-organized into new ones.

Since, then, the Bible, though the directory of Faith and Practice, is one thing to one man and another to another, according to what each understands it to teach; since there is variance of belief even touching fundamental points,—what is done by all, but to fall back on their own minds, enlightened by Revelation, as the last criterion. Each one claims and allows the supremacy of the Scriptures, but he must rely on his own mind to tell him what they teach. Probably no two persons, who have read the Bible understandingly, and reflected earnestly on religious subjects, think exactly alike. The more men reflect, the more they differ, and the smaller their differences become, because they approximate continually nearer to absolute truth. Modern civilization and free thought multiply sects in profusion, but their influence is to make "the crooked straight, and the rough ways smooth," and to unite all upon the essentials of Christianity.

From these remarks, it will be clear to every candid mind, that in regard to the interpretation of the Scriptures, as well as in matters of Faith, Unitarians proceed upon no novel and dangerous principle of using their reason, which is not equally adopted by others as their rule. Precisely like other denominations, they refer to the Bible as their standard, and to their minds to inform them what that standard requires. They would not only read, but understand the word with the faculties God has bestowed for that purpose. They hold that He intended his Revelation should be understood, as indeed with what propriety could it be called a Revelation, if it was not intelligible. Where were the value of Faith if it were placed at random?—where the merit of conduct, if action were indiscriminate?

In pursuance, then, of what has been intimated, it is proper to repeat, that Unitarians differ from other Christians, not in their using Reason, or exalting it above Revelation, but in their coming to different conclusions by the exercise of that faculty. "This is the front and forehead of their offending." Reason teaches them to believe in the inspiration of the Scriptures; the miracles of Christ; his inquestionable authority as the Son of God and Saviour of men; in the reconciliation, or atonement, of men to God through him; in the influences of the Holy Spirit, the immortality of the soul, and future retribution. These they receive and cherish, as their guide in life, their hope in death. These, and other subsidiary doctrines, kindred to them, seem to be as clearly taught in the Scriptures as language allows. They cannot believe in the Trinity, in total depravity, in the popular doctrines of the atonement and of election, because they do not find them in the Bible to believe. Revelation, as well as Reason, disowns them. But they would rather their "right hand might forget her cunning," and their "tongue cleave to the roof of their mouth," than do any violence to the blessed charter of their privileges and their hopes. They would not for worlds be guilty of perverting one word that fell from the sinless lips of Jesus, or the inspired tongue of the Apostles. They use their own minds in determining what the book of heaven teaches, because they deeply reverence, not because they "lightly esteem" that volume. But with Paul, they had rather speak "five words with their understanding than ten thousand words in an unknown tongue." They feel that Reason is fallible, therefore they cannot trust another man's, but must hearken to their own. Reason is fallible; therefore they would use it with great care and activity, that it might become more and more trustworthy. Reason is fallible; it may be dimmed by worldliness, or warped by prejudice, or stormed by passion; therefore they cannot dogmatize, for they may be in the wrong, and others in the right. They marvel how others can dogmatize, for *they* must be in the wrong, and themselves in the right. They see no danger in the use of Reason, they see every danger from its neglect and abuse.

Finally, they feel a solemn and awful responsibility, resting upon every individual soul, to decide for itself, according to its best light, what it shall believe and do. The interest here is personal, not social. Human authority is not admissible. Calvin cannot decide, Arminius cannot decide for me; I must decide for myself. God has put it upon me, and I cannot, I dare not, shake off the responsibility. It will not do for the council of Nice, nor the synod of Dort, nor the assembly of Westminster, to step in between me and my master, and determine for me what he taught, and what I must receive. Solemn interests I have at stake. A mighty business is upon my hands, which cannot be done by proxy, though popes and councils should tender their aid. The soul, in such high matters, must do its own work with God's assistance, not with man's interference. My own free mind is worth more to me in settling the grounds of my duty, and my destiny, than the wisdom of the whole world besides, backed by all its great names, and its vast authority. My conscience, my judgment, my reason— these living principles in my soul, set there by God, kindled by his inspiration, fanned by his Spirit,—these hold me accountable to him with an adamantine strength. If through them I have approved myself to him, my Almighty Father, what are the reproofs of friends, and the slanders of enemies, and the thunders of councils and assemblies?—the mere blast of an adverse wind, the peltings of the outward storm,—they cannot touch the quiet peace of the heart. But—fearful contrast!—if I have from the motives of temporal expediency, from the fear or the favor of man, wrested my conscience, done despite to the good spirit, and embraced a creed, or led a life, which is condemned by that mind God gave me as a governor, wo is me, I am undone, the sweet approval of the heart is gone. "If our heart condemn us, God is greater than our heart and knoweth all things. Beloved, if our heart condemn us not, then have we confidence toward God."

❧ The Incarnation

OLIVER STEARNS (1807–1885)

Christmas, the festival of the Incarnation, was not recognized in the old Congregational churches of New England. "It does not seem to me that I ever heard of Easter or Christmas till I reached manhood," declared Grindall Reynolds, Congregationalist turned Unitarian, as late as 1889.[1] Nor was his case unusual, for it was not until the 1850s that the old Yuletide traditions began to reappear. Unitarians were quicker to throw off such Puritan restraints than the orthodox, being more inspired, no doubt, by romantic, tradition-loving Unitarian laymen like Henry Wadsworth Longfellow. It is important to realize, however, that the abandonment of a strictly Trinitarian understanding of the Godhead by no means made the historic Christmas texts a source of embarrassment to Unitarians. The interpretations they made naturally varied, ranging from those of Socinus to high Arianism and modalistic Trinitarianism. The boundaries with orthodoxy on the right and Transcendentalism on the left were often blurred. Yet there was a center position, and Stearns voiced it in the following selection. (Edmund H. Sears's position in the succeeding selection was possibly somewhat right of center.)

When Stearns delivered this sermon on December 6, 1854, he was minister of the Third Church in Hingham, Massachusetts, where he had served since 1840. Before that, he had been minister to the Second Church in Northampton, from 1831 to 1839. Born in Lunenburg, Massachusetts, Stearns had been graduated from both Harvard College (1826) and its Divinity School (1830). In 1856 he was called to succeed Rufus P. Stebbins as president of Meadville Theological School. To this task he brought great energy and resourcefulness, and his erudition and philosophical acumen soon made him the center of the school's intellectual life. It was a tremendous blow to Meadville, therefore, when he accepted the Parkman Chair at Harvard in 1863. From 1870 to his retirement eight years later Stearns served as dean of the Harvard Divinity School.

When compared with Dr. Stebbins, his predecessor at Meadville, Stearns was regarded as a liberal. Francis Christie, moreover, credits Stearns with being "the first academic theologian in America to announce a belief in evolution as a universal cosmic law."[2] In this Stearns is also said to have

1. Grindall Reynolds, "Ecclesiastical and Denominational Tendencies," in Channing Hall Lectures, *Unitarianism: Its Origin and History*, p. 362.
2. Francis Albert Christie, *The Makers of the Meadville Theological School*, p. 79

preceded Spencer. His teaching at Harvard, however, showed a constantly growing emphasis on fundamental theology, especially Christology, soteriology, and eschatology. His published writings were very few in number, but there are many testimonies to his power as a teacher, and two decades of graduates from one or the other of the two Unitarian seminaries extended throughout the denomination his moderate and deeply rooted conception of Unitarian theology. The ordination sermon which follows may be taken as representative.

LUKE ii. 11:
For unto you is born this day, in the city of David, a saviour, which is Christ the Lord.

The beautiful prayers and collects of the ancient Church, in all this month of December, point to the Incarnation. They very appropriately, as it seems to me, turn the thoughts of believers to the moment which marks the beginning of the New Despensation, to the Saviour's birth, to the shepherds watching their flocks by night on the Judaean plains, to the angels choiring peace and good-will, and to the mother bending with new-born interest and inexpressible hope over the unconscious babe. He who took little children in his arms and blessed them, with words which are his eternal benediction to childhood, himself lay a little child in the manger at Bethlehem. In that infant form was inclosed a spirit which should look through the windows of sense as with the eyes of God upon the life it came to exalt and the world it came to redeem, and be the medium of disclosing in its full brightness the Father's grace and truth. In that helpless babe lay wrapped the germ of a love which would infold the race of men in its embrace, and devote its unabused body to the bitter cross for their deliverance from sin. In the wailing child trembled a voice whose articulate speech, the word of God, would be echoed from the most distant ages of future history, and from men's immortal destiny.

I shall attempt to speak of this Incarnation. And I observe, first, that the ministry of the Holy Spirit by this Incarnation commenced with Jesus's birth. The mother and the child of Bethlehem have become the sacred images of maternity and infancy throughout Christendom. As men in rude times looked upon the picture with a simple faith, albeit mingled with something like adoration, they felt more the dignity of the maternal office, the worth of childhood, and the sacredness of the mystery of a soul's birth in a form of flesh. . . .

It seems to have been one of the functions of the Redeemer to shed a new light, by his history from his birth to his ascension, upon the origin, uses, relations, and end of human life. All this was wrapped in darkness to most of the world, when his earthly course began. . . . So they are now where Christ is despised and rejected. It was one of his functions, in delivering us from sin and the power of the senses, to rid human life and its prominent stages and experiences from trivial and debasing associations. . . . So I think the miracle of his introduction into the world was designed in part to give to the sceptical or grovelling minds of men higher suggestions respecting all human origin. It was, perhaps, needed, to lift men's thoughts directly to the Creator; to teach that, as his unsullied soul was the direct creation of the Divine Spirit, and thus fitted to be the instrument of the Divine Word, to express God, so all souls are divine offspring, breathings of the effluent spirit, even if corrupted by descending through ancestral channels; that all are impressed with the Divine image, however worn dim with the streams of human offence. . . .

The Incarnation has consecrated human birth. Every child springs from a divine lineage; it is not only a son or daughter of Adam, but of God. It has the impress of the Father, which, however overlaid it may seem, can be renewed and made distinct. It has the essential human faculties, the one original constitution which makes a human soul, by whatever peculiarities modified in the individual. This is a capacity to become the servant of the Most High. This makes it a subject for Christian nurture and for divine grace. This makes it capable of redemption from the tendencies and forces hostile to its integrity. The Christian child is born within the bosom of Christian beliefs and sanctities. It comes to pass through some or all stages of this life as preparatory to another. It comes to take life's events and relations as a ministry of God. It comes to meet tempters, to love, to rejoice, to weep, and if it grow up a disciple of the Crucified, to take up the cross, to conquer self, and to ascend at last into a higher being. It is born to be instructed in God's providence, and to grow in the knowledge of human and divine things. It is born to teachers and guides refined by holiness, schooled in the faith to hallow as they tempt forth its soul, and to minister to it as unto an heir of salvation. It is born to all which is symbolized by baptism. It comes to be baptized into those influences of the effluent spirit, which, as water flows in all countries, flow in the vicinity of every soul. It comes to have its plastic nature bathed, penetrated through religious education with that remoulding and corrective life from God, which dwelt in Jesus, which dwells in every society of redeemed souls; and thus to be led, reconciled and happy, to the bosom of its Father's love. This is the significance of human birth under the Christian dispensation, and Christ's birth may teach it still.

The birth of a soul in the corporeal form and life, amidst means of grace and religious opportunities, is the prelude to the spirit's birth into an inward life of holiness. It is the vestibule to the religious life, which is hid with Christ in God. Yet it is only the portal; it is not the very birth in the spirit of holy principles and affections; that comes we know not how nor whence, except that it must come from the fountain of original energy. We are not to confound occasions with the Omnipresent Spirit which works by them. Using opportunities, we are yet not to ascribe to human agencies that which is wrought by the Divine power. Train the child in the nurture of the Lord, but remember that its spirit cannot be redeemed from the besetting presence of evil, and born to holiness, without the inspiration of the Almighty breathing through its nature; and pray for that to work through your agency. Christ's supernatural advent instructs us to look above nature for the coming of spirit in nature, and to see God in the spiritual as well as in the natural birth. The holiest leadings and most blessed exercises of our souls, intelligible in experience, are mysterious in their causation, and we can rest only in the thought that all good desires do proceed from the Central and Underived Being; and the ripe saint who has done most with opportunities, and put to best uses nature and life, will bend with awe and humility before an inward Redeemer, and say with Paul, "By the grace of God I am what I am."

II. The course of our meditation has brought us to the great fact of redemption, the birth of Christ in consciousness and the soul. There follows necessarily the regeneration of humanity, the coming of Christ's spirit in society, in human laws, ideas, usages, and institutions. But first in order is the birth of the Redeemer in the individual soul. "Unto you is born a Saviour, who is Christ the Lord." This Saviour must be in us, generating a life opposed to the life of self. He must be the inward Lord and Sovereign of our affections and desires. . . . This is the great fact of redemption. This meets the deep, central, indestructible want of the soul. As soon as it becomes in some degree conscious of its spiritual relations, the soul finds itself in spiritual helplessness. The deepest religious experience is marked at some time by a profound sense of deficiency. The Divine will has not been done. The Divine law utters its condemnation of us. Abuse has crept into our being. A life of self lies hidden at its centre, as a power of sin holding us at its mercy, and balking our better aspirations. Natural inclinations, grown tyrannous, may have intrenched themselves as hurtful passions and lusts in our souls. The evil spirit of the world may have passed into us. The evil spirit of those who lived before us may reappear in us. The moment the holiness of God and the Divine requirement shine in upon the soul in full radiance, sin, seen to be a fearful tendency, is felt to be our chief enemy,—our only danger and misery. How it came we may not know. But its power is felt. It seems to beset us behind and before. When this conviction of sinful tendency and spiritual weakness is wrought in the soul, to be delivered from it is the greatest joy. Human nature, arrived at this stage of the consciousness of its relation to the spiritual order of the universe, craves a more than human help. It wants more than human wisdom, affection, or pity can do for it. It wants harmony with its own highest law written upon itself. It wants reconciliation with offended holiness. It wants atonement between itself and the spotless rectitude. . . . It turns to conscience, and conscience cries, One thing thou lackest. It turns to the natural creation: *that* is beautiful; but its beauty does not meet this deepest need; its order chills the spirit longing for Divine pity. That order feeds and protects, but sometimes it famishes and destroys. It is inexorable law. Wisdom and mercy, we may come to trust as Christian believers, are its rule. But to us in its natural aspect it is inexorable law. It goes on with its ceaseless and mighty retributions. Its wheels never turn out of the eternal ruts. It sheds bounty and scatters flowers; but it crushes us at last bodily in its fingers, as the moth perishes in the blaze of your evening light. . . . Man, bowed by the consciousness of weakness and sin, if he could turn nowhere else, might stand in prayer, in almost the cry of despair, "Speak, Almighty Power! in some accents of compassion. Break through this dread order, and say if thou lovest my soul. Declare thyself mercy as well as law. Solve for me this mystery in which I am encompassed. Tell me of forgiveness and eternal life and help for my spiritual conflicts." And that cry from the depths of the want like no other, and of an anguish like no other, that of a weak and wounded spirit, has been answered on the shores of the Galilæan lake, by the voice which broke upon its storm, the voice of the Father in him who walked upon its waves, "It is I, be not afraid." I am with you always, the Paternal Spirit, in and above the natural order, adjusting your discipline, cognizant of your trials, and instantly present to your prayer. The Almighty has broken through the natural order to reveal the spiritual order. While we were yet sinners, that cry of the soul's great want had been already answered; for Christ had been born and had fulfilled his ministry; his story had been written in light in the world's history; mercy had anticipated the crisis of the soul. It was answered by the word incarnate in Jesus, at Bethlehem and Bethany, and at Olivet and Calvary. It is answered now, by Christ born in the regenerated soul, dwelling in the heart by faith, its purifier, its forgiver, its Comforter, the life of its holiest affections, its assurer of immortality, the indwelling pledge and fulness of the Father's power and love.

III. As the fact of redemption first in order is Christ spiritually united with the individual believer, so the fact consequent upon it is Christ dwelling in many united in him. The Word first has form in the single disciple, and then it takes form in worship, laws, and social life. All advance in the social spirit and condition of man is the embodiment of Christ in social institutions and dealings, the incarnation of the Divine Word in mankind. A perfect Christian society or state would be the realization on earth of one of the grandest thoughts of God. . . . From the ascension till now, men have looked for a form of social life, which should be the Shekinah assuring them of marching under the leadership of Jehovah. And in a time of universal ferment and undefined expectation like ours, many share the impatience of the first disciples, and ask if the Lord will now descend, and the reign of truth and righteousness come with some decisive transforming stroke upon the kingdoms of the world. And the answer of Jesus has been ever, "Ask not of times, but watch for the duties which the Spirit shall disclose, and do them in their order, and power shall go with you." *There* is the sole power for the social regeneration of man, in the Lord Christ descending into upward-looking souls. I say not that one civil constitution is as good as another; but evil will creep in under any constitution, if Christ be cast out from those who under it constitute a state. Representative legislatures and elective magistrates will not enact and execute justice, if Christ be not in the heart of the people. Liberty, equality, and fraternity, the watchwords of the people, mean no good, out of Christ; for liberty is but animal passion at large, equality but the equal chance of brutes in confused scramble, and fraternity but the association of robber bands. Christ renewing men reforms society. The Church—the invisible Church—must keep or deliver the State. Not that any formal union of Church and State is expedient. But Church and State are always vitally united,—the heart and arm of one organizing life; and the limb will wither as soon as it ceases to throb with pulses thrown into its arteries from the centre of a vitality replenished from God. . . .

IV. The incarnation of a Divine Word to communicate large measures of the Holy Spirit to the human family, was a demonstration of supernatural grace. It stands in the centre of all the Divine Providence, and stands out from it, supernatural in its method, and special in its intent. It was costly to the Divine mind and heart. It involved necessarily a sacrifice of the Mediator; and this involved a sacrifice on the part of the Father, of whom he was the voice and image. In the fact of that sacrifice resides the chief power to convince the world of sin, and to prepare man's heart for the renewing contact of the Divine Spirit. It was not substituted punishment. It was sacrifice inevitably incident to a Divine mediatorship. It was essential to God's expression of himself, to bringing on earth the Gospel of truth and forgiveness. The person who should institute this redemption by a life on earth must unite in himself, perfectly, the Divine and the human. The Father must dwell in him; how, we know not; but it is a rational conception that the Father should dwell in him, so that he and the Father should be one in the impression made on man; so that his word and act should be his own, and yet should exactly express God, and as fully as God can be expressed to finite apprehension. He must also be truly human, in human form and with susceptibility to human feeling. The Divine fulness in him must make him, not more impassive, but more alive to the proper impressions of things. It must be an inlet of vast joy. It must be an inlet of vast suffering. This was the fact. The marvel of the evangels is the blending in him of the supernatural and the human with a perfection of which the prototype must have been a real person; and which puts the question of the mythical origin of what is peculiar to them almost out of the pale of argument; for the conception of it seems impossible to any mind but that which conceived it before the world was. A sinless man, who, let me ask, would suffer from proximity to human sin and collision with it, like him whose immaculate nature reached into the depths of the indwelling Father? In the form of God, he could not jealously assert his Divine dignity, nor selfishly claim any exemption from the stroke of evil; he must rather, as it were, empty himself of divinity, that the suffering of a genuinely human condition might come in upon him. . . . He who should bring a redeeming power down to mankind,— who should become man's hope, his object of contemplation, his standard of truth, his leader for all generations, the trust of his weak heart, and its uplifter to a forgiving God,—must be on the one side a representative of human life victorious and pure, and on the other the representative of God to men,—Son of Man, and Son of God, a special and beautiful creation. Through his celestial spirit and his divine insight he must be capable of unfathomable suffering, and sink in Gethsemane under an agony which has amazed the world with its mystery. Should God decree that incarnation? Should God expose an immaculate soul, his beloved Son, to the stroke of evil?

The tone of the introduction of the Gospels, the tone of amazing expectation, and of wonder at the Divine grace, as if the destiny of our race hung upon that moment, is a fit prelude to the sequel. "Unto you is born this day a Saviour." It *was* a crisis in man's history. There was need of a being who, under the forms of a human presence and condition, should manifest God,—who should draw men's minds to himself with a new veneration, and give them higher thoughts of Divine pity and Divine purity. There was need of interposition, as we express it. Not that a point of time had arrived in history unforeseen by Divine prescience, an emergency to be suddenly provided for. Not that the order of the universe so far had failed, and something originally forgotten must be appended as

supplementary. The provision for the crisis was a part of the eternal order. It was the predestined complement of the creation up to that point.
We may call the fulfilment of this provision an interposition, to give it a
proper relief on the plane of Divine operations, to express the speciality
of the Divine purpose in adapting it to its place in the Divine order. Why
God chose to create a race with spiritual faculties, yet to grope so long in
a dim apprehension of their objects, and at length to reveal those objects
fully in one person,—why He so slowly pushes this lamp of truth into the
dense pagan darkness,—is one of the secrets of his incommunicable being.
But the actual method of the Divine procedure we see and know. It is unfolded in the history of the world, which may be looked at as the history
of God's thought. That procedure and that thought we think and speak
of in human modes of conception and in forms of human language. God
has addressed, in history, and especially in Christ, our human modes of
thinking and feeling, to convey to us some portion of his thought and
character which is otherwise incommunicable. And as we humanly apprehend the matter, there was need of interposition, of a way in which Divine
love should make itself more felt in sinful human hearts, and of a life
adequate to represent Divine truth to man. That love and that truth must
be embodied in the purest person. And that person must fall a victim to
human cruelty. For Divine truth could not be incarnated on the stage of
human action without coming into conflict with sin. That conflict was indispensable, also, because the Divine mercy or spirit of sacrifice in God,
to be imaged to all the generations of men in that person's love, could
find such expression as the case needed only by meeting contumely and
death at the hands of the Spirit of Evil. Should such a person be sent?
Thus we may humanly represent the matter as a question of the Divine
mind to itself. And in the eternal thought there was no other way of
communication between the wandering child and the Father's feeling.
This way God chose, because it alone satisfied his perfection. Thus, we
may say, Christ alone satisfied God's hatred of sin, and his holy nature;
Christ alone expressed the yearning of the Divine heart. God *spared* not
his beloved Son. This is a form of human speech and human conception.
But it states a fact in providence and history, and a fact which is a standing revelation of something—the spirit of sacrifice—in the Divine character, incommunicable in all other modes.

There was a crisis in the history of our race at Jesus's birth. Man had
not the sufficient, all-reconciling truth, and he could not work his way to
it alone. The "word made flesh" was the demonstration of that truth;
Christ crucified was the price of it. I see little danger of exaggerating the
world's debt to the Gospel as a medium of religious truth. We can scarcely
imagine that debt. . . . It is easier to see how unworthy we are of this

light of the world, than to show what would be our condition now without the Incarnation and its fruits. I see no probability that natural and moral science would have given us the essential truth. . . . In ancient literature there is no recorded sentiment, no strain of conversation, which rises to the level of the Evangelist's doctrine of a spiritual Father, or Paul's bold lyric announcement of the resurrection. Why was it? Because Christ embodied these truths in himself, and brought them to man's spiritual perception. If that accomplished Roman who in the midst of public affairs found time for philosophy had sat with the band around the paschal board, and had asked, "Show us the Father,—tell us whither thou goest," Christ could have answered him only as he answered Philip and Thomas, "I am the way,"—"He that hath seen me hath seen the Father." And if Cicero had communed with Jesus personally in his ministry, had seen him suffer on the cross, and then had pondered the words and deeds of that One, and by the touch of that spiritual power his intuitional faculties had been waked, a new object would have been presented to his thought and love; Christ would have stood forth to his anointed vision a representation of Infinite Holiness and Love; and that new object would have shed on every relation and act, and on the issues of things, a light for which he longed. Conviction of sin would have crucified vanity. Love would have widened into more than Roman patriotism. Humanity would have superseded glory. Loose thoughts of providential powers would have concentrated into the burning thought of God as a benign and holy Father, and of himself as a child sustaining through love and duty a relation to that Father, of which only eternity could fulfil the obligations and hopes. Thus the mortal gulf would have been spanned by a spiritual arch, and the unseen Divine hand felt extended for him to grasp and hold by as he walked through the shadow of death.

It was not Jesus's speech only which taught man Divine truth, not his outward miracles alone which proved it, not his resurrection alone, but all together, all that he was. The life and sacrifice which he wrought through a human body lifted the Divine character and human destiny into the world's view. They made this character, this destiny objective, and thus informing and quickening to man. They still do this. And it is the office of the Church and the ministry to give prolonged effect to this mediation; to repeat in ritual and in speech this voice of Jesus out of the Divine heart, beseeching the sinner to be reconciled to God. Therefore neither mountain nor ocean, no aspect of nature,—no crystal palace or monumental pile, or victorious battle-field, or eloquence in high debate at the organizing of a nation's life,—no work, act, or art of man,—is the token of anything so grand and affecting as that of which the lowliest Christian temple is the symbol. . . . There is no work which reaches to the height and depth of the preacher's,—that of him who is an ambassador to men in Christ's stead. . . . He is to be the tongue of the Incarnation, the medium by whom the Comforter will come and bring earth's child and heaven's Father together. If he have felt the proper power of the Word made flesh, that power will go out on his word; for the Son of God will be with such preachers until time shall be no more. Let him never attempt to reduce the Gospel to a mere result of the operation of natural laws. Let him preach the supernatural grace. Let him preach Christ, with whom the Father was one.

 Christ the Divine Word

EDMUND HAMILTON SEARS
(1810–1876)

Edmund Hamilton Sears is probably the only Unitarian minister whose words are known and repeated by almost every man, woman, and child in America, for he wrote "It Came Upon a Midnight Clear." No doubt millions of others at Christmastime have also sung and loved another of his many hymns, "Calm on the List'ning Ear of Night." That he should be thus remembered is altogether appropriate, for he was essentially a religious poet whose mind was occupied with the transcendent themes of the spiritual life. His sermons, it was remarked, became prayers without any break in the sequence. He found the secret of his power in what he called the holy ministries of solitude and silence, and these ministries were brought near to one who spent his whole life in rural surroundings. Born in Grandisfield, in the Berkshire hills of western Massachusetts, he was educated at Union College in Schenectady, New York, and the Harvard Divinity School. After a year as a missionary in the West he was ordained in 1839, and all of his pastorates were in Massachusetts country towns (Wayland, Lancaster, and Weston).

Sears was not a recluse, however. During the years 1859 to 1871, so fateful for Unitarian history, he and Rufus Ellis edited the important *Monthly Religious Magazine* and through it supported the conservative cause in the intra-Unitarian controversies of the day. Though no advocate of narrow exclusionism, he was among those who wished to commit the movement to a more explicitly evangelical platform. Yet Sears is remembered as a seer and a poet, not as a controversialist; and this is as it should be for one who aligned himself with that great tradition of mystic piety nourished by the Fourth Gospel.

Characteristic of his time, Sears gave the Johannine literature a heavily Platonic reading. Following Andrews Norton and Ezra Abbot of the Harvard Divinity School, he accepted the traditional authorship of the Fourth Gospel and interpreted it in a fervently Christocentric way. Sears wrote to edify and arouse the Christian. This is not to imply, however, that his reading of contemporary critical literature was limited. Considering the rural setting of his researches, he was remarkably abreast of contemporary Biblical criticism. He also sought by his own scholarship to counteract the naturalistic accounts of Jesus and New Testament religion which Unitarians were writing and reading (see, for example, the various major works by William Henry Furness). This purpose is apparent from Sears's insistence on the unity of the Gospels. He denied the possibility of an escape from the Christ of John to the human Jesus of the three synoptic Gospels or from the theology of John and Paul to the simple ethical message of the Sermon on the Mount. Reprinted here is a central section from his most thoughtful and scholarly work, *The Fourth Gospel the Heart of Christ*, the title of which was adapted from a statement of the great German Biblical scholar Johann August Ernesti (1707–81).

Chapter II. Jesus of Matthew Is the Logos of John.

Matthew and Mark dwell primarily on the humanity of Jesus; but his natural life is not described as unfolding under conditions which are merely normal. It is described as the ground and the ultimate manifestation of a life which is more than human. Not only in what Jesus teaches but in his manner of teaching this is always to be observed. He speaks with that tone of command and authority which, with men giving their natural intuitions or the deductions of their private reason, would be intolerably offensive. The sermon on the mount amazed his hearers, not so much on account of its subject-matter, as on account of his method and tone, for he appealed not to the law and the prophets for his proof-texts, as the scribes were wont to do, but made his utterance out of that original divine sovereignty whence law and prophets derive their authority. What to him were Moses or Solomon,—"a greater than Solomon is here." Mark dwells less than either of the synoptics on the proper divinity of Christ; but all through his narrative there is an air and manner on the part of the subject of it which would be intolerable self-assumption for Moses or Solomon, or for any prophet or lawgiver, and which presuppose a divine epiphany in Jesus. We can cool down these passages by a process of criticism into figure and rhetoric, but the whole air and method will remain, and they are such as fit in with the natural coursings of no human biography before or since.

But we come now to remark another of the boldest characteristics of Matthew's Gospel. If we imagine that because Matthew was concerned primarily with the humanity of Christ, he was forgetful of his divinity, and presents him to us as a fine specimen of the best culture of his times, we shall not read far before we find our imagination melting away. Not merely Jesus but the Christ—the Christ of authority from above—is presented with a sharpness and boldness made more uncompromising by the intense realism of the first Gospel. Many illustrations of this fact are crowding upon us, but we will select only three.

1. The doctrine of John's Proem is explicitly asserted in Matt. xi. 27. After rebuking the cities where his Word had been delivered and his works had been done, Jesus tells them that their guilt in rejecting him was greater than the guilt of Sodom, and that it would be more tolerable for Sodom in the day of judgment. Then falling into a strain of indescribable tenderness, he subjoins: "All things are delivered unto me of my Father, and no man knoweth the Son but the Father, NEITHER KNOWETH ANY MAN THE FATHER, SAVE THE SON, AND HE TO WHOMSOEVER THE SON WILL REVEAL HIM. Come unto ME all ye that labor and are heavy laden, and I will give you rest." It has been asserted that the Logos-doctrine is peculiar to John. We find it not so, but only its metaphysical form of statement. It is set forth here in Matthew, with a clearness which no human language can improve upon, coupled with invitations out of the very heart of the Divine mercy which no fabricator would invent or imagine.

2. Christ, as the judge of men, is unquestionably the burden of the fourth Gospel. But if found in John asserted in more metaphysical language, it is found in Matthew drawn out with more than dramatic power, and with a sublimity unsurpassed anywhere in the New Testament. And it is not found in Matthew as exceptional as if some interpolater had put it in. It is found at the conclusion of the discourse from the heights of Olivet, when, as the doomed city lay at his feet, the vast future opened to the eye of Jesus, even to the retributions of an eternal world. The discourse rises in grandeur to the final announcement, "When the Son of Man shall come in his glory and all the holy angels with him, then shall he sit upon the throne of his glory. And before him shall be gathered all nations, and he shall separate them one from another as a shepherd divideth his sheep from the goats." There is no such passage as this in the fourth Gospel. The same doctrine is variously asserted. The incarnate Word is to be the Judge of men. "All who are in the graves shall hear his voice, and shall come forth." But it is stated in a more colloquial and supplementary way, and is no more than a commentary on the grand and sustained utterance from Mount Olivet reported in the first Gospel.

3. But there is another passage, if possible still more significant, in the first Gospel, asserting the Divinity of Christ with a power to which neither John nor any other writer has given any additional strength. It is the final charge of Jesus to his disciples, involving the formula of baptism. It was given as Matthew reports, at the last post-resurrection appearance of Jesus to his disciples. "All power is given unto me in heaven and

in earth. Go ye therefore and teach all nations, baptizing them in the name of the Father and the Son and the Holy Ghost, teaching them to observe all things whatsoever I have commanded you: and lo! I am with you alway, even to the end of time."

The passages we have cited are not exceptional in Matthew's Gospel, but with others of similar import they connect themselves organically with the whole narrative. The fact then stands thus: that the first Gospel dwells primarily on the humanity of Jesus, for it comes first in the order of time. The whole doctrine of the incarnation is baseless without it, and would only be a Gnostic theosophy floating in air. But Matthew, in consequence of those very qualities of his mind and style which give his narrative this intense and uncompromising realism, has also made the Divinity of Christ stand out with corresponding distinctness of outline. John writes thirty years afterwards with the synoptics before him, professedly to complete them. He does complete them, not undertaking to lay the foundations anew, but telling us a great deal about the Divinity of Christ, which explains, illustrates, and enlarges what the others had reported, showing the sublime peaks of doctrine which they had left in rugged outline, bathed in a sweeter and softer splendor from the morning sky.

If the reader, however, is in any doubt as to whether the Jesus of the first Gospel is the Christ of the fourth, if he thinks the first may be a man developed like other men out of the culture of his times, while the other was the factitious invention of a later day, he can easily bring this matter to the test. Summon the best man you can find, the most advanced prophet of to-day, and let him stand in the position of this same Jesus, the *mere man* of the first Gospel. Let him see if he can grasp his thunders. Let some prophet of to-day who ought to have grown up to the stature of Jesus,—the mere human development, declare in the face of the world that no man knoweth the Father but himself, and those to whom *he* shall reveal him; let him assume to sit on a throne of glory with all the holy angels around him, and part the nations to the right hand and the left, to everlasting punishment or to life eternal; let him announce that all power is given to *him* both in heaven and earth; let him put his own name into a formula of baptism, and charge his followers to make disciples, in the name of the Father and the Holy Ghost, and—himself. Would the world be converted by such preaching at the rate of three thousand in a day, or would they regard it as self-conceit and self-assertion, passed into the stage of monomania, and fit only for an asylum for the insane?

Chapter VI. The Logos Doctrine.

To void idolatry from the cultus of Christianity, two ways are open to us. One is, to apply to the record such destructive criticism as will cut out from it all that asserts the essential divinity of Jesus Christ. Such criticism assumes that this supposed divinity is a factitious halo which has been thrown about him from the warm and idolatrous imaginations of his followers. Take all this away, and we should find a remarkable preacher and reformer, a man developed probably from the best spirit of his times, who was born and who died like other men, but who like some other men received an apotheosis after death. He was divine, says Baur, speaking from the stand-point of his Hegelian theosophy, only as all human nature is divine; and the doctrine of the incarnation is passed over to the interest of the race, serving only as a type of the divine incarnation in all humanity, evolving the Christs of every age, according to the nature and fullness of its inspiration.

Try this theory and see how it applies. Beginning with Matthew and ending with the Apocalypse, go through and sift out from the record everything which imports the superhumanity of Jesus Christ. Go over those passages which we cited in the last chapter, and all the Scripture essentially involved with them, including the discourses of Jesus, which put forth claims such as no prophet or sage could do; go over these and eliminate them all, and what have we left? We have not a "mere man" left, nor the ghost of a man which can be outlined to any rational criticism, however microscopic and keen. The Johannean writings must be voided almost entire, as the German critics very well see. So much of the synoptics as constitute the very frame of their history, must be ignored (for example, Matt. i. 8–25, xi. 27, xxv. 31–46, xxviii. 18–20). The Apocalypse must be rejected,—a book whose genuineness is past all reasonable question,—as a vision which has no objective reality answering to it. Whatever is merely natural and human in the life of Jesus as given in the New Testament, so interblends with the supernatural and superhuman, and makes so complete a whole, that if you pull away the latter, the former comes with it, or else gives a remainder of shreds which belong to no history human or divine. For instance, the birth accords with the resurrection and ascension; the incarnation with the excarnation, the ingress into the world with the egress from it. These mutually explain each other, and explain the miracles as well. Again, the discourses of Jesus constantly forecast just such a death and coming again, and imply their necessity, and they give tone to his divine eloquence and to that inimitable and tender pathos that swells through every sentence of his later utterances. . . .

We must seek some other and more rational method to clear away this supposed idolatry from the cultus of Christianity. We must find it in the key of interpretation offered to us freely and constantly in its own unmutilated records. The proem taken as the grand postulate of Christianity, and not resolved into mere rhetoric, gives us an open way into the heart of the divine revelations, and justifies the egoism of the fourth Gospel. The Word, the Divine Reason itself, which is God in the act of utterance, God coming into personal manifestation, was incarnate in the Lord Jesus Christ. It was not an inspiration merely, it was not a vision of God like that of Isaiah or of St. John. It was a more interior union of natures, the divine within the human. By conception and birth the divine was nearer in degree to the human, and dawned through the consciousness more clearly until Jesus speaks from it and acts from it as the normal condition of his own being. Then it is not the finite, tempted, suffering man who speaks; it is the Divine Logos itself, God revealing himself with no admixture of our mortal fallibility and infirmity. Jesus in his full Messiahship has passed into this consciousness of the divine and speaks from it, and the I is no longer the man Jesus, but the Word that existed before Abraham was, which was always with God, which always was God in the act of self-revelation. Even so would the Word ever speak of himself as derived from the Father, as less than the Father, as begotten of the Father, and his only Son. Because the Father is the infinite deeps of Divine Being; in its infinitude unrevealed and unrevealable to any finite mind. The Word is God so far forth as He is revealed; forthgoing from the depths of his infinitude; eternally born of the divine nature, and bringing God into personality and into blissful relations with the creatures He has made.

Let no one say that this is Sabellianism or Arianism, or Trinitarianism, if that means the worship of three persons. The well-informed reader knows it is neither. It is THE LOGOS-DOCTRINE of the primitive church, found roughly in the synoptics and in Paul's fervent metaphysics, but found in the Johannean writings in a continuous blaze of light, the central sun of the whole system of Christian doctrine whence all its other truths are harmonized. It affirms an essential distinction in the divine nature of Father and Son; that these are not merely modes of manifestation in time, but were "in the beginning," and therefore timeless and eternal. God as the Father is the infinite deep of divine being, beyond finite apprehension, beyond the reach of human thought; what "no man hath seen or can see." But left here we are in blind worship, and can only build an altar to the Unknown. Left here we should not know God as a self-conscious intelligence, or as a being who felt the yearnings of an unchanging and tender affection. But the Word is God speaking, the divine Reason in self-revelation, ever on the bosom of the infinite deeps, and bringing forth their treasures of truth and love. This is the Logos-doctrine. We grope towards it in nature, for nature, the more its forces are analyzed, resolves itself into one primal force, a supreme intelligence with unknown depths beyond. The nature-religions groped after it and sometimes saw it in dim twilight. But not till the Word was made flesh, and dwelt among us in Jesus Christ, full of grace and truth, did this benign personality of God appear in its unclouded splendor and break as a new sunrise upon the world.

We see no possibility of missing the doctrine the moment we listen to Jesus as his own interpreter. When the Jews charge him with making himself God, he meets their accusation by saying, "Believe the works, that ye may know and believe that the Father is in me and I in him;" and to one of his own disciples, as if guarding him from a like misconception of making the Christ a God exterior to another or a higher one, he says, "He that hath seen me hath seen the Father. Believest thou not that I AM IN THE FATHER, AND THE FATHER IN ME? The words that I speak unto you I speak not of myself, but the Father that DWELLETH IN ME he doeth the works." The preëxistent sub-deity of Arianism, we do not find here. The coeternal second person in the Tritheism of the modern church, we find not here nor anywhere. Personal preëxistence, claimed by Jesus, construed as of another person exterior to the Father, is a doctrine rigidly excluded by his own explanations of his own language. But the church-doctrine, ancient and modern, of "the hypostatic union," an interior UNION AND INEXISTENCE OF NATURES, we do find such as justifies language on the lips of Jesus, which on any other lips, angelic or human, would be insufferable, and would be blasphemy indeed. And so, in his full Messianic consciousness, the Divine Word so possessed his being, that he could identify himself with it and say, "I came down from heaven,—I *am* the Word." Or again, the Absolute Truth was inorbed within him so complete, the truth that was to feed the world forever, that he could speak as the absolute Truth itself, and say, "I am the bread that came down from heaven." Tripersonality, we do not find. But the three central doctrines of Christianity,—the uncomprised Oneness of God, the essential divinity of his Christ consubstantial with Him, and the complete humanity of Jesus, making all humanity sacred,—we do find in their full consistency and harmony.

The Eternal Word, which was in the beginning and in which God ever is, was so embodied and impersonated in the Christ that in his full Messianic consciousness he calls it himself. As such he came forth from the Father, and returned to the Father; as such he comes down from heaven, ascends to heaven, and is the Son of Man in heaven; as such he created the world, and judges the world; as such he raises the dead; as such he was before Abraham, and as such he promises, "Lo! I am with you always." This we understand to be the doctrine of the Logos which, carried through the Johannean writings, and the whole New Testament as well, makes a continuous line of light. . . .

 *The Holy Spirit*

ANDREW PRESTON PEABODY
(1811–1893)

Andrew Preston Peabody's prodigious activity began early. He could read at the age of three and passed Harvard's entrance examinations nine years later. Given private instruction for a year, because of his immaturity, he did two years of college work and was thereupon admitted as a junior. He received his A.B. in 1826, as, except for Paul Dudley in 1690, the youngest graduate in Harvard's history. After serving variously as teacher, tutor, and schoolmaster, he prepared himself for the ministry at the Harvard Divinity School, graduating in 1832.

From 1833 to 1860 he was a minister in Portsmouth, New Hampshire. During these years he delivered and published his *Lectures on Christian Doctrine,* which, along with William G. Eliot's similar series, was regarded throughout the denomination as a standard exposition of theology. From 1853 to 1863 he was also editor of the *North American Review.* Peabody resigned his pastorate in 1860 to become Plummer Professor of Christian Morals and Preacher to the University at Harvard. Until his retirement in 1883 he taught more or less continually in the philosophy department, filled in frequently in the Divinity School, and served twice as acting president of the university (1862, 1868–69), being a prominent candidate for the permanent post in 1869 when the young Charles William Eliot was finally elected.

Peabody made his position as chaplain at Harvard one of deep influence on student life; and during an age when Unitarianism was gradually being transformed by idealistic and critical currents from Germany, he remained a defender of the point of view held by his professors in the Divinity School, the two Wares and John Gorham Palfrey.

Dr. Peabody was in every way a conservative. Just as he lamented the curriculum reforms of President Eliot, he resisted the theological transformations being accomplished in the name of Transcendentalism. He grounded his thought in the Scottish philosophy and the Unitarian doctrines of the early period. Even what yielding to idealistic trends he allowed was accomplished through a careful and selective acceptance of guidance from Sir William Hamilton.

During Peabody's period of greatest effectiveness—from 1840 to 1870—he was a major voice in the Unitarian movement. The selection reprinted here from his *Lectures* dates from that period. So lucidly does it indicate the basis of Unitarian thinking on the Holy Spirit that no editor's comment is needed beyond what is said in the Introduction to this volume. Peabody's lecture, to be sure, does not suggest what the doctrine could mean experientially, but it does reveal very clearly the nature of early Unitarian Biblical argumentation.

LUKE XI. 13:
If ye then, being evil, know how to give good gifts unto your children, how much more shall your heavenly father give the holy spirit to them that ask him?

The Holy Spirit is my subject this evening. I will commence my lecture by a word of explanation, which will be necessary for but few, yet which some may need. We sometimes read in the New Testament of the holy *spirit,* and full as often of the holy *ghost.* The original word is the same in one case, as in the other; but, at the time when the Bible was translated, *ghost* and *spirit* meant the same thing, and were used indifferently to express the same idea. Since that time, the word *ghost* has become so restricted in signification, as to denote only a *spectral apparition;* while *spirit* means the same now that it did then.

The controversy with regard to the holy spirit is, not as to its reality, or its divinity, but as to its *personality.* No christian denies that there is a holy spirit, or maintains the holy spirit to be an inferior and subordinate person. But the Trinitarian maintains, that the holy spirit is a distinct and equal person of the Godhead. We, on the other hand, believe that the holy spirit is but a name, and a most appropriate name, for divine influences and operations, and, especially, for the influence of God upon the soul of man. In the present lecture, I shall first give you my reasons for not embracing the Trinitarian view of the holy spirit, and then shall expound and illustrate my own view of the nature and influences of the holy spirit.

I could name with great sincerity, as my first and sufficient reason for not embracing the Trinitarian doctrine on this subject, that I see not the shadow of an argument in support of it. I confess, that, while I cherish no disrespect for minds so constituted as to perceive the force of the arguments employed in defence of this doctrine, I myself am unable to appreciate them, and should hardly know how to refute them better than by a simple statement of them.

But, in pursuance of the plan marked out for these lectures, I shall go over the whole ground of the argument on both sides, as thoroughly as I can in a single discourse.

At the outset, in the way of regarding the holy spirit as a separate and independent person of the Godhead, there stand several scores of passages in the New Testament, in which the holy spirit is spoken of as subject to, or conferred by God and Christ. Such passages are the following: "I will *put* my spirit upon him." "How much more shall your heavenly Father *give* the holy spirit?" "God *giveth* not the spirit by measure unto him." "God, who hath also *given* unto us his holy spirit." "The holy ghost *sent* down from heaven." "The Comforter, whom I will *send* unto you from the Father, even the spirit of truth." Who can send or give the supreme and eternal God? The very idea is unspeakably absurd.

I am aware of the usual mode of accounting for phraseology of the kind just quoted. It is maintained that the three equal persons of the Trinity entered into a covenant, by which the Son agreed to be subject to the Father, and the Holy Spirit to move at the bidding of the Father and the Son. But this covenant is not mentioned in the Bible. Moreover, it is a covenant of falsehood,—a covenant, by which the Son and the Holy Spirit agree to act a lie,—to represent a state of things, which has no actual existence,—to play an assumed part. But, were we to admit this incongruous idea, (which I know not how to entertain for a moment,) of a covenant between the three persons of the Godhead, I still should maintain, that, whatever reason existed for the assumed inferiority of the second and third persons, the same reason must needs exist for our receiving and regarding them in the characters, which they have assumed. It is far more reverent and pious, to receive them as they are offered to us in the gospel, than to insist on rending off the disguise which they have chosen to wear, rescinding the covenant which they have sealed, and regarding them in a light, in which they have agreed not to be regarded.

Again, were the holy spirit a person, especially, a person of the Godhead, we should at least expect to find him designated by the use of a masculine noun, and masculine pronouns. We should hardly expect to find a divine person generally designated by a noun in the neuter gender, with articles, pronouns, adjectives, and participles in the neuter, (for in the Greek, all these parts of speech are distinguished by gender.) Yet the Greek word rendered *spirit* or *ghost* is neuter, and is invariably connected with neuter articles, pronouns, adjectives, and participles. There is not an instance, in which, in the Greek of the New Testament, a pronoun corresponding to our word *he, his,* or *him,* is used in connection with the holy spirit; but always a pronoun corresponding to *it* or *its.* Now, in the Greek language, the only cases, in which living beings are denoted by neuter nouns and pronouns, are those of certain diminutives, the smallness of which is expressed by the use of this gender,—an idiom like that, by which we, though in bad taste, call a very little child *it,* instead of *he* or *she.* Is there then the slightest probability that the sacred writers should have employed the neuter gender to denote a person of the most exalted dignity,—a person of the Godhead?

But the holy spirit is, *four* times in the gospel of John, called the *comforter* or *advocate,* and in connection with this term, are employed words in the masculine gender; and, it is asked, must not that, which is called by a word so manifestly the name of a person, be a real person, and not a mere influence? I reply, that, either the word *spirit,* and the neuter words used with it, are employed figuratively, or the word *comforter* is so employed. Now which is the most probable,—that this divine person should be spoken of literally in the New Testament but four times, and figuratively several hundreds of times, and that too in a figure, which diminishes, instead of amplifying his dignity; or, that a divine influence, which is spoken of literally several hundreds of times, should four times be personified? We must, in answering this question, bear it in mind, that the personifying of things without life, whether outward objects, or conceptions of the intellect, is an exceedingly common figure of speech, and one which always gives dignity to the things personified; while the opposite figure, namely, the use with regard to a person of language applicable to an inanimate object, is exceedingly rare, and is seldom employed, except in derision or irony, or to indicate the exceeding littleness of the person spoken of.

To show the true value of the argument for the personality of the holy spirit, based on the use of the word *comforter,* let us suppose a parallel case. Suppose that a volume of American sermons were put into the hands of a heathen, who understood our language, yet did not know the import of the word *Bible.* He would, it is to be hoped, often meet with that word, perhaps several times in each sermon. He would find it always treated as a neuter noun, and would see its place supplied by *it* and *which,* not by *he* and *who.* For the most part, there would be nothing said about the Bible, which was not literally applicable to a book. But in an exhortation towards the close of one of the sermons, something would perhaps be said about the duty of taking the Bible for a *guide;* and we will suppose the word *guide* used with regard to the Bible *four* times in this one passage. Now, were the heathen reader to insist that the Bible was a person, because in this volume of sermons it was *four* times called a *guide,* he would reason precisely like those, who infer the personality of the holy spirit from the use of the word *comforter* concerning it, *four* times in a single discourse of our Saviour.

Again, any possible inference, which might be drawn in behalf of this doctrine of the personality of the holy spirit, from the use of the word *comforter,* is entirely precluded by the fact, that in each of the *four* instances,* in which this word is used, it is defined by the neuter noun *spirit,* with a variety of words in the neuter gender connected with it. The first instance reads thus: 'I will pray the Father, and he shall give you another comforter, that he may abide with you forever,—even *the spirit* of truth, *which* the world cannot receive, because it seeth *it* not, neither knoweth *it;* but ye know *it;* for *it* dwelleth with you, and shall be in you.' Every one of these pronouns in the original is in the neuter gender. The next instance reads thus: 'The comforter, that is, *the holy spirit, which* the Father will send in my name,' the relative in the Greek being neuter. The next is this: 'When the comforter is come, whom I will send unto you from the Father, even *the spirit* of truth, *which* proceedeth from the Father.' In the fourth instance also, the comforter is defined to be *the spirit* of truth.

I would next remind you of other forms of speech in the New Testament, entirely incompatible with the personality of the holy spirit. The holy spirit is repeatedly said to be *poured out, shed, quenched,* and the like, and Christians are said to be *anointed* with the holy spirit,—expressions never used with regard to persons, but entirely applicable when used with regard to influences.

Another most decisive argument against the distinct and personal divinity of the holy spirit, is to be found in the offices ascribed in the Scriptures to the Father, Son, and Holy Spirit, respectively. The Trinitarian theory is, that there is a partition of divine attributes and offices between the three persons, whose respective functions are entirely distinct and separate from each other. The Father is the Creator, the Son the Redeemer, the Holy Spirit the Sanctifier. Now it might with much reason be objected to this partition, that the two last-named offices are one; that sanctification is man's only redemption; that sin is precisely what Jesus came to save men from; and that he can do this only by making them holy. But we will not insist on this. We will suppose these three offices of creator, redeemer, and sanctifier, in themselves entirely distinct from each other. Now if it appears that the three persons of the Godhead, (so called,) discharge each other's alleged functions, the distinction of persons can be no longer maintained. This, I think, will appear; and, in particular, we shall see that sanctification, deemed the special function of the Holy Spirit, is ascribed both to the Father and to the Son, and, on the other hand, that creation and redemption, regarded as the prerogatives of the Father and the Son, are ascribed to the Holy Spirit.

Sanctification is ascribed to the Father. In a prayer addressed expressly

* John xiv. 16, 26; xv. 26; xvi. 7.

to the Father, Jesus says: "Sanctify them through thy truth." St. Paul prays: "The very God of peace sanctify you wholly." St. Jude addresses his epistle "to them that are sanctified by God the Father."

Sanctification is also attributed to Jesus. Says St. Paul: "Of him are ye in Christ Jesus, who of God is made unto us wisdom, and righteousness, and sanctification." And, again: "Christ also loved the church, and gave himself for it, that he might sanctify and cleanse it." Says the writer to the Hebrews: "We are sanctified through the offering of the body of Christ once for all." And, again: "Jesus also, that he might sanctify the people with his own blood, suffered without the gate."

To the holy spirit also, creation, the Father's alleged prerogative, is ascribed, as in these passages: "By his spirit he hath garnished the heavens." "The spirit of God hath made me, and the breath of the Almighty hath given me life."

Every stage also in Christ's work of redemption is ascribed to the holy spirit. He ascribes his own miracles to "the spirit of God;" and he is said to have "offered himself through the eternal spirit."

The scriptures then leave no ground for the distinction of attributes and offices between the three persons of the Trinity, claimed by our Trinitarian friends; and, in ascribing to the holy spirit the same, and only the same attributes and offices ascribed to the Father and the Son, they make the distinct personality of the holy spirit a theory utterly without foundation.

The texts, usually quoted in support of the personality of the holy spirit, are those, in which the holy spirit is spoken of as being *sent, blasphemed, tempted, grieved* or *resisted,* all which are not unusual instances of personification, and represent a style of language constantly employed with regard to objects without life. Thus we say, that a *shower* is *sent,* that *divine mercy* is *blasphemed,* that one's *integrity* is *tempted,* that *good counsels* are *resisted.*

The only text, that demands distinct notice, is the following: "Likewise the spirit also helpeth our infirmities; for we know not what we should pray for as we ought; but the spirit itself maketh intercession for us with groanings which cannot be uttered. And he that searcheth the hearts knoweth the mind of the spirit, because it maketh intercession for the saints according to the will of God." It is surprising that this text should ever have been quoted as favoring the idea of the supreme, independent divinity of a spirit, which *intercedes,* that is, offers prayer, of course to some superior being; nor does the idea of *groaning* accord with the serene and perfect happiness of an almighty being. I do not think, that the spirit of God is referred to in this passage. It is the spirit or soul of *man,* of the *christian,* that is here spoken of. The apostle has alluded, in the preceding verses, to the infirmities of an earthly condition, which are to be borne with patience and hope. He adds: "The spirit, the soul, also, fixed on God and on eternal things, helps our infirmities,—sustains our frail bodies. We indeed often know not what is best for us,—what we ought to pray for; but the soul still prays,—pours itself out to God in aspirations and longings, deep and fervent, though often vague and indefinite. And he, that searches the hearts of men, knows the mind of the spirit,—knows the meaning of its groans and supplications,—knows the wants, which it does not know itself; for the souls of the righteous intercede for them according to the divine will,—long and yearn, in these groanings that cannot be uttered, for such spiritual favors, as God is always ready to bestow." The idea of the passage is, that the devout soul, in all its infirmity and its ignorance, will still be sustained, for it will still press to the mercy seat; and that, if it knows not even what to ask for, and cannot shape its own supplications, God, knowing the rectitude and earnestness of its desires, will satisfy all its real wants.

The holy spirit is not then a distinct person. What is it? What does the phrase mean? How are we to account for its use? We shall not, it seems to me, need to look far for our answer. Our common use of the word *spirit* will sufficiently explain its use in the sacred writings. What do we mean by the *spirit* of a man? A man performs two kinds of works,— exerts two kinds of agency. Some things he does expressly,—visibly, or audibly,—by word, or hand, or writing. Other, and often much greater things, he brings to pass by his influence,—by silent outgoings from his character,— by the power of his example,—by an agency, which far transcends his sphere of immediate action, and often outlasts the period of his mortal life. This influence, this agency, we usually denominate the *spirit* of the man; and its effects, its fruits, whether in the character of individuals or in the state of society, we also designate as his *spirit.* For instance, we call the influence, which the efforts and example of Howard the philanthropist had, and still have, the *spirit* of Howard; and, whenever we see works like his wrought, or persons engaged in works like his, we say that the *spirit* of Howard is in those works, or in those men. We then habitually use the word *spirit* to designate, *first,* a man's *influence,* and, *secondly, the effects of that influence.*

Now I conceive that we have no need of going beyond these common, well known uses of the word *spirit,* to explain its use in the Scriptures with reference to the Almighty. We find the phrases, *spirit of God, spirit of truth, holy spirit,* and the like, constantly used in these senses; and there is not a passage, as seems to me, in which it is necessary to look farther for a signification both obvious and satisfying.

The *spirit of God,* the *holy spirit,* and like phrases, most frequently denote simply the divine influence, sometimes in creation, and in outward events, but, in the great majority of instances, on the soul of man. They denote indeed a great diversity of divine influences, just as, by the spirit of a man, we denote every variety of influence, which a human being can exercise. We trace the spirit of a man in the building of a city, in the planning of a voyage, in the diffusion of literary taste, in the establishment of any public institution, in the tone of moral feeling cherished by his influence, in ideas or sentiments, to which he gave the first development, in fine, in any way, in which, without his direct bodily action, his character has impressed itself on objects, events, or the minds and hearts of others. An equally wide ground does the phrase *spirit of God,* with its cognate phrases, cover. It is used with reference to the plenary inspiration and the power from on high, which rested upon Jesus. To him, we are told, God 'gives not his spirit by measure;' but on him bestows every form of divine influence and endowment, of which a created being is capable. Then it is used concerning the peculiar communications of light and power vouchsafed to the apostles and their converts. Those, who were thus endowed, were always said to have received the holy spirit. It is used of particular divine intimations and impressions, as when the spirit bade Philip join the Ethiopian, and sent Peter to the house of Cornelius. Then, too, it is often used, as in our text, to denote those aids in the religious life, which 'whosoever asks, receives, and he that seeks, finds.' And it is used, in all these cases, with regard both to the influence and its effects, that is, it is employed to designate the spiritual gifts of God, both as they come from him, and as they rest upon the minds and hearts of men.

Now it is self-evident that there is the same room for the use of this phraseology with reference to God, that there is with reference to man. There is the same distinction between the modes and forms of divine action, that there is with reference to the deeds and agency of man. There are some things, which God confers, utters, or brings to pass, visibly or audibly. There are other things, which he gives or brings to pass silently, without any interposing cause that can be seen or traced; and all the various influences of this kind, with their results or effects, are what are termed in the Scriptures the *holy spirit.*

But, while we find no ground in reason or Scripture for believing in the personality of the holy spirit, we regard the influence of God upon the soul of man as an indisputable, essential, fundamental doctrine of religion. What distinguishes us from our Trinitarian brethren on this point, is, that we regard this influence as flowing, not from a fragment of the divine nature, but from the whole undivided Deity. And least of all, can we sympathize with believers in the Trinity, in separating God the Father from the divine influence upon the soul. We feel that it is peculiarly in his fatherly relation and attributes, that God is present with the soul of man. We find the full promise of the holy spirit in these words of Jesus: 'If a man love me, he will keep my words; and my Father will love him, and we will come unto him, and make our abode with him.' It is the spirit of the Father, and the Son, and this alone, that we desire and seek, not a spirit in any respect or degree distinct from either the Father or the Son.

Let me employ the few moments, for which I yet can claim your attention, in developing what I conceive to be the scriptural doctrine of spiritual influences.

In the first place, the spirit of God is in his works. We accord in full with the declaration of the Wisdom of Solomon: 'Thine incorruptible spirit is in all things.' Well has it been said: 'This fair universe, were it in the meanest province thereof, is in very deed the star-domed city of God. Through every star, through every grass-blade, the glory of a present God still beams. Nature is the time-vesture of God.' With equal truth and beauty, does Goethe put into the mouth of the earth-spirit the words:—

> 'Tis thus at the roaring loom of time I ply,
> And weave for God the garment thou see'st Him by.

Our first parents heard the voice of the Lord God in the garden; and they, no doubt, miraculously, but not one whit more distinctly, than we may hear it this very night. There is no poetical fancy, but literal truth in the beautiful words of the hymn just sung:—

> Hark! on the evening breeze,
> As once of old, the Lord God's voice
> Is heard among the trees.

Such is the constant testimony of Scripture. God is spoken of as actively present in all the forms and agencies of the outward universe. Does a tempest rise? "He maketh the winds his angels." Do the thunders roll? "The voice of the Lord is upon the waters; the God of glory thundereth." Do showers bless the harvest field? "He watereth the hills from his chambers." Does verdure clothe the plain? "He causeth the grass to grow for the cattle, and herb for the service of man." And in all these forms, in myriads of ways, is he speaking to the hearts of his human family, claiming their worship, casting deep reproach upon their coldness and indifference, and awakening in every thoughtful soul the resolution of the psalmist: "I will sing unto the Lord as long as I live: I will sing praise unto my God while I have my being. My meditation of him shall be sweet: I will be glad in the Lord." There is, I believe, a perpetual communion on God's part with man, in the order, harmony, beauty, and majesty of creation. I believe, that I no more truly address loving words day by day to the children dearer to me than my own soul, than God has this day directly spoken to each and all of us, his children, in the sunshine and the flowers, in the mellow twilight and the gentle breeze. I sincerely believe, that the express design of this fair and wonderful creation is to bring the Creator near, and to make his presence felt by the living souls of men,—to supply a medium of communication between the Infinite and the finite,—to render visible and audible those thoughts of love, fathomless as the ocean, numberless as its sands.

In the same light do I regard the whole course of Providence. The events of life, ordered by the close and constant care of the Almighty, have each a voice from him for the spirit's ear, a lesson of truth, a message of duty, a word of warning or rebuke, comfort or encouragement. How near, how incessant the watchful presence indicated by our Savior's words: "The hairs of your head are all numbered." In the mercies so thickly strown along our daily path, are fulfilled, in every one of our thoughtless moments, the words of holy writ, "God hath spoken once, yea, twice, but man perceiveth it not." In every sorrow comes the voice, "Hear ye the rod, and who hath appointed it."

But, yet more, apart from outward forms and events, I believe in the intimate presence and communion of God with the soul of man. His hand-writing is on our innermost shrines of thought; his voice thrills through the deepest recesses of our being. As the builder of a house may construct for himself a secret passage, opening by springs which no one else can find, so has the Almighty architect of the soul of man reserved his own hidden avenues of access, by which he visits the soul in its days of gladness and its night seasons of sorrow, in its health and its sickness, giving it meat to eat, of which the world knows not, letting in the day-spring from on high upon its darkened chambers, filling with the oil of joy its empty and shrunken vessels. None can shut out the thoughts that God sends; but, unsought, unsuggested by the ordinary laws of association, nay, often unwelcome, they remain, return, haunt the soul, knock at the heart's door, and often forsake it not, till they are cherished and obeyed. How true to human experience are the psalmist's words: "Whither shall I go from thy spirit?" Not we ourselves can hold so close communion with our own souls, as God can; for how often does his spirit reverse our own inward thoughts, and say the opposite of what we were saying within ourselves! We are whispering peace to our souls; but the spirit cries, in a voice which self-delusion cannot drown, "No peace without repentance and the fruits of love." We flatter ourselves that we are rich and full; but the spirit cries, "Nay,—ye are poor and naked, hungry, and thirsty,—come, drink of my cup, and eat of my bread, and put on my beautiful garments." Or, on the other hand, though in the way of duty, we doubt and fear; and, in the hour of sad self-communion, the spirit enters, and says, "Peace be with you," and the cloud rises from our souls and melts away, our hearts grow warm, and burn within us, and we perceive that it is the Lord.

Whence too, when we have trodden the path of transgressors, those unsought warnings, presentiments of evil, forebodings of penalties that we have defied? Whence that uneasy, restless feeling, that will ever intrude itself, when we linger too long on the roadside of our heavenward pilgrimage, when we forsake duty for pleasure, when we serve Mammon instead of God? Whence those preparation seasons for the trial of faith or virtue, which every Christian has experienced,—seasons, when, without any outward cause, impressions have been borne in upon our minds, spiritual exercises have been induced, and views and purposes cherished, precisely adapted to exigencies just at hand, yet unforeseen, as if our Father, when he saw the storm gathering, had hastened to wrap us beforehand in the mantle of his love, and to set our feet in a straight and safe path? Whence that serene satisfaction, that joy in the Lord, that inward repose and harmony, which flow from trials well sustained and duties nobly done, and which give us the surest foretaste of heaven that we can have below? Has there ever been a day, whether of duty or of sin, of joy or of sorrow, of levity or of seriousness, when, if we had strictly reviewed our heart's history for the day, we should not have been constrained to confess that God had been there, and that his spirit had borne witness, either with, or against our spirits? No. The divine spirit has always sought to draw us. God has been unceasingly near. "Behold, I stand at the door and knock," is his voice to each of us. There lives not the man, who has ever succeeded in shutting God from his heart. Though we take the wings of the morning, he is before us. Though the darkness cover us, it hides us not from him.

It is of these influences of the divine spirit upon the soul of man, that it is written, "Quench not the spirit,"—"Grieve not the holy spirit of God." For these influences, the Scriptures teach us, are not irresistible; but, like the counsels or the influence of a faithful human parent or friend, may be disobeyed and disregarded.

To these same spiritual influences, welcomed and obeyed, the Scriptures ascribe all that is good and holy in man,—all the graces and virtues of the regenerate heart. It is by the help of God, that we discharge our duty, that we grow in grace, that we become followers of Jesus,—all which is sufficiently indicated in such Scriptures as these: "By the grace of God I am what I am,"—"It is God that worketh in you to will and to do of his good pleasure,"—"As many as are led by the spirit of God, they are the sons of God,"—"The spirit of God dwelleth in you." In accordance with this idea of the helping spirit of God, as essential to the Christian life, those, who yield themselves to the divine influence, are styled "born of the spirit,"—"baptized with the holy spirit;" and are said to "walk after the spirit," to "live in the spirit," and to "have the spirit of God resting upon them."

Such is the Christian doctrine of the *holy spirit*,—the influence of God in nature, in providence, and, more than all, his direct, immediate influence upon the heart of man,—not a constraining, irresistible influence, but an influence, which may, on the one hand, be grieved and quenched, or, on the other, welcomed and obeyed; and which, if yielded to, becomes the source of every thing worthy and holy in the character,—the fountain of renewed and sanctified affections, and of a Christ-like walk and conversation.

For this spirit, for these influences, prayer prepares the soul, so as to render them availing and enduring. By prayer man opens the door of his heart to the spirit, that always seeks an entrance and a home there; nor can any earthly parent so promptly meet the wants of an only child, as God, by his ever present spirit, fulfils the desires of the praying soul.

I am happy to believe, that, with regard to these fundamental, practical views of spiritual influences, there is no essential difference among Christians. On this subject, the religious phraseology of Christians of different modes of faith, for the most part, coincides; and all true religious experience must of necessity be coincident. This experience of the welcomed influences and the blessed fruits of the spirit, may God grant us all, through Jesus Christ our Savior.

 Baptism

LEONARD JARVIS LIVERMORE
(1822–1886)

The sacrament of baptism had always been a stone of stumbling to the Congregationalists. They believed unreservedly that the visible Church was rightly a congregation of the elect, of those who had experienced conversion as responsible, thinking Christians. At the same time they believed in infant baptism and opposed the doctrine of Baptists that this initiatory rite was only for the confessed and converted Christian. As a concession to the strict views of Baptists, the Puritans tended to agree that only the children of the elect could be baptized—and it was this that opened them to the charge of being familial tribalists. The early Puritans, in other words, experienced great tension between their ideas of church membership and their ideas of baptism. The same was true for the founders of the Puritan commonwealths in America. The first president of Harvard, Henry Dunster, became a Baptist and resigned; the wife of New Haven's founder, John Davenport, also became a Baptist and was excommunicated. Roger Williams and Anne Hutchinson evidence the same trend. The force of logic plus a number of complex social factors led to a steady increase of Baptists throughout New England. The Great Awakening produced similar results, and many if not most of the strict Congregationalists who then separated themselves from the Standing Order (Isaac Backus, the father of the New England Baptist movement) became Baptists.

Some Puritans resolved the tension by moving in the opposite direction. The First Church in Boston very early relaxed the strict rule of baptizing only the children of converted saints; the problem was an important reason for calling the synod which prepared the Cambridge Platform (1648). The Half-Way Covenant of 1662 officially allowed the baptism of the children of half-way members (i.e., those who had been duly baptized but not converted). In Connecticut, the Saybrook Platform of 1708 took this same position, and the practices thus allowed became widespread. In the new Brattle Street Church of Boston (1699), which was to become a stronghold of Unitarianism a century later, the half-way idea was made a formal constitutional rule. Among the liberal churches of eastern Massachusetts the precedent set in Brattle Street gradually became normative.

In practice, therefore, Unitarians tended to return to views more closely approximating those of Presbyterians, Anglicans, Lutherans, and Roman

Catholics. As to the significance or meaning of baptism, however, they were only in very heavily qualified agreement with traditional views. In the selection that follows, Livermore says that "the significance of infant baptism depends much on our faith in the Church as the organic and perpetually renewed body of Christ,—one, though ever changing." Revisions of traditional doctrines of original sin also affected the meaning of baptism. Consequently baptism was usually held to be only a symbol, an act which does not make the bond but simply declares it. It was, in other words, a "pledge" made by an adult or by parents for their children.

Leonard Jarvis Livermore was born in Milford, New Hampshire, and educated at Harvard. He was minister successively in Unitarian churches at East Boston (1847–57), Lexington (1857–66), and Danvers (1867–86). He was a secretary of the Unitarian Sunday School Society and the compiler of the long-used *Hymn, Tune, and Service Book*. His published writings were not voluminous, and when he is remembered at all it is chiefly for a long, devoted, and useful pastoral career.

The practice of baptism, as a symbol of moral purpose and religious conviction, is supposed to have originated from the use of water in bathing, and as a means of ceremonial cleanness. . . . That it was a rite already in use among the Jews, and with a somewhat definite religious signification, appears from the way in which John is said to have come baptizing, without any thing to intimate or suggest that it was a novelty originated by him. The same is also indicated by Christ's words to Nicodemus, in John, third chapter, fifth verse. . . .

When John came preaching in the remoter country regions of Judea,—conscious of a religious inspiration and mission, and looking for the speedy appearing of the Redeemer,—he found this symbol of moral and religious renewal already familiar to the people. It was well adapted to give point and permanence to the religious feelings he awakened. It defined the nature and purpose of his call to them, in a clearer and more effective way than verbal statements alone could do it. . . .

The same reasons which made this rite suitable for John's purposes commended it to Jesus. Almost as soon as he began to have disciples, the disciples began to baptize. There is no reason to doubt this baptism was in the name of Jesus; that is, it implied a receiving of him so far as his work was then manifest. When the Lord's earthly task was completed, he left this to his disciples as the plainest outward sign of faith in him. Its meaning to the Christian convert lay not in any implied confession of past sins, or any supposed power in the rite to make him clean. It was his formal reception of a new teacher, and a new life,—a life of moral purity and of religious consecration. By receiving baptism in the name of Jesus, he signified that the purer life to which he pledged himself was made to appear to him his duty through the teachings of Christ; that he believed in Jesus as one sent from God, as his Lord and Master; and, because believing so, that he took on himself the duty of living according to the commands of Jesus. The ordinance carried with itself a meaning varying according to each convert's measure of Christian faith and understanding. It stood for his pledge of faith and duty, and was equally the symbol of his participation in the grace and privileges of the gospel.

Baptism came to be an ordinance of the Christian Church, not because of any essential value in itself,—not because Jesus Christ saw in it, of itself, any spiritual value,—but as a form or symbol, the meaning of which was already familiar to those around him, and therefore well adapted to serve as an expressive, intelligible, and visible sign and confession of faith in him as the Teacher and Redeemer of men. There is no proof that Jesus regarded the rite as an indispensable condition of salvation, or of a Christian faith and standing. The words already referred to, spoken to Nicodemus, are most reasonably explained, not as enforcing a double necessity of baptism and of spiritual regeneration, but one necessity,—the moral and religious birth, of which the washing of water was the recognized symbol and the spirit of God the efficient cause, in opposition to the Jewish trust in natural descent from Abraham. Any thing so contrary to the general tenor of Christ's teaching as the absolute necessity of an outward and ritual observance can be received only on the authority of an express declaration. There is no such express declaration of the indispensableness of baptism. If Paul had regarded this rite as the invariable and necessary condition of a Christian position and salvation, expressly enjoined and instituted by the Lord, he could not have said, "Christ sent me not to baptize." His way of speaking of it shows that he looked on it as a thing of subordinate importance,—as a sign, which, being in use and well understood, and approved by the Lord, should be observed, but to be carefully restrained to its proper use as a symbol only; that he avoided any views that seemed to attribute to it any efficacy other than as a sign and pledge of a new and better life after it.

With regard to the method of baptism, there is nothing to prove that the form was considered material,—nothing to make it certain that any one form was exclusively used. It is not improbable that it was often by immersion. Habits and conditions peculiar to that age and climate made this a far less inconvenient and otherwise objectionable form than in our time and situation. . . . We believe it is actually following Christ, to assert our freedom from an unvarying rule of form, while we aim to preserve the moral and spiritual significance.

With regard to the baptism of children in infancy, we hold that the New Testament does not give any explicit information. The words in Acts viii. 16, taken in connection with what immediately precedes, and interpreted in the light of what is well known to have been the custom of the Jews, create a strong presumption that children were baptized then and there by the apostle, or under his immediate direction. . . . The several instances where households are said to have been baptized, as if following the lead and example of the head of the family, strengthen the presumption. Moreover, this has been the practice of the Church from the earliest times of which we have record. The first fathers allude to the custom, as that which was in general use, and derived from the traditions of the apostles. They discuss questions as to time and other conditions, but not as to the fitness of the custom itself. We favor this practice also on grounds of reason, which are good in the absence of express precept to the contrary, as significant of the divinely ordained connection between the life of the parents and that of the children; and symbolic of the natural law, that children of faithful Christian parents grow up believers in the Lord Jesus Christ.

We do not regard the baptism of the young as a completed thing, until, being brought up in the knowledge of God and the Saviour, and having attained to the power of acting and judging for themselves, they openly and freely adopt the act of their parents as their own. The significance of infant baptism depends much on our faith in the Church as the organic and perpetually renewed body of Christ,—one, though ever changing,— and resting on the divinely appointed continuity of human life. The children of Christian parents are born into the Church of Christ. They are the Lord's. Baptism does not make the bond. It declares it, and pledges the parent to fidelity in his efforts to make it a lasting and complete union by the Christian nurture and instruction of his offspring.

We regard baptism as only a symbol, in itself of no effect, as signing the pledge is in the case of one who abandons the use of alcohol. This symbol is of higher respect than any other, as having come to us through ages of Christian observance, as pertaining to the most momentous interests and duties, and as sanctioned by the example and authority of the Head of the Church. It is not formality to adhere to it, there being no objection to it, when it is held free from superstitious notions, either as to its efficacy or its form; and, on the other hand, there being many good reasons for continuing it. Those rather are formalists, who, like the Quakers, make a *point,* and therefore a *form,* of rejecting all forms. It is the only visible mark of the unity of the Church,—one Lord, one baptism. It is a plain, easy, intelligible way of performing a universal duty, that of openly confessing faith in Christ; an equally intelligible sign of the pure and righteous life to which the Christian pledges himself. Coming to us from Christ, and administered in his name, it is a means of expressing, and therefore a means of strengthening, the sense of our union with him. It continues and visibly expresses the unity of the Church as the fellowship of believers in one Saviour, believers in God the Father through Christ the Son. We offer and urge it on the unbaptized, not as an avowal of holiness attained, or a saving change already wrought, but, after the apostles' custom, as a simple act of faith in the Lord Jesus Christ as our Teacher and Redeemer; the law of our higher and better life, when life in its strength is ours; and the ground of a hope triumphant over sickness and the fear of death.

❧ On the Uses of the Communion

ORVILLE DEWEY (1794–1882)

Orville Dewey's background was rigorously orthodox. Born and reared on a farm in Sheffield, Massachusetts, a rural community in the Housatonic valley, he was nurtured in a strict tradition even though his father, on periodic visits to Boston as a state legislator, had been much affected by the preaching of Channing. In 1814 he was graduated from Williams College at the head of his class despite serious difficulties with his eyes. During the next three years he attended Andover Theological Seminary, and it was there (ironically in the exegetical classes of Moses Stuart) that his orthodoxy began to weaken. After graduation, when faced with a call to the Congregational church in Worcester, he declined ordination on grounds of doctrinal indecision and took on a year's preaching duties instead. An immensely serious and conscientious person—given, as he said, to long periods of Carthusian silence and meditation—Dewey spent the year making up his mind. The nature of his decision is indicated by his becoming an assistant to Channing at the Federal Street Church in Boston. In 1823 he accepted a call to the New Bedford Unitarian church, where he served until 1833 when ill health forced upon him a recuperative period of rest and foreign travel. (His impressions of Europe and America are presented in *The Old World and the New.*) Improved in strength, he accepted another call in 1835, this time to Second Congregational Church (Unitarian) of New York. This flourishing society had an imposing church building at the corner of Mercer and Prince streets. Unfortunately, it burned in 1837, but in the newly named Church of the Messiah on Broadway, Dewey reached an even larger and more influential congregation. Among his parishioners were Peter Cooper; William Cullen Bryant; and Charles Curtis, the civic leader, reformer, and father of George William Curtis, an important political leader. During his first six years in New York, Dewey was extraordinarily effective in his preaching ministry, but thereafter his health declined. Another journey abroad in 1841 to 1843 did not bring any great improvement, and after various other unsuccessful expedients he retired in 1848 to the family home in Sheffield. Here he pursued intensive studies in the philosophy of history and related subjects and sallied forth repeatedly as preacher and lecturer.

His daughter said Dewey was greatest as a preacher, and it was in this role that he made the Church of the Messiah a center of liberal religion, ethical concern, and active philanthropy. He thought no one person should either deliver or hear two sermons a Sunday. On Sunday evenings, therefore, the throngs who crowded his church heard lectures on a wide gamut of subjects. He was a strong champion of many civic reforms, an outspoken critic of slavery, and an advocate of gradual emancipation. To his Whig parishioners he was also a steady defender of Bryant's Democratic views.

Dewey's great power as a pulpit orator never overshadowed his deep concern for corporate worship. Like many Americans of his day, he found that visits to the great churches of Europe deepened these convictions. In 1839, when his congregation moved into their new edifice, he sought to introduce the King's Chapel Liturgy. He ceased to press for the change when a considerable minority of his parish opposed it, but he expressed a hope that a liturgy greater than any then existing would ultimately be forged from the German, English, and Roman traditions.

Dewey also felt a profound respect for the historic sacramental ordinances of the Church. On the subject of the Lord's Supper, particularly, he sought to reform the tradition and practices that had grown up in New England. In his *Autobiography* he reflected on that tradition: "I remember looking down from the gallery as a boy at church upon the celebration of the Lord's Supper, and pitying the persons engaged in it more than any people in the world,—I thought they were so unhappy."[1] As a pastor and with a Unitarian theology far different from that which ruled his childhood church, he sought to reinvest the observances with spiritual meaning and to encourage every professing Christian—not just a small spiritual elite—to partake. In this effort he joined hands with, for example, Cyrus A. Bartol, who in a major work on ecclesiastical polity sought to eliminate the old distinction between church membership and society or parish membership that Unitarians had inherited from the Puritans. The homily on the Holy Communion reprinted here was first delivered in the Church of the Messiah to further this end.

I wish to offer some thoughts in this Essay, upon the uses of the Communion, and the propriety of a general attendance upon it. From various causes, some of which are to be traced to historical events, others to doctrinal errors, and others still to a superstition ever lurking in men's minds,—from various causes, I say, it has come to pass that a ritual service, intended for the edification of the whole body of believers and worshippers, has been consigned over to the charge of a few. That which was meant to be a bond of union has become a badge, not of sectarian, but—

1. Orville Dewey, *Autobiography and Letters,* p. 16.

what is worse—of personal distinction. A symbolic observance, of easy interpretation and of wide comprehensiveness, designed to be a common ground among different nations, and a common expositor of the faith among differing languages, has been made a peculiar and a profound mystery. A broad and generous institution is turned into a mystic singularity. And that, which by the tenderest pleadings was set forth to draw all men to Christ,—to be a rite of Christ's love and compassion and fellowship, is made to multitudes to be a rite of repulsion and estrangement. I verily believe, that if there were no such rite as the Lord's Supper, in our churches, many would feel that they have a part and an interest in religion, which they now consider as denied to them. I do not say that this is a good reason for abandoning the ordinance; but I say that it is a good reason for considering most seriously the views that are entertained of it. And I do say also, that so it was not in the beginning. It is observable, indeed, that in the founder of this institution there was none of that extreme sensitiveness about its profanation, that has prevailed in later days; for he did not forbid Judas from partaking in it, though he knew that murder and betrayal were in his heart. And when it fell into the hands of Apostles, when the early Christian congregations were gathered, we know that all who believed in Christ, and desired to place themselves under his discipline,—that is to say, that the entire company of Christian worshippers,—were communicants; that they as much and as freely participated in the act of communion, as in the act of prayer. The table of the Lord's Supper was spread; and the only condition of approach to it was faith in Christ,—a hearty reception of him as a heaven-commissioned Master and Saviour. There is no evidence that there was any church vote, or any exertion of the Apostolic will, in the matter. A credible expression of faith was the unquestioned passport. And when the children of these primitive confessors grew up, and took the places of their fathers, they all succeeded to the inheritance of their privileges. So it continued to be, till the time of the Reformation; so it is in the Catholic church to this day.

It is upon this primitive ground of general participation, that I would wish to see the Communion placed in our congregations. I could wish that every person, who believes in Christianity, and seriously purposes to lead a life in accordance with it, would come and engage in the acts and offices and meditations of this holy season. If there be any person among us of infidel principles, or vicious life, it is true that I could not advise his coming to the table of the Lord; there would be an utter impropriety in his coming. So far, doubtless, the act of communion is a profession of religion. It is a profession of Christianity, and of Christianity as the law and guide of life. But it is not the profession of any peculiar sanctity, of any superiority to others; it is only the avowal of a sincere desire to attain to the elevated virtues of Christianity; to follow Christ as the heaven-ordained Master. Every person, faithfully entertaining such a desire is fully entitled thus to come and express it; and to seek to seal and confirm it. It is to such emphatically that the Communion offers its aid.

Were the ordinance arranged as I would wish, the whole time of the Morning Service should be given to it. It should not be set aside in a corner, nor brought in at the close of another service, by which our minds had been already exhausted. The whole congregation,—that is, of the serious, thoughtful, and religiously disposed, who believe in Christ,—should gather around the table, and the pastor should from time to time, during the service, utter such thoughts as the occasion would suggest to him; thoughts which would occupy as much space in the delivery as a sermon, and would be, I believe, not less useful, but more so.

But what, it may be asked, is the advantage of having any such particular occasion, any such special meditation at all? Why should Christ, and the death of Christ, be made the subject of this peculiar consideration? What propriety has it, and what advantage would it offer to us, over and above what belong to the ordinary devotions and meditations of the sanctuary?

This question I shall attempt now to answer; and the rather, because I fear, that only a kind of demure and unbelieving assent is frequently yielded to the expediency and importance of that commemoration of Christ, which obtains in the Christian church. That the name of Christ should be frequently named in the churches; that constant references to the Saviour should mingle with our prayers and our meditations; that times and seasons should be set apart for the special remembrance of his sacrifice; all this is admitted to be proper, and has been so long admitted to be proper, that assent has lost much of the character of an original conviction. Faith, when it loses sight of its original grounds, is apt to die out; and hence it is, that not only this or that particular ordinance, but even all general worship is sometimes brought into question. The old faith is dead, and there is no new one to replace it. It is therefore important to go back, from time to time, to the primary reasons for certain institutions; and this is what I now propose to do in reference to the observance of the Lord's Supper. . . . Every rite is designed to teach something that is worth knowing or remembering; and to impress what it teaches by fixing attention. This is the whole theory of ritual usages. Most ritual observances are but forms of meditation. The uplifted eyes and bended knees, or the head reverently bowed and the eyes closed in prayer, are thus far ritual; they help the mind by fixing attention. Grant, indeed, the original propriety of the act; but its *use* is to fix attention.

With these preliminary remarks, I proceed to consider the original and the still existing grounds and reasons for the commemoration of Christ, in the rite, which for that express purpose he instituted.

1. Let it then be observed, in the first place, that the chief means of religious progress is to be found in this one thing,—that is to say, a just, clear, and impressive idea of what religion is. The grand instrument of improvement is admitted to be *truth*. "Sanctify them," said our Saviour, "through thy truth." But what especially is this truth? I say, it is truth with regard to what a pure and religious life is. It is the lofty ideal of virtue that carries us to the lofty practice of virtue. Of course we cannot be good at all, unless we know what goodness is. And in proportion as our idea of goodness is elevated, are we provided with the efficient means that most powerfully teach and impel us to advance in goodness. . . .

Indeed to see the wisdom and blessedness of a right life,—to apprehend it clearly and deeply,—to have the truth of this wrought out in the soul,—beyond all question and doubt,—this is one of the most momentous of all convictions. The learning of a hundred sciences were nothing to a man's happiness and dignity, compared with this. It is the very business and con-summation of a wise man's enquiries to know this. Let this be once fixed in his mind, and with what disdain can he tread upon all the baits and allurements of passion and the world; how calmly can he meet all the calamities of life,—feeling that he has an aim and a treasure superior to them all. . . .

But what now is to help him to that conviction? I answer, nothing, instrumentally, but meditation. God will aid his true endeavor; but there is nothing within his own reach to do, but to meditate. He must fix his mind upon the divine ideal of a holy life, in order to realize it. He must go down into the depths of his soul; he must study its nature, its capacities, its wants; he must find out what it was made for. He must become familiar, by contemplation, with the beauty of rectitude, with the divinity of good-ness, with the venerableness of sanctity, with the majesty and humbleness of prayer, with the heroism of virtue, with the sublimity of devotion. Thoughts, glowing thoughts of purity, and gentleness, and candor, and forbearance, and disinterestedness, and love divine, must become his bosom companions. Where these thoughts dwell not, there will be no improvement,—there can be none; where they abide and live,—where they live in self-reproach, and struggle in prayer, there is garnered up the whole magazine of means,—the very means of salvation.

2. All this being admitted, and being indeed most evident, the next observation I have to offer is, that all this ideal of excellence is perfectly realized in Christ.

It is a wonderful thing to contemplate,—upon the high table-land of human history,—this image of perfect spiritual beauty. There it stands, in the sight of all men; and from whatsoever age or country the eye hath been directed, it hath never discovered in that living excellence one single fault. No picture of such a life, of such immaculate excellence, was ever imagined, till the living original appeared, and drew from the pens of simple fishermen, such a story of wisdom, and goodness, and grandeur, as human genius and inspiration had never before reached,—have never since equalled. . . .

Now the great difficulty about this excellence is its inaccessibleness. Its own elevation might have presented a sufficient obstacle to weak and erring creatures; but this obstacle has been incalculably increased by causes, lying, not in the object contemplated, but in our manner of viewing it. If we clothe Christ with the attributes of Divinity, it is difficult to see how he can be an example to humanity. For, although his manhood be held as well as his godhead, yet the supposed intimate union of both, so as to make one, only one self-conscious being, must impart such a peculiarity to his human virtue as almost entirely to remove it from all approach and imitation. This, it may be thought, with our creed, does not concern us. But believe me, the remnants or relics of all the prevalent creeds, that ever were in the church, are still lingering in our minds; the influence of a creed is not dismissed with an act of disbelief, nor is it worn out in one generation. Still the force of Christ's example is immensely weakened,—is, in many minds, reduced almost to nothing, by the mystery that has surrounded his person. . . . As men generally conceive of Jesus, there is a want of imitableness, of tangibility, almost I fear of reality, in his example.

Now, I have said, in the first place, that the way to gain excellence is to meditate upon it, and thus to fill our minds with the glow of admiration and desire. And, in the second place, I have said that the character of our Saviour is the very realization of all our ideas of wisdom and goodness. And I have said it, of course, with the implied inference that this is, above all things, worthy of our meditation. . . .

3. And, I proceed now, in the third place, to observe that there is a yet further and more especial propriety in the meditations to which this ordinance calls us, because our hardest struggle in life is with suffering and sorrow, with injury and wrong, with calamity and death.

Let us cast away all mystical ideas of this occasion, all preconceived ideas of the Gospel, and all visionary ideas of life, and come, on each point, to the reality.

I find my lot cast in, whether I will or not, with a life of change and trial and many pains. I would be happy; but alas! I do not easily learn to be happy. Peace of mind, calm repose, sustained and unbroken satisfaction—how hard is it to reach them? Many burdens press upon every man; many collisions with untoward events, or uncongenial persons, cut us to the quick; many wrongs and oppressions in society distress, and perhaps exasperate us. . . . No reasoning can reason this away. It is sad reality. It is "the still sad music of humanity," sounding through the world.

Now, suppose any one thus conscious of what life is, to have fallen upon the readings, for the first time, of the life of Christ. Instantly he would feel that this was something to him,—was much,—was everything to him. "Here," he would say, "is the very type of my own humanity. Here is affliction, suffering, sorrow, injury, detraction, wrong,—a struggle with temptations and difficulties; and all sustained with an evident inward serenity, courage, and joy. What meekness armed him against hostility; what divine trust against calamity; what triumph bore him up amidst the depths of agony and the shadows of death! Neither surrounding tumult nor gathering terror entered into his *soul; there* all was calm, while the storm raged without; *there* all was blessedness, though the miseries of life, from a full cup, were given him to drink. But it was the cup which his Father gave him; it was the misery which Heaven's will ordained for his trial and his triumph; and it was received with a filial reliance,—it was received, as if he knew that which was afterwards recorded of him, that he was to be made perfect through sufferings." "Could I live like this being," would the meditative reader say,—"could I breathe his spirit; could I enter into his joy; surely then would the dark and painful problem of my life be solved into perfect light; the cloud would be lifted up, and the way of life—filled with care and toil and grief, and trodden with many heavy steps—would show like a way of triumph and glory."

I beg the reader to bring his mind to this point. I cannot go into instances of what Jesus was as a sufferer. But do you not see that whosoever should meditate upon the life of Christ, with a living sympathy; whose mind soever should be brought into a glowing admiration and love of his patience, gentleness, serenity, and holy self-forgetfulness and self-sacrifice;—whosoever should lay his heart, if I may speak so, to the heart of that divinest friend and Saviour, would be fast growing into his likeness—would be rapidly attaining to the truest wisdom and happiness of life? Christ's life is the exemplar of our life; and our special concern with it is to see in it the model of our own—to see how to live—to see it, in everything, save its official grandeur, and, if I may so say, its circumstantial shadings—for there was in it, the high resolve, and the subdued, almost the saddened tone of a great enterprise,—to see it, I say, saving in some peculiar traits, as our example. The happy dwellers in a country are not to live precisely as did the solemn, sad, determined patriots, who, through suffering and death, wrought out its deliverance; but who would not pray that the essential virtues of those heroic and martyred fathers might dwell in their children?

Now, it is especially to a meditation on the sacrifice of Christ, on the truths disclosed and the virtues manifested in it, that the communion season invites us. "This do," says our Saviour, "in remembrance of me." And let me say, distinctly and emphatically, that it is only through this meditation, this remembrance of Christ, that we can receive the blessing he designed to communicate. It is not in any mystic way. There is no mysterious virtue in the act of communing. It is only by meditation, by fixed attention, that we can receive anything into our minds. Would you possess any virtue? Would you drink in the spirit of any life? What have you to do,— what *can* you do, but earnestly contemplate it.

Therefore does it seem to me good and meet, that all Christians; all who would indeed be Christians, should gather together, from time to time, in commemoration of the sacrifice, the patience, the forgiveness, and love of Jesus. Could but these simple virtues be wrought into any heart— how would all settle into peace there—into calm repose, and deep satisfaction, and divine blessedness!

Good has it often seemed to me, to enter into some ancient and venerable temple, whose altar-steps had been worn by the knees of pilgrims and penitents from far distant countries and ages; whose pavements had been trodden by successive generations; whose walls had grown hoary amidst the flight of centuries. An odor of sanctity seemed to fill the place. A solemn presence seemed to be there; the mind was carried up above the world; it was translated out of its ordinary and earthly frame; all worldly strifes and griefs died away; *that* was none other than the house of God,— it was the gate of heaven. But how much more do all earthly, all unholy passions die away, amidst that scene, brought down from the birth-time of Christianity itself, consecrated to its sublimest theme, its tenderest recollections, and its most inspiring promises! "For, as often," says our Saviour, "as ye do eat of this bread and drink of this cup, ye do show forth the Lord's death till he come." Let any one approach this scene; let him come, from whatsoever state or condition where the hard conflict of life is carried on; from the house of merchandise or from the abode of affliction,—from strifes with his neighbor, from contests of ambition, or the bustle and bitterness of a political canvass,—yes, let him come *with* his neighbor to this holy communion and commemoration; and will not the mild countenance and voice of the common Master, of the crucified one, speak to him salutary, solemn, and gracious lessons? Will it not be good for him to be here? Will not the spirit that breathes around this holy rite—this gathering place of all the Christian ages—this altar place for

prayer and penitence through centuries—this great symbol-rite that cele-
brates redeeming sorrow and peace-speaking blood, that sets forth the
prostration of all earthly powers and principalities before the majesty of
forgiveness and love—will not all this raise the man above the world?
Will it not make him feel the littleness of all human strifes, of all worldly
pretensions, of all the passing fashions of this world? Truly, and strictly
speaking, it is true—all that is evil in the world nowhere finds its grand
antagonist principle so clearly and powerfully set forth, as in this very
altar of communion.

Meet it is, then, that we gather around this altar. It is no vain, no idle
ceremony; no arbitrary, no merely commanded institution. It is a simple
commemoration, a simple meditation; so do I regard it; but no meditation on earth seems so needful, so pertinent to me, as a sinful and suffering creature, as that which is commended to me here. Neglected may this
scene be, as unnecessary; or rejected, as unauthorized; yet, if I were left to
the simple determination of my own judgment, of my own conscious
needs, I should say, that nowhere in the world is there such reality to my
feelings as here. I speak not of a form now, but of that which the form
meaneth. And I say and verily believe, that the meanings of this holy rite
have more to do with my happiness, than any other event, any other
transaction, any other era, in the great train of human history. Suppose me
only to feel these two things—that I must have this excellence of Christ,
that I must have the spirit of the cross, or I cannot be happy; and that I
can have this excellence only by meditation—that it can by no possibility
be got in any other way—and then is not my conclusion, and my course a
very plain one? And that I feel that I want this spirit, that I am sinful and
unworthy—that my mind is daily exposed to break out into anger, or to
sink in worldliness and sense,—is that any objection to my coming to bow
my soul before the great example of purity and meekness, and the great
testimony of God's forgiving pity? Nay, it is the very argument for my
coming, provided I sincerely desire to conquer my pride and passion and
sin in every form. . . . In the Lord's Supper we celebrate the greatest
event in the world; the consummation of the grandest story that the world
ever heard; we celebrate it with less ministering to the body indeed, but
in a manner nevertheless substantially accordant with the usages, not only
of ancient but of modern times.

In the next place, I pray you to consider whether there is not something
too generalizing in the religious feeling that is averse to the Communion?
Does it come sufficiently near to Christ, I will not say in the Communion,
but in any way? A personal reference and regard to him, is a part of our
religion. To bring near to us his very life, his very death, and the very
spirit and manner of his living and dying, is a leading feature of the great

discipline of Christianity. Abstractions of truth there had been before; the world wanted a Saviour: systems of truth; the world wanted a life. Doubtless, at first, the danger was that of making too much of Christ as a mere person, and that danger has continued long. But now, in the reaction from those views, the danger is of too much generalizing; of sinking the historical view of Jesus into a vague spiritualizing about him, and of thinking this spirituality all-sufficient. The truth of Jesus is not all that commends him to us; the life of Jesus is more. Not then, when Jesus taught, was spiritual truth first taught; but then was it first lived in perfection. To the living and dying Jesus, therefore, must the disciples of Christianity especially and stedfastly look; and to this view are they emphatically held by the rite of the Communion. It dismisses abstract excellence, and sets before us the model of living and dying virtue. It bids us have done with generalities and follow Christ. Good Christians enough are we perhaps, *in the general;* but do we follow Christ? Many admire him, but few follow him. "Many are called, but few are chosen."

Once more, and finally, I have asked if there are not deeper views of life, which commend to us the meditation and the vow which are implied in the Communion. In nothing does life seem to me to be less understood, than in the depth, the power, the might, the awfulness that belong to it. We think it something trivial, superficial, worldly; but it is not so, and never can be. The wisest of us are apt to be fancy-beguiled in this matter. Look at yonder country cottage, on a green bank; a sheltering wood on one side; on the other a sparkling stream; and around, a small domain of waving grain-fields, and pastures covered with flocks! Does it not seem to you that it is the very bosom of peace and quiet enjoyment? Does it not seem to you as if worldly passion had retired from that peaceful spot, and all within were serenity and happiness? And so you think, perhaps, that you will one day go and live there. But be not deceived. There, even there, is carried on the inward strife of passions, desires, hopes, fears, that fill every human bosom. There, every day, is a spiritual struggle; conscience and pride and sense and, perhaps, tongues of discord are in fearful contention. And what is *there,* is *here,*—is everywhere. Everywhere life embosoms an awful experience. Everywhere it is beset with dread foes. Everywhere a fearful destiny presses upon it. It is a land of probation and of peril through which we walk.

Now, in such a pilgrimage, I deem it good to come, from time to time, to a place—to an altar, which sets before me the consummation of that great work by which God has designed to redeem us from the greatest evils of life—from that which only, in comparison, is evil—from the power of evil passions. I deem it good to come there to meditate and pray. I deem it good to come there, and to vow obedience to my life's leader and

Redeemer. I would come to it, and would say, "O altar, on which my Saviour was slain! upon thee would I swear fidelity; erring, wandering, forgetful, here would I renew the great vow of life; here, in suffering, in sorrow, in death, did Jesus conquer—through meekness, through love, through forgiveness; so let me conquer; I am poor, I am weak, I am unworthy; help me, O thou mighty power of God, according to the promise which thou hast sealed in blood upon this holy altar;—

'Guide me, O thou Great Jehovah!
Pilgrim through this barren land:
I am weak, but thou art mighty;
Hold me with thy powerful hand.
Bread of Heaven! Bread of Heaven!
Feed me till I want no more.' "

 # Regeneration

WILLIAM GREENLEAF ELIOT
(1811–1887)

In our present day the most effective way of calling attention to the significance of William Greenleaf Eliot is to point out that he is the grandfather of T. S. Eliot. A century earlier he stood in his own right as a public figure. To the Civil War generation he was known as the instigator of the Western Sanitary Commission (the Red Cross of that time), the founding spirit and chancellor of Washington University in St. Louis, and one of the great champions of the Union in Missouri. To Unitarians he was the bishop of the West, a founder of the Western Unitarian Conference (1852) and one of the Liberal Faith's most adventurous apostles beyond the Alleghenies.

He was born in New Bedford, Massachusetts, the son of a prosperous merchant with both maternal and paternal ties to many of the Bay Colony's oldest and most distinguished families. His father was ruined financially by Jefferson's embargo, however, and after a brief stay in Baltimore, made his home in Washington, D.C., where he was chief examiner in the auditing office of the Postal Department. William, Jr., received his A.B. from Columbian College (now George Washington University) in that city in 1830; then after a year's employment in the Postal Department, he entered Harvard Divinity School, where his informal reading in German philosophy (especially Fichte) did much to establish him in his faith. Following the example of his dear friend, James Freeman Clarke, then in Louisville, Eliot was ordained in 1834 as an evangelist, whereupon he set out for St. Louis.

Eliot's zeal was richly rewarded in that frontier city of seven thousand turbulent souls. A year after his arrival a Congregational Society was formed; three years after that a new meeting house was dedicated. In 1851 a second edifice, seating twelve hundred people, was built and named the Church of the Messiah. During the antebellum years the church became a center of organized charity and philanthropy. Eliot was especially active in educational reforms, and in 1854, when a group of his parishioners founded Washington Institute (later University), he became president of the board and remained so for the rest of his life. When he resigned his pastorate in 1870, after thirty-six years of service, he became chancellor of the university.

On the great issue of the day, Eliot was a firm but patient gradual emancipationist. Voluntary manumission was the heart of his advocacy, and among his large and influential congregation his success in obtaining it was virtually complete. In 1856, when the Western Unitarian Conference took more radical ground, Eliot withdrew his personal membership.

Eliot was always a moving preacher, and his chief literary remains are collected sermons. "Dearer to me than life itself," he wrote, "is the precious ministry of the Lord Jesus Christ. Most sacred of all commands is his word, 'Feed my sheep.' "[1] Notwithstanding the heady German wine of seminary days and his early support of James Freeman Clarke's avant-garde *Western Messenger,* he became known as a conservative in theology. Christ's life and teachings, with many ethical applications, formed the center of his message, and he attached great significance to baptism and the Lord's Supper. He considered the communion table the center of the religious life of a church.

The sermon reproduced in this selection was part of a series first preached in the Church of the Messiah. It is a faithful presentation of the Christian Unitarian view and utterly consistent with Eliot's other recorded sermons, lectures, and prayers. Its evangelical spirit requires no editor's underlinings; yet the Liberal Faith is clearly expressed. Unitarianism's traditional Arminianism is explicit—and likewise its deep-seated distaste for camp-meeting revivalism. One also sees the influence of Friedrich Schleiermacher and perhaps more immediately of Horace Bushnell's *Christian Nurture.* Eliot notes carefully and approves the gradual liberalization of orthodox interpretations of sin, depravity, and conversion, yet the Unitarian stand is clearly taken.

In view of this comprehensiveness in coverage, as well as the prestige of the author, it was both judicious and natural that the American Unitarian Association should have published this lecture and the others in the series separately as tracts, and then together, as an epitome of Christian doctrine.

JOHN iii. 3, 6:
Jesus answered and said unto him, Verily, verily, I say unto thee, Except a man be born again, he cannot see the kingdom of God. That which is born of the flesh is flesh, and that which is born of the Spirit is spirit.

1. "In the draft of an anniversary sermon prepared for the meeting of the National Unitarian Association in 1870 appears a statement afterwards suppressed in the copy, . . . Dearer to me, etc.," from Charlotte C. Eliot, *William Greenleaf Eliot,* pp. 329–330.

Our subject . . . is the Christian doctrine of Regeneration, or the new birth; the nature of the change implied in those words, the means and agency by which it is produced, and the evidences by which we may judge of its reality. It is a subject whose importance all Christians acknowledge, for whatever views we take of it, as theologians, we must admit that in practical religion every thing depends upon its application. To ask who is regenerate is to ask who is a Christian. To become regenerate is to become a Christian. We may dispute as to what the new birth is, but we cannot dispute the Saviour's words, that "unless a man be born again, he cannot see the kingdom of God." There are some persons who suppose that Unitarians deny this doctrine. But there could not be a greater mistake. It would be the same as denying that a man can become a Christian, or that there is any real difference between good men and bad, between those who serve God and those who serve him not. There are some explanations of the doctrine which we reject, because they are unsound and unscriptural, but we do not reject the doctrine itself.

For example, we do not believe in an instantaneous and miraculous change, by virtue of which he who is at one moment totally depraved can become in the next one of God's saints. But we do believe, that by the blessing of God a radical change may begin at any time, by which the *direction* of a man's life may be changed from that which leads downward to that which leads upward.

We do not believe that this change will always be accompanied, either with the panic of an agonized conscience, or the ecstasies of rejoicing, but that its inward experience will be different in different individuals, according to their various temperament and education, to the degrees of their guilt, and to the influences under which they have been placed. The outward evidences of the change will also differ in an equal degree. I have seen men at a camp-meeting under such strong excitement, that they have been tied, hand and foot, to prevent them from some bodily injury; others pass through an equally strong experience, to whom the kingdom of God comes without observation. We do not deny the reality of the change effected in either case. We must judge of them both, as we judge of the tree, by its fruit. We give our preference indeed to the latter, because observation leads us to distrust all violent excitements. . . . We have greater confidence in the change which comes through the quietness of thought. It may promise less at first, but will accomplish more in the end. It may be accompanied with less of the rapture of religious triumph, but it is more likely to bring us to that peace which passeth all understanding. For such reasons, we do not enter into what are called "revivals of religion," and the protracted meetings by which they are generally excited. Our observation of them has not been favorable to their permanent usefulness.

It is not that we deny the change of heart which is needed in becoming a Christian, nor that we would limit the action of God's spirit in producing it. We may rightly pray to him, "Revive thy work in the midst of the years"; and in the progress of every religious society, as in the experience of every individual, there will be times of awakening, in which the luke-warm becomes zealous, and the cold-hearted and sinful are rebuked. Such seasons of refreshing, when they come from the use of the ordinary Gospel means, are always to be welcomed, and their result is always good. But when they are brought on almost forcibly, by the use of what we may call religious machinery, it is quite a different thing. They are artificial in their origin and unnatural in their result. . . .

Once more: we believe that every real change in the character and in the heart must be begun, continued, and ended in God. It is he "who worketh in us both to will and to do, of his good pleasure." In the Christian course from the very first to the last, we are dependent upon him. As in the natural world, the seed is formed by his creative power, and germinates and grows up and is developed into a plant or tree, through the benign influences of nature, which are only another name for the Divine working, so it is in the human soul that the seed of righteousness is at first planted, and is developed by the sweet influences of God's grace. With this difference, however, which should be carefully remarked, that in the latter case the soul must acknowledge the working of God and feel itself sustained by his presence. In proportion as we feel our dependence on God, we become strong. If we rely upon ourselves alone, we become weak. We are never so much in danger of falling, as when we boast in our hearts that we stand firmly. It is thus that God teaches us, by the practical experience of life, that we depend on him, that we are not sufficient to ourselves.

But while we receive this as the Scriptural doctrine of God's grace, we do not the less insist upon the necessity of our own working. In one sense, we depend for the whole work of our salvation, from the first dawning thought of goodness to the last complete triumph of Christian faith, upon the awakening and saving influences of God's spirit. . . . But on the other hand we too must work; we have no right to expect miracles to be done for us. We have no right to expect that the spirit of God will come to us unsought. God helps those who try to help themselves. He will not save us in spite of ourselves. It is of those who are striving to work out their own salvation with fear and trembling, that the Scripture says, "God worketh in them both to will and to do." To those only who use what they already have, is it promised that more will be given.

Nor can we separate the Divine working from that which we call the natural operation of our own minds, and the natural influences of our daily life. A thought of righteousness comes to the hardened sinner, he scarcely knows how, nor is it important that he should know. It is of God's sending, whether you call it the direct suggestion of his Spirit or not. It is an angel visitant, and if cordially received others will follow in its train, until the heart becomes the temple of the living God, full of his ministering spirits. From that first impulse towards goodness, as he advances, step by step, contending against sin, reaching towards heaven, the Christian can never tell exactly how much depends upon his own exertion, and how much upon a higher power. He knows that when his heart is full of prayer, he progresses most rapidly; but he also knows that a blessing never comes upon his indolence. He finds no encouragement to wait until God does his work, but no sooner does he take hold of it than he feels sure that God is helping him. He thus feels the equal necessity of his own exertions and of the Divine blessing, and is kept in that healthy progress of mind and character, which belongs to the true Christian life. Such we think is the wise ordering of God. In the influences of his Spirit upon the soul we cannot say, "Lo here! or Lo there!" "he cometh down like rain upon the mown grass, as showers that water the earth," and the proof of his coming is found in the fruits of righteousness, in pure and holy thoughts, in heavenly aspirings, and in every Christian grace.

It is supposed by many persons, that the doctrine of Regeneration depends upon what are called the doctrines of Original Sin and Total Depravity. This is a mistake which it is important to remove. We must therefore consider these doctrines for a few moments before going further. In fact, there are few persons who explain them at the present day in the same manner in which they were taught fifty years ago. The Calvinistic doctrine of original sin is, that in the fall of Adam the whole human race were made sinners; that in consequence thereof, sin is *imputed* to every human being at his birth, in such a sense that he is under the wrath of God and is subject to eternal damnation; that his nature, being essentially corrupt, is capable of no good thing, not even to wish or pray for good. Its best actions therefore are hateful in the sight of God, and absolute, total depravity is the necessary result of its development. For a nature such as this, there is but one hope of salvation, which is in the miraculous and irresistible grace of God. The change of heart is therefore, according to this view, an absolute change of nature, it comes not because of a man's own seeking, but irrespectively thereof. Those to whom it comes are thereby God's elect. Those to whom it does not come remain under the sentence of condemnation, from which they cannot by any means escape.

Such is the theory which Calvin taught. But I think very few of his adherents now receive it. It is so much modified, that, even when the same words are used, different ideas are conveyed. By original sin, the majority understand no more than original imperfection; and by the imputation of

Adam's sin, no more than the evil consequences which the child inherits from his parents, in an impaired physical and mental constitution. In this sense, we believe in original sin. We are certainly born imperfect, with many tendencies to evil. These tendencies are also, to some extent, inherited. In this sense, the sins of the father may be said to be visited on the children, as I have known whole families to be born with depraved appetites, which have followed them to their graves. But if, on the one side, there are evil tendencies, there are, on the other, equally strong tendencies to good; amiable dispositions and a natural love of truth and purity. These also come to us in part as our birthright. We do not call them virtue or religion, nor do we say that these alone make us acceptable to God. Nor, on the other hand, do we say that the evil tendencies with which we are born make us hateful to God. In both cases, the natural constitution of our minds, together with all the circumstances of our birth and education, will be taken into account by a just and merciful God, in his final judgment of us. To whom much is given, of him much will be required. To whom little is given, of him little will be required. No one will be condemned because of the sins which his father committed, although he may suffer in consequence of them. "The soul that sinneth, it shall die." Such is the theory of original imperfection, which is sometimes improperly called original sin.

With regard also to total depravity, most persons who profess to believe it mean nothing more than this, that the best actions of a selfish and worldly man partake of his selfishness and worldliness; that until we have learned to deny ourselves and to take the law of God as our supreme law, our most amiable qualities partake of the character of sin. In such a sense, therefore, you may say that the unregenerate man is totally depraved, because there is no part of his conduct or his character which is fully conformed to the Divine law. The pervading principle of his life is wrong, and, in this sense, all is wrong. Change that pervading principle, and you change every thing. It is like infusing healthy blood into the physical frame. It will gradually, but certainly, change every part of the physical and mental constitution.

We shall not follow this train of thought further. What I have said will serve my purpose to show, that, while the doctrines in question continue the same in words, they may be very different in idea.

The truth concerning our nature by birth, and the spiritual condition to which we are brought by regeneration, or the new birth, seems to be this. We are born with a mixed constitution, physical, intellectual, and moral. These, as they originally came from the creative hand of God, were pronounced to be good. The moral nature is the highest, that is the soul, and to this the physical and intellectual, the body and the mind, should minister. But, by the necessity of the case, the physical is developed first, "the first man is of the earth, earthy." Our first wants, our first enjoyments and sufferings, are purely physical. The first exercise of the faculty of thought takes that direction. Self-love, which is needful for self-preservation, is thus early developed. Self-indulgence in what is pleasant, and angry resistance to what is unpleasant, are the natural consequences. All this is not sinful, it is simply of the earth, earthy. It is our physical nature. Gradually the higher nature begins to appear. The sweet affections of the child, pure and truthful, begin to expand. A sense of right, of justice, and of truth, gradually shows itself. At first very weak, but also very correct, for the instincts of childhood upon all moral subjects are sure to be right. In the progress of development, the intellect adds strength either to the physical or moral constitution, according to the natural temperament and the circumstances of education and example.

The period when moral responsibility begins is hard to determine. It certainly does not begin until there is a clear perception of right and wrong, and a choice of one or the other; but whenever it begins, the child is conscious of difficulties. His first exercise, as a moral being, is a struggle, a conflict. There is an enemy to be conquered, a victory to be won. Conscience claims the supremacy; it says, Thou must, or Thou must not; but the body, with its wants and its enjoyments, resists its commands. Reason pleads for the right, passion and appetite for the wrong. It is the struggle of life commenced, the spirit against the flesh, and the flesh against the spirit. The result, if human weakness receives no heavenly aid, is but too evident. The physical, that is to say the powers of the flesh, being first developed, is strong and vigorous, while the moral has but an infant's strength and soon gives way. The passions gain strength by what they feed on; the intellect is brutalized and brought into their service; the conscience is buried under the accumulated rubbish of sin.

Even in Christian lands, and under the influences of Christian education and Christian example, which is a strong divine helping to the principle of right, the great majority of men and women, when they come to the age of mature life, find that the work of moral discipline is still to be accomplished. There is a difference in their degrees of sinfulness; but with nine out of ten, the pervading principle of conduct is self-love, or self-indulgence, or worldly ambition. In nine cases out of ten, therefore, a radical change is needed, before they can properly be called Christians. I call it a radical change, for if you change the principle of life, as I have already said, you change every thing. It is not only an outward change, for the proprieties of life may already be observed. It is chiefly an inward change, which concerns the motives and the affections. In many instances where the outward conduct continues the same, the real change of character is equally great.

I have said, in nine cases out of ten, that such will be the result; perhaps I might have used even stronger language, for there are very few persons who are not under the necessity, sooner or later, of that strong moral exercise, through which, by the blessing of God, the worldly and selfish heart becomes religious. Sometimes it is a violent and short struggle, sometimes a slow and laborious self-discipline; sometimes we can tell the day and the hour when it begins, and sometimes we almost doubt whether it has commenced or not, until it is accomplished. But with nearly all, in some way or other, the change must be accomplished from the earthly to the spiritual, from the worldly to the religious, from the selfish to the self-denying character, after we have come to the years of conscious self-direction.

In a few instances, equally rare and beautiful, the development of our nature is so healthy, that the soul, almost from the first, asserts its rightful supremacy. This is sometimes the result of pure Christian influences, the wise training of parents, the example of good and pious teachers, which may be called the human agency by which the Divine Spirit is working. Sometimes, even when surrounded by the worst influences of sin, in the dens of iniquity, or in the high places of worldliness, the child is seen to grow up with almost stainless purity, through some mysterious guiding of which it is not conscious, but which leads heavenward, as by an angel's hand. In such cases there seems never to be a struggle between the flesh and the spirit. The soul grows up to the heavenly life, almost as the seed grows up to its appointed beauty. Yet I believe that, even in such cases, if we could understand the full working of the soul, we should find here, as elsewhere, what is called the new birth, which is the passing from the earthly or natural state to the spiritual or heavenly. It may take place very early and very gradually, but I think that it is not the less real. The life of the spirit is not that to which we are first born, but the life of the flesh. The second man, and not the first, is the Lord from heaven. When Christ is formed in the soul, it is the redemption of the soul from the natural earthly influence. If it is effected before that influence has brought degradation, the thanksgiving to God may be greater, but it is not less a redemption.

Upon this subject, however, I would not dispute. Such instances are as rare as they are blessed. With by far the greater part of the human family, the experience is very different and far more painful. We find ourselves laden with sins, we scarcely know how. We are walking in a wrong direction, almost before we have thought whither the path leads. Our first serious thoughts of heaven are awakened, by our seeing that our faces are not turned heavenward. It is the restlessness of the soul under the bondage of sin, that arouses us to assert its true dignity. Through some human agency, or through the working of our own mind, God speaks to us, and if we hearken, the conflict begins, the result of which is properly called a deliverance and a victory.

From what has been now said, although in a desultory manner, you will understand my views upon this important topic, the doctrine of Regeneration. By this new birth, we mean a change from the carnal to the spiritual; that is, not an absolute change of nature, which would be the creation of a new soul, but the subjection of the lower principles of our nature, which are of the flesh, to the higher principles, which are of the spirit. It is a change, therefore, in the motives and the affections, that is a change of heart. It is a new direction given both to the inward and outward life, and the whole meaning of life is thereby changed. I do not mean any thing mystical or mysterious by this; in proportion as we become religious persons, we shall understand it.

Secondly: It is a change needed by all. Sooner or later it must be experienced by all, before they can be called the followers of Christ. For we are not born Christians. Innocence, or freedom from actual transgression, is the utmost we can claim, which is a very different thing from moral excellence or righteousness. This must come from the discipline of life, and to accomplish it is precisely the purpose of our being placed in the present state of probation.

Thirdly: The manner and process of this change, of this spiritual development and growth, are very different in different individuals;—as different as men's natural constitutions and the circumstances under which they are placed. To prescribe an invariable rule by which the spiritual experience of all shall be governed, is nothing but religious empiricism, and is the mark of a narrow-minded teacher. It is not necessary that all should walk in the same company and wear the same badge, to be followers of the same Master.

Fourthly: In the formation of our religious character, which is our Regeneration, we are chiefly indebted, as we are in every thing, to the Divine guidance and help. Without God, we are nothing and can do nothing. But we too must work. His working is through our working, nor can we, generally speaking, separate the one from the other. The operation of the Divine Spirit is real and effectual: but as "the wind bloweth where it listeth, and we hear the sound thereof, but cannot tell whence it cometh or whither it goeth, so is every one born of the Spirit."

Finally: The proof of Regeneration is in the life. "Let no man deceive you; he that doeth righteousness is righteous, even as he is righteous."

(1 John iii. 7.) It is not in professions, nor in ecstasies, nor in flaming zeal, much less in the self-righteous condemnation of others; but in a life of genuine goodness, purity, and truth. The evidence of the Christian spirit is in the Christian character. By their fruits shall ye know them. "Pure religion and undefiled before God the Father is this, To visit the fatherless and widows in their affliction, and to keep ourselves unspotted from the world."

The Apostle Paul and the Epistle of Paul to the Romans

ABIEL ABBOT LIVERMORE (1811–1892)

No serious treatment of Christian doctrine can evade the problem of dealing with St. Paul, and Unitarians attempted no evasion. They agreed with St. Augustine and Luther that the Epistles were veriest gospel and that in them were to be found the great truths of justification and sanctification, faith and love, human nature and human destiny. Paul was, indeed, a chief source of inspiration, and far from arguing that he had altered, or worse yet corrupted, the message of the Gospels, they found in him the verification for all their central convictions. That they took a firm stand even on the Epistle to the Romans is very important. It also leads to interesting consequences because they thus deal with the great scriptural foundations of Reformation divinity. In their commentaries, one sees Unitarians coming to grips, verse by verse, with all of the major exegetical problems, revealing as they do so not only their own doctrine but their methods of Biblical interpretation.

Abiel Abbot Livermore was perhaps the most important of the Unitarian commentators on the New Testament, although he was by no means their most intensive Biblical scholar; George Noyes, for example, commanded much attention at the Harvard Divinity School as the Hancock Professor of Biblical Languages and Literature. Livermore, though, is a pulpit voice from the center of the Christian Unitarian tradition, and in his commentaries he gives the clearest expression we have of this point of view as it relates to sustained scriptural interpretation.

His six-volume New Testament commentary, which included revised translations, was published from 1842 to 1881, the volume on Romans coming out in 1854. As the selection reprinted here reveals, he was an admiring follower of Channing and a critic of his Divinity School classmate Theodore Parker. Like Parker, however, he was interested in comparative religion. He delivered the Lowell Lectures on the subject in 1868, and later he introduced such studies at Meadville Theological Seminary in Pennsylvania. In Biblical scholarship he was uninfluenced by the more radical German criticism, following instead the lines laid down at Harvard by Norton and Noyes. Of this position he is one of the finest representatives, and although many technical points of his exegesis have been corrected by subsequent discoveries, his commentary—a lifelong labor of love—can still be read with much profit.

Essay III: The Apostle Paul

St. Paul, though chosen last, is the first in rank of the "glorious company of the Apostles." The Twelve, striving among themselves who should be the greatest, little thought that a native of Tarsus, a city of an insignificant province of Asia Minor, would bear off the palm from the children of the Holy Land. They were appointed to a general office, but he was singled out for a peculiar mission, for which neither the zeal of Peter nor the love of John was adequate. To overstep the limits of Palestine, and carry the Gospel to the vast Gentile world, required a rare combination of gifts, and in Paul that combination was found. The chosen one must be born as it were between Judaism and Gentilism, that he might not be too much tyrannized over by either system. He must be conversant, too, with the old, that he might better measure and appreciate the new. Paul was a Greek by nativity, a Roman by citizenship, and a Jew by religion. Versed in Gentile lore, and taught at the feet of Gamaliel, he was prepared to see, when his eyes were opened, the perfection of the truth as it is in Jesus. With a profound sense of duty inwrought by the Jewish faith, with the culture of a Grecian city, and under the shield of that magic citizenship by which Rome was then opening privileges to the traveller who possessed it over the habitable globe, Paul was furnished in a remarkable manner for his work, by birth, education, and position.

In considering also the "final causes" of the selection of Paul by that Infinite Intelligence, who adapts now an insect to its element of air or water, and now a planet to its orbit, we discern much of fitness and foresight. There is a great work to be done, and a mighty workman is chosen for its execution. The original nature of Paul fitted him to perform a sublime mission. Without question, he is the leading intellect among the sacred writers. He had a too sharply defining imagination for a poet, too logical an understanding for a psalmist, and too impassioned a nature for a philosopher; but he nevertheless combined in himself much of all these characters. His illustrations are often beautiful, his soul is constantly attuned to praise, and by single flashes of thought he compasses results which others attain by long processes of argumentation. Whatever there might be of ruggedness of outline in the forms in which he presented his thoughts, those thoughts themselves burned with an inextinguishable fire of conviction. He was no quoter nor second-hand repeater. Whatever might go into his mind came out personal and Pauline. Wide in his outlook, yet distinct in his aim; indomitable of will, but flexible when that will must bend or break; profound in his thought, but practical in its application; zealous in temperament, yet imbued with a charity that would clasp the world in his embrace; loving controversy, but loving the truth better than victory; highly intellectual, yet always paying allegiance to the supremacy of the moral powers,—the Apostle presented an ample range of contrasts in his genius and character. . . .

The Apostle's life also possessed a remarkable unity. He believed Judaism divine, and he advocated it with his whole soul. And when new light came, and he recognized the higher divinity of the Gospel, he was "not disobedient unto the heavenly vision." His notable conversion, therefore, was a change in direction, not in motive, or zeal, or conscientiousness, or devotion to the service of God. It was like the change of his name, the substitution of one, and that the first, letter for another, changing, but not annihilating, the original sound.

Yet Paul had passed through very different religious experiences from those of the other Apostles, and he derived new power from this source. It has been said, that we cannot fully know the strength of an opponent's argument, unless we have at some time been of his belief. Paul was a Hebrew of the Hebrews. A Jewish doctor could tell him nothing new. He had been a Jew after Christ had lived and died, a Jew in opposition and persecution, and he had tasted the guilt of that passion and the force of that prejudice. Men and women he had hauled to prison and to death. In his inhuman bigotry he "breathed out threatenings and slaughter against the disciples of the Lord," and persecuted them from city to city. The very existence of the Christian Church was endangered by this arch-enemy. But in the height of his career, he is arrested by a voice from heaven; a voice, not of vengeance, but of mild expostulation and warning from the Lord, whose cause he was pursuing with rancor and murder. Every circumstance connected with the conversion of Paul substantiates its miraculous origin. But within the precincts of his own mind, we detect no compulsion or violation of his free agency. The blow by which he was stopped in his course of persecution was sudden, but the process of mind through which he became fully imbued with the Christian faith and charity was progressive. For a season he sits in blindness and prayer, neither eating nor drinking. For three years he dwelt in Arabia and foreign places, and only once during fourteen years visited Jerusalem, the head-quarters of the new faith. Though no one, accordingly, was more active in proclaiming Christianity to the world, or entered so fully into what might be called the missionary cause of that period, no one, again, had a more personal, peculiar, and vivid religious experience. From a persecutor he had been raised to the glorious office of an Apostle; the chief of sinners, he had found mercy. Hence there is a vividness of emotion, an intense yearning of love and gratitude, that can find no words strong enough to do them justice. Jesus had not been known to him personally in his daily walks and familiar conversation and travels, as he had to the other disciples. He had spoken to him from heaven, and communicated in visions. He was, therefore, a more solemn and awe-inspiring being, a more transcendent benefactor, to Paul, than to John who reclined in his bosom, or to Peter who denied him and was pardoned. Paul was very far from regarding or speaking of Jesus as God, but he more constantly calls him Christ and Lord. The events of his own life became the background on which his rescue from the guilt and fate of a persecutor of the Church stood out in strong relief. His own experiences became motives to prompt him to save others. He had measured the depth of that pit out of which he had been drawn, and he spared no toil or suffering to lift up others also from its dark recesses into light and liberty. The line kindles with personal emotion when he speaks of sin and pardon and salvation, and he added to the power of argument the intensity of personal consciousness and conviction.

Then, too, his life subsequently to his conversion furnishes abundant materials to illustrate and vivify his discourse. He had sounded all the depths of the inward life, and he had traversed all the regions and scenes of its objective manifestations. Hence his character was one of no halting or half-way quality. The pendulum of its movement had a wide swing, and it passed through many arcs of a complete circle. What the Apostle said, he said with all his heart, and what he did, he did with all his might. His faculties have totality of action, and when they enter into battle they give their whole momentum to the charge, without fear or misgiving. He could speak like a prophet, because he had lived like a hero. He could write with the enthusiasm of poetry, though without its form, because in his history were the elements of romance. His journeys, his perils, his shipwrecks, his scourgings and stonings, his chains and imprisonments, his joys and his triumphs, all afforded vivid figures of speech, with which his glowing mind clothed itself in the act of composition. He had touched the extreme points of earthly vicissitude, and measured the length and breadth of hope and fear. One day on the point of being adored as a god, he was liable on the next to be killed as a common malefactor. Now the object of the most affectionate confidence, and revered as holding the sceptre of an Apostle's authority, he was exposed by the sudden turn of the wheel of his fortunes to the suspicions of his friends or the malignity of his enemies. Under such circumstances, his words are laden with the unction of the truth for which he lived and suffered. His language becomes action rather than the medium of meditation, and the page seems to heave with the throbbings of a living heart. It thrills and trembles with the exultations and agonies of his powerful emotional nature. "Who," he exclaims, "is offended, and I burn not?" "I glory in my infirmities, that the power of Christ may rest upon me." The writings of Paul, as said by a brother Apostle, "are hard to be understood," but he himself is transparent and intelligible. His weaknesses and his excellences are depicted with all the accuracy of legal testimony.

In analyzing, therefore, the sources of his power, we detect as one of the greatest charms of his writings their vigorous and vital personality. His epistles are an autobiography. They might be called "The Confessions of St. Paul." However abstruse the point of controversy, the face of Paul himself looks out from amidst the arguments. We feel that it is a warm and living hand, fed from a great heart, that is leading us through the labyrinth of free will and foreknowledge. Paul will ever stand within the circle of our human sympathies, for if we cannot in every instance trace the line of his thoughts in their logical sequence, though we never can doubt that that sequence exists to his own mind, we always feel the electric shock of his enthusiasm. His tears and bloody stripes wet the leaf we read, and the resonance of his gratitude echoes and reechoes from side to side. His dangers and sufferings, his joys and triumphs, his glorious self-sacrifice and his poignant self-reproaches, his scathing moral indignation and his sweet and earnest charity, are portrayed on every page as by the colors of the painter, more than the words of the writer. This autobiographical characteristic of his writings may diminish in some measure the perfection of that "dry light" in which a more impersonal writer would look at his subject, but it will ever add an inexpressible charm of the earliest controversies of the Christian Church, that they were incorporated into the living experience and interest of so large and vital a soul as that of the Apostle to the Gentiles. To this quality especially we may attribute much of the interest which attaches to his writings in the churches of the Reformation, because in him more than in any other Apostle is manifested that marked and self-relying independence which constitutes the genius of Protestantism. . . .

As the characteristics of Paul differ from those of his apostolical associates, so has he had a peculiar influence and destiny in Christian history. He may be called the Apostle of the Protestant Church, if John be that of the Oriental and the Greek, and Peter of the Roman Catholic. The Cathedral of St. Paul stands in London, the Protestant metropolis, and St. Peter's is in Rome. The mysticism of John, the zealous but compromising spirit of Peter, and the strongly marked intellectual and controversial qualities of Paul, have unconsciously given a cast and coloring to the great bodies of Christendom. As Christ has not yet become the real head of his own Church, those who stood as it were in the capacity of mediators between him and the world have given, not merely a local name and habitation, but an intrinsic spirit, to the churches of nations and ages. Orientalism delights in the Johannine love, and the mystic union with the divine. The Romish Church has too readily coalesced with the existing faith and ceremonies of its converts, whether in ancient Rome or in modern China, as Peter is accused of doing with regard to Judaism. But the Apostle Paul is essentially a controversialist in the good sense of that term, an evangelical dialectician, a tenacious advocate of the truth, ready at all times to do good battle for its smallest iota, whether in theology or morals. The mystical and the ceremonial sects receive Paul with qualification. The followers of Swedenborg do not regard him as canonical, and the liturgies of Greece, Rome, and England contain scarce a sentence from his glowing utterances of truth and love. But the Protestant chiefs have held Paul in great repute. Luther found in him the doctrine of justification by faith, which he hurled as his most effective missile at the Vatican. Calvin took, as heads to his sermons, hundreds of texts from the Epistles of Paul, but scarcely one from the Gospels, and the confessions of faith of all those churches which hold the Trinitarian dogmas and the doctrines of grace, technically so called, bristle with weapons, offensive and defensive, from the same grand armory.

In order to understand the causes of the somewhat exclusive and despotic influence which the writings of Paul exercise over the majority of the Protestant world, we must take into consideration a variety of facts. Paul's writings are argumentative, and Protestantism, in coming out of the errors of the past and remonstrating against them, necessarily lives and moves and has its being in controversy. Then the vitality of Paul was great; great in his person, great in his mission, and great in history. He has none of the Oriental repose. Paul never could be imagined as the father of monkery. The Protestant and American age, therefore, with all its energy, inventiveness, and restless progress, finds itself mirrored in him as its congenial representative. His vast circumference of intellectual vision, and the strange contrast of his spiritual experiences, that seemed to be almost too many to be comprehended in the life of one man, place him in contact at innumerable points of sympathy with the many-minded soul of Protestantism. He is decided, and perhaps sometimes borders on dogmatism, though he gives sufficient scope to the speculative faculty. And those very qualities which, to our minds, mar him as an image of absolute perfection, make him all the more the Apostle of a peremptory, doctrinal, and yet inquisitive age. His zealous and practical characteristics also, his earnest exhortations and rousing appeals, are much in harmony with modern religious methods, and especially with that great moral crusade in which Christendom is now precipitating itself upon the heathen world. Paul the man of facts and of business, Paul the itinerant preacher, Paul the traveller from city to city and country to country, Paul the writer of epistles to the churches and calls for contributions of charity, Paul the foreign missionary, must excite unusual interest in an age of locomotion, philanthropy, and missions. He has, as we most firmly believe, been marvellously misinterpreted, looked at, so to speak, microscopically rather than telescopically, and of course made to preach doctrines which he never held, and the incipient element of which in the Christian Church it was one of the leading aims of his letters to extinguish. Still, in certain preliminary and inferior stages of the progress of the individual and of mankind, we can easily conceive that Paul, with his highly-colored peculiarities, would exercise a more potent sway than Jesus Christ, with his stainless perfections. Paul was chosen to be the Apostle to the Gentiles, and the Gentiles make up the greater part of the world.

We believe that there is a new age of Christianity to come, when they who have been so long striving, as did the Twelve, who should be the greatest, will return to Him who *is* the greatest, and when the churches of the Fathers shall give way to the churches of the Epistles; and the churches of the Epistles to those of the Gospels; the churches of the Apostles to the Church of Christ. Those who call themselves *evangelical* would be better characterized as *epistolical,* for they draw, as did Luther and Calvin, more largely from the Epistles than from the Sermon on the Mount. The true order is Patristical, Apostolical, Christian. The reform which still remains unaccomplished in theology is to recede from the commentaries of his followers to the text and spirit of the Infallible Teacher.

But if we complain of the errors of interpretation, it devolves upon us to show why and how all was obscure, and how it happens that he who said, "In the Church I had rather speak five words with my understanding that I might teach others also, than ten thousand words in an unknown tongue," should furnish in his own writings the chief debatable region of theological controversy.

In the first place, if Paul was an Apostle of inspiration, he was also a being of impulse. His genius was regulated not by rule, but it swayed and vibrated under a powerful enthusiasm of a healthful description. In rhetoric, he cannot conclude one figure of speech before he enters upon another. He is full of allusions, suggestions, and hints, and is dramatic without marking distinctly the changes of the dialogue. In logic, his power of argument is unquestionable, but a clew is needed to guide us through the labyrinth, where aisles and side passages are constantly diverging from the main corridor. Paul is abrupt, emotional, parenthetical; he makes rapid transitions and obscure intimations, and repeats in one connection what he has said in another. He reasons, allegorizes, narrates, and exhorts, in the same breath, and makes his page, not a homogeneous texture, but a rich mosaic. And like the ancient orators and philosophers, in general, he writes informally and unsystematically; not announcing his subject and its divisions when he begins, nor marking the successive stages of its advancement, nor pausing to recapitulate when he is done. We can conceive a close logical thinker, a severe legal understanding, a profound and far-sighted intellect, taking great pleasure in unravelling the tangled skein of his discourse, and in following the one consecutive thread of his argumentation, until it should be confessed, what we believe to be true, that the last charge that can be sustained against the Apostle is, that he is a loose and illogical writer. If he break the rules of composition, it is to follow the higher laws of his own transcendent intellect.

Then his writings are all epistolary. Judging by his speeches reported in the Acts of the Apostles, his oral discourse was sufficiently intelligible. But a letter is necessarily a blind composition except to the correspondents themselves. It refers to many things known only to the parties concerned, is filled with obscure allusions, and takes many points for granted. It is unexpected in its transitions, informal in its statements, bold in its liberties, familiar and personal in its illustrations, careless in its diction, and loose in its arrangement of topics; a production written on the spur of the moment, rather than by mature study and careful review, and often most successful as a letter when least capable of being classed with any other composition.

In writing to public bodies, as he generally did, Paul escapes some of the infelicities of the epistolary style, and raises his letters more into the rank of set treatises. His subject, too, the wonderful new religion, and his object, the conversion to the Gospel of all mankind, imparted of course a gravity and dignity not common to ordinary correspondence. His salutations are Christian greetings, and his compliments, exhortations to love and good works. He is lyrical, percussive, impassioned, and at times satirical, but all in earnestness and good nature, and all the filaments of the discourse are woven into a complete whole. With the principles he held, and the end he had in view, the letters of Paul are works of artistic beauty, and full of unity and life. They are the flower of his genius, dashed with a heavenly odor, and imbued with a quick contagion to all true souls of like divine sentiments. They burn, they glow, they are warm and heaving with life-blood.

Besides these qualities of an informal style and an impassioned soul, the Epistles have the length, the stress of argument, and the range of thought, essential to works of a larger calibre. For whatever Paul did must bear the stamp of a strong and earnest nature. He was not one to trifle or bandy words with friend or foe, but threw his whole soul into every thought and action. The bright blade of his falchion is always unsheathed. His mind is ever at its full tension. Hence his letters, though written for a transient purpose, bore his spirit like a rushing wind to distant cities, and diffused it throughout humanity. He alludes, in one instance, to the weightiness of his epistles, as not being matched by the authority of his personal presence. But none except himself has disparaged his oral address. His discourses in the Acts of the Apostles are full of beauty and power, and we read of the effects of his eloquence, when, standing as a defenceless prisoner before the proud and titled of the earth, "he reasoned of righteousness, temperance, and judgment to come."

We must remember, likewise, that all was not as clear to the Apostle, though miraculously illuminated, as to those who have lived later, and possessed in Christian history the key of interpretation. We behold the Gospel in its diffusion, he beheld it in its cradle. Though less subjective than the other Apostles, he might be said to be too near the object to see it well. Granted that he was a prophet, yet it is one of the conceded points of his office, that he does not fully comprehend the burden and bearing of his own predictions. Granted that he was inspired, yet inspiration is help, not substitution; a gift of degrees; and it is not of universal infallibility any more than it is of absolute sinlessness, and does not forego individual thought, style, argument, and illustration. Paul again and again announces himself as speaking as a man, as well as from the Lord. He is evidently and professedly his own free agent, as well as the servant of Jesus Christ; the personal pronoun often occurs in his writings, and he utters himself, not with a servile dictation forced upon his mind, but with a truth-seeking aspiration rising from it. He drew the water of life from the fountains of his own being, though those fountains were as the rock in the desert until smitten by a divine rod, and bitter as those of Marah until sweetened by the branch of Christian charity.

In reviewing the actions and writings of historical characters, we are too prone to imagine that they judge themselves from our point of view instead of their own. We attribute to them an anticipation of all that has since befallen them of fame and influence. We do not sufficiently consider, that to them, as to us now, the future spread out a cloudy curtain; or if, as in the case of prophet and apostle, they could discern the faint shadows of events to come, yet their perspective was very imperfect. Time, that brought the fulfillment, must also bring the explanation. There is no reason to suppose that Paul foresaw that his Epistles would constitute more than a third part of the permanent Scriptures of the Christian Church. Many believe, and not without plausible reasons, that he viewed the catastrophe of all things as then impending, and that his own were some of the last zealous words that would be spoken to arouse dormant consciences. Paul gives no intimation of having foreseen Christian Europe and Christian America. Much less, probably, did he suspect that the hurried and impassioned letters which he dictated in the intervals snatched from tent-making, travelling, and preaching, and which bore the form and imperfection of the hour in some respects, would be exalted into permanency and universality, and that one hundred and fifty languages at the end of twenty centuries would repeat his exhortations and arguments to all the tribes of men. He wrote, if we may say so, instinctively, rather than intentionally. As he himself said, "necessity was laid upon him," and a zeal, all absorbing and unselfish, urged him onward. Thus writing for the time, he has doubtless written the best for all times, though, had he foreseen his fortune as an author as well as an Apostle, he would probably have re-edited his letters, to use the modern phrase. But it is well that he did not know the boundless sphere of his influence, for it might have proved a disturbing cause even to his apostolic singleness of heart. It is well that the great do not ever anticipate at the moment the consequences that are to flow from their words and deeds. With all their obscurities, therefore, the Epistles accomplish a greater mission for universal humanity, because they speak so individually to Timothy and Philemon, Romans and Ephesians. The cases of his churches in fact generalized the world. But being "Tracts for the Times," and all the better for that reason, we must not complain that these letters contain some riddles when read in our times. Paul had in his mind, when he wrote, men and women living in a totally different state of society from the present, and the whole warp and woof of whose social and traditional existence were otherwise compounded and colored. It is indeed wonderful that, in this view, while the form and occasion of the Apostle's works were thus peculiar and temporary, their spirit is so central, and their adaptation so comprehensive and eternal.

Another cause of obscurity lies in the controversial character of the Epistles. We have not the statements of the other side, except by implication. We are obliged to read Paul's opponents through Paul. Most of that world of thought and manners which Paul had in his eye, which shaped his arguments, gave complexion to his style, fired his enthusiasm, and aroused his energy, is irrevocably dead and buried, and not even the best trained and most creative moral and historical imagination can raise it again to life. We have glimpses here and there of customs and characters then prevalent, and of the agitating questions of the Church, but they are pale and ghostlike. If the Apostle were hard to be understood in his own day, and his reasonings began so early to be wrested to prove another doctrine than he intended, how significant was that fact of the fortune of subsequent ages, when whole systems of theology would be built upon his authority, that are alien to his spirit!

We are not inclined, again, to make sufficient allowance for the barrenness of language at that period for communicating such truths as Jesus and his Apostles taught. The Hebrew tongue was very limited in its vocabulary, and stiff and circumscribed in its idioms. The Greek, though in some respects the most perfect of languages, had yet sprung from a people rather volatile and witty than spiritually-minded, and more aesthetic than moral. And the Jewish Greek, or Hellenistic dialect, though richer than either Hebrew or Greek alone for the purposes of the sacred writers, was yet too confined and sensuous to give a distinct and luminous outline to that new cast of moral thought, and those higher spiritual conceptions, which it was the mission of Paul to introduce into the Gentile world. Old words must be filled with a new sense. Old idioms must dilate with a grander style of spiritual imagination. Hence we often feel that the writer was obliged to resort to circumlocutions, and multiplicity of terms and sentences, to do himself justice, and that his language sometimes breaks down under the weight of his thoughts. Then the translation into English has still further complicated the difficulties of language. Paul, though rendered in the tongue of Shakespeare and Milton, is obscure, with the best helps of modern criticism. But we can easily imagine, that, if he had originally possessed such a rich and powerful instrument of spiritual expression as the English or German of our day, the demands of so many-sided and profound a soul as that of Paul to defend and embody itself in words would have been more adequately supplied.

From these remarks upon the general obscurity of the Apostle, we would descend to some specific points in which he has been, as we think, greatly misunderstood. Unhappy Paul, crucified in the body in his day, crucified in the spirit in ours! He is constantly made to prove what he never believed, to uphold what he spent himself in overthrowing, and quoted continually as authority for sentiments on which he would have bestowed a hearty *anathema maranatha*. Cant recites, with measured tone and dogmatic purpose, sentences that came glowing in a white heat from his ardent soul. Bigotry is intent upon digging up the flowers which he planted to adorn the garden of God, to find some root of bitterness. Theologians express their ideas in his words, rather than his ideas in their words. The most free from technical or philosophical limitation of any of the writers of the New Testament, unless it be John, recasting the Gospel in his own forms of phraseology, Paul is the last man to be quoted to justify any sort of exclusiveness or uncharitableness in religion, or to tie down all the world to the same formularies of faith, worship, and works. A freely living and a freely moving soul, airing himself in the atmosphere of different countries and continents, conversant with the works of God and the philosophies of men, touching at one point the culture of the intellectual Greek, and at the other that of the believing Hebrew, commissioned to proclaim and estab-

lish in new regions so loving and liberal a system as the Gospel, love from
God, and good-will to men, with his bosom heaving in sympathetic beat-
ings to every pain and wrong of the race, and with his tears flowing like a
fountain whenever ill betided any portion of the Church, Paul is made to
utter a language at variance with every emotion of his heart, and every purpose of his life, when he is interpreted as the teacher of doctrines inconsistent with the fatherly character of God, condemnatory of human nature,
and darkening its destiny here and hereafter. Paul has given us, not a body
of divinity, rigid and narrow, but a soul, and that soul consists in faith,
hope, and charity. With what amazement would he have looked upon the
spectacle of modern textual theology! With what severity would he have
lashed that principle of interpretation that can at one time torture out of
his writings justifications for exclusive creeds and persecuting churches,
and at another, licenses for social inhumanity and public wrong! Would
he recognize, indeed, and own as his writings, those espistles, crumbled up,
almost without regard to connection, into chapters and verses, compacted
sentences divided and subdivided into separate propositions, sometimes mis-
translated, and shaded with the expressions and biases of a dark age of society and theology,—when read, read piecemeal, as if constituting a charm,
not a composition,—and when quoted, quoted in fragments, broken from
their place and connection, to point a sentence or prop up a doctrine, as if
they were independent proverbs, not closely jointed limbs of a living and
inseparable body? There is no part of the Sacred Scriptures so much injured by this mode of treatment as the long sentences and close argumentation of the Apostle Paul. No book but one so potent and vital as the
Bible could survive for any considerable time such a Medean process. As
it is, a new translation can hardly be expected that will secure so generally
the suffrages of the Protestant sects in England and America as the imperfect one of King James's reign. But in the mean time, paragraph Bibles, and
editions with here and there an explanatory note in the margin, like those
of Shakespeare and other English classics, to say nothing of commentaries,
might do something to remove the veil from these glorious works. The
Epistles are a mine still to be worked, and capable of yielding new supplies to the golden currency of truth.

One very important question in regard to these writings is, whether
they really make any essential doctrinal addition to the Christian religion,
or not. They no doubt contribute many new illustrations, applications, and
developments of the truth, but do they impart what is absolutely new, and
what cannot be found in the Gospels and the Acts of the Apostles? On
this subject theologians have differed, but even those who take the negative still concede a species of new revelation to Paul, inasmuch as he
gives more fully than any other the philosophical explanation of the

concluding facts in the life of Jesus, the crucifixion, resurrection, and ascension, and his posthumous influence upon his Church. . . .

We believe, on the other hand, that Paul was not a revealer, but an analyzer, applier, commentator, of the Gospel. He philosophized about its facts and truths, but he did not originate a single essential one. If any distinct principle of Christianity were disclosed in the Epistles alone, we should regard it as a matter of great wonder, if not of questionable authority. We cannot believe, with Bolingbroke, that the Gospel of Christ is one thing; and that the Gospel of Paul, and of all those who have grafted after him on the same stock, is another. But if the *doctrines of grace,* so called, do depend solely or chiefly upon the words of Paul, then we submit that they occupy a secondary, and not a primary, place in Christian theology. That Jesus should be born and sent into the world to bear witness to the truth, and should leave that truth unspoken, and that it should devolve on one who had not been imbued with the spirit of his Master's personal intercourse and instructions, but converted from the ranks of his enemies, to consummate the glorious design, is utterly incredible. We believe the character of God, and of his Son, the need of the Gospel, and all its leading features, its succession to Judaism, and its universality for the race, are all taught in the Gospels and Acts of the Apostles. The miracles, parables, and conversations of our Lord are not distinctly dwelt upon, though they are referred to by Paul, but the primal truths which underlie them are the basis of his every argument and exhortation. If the doctrine of the Trinity, the total depravity of human nature, justification by faith, election, effectual grace, and the final perseverance of the saints, or any other dogma, were actually to be found in Paul, we should regard it as wonderful indeed that our Saviour had not even lisped of it in his Sermon on the Mount, his commission to the Twelve or to the Seventy, his parables, or his farewell discourses and prayers with his disciples. But the proof-texts which are employed to defend the above doctrines are more largely drawn from the Epistles of Paul than from other portions of the Scriptures. The Apostle settled some controversies, but he has originated many more. For the sake of maintaining the value of tradition, the Roman Catholics and the Puseyites contend that the doctrine of the Trinity cannot be upheld on the authority of the New Testament alone. The Fathers must be brought in to complete the structure which the Apostles left unfinished. Were that ground tenable, it is evident that, so far as you thus strengthen tradition, you really weaken the word of God. It is a dangerous concession to make respecting any Christian doctrine, that it is defensible upon some other grounds than those of the Bible. And so we may say of Calvinism, that if it be, as some say, in the Epistles of Paul, but not in the discourses of Christ, so much the worse for Calvinism, to say nothing of Paul. It is pretty conclusive evidence that Christianity and Calvinism are discordant systems. But we hold that there is no such unfortunate clashing of authorities; that the New Testament is a homogeneous book; that all its witnesses yield a harmonious testimony, and that the Gospel is one and the same in essence, though differently cast and colored in passing through finite minds, and that the Christianity of Paul is easily seen to be identical in all its substantials with the Christianity of the Evangelists.

Dr. Channing justly says, in a letter to a friend: "You must show that the passages in the Epistles which are thought to teach other and higher doctrines than Jesus taught are in fact only different forms of the same truth,—and narrower forms, being adaptations of it to a particular age, and very peculiar state of the Church. As long as men think they find in the Epistles great principles not communicated in the Gospels, the latter will pass only for initiatory teaching. Here, I apprehend, is the chief use of Biblical criticism,—not to disclose new truths, but to show that the darker parts of the New Testament, which belong almost wholly to the Epistles, contain the same doctrine with the simple and luminous teaching of Jesus." . . .

Essay IV: The Epistle of Paul to the Romans

. . . It has sometimes been asserted that Paul raised as many questions as he laid, that his writings are the debatable land of theology, and the grand armory of the theological warfare, from which every combatant may pick out the weapon that pleases him best. But it is plain that Christianity came to arouse dormant human nature, and it is but natural that the first exhibitions of its activity should be somewhat irregular. Jesus said, he came to bring, not peace, but a sword. Discussion, argument, controversy, are inseparable concomitants to the progress of truth. We may deprecate justly the angry jars of the conflict, but we cannot help being gratified with the victories of truth, and hailing its champions as among the most illustrious benefactors of mankind. Paul has indeed awakened much controversy, but it has resulted from misinterpretation of his writings, from preconceived theories, and stubborn prejudices, and philosophy, falsely so called, and we cannot but rejoice to see these slowly yielding the field to the mighty prevalence of truth. "The Conflict of Ages" has not been in vain, and the Apostle, though quoted too long on the wrong side of the question, is truly the Achilles of the host. He was the sublime vindicator of spiritual freedom in his day, and he is the legitimate father and forerunner of Luther, who has led the way to civil and religious independence in our age. Paul and Luther have many spiritual features alike, but not less did the mission they came to perform in ages wide apart bear a kindred resemblance.

The single key, in few words, we conceive, which will unlock the Epistles of Paul to the Romans and the Galatians, is not, as has been stated, "justification by faith," as if the great question were, how a man is judged or estimated on the side of God, but "righteousness by faith," faith-righteousness, or how a man really is in his own character, on the side of himself. The Apostle shows conclusively, that neither Grecian wisdom nor Hebrew law could be trusted as adequate to produce this superior, spiritual faith-righteousness; that, in fact, they had both been tried, and found wanting, but that the religion of Jesus was chartered, treasured, and energized with powers adequate to achieve the grand result. It was the wisdom of God, and the power of God unto salvation. . . .

❧ The Christian Church

JAMES FREEMAN CLARKE (1810–1888)

James Freeman Clarke reached as large a general American audience on topics of religion and theology as any Unitarian of his generation. A grandson of James Freeman of King's Chapel, a graduate of Harvard College (1829) and Divinity School (1833), he was well fitted to become an illustrious apostle of the Liberal Faith. The first seven years of his ministry were spent at the Church of the Messiah in Louisville, which he helped found. While there he edited the *Western Messenger,* wherein he expressed his enthusiasm for romantic conceptions of religion and published for the first time some of Emerson's early poems.

Upon returning to Boston in 1841, Clarke indicated his growing concern for Church reform by founding the Church of the Disciples along principles that marked, perhaps, a more revolutionary step than Boston Congregationalism had seen since the founding of the Brattle Street Church in 1699. Pews were not sold in the established manner, but seats were free and members contributed on a voluntary principle. Members were also involved more than usual in the congregation's work and worship.

Clarke was active in Unitarian affairs and a prodigious writer and translator in many fields of literature, history, religion, and philosophy. His work as an apostle of German culture is of lasting significance, but his greatest contribution to American religious thought is, no doubt, his two-volume *Ten Great Religions.* In it the new and increasingly important science of comparative religion was intelligently and successfully popularized, and the work went through many editions. Within his own denomination Clarke was a great mediator whose basic conservatism did not preclude sympathy for and understanding of the Transcendental movement. He was a charter member of the Transcendental Club, yet in 1866 his eloquence was instrumental in maintaining an explicitly Christian avowal in the preamble to the National Unitarian Conference.

Ecclesiology—that branch of theology concerned with the nature and role of the Church—was never prominent in the writings of Unitarians. Quantitatively they spoke more on most of the other major topics represented in the present anthology. In this they were typical of American liberal theology, which maintained comparative quiet on these matters well into the twentieth century despite the fact that the Church question was a much agitated one among Anglicans, Lutherans, and the German Reformed.

New England Church leaders of the past had been enormously concerned with problems of polity and the ministry. The very names "Congregational," "Presbyterian," and "Episcopalian" reflect these highly divisive issues; even in the mid-eighteenth century two of the four Harvard Dudleian Lectures had been devoted to these questions. But in the Unitarian tradition ecclesiology was reduced to a secondary status. Men simply did not dispute about polity, the ministry, or the nature of the Church.

William R. Hutchison in his extremely valuable *The Transcendentalist Ministers* has shown that the Transcendental movement contained an important current of Church reformism. This development had only the most limited impact on Christian Unitarians, though it did force them to define their position more explicitly. One could find many Unitarian writings, to be sure, that take firm and tradition-oriented positions on these issues, especially the earlier Unitarian writings of men like H. H. Hepworth, Samuel Osgood, or F. D. Huntington, who later entered the Congregational or Episcopal ministry. But these would not be typical. The central Unitarian tradition is best represented by Clarke's exposition, which follows, and by the selections on baptism (Leonard J. Livermore) and communion (Orville Dewey), as well as by the unclassifiable address of Henry W. Bellows. Clarke voiced the irenic and inclusive spirit of Unitarian thinking on the Church and many other issues in the oft-reprinted work from which the present selection is taken. It was a volume in which he showed his profound respect for the entire history of the Church without muting the particular emphasis of Unitarianism.

One of the most interesting questions of the present time, in practical theology, concerns the nature, authority, organization, functions, and future of the Christian Church. . . . The question is, Is a Christian Church needed for the permanent wants of man? Was such a Church established by Christ? If so, which Church is it? And what is to be its future character and mode of organization.

It is scarcely necessary to discuss here the abstract question—Is a church an essential want of man, so as to be needed by him forever. It is enough to show that a church is needed now, and will be, for a long time to come. . . . Without asking, therefore, for any other authority for the Church, than its adaptation to human wants, we may safely say, that it is a great mistake to suppose we can dispense with churches. . . . No; the Church is not to be destroyed; it is to be renewed with a deeper and fuller life. . . We want an apostolic Church, fitted to needs of the nineteenth century. The theological preaching which satisfied our parents is not what we wish now. We need Christianity applied to life—the life of the individual and of the state. . . .

The Roman Catholics [have] made the visible Church, or outward Christian community, the central idea of Christianity, and having changed this into a close corporation of priests, it was natural, perhaps, that Protestants should go too far in another direction. Accordingly, the central idea in Protestantism is not the Church, but the salvation of the soul; not social, but personal religion; not the kingdom of heaven, but heaven in a future life. Yet it is true, and has been shown lately with great power, that the direct and immediate object of Jesus was to establish a community of believers. This was implied in his being the Christ,—for the Christ was to be the head of the kingdom of heaven,—and the kingdom of heaven was to be an earthly and human institution. Jesus took the idea of the kingdom of God, as it was announced by the prophets; purified, developed, deepened, and widened it; and it resulted in his varied descriptions of the "kingdom of heaven." This phrase, in the mouth of Jesus, expresses essentially what we mean by "the Church."

This will appear more plainly if we sum up the principal meanings of the phrase "kingdom of God" in the New Testament. It is,—
1. Something near at hand (Mark 1:15; Luke 9:27; Mark 9:1).
2. It was already beginning (Luke 17:20).
3. It was not of this world (John 18:36).
4. But was to be in this world (Matt. 6:10).
5. In some respects it was to be an outward and visible kingdom, or an outward institution (Parable of the mustard seed. Matt. 13:31, 32).
6. It would contain good and bad (Parable of the net. Matt. 13:47).
7. It would belong to Christ (Col. 1:13; Luke 22:30; John 18:36; Matt. 16:28).
8. It would be finally given up to God (I Cor. 15:24).
9. It is a spiritual kingdom (Rom. 14:17).
10. Flesh and blood cannot inherit it (I Cor. 15:50).
11. The conditions of admission are spiritual (John 3:3, Matt. 5:3; I Cor. 6:9; Gal. 5:21; Eph. 5:5).
12. The kingdom was to be established by the Son of man at his coming (Matt. 24:30; Matt. 25:1).

Christ, therefore, had in his mind, as the direct object of his coming, to cause God's kingdom to come, and his will to be done on earth as in heaven. It was not his direct purpose to teach the truth in abstract forms, like the philosophers, nor to make atonement by his death for human sins; nor to set an example of a holy life; nor to make a revelation of God and immortality; nor to communicate new life to the world. These he did; but they came as a part of the kingdom of heaven. They were included in his great idea. His kingdom was a kingdom of *truth,* in which his *word* was to be the judge. He was to reconcile the world to God by his death. He was to show what man was made to be and could become. He was to reveal God as a father to his human children. He was to set in motion a tide of new spiritual life. But the METHOD by which all this was to be done was the method of a community of disciples and brethren, who should be his apostles and missionaries. They were to be an outward, visible association with the symbols of baptism and the supper. They were also to be an influence in the world, a current of religious life. We find that such was the result. We see the disciples embodied and united in a visible community, which spread through all the Roman empire, which soon had its teachers, officers, its meetings, its worship, its sacred books, its sacred days. But we find also the larger and deeper current of life, which constitutes the invisible Church, flowing, like a great river, down through the centuries. All Christians in all Christian lands drink from this stream, and all their ideas of God, man, duty, immortality, are colored and tinged by it. We read the Bible by the light of the convictions we absorbed at our mother's knee in our infancy. We carry on our churches in the power of the holy traditions which have become a part of our nature. There is a Christian consciousness which grows up in every child who is born in Christendom, and is the best part of his nature. This makes him a member of the invisible Church before he outwardly becomes a member of the visible Christian community.

There are two parables of Christ which apply to the Church visible and invisible. The Church Visible is the Church of the Mustard-seed; the Church Invisible is the Church of the Leaven. The former is an organization, the latter an *influence;* the one is body, and the other spirit. The Visible Church is limited by certain boundaries; defined by its worship, creeds, officers, assemblies, forms. It has its holy days, holy places, holy men, holy books. But the Invisible Church is not limited by any such boundaries; it exists wherever goodness exists. . . .

Get out your catechism, my Orthodox friend; establish, dear Methodist brother, your experience to determine whether one is converted or no. Settle for yourself, excellent formalist, the signs of the true Church, out of which there is no salvation; and when you have got all your fences arranged, and your gates built to your satisfaction, you are obliged to throw them all down with your own hands, to let *the Church of the Leaven* pass through. . . . Here are the three fences of the Church of the Mustard-seed. But see! Here comes an innumerable multitude of little children, who have never believed in Trinity or Atonement; have never been baptized at all; have never been converted. Yet neither Dogmatist, Sentimentalist, nor Formalist dares to exclude them from heaven. Logic steps aside; good feeling opens the three gates; and the little ones all walk quietly to the good Shepherd, who says, "Let them come to me, and forbid them not;" gathering the lambs in his arms, carrying them in his bosom, and tenderly leading them in the green pastures beside the still waters. . . .

The Church of the Mustard-seed . . . is not the spirit, but the body; not the life, but the organization of that life. There is no doubt that we need a Church visible as well as a Church invisible; need a body as well as a soul; and it is a very important question what sort of a body we shall have. . . . [To this end we may consider the Church visible from four points of view:]
  1. The Primitive Church, or Church as it was.
  2. The Church Actual, or Church as it is.
  3. The Ideal Church, or Church as it ought to be.
  4. The Possible Church, or church as it can be.

If we study the nature, organization, and character of the primitive Christian Church, as it appears in the book of Acts and in the Epistles, we recognize easily the warm, loving life which was in its spring time, when all buds were swelling, and all flowers opening. It was far from being a perfect Church. It had many errors, and included many vices. Some persons in the Church did not believe in the resurrection of the dead. (I Cor. 15:12) Some disciples had not heard there was a Holy Ghost. (Acts 19:2) Some even became intoxicated at the Lord's Supper. (I Cor. 11:21) Some Christians had to be told not to steal (Eph. 4:28); nor to lie, (Col. 3:9); nor to commit other immoralities. Peter (supposed to be the infallible head of the Church) was rebuked by Paul for dissimulation. Paul and Barnabas could not get along together, but quarrelled, and had to separate. Part of the Church Judaized, and denounced Paul as a false prophet. Another part Paganized, and carried Pauline liberty into license. And yet, though there was so little of completed Christian character, there was a great amount of spiritual life in the apostolic Church. . . . They were full of faith, zeal, enthusiasm, and inspiration; so they had in themselves the promise and expectation of saintship, if not its reality.

Directly after the ascension of Christ, and the wonderful experiences of the day of Pentecost, we find the Christian community in active operation. Its organization was as yet very indefinite; that was to come by degrees.

It was a Church without a creed; its only creed was a declaration of faith in Jesus as the Christ, the Son of God. It was a Church without a bishop, or a single head of any kind; for Peter, James, and John seem all three to have possessed an equal influence in it, and that influence was derived from their character. . . . No mention is made anywhere in the book of Acts of a single bishop presiding over the Church at Jerusalem, or over any other Church. And as to the Roman Church, which claims to be the oldest Church, and the mother of all the rest, it was not yet founded at all, when the Church at Jerusalem was established. Nor was the Church at Rome as old as the Church at Antioch, at Lystra, at Iconium, and elsewhere, for Paul and Barnabas ordained elders in all these churches, as we are expressly told in Acts 14th; and in Acts 15:7 we find Peter still at Jerusalem. If there was any church at Rome, Peter was not its bishop; then either it was a church without a bishop, or Peter was not its first bishop.

We find also that as the apostolic Church had no creed and no bishop, neither had it any fixed or settled forms. Its forms and usages grew up naturally, according as convenience required. . . . That they had no form of service, no fixed liturgy, in the apostolic Church appears from I Cor. 14:26. . . . But though the apostolic Church had neither bishop, nor creed, nor fixed forms, nor fixed body of officers, it had something better— it had faith in God, and mutual love. . . . The apostolic Church was a home of peace and joy. Whatever tribulations they might have in the world, when they met together, they met Christ, and ate their meat with gladness and singleness of heart. They were in an atmosphere of love and freedom. We hear of no rules, no laws, no constraining forms; but all were led by the Spirit of God. Even in their public service, as we have seen, though Paul recommended a greater order, it was not based on authority, but on the sense of propriety of each individual, because God was not the God of confusion, but of peace.

Such was the original Church, as described in the Acts and Epistles. It sprang up because it was wanted, and Christ foresaw that it would be. It was founded not on an arbitrary command, but on the needs of human nature. Man is not a solitary, but a social being. He needs society in his labors and in his joys; society in study, society in relaxation. Even in the highest act of his life,—in the act of prayer, in communion with God— . . . even then he cannot be alone. . . . Thus we see that the apostolic Church was a home for Christ's family (Matt. 12:49); a school for his disciples; a fraternity of brethren. For discipline, it had officers, but no clergy, nor priesthood, for all were priests, and all took part in the services. . . . The unity of the Church was not the unity of opinion, nor the unity of ceremonies, but the bond of the Spirit (Eph. 4:3), and the central unities of faith, not of doctrine (Eph. 4:5.) The object of Church service was not merely to partake the Lord's Supper together, nor to maintain public worship, nor to defend and propagate a creed, nor to call men into an outward organization, nor to gather pious people together, and keep them safe as in an ark, but to *do good* and *get good*—to grow up in all things into Him who is the Head. And the condition of membership was to wish to be saved from sin, and to have faith in Christ that he could save them; it was to hunger and thirst after righteousness.

Now, if we turn from the Church as it was to the Church as it is . . . we see a difference. Instead of the freedom and union which were in the early Church, we find in the Roman Catholic communion union, but no freedom; in the Protestant Churches freedom, but no union. In both we find the Church built on the ministry, instead of the ministry on the Church; the priests everything, the people nothing; fixed forms, instead of a free movement; dead creeds, instead of a living faith. The spirit of worldliness has entered the churches, and they try to serve God and Mammon; God on Sunday, and Mammon on the week days. The members of the churches are more devout and more religious, but not more moral or more humane, than many who are out of their body. And because they do not love man whom they have seen, they find it hard to love God, whom they have not seen. Their want of humanity destroys their piety.

A vast amount of good is done by the churches, even in their present state; but when we think of what they might do, it seems nothing. Yet it is *not* nothing. . . . Could we see as God sees and the angels see . . . we should feel that the churches, in their greatest feebleness, are yet the instruments of the incalculable good. But when we look at what *is* to be done, what *ought* to be done, what *could* be done by them, their present state seems most forlorn. . . .

The Church Ideal is full of life, power, love, freedom. It is a teaching Church; calling men out of darkness into marvellous light, throwing light on all the mysteries of human existence. It takes the little child and teaches it concerning its duty and destiny. It organizes schools through every Christian nation, so that all Christian children shall be taught of God, and that great shall be their peace. It teaches systematically and thoroughly all classes of society; so that all, from least to the greatest, know the Lord. It organizes missions to all heathen lands, and its missionaries are so true, noble, kind, so reflect the life of Jesus in their own, that the heathen come flying like clouds, and like flocks of doves to the windows of the holy home. . . . Enter its gates, and you find yourself in an atmosphere of affection. The strong bear the infirmities of the weak. Each seeks the lowest place for himself. They love to wash the disciples' feet. . . .

But where is the Ideal Church? We have seen it is not in the past, where many look for it. The Ideal Church is before us, not behind us; it is to come. . . .

Is any Church possible but the Actual? We think there is. We think that a Church may be something more and better than any we have now. Without reaching the ideal standard we can yet do something.

We think it is possible for the Church to be united on a basis of study and action rather than on that of attainment. Instead of having it consist of those who have formed opinions, let it consist of those who wish to form them. Instead of having it consist of those who have been converted, and who believe themselves pious, let it consist of those who wish to be converted, and who desire to be pious. . . .

We think it possible to have a Church, and even a denomination, organized, not on a creed, but on a purpose of working together. Suppose that the condition of membership was the desire and intention of getting good and doing good. The members of a church are not those who unite in order to partake the Lord's Supper, but to do the Lord's work. The Lord's Supper is their refreshment after working. They come together sometimes to remember his love, and to get strength from him. . . .

We therefore think it possible for a Church to be built on Christ himself, not on a minister. The Church might even do without a sermon; the members might pray together and sing together, when they had no minister, and be a true family of Christian men and women, brothers and sisters in the Lord. The lowest view of a Christian Church is that which makes it a body of pew-holders; the next lowest, that which makes them an audience met to hear a sermon; the next lowest, a mere congregation or assembly of worshippers; a little higher is that of a body of communicants, bound together by a desire of knowing Christ; but highest of all is that which regards a Church as the body of Christ. Such a Church is to learn of him, and to do his will; it is his eyes, to look on all things with a Christian vision; his hands, by which we shall still touch and heal the wretched; his feet, to go through the world, to search out its evils and sins; his mouth, through which he shall speak words of divinest help and encouragement. "The body of Christ, and members one of another." The body of Christ; always active, always progressing, always advancing; advancing into a deeper and better knowledge of his will, into a purer love of his kingdom, into a further and divine life of union with him; the body fitly joined together, and compacted by that which every joint supplieth, making increase of the body to the building of itself up in love.

It is possible to have a Church which shall be ready to teach and preach the gospel, not to a few pew-holders only, but to the whole community. . . . It would seem to be possible, since we have free schools, to have also free Churches, and so really to have, what we profess to maintain, *Public Worship!* There is no such thing now as public worship. The churches are not public places—each belongs to a private corporation of pew-holders.

It is possible to have a Church which shall consider it its duty to obey its Master's first command, and "preach the gospel to every creature." Its mission shall be to go out into the highways and the hedges, to seek and save the lost. It will regard the world as its field, and the whole community as its sphere of labor—the whole community, according to its needs, to be taught, helped, comforted, and cured by the gospel.

It is possible to have a Church which shall be united, not on ceremonies, nor on a creed, but on study and labor, on loving and doing. The condition of admission should be the purpose to get good and do good. They should enter this school to learn, and not because they were already learned; to become good, and not because they were already so.

It is possible to have a Church which shall make it its purpose to educate the whole man—spirit, soul, and body; and not merely the spirit; to present the human being to God perfect and entire, wanting nothing.

It is possible to have a Church which shall combine union and freedom. . . . Union without freedom is not union; freedom without union, not freedom. There is no harmony in the juxtaposition of similar notes, but in the concord of dissimilar ones. Difference without discord, variety in harmony, the unity of the spirit with diversity of the letter, difference of operation, but the same Lord, many members, but one body,—this is very desirable, and wholly possible.

The day is coming in which our dogmatic Churches, formal churches, sentimentally pious Churches, and professedly liberal Churches, shall be all taken up into something higher and better. The very discontent which prevails everywhere announces it. It is the working of the leaven—mind agitating the mass. In Protestant countries there is a tendency to Rome; but in Roman Catholic countries an equal or greater tendency to Protestantism. Orthodoxy tends to Liberal Christianity. Liberal Christianity tends to Orthodoxy. Each longs for its opposite, its supplement, its counterpart. It is a movement towards a larger liberty and a deeper life.

❧ The Day of Judgment

JAMES WALKER (1794–1874)

Roland Bainton once wrote that the great established churches, perhaps precisely because they were established, have been less disposed to look for the end of the world. In short, chiliasm has always tended to find more favor among the disinherited. This observation may help to explain why New England Congregationalism revealed a decreasingly radical concern for last things and why Unitarians tended to have even more moderate views on these subjects. Both groups were until 1833 formally established, in Massachusetts at least. The Unitarians, furthermore, enjoyed a sound and stable social establishment long after constitutional revisions had been ratified. They were certainly not among the disinherited! Given so many outward manifestations of economic and social felicity and inducements to optimism in the areas and among the peoples of Unitarian tendency, it is perhaps only natural that an enthusiastic acceptance of the idea of progress should provide the basic structure for eschatology. Traditional views of divine judgment were correspondingly modified but were by no means rejected.

James Walker's interpretation of "The Day of Judgment" accurately expresses the Christian Unitarian view. So great was Walker's prestige, moreover, that even if he had deviated from the central tendency in this sermon, he would certainly have carried many leaders of the denomination with him. After the death of Channing he was very nearly the spiritual leader of Unitarianism. Born in Burlington, Massachusetts, he had been graduated from Harvard College in 1814 and the Divinity School in 1817. For the next two decades he served the new Harvard Church in Charlestown, whose socially prominent membership had withdrawn from Jedidiah Morse's First Church in 1815. Here he distinguished himself as a preacher, scholar, and controversialist, serving also as an editor of the *Christian Examiner* during the strife-filled years from 1831 to 1839. In the latter year he was rewarded by a call to be Alford Professor of Natural Religion, Moral Philosophy, and Civil Polity at Harvard. In 1853 his further attainments won him the presidency of the university, in which capacity he served until his voluntary retirement in 1860. He delivered an extremely well-received series of Lowell Lectures shortly thereafter on the subject of natural religion, but his reputation scarcely survived his death in 1874.

Walker suffered the fate of a moderate in times of religious extremism, and consequently he was cherished neither by the Transcendentalists nor by the conservatives. He was indubitably touched by the new currents of thought and scholarship that transformed New England theology during his lifetime. For example, though one of the founders of the American Unitarian Association in 1825, he was also a member for a time of the Transcendental Club. He was convinced, however, that the proper corrective for the deficiencies of Lockean sensationalism and its theological corollaries was to be found not in German romanticism but in the Scottish philosophy. He indicated his solution for the agitated theological problems of his day by editing two volumes of the writings of Thomas Reid and Dugald Stewart. Faced with the facile demands for moral self-reformation being uttered by many in his day, he insisted in 1855 that the Christian life was not a development of human nature, but something superinduced upon it, and wholly the work of grace. With such views it is only to be expected that his words on "The Day of Judgment" should reflect the affirmation contained in the fourth article of the creed he submitted to the Charlestown church before his ordination: "I believe in the divine institution of the visible Church, in the resurrection of the dead, man's future accountability, and life everlasting."

REVELATION XX. 12:
And I saw the dead, small and great, stand before God: and the books were opened: and another book was opened, which is the book of life: and the dead were judged out of those things which were written in the books, according to their works.

It belongs to man, in which he would seem to differ essentially from the inferior animals, to make himself and his own thoughts an object of thought; not only to know what he is doing, but to be able to review his conduct and compare it with an ideal standard of expediency and right; in one word, to call himself to account. Not only is he able to do this, but through his intellectual and moral constitution it is forced on him as a practical necessity. In every human mind, according to its measure of activity and self-consciousness, this process of self-judgment is continually going on; and no small part of our happiness and misery on earth is traceable to it,—that is to say, to the pleasures of self-approbation, and the pains of remorse. There is, therefore, an important sense in which the whole of human life is one continued Day of Judgment.

Moreover, the self-judgment here referred to is understood and felt to be of an authority and sanction higher than that of man. We cannot shake off the conviction that there is a divine, as well as a human, element in

conscience. The opinion which we form as to what is right in any particular instance, is a mere human opinion. It may be true, and it may be false;
one thing to-day, and another thing to-morrow. But the sense of obligation under which we are all laid to judge ourselves by some acknowledged
standard of right, and to bring ourselves into conformity to it as we best
can, is not human. It does not depend on our own will. It is the decree of
our nature; and our nature is the decree of God. It is the voice of God
speaking to us through the human faculties, ordained by him for that
purpose. Who can believe that God has so made us, that we cannot help
judging ourselves by the law of right, without believing, at the same time,
that he intended us to be judged, and rewarded or punished according to
that law?

On looking round, however, we see that this law is very far from being
universally applied, or fully carried out *in the present life.* Nothing is
easier than to say, that virtue is its own reward, and vice its own punishment. So perhaps it would be, if the natural and legitimate tendencies of
virtue and vice were never obstructed, or turned aside; but, as things go
in this world, we know that in point of fact they are obstructed and
turned aside in a thousand ways; and the consequence is, that in cases
without number the wicked prosper, and the righteous are trodden down.
Let no one think to shake this conclusion by insisting that the tendencies
of virtue and vice, referred to above, are natural and eternal, whilst the
obstacles to their becoming effect in this world are accidental and temporary. It is enough for the argument to know, that the obstacles in question, whether accidental and temporary or not, will last as long as this life
lasts. Thus much being conceded, it follows incontestably, that, if there
is ever to be a perfectly righteous retribution, we must look for it beyond
the grave. Clement of Rome has handed down a tradition in the Church,
that the Apostle Peter was so much impressed by this view of the subject
as to be in the habit of exclaiming, "God is just; therefore, the soul is immortal."

By such natural intimations as these, almost every people, with or
without the aid of revelation, have been led to entertain, with more or
less distinctness and confidence, the presentiment of "a judgment to
come." Even in Homer there are unmistakable traces of a popular belief
in a future state of existence, where the fate of the individual is made to
turn, more or less, on his previous character, and especially on his conduct towards the gods. The same is also laid down as a practical doctrine
of great moment by the best among the pagan philosophers and moralists;
and sometimes, as in the apologue of Erus the Pamphylian, given in
Plato's Republic, in language bearing a striking resemblance to that used
four hundred years afterwards in the New Testament. A brave man, hav-

ing fallen in battle, was permitted to return to the earth on the twelfth day, in order to warn the living by a revelation of what he had seen. He had seen the dead arraigned, and when the judges, to borrow the words of the apologue, "gave judgment, they commanded the just to go on the right hand, and upwards through the heaven, having fitted marks on the front of those that had been judged; but the unjust they commanded to the left, and downwards, and these likewise had behind them marks of all that they had done."

There are those, I am aware, who make no account of pagan notions of a future retribution, on the ground that they neither amounted to a proper faith, nor had the influence of a proper faith. We are told, for example, that Cicero, though he insists on the doctrine in his philosophical writings, takes occasion in more than one instance to deride or disown it in private correspondence with his friends. The argument, however, is not of much weight; for, in the first place, what Cicero derides and disowns is often, not the fact of a future retribution, but the popular superstitions respecting it; in the second place, even if his misgivings occasionally go deeper, is it without precedent that very good and pious men should be subject at times to moods, during which they can hardly be said to believe in anything? and, lastly, the individual selected as a representative may be objected to, for it has never been understood that Cicero was a very good, and much less a very pious or religious man, even for the age in which he lived. If, then, a still broader ground should be taken, if it should be contended that the life of pagans cannot be reconciled with a sincere belief in a righteous retribution, I freely admit the difficulty: but it is a difficulty which does not end with the pagans. I ask you to reconcile, if you can, the actual life of Christendom itself with the general acceptance of that doctrine. Probably the solution of the difficulty is the same in both cases. As a general rule, men do not act out their opinions, their theories, their real convictions, certainly not with much strictness, whatever they may be: they act out their passions, propensities, and habits; and these again depend, in no small measure, on organization, and on the customs and institutions of society, that is to say, on physical and local causes, many of which it is impossible either to trace or explain.

From the pagans we pass to the Jews, among whom Christianity arose. Moses, their great Lawgiver, aimed to establish what is called a theocracy, that is a government of God *upon earth,* in which perfect righteousness was to be fulfilled. Of course, in such a state of things, as they had a *present* Divine judgment, there was the less occasion to appeal to a *future* Divine judgment. Nevertheless, I cannot help thinking that those who go so far as to deny a distinct recognition of another world in the Old Testament, and even in the earlier parts of it, must find extreme difficulty in explaining certain passages, especially such traditions as those respecting the translation of Enoch and Elijah. Be this, however, as it may, there can be no doubt that in the time of our Lord the great body of the Jewish people had become believers in the doctrine of a future state of rewards and punishments. In the apocryphal "Book of Wisdom," supposed to have been written about a century before Christ, we find a passage on this subject which might have come from an apostle: "But the souls of the righteous are in the hand of God, and there shall no torment touch them. In the sight of the unwise they seem to die; and their departure is taken for misery, and their going from us to be utter destruction; but they are in peace. For though they be punished in the sight of men, yet is their hope full of immortality; and having been a little chastised, they shall be greatly rewarded: for God proved them, and found them worthy of himself."

Accordingly, the doctrine of a future state of retribution cannot be accounted a Christian doctrine in the sense of being first taught in Christianity. How, then, it may be asked, are we to understand that passage in St. Paul's Second Epistle to Timothy, in which he speaks of "the appearing of our Saviour Jesus Christ, who hath abolished death, and hath brought life and immortality to light through the Gospel"? I answer, that to bring a subject "to light" does not necessarily mean to make it known for the first time, but to make it more generally and fully known,—to illustrate it, to clear it up, to set it in its true light, so that all may see it as it is. And this is precisely what Christianity has done for "life and immortality." It has given us new evidence of the facts in the case; it has enabled us to see these facts in new lights, and under new aspects and relations: so that the whole doctrine, in itself considered, has become substantially a new doctrine.

This being the case, it remains for me to speak of what may properly be considered as *peculiar* and *original* in the Christian doctrine of the judgment to come.

In the first place, I attach but little, if any, importance to the distinction insisted on by Bishop Butler. According to him, "all which can positively be asserted to be matter of mere revelation, with regard to the future judgment, seems to be, that the great distinction between the righteous and the wicked shall be made at the end of this world; that each shall *then* receive according to his deserts." On the contrary, the whole doctrine of a *day* of judgment—of a single day or a set time for all mankind—seems to me to have originated in the mistake of construing passages literally which were intended to be understood figuratively. If we insist on construing these passages literally, consistency would seem to require us to go further still. We must believe not merely in a day, but also in a place,—nay, more, in real books, in a real consultation of records; in short, in all the paraphernalia of a human tribunal. Let me not be suspected of objecting to or undervaluing those representations of Scripture which bring up the vision of all mankind standing before the judgment-seat of Christ, "that every one may receive that things done in his body, according to that he hath done, whether it be good or bad." In no other way would it be possible sufficiently to impress the imagination and the feelings with that greatest and most solemn of realities,—namely, that you and I, and every one that lives, will have to answer in the spirit for what is done in the body. It is only necessary, that, in our sober thinking, we should not confound the truth which is conveyed under the images in question with the images themselves.

On the whole, the most natural and Christian view would seem to be, that, with every individual, as soon as this life ends the next life begins. Else how could our Saviour say to the penitent thief on the cross, "To-day shalt thou be with me in paradise"? or Paul, of Christians generally, "We are confident, I say, and willing rather to be absent from the body, and to be present with the Lord"? or Stephen exclaim in the agonies of death, "Lord Jesus! receive my spirit"? Without pretending, therefore, to be wise above what is written, I think we may safely hold, that the day of judgment to every individual will be the day of his death. It will *begin then;* by what processes and instrumentalities it will be carried on, and how or when it will end, are among the secret things which belong to the Lord our God. If you wish to be told the details of what is to be in the life to come, you must not go to the Gospel; you must go to the Koran, which is full of it. As regards everything pertaining to the form and manner—or, so to speak, the outward appearance—of the invisible world, what most distinguishes Christianity when compared with other and false religions,—what indeed, on the negative side, may be regarded as *peculiar* and *original* in it,—is, not the fulness of the information it conveys, but its discreet and solemn reserve. In the not very frequent allusions to the subject the language is purposely varied, so that the most cursory reader might not fall into the mistake of understanding it to the letter. One thing, however, is put beyond question,—happiness to the good, misery to the bad; that is, all that can give moral effect to the revelation: not a word, not a syllable, either to stimulate or gratify an idle and impertinent curiosity.

But these things are comparatively of small moment. What chiefly and essentially distinguishes the Christian doctrine of the final judgment has nothing to do with the time and circumstances of that event; it relates to the principle, to the law by which everything is then to be determined. "Who will render to every man according to his deeds: to them who, by patient continuance in well-doing, seek for glory and honor and immortality, eternal life; but unto them that are contentious, and do not obey the truth, but obey unrighteousness, indignation and wrath; tribulation and anguish upon every soul of man that doeth evil,—of the Jew first, and also of the Gentile; but glory, honor, and peace to every man that worketh good, among men, and applied to human affairs. And finally, the Gospel is the Judge, inasmuch as it is the expression of the Divine justice, that is, it sets forth the laws and conditions of spiritual life and spiritual death, according to which every soul will take its appropriate place in the eternal world.

The last-mentioned statement makes it necessary to glance at one question more. We say, every soul will take its appropriate place in the next life; but why do so in the next life, any more than in this?

There may be agencies and appliances to carry into effect the righteous retributions of eternity, of which, with our present faculties and experience, we can form no conception. But it is hardly necessary to resort to what may be termed the argument from ignorance. There is one thing which we *know*. We know *why* it is that a righteous retribution is not more generally reached in the life that now is. We know, for example, why it is that a mean man lifts up his head in good society; why it is that a designing politician often passes for a sincere patriot; why it is that showy manners often go for more than substantial virtues; why it is that, in the struggle for wealth and honor, the bad man often succeeds, and the good man often fails. It is because *the purely moral* aspect of things has comparatively little to do in determining our condition here. It is because a multitude of influences, having little or nothing to do with virtue or vice are constantly at work in this world to modify the opinions entertained of us by others, and even by ourselves. Here things are not as they seem. We walk in "a vain show." It is only necessary to suppose, therefore, that death will have the effect to strip off these disguises; it is only necessary to assume that this imposing but hollow masquerade will come to an end, and then every soul will *seem to be what it is, and take its place accordingly*. Glimpses are sometimes given us of what is to be expected when the world is judged in righteousness, and the secrets of all hearts are laid bare; and it is always, as our argument would lead us to anticipate, when for some reason moral causes have become for the time all in all. It is when man forgets everything else, and thinks only of his relations to a holy and merciful God;—as in the joy and peace of the new convert, and in the remorse and despair of the stricken soul. Let such a state of things become general, universal, and the dark and perplexing riddle of human destiny is solved:—the judgment is past; heaven and hell have begun!

It may be said, that the guilty soul will still be in the hands of a compassionate God; and this is true. Beware, however, of making compassion in God what it often is in man,—a mere tenderness, I had almost said, a mere weakness. Nor is this all. We must not expect in the next world what is incompatible with its nature and purpose. We are placed here *to make a beginning.* We can begin here what course we please; and if we do not like it, we can go back, and begin again. Are you sure it will be so in the world to come? Why first a world of probation and then a world of retribution, if after all both are to be equally and alike probationary? Let us not run risks, where the error, if it be one, is irretrievable, and the stake infinite. How much better to be able to say, with the Apostle, "Therefore we are always confident, knowing that, while we are at home in the body, we are absent from the Lord: we are confident, I say, and willing rather to be absent from the body, and to be present with the Lord. Wherefore we labor, that, whether present or absent, we may be accepted of Him."

Let us now go one step further, and ascertain, if we can, precisely what is meant when it is said, that men are to be judged "according to their deeds." I believe there are those who interpret it to mean, that a sort of moral account current is opened with every man, as soon as he comes to years of discretion, in which he is credited for all his virtues and charged with all his sins, and that he will be rewarded or punished in the end for each particular act. Mr. Locke must have entertained some such notion when arguing that, before a man can be justly punished in the next life for the sins committed here, those sins must be brought to his remembrance; that is, he must be conscious of having committed those particular sins. And so Coleridge, who, after advancing the conjecture that "the resurrection body" may so stimulate the memory, as to bring before every human soul the collective experience of its whole past existence, adds: "And this,—this, perchance, is the dread Book of Judgment, in whose mysterious hieroglyphics every idle word is recorded." All such speculations originate, as it seems to me, in the common error of pushing too far the analogy between the human and the Divine administrations of justice. The distinction here to be taken into view is sufficiently obvious. We were told long ago, that "the Lord seeth not as man seeth; for man looketh on the outward appearance, but the Lord looketh on the heart." If, therefore, there is one thing clearer than any other in Christian ethics, it is this,—that every man is to stand or fall according to what he is in himself;—not by what he *does,* except in so far as it expresses what he really *is.* Acts of worship in a hypocrite, munificent gifts merely for the name of it, solemn make-beliefs of the would-be worshipper of God and the world at the same time, go for nothing. The question continually returns, What is the man *in himself?* Not that the language used in Scripture in speaking of the final judgment is to be excepted to or set aside, in any manner or degree. It is still as true as ever that we shall all be judged at the last "according to what we have done, whether it be good or bad," because this *will have made us to be what we are;* nevertheless everything at the Judgment Day will depend on what we *are.* There is, therefore, no occasion for the nice balancing of accounts, item by item, referred to above; neither is there any occasion for a miraculous memory to enable us to call to mind every thought we have indulged, every word we have uttered, and every action we have performed. It will be enough, if we know in what moral and spiritual state *all these have left us;* and to know this it will be enough, if we are made conscious of what we are.

This view of the case—distinctly apprehended and firmly held—will help to reconcile an apparent discrepancy in the Scriptures as to *the person of the Judge.* Thus, in one place we are told that *"God* shall bring every work into judgment, with every secret thing, whether it be good or whether it be evil." In another place it is said, "the Father judgeth no man, but hath commited all judgment to *the Son."* And, in still another place, our Lord himself is represented as saying: "And if any man hear my words, and believe not, I judge him not: for I came not to judge the world, but to save the world. He that rejecteth me, and receiveth not my words, hath one that judgeth him; *the Word that I have spoken,* the same shall judge him at the last day." Now there is plainly no contradiction, no difficulty here, provided only that we dismiss the imagination of a formal trial, and make the future judgment to consist in the fact, that every soul will become happy or miserable at death, according to its conscious deserts. The judgment thus understood, we may say with equal truth, looking at the subject under different points of view, that God is the Judge, that Christ is the Judge, or that the Gospel is the Judge. God is the Judge, inasmuch as all justice has its origin and foundation in the absolute holiness and rectitude of the Divine nature. Christ is the Judge, inasmuch as he is the dispenser of Divine justice on earth; it is in and through Him that this justice is made known—to the Jew first, and also to the Gentile; for there is no respect of persons with God. The same ground is also taken by another apostle: "Then Peter opened his mouth and said, 'Of a truth I perceive that God is no respecter of persons; but in every nation he that feareth him, and worketh righteousness, is accepted with him.'" A multitude of such passages might be cited from the apostolic writings; and they do but reassert what our Lord himself had expressly taught in the Sermon on the Mount: "Not every one that saith unto me, Lord, Lord, shall enter into the kingdom of heaven; but he that doeth the will of my Father which is in heaven. Many will say to me in that day, 'Lord, Lord, have we not prophesied in thy name? and in thy name have cast out devils? and in thy name have done many wonderful works?' And then will I profess unto them, I never knew you: depart from me, ye that work iniquity."

We are so accustomed to language like this in the New Testament as to be hardly in a condition to see in it anything *peculiar* or *original*. But where will you find its parallel? Certainly not in any of the thousand forms of polytheism which have prevailed in the world. I do not say, I have no right to say, even of these, certainly not of the best of them, that they entirely exclude moral ideas or a moral accountability. But need I remind you how often even the purest of them represent justice as interfered with by jealousies and rivalships among the Divinities themselves, or by partiality or favoritism for particular communities or particular individuals? how often they speak of the anger of the gods as directed, not against unrighteousness, but against some personal slight or neglect? And what shall I say of Judaism? Every thoughtful reader must be struck with the lofty tone of monotheistic morality pervading the Old Testament; but it was never understood to come up to the Christian standard; it is expressly said in the Sermon on the Mount not to do so. Judaism is marred throughout—sometimes in principle, and still oftener in spirit—by the narrowness and arrogance of a people educated in the belief that God was *their* God in a sense in which he was not the God of all mankind. Nowhere but in Christianity will you find it distinctly laid down, as of Divine authority, that every man is to be judged at last by what he has himself done, whether it be good or bad.

🎜 Unitarian Hymns

Eric Routley writes in his *Hymns and Human Life* what amounts to a concise statement about the role of hymns not just in worship but in the theological awareness of the worshippers: "Every movement has its songs, and always for the same reason—to place its experience and vision outside itself and make it public; to bind itself together against adversaries; and to urge itself on in its daily task towards the goal for which the movement was founded."[1]

Routley goes on to indicate that it was actually the followers of Arius who wrote the first hymns. Denied the right to hold public worship, the Arians paraded through the streets singing. The first hymns composed concerned God and Christ. In the centuries following, especially since the Reformation, the material has become even more complex.

Unitarians used their music to proclaim their faith. Many people may be surprised to know, for example, that Frederic Henry Hedge translated "A Mighty Fortress Is Our God," the classic hymn by Martin Luther, from the German into English. But Unitarian contributions were also original, ranging from Edmund Sears's "It Came Upon the Midnight Clear," to Elizabeth Lee Cabot Follen's "Remember the Slave" and Sarah Adams's "Nearer, My God, to Thee." Even President John Quincy Adams, a Unitarian, was a composer of such works as "The Death of Children."

Daniel Walker Howe's *The Unitarian Conscience* has provided the best modern argument that the Unitarians were not the corpse-cold rationalists Emerson rejected. Rather, there was a genuine emotional, almost sentimental, dimension to much of their work. In reading their hymns, one can appreciate this aspect of their Church life. Henry Ware, Jr.'s "Resurrection of Christ" is a vivid example, as are Nathaniel Frothingham's two hymns on communion and John Pierpont's beautiful and simple "O, Bow Thine Ear, Eternal One."

The Death of Children

> Sure, to the mansions of the blest
> When infant innocence ascends,

1. Eric Routley, *Hymns and Human Life,* p. 18.
Sources for hymns are listed in a separate section of the Bibliography.

Some Angel brighter than the rest
    The spotless spirit's flight attends.

On wings of ecstasy they rise,
    Beyond where worlds material roll,
Till some fair sister of the skies
    Receives the unpolluted soul.

There, at th' Almighty Father's hand,
    Nearest the throne of living light,
The choirs of infant seraphs stand,
    And dazzling shine, where all are bright.

That inextinguishable beam,
    With dust united at our birth
Sheds a more dim, discolored gleam,
    The more it lingers upon earth.

Closed in this dark abode of clay,
    The stream of glory faintly burns,
Not unobscured the lucid ray
    To its own native fount returns.

But when the Lord of mortal breath
    Decrees his bounty to resume,
And points the silent shaft of death,
    Which speeds an infant to the tomb,—

No passion fierce, no low desire
    Has quenched the radiance of the flame;
Back to its God the living fire
    Returns, unsullied, as it came.

John Quincy Adams, 1807

Resurrection of Christ

Lift your glad voices in triumph on high.
    For Jesus hath risen, and man cannot die;
Vain were the terrors that gathered around him.
And short the dominion of death and the grave;
He burst from the fetters of darkness that bound
    him,
Resplendent in glory, to love and to save:
    Loud was the chorus of angels on high,—
    The Saviour hath risen and man cannot die.

Glory to God, in full anthems of joy,
    The being he gave us death cannot destroy:
Sad were the life we must part with to-morrow,
If tears were our birthright, and death were our
        end;
But Jesus hath cheered the dark valley of sorrow,
And bade us, immortal, to heaven ascend:
    Lift, then, your voices in triumph on high,
    For Jesus hath risen, and man shall not die.

Henry Ware, Jr., 1817

It Came Upon the Midnight Clear

It came upon the midnight clear,
    That glorious song of old,
From angels bending near the earth,
    To touch their harps of gold:
'Peace on the earth, good will to men,
    From Heav'n's all gracious King.'
The world in solemn stillness lay
    To hear the angels sing.

Still thro' the cloven skies they come,
    With peaceful wings unfurled;
And still their heavenly music floats
    O'er all the weary world:
Above its sad and lowly plains
    They bend on hovering wing,
And ever o'er its Babel sounds
    The blessed angels sing.

But with the woes of sin and strife
    The world has suffered long;
Beneath the angel-strain have rolled
    Two thousand years of wrong;
And man, at war with man, hears not
    The love song which they bring
O hush the noise, ye men of strife,
    And hear the angels sing!

Edmund Hamilton Sears, 1849

Calm, On the List'ning Ear of Night

Calm, on the list'ning ear of night,
    Come heav'n's melodious strains,

Celestial choirs, from courts above,
   Shed sacred glories there;

Where wild Judea stretches far
   Her silver mantled plains.
And angels, with their sparkling lyres,
   Make music on the air.

The answering hills of Palestine
   Send back the glad reply;
And greet, from all their holy heights,
   The Dayspring from on high.

O'er the blue depths of Galilee
   There comes a holier calm;
And Sharon waves, in solemn praise,
   Her silent groves of palm.

'Glory to God!' the sounding skies
   Loud with their anthems ring;
'Peace to the earth, good will to men,
   From heaven's eternal King!'

Light on thy hills, Jerusalem!
   The Saviour now is born!
And bright, on Bethlehem's joyous plains,
   Breaks the first Christmas morn.

Edmund Hamilton Sears, 1834

Beneath Thine Hammer, Lord, I Lie

Beneath thine hammer, Lord, I lie
   With contrite spirit prone;
O, mould me till to self I die,
   And live to thee alone!

With frequent disappointments sore
   And many a bitter pain,
Thou laborest at my being's core
   Till I be formed again . . .

Smite, Lord! thine hammer's needful wound
   My baffled hopes confess;
Thine anvil is the sense profound
   Of mine own nothingness

Smite, till from all its idols free,
    And filled with love divine,
My heart shall know no good but thee,
    And have no will but thine.

Frederic Henry Hedge, pub. 1853

Communion Hymn

"And he took bread, and gave thanks."

The Son of God gave thanks,
    Before the bread he broke.
How high that calm devotion ranks
    Among the words he spoke!

Thanks, mid those troubled men;
    Thanks, in that dismal hour;
The world's dark prince advancing then
    In all his range and power.

Thanks, o'er that loaf's dread sign;
    Thanks, o'er that bitter food;
And o'er the cup, that was not wine,
    But sorrow, fear, and blood.

And shall our griefs resent
    What God appoints as best
When he, in all things innocent,
    Was yet in all distressed?

Shall we unthankful be
    For all our blessings round,
When in that press of agony
    Such room for thanks he found?

O shame us, Lord!—whate'er
    The fortunes of our days,—
If, suffering, we are weak to bear,
    If, favored, slow to praise.

Nathaniel L. Frothingham, 1855

Communion Hymn

"Do this in remembrance of me."
"How he was known of them in breaking of bread."

"Remember me," the Saviour said,
    On that forsaken night,
When from his side the nearest fled,
    And death was close in sight.

Through all the following ages' track
    The world remembers yet;
With love and worship gazes back,
    And never can forget.

But who of us has seen his face,
    Or heard the words he said?
And none can now his look retrace
    In breaking of the bread.

O blest are they, who have not seen,
    And yet believe him still!
They know him, when his praise they mean,
    And when they do his will.

We hear his word along our way;
    We see his light above;
Remember when we strive and pray,
    Remember when we love.

Nathaniel L. Frothingham, 1855

O, Bow Thine Ear, Eternal One

This is none other but the House of God
—Genesis 28:17.

O, bow Thine ear, Eternal One!
    On thee our heart adoring calls;
To Thee the followers of Thy Son
    Have raised and now devote these walls.

Here let Thy holy days be kept;
    And be this place to worship given
Like that bright spot where Jacob slept,
    The house of God, the gate of heaven.

Here by Thy praise devoutly sung;
    Here let Thy truth beam forth to save,
As when, of old, Thy Spirit hung,
    On wings of light, o'er Jordan's wave.

And when the lips that with Thy name
    Are vocal now to dust shall turn,
On others may devotion's flame
    Be kindled here, and purely burn.

        John Pierpont, 1823

Doxology

All glory to Thy wondrous name,
    Father of mercy, God of love
Exalted be the Lord, the Lamb,
    And thus we praise the heavenly Dove.

        John Pierpont, 1823

Remember the Slave

Mother! whene'er around your child
    You clasp your arms in love,
And when, with grateful joy, you raise
    Your eyes to God above,
Think of the negro mother, when
    Her child is torn away,
Sold for a little slave,—O, then
    For that poor mother pray!

Father! whene'er your happy boys
    You look upon with pride,
And pray to see them when you're old,
    All blooming by your side,
Think of that father's withered heart,
    The father of a slave,
Who asks a pitying God to give
    His little son a grave.

Brothers and sisters! who with joy
    Meet round the social hearth,
And talk of home and happy days,
    And laugh in careless mirth,

Remember, too, the poor young slave,
    Who never felt your joy,
Who, early old, has never known
    The bliss to be a boy.

Ye Christians! ministers of Him
    Who came to make men free,
When, at the Almighty Maker's throne,
    You bend the suppliant knee,
From the deep fountains of your soul
    Then let your prayers ascend
For the poor slave, who hardly knows
    That God is still his friend.

Eliza Lee Cabot Follen, 1831

Nearer, My God, to Thee

Nearer, my God, to thee,
Nearer to thee,
E'en though it be a cross
That raiseth me;
Still all my song shall be,
Nearer, my God, to thee,
Nearer to thee.

Though like the wanderer,
The sun gone down,
Darkness be over me,
My rest a stone;
Yet in my dreams I'd be
Nearer, my God, to thee,
Nearer to thee.

There let the way appear
Steps unto heaven;
All that thou sendest me
In mercy given;
Angels to beckon me
Nearer, My God, to thee,
Nearer to thee.

Then with my waking thoughts
Bright with thy praise,
Out of my stony griefs
Bethel I'll raise;

So by my woes to be
Nearer, my God, to thee,
Nearer to thee.

Or if on joyful wing,
Cleaving the sky,
Sun, moon, and stars forgot,
Upwards I fly,
Still all my song shall be,
Nearer, my God, to thee,
Nearer to thee.

   Sarah Flower Adams, 1841

III ETHICS AND MORAL THEOLOGY

❧ Of the Nature and Principle of Evangelical Obedience

JONATHAN MAYHEW (1720–1766)

Jonathan Mayhew has been rightly regarded as the orator of the liberal movement. His strength of religious conviction, combined with a mind that spoke what it believed in no uncertain terms, made him one of the formidable figures in pre-Revolutionary War America. The son of the Reverend Experience Mayhew of Martha's Vineyard and descendant of several generations of Indian missionaries, he was graduated from Harvard College in 1744. After several years of theological study, Mayhew was called in 1747 to the West Church in Boston.

The West Church had been known for its liberality since its establishment a decade before; and Mayhew was the perfect choice for minister because of his vocal dissatisfaction with a number of theological issues. Even his installation was controversial, since few ministers from Boston would participate. Only by inviting a number of ministers from rural churches to assist in the service was the necessary quorum gathered and Mayhew installed. He never became a member of the Boston Association of Congregational Ministers and thus could not exchange pulpits with many of his colleagues. This placed a large burden of preaching on him.

Mayhew's Arminianism was pronounced at a time when the liberal thought of others, including his two friends Charles Chauncy and Ebenezer Gay, was much more restrained. He was known for his forthrightness from the beginning, and this selection from a 1755 sermon, "Evangelical Obedience," demonstrates his command of his Christian faith with its stress on the unity of God and unabashed unwillingness to indulge in metaphysical abstractions. Mayhew attracted much attention for his theological articulations, although it is clear that an increasing number of his colleagues were also silently questioning the existing statements of faith in New England. Forty years later a visiting Presbyterian could remark disconcertingly after observing the Boston Association of Ministers that some were Calvinists; some, Universalists; some, Arminians; some, Arians; and one at least was a Socinian. Jonathan Mayhew was indeed one of the first individuals to represent the Liberal Faith.

Having observed in *general,* that christian obedience consists in conforming our tempers and behaviour to the laws of Christ; it may be proper, for the better understanding of what is here intended, to show more *particularly,* how this obedience is distinguished from any other.

And it certainly differs very widely from obedience to the law of nature, or the moral law; especially in that narrow, partial sense and acceptation of this law, which confines *morality* to men's behaviour towards each other in civil and social life: and to the private virtues of temperance, and the like, without any regard to *Deity,* and a *moral Governor.* The ancient pagan Moralists generally considered morality only in this light. When they teach that the law of reason, or the law of nature, is to be followed and observed, (on many branches of which, they treat with great propriety) they usually mean no more, than that men are bound to practice justice, benevolence, sobriety, and the other virtues of private and social life, as being, in their own nature, convenient, fitting and decent. This is a notion of virtue and obedience, which falls vastly short of the Christian idea; not only because Christians are under obligation to practice other duties besides those which nature dictates; but also because christianity ultimately resolves all duties into the will of God, considered as the all-wise, good, and righteous Lawgiver, and the moral Ruler of the world. "There is one Lawgiver, says St. *James,* who is able to save and to destroy." And "He that said, do not commit adultery, said also, do not kill." Our obedience is, "doing the *will* of our Father which is in heaven." Whatever duty we are bound to practice, it is considered as injoined upon us by the authority of almighty God. All our good and virtuous actions, are considered as a tribute which we owe to Him; as a *sacrifice* offered to Him; and with which He is *well pleased.* And, on the other hand, whenever we transgress our duty, this is considered as transgressing the law of God: against *Him, Him* only do we sin. For the divine will and authority, does, as it were, involve and swallow up all other obligations; even the laws of nature and reason, as they are sometimes called, being the laws of Him who is Lord of nature, and the Fountain of all reason.

But what has now been said, only distinguishes the obedience of Christians from such virtue as a mere *Atheist* may, in some degree, be the subject of. For a man may be, in some measure, just, beneficent, temperate, &c. from an internal sense of the reasonableness and fitness and advantage of being so; altho' he is so far from obeying and honouring God therein, that he does not even believe his existence. Our modern *Theists* profess to go much farther than this; tho' their obedience, if they really practised agreeably to their principles, (which they seldom do) would fall much below that of Christians, who act up to their profession. The *Theists* profess to reverence God as the moral governor of the universe, whose will and laws are to be read in men's hearts, and in the volumes of visible nature. And the dictates of nature and reason, it is said, ought to be obeyed, not merely considered as in themselves fit to be observed; but also because they must be supposed conformable to the will of the *Deity;* and to have all the force of laws enacted by *Him:* So that it may be concluded, men will be rewarded or punished by *Him,* as they obey or disobey these laws. I speak now only of the more sober and rational part of modern *Theists.* There are others of them, who while they profess to believe in God, deride all this as mere *superstition* and *enthusiasm;* and with whom it is nothing but the *inherent* amiableness of virtue, that claims regard; virtue not being rewarded, nor vice punished, as such, by a moral *Governor* and *Lord;* tho' it is owned they have a tendency, in the very nature of things, to render the subjects of them happy and miserable, respectively. Whether these nominal *Theists,* are not really *Atheists* at the bottom, or, at best *Epicureans,* which comes much to the same thing at last, I will not pretend to determine. Only it is evident, there is but very little difference betwixt saying, that there is no God at all; and saying, that there is none who is to be regarded and reverenced, as the righteous *governor* of the world; none, who rewards and punishes men for their actions.

But as to the more sober and religious *Theists,* who consider the natural laws of virtue, as the laws of God; and who not having, or not acknowledging any *revealed* law, yet "do by nature the things contained in it," in some measure; even *Their* obedience falls far short of the Christian standard. Christian obedience differs from *Their's,* not only as Christians make a revealed law the rule of their obedience; and *They,* only the light of nature: (which would not, of itself, be sufficient to constitute a very essential difference, provided the *matter* of these laws were exactly the same.) But it differs in divers other respects. The catalogue of Christian duties and virtues is considerably longer than the *Theist's.* Every duty of natural religion, is indeed a duty of christianity; of revealed religion. But the gospel moreover injoins upon us divers things, which are not contained in the law of nature; and are no part of it. And the obedience paid to these different laws, *viz.* of mere nature, and of Christianity, must differ as much, at least, as the laws themselves differ.

Besides: Whoever duly attends to the Christian doctrine of a *Mediator,* will find, not only that various duties result from, and are injoined upon us in consequence of, that supernatural interposition of providence; but also that our obedience in general is put upon a different footing thereby, having, in the whole of it, a reference to this great dispensation of divine grace to a sinful world. All the precepts of the gospel, tho' they are truly the *laws of God;* yet they are not to be considered *only in that light;* but as his laws promulgated by His only begotten Son, who has redeemed us, and whose *servants* and *subjects* we more immediately are. Agreably whereto it is said, that we are "not without law to God; *but under the law to Christ.*" God has subjected us to the rule and authority of His Son, in consequence of his undertaking and executing the mediatorial office. In our Saviour's own words, "The Father loveth the Son, and hath given him authority to execute judgment, because he is the Son of Man:" i.e. because he became incarnate. And in the language of the Apostle *Paul,* He "took upon him the form of a servant, and was made in the likeness of men;— and became obedient unto death, even the death of the cross: *Wherefore* God also hath highly exalted him, and given him a name, which is above every name; that at the name of Jesus every knee should bow." &c. Now it is as invested with this royal power and dignity; as being the *King whom God hath set upon his holy hill of Zion,* that Christ gives laws to men; not merely as a prophet, or divine messenger. He is "made Head over all things to the church" and we are put under his authority, in a sense wherein we cannot be said to be under that of any other messenger or minister of Heaven, whether human or angelical. From which considerations it is manifest, that our obedience is more *immediately* due to the *Son,* than to the Father; it being more *immediately* by *His* authority, that the various duties of the gospel are enjoined upon us; and to him, that we are more *immediately* accountable for our conduct.

Allowing for the present, (what is far from being true, *viz.*) that the laws of christianity are, in all respects the same with the laws and religion of nature, and only a republication of it; yet, surely, we could not be said to pay a proper obedience to them, without considering them as being the laws of Christ, our Redeemer and Sovereign. And this is what constitutes one essential difference betwixt christian obedience, and any other. In order to a person's obeying as a Christian ought to do, it is not only necessary that he performs the duties *peculiar* to Christianity; but also that he performs all others, which may be *common* to this and other religions, in obedience to Christ, as his Lord and Master and final Judge: *doing all things whatsoever he does in word or deed, in the name of the Lord Jesus.*

However, Christians do not (at least they ought not to) set aside the supreme authority and dominion of God, the FATHER Almighty: or, by attempting to divide, really destroy, the *Monarchy* of the universe; which is still in HIM alone; the mediatorial authority of Christ, being derived from HIM, and subordinate to HIS. Tho' our obedience as Christians, is due more *immediately* to our Lord Jesus Christ; (as was said before) yet it is *ultimately* referred to *His Father, and our Father, to His God and our God;* who "is greater than ALL;" and who has conferred this dignity and authority on the Son. And of this important truth, *viz.* that all the homage and obedience which we pay to the Son, should thus be referred to, and terminate in, the *Father;* of this important truth, I say, the apostle admonishes us, when he tells us, that God *highly exalted* his Son, that every tongue might confess him to be Lord, "to the glory of God, the FATHER."

So that Christians ought not, surely, to pay any such obedience or homage to the Son, as has a tendency to eclipse the glory of God the Father; who is without Rival or Competitor. The Dominion and Sovereignty of the universe is necessarily *one,* and in ONE;—the *only* living and true GOD, who delegates such measures of power and authority to other Beings, as seemeth good in his sight; but "will not give his [peculiar] glory to another." Our blessed Saviour does indeed assert the rights and prerogatives of *his own* crown; but never usurped those of His *Father*'s: On the contrary, He constantly and uniformly tells us, that his authority was *given* to him of the Father; and is exercised in subordination to His will; not independently of it. He claims no authority, besides what he claims by virtue of the *Father*'s grant, and the commission which he received from *Him.*

What is said above, seemed needful to prevent mis-construction; to suggest the true ground of that obedience which we owe to our blessed Lord; and to show the perfect consistency of paying it, with the *Unity* and the *Supreme* glory and dominion of God, the FATHER: The not sufficiently preserving of which *Unity* and *Supremacy* amongst Christians, has long been just matter of reproach to them; and a great stumbling-block both to *Jews* and *Mahometans.**—But to return,

As christian obedience is distinguished from that of mere *Theists,* by our making a written *revelation* the rule of it; by the *peculiar* duties of the gospel; and by our paying all our obedience more *immediately* to Jesus Christ, as our Redeemer, Lord and Judge; so it is still farther distinguished therefrom, by the *motives* from which it is performed.

* With the metaphysical abstract nature, or essence of the Deity, I am not bold enough to meddle. Disquisitions of this kind, and denunciations of God's vengeance against those who do not affect to be *wise,* or are not willing to believe, *above what is written,* are left to the unaccountable Temerity of the *Athanasians.* I can, for my own part, freely acquiesce in St. *Paul's* doctrine, in the most obvious sense of his words, *viz.* That "tho' there be that are *called* Gods, whether in heaven or in earth; (as there be gods *many,* and lords *many*) but [yet] *to us* there is but ONE GOD, the FATHER—and *One Lord,* Jesus Christ."—I *Cor.* 8, 4.—"There is ONE GOD, and *One Mediator* betwixt GOD and men, the Man Christ Jesus"—I *Tim.* 2, 5. Who the *only true GOD* is, we may farther learn from our Saviour's prayer, *John* 17 begin. "These things spake Jesus; and lift up his eyes to heaven and said. FATHER, glorify thy *Son*—This is life eternal that they might know THEE, the ONLY TRUE GOD, and *Jesus Christ,* whom THOU hast sent."

The obedience of a mere *Theist* may be excited by a contemplation of the divine goodness, and other attributes, as manifested in the creation of the world; and in that providence which sustains and governs all things. But a Christian's obedience is moreover, excited, I might perhaps say, more especially excited, by a contemplation of God's perfections, as manifested in our redemption: And we are *constrained by the love of Christ,* who "died for all," when all were dead. The *Theist* may do acts of charity to his neighbours considered as his fellow-creatures, the creatures of God. But a Christian moreover considers the relation in which all men stand to Christ, who so loved them, as to give his life "a ransom for all:" And if he gives ought to a disciple, it is *in the name* of a disciple that he does it, and *because he belongs to Christ.* The *Theist* may be sober and temperate because this is reasonable, and conducive to health. But the Christian moreover, considers himself as "the habitation of God thro' the spirit;" and will not *defile the temple of God,* lest God should *destroy* him. The *Theist's* virtue and obedience may be excited by some general confused notions of a future state of retribution. But a Christian lives under the habitual expectation of a resurrection, and a future judgment; when all they that are in their graves shall hear the voice of the Son of God; and come forth, *they that have done good, to the resurrection of life,* and *they that have done evil, to the resurrection of damnation.* The *Theist* may obey, because he imagines his virtue (notwithstanding all it's defects) so valuable in itself, that it will fully and sufficiently recommend him to the approbation of his Creator. But the Christian obeys, because this will be acceptable to God thro' his Redeemer, and be rewarded for *his Sake.* In fine, the obedience of a Christian, in all its parts and branches, receives a peculiar tincture and complexion from his profession; and is animated by the faith of the Son of God, who has redeemed us by his blood; *and made us kings and priests unto God, to offer up Spiritual Sacrifices, acceptable to Him by Jesus Christ.*—These things are sufficient to show the wide difference which there is betwixt the obedience of a Christian, and that of a mere *Theist,* even supposing the latter of them to live up to his principles.

But it may be inquired, How christian obedience differs from that of good men under the law of *Moses,* before the coming of Christ in the flesh? The resolution of which inquiry, depends very much upon another question, *viz.* How far the mediatorial scheme of our redemption and salvation, was opened to *Their* understandings, during that preparatory dispensation? If we suppose this scheme to have been as clearly revealed to *them* in general, as it seems to have been to some of the *Patriarchs* before the law, and to some good men after, and under, it, the difference will not be so great as some may perhaps imagine. For it will then consist chiefly in these two things:

1st. In the externals, the modes and rituals of religion; which, to be sure, were very different under the *Mosaic,* and the *evangelical* dispensation; the morality of the law and of the gospel being still the same. And

2dly. Whereas We believe and trust in a Redeemer already come; and are hereby excited to obey: *They* believed in the same Saviour, as promised, and looked for; and were, by this expectation of a Deliverer, stimulated to the service of God.

We are told expressly, that the *gospel was preached to Abraham,* who *rejoiced to see the day of Christ* approaching. And he, together with others both before, and after the *Mosaic* oeconomy took place, were justified in the same way, and upon the same footing of grace, that we are now; *Abraham* being the *father of the faithful* in all succeeding generations. And the Author to the *Hebrews,* having enumerated divers of these ancient worthies, tell us, that "these all died in *faith,* not having received the promises; (i.e. the fulfilment of them) but having seen them afar off, and were perswaded of them, and embraced them; and confessed that they were strangers and pilgrims in the earth." And of *Moses,* it is said afterwards, that he "esteemed the reproach of Christ, greater riches than the treasures in *Egypt:* having respect unto the recompence of the reward." Now according to these, and such-like representations in the new-testament, one would think that, excepting the two particulars mentioned, there could be no considerable difference betwixt the obedience of good men before, and after, the coming of Christ.

But whether this knowledge of a Saviour to come, were common to all good men, under the *law,* or not, there is some ground of doubt. For tho' one great end of the law was, that it might *shadow forth good things to come;* that it might at once admonish those who were under it, of their *need* of a *Spiritual* deliverer and Redeemer, and lead them to *expect such* a One; yet it is manifest that the generality of the *Jews,* for sometime before our Lord's nativity, had no notion of this spiritual meaning, and typical reference of the law; and therefore interpreted all the prophecies concerning the *Messiah,* of a *temporal* Prince and Saviour. And whether some truly pious and virtuous men, were not carried away with this prevailing error, I will not pretend to determine—Nor can we fully and thoroughly discriminate betwixt the obedience of good *Jews,* and good *Christians,* unless we knew more exactly than we do, what the ideas and sentiments of the *former* generally were, respecting the promised Saviour.

To conclude this head, concerning the *nature* of christian obedience— This obedience is not only *that* which, for the matter of it, is agreable to the precepts of the gospel; but *that* which is performed with a due regard to Christ, as our great Prophet, Priest and King; *the Captain of our Salvation;* the *author and finisher of our faith: That* obedience, which has the gospel revelation for its basis and rule; and which is performed from views and motives proper and peculiar to this dispensation of divine grace. However right and reasonable men's actions are, considered in themselves; however corresponding to the *law of liberty;* yet there is not, in strict propriety, any thing of christian obedience therein, any farther than they are done with reference to the gospel of Christ. This is the *characteristick* of the obedience we are considering: hereby it is distinguished from any other. And this will be farther evident from a consideration of the grand *principle* of this obedience, which was the *second* thing proposed in the beginning of this discourse, and to which I now proceed.

The great *principle* of christian obedience, is *christian faith;* faith in Christ, and in God thro' him. I add—*in God thro' him;* because the faith of Christians does not terminate in Christ as the *ultimate,* (tho' he is the *immediate*) object of it: but it is extended, thro' him, to the *one God and Father of all.* And to beget in men that belief and trust in God, which is here intended, was one grand design of the mediatorial undertaking. Christ came into the world in his Father's name, as sent and commissioned by Him, to declare and reveal Him. And in His name he spake to the world concerning God, and His kingdom. All he taught, did and suffered, refered ultimately to the Father; the end thereof being to *bring us to God.* A passage in the apostle *Peter* will both illustrate and confirm the thing here intended; where, speaking of our Saviour, he says, that he "was foreordained before the foundation of the world; but was manifest in these last times for us, who *by him do believe in God* that raised him from the dead, and gave him glory, that our *faith and hope might be in God."* From hence, and from many other passages of scripture, it is evident that christian faith is not merely a belief in Christ, or relying upon him for salvation; but rather a belief and hope in *God* thro' him; a belief that *He* is what Christ has declared him to be; that *He* is that righteous, that good and gracious Being, which the gospel represents him to be; that He is *reconciling the world unto himself,* by such means, and upon such terms, as are therein mentioned: A belief, that Christ is "the way, the truth and the life; that no man can come unto the Father, but by him;" or that sinners can obtain eternal life in that method, and that alone, which he has opened and revealed.

This is the proper notion of christian faith: And, indeed, to suppose that faith terminates in Christ, as the *ultimate* object of it, is inconsistent with his being a *Mediator* at all. We lose the very idea of a *Mediator* upon this supposition. If Christ is really "the Mediator betwixt God and

Man;" he is to be believed on as such; and our faith must terminate, as was observed before, in *that God,* betwixt Whom and us, he *mediates.—* And having premised thus much concerning the nature of christian faith in general; (which is much mistaken by many) I am now to show, that this is the great *principle* of christian obedience. I do not mean, that all who thus believe in Christ, and in God thro' him, do actually obey the gospel; (which is contrary to fact and experience) but, that all who obey it, obey it from this *principle.* It is this faith that purifies their hearts; and animates them in the discharge of all the duties of the christian life—Let me explain myself a little more particularly upon this point.

It is very evident that no man can obey as a Christian, who has not the faith of a Christian. It is supposeable that a *Mahometan,* or even an *Atheist,* might *externally* perform any duty which the gospel injoins upon us. But if a *Mahometan* or *Atheist,* known to be such, should perform many of these duties, no one, surely, would call this *christian* obedience. Evangelical faith being wanting, there cannot, properly speaking, be any thing of evangelical obedience in any actions whatever.

Such faith in Christ, and in God thro' him, as is mentioned above, has a very natural and apparent *tendency* to make the subjects of it truly pious and virtuous; and to yield that obedience to the gospel, which is required of them. As far as the belief of any thing; as far as any faith, in the primary and most proper sense of the term, can influence the tempers and practices of men; such a faith as I am speaking of, bids the fairest of any, to have a good influence upon men's hearts and manners; to turn them from sin to God; and to induce them to obey his commandments. . . .

❧ The Comparative Moral Tendency of the Leading Doctrines of Calvinism and the Sentiments of Unitarians

JARED SPARKS (1789–1866)

Morality was an important issue during the whole course of the Unitarian Controversy. Channing's Baltimore Sermon served as one occasion for debate on this subject. One year after it had been delivered, Samuel Miller, a diehard Calvinist and the first professor of ecclesiastical history at conservative Princeton Theological Seminary, also preached an ordination sermon in Baltimore, in the course of which he noted that American Unitarians were not Christians and therefore that their morality could not lay claim to a religious basis. That remark led to a lengthy exchange, which brought Miller and Princeton into the Unitarian Controversy.

Miller's opponent was Jared Sparks, the first minister of the Baltimore Unitarian church. Sparks, born in 1789 in Willington, Connecticut, was first trained as a carpenter, but several ministers, impressed by his intellect, helped him gain entrance to Phillips Exeter Academy. From there he went to Harvard College, and was graduated in 1815. For several years he tutored the sons of the Reverend Nathaniel Thayer in Lancaster, Massachusetts; he then served at Harvard as a tutor in mathematics for two years. In 1819 he was called to the Baltimore Unitarian church.

Sparks served that congregation for four years, during which period he was for a time the chaplain of the U.S. House of Representatives. He founded the journal *Unitarian Miscellany* (1821–24), which extended the spread of Unitarian views beyond New England. For six years after leaving Baltimore he served as editor of the *North American Review*. In 1838 he was appointed professor of ancient and modern history at Harvard and in 1849 became president of the university. During these years he published extensively; notably, valuable biographies of American leaders, some of whom were his close friends.

The selection which follows, on the comparative moral tendencies of Trinitarianism and Unitarianism, demonstrates well the bitter controversies of the times. Andrew Fuller had published in England *The Calvinistic and Socinian Systems Examined and Compared as to Their Moral Tendency* (1794), a carefully reasoned effort to distinguish the two systems. But

Sparks sought a practical approach, which showed the innate moral dignity of man. His book was not academic or philosophical, but, rather, polemical, a deliberate effort to make Miller respond. Their exchanges continued as pamphlet followed pamphlet, and book answered book. However, the practical nature of Sparks's writings did not attract a learned following, and thus the exchange did not have the impact of the earlier Woods and Ware debates.

Letter I

CALVINISTIC AND UNITARIAN VIEWS OF THE
DEPRAVITY OF MAN.

Sir,

We come now to a consideration of the more peculiar doctrines of Calvinism; or those doctrines which owe their origin to the metaphysics of Austin, their growth and strength to the genius of Calvin, and their maturity to the deliberations at the Synod of Dort. They may be arranged in the following order, namely, *total depravity, irresistible grace, divine decrees, particular redemption,* and *final perseverance.* These are the five links in the Calvinistic chain, and so closely depending on each other, that, should one be broken, all the rest must fall. According to Calvinists, this chain constitutes the entire system of Christianity; it comprises faith, charity, virtue, piety; it embraces the whole compass of the divine dispensations to the moral creation, and points out the only possible method by which the Maker of the universe could bless any portion of his creatures with salvation and eternal life.

Some of these doctrines you enumerate, and you profess to account it an evidence of the immorality of Unitarians, that they do not believe and preach them. Whether this be a just conclusion we are now to examine.

It is but fair to premise, that you acknowledge some friends among Unitarians, whom you esteem, and who "set an example of integrity, benevolence, and active virtue." But lest it should be thought that you allow even these to have the virtues of *Christians,* you immediately ask, "may not the same be said of many Deists, from Lord Herbert down to the present day?" Whether your unitarian friends will take this as a compliment or not, this is no place to inquire. If it has been your ill fortune, however, to find none among them, who showed from their professions, lives, and conversation, that they acted from higher motives than those of deism, I must think your acquaintance has been extremely limited, and must lament, that you should feel warranted from information so slender, in denying the christian name to a whole denomination of professed Christians. Every sincere unitarian must hope, that those who differ from him in faith, will hereafter be more fortunate than you have been, in the friendships they may form, and the acquaintances they may contract, with his brethren. I am willing to grant, however, in passing, that so far as you have testified, that the Unitarians, who, most unluckily for their brethren, have enjoyed your friendship, are without *christian* morals, you have proved the fact of your charges. But your premises are too narrow for your conclusions. If you had said, that all Unitarians, whom you ever knew, were no better than deists in principles and practice, the subject would stand on a very different footing. It would be an affair exclusively between you, and your private unitarian friends. But now it comes in another, and a vastly more important shape. You embrace Unitarians "all over the world," and consequently all must feel themselves implicated in your charges.

After some preliminary remarks you go on to speak as follows.

"The Unitarian mode of preaching is more acceptable to the taste of carnal, worldly men, than any other kind of preaching. And can any one, who reflects a moment, or who has eyes to see, and ears to hear, doubt that this is the fact? All unitarian preachers, that I ever heard of, teach their hearers, that human nature is not so depraved, as calvinists believe; that regeneration is unnecessary; that the various exercises of mind, supposed by many to be essential to piety, are mere dreams of enthusiasm; that the strictness and seclusion from fashionable amusements, such as the theatre, the ball room, and the card table, which some inculcate, are uncommanded austerities, and being 'righteous over much,' and that all men, whatever may be their character, will finally be saved, or annihilated."

This you state as a "fair specimen of the doctrine inculcated by unitarian preachers *all over the world,*" and then infer, that those, who can preach thus, and approve such preaching, must necessarily be among the more immoral part of the community.

It cannot escape observation, that you profess to build this description of unitarian preaching upon *hearsay.* You produce no authority to confirm your statement, nor do you pretend to derive your knowledge from personal observation, or enlarged inquiry. But admitting you sincerely believe your impressions to be correct, which I certainly do not doubt, are you willing to take upon yourself the responsibility of bringing reproach and censure on the whole body of Unitarians, with nothing better to sustain you, than idle rumour, and the poisoned breath of evil report? Nay more, suppose you can make it appear, that some individual among them has actually been known to preach exactly in the manner you describe, do you think it fair to judge them all by this example? Is there a single sect in Christendom, who would think themselves well used to be judged as a body by the opinions, preaching, and conduct of some one, two, or half a dozen prominent men, who might be selected from among them? Would you think it just, or honourable, in a Unitarian to judge Presbyterians in this way? And especially, would you think it just, or honourable, or christian-like in him, if he had never listened to the preaching of Presbyterians, and relied on what he had heard for his knowledge, to charge them as a sect with preaching to please the immoral and licentious? This is a fair test, and one which you can apply to your own conscience and sense of propriety.

All Unitarians sincerely believe, that the peculiar doctrines of Calvinism, if allowed to have their full effect on the mind and principles, are of the most immoral tendency. They consequently believe, that preaching these doctrines will have, and does have, a bad influence on society. But would you think them justified by this belief in maintaining that all persons, who are fond of hearing these doctrines preached, thereby give unusual tokens of the depravity of their hearts, and looseness of their lives? It is presumed you would not. Why then judge others upon principles, which no man is willing to have applied to himself? Unitarians believe it possible for Calvinists to be good people and good christians, even in defiance of their principles. Conscience, reason, common sense, and the plain practical parts of scripture have a stronger power, for the most part, than the dark dogmas of theologists; and however the latter may pervert the former, it is no easy thing for them to assume an entire ascendancy.

For this reason, Unitarians do not call Calvinists deists, when they find them departing, as they think, most deplorably from the true faith of the Scriptures, or showing in their conduct little respect for their principles. We consider them christians, not for their virtues alone, nor their distinctive tenets, but because they believe in Jesus Christ as their Saviour, and profess to be guided by his Gospel. Nor do we think we ought to deny them the christian name, because, in addition to the essential articles of faith, they hold to many errors dangerous to morals, and holy living. Nor, because we find deists apparently as moral and virtuous as many Calvinists, do we think it the part of charity, or an evidence of a christian spirit, to rank them together in regard to their principles, motives, expectations, and the ground of their hopes. And yet we feel, that we may with just as much propriety take this course against Calvinists, as they can do it against us.

We are induced to embrace our views of the christian doctrines, not simply from the conviction, that they are more rational and scriptural than the prevailing notions of many of our christian brethren, who differ from us, but because we are fully persuaded that they are vastly more efficacious in promoting vital godliness, and keeping alive the pure spirit of religion, the essential duties of piety and morality. They are calculated to draw us to a more fervent love and reverence of God, and make us more devoted to the interests of our fellow-men, by kindling our sympathy, strengthening our good affections, and enlarging the bounds of our benevolence. This obvious tendency of our principles we think a very strong confirmation of their truth, and it is one of the chief reasons, why we value them so dearly, and adhere to them with so much confidence and joy.

You have taken much pains to exhibit the picture in another light, or rather to show it in darkness: and it is your efforts in this work on which I am now about to make a few brief remarks. But the comparative moral tendency of Unitarianism and Calvinism, as you have stated the subject, is too large a field to think of compassing in the narrow limits prescribed to these letters. To trace out the mischievous consequences of the calvinistic doctrines, both as they affect the character of God, the nature, ability, and agency of man, the happiness of society, the rules of virtue, the principles of piety, and the practice of holiness, would not be a work of limited extent. I can only touch upon some of the more prominent particulars, in the order in which you have brought them forward; by which it will be seen, in the first place, that you have very imperfect notions of what Unitarians actually preach; and in the second place, that you have false conceptions of the tendency of their preaching.

You begin by saying, that *unitarian preachers teach their hearers, that human nature is not so depraved as Calvinists believe.* This is not denied. But the inference, which you would draw from it, is denied, namely, that the doctrine as taught by these preachers is less moral in its influence, than it is as taught by Calvinists. In the opinion of all, but Calvinists themselves, the fact is the contrary. After the doctrine of election and reprobation, which is the combining and sustaining principle, the life and soul of Calvinism, there is none, which derogates more from the highest moral attributes of the Deity, or more completely destroys all moral ability in man, than the notion of *total depravity,* as explained by Calvinists. Allow me to state this doctrine in the expressive language of the symbol adopted by the Presbyterian Church. "From this original corruption, whereby we are utterly indisposed, disabled and *made opposite* to all good, and *wholly inclined to all evil,* do proceed all actual transgressions." Again, "Man, by his fall into a state of sin, hath *wholly lost all ability of will to any spiritual good* accompanying salvation; so as a natural man, being altogether averse from that which is good, and dead in sin, is not able, by his own strength to convert himself, or to *prepare himself there-*

unto." From this statement, which is sufficiently perspicuous, it would seem, that from our very nature we have no power to do any good thing; that, notwithstanding our endeavours, every word, thought, and deed, is a heinous offence in the sight of God, adds new violence to the flames of his wrath, and sinks us deeper and deeper under the curse of his law. And what is worse, not only every act is a sin, but every sin is equally aggravating. There can be no gradation in crimes, which proceed from a heart perfectly depraved. Hence, the infinitude of sin is a calvinistic doctrine. Every effort we make to please God, by seeking holiness and obeying his laws, only helps to sharpen the fierceness of his anger; every step we take in what we think to be the path of duty, virtue, piety, and a good life, carries us so much further towards the wretchedness and ruin, which, it would appear, are our just portion for being what God has made us.

To say nothing of the extreme absurdity of this doctrine in the abstract, what effect *ought* it to produce on him, who fancies he sincerely believes it? What must necessarily be his feelings towards his Maker? Can you love him, who punishes you for an offence, which he compels you to commit? What is there amiable, or benevolent, or glorious, or lovely in such a Being? Can we feel gratitude to him, who has created us to be wretched, not by reason of our own follies, or transgressions, but by his arbitrary appointment? If it were possible for us to realize these traits of his character, could we approach him with thanksgiving, reverence, and praise? Should we not detest a human magistrate, who would be so unreasonable, vindictive and cruel? And how can we love that in God, which is so abhorrent to every principle of our nature in men?

Preach this doctrine of total depravity, and total inability to any man, and if he believes you, and is in his senses, he certainly will not strive to do what you tell him it is utterly impossible for him to do. He will not cultivate the love of God and man, the mild, amiable, and exalted virtues; he will not cherish the kind affections, the spirit of meekness, forbearance and charity; he will not administer to the necessitous, nor console the afflicted; he will not subdue his passions, restrain his desires, resist temptation, nor avoid evil,—he will make no attempt to do any of these things, and for a very good reason,—all such attempts would be vain, and only prove his folly and weakness. What is there in this doctrine, preached in its true spirit and full extent, which would be likely to make any one a virtuous, holy man, a good citizen, or a candidate for heaven? Let it be generally understood in the world, that no man can possibly do any other than a wicked action, and that every action, or crime, is equally wicked, and do you believe such a doctrine, reduced to practice, would contribute much to the peace of society, or the establishment of morals and religion? Is it not evident to a demonstration, that it would dissolve all social order,

break the cords of the strongest compact, poison all that is pure in principle, and destroy all that is holy in practice? Such is the calvinistic doctrine
of depravity, when exhibited without sophistry, and divested of the clouds,
which have been gathered around it in the misty ages of school theology.

Unitarians, it is very true, preach no such depravity as this. They dare
not pamper the evil propensities of men by preaching to them, that they
sin from necessity, and have no power to amend their lives, and please
their Maker. They dare not preach a doctrine of such mischievous tendency, which they do not find supported in the Scriptures, and at which
every principle of the understanding revolts. They preach, that all men
are depraved, deeply depraved, and sinners in the sight of God—not by
the will and appointment of their Creator, but by their own choice, their
neglect of duty, and their obstinate disobedience.

There is no theme, in fact, on which unitarian preachers dwell more,
than on the moral depravity of man. This is the moral disease, which they
believe the religion of Jesus was intended to heal. As a free agent, man
has contracted this disease, and as a free agent he has the power of applying an effectual remedy, by using the means granted in the religion of
Christ. They describe the wretched state of the sinner, as the result of
his own follies, his abuse of his better faculties, his disregard of the counsel and chiding of conscience, and of the obligations of the divine laws.
They call on him to awake from his slumbers, to seek light rather than
darkness, to renew his depraved heart, to lay hold on the promises of
Christ, and to establish the hope of their fulfilment, by studying the will
of God as revealed in the Gospel, by giving strict heed to the perfect law
of faith, love, and righteousness, which this Gospel contains, by walking
resolutely and undeviatingly in the footsteps of Christ, and by making
his precepts, and these alone, the rule of their lives. They urge these duties
by all the motives set forth in the Gospel, by the perfections of God, the
dependence of man, the promise and prospects of joy to the righteous, the
threatenings of despair and suffering to the wicked. They afford not a
single palliative to the sinner's conscience, not a single excuse for his
shameful irresolution, or his rebellious obstinacy, by telling him, that his
Maker has formed him with a total, inherent, irremediable wickedness of
nature, which no effort of his own can remove. Why should you preach
repentance and holiness to such a being, unless it were to deride his im-
potency, or to make still deeper the shades of despair, which you have
caused to brood upon his soul? Why suspend the awful judgments of
God over the impenitent sinner, and then aggravate his misery by assuring him, that he has no power to escape?

It is unnecessary to pursue the parallel farther. I am willing to let the
decision rest on these short hints. With these alone let the question be

submitted to the understanding and common sense of every reader, whether the doctrine of depravity, as taught by Calvinists, of Unitarians, is the most likely to strengthen the cause of morals? Whether the doctrine, which makes men radically, necessarily, and perfectly wicked, and takes away all ability of improvement, is better calculated to fix the principles of religion in the soul, and to produce the fruits of piety, righteousness, and a good life, than the one, which lays the sins of every man to his own charge, which exhorts him to throw off the shackles he has thus forged for himself, confess his follies, repent of his wicked deeds, seek God, and live?

❧ Two Selections on the Christian's Social Responsibility

JOSEPH TUCKERMAN (1778–1840)

Daniel T. McColgan, the Roman Catholic historian who has written the only substantial biography of Joseph Tuckerman, compares his subject with St. Vincent de Paul. He makes very clear that Tuckerman was an important pioneer in American social work. He was also a pathbreaker for the social gospel in American Protestantism. Drawing inspiration and rationale from his friend and college classmate William Ellery Channing, Tuckerman personified the practical concern for the social order which was repeatedly insisted upon by the early Unitarians. The loneliness of his labors testifies to the degree to which theory tended to supersede practice in the movement as a whole. He was more a prophet than the founder of a continuing tradition of social concern.

Tuckerman was born in 1778, the son of a successful Boston merchant. He was educated at Phillips Andover Academy and at Harvard College (class of 1798) and, in preparation for the ministry, under the Reverend Thomas Thacher of Dedham. In 1801 he was settled over the church in Chelsea, then a rural town adjacent to Boston. Here he took his stand with the liberals in the Unitarian Controversy. He celebrated the silver jubilee of his ordination in the same parish and was praised at that time chiefly for his devoted pastoral work.

In 1826, however, Tuckerman entered upon a new career by resigning from his church in Chelsea (for reasons of ill health) and then accepting an invitation offered by the executive committee of the American Unitarian Association to be their missionary to Boston's poor. At this time he had no mature plan for urban social work; but as his visitations continued, he became passionately concerned with the problems of the rapidly growing slums, with the unchecked menace to religious and democratic nurture they presented, and with the tragic physical and moral plight of their inhabitants.

Through his efforts, an active ministry-at-large was established, chapels founded, and ministers of other denominations attracted to joint labors. An accompaniment of this work was his growing conviction that the care of the poor and kindred problems were a science. Yet in his social advocacy Tuckerman was not a radical. His was a conservative social gospel,

340

with its individualistic and moral emphasis and its preference for private philanthropy rather than public relief. His sense of injustice, however, precluded anything like the latter-day rationalizations of the Social Darwinians, who opposed social reform on the theory that moral fiber would win its reward, and the fittest would survive.

Tuckerman's regular reports to the American Unitarian Association are outstanding examples of early social reporting. A half-century after his death they were edited for publication by Edward Everett Hale, who then belonged to the activist element in the Unitarian movement that looked back on Tuckerman as a hero. The first part of the present composite selection is taken from Tuckerman's only full-length reflective work on the subject of social action; the second part is from Hale's selections from the reports.

Letter IV (from *The Principles and Results of the Ministry at Large in Boston*)

Poverty, or dependence upon alms, is, I think, one of the intended conditions of man in this world. I believe there will be those who will be thus more or less dependent even in the most advanced stage of christian improvement to be attained in this world. Who knows not that there are those, who, from original defects in their physical conformation are incapable of labor, and others who were born without the intellectual capacity required for self-support, each of whom is therefore cast by God's providence upon the care and kindness of others? And greater still is the number of those, who by disease, or accidents, or misfortune in business, or by old age, are deprived of the resources once had for self-subsistence, and are reduced to the necessity of asking alms. And not only may the poor of this class be virtuous, but they may be descendants of parents as virtuous as are to be found in any christian community. . . . These indeed, when taken together, are few when compared with those who now ask and receive alms. But few as they may be, they have their peculiar and distinctive claims; and one of the means, and an important one, of securing a due regard to these claims, is a clear development of the principles upon which they rest. I have stated these principles, and to yourself, Reader, I leave their application.

Yet think not that I would encourage an unnecessary dependence. Man is a creature too excellent in the constitution and objects of his nature for any other dependence than that which will minister to virtue. There are times, occasions, circumstances in which he needs, and in unnumbered

ways needs the aid of others. He has physical, intellectual and moral weaknesses, and wants, and tendencies which lead to a necessary and a widely
extended dependence both upon men and things around him. And our
common Father intended this dependence. It is a principle of the constitution both of the individual, and of society in this world. In every stage of
his being here, from the first breath of infancy to the last of the extremest
old age, every one is scarcely less dependent upon his fellow-beings, than
he is upon the vital air, and upon food. And so in this world will our race
ever be. This is among the most beautiful of the moral ordinations of our
Father's providence. A very large proportion of all the virtue of which
we are capable arises out of, and is indissolubly connected with this dependence. But it is also equally a law of our moral nature and condition,
and a law not at all less important to our moral progress and moral happiness, that to as great an extent as may be, we are to be a law to ourselves, in the high sense that we are to be self-determining, self-directing,
and self-supporting beings. . . . Let us do what we may to restrain it,
and there will still be the hungry who must be fed, and the naked who
must be clothed. And there will be those also who will be without the
bread of life, if it shall not be carried to them; many who will mourn
without comfort, if there shall be no one who will seek them out for the
very purpose of carrying comfort to them; many who will enter the ways
of sin and death, unless others than those immediately connected with
them shall take them by the hand, and lead them into the way of virtue
and life; and many will be lost whom Jesus came to seek and to save, if
there be not ministries for the very purpose of seeking, that they may
save. Nor will a greater good be received in either of these cases, even by
the most necessitous of those who need and claim it, than awaits those
also, who, according to their means and opportunities shall faithfully contribute to the support, comfort and salvation of their fellow-beings. . . .

Here also let me offer a remark upon the words poverty and pauperism,
as interchangeable terms. If we look only at their derivation, they have
indeed the same import, and are therefore very properly interchangeable.
Words however become modified, and more or less changed in their
signification, by the change of circumstances under which they are applied. . . . Let pauperism then, I would say, have its recognised technical sense, and be understood to imply a preference of support by alms, to
support by personal labor. Or yet further, let it be understood to imply
not only a union of debasement with want, but want produced by vice.
This is indeed a sore evil both to those suffering it, and to the community.
And never did God intend this condition of poverty, any more than he
intended intemperance, or idleness, or theft, or profligacy. . . .

I would add a word also in behalf of the pauper class, strictly so called.

The judgment and condemnation which are passed upon this class of our fellow-beings is often a most unjust one. They are indeed vicious, and their degradation is to be ascribed to their vices. But often it has seemed to me that these vices, and the dependence consequent upon them, are almost as necessary results of the outward condition, and the moral neglect of the early life of this class of the poor, as they could be even of a divine decree. It is one thing to look upon these victims of sin and want one by one, as we occasionally pass them in the streets, or see them as beggars at our doors, or in an alms-house in which they are brought before us as an isolated part of the community; and quite another thing to know them in their homes; in their personal history; in the moral exposures and the direct excitements to vice amidst which they were reared; in the workings of their minds under their wants and difficulties; in the necessary confinement of their social intercourse to those of their own class, and in their almost equally necessary influence upon one another. Let me say, then, that I have known much of them in these respects by having lived among them; and I do not hesitate to declare, that strongly as I have been made to feel their accountableness for their dependence and sufferings, yet very often have I been equally made to feel that this very dependence, with all its concomitant evils, comes not more in the form of retribution to its immediate subjects, than to the society of the prosperous around them, and in the midst of which they have been reared. Nay. In view of the moral exposures and difficulties of the children of this class of the poor, it is a matter of wonder that there are any among them who are not as deeply corrupted as they might be. In a land of Christians, and in a city of Christians, they were born, and have been reared as if they were of a recognised Pariah caste. They have been debased and corrupted by circumstances within the control of those in more favored conditions, but not within their own control, or that of their parents. In view, then, both of their dependence and their vices, have they not, I ask, high and strong moral claims upon society around them? Here they are; and, as I have said before, here they and their children will be. And here too, if they shall be left only to the provisions of law, and of a police, and to the casual kindness of the susceptible and the sympathising, they will not only continue to increase in numbers, as they have increased under the influences incident to the moral neglect in which they have been left, but in a dependence and recklessness which will increase with their numbers. Would that I could awaken in the prospered, secure and happy families of our community, a Christian sense of their responsibility for the condition of the parents of this class; and for the moral exposures and the vices of their children! . . .

Reader, had you been reared in circumstances like these, how much better now might have been your condition than that of these parents? And what better hopes could be had of your children, if they should be reared as are these children? Think you that the evils of that condition, and responsibility for them, would then have been wholly attributable either to yourself, or to those of the class to which you would have belonged? Surely there is some great and radical defect in that administration of the gospel in a city, which comprehends no agency by which the sympathy and interest of Christ shall be extended to fellow-beings so much in need of them as these are.

Here let me offer one or two remarks upon the subject of wages. . . . The natural principle,—for such it seems to me,—of a rate of wages for labor, like the rate of price for any article in the market, proportioned to the amount brought into the market, and the demand for it, is that on which we shall be compelled to fall back after all our discussions of the question as a general one, of the just rate of wages? I admit that there are great incidental evils, or I should rather call them, sufferings, under some of the operations of this principle, which in their results may, or may not on the whole be regarded as evils. But all classes, in a greater or less degree, are exposed to these sufferings, and actually incur them. They indeed generally bear much harder upon the labor capitalist, than upon the money capitalist. And yet it is often doubtful which of these classes actually suffers most from the fluctuations which bring down profits. The truth is, that the condition of the laborer is to be improved, not by any artificial system for the advance of wages, but alone by the advancement of high moral and religious principle and character throughout society. Here, I believe, is our only remedy in the case. Let Christianity have free course, and exert the intended influences of its principles of love and righteousness, and there will be no insurmountable difficulties upon the questions of wages, or rent, or price; or in respect to any of the circumstances of human dependence and necessity. Let those of us who pay wages, pay as freely and generously as we consistently can for the labor which is done for us. Much may thus be done for the relief of the laborer. Grudge not the full amount of all that he shall have earned. Seek not, by availing yourself of his pressing necessities, to obtain his services at the lowest rate at which you can purchase them, or at as low wages as he can be induced to receive for those services. It is unspeakably mean to do so; and the poor *feel* all the meanness of it, and estimate accordingly those by whom they are so treated. . . . This is an object beyond the scope of political economy. But it is within the scope of Christianity; and Christianity is alone sufficient for all the good to be obtained in this, and in every other department of philanthropy.

I have spoken of poverty as an intended condition of man in this world. . . . This inequality of property, or of wealth, seems to me indispensable to the maintenance of civil society. . . . But distinctions, and great distinctions in this respect seem to me to have been intended by him upon the same principle, and for similar ends, for which he has appointed the unequal capacities of men, their means and opportunities of intellectual acquisition, and of power in the various kinds of it which are required for the diversified necessities and wants of human society. . . . The question then arises, what are Christian views of wealth?

Both the conduct of our Lord, and his teaching in respect to riches and to the rich, were certainly very remarkable. . . . What is its import in application to yourself? I know, indeed, of no trial of human piety and virtue from which so few have come out uninjured,—may I not even say unindurated and undepraved by the very trial itself, as from the trial of great wealth. Looking at man in the lights of the gospel, I know of no condition of humanity less to be envied, than that of the very rich. Were Christian principles of riches carried out by the rich, not one necessity which Christian benevolence could supply would be unsatisfied, and not one social improvement it could make be uneffected. . . .

It is indeed a first principle of social morality, that every human being has a right to life, to liberty, to property, and to the pursuit of happiness. But not one of these rights is illimitable; and just conceptions of their limitations in every case are as important as are just conceptions of their reality. . . .

I ask then in this connexion, have not the poor who apply to us for alms *a right* to the alms which they seek? . . . The right of one party, in this case, seems to me a most clear limitation of the right in the other. Right and duty here, I think, rest upon the same principles of the divine government, and are perfectly reciprocal. . . .

God, as the universal Father, has an equal love for each one of his children *as such*. This is an elementary principle of all fair reasoning among Christians respecting the relation of man to man, and of man to the world. Inequality in this case would imply not only imperfection, but injustice. . . .Why then has he made us to differ as we do in our means of subsistence, improvement and happiness? Why but that man may be made the minister of his equal love to man? And if this be God's design, what are rights and duties in the case?

I beg to proceed one step further, and to say that it is a principle or ground to be asserted for reasoning and for action upon the subjects of human relations, rights, and duties, that the world in which we live is *God's world*. Men often thus speak of it, without any apparent consciousness of the importance of the truth of which their words are a recognition. But if this be God's world, then neither as a whole, nor in any of its parts, nor in anything belonging to it, can it rightfully become in any degree or respect the property of man individually, or collectively, nor by any other means, nor for any other uses, than in conformity to the known will of God. . . .

In view then of these principles, it seems to me that the right to accumulate property is a most distinctly limited right. . . . God intended that there should be individual property or wealth, and even great disparities of property. But his purpose in the appointment of riches and poverty, as of all the distinctions of human capacity and condition, is *virtue*. Virtue is an end, and not a means to an end. 'Virtue,' I repeat, 'is the beginning of heaven, and heaven is the perfection of virtue.' That accumulation of wealth, therefore, by any individual, which shall be extended beyond the limits which that individual's conscience will finally recognise as its just limits, when he shall stand before God to be judged by the precepts of the gospel, is to be held unchristian, and not to be classed among the rights of Christians. . . .

The Means Most Effectual for Relieving the Wants of the Poor (from On the Elevation of the Poor)

It is asked, then, how should we act, or what is it our duty to do in this difficult work of provision for the poor of our city?

Before I give my opinion upon this question, I may be allowed to exonerate myself from a suspicion to which I feel that I may be exposed by the precautions which I have suggested in relation to the exercise of our charity.* It may be said that I have learned to look upon the poor rather in the light in which they are seen by the political economist than as a Christian. But I answer, that I should esteem that to be a false and injurious principle in political economy which is not in perfect consistency with Christian morality. I would, however, consider the Christian precepts in regard to the poor as I would the language of the New Testament respecting the rich, in connection with those qualifications which other precepts of our religion as well as good common sense require us to employ in the practical interpretations of them. While, therefore, I would understand and feel that the poorest of human beings, equally with the richest, is a child of God; that every human being, however poor and

---

* On preceding pages [in Hale's book, Tuckerman] had criticized proposals to relieve the poor by artificially reducing their rent, by developing new modes for employing the poor or providing houses for employing the female poor, and by establishing soup-houses or depositories of vegetables to which "the suffering poor might go for small supplies." [Eds.]

however degraded, has a common nature with him who is the most favored, and is his *brother;* that for our means and opportunities for instructing the ignorant, of supplying the wants of the destitute, and of recoving the most debased to virtue and to God, we are finally to give account to him who has made us to differ, and who has intrusted us with these means that we might be the instruments of his benevolence to our fellow-creatures; and while I would feel all the power of the words of our Lord Jesus Christ, and the blessedness of the privilege to which we may be advanced by them, "inasmuch as ye have fed the hungry, and clothed the naked, and visited the sick and the prisoner, ye have shown this kindness unto me." I would yet remember also that our religion with equal distinctness teaches us, if not in its letter, yet in its spirit, that we are not by our charity to encourage idleness and vice, and thus to increase and perpetuate pauperism and misery. As we are not to do evil that good may come, so neither are we to mistake that for goodness which a little judgement and foresight might teach us would inevitably lead to evil. As, therefore, I think it to be the Christian duty of parishes in the country to take the charge of their own poor, I would say let us act upon this sentiment. And I think that the inhabitants of a city are acting for the best good of that part of the very poor among them who belong to the country by using all fair and Christian means of inducing them to return, or of sending them to the places from which they came, where they will be at least equally well supplied. And let us do what we may for the relief of the city, we shall always have a great number of poor among us, to whom it will not be more our duty than it should be our happiness to do good as far as God shall enable us. Nor is it desirable that we should have no poor among us. Nay, it is even desirable to awaken more of the spirit of Christian charity than now exists among us. The more favored classes of our society are far behind the requisitions of our religion in regard to their duties towards the poor. But I comprehend in the term "charity" far more than alms-giving. We should aim not alone at the greatest immediate but at the greatest ultimate good. We should do good at the expense and even at the hazard of the least possible evil. We should make alms-giving, as far as possible, minister not only to comfort but to piety and virtue. This will be found at once the truest economy.

That we may most effectually meet the wants of the poor, I would say then, *first,* that it should be insisted upon that there shall be *a discrimination in the distribution of alms by our charitable societies.* . . .

It should be known that our benevolent societies endeavor to maintain the principle of discrimination in the exercise of their charities. They *visit* the families which apply for their bounty, and learn what they can respecting their characters as well as their wants. The difficulty, however, is, that as they now act, without any communication with each other, they do, and necessarily must, interfere with each other. . . .

It is asked how we shall obviate these evils. The most simple measure of which I can conceive for the purpose, and the only one by which I believe the object can be gained, is, that a registry shall be made every week in a book kept for the purpose in the office of the overseers of the poor of the persons relieved by them in their several wards, and that similar books be kept at this office by the agents of all our benevolent societies.

In the *second* place, I think it to be of great importance that *immediate and more vigorous measures should be adopted for preventing the accumulation of foreign poor in the city.*

There would be no difficulty in providing for our native poor, if it were for them only that we were called upon to make provision. But vast numbers of the poor of other countries are thrown upon us. I say it not in the spirit of reproach,—they are taking the bread of our own children. They are here, and must have their share of the labors of the poor and of the bounty which we have to bestow upon the poor. Unhappily, it has been thought to be good policy to encourage emigration to our country; and we have held out the lure to the restless and discontented throughout the world as well as to the enterprising and virtuous. It is asked, what remedy is proposed for this evil? I answer, we require new legislative measures in regard to the foreign poor who come to us. . . .

And in the *third* place, I would say, *that means should be taken to impress our community with a deeper sense of the relation which Christianity recognized between the more and less favored classes of society,—between the more and less favored classes of society,—between the rich and poor.*

It is not to be forgotten that after all the vigilance that can be exercised and all the judgement and caution that can be maintained for the prevention of pauperism and for security against deceptions and the abuse of charity, there will still be very many, in a city like ours, who will be more or less dependent upon the care and kindness of others for subsistence. And in view of the Gospel of Jesus Christ, if not of the doctrine of political economists, these *have claims* upon those who are able to provide for them. I go further,—there are many who are comparatively unworthy of the bounty which they seek, and yet have, if Christianity be true, strong claims upon the consideration of their fellow-beings in happier conditions than their own. These claims may, in part, be answered by public and by private benevolent institutions. But there is no *public* provision or *associated* exercise of charity that can supersede or be substituted for *individual obligation* and *individual responsibility*. This obligation and responsibility is felt to an important extent among us. But if it were felt as it should be, there would be no need of benevolent societies. *Here, then, is the great end at which we should aim.* And I am doubtful whether the blessing so obtained would be greater to the object of charitable regard and care or to the favored instruments of such charity.

It is asked, what are the duties of the intelligent and the rich in regard to the poor? What is demanded of us as private Christians?

I answer, I think it is contemplated by our religion that the more favored classes should strongly feel that they have a common nature with those in less favored conditions of life; that opportunities and means are responsibilities; and that it is God's will that they should be his instruments for accomplishing the purposes of his benevolence to the poor. They should therefore *visit* them, and do what they can to help and improve them. To be more explicit, every individual who has the means of assisting a few families should feel his obligation to seek out and to know a few families with which he shall connect himself as a Christian friend. Every man *who is disposed for this intercourse* may find leisure for it. Let him visit these families once a week,—and if he cannot do it at other times, do it on Sunday. And let him feel that in forming this connection he has taken upon himself a moral charge; that he is to be the adviser, and to seek the improvement of parents and children,—to aid the parents in keeping their children at school, and in placing them out as apprentices; to promote temperance, industry, order, and cleanliness among them; to connect them, when practicable, with some congregation of worshippers; to inspire them with a proper self-respect; in times of sickness and sorrow to be their comforter; and in seasons of want so to minister to their necessities that their energies for self-support may be increased rather than lessened by the bounty they receive. The simplest principles of Christianity carried into full exercise would perfectly secure the permanency of all this good among us. We have means enough, intellectual, moral, and pecuniary, to meet all the demands of our city in regard to the poor. The whole difficulty is to bring these means into use for the purpose. Our great want is a greater prevalence of the true spirit of our religion among the intelligent and the rich in regard to their relation to the poor and the duties that grow out of this relation.

❧ The Christian Theory of Life

WILLIAM ROUNSEVILLE ALGER
(1822–1905)

William Rounseville Alger was born in Freetown, Massachusetts, three years after Channing's Baltimore Sermon. He entered the Harvard Divinity School without a college degree, and was graduated in 1847. (He received an A.M. from Harvard College five years later.) He was ordained to the Mount Pleasant Unitarian Society in Roxbury in 1847 and served there until 1855, when he accepted a call to the society in Bulfinch Street, Boston. This society merged with Theodore Parker's old 28th Congregational Society two years later, whereupon Alger became an exceedingly popular preacher in the Music Hall. In 1874 he began a four-year ministry at the Church of the Messiah in New York, which was followed by three other brief pastorates (in Denver, Chicago, and Portland, Maine). He retired from the ministry in 1882.

Alger's literary productions were diverse. An antislavery Fourth of July address delivered in Boston in 1857 was even at that late date regarded as so intemperate by the board of aldermen that they refused the customary vote of gratitude. But in 1868 he was made chaplain of the Massachusetts legislature and in the following year was requested to publish his prayers uttered before that body. He published a great many sermons and works of edification, as well as works of scholarship ranging from a volume of Oriental poems and a life of Edwin Forrest to *A Critical History of the Doctrine of the Future Life,* which, with its enormous bibliography compiled by Professor Ezra Abbot of the Harvard Divinity School, remains a valuable reference work.

Although Alger inherited the mantle of Parker by becoming a preacher at the Music Hall, his true place in the denomination is better indicated by his following in the succession of such conservatives as Orville Dewey, Samuel Osgood, and George H. Hepworth at New York's Church of the Messiah. His theological orientation is well set forth in his early *Sources of Consolation in Human Life* and in his *History of the Cross of Christ.*

It would be difficult to find—or even to imagine—a brief essay that expressed more succinctly the Unitarian outlook on man's nature, destiny, and immortality than the short compendium reprinted here. Its focus, to be sure, is on ethics, but very few essential elements of the Liberal Faith escape notice or mention. Clearly set forth are both the view, taken wholeheartedly from the Scottish philosophers, that man is inherently a seat of original, creative moral power and the belief that all kinds of hedonistic ethics (including by implication the otherwise useful works of William Paley) and every sort of determinism (including what was to Alger the same thing, predestinarian doctrines of Christianity) are unacceptable. One sees here, moreover, a well-rounded exposition of the argument from design elaborated by the same Archdeacon Paley and the other natural theologians of the eighteenth century. Alger's profound confidence in man's goodness and perfectibility and in the inevitability of progress reflects Channing's fervent optimism. The argument by which Christianity is understood as a pleroma encompassing and expressing all that is good and true in the other great world religions is the one later to be set forth in greater detail by James Freeman Clarke in his widely read work on the world's ten great religions. The present selection is also an incisive statement of those views (later the subject of much examination by Max Weber and others) according to which Christianity is seen as the stimulating factor in the dynamism of Western civilization, and therefore that the Protestant ethic is vital to the rise of commercial and industrial expansion.

There are, and can be, only three different theories of life. One of them is, that man can complete his destiny here, in this world. This makes enjoyment the true end and aim of human existence. Whatever form it may assume, this is the essence of the Epicurean philosophy. It is the faith which the world and its evil allies would ever impose upon mankind. It is the natural theory of the senses. It is the first scheme devised by the reasonings of an unrefined selfishness. It is the false conclusion and the hasty induction of ignorance, and a narrow, barren soul. It is outgrown by the development of the holier affections, finer sentiments, profounder wants, and loftier faculties of our nature.

The principal objections to it are these. It can only answer for the young, the vigorous and joyful, to whom the senses are fresh, the world fair, and the founts of pleasure flowing freely; and it is not sufficient for any, even the gayest and most thoughtless. It considers but a part of the facts in the case; takes into account only the mechanical forces and the animal elements, leaving out of view the causal energies and the spiritual portions of our being and experience. It proposes as the chief end happiness, which no man can be sure to win. It makes its disciples miserable by causing them to forsake high duties and aims for paltry expediencies and hollow pleasures, followed by inevitable retributions. It is the very root and core of selfishness, preventing any self-sacrifice or public beneficence.

It is most dangerous, as the secret but fatal path to sin and spiritual ruin; for when virtue is guarded by vice, it is easy to corrupt the sentinel. It is refuted by the existence of the absolute moral law, binding upon all, without regard to consequences. It is disproved by the evidence of immortality, accumulated from all quarters until it overwhelms us with the glorious burden of its proof.

Another theory of life is, that man cannot in this world fulfil any part of his destiny. This makes passive submission his true aim in the present state. All labor is, of course, useless. His only wisdom is to fold his arms in dreamy contemplation of the phenomena he cannot avoid, and, idly waiting a change, say within himself,—"Vanity of vanities, all is vanity." This is the substance of various theories of the Oriental mystics, and is also fairly involved in those theological systems extensively prevalent in Christendom, which deny that there is in man self-determining power,— those schemes of faith which deny the necessary continuity of spiritual life, and sever the moral connection of the present with the future. It has its origin from different sources. It is inferred from the false philosophy of fatalism, in which all men sometimes believe, and some men always. It is suggested by the mighty power of evil, the necessary warfare between the good and the bad principles and tendencies in the world. It is seemingly taught by the finiteness and weakness of man, the frequent futility of his desires, and failure of his most arduous labors. It is insinuated by languid indolence, by feebleness and despondency. It is a necessary consequence of the Eastern doctrine of final absorption in the essence of Deity.

On the other hand, it is refuted by the consciousness of freedom, of an inherent causative power, and of a law of obligation. It is instinctively denied by men of a strong and ardent personality,—by ambitious and creative men. It is disproved by the actual existence of those laws of cause and effect with which we are acquainted, involving all the phenomena and experience of immediate and lasting personal retribution and reward; and of which we may avail ourselves or not, as we please, but which, at any rate, rule the world and all it holds. It is overthrown by the consideration that God is the universal Creator, and is almighty; and that, therefore, it is absurd to suppose a world and all its inhabitants to exist for no purpose; for upon the view that man can fulfil no destiny here, this life might just as well all be blotted out. It cannot be so. This life is a fact; God's hand is therefore in it, and it must have a present meaning and a present purpose. It is demolished by the cumulative argument from analogy, showing that throughout the realm of nature there is not a living creature that wastes its life like the idle Hindoo, who maintains that work is folly, as if it were not an ordinance of God, or that torments itself voluntarily, like the self-scourging ascetic, who asserts the essential hostility and eternal opposition of spirit and matter, earth and heaven, as if God did not make them both, and they were not each the complement of the other. And, finally, its falsity is clearly shown by its actual effects. It leads to indifference, stagnation, physical degradation and wretchedness, moral and intellectual death. Compare the principal portions of Asia with those of Europe or America. In the former, age after age passes away with no favorable change, with but little save monotony and decay. In the latter, each generation beholds a marked improvement and advance. There the dead sea of sloth lies putrid and silent. Here the hurrying river of industry bears health, fertility, and commerce through its course, and pours their tribute into the general mart of nations. Wherever this theory prevails, you will find idleness, debasement, cowardice, torpidity, and despotism. Into this miserable mixture, that has stood so long, only introduce one new truth which it wants,—the Christian doctrine, that man as an individual is immortal, and has a destiny to fulfil in this world preparatory to the one which awaits him in another,—and, at once, it will crystallize, shooting into the sparkling forms of activity, enlightenment, and joy; the elements of its life—to vary the figure—will be changed into nutriment for a higher and clearer life, as when a foreign branch is ingrafted into a tree, the juices from the old roots and trunk are converted into a different and superior fruit.

For the reasons now given, these two theories of life—the one, that man's destiny is personal enjoyment, and that he must finish it in this world; the other, that in this world he can do nothing of any lasting use, but is the victim of an evil fate—must be rejected alike.

There remains but one more theory, and that is the one embodied in Christianity. This declares that the destiny of man is endless; that he can fulfil a portion of it here, and continue it hereafter, for it stretches through eternity and will be fulfilling for ever; that it is the purpose of his being to constitute a conscious and ever-rising portion of the universal order. This work he can commence in the present, carry on in the future, but never finish, since, being a child of God, he is an heir of immortality. The Christian theory is well stated by Paul, when he says,—"For to me to live is Christ, and to die is gain." That is, to live is useful labor, to die is glorious reward. It may be summed up as follows.

This life on the earth is no delusion, but a substantial reality. It is under the direct superintendence of an Infinite Father, who numbers the hairs of our heads and provides for the little sparrow. Its labors are ennobling and preparatory. Its duties are great, reaching up to heaven, and going down to hell. Its temptation, weariness, and agony shall work out for us a far more exceeding and eternal weight of glory. Its mysteries, so dark and unfathomable now, shall be clear hereafter. God never forsakes us, for in him we live and move and have our being. He freely forgives us our sins, whenever we sincerely repent of them, and forsake them. He never ceases to love us, for that would be to hate himself, since we are all his offspring. And to those who love him and keep his commandments, all things shall be seen in the end to have worked together for good. The object of this life is, through toil, trial, sin, sorrow, and their opposites, to develop in man virtue and strength, wisdom and love, those traits and tastes which will fit him for the more exalted and ethereal experience of the spirit-world. Moral freedom, and the consequent exposure to evil and its punishment, are an unavoidable part of the discipline in such a scheme as this, which is the only one fitted to man and truly worthy of him, and is the best possible one for him. Death is but the transition from this state of existence to a higher and freer one, to endure for ever. Where earth and this life set us down, there heaven and immortality will take us up. When man lays his body in the grave, that he himself enters into open relations with a grander sphere is no baseless dream, but a sublime verity. The experience of that untravelled world will, still more evidently, be directly in the hands of God's good providence. It is a continuation of the soul's life, under new circumstances. It opens a scene and an experience of greater dignity and delight, filling the good with bliss by its divine revelations, purifying and elevating the bad by its remedial retributions. It removes the clogs of the body, the temptations and evils of sense. It leads to spiritual employments of nobler use and purer joy. With the progressive spirits of all the just, it soars and aspires along the line of perfection through endless ages. Therefore, to live is Christ, and to die is gain; this life is well, but the heavenly life is still better.

Such, in plain terms, is a brief outline of the Christian theory of life. The most striking, conclusive evidence of its truth is afforded by the singular precision with which it fits in to the facts, meets the emergencies, and supplies the wants of human nature and mortal experience. Had a wise man, taking all the experience of life as we actually find it, set himself down to invent a theory to interpret the phenomena in all respects, it could not harmonize with the state of the case more completely, or appear more consistent throughout. With the deliberate emphasis of a fixed conviction, we say that the reality of this view is proved by the wonderful exactness of its adaptation to the real wants of men and nations,—the beneficence of its practical workings. . . .

The pagan and the Mohammedan portions of the world give few indications of improvement. Heathen life universally is losing ground, its vigor is waning, it shows symptoms of burning low, of flickering and expiring in its socket. The eyes and the hopes of humanity are fixed upon Christendom, and there alone is true progress made. These facts are no faint indication that the life-philosophies of heathendom are false, and that they are fated to perish; that Christianity is divinely true, and that it is really destined, as has ever been prophesied and hoped, to number among its subjects all the children of men, stretching its dominion from shore to shore, till its Promulgator shall indeed have a name that is above every other name. The priests and devotees of the religions of Brahma, Zoroaster, Confucius, and Buddha, all sit with their backs to the rising orb, gazing reverently upon a mighty past wherein their systems were triumphant powers. Backwards they point and adore. But the religion of Jesus is the promise and the energy of the future. Its history is the account of human progress. It stands upon impregnable realities, and points to heaven with humble piety and sublime trust. It looks along the vista of coming ages with prophetic exultation, and flings over all the earth this voice of cheer,—"Leave the Past with repentance; improve the Present; press on to conquer the Future for God and for man, for in it the Golden Age lies waiting!" . . .

The Christian theory of life combines in itself every truth contained in the other theories, at the same time correcting their errors and supplying their deficiencies. Consider if it be not so. There is, for instance, a truth in the theory that man can accomplish his destiny on earth; but the Epicurean exaggerates it into a falsehood. This truth Christianity acknowledges, with the necessary qualifications, saying, Man can fulfil, but not finish, his destiny, in this life, for it is endless. It also admits that happiness is an important and innocent fact in life, only adding, that it is not the object, but the attendant, of labor; that virtue is the end, and happiness the concomitant, of true life.

The Epicurean philosophy, moreover, has a fatal defect. It cannot satisfactorily account for sadness and suffering. It cannot give them any relief. It can see no good in evil. If happiness be the great aim of life, there can be no possible consolation for its deprivation, or for the anguish of misery! This deficiency Christianity supplies, declaring virtue, spiritual growth and strength, to be the end of living, and this object can be effected as well, and often far better, by the ministries of affliction, as by ease and enjoyment; and thus the darkness of melancholy and repining becomes the light of joyful faith. . . .

IV UNCERTAINTIES AND CONFLICT

❧ Philosophical Difficulties in the "Unitarian Controversy"

HENRY WARE (1764–1845)

Two phrases pervaded New England's thinking about God in the eighteenth and nineteenth centuries: the sovereignty of God, which is, of course, a central thesis of all true Reformed theologies; and the moral perfection of God, which was central to virtually all liberal theologies, including some which are not ordinarily considered liberal (e.g., Jonathan Edwards's). As a matter of fact neither side, Reformed nor liberal, ever denied God's omnipotence or his moral perfection, but the emphasis given to one attribute generally conditioned the interpretation given the other. If sovereignty were emphasized, then God was seen as beyond human, finite moral judgments and as inscrutable or even arbitrary. If moral perfection were emphasized, as by Channing in his important essay of 1809, then God was understood as acting according to the moral values and precepts which people could and did know. These phrases and the consequent arguments represented the alternative between theocentric (God-centered) and anthropocentric (human-being-centered) theology. Each position had its difficulties, but they were difficulties of different kinds.

Henry Ware points out in the brief passage which follows that Unitarian difficulties are logical or metaphysical, whereas orthodox difficulties are moral. Ware added considerably to his stature by openly stating his awareness of the issues, as he does in this selection. He reveals another important fact: the close relationship between views about man's nature and views about God. In this way he entered into the classic Christian debates about metaphysics, morality, and theology which have concerned such theologians as Augustine, Aquinas, and Calvin in centuries past and, in more recent days, ones such as Barth, Brunner, and Tillich. Henry Ware represents the Unitarian ethos when he declares, "we [Unitarians] are far more competent to judge upon moral, than upon metaphysical questions."

. . . I have something . . . to observe, with respect to these *metaphysical difficulties* [of the Unitarian doctrine] on the one hand, which have so much weight with the orthodox; and moral difficulties [of the orthodox view] on the other hand, which Unitarians think so important. There can be no doubt, that each of them is deserving of consideration; and no one can be intitled to the character of a fair and liberal inquirer, who wholly overlooks either of them, in making up his mind, as to the foundation of the two opposite systems. But suppose the direct evidence from experience and scripture were equal on both sides, (which I am fully persuaded, however, is very far otherwise, and that it is decisive on the side of the Unitarian faith,) suppose it were equal, I say, and our opinion were to be decided by our estimate of the weight, which we think should be allowed to the respective difficulties, by which each system is pressed; the question then for us to decide will be, to which of the difficulties it is reasonable for us to allow the most influence in determining our choice.

Now the difficulties, as I have stated, which press upon the Calvinistic scheme, are wholly of a *moral nature;* those objections which the opposite scheme has to encounter are *metaphysical only.* The Calvinist has to reconcile his scheme with the moral character and moral government of God, and with the moral and accountable condition of man; and this, he will not deny, is an arduous task, and one that requires him to subdue the feelings of nature, and to silence the voice of reason. The Unitarian, on the other hand, can never so fully explain the nature of moral liberty, the influence of motives, the consistency of contingency with foreknowledge, and the existence of certainty without necessity, that the scheme shall be pressed with no remaining difficulty. But it seems to me, that a little just reflection will decide for us, which of these difficulties ought to have the most weight, on the supposition that the direct and positive evidence on that side be not absolutely conclusive, nor invalidated by opposite evidence. And the single reflection I think is this, that we are far more competent to judge upon moral, than upon metaphysical questions, being capable of the most clear and satisfactory knowledge of moral truth, while we can only arrive at uncertain conclusions in our metaphysical inquiries. And this is particularly the case, as to the great metaphysical and moral questions, which are brought into view in this controversy.

Of the nature of efficient causes, of the manner in which the will is influenced by motives, and what degree of power the agent may or may not have over the will, independent of motives, or in limiting their influence, we can have but imperfect knowledge, and ought to be modest in our decisions: but we may be perfectly confident in pronouncing what is, and what is not, consistent with moral rectitude. We are certain that malevolence, cruelty, injustice can never be right, and can never be the attributes of a holy being.

How it is possible for God to make a being capable of moral freedom, and how he can foreknow the free actions of such a being, we may not be able to explain; but we can certainly know, that a being morally good, will not make a single creature, much less a whole race of beings, so inclined by nature to evil, and indisposed to good, as to be from the first the objects of his hatred and wrath, and continue so till their nature is changed by a divine influence, which he never grants them. And we are sure, that he will not require of such beings a change, which he has made it *morally impossible* for them to experience, and yet inflict eternal punishments upon them for failing to do it. Yet this I think is nothing more, than a fair statement of the moral difficulty, under which the orthodox system labours.

❧ Sober Thoughts on the State of the Times

HENRY WARE, JR. (1794–1843)

By 1835 it was clear to any acute observer that a major phase of the controversy between Unitarianism and orthodoxy was a thing of the past. Earlier Channing had called attention to the rapid growth of liberal churches when farmer and judge alike embraced Unitarianism. In a famous phrase included in the selection that follows, Henry Ware, Jr., pronounced: "We are a community by ourselves." Yet all was not well with the Unitarian community so lately established, as the sensitive mind of the younger Ware perceived. He, like so many of his brethren, was alarmed and concerned that the liberal movement was not making the advances which at one time had been so glowingly predicted.

Looking about him, Ware saw the weakness of the American Unitarian Association and recognized the feeble evangelistic impulse that its impoverished treasury denoted. He remarked, too, the disturbing need for a larger ministry and the paucity of theological students. Most serious of all, he saw everywhere the apathy and complacency which it had been his particular purpose to root out of his own parish. To attack these numerous sins of omission he published in October 1835 his *Sober Thoughts on the State of the Times*. The pamphlet was sent forth anonymously, but its authorship, suspected immediately by some, was soon generally known. The essay was and remains a major work of Unitarian self-analysis.

Twenty years of controversy have just passed by. It has been a season, we may suppose, much like that of all controversies; but it has had its own characteristics, and, what is worthy of special observation, it is likely to be followed by more distinct and lasting results than generally happens. A theological discussion of great severity is oftentimes carried on for years, and yet it would be difficult to trace its consequences any where, excepting in the books which have been written, and which are themselves soon forgotten. But in the present instance, a broad mark has been left upon the very face of society; a permanent change has been effected in some of its institutions, and in the relations of its members. For it has been one of

362

that series of struggles for liberty and light, which began at the opening of the Reformation in Germany, three hundred years ago, and which is pushing on step by step toward the completion of that immortal work. Society advances in opinion, in knowledge, in institutions, by some great effort of its powerful minds, and then pauses for a time, as if to secure and consolidate what is gained. Then another effort, agitation and advancement, and again another pause. During these pauses it may seem stationary; it may even appear to the apprehensive mind retrograde; but it is certainly true that revolutions do not go backward; and though the tide of improvement, as it rolls up its glorious waves, may appear to be occasionally retreating, it is only to gather up its might, and come on with a firmer swell; while Dame Partington and all her maids brandish their ancient mops in vain.

It is the rolling in upon the shore of one of these larger swells that has attracted our attention during the last twenty years. The Reformation has been making a vigorous advance. The commotion has been extensive, the tossing has been fearful, the alarm and bustle of those exposed to the spray have been loud and earnest. At length the height of the swell seems to have passed. There are symptoms of greater quiet and repose. To change the figure, the heat of the warfare is over; the great battle has been fought; and it is time to look about us, and see what is the result, where the world stands, and what use is to be made of the losses and the acquisitions of the contest. I know no more instructive inquiry to the impartial seeker of truth. Who will undertake the investigation? Perhaps the day for it is not yet fully come: in order to a satisfactory decision, we must perhaps wait for the termination of several most interesting discussions in various unconnected portions of the Christian church, which are now in fervent progress,—all of them growing out of the great action of the principles of the Reformation, all a part of the mighty struggle of the times for liberty and light, all portending salutary change throughout the religious world, and giving to the thoughtful observer auspicious pledges of the sure advent of a day of complete and established reform. "Let the people praise thee, O Lord! let all the people praise thee!"

It is no part of my design to look at the whole of this most extensive subject. I confine myself to that division of the church which has stood in the front rank during the recent contest, which has carried farthest the principles of the Reformation, and has consequently suffered (as the leading corps in this cause have always done) from the suspicions, the opposition, and the anathema of the general body of the believers. The majority of those who have reformed to a certain extent has always been seriously inimical to those who desire to reform further. "They have come to a period in religion," to quote the significant expression of the immortal

Robinson, and they call it Orthodoxy. To go a step farther, and read the next sentence, is heresy, and heretics, of course, are not to be tolerated. This intolerable class, at the present age, is that of Unitarians. They are desiring to press the Reformation beyond the orthodoxy of the present times, just as the Puritans desired to press it beyond the orthodoxy of the English church, and are therefore to be regarded and treated no better than those unfortunate schismatics were treated by the powerful sects around them. Happily, indeed, no *secular* persecution is possible in these days; but doubtless the wicked Puritans of King James's time were not worse, in the eyes of the monarch and the church, than the wicked Unitarians now are in the view of the leading powers in church and state.

The recent controversy has been, not simply a discussion of opinions, but a contest for rights; it has involved questions of reputation for piety, claim to the Christian name, and, in some instances, questions of property. It has been the cause of various trying changes in the domestic and social relations; it has rent asunder long-united communities; it has touched, in all parts of the land, and sometimes with a most ungentle hand, many of the tenderest interests and charities of life. With so many circumstances and occasions of exasperation, is it strange that it sometimes, on both sides, took an unhappy tone of bitterness and recrimination? Are we to wonder, when the excited disputant sat down to his task of argument or defence, and remembered that not only his most sacred opinions were to be shielded, but that momentous results of immediate, tangible good and ill, happiness and wretchedness, were at stake—are we to wonder that he sometimes spoke too warmly, accused too fiercely, answered too indignantly, and was over-valiant in the use of provoking and irritating missiles? There is much of this to be lamented and forgiven on both sides. . . .

Yet, upon the whole, there is much upon which the mind may look back with satisfaction and devout gratitude. Those to whom I write will not fail to recognize the hand of a wise and gracious Providence in much of the fiery trial through which they have been called to pass. "If the Lord had not been on our side when men rose up against us, then they had swallowed us up quick, when their wrath was kindled against us. Blessed be the Lord, who hath not given us as a prey to their teeth." We have much to be thankful for, in the manner in which the discussion, on the whole, was conducted; for the vigor, manliness, strength, and sobriety,—for the fairness, seriousness, love of truth, and spirit of piety, by which it was sustained and imbued; and for the lofty eloquence of faith, and fervent attachment of heart, with which the SOUL of Christianity—its vital and life-giving essence—was clung to, advocated, appealed for, in the midst of this confounding din about the outworks of opinion. Now that it is so far past, let us gratefully adore the goodness which has brought us through, purified, improved, and advanced as a people, rather than consumed, dwindled, deteriorated. We had a conscientious and extreme dislike to controversy. We dreaded its operation as a blight on the kindliness of the affections and the devoutness of the spirit. We entered its perilous way with anxious alarm. But we now find that our fears did not prophesy truly. Piety has not decayed, religion has not languished, the charities of life have not perished. On the contrary, we seem to have clasped the more closely to our bosom the spiritual treasures of our faith, and to have valued them more highly than ever. We tested and felt anew their unspeakable worth. And, probably, practical and vital religion was never more esteemed and prevalent, than at this very time, when we are issuing from a storm which seemed destined to destroy it.

This, then, is the present aspect of our religious affairs. We have discussed with our differing brethren the doctrines respecting which we differed, and the questions are at rest. *The result is, that we are a community by ourselves.* When we began the debate, we were members of the general Congregational body, communicants at the same tables, and sheep under the same shepherds. (I speak in general terms.) Now, a separation has taken place. We have our own congregations, our own ministers, our own institutions and instruments of religious improvement. It is a crisis of unspeakable interest to us. We are deeply concerned to know what is the character and power of those institutions, what the nature and operation of our distinctive faith, and how far we are faithful representatives, advocates, stewards, of that pure and glorious gospel on whose behalf we have been allowed to contend. . . .

I must begin with a statement respecting our community, which is necessary to be carefully considered, in order to a just appreciation of what shall follow. We are familiar with the distinction between *real* and *nominal* Christians. Every sect, every congregation, has its nominal adherents,—those, namely, who, from birth, or residence, or policy, or other accidental circumstances, are attached to it, but are not deeply pledged to it as a matter of conscience and salvation. There are such nominal Christians every where. They are found in our community, as well as in others. Generally speaking, they are regarded in any community, not as a part of the actual, efficient force of the camp, nor as the fair representatives of the character and principles of the body. *Neither are they to be accounted such in ours:*—and this is a position to be insisted on. It unavoidably happens, from the circumstances of the case, that our community is encumbered with rather an unusual proportion of these irregular adherents; and it is a fact, not only not to be overlooked, but to be carefully explained, if we would understand aright our situation and our duties.

Let us recollect, then, that there are among us two classes of congregations,—the old and the new,—originating under different circumstances, and existing beneath different influences. The old congregations are, many of them, equal, in point of antiquity, to the country itself; they have very gradually receded from the Orthodoxy of the forefathers, and have become what they are without passing through any period of effervescence or convulsion. Such societies, in point of steadfastness, order, and general quietness of faith, do not differ from other old societies. But the new congregations have been the creation of the times. They have been formed by schism and secession; and, like all seceders, have something of a spirit not perfectly accordant with the best condition of personal religion. Some of them are the offspring of an open rupture and a violent contest with friends and neighbors, when the spirit of religion was mingled with personal animosity. Some have more calmly withdrawn from the places in which they were brought up, where they had long silently listened to doctrines which they disbelieved, and had sat, for the sake of peace, among religionists with whom they had no sympathy. They have always been in opposition to the minister, and to the current theology, of the place; consequently, they have received into their souls none of those wholesome influences which come from early attachment to the institutions of the gospel, and are very likely to be void of that deep sense of their worth and necessity, which leads men to struggle for them and maintain them, at any cost and at some sacrifice.

And, next, in all our congregations, and throughout every part of the country, there is a class of men who have attached themselves to us simply because we are not Orthodox; men who dislike Calvinism, but like nothing else; who think religion a good thing, that ought to be supported, and are glad to find some form which they can support, different from that which they have been taught heartily to hate. They are anti-Calvinists, anti-Orthodox, anti-zealots, anti-every thing severe and urgent in religion. They will not forsake it, because to do so would put them out of good society; indeed, they are not without a vague traditional respect for it. They maintain a pew in the church for the same reason that the worldly-minded merchant asks his minister to say grace when he has company to dine. It is decent, and is expected of him. Such men are found among the loose hangers-on of every sect. A sect in the church militant is made up like an army going forth to war. There is the select body of the wise and hearty, who enter zealously into the merits of the cause, and give themselves to it soul and body. There is the larger number of considerate and faithful adherents, bound to it unflinchingly, but who are merely followers of the opinions of their betters, and take on themselves none of the responsibility of judging the merits of the case, or deciding on the propriety of the measures. There is still another class, who care little about the matter, who are in this army merely because it so happened, but are no more interested in its movements or success, than as they increase or diminish their own personal comforts. And, lastly, there are the loose retainers of the camp, now here, now there, now nowhere, who like the protection of the flag and swell the numbers of the march, but who own no allegiance, perform no service, and are but a pestilent hindrance to those who are earnest in the cause. Such men, I say, are hanging about the skirts of every sect,—they hang about ours; would to God we could make good Christians of them! they are far enough from it now.

There are others, too, far enough from being good Christians; forward and respectable men, who, for worldly reasons merely, whether of public good or of personal credit, take a zealous part in the secular concerns of the congregation, and identify all its interests with their own character,— very earnestly devoted to a cause to which they bring disrepute by their own characters,—sincerely wishing to strengthen the hand of religion, and by the very act calling forth the sneers of the ungodly, and encouraging the ribaldry of the vain. Would to God that such men would either leave the ark of the Lord to itself, or purify themselves before they touch it! . . .

Let us look at the Unitarian community, with this reference to the circumstances in which it is placed. What has it assumed as the universal principles of truth and duty? and how is their practical operation affected by the posture of the times? and what are the peculiar obligations thence resulting? I could not answer these questions in a volume; in this pamphlet I only pretend to hint at an answer.

In respect to *principles,* what is most worthy of observation seems to me this: It professes to have adopted as the universal principles of truth and duty those fundamental, everlasting principles, which are received by all Christians as the basis and substance of their faith, and which comprise the essence of all religion, morality, and philosophy. The process by which these principles are arrived at is very simple. It has, in following out the doctrines of the great Lutheran reform, stricken off from its list of theological articles those which were *peculiar* to the Romish church, and had made that church distinctively what it was; then, it removed those which formed the *peculiarities* of the Lutheran and the Calvinistic bodies; then it set aside those which were peculiar to the Church of England, and the Kirk of Scotland; and, in a word, it excluded whatever, in any one narrow body of believers, formed *the distinctive badge of that body,*—Moravian, Methodist, Baptist, Swedenborgian, &c.,—reserving to itself whatever, by being found in each, was proved to be common in all. All that illustrious and unquestionable truth, which is so divine, so essential, so undeniable, that no one of those numerous companies of the holy and good has been led by any philosophy or interest to withhold assent from it; all that glorious and comforting doctrine, which brings to consent and sympathy the purified spirits of our Pascals, Leightons, Doddridges, Wesleys, Cappes, and Penns,—this, separated from all accompanying admixtures, is that truth which the Unitarian community professes to receive as the binding, authoritative guide to the human soul. This is that to which the study of the Scriptures, unbiased by the authority of ages or of churches, naturally conducts. It places those who receive it at once in harmony with all the diversities of the church, as respects the essentials of religion, and in contrast to them, as regards the non-essentials. As if the sacred metal of truth having been coined up for current use by the different Christian peoples with various proportions and qualities of alloy, this people had proposed to separate from it, and cast away those meaner ingredients, and receive in circulation none but the original and unadulterated.

This is the IDEA. This is what they profess to desire, and to aim after. This is the image of full attainment, the mark of the high calling in Christian doctrine which is set up before us. Not that it has ever been reached; not that, in any community among us, this great perfection has been realized. Far from it. It is the glorious aim of many, but probably the actual attainment of none. And when we consider how glorious it is, and what incitements we have to strive after it, it is mortifying and humbling to observe how far short of it even they fall who have the clearest perception of its grandeur and excellence. . . .

This is the result to which the sublime principles of the Reformation conduct. Those principles insist on freedom of thought, liberty of conscience, the right of private judgment, independence of human control, in the strictest sense. They permit and require every man to inquire of the Scriptures, and decide for himself—with unqualified submission to God, with absolute independence of man. That denomination has most consistently adhered to them, which has thrown away every creed but the Bible, and unseated every judge but Christ.

If I understand the subject aright, this is what Unitarianism claims to have done. What a responsibility does it imply! What honesty of mind, what singleness, directness, and steadfastness of will, what resolute allegiance to conscience and God, does it demand of its disciples! It might be excusable for other men to inquire dilatorily for truth, and with an indolent foot follow the path of their convictions; for they have cast a portion of their responsibility upon others, and professedly learn much from human teachers. But for those who claim to be free from the interference of every human mind, to plant their faith and risk their salvation on the word of God alone,—they are guilty of most inexcusable madness, if they stop short at any secondary knowledge, if they do not draw industriously from that infinite fountain, if they be not as absolutely subjected to God as they are freed from man. For the object of their liberty is not, that they may follow wildly their own momentary and undisciplined impulses,— that they may take up and lay down at pleasure the thoughts and pursuits which expediency may suggest. They are set free from the control of man, as the planets are, that they may the more exactly and blissfully observe the true orbit appointed by their Maker; made free by the truth, that they may obey the truth, by the truth be sanctified, and thus arrive at that only honor which a rational soul should desire, or in which it can find its well-being.

Has any one fully realized this great idea in his own mind and history? Is there any ONE who has been thus gloriously true to his trust? Let us believe that there have been many such. We think that we have known them,—some, shining out illustriously to brighten and shame the world— some, in the humblest retirements of life, to call forth the admiration and eulogy of the few who see them there, and who marvel that God should not have placed them on high among men. Let us hope that there are many beyond what is supposed, who have arrived at this singular attainment. But does it characterize any *community?* Do we see the community, which bears upon its very front the token of this holy and resolute independence, which is imbued throughout with this heavenward and indefensible allegiance to conscience, unswayed by human opinion, reputation, and fashion, consecrated to duty, and sacrificing to duty all selfish and worldly ends? Do we see the community, which has so thrown off the dominion of man, that it is led neither in its opinions nor its practices by the fluctuating standard of the popular breath, but is palpably subject to the supreme and unbending law of God? I think not. Liberty of thought and opinion is strenuously proclaimed; in this proud land it has become almost a wearisome cant; our speeches and journals, religious and political, are made nauseous by the vapid and vain-glorious reiteration. But does it, after all, *characterize any community among us?* Is there any one to which a qualified observer shall point, any say, *"There,* opinion is free?" On the contrary, is it not a fact, a sad and deplorable fact, that in no land on this earth is the mind more fettered than it is here? that here, what we call public opinion has set up a despotism such as exists nowhere else? Public opinion—a tyrant, sitting in the dark, wrapped up in mystification and vague terrors of obscurity; deriving power no one knows from whom; like an Asian monarch, unapproachable, unimpeachable, undethronable, perhaps illegitimate, but irresistible in its power to quell thought, to repress action, to silence conviction,—and bringing the timid perpetually under an unworthy bondage of mean fear to some impostor opinion, some noisy judgment which gets astride on the popular breath for a day, and controls, through the lips of impudent folly, the speech and actions of the wise.

From this influence and rule, from this bondage to opinion, no community, as such, is free, though, doubtless, individuals are. But your community, brethren, based on the principles which you profess, is bound to be so. Each for himself in faith, each for all in action; men to be loved and served, but not to be followed or obeyed; no master but Christ, no Father but God;—these are your maxims. Man seems something more than human when these principles are stated; but he becomes something less, if, professing them in form, he falsify them in fact.

❧ The Suspense of Faith, A Discourse on the State of the Church

HENRY WHITNEY BELLOWS
(1814–1882)

During the two middle decades of the nineteenth century, Unitarianism experienced an acute but extended crisis in both theology and polity. The doctrinal inroads of Transcendentalism, the disorganization wreaked by extreme congregational independency, and the apathy following upon the achievement of accepted denominational status all conspired to darken the prognosis for a movement that had dreamed of nationwide influence. A campaign of revitalization was urgently needed, and Henry W. Bellows was unquestionably the most important among the men who made this campaign an actuality. Born in Boston in 1814, graduated from Harvard College (1832) and Divinity School (1837), he became minister of the First Unitarian Church of New York City in 1839. During his forty-year pastorate All Souls Church became prominent in the city's religious life, and Bellows, especially through his activities during the Civil War as founder and president of the U.S. Sanitary Commission, gained enormous personal prestige.

His assault on larger Unitarian problems can be said to have begun in 1846 with his founding of the *Christian Inquirer,* and widened through his affiliations with other Unitarian periodicals, the *Liberal Christian,* the *Christian Register,* and the *Christian Examiner.* In his address to the alumni of the Harvard Divinity School in 1859, reprinted here, he made explicit his basic critique of Unitarianism as well as his program for ecclesiastical reform. After the Civil War he was instrumental in setting in motion the plans for organizing a National Unitarian Conference. In April 1865 this end was accomplished, and Bellows was made president of the new organization.

Bellows was a natural leader. "He was our Bishop, our Metropolitan," said Frederic Henry Hedge in a memorial address, "the office has no place in our acephalous, isocratic polity. But this once in our history . . . the function was exercised. . . . He took possession of his see by supreme right of natural leadership and self-evident vocation. . . . He ordered us

371

hither and thither, and we surrendered ourselves to his ordering."[1] Because of Bellows's forcefulness, *The Suspense of Faith* is unquestionably one of the half-dozen most important public pronouncements in the history of American Unitarianism. It is also an unusually penetrating diagnosis of the American religious situation in the mid-nineteenth century. But its special significance stems from the fact that Bellows went on to give it concrete, though by no means literal, application.

Almost immediately after its delivery, the address provoked outspoken criticism. To his own congregation Bellows even felt required to deliver and publish *A Sequel to "The Suspense of Faith"*, which was longer than the initial address. In this follow-up statement Bellows made clear that he did not have revolutionary intentions either for his own society or for his denomination. And as Bellows continued to qualify his assertions, the furor gradually subsided. By 1864 a point of balance had been reached, and in 1865 Bellows was inclined to desire no basic changes in Unitarian Church practice, though he did work for the Christian preamble to the National Conference constitution. By 1868 he had come half-circle and was opposing men like George H. Hepworth, Edmund Hamilton Sears, and others who wanted a confessional platform for the denomination.

However, Bellows is not likely to be put down as a vacillating opportunist. There was a consistent demand underlying all that he asked of his denomination and motivating all of his organizing labors. He wanted a Church that was alive and doing things; he wanted a sense of purpose and a commensurate organization of resources. Seen in this light, *The Suspense of Faith* is an invaluable index of potential Christian Unitarian forcefulness.

The subject I propose to treat at this time is large, and will stretch your patience; it is disputed, and will need your charity; it is, in some measure, new, and not sure of your sympathy. I cannot, perhaps, introduce it better, than by confessing the difficulty of naming it; and the difficulty is intrinsic. To raise a question, and not answer it; to object to what exists, and present nothing better; to start a discussion, without much advancing it, is, of course, more or less, to beat the bush without being able to foretell the game. And yet, how can a Unitarian Christian, amid the honest antagonism and divergent tendencies of his own people, treat of our reli-

1. "Memorial Address, Spoken on the 30th of May 1882 (Decoration Day), at the Annual Meeting of the American Unitarian Association," cited in Joseph Henry Allen, *Our Liberal Movement in Theology*, p. 204.

gious times, our denominational experiences, wants, and prospects, with candor and largeness, and yet claim wholly settled convictions, clear views, and a fixed policy? Nay, how can our history, position, and future, be considered at all, apart from the history, position, and future of the Protestant era itself: that is to say, without a consideration of the mental and ecclesiastical attitude of the nineteenth century? To search out the characteristic ideas, positive and negative, of this epoch, with special reference to the good or evil influence they have exerted upon our own faith and its embodiment, is what I undertake. And before I conclude the discussion of my theme, I shall hope to justify its title, which is this:—The Suspense of Faith.

Let me preface what I have to say, with a single word more. I am about to speak of *tendencies;* and the most liberal exceptions are to be allowed for, in favor of those who resist them. I am about to enter complaints against what I could spend the whole time in praising, and yet leave the ground of these complaints as solid as ever. Let no one, then, imagine me to be ungrateful to the services, insensible to the merits, or cold to the fellowship of the Unitarian Body, or the Protestant era, because my present business is to examine their defects. If I criticize Unitarianism, it is as a Unitarian; or Protestantism, it is as a Protestant. If I show the wants of our own system, it is not as advocating a return to the systems we have abandoned; if I question the finality of Protestantism, it is not in the interest of Romanism; if I speak in the language of a Churchman, it is not as an Episcopalian, much less as one aiming at the re-establishment of a hierarchy; if I use some tones of despondency, and point to some clouds big with threats, it is not in forgetfulness of the everlasting bow that spans the storm that evokes them. I place this *caveat* at the threshold to avoid the necessity of a fatiguing caution in every step beyond it.

What, then, is the present condition of our Unitarian body? Considered numerically, or with reference to social position and moral influence—considered relatively to its age and opportunities—considered with reference to any obstacles to its spread in public sentiment, or from external quarters, it is impossible not to concede to it a fair degree of prosperity. There was never less reason for despondency, so far as a rivalry with other religious sects could breed it; never less to fear from the arguments, the exclusiveness, or the reproaches of others. Our ministers, churches, charities, public gatherings, manifestations of all sorts, were never so numerous and so popular as at present.

And yet, spite of increasing numbers and increasing moral vitality, of growing earnestness and activity, of larger acceptance and easier advance, there is an undeniable chill in the missionary zeal, an undeniable apathy in the denominational life of the body; with general prosperity, in short, there is despondency, self-questioning, and anxiety. It is a singular, and, to many, perhaps an unaccountable phenomenon.

What is the explanation of it?

It will be found in a consideration of—

I. The particular,

II. The general,

III. The universal, Reason, of what, in the course of this discussion, will show itself to be a common *suspense of faith*.

I. Is it not largely due, in the first place, and particularly, to the fact, that our missionary and denominational work, through the changed aspects of the theological world—the decay of intolerance, the softening of the current creed of Christendom, and the spread of mild and practical views of religious duty—has lost much of its urgency and point? Is not the work of emancipating the community from bigotry and superstition, so much more rapidly and successfully carried on by political and democratic life, literature, and the public press, that our vocation in this direction is mostly gone? Doubtless, in the newer parts of the country, there are thousands of small communities, where the polemic instructions of the Unitarian pioneers would be a great blessing still; but before such wants could be met by us, they are so sure to be overtaken by more general influences—the spirit of the country, the age, and the Church,—that we instinctively feel the inexpediency of wasting our energies upon them. The propagandism of Unitarian ideas is essentially paralyzed by the feeling that they are sowing themselves broadcast, not in the formal, but the essential religious thought of the country and the time; and the indifference to increasing our ministers and our churches is very much due to the conviction that many ministers and churches, of all names and orders, are now doing our work, if less directly, yet more thoroughly than we could do it ourselves.

I do not wish to take this first position, which lays no claim to originality, without careful discrimination. It is, otherwise, liable to misconstruction, and justly offensive, both to earnest Unitarians, as disparaging the importance of our formal controversy, and to the great orthodox public, as a boastful calumny upon its sincerity and actual self-knowledge. I do not affirm, therefore, that the spirit of the age and the providence of God, are making the world Unitarian, in the sectarian sense of that word, or that an inevitable abandonment of those formulas of the Church against which we have openly protested, is in the near, or even the distant prospect. But I do maintain, that the principles and sentiments, the rights of conscience, the rationality of method, the freedom of inquiry, the practical views of religion, which we have been contending for under the name and colors of our Unitarian theology, are under other names and colors so rapidly conquering the mind of our American Christendom, that it is no longer felt to be necessary to maintain a stringent denominational organization for their sake; and thus that the original and animating spirit of the denomination is taken away, by the success of the principles for which it stood. On the other hand, while not prepared to claim that the Unitarian movement has caused this general advance, or that its present position indicates the final stand of the Church, I believe that it has providentially led, and historically signalized, a forward movement of the whole Protestant body; and that universal Christendom will heartily own in due time the urgent necessity of the correlative ideas for which we have so boldly stood. I thoroughly believe that the Trinitarian theology of the historic Church, outworn and embarrassing now, was helpful, because relatively true, to the times in which it arose; and that the ideas which lay in the minds of the authors of the Athanasian and Nicene Creeds—to emphasize and defend which against the swelling and encroachment of other and mischievous opinions they erected the bulwarks of those mighty affirmations and solemn protests—were essential ideas; but ideas, which, if they add anything to a devout and scriptural Unitarianism, (which is doubtful,) contradict nothing in it. It was because, in course of time, the heirs of those creeds, ignorant of their origin, or forgetful of their purpose, came to hold them in a way that did contradict the common sense and self-evident principles touching God's sovereignty and Fatherhood, Christ's humanity and subordination, and Man's uprightness of nature, which Unitarianism has so triumphantly vindicated and re-established, that our mission became imperative.

Mazzini lately refused the programme of the Allies, because the Piedmontese government substituted the unification for the unity of Italy; thus admitting its division under different rulers. We refused and refuted the programme of modern Orthodoxy, because a degenerate Trinitarianism had substituted the unification for the Unity of God. The Church Universal will, in due time, bless us for this service to the common cause.

No view of ecclesiastical history is respectable which allows much place to self-will in the origin of considerable sects and heresies, still less in the grander movements of the Church. There is a providential necessity in the rise, progress, conflict and confluence of all religious bodies. As our Saviour's robe was parted among his enemies, so his truth is divided among his friends. Sects are complemental of each other, and none of them are anything more than relatively right. To speak of Unitarianism independently of Trinitarianism, conveys no correct, and no valuable ideas; and the purely denominational theology of our body has no worth in the decline of the errors or extravagancies it was born to balance or compensate.

It is for this particular reason that we are now experiencing our loss of interest in it, and its consequent languor as a missionary impulse.

II. But, in the second place, to come to the *general* reason. There is a broader view to be taken of the general cause of the pausing posture and self-distrust of our Body. Since we began our career, a fact of decisive influence upon our destiny has unexpectedly disclosed itself. The underlying principles and sentiments of the Unitarian body have turned out to be the characteristic ideas and tendencies of the religious epoch we live in. Protestantism produced us, not we it. Whatever is good or bad in our spirit and direction, was latent in the Reformation, and is fast becoming patent in the whole product of that world-movement. The peculiar identification of Protestant tendencies with our special theology is partly accidental, partly historical; the tendencies themselves are the great fact. Thus no criticism of Unitarianism is radical which is not also a criticism of Protestantism; nor is it possible to understand our position and prospects, without considering from a high point of view the general drift of Protestantism itself. Our eddy or rapid is to be explained only by a survey of the main current; our drought or freshet only by an examination of the common water-shed. If I say, then, that our pause as a denomination is the pause which Protestantism makes on awakening to the full consciousness of her own tendencies, I shall best express my second and most important idea.

These tendencies have only recently cleared themselves to view, and are not by the boldest faced without some concern. Yet it is best to look them full in the front; to acknowledge them for just what they are, and rely upon God and the truth to deliver us from evil at their hands. Permit me, then, for the moment, to state in unqualified, and even in offensive terms, what the logical product of Protestantism is.

If, then, with logical desperation, we ultimate the tendencies of Protestantism, and allow even the malice of its enemies to flash light upon their direction, we may see that the sufficiency of the Scriptures turns out to be the self-sufficiency of man, and the right of private judgment an absolute independence of Bible or Church. No creed but the Scriptures, practically abolishes all Scriptures but those on the human heart; nothing between a man's conscience and his God, vacates the Church; and with the Church, the Holy Ghost, whose function is usurped by private reason: the Church lapses into what are called Religious Institutions; these into Congregationalism, and Congregationalism into Individualism—and the logical end is the abandonment of the Church as an independent institution, the denial of Christianity as a supernatural revelation, and the extinction of worship as a separate interest. There is no pretence that Protestantism, as a body, has reached this, or intends this, or would not honestly and earnestly repudiate it; but that its most logical product is at this point it is not easy to deny. Nay, that these are the *tendencies* of Protestantism is very apparent.

Let us not be too much alarmed at this statement, assuming it to be true. Tendencies are not always ultimated. They encounter resistance. They meet and yield to other tendencies. The tendencies of an epoch, religious or political, do not decide its whole character. There are forces in humanity stronger than any epochal powers—the permanent wants, the indestructible instincts of our nature. It is safe, and it ought not to be alarming, to see and confess that the tendencies of political and religious speculation and sentiment, in the universal Church of our day, are to the weakening of the external institutions of Christianity, the extinction of the ministry, and the abandonment of any special interest in religion, as a *separate* interest of man or society. If our Unitarian body understands this better than the inner ranks of Protestantism, it is only because the squadrons behind have pressed it nearer the brink towards which they are unconsciously advancing. With great temporary superiority and advantages, one over another, there is really nothing to choose between the Protestant sects in general direction, and ultimate destinies; logically, and what is more, practically, they are shut up to one conclusion. All alike in this respect, they represent human liberty, self-assertion, and man's power to choose and enthrone his own God. The differences between them are chronological, circumstantial, accidental; the likeness is logical, essential, and absolute. We need not fancy that our peculiar theology is responsible for the latitudinarianism, the negation, the undevotionality, complained of in the Unitarian body. The same qualities belong to all Protestant sects, to the degree in which their culture and opportunities establish positive and logical relations between their principles and their characters. The Unitarian body, not as being more learned or more thoughtful than other Protestant bodies in its leaders and ministry, but as having a laity on the same intellectual level with its leaders, and no dead weight of mere instinct and affection to drag along with it, has carried out and experienced in its denominational life, what no other Protestant sect has yet been sufficiently conscious of itself, and enough under the dominion of its own ideas fully to experience. We have shown the world the finest fruits and the rankest weeds of the Protestant soil; we have most freely felt and most plainly indicated the main Protestant current; and the criticisms we have suffered from our Protestant brethren have owed much of their edge, to the anxiety of fellow-passengers, bitterly upbraiding the officers of the ship because they could not resist the force of the stream that set towards the rapids and the precipice. The same sympathy, taking often the form of antipathy, that connects the conservative and historical rank of our own body, with the front-rank of avowed rationalists, connects us all, as the front-rank of Protestantism, with the whole body behind; and we must pardon the severity of its criticism upon us, when we consider that it is an unconscious self-criticism—a parent's blame of the hereditary taint it has communicated to its child.

Let us not deceive ourselves in respect to the tendencies of Protestantism, as such, by crediting it with the resistance which is constantly made to its logical and its spiritual impulses, by the permanent instincts of humanity, or by the still unspent force of past epochs of a diametrically opposed quality. It is not the devout and virtuous class which, in any community or sect, best expresses the animating tendencies of the time and place. Catholic saints do not properly measure and represent the level of Romanism, or its characteristic influence and sentiments, but rather the common people of that Church any and everywhere. And Unitarian saints—of whom, thank God, many as pure and noble as the calendar of any Church can produce have shed their fragrance upon us and gone up in clouds of glory—do not exhibit the tendencies of our liberal faith. Nor is it the religious portion of Protestantism that shows the influence of Protestantism. Exceptional and marked piety, is, in all Churches, constitutional; due to the devout nature of its subjects, independent of the theological opinions or the special era and circumstances with which it is associated. Men and women, pious by nature, are pious as Heathen, Jews, or Christians; as Catholics or Protestants; and it matters little under what religious influences they are brought, or on what times they fall. The religious tendencies of an era are indicated satisfactorily only by the ideas and sentiments that sway the unthinking, unspeculative, unconscious masses. No opinions are efficacious over society at large, which are held as opinions, or voluntarily taken up and inculcated. We inculcate opinions for the benefit of future generations, in which we may hope they will appear as blessed prejudices of the blood. For, as a rule, it is only ideas from which men cannot get away, sentiments that are spontaneous, natural, and constant, that exert any shaping and decisive influence over them. "Opinion," says Milton, "is knowledge in the making;" and until it has passed the stage of intellectual effort and conscious will, it is inoperative to any degree worth considering in a large view of things. If we would know the religious tendencies of our Protestant age, (for I deny the existence of any living Catholic Church in an estimate of the world-movements of the time,) we must go outside the Churches, to the vast population, said to be much more than half, perhaps three-quarters, of every considerable community, that goes to Church nowhere; we must notice the deepening hostility of all States to established churches; the disjunction between science and faith, literature and theology; the transference of the faith of the people from the church to the school-house; the popularity of all attacks upon the clergy; the acceptance and elevation of those ministers, understood to be suspected and discountenanced by the rest; the open and extensive sale of infidel books; the growing use of the Sabbath for recreation—not, as abroad, under the smile of the Church, but in direct contempt of its frown; the easy conscience of the people in the profound secularity of their lives—indicating their contentment in a condition of alienation from religious relations and ideas; the frequency of suicide; the increasing laxity of the marriage-bond; the defence of scortatory love—all marked indications of the decay of religious ideas; the peculiar interest attached to preaching in contradistinction to worship, and the necessity of keeping together the church-going class by the extra allurements of gifted speech; the general inculcation of morality on utilitarian grounds; the excellence, as citizens and neighbors, of an avowedly irreligious class; the popular and applauded hostility of the philanthropy of the day to the Churches—the most accomplished orators of the times, being hightoned, virtuous, respected men and virulent assailants of the religious creeds and customs and institutions of the community; the existence of a vast and governing class in this country, felt in all our elections, and more and more shaping our institutions, with whom not only is the higher law in its refined form unknown, but whom religious considerations of any kind seem to sway not at all; so that an infidel, as such, would not perhaps stand a poor chance as a candidate for the presidency. I do not forget that religious or sectarian prejudices exert a considerable influence in our politics. But when we remember how numerous and powerful the great religious sects in our country are, it becomes still more striking to think how large must be the body of citizens, without *religious prejudices,* that is, for the masses, without *religious ideas,* when they are the regular reliance of the democratic (which is the logical) party, in all our great elections. I call it, then, an *un*religious age—I do not say *ir*religious, for that implies active opposition to religion; not a bad, or an immoral, or a discouraging, or a wicked age—better, doubtless, on the whole, and in respect of the general interests of society, than any that has preceded it—but nevertheless characteristically an unreligious age—despite its philanthropy and its throes of sectarian piety, its rights of man, and its self-complacency toward God.

Nor is this all. It is not only an unreligious age, but it is becoming more and more unreligious. For religious institutions and ideas in our day flourish mainly in the strength of their roots in a religious past, a strength which is constantly diminishing. As respect for rank in England, the remnant of an honest aristocratic system ages in power, is the wholesome *vis inertia* which prevents the democratic instincts of the age in that country from hurrying precipitately to their inevitable goal, so the genuine religiousness of ages gone by, whose flavor lingers in our blood, is the most vigorous support the worship of this age enjoys. Whatever public nourishment besides, distinctive and essential religion has in our generation, is due to the exceptional devoutness of spirits born out of due time, and to the *esprit de corps* so characteristic of the day—the love of joint action, the fondness for educational, moral and ethical institutions, the emulation of communities with each other, the partisan rivalry of sects, and the fact that, under the name of religious institutions, we sustain a vast and valuable system of adult education, in thought, humanity and manners. Our churches, to a great extent, and constantly more and more so, are lecture-foundations—in which the interest is less and less religious, more and more political, social and ethical. The one thing the people are interested in is life, themselves, each other, and the relation of the inside to the outside—of man to his dwelling, of man to man, of man to himself. To make a religion out of self-respect, right-living, self-culture—to insist that aspiration is worship, that truth is God, that goodness is religion—is the highest ambition of our modern pulpit. I do not say it in blame, nor in scorn; for, under the circumstances, it is an honorable ambition, laid upon men by the necessity of justifying their own faith to themselves. *God* is too sacred a word to be lost out of the language; worship too holy a thing not to be held on to on some pretence or other; piety too profound and indestructible an instinct to be abandoned; and therefore the political and social idealism of our age clothes itself in religious phraseology and forms, out of an honest respect for the past, a sincere self-delusion, and, what is best of all, under an instinctive or a providential guidance. But to say that the animating and characteristic quality of the American people of the nineteenth century is religion, worship, faith, or that whatever is theological and ecclesiastical in our terms and usages represents a living spirit, and not a revered memory, is more than a just discrimination will allow. On the contrary, the science, philosophy and literature of the day are busily engaged in creating substitutes for religion—and authorizing the continuance of the names and forms and symbols of worship and faith, after asserting, in more or less obvious language, the irrelevancy of the things themselves.

When the Head of an American University, from whom I had the anecdote, inquired of a professor in Berlin, what Humboldt would probably answer, if asked what was his religious faith?—He said, his reply would probably be: "I am of the religion of all men of science."

Doubtless he meant what the lively Frenchman, the excellent Catholic! who has just treated the Roman question, means, when he says in praise of the Bolognese as compared with the Romans, "They know all that we know; they believe all that we believe, and nothing more."

We owe a recognition to the actual and serious faith of science in our day. While Oersted, Whewell and Hugh Miller, and names nearer home, are remembered, we are not likely to forget our respect for the union of science and faith.

Yet the actual weakness of positive faith is visible in nothing so much as in the eager welcome yielded by the professed friends of Christianity to any succor which the science or literature of the day may see fit to bestow, in charity, upon the Church. The times, indeed, are changed, since science and literature were humble suppliants at the Churchgate, asking her permission to set up their conclusions within her palings; and now religion is thankful if geology, scornfully passing by, does not throw her hammer at her head, and literature lampoon her in her own pulpit.

I have been speaking, you will observe, not wholly, yet mainly, of tendencies; and tendencies may be dangerous and extravagant, and yet necessary and providential—a wholesome reaction upon other tendencies still more alarming. There have been perilous tendencies to excess of ritual and positive religion in Oriental regions, in past eras, ending in paralysis of the private will, and deterioration of humanity. At times, even in the Christian world, there has been too much worship, too constant and formal a reference to God's will to admit of a proper degree of human freedom. You will not understand me, then, as generally questioning the merits of the age we live in, by calling it an unreligious age, or as disparaging Protestantism, as if it had not been, and were not still, until honestly exhausted, a valuable and indispensable movement. And for a psychological reason of the utmost importance, to explain which is the third step in our journey. I have shown, first, the particular, and next, the general historical reason of the pause of faith; I wish now to set forth the still more fundamental or psychological reason of this pause—the *universal* reason.

III. There are two motions of the spirit in relation to God, his Creator and upholder, essential to the very existence of generic or individual Man—a centrifugal and a centripetal motion—the motion that sends man away from God, to learn his freedom, to develop his personal powers and faculties, relieved of the over-awing and predominating presence of his Author; and the motion that draws him back to God, to receive the inspiration, nurture, and endowment, which he has become strong enough to hold. For man, though a creature of faculties, is still more characteristically, a creature of capacities; and his capacities must be developed before they can be filled—his vessel shaped before it can go to the fountain.

He must have freedom before he can yield obedience; he must possess a will before he can surrender it; affections, trained to love visible objects, before they can love the unseen Source; intellectual and moral independence, to make his loyalty significant, and his service blessed. Accordingly, the origin and history of the race exhibits the care with which God has hidden himself away from his creatures in the infancy of their existence, lest they should be scorched and shrivelled in the glory of his presence. And yet his whole purpose is to create a race that can live in his conscious society, without losing their individuality and freedom in gaining his inspiration and guidance. The whole vexed question of the tardiness of the great Dispensations, and of the necessity of Revelation itself, is to be solved only in the light of this law, the sistole or disastole, or double motion of our spirits. Man is not made acquainted with God by nature, and God does not come into his earliest stages of existence with distinctness, because spiritual creation must precede spiritual salvation. The first man is of the earth, earthy; the second man, is the Lord from heaven: the first Adam was created a living soul; the second Adam a quickening spirit. Man's creation is not complete at his birth, but continues on in his development as an intellectual and moral being; and this development is primarily more important than the use to which his faculties are put; as the life, health, and growth of our children are more important than any thing they can do for us, or any affections they manifest towards us, in their infancy and youth. If we view the history of the race in a comprehensive way, we shall observe that it has been providentially occupied in all its earlier eras with itself, establishing what may be called its selfhood; and that what is termed natural religion—which is only an inverted self-worship, in which man makes his own deity to suit his tastes and feelings, and, of course, does not make him too strong for his own self-will— is then the only witness of the living God—a witness so meek, as not to interfere with the providential process of setting man up in his own right and liberty. Revealed religion—the only religion that ever has had authority, or which, by the nature of the case, can have power to awe, restrain, and elevate man, or to overcome the congenital bias of his nature—being something outside of, and independent of his personality—has necessarily been subsequent to his creation; confined to special representative races and eras; and has applied itself through the slow form of institutional influences, in order to gain a greater power in the end, because over a more freely and fully developed being, surrendering himself voluntarily to a control which enlarges his true freedom, and accepting a liberty in divine dependence, of which his previous independence has been only a fictitious foreshadowing.

Thus, taking in all history, we may consider the educational orbit of the race, as completing itself under natural and revealed religion, as its centrifugal and centripetal forces; natural religion being, as I have said, in its last analysis, self-worship—and of course intensely favorable to self-assertion, individuality, and self-development, or alienation from God as a necessary preparation for the worship of God in the end—and revealed religion, being the essential condition of emancipation from self and connection with God, as a power outside of and independent of man—or, God coming to possess, and fill, and occupy the soul he has been making for his dwelling.

But within the domain of revealed religion, and in Christendom, the same centrifugal and centripetal forces continue to act; of course under the modifying influences of revelation. Here, the World represents the centrifugal, the Church the centripetal force; the world upholding, asserting, and defending Humanity, its freedom, the unimpeded play of its tastes and faculties and desires—favoring the development of the utmost energy, enterprise, and individuality;—the Church steadily denouncing humanity, as depraved, corrupt, unclean, partial, condemned—its freedom, license; its independence, rebellion; its only hope and salvation in and from God. Thus the world, and the Church, notwithstanding, or rather because of this disagreement, has each had truth on its side, and each been performing indispensable duties—one *making* man, and the other *saving* him; one giving him a Being to *be saved,* and the other putting salvation into his being—one making him "a living soul," the other, "a quickening spirit." The world, and that portion of the Church, which has been with the world in this quarrel, has been mainly right in asserting the dignity and rectitude of human nature; the Church mainly right in asserting the destituteness and depravity of human nature—for one looked at man with reference only to his faculties, the other with reference only to his destiny. One looked at him, as a vessel of honor, in the shape originally given it by his creator, finished and perfect; the other as a vessel, empty and waiting for a divine fullness, which should prove its true ennobling. There was nothing inconsistent in these ideas. Both were true—and each did injustice to the other's real meaning, but not to the other's terms—and, greatly as the earnest discussion touching the import and the fitness of the phrases used to convey the ideas of these opposite parties was needed to clear up the real truth, we can afford now to drop it, if prepared, on both sides, to acknowledge the halfness of our antagonistic statements.

And within the Church, as well as within Christendom, these two forces have been at work, under the names of Romanism and Protestantism; Romanism representing the centripetal force of Christianity, Protestantism the centrifugal; Romanism standing for external or divine authority, Protestantism for internal liberty and individual freedom; Romanism representing God's condescension to man, Protestantism man's aspiration toward perfection; Romanism leading to worship, Protestantism to work. But there is no doubt that Romanism, merely as a religion, fulfilled its function more perfectly than Protestantism, whose main services have not been to religion, but directly to humanity, and to religion only indirectly. Not that her influences were not vastly, nay, indispensably necessary, even to the ultimate triumphs of faith; but they have not been in the way of bringing man's soul more under the idea or the inspiration and sway of God, but rather of conscience, and intellect, and will—a magnificent development of human faculties and powers—but not, as experience proves, adequate to the religious wants of man; to the peace and rest of the soul, the nurture of the sweet and unselfish affections of the Gospel.

Is it not plain, then, that as Protestants of the Protestants, we are at the apogee of our orbit; that in us the centrifugal epoch of humanity has for this swing of the pendulum, at least reached its bound. For one cycle we have come, I think, nearly to the end of our self-directing, self-asserting, self-developing, self-culturing faculties; to the end of our honest interest in this necessary, alternate movement. We see it to be so well established in Protestantism at large, that it does not need our leadership—that it is sure to do its work and complete its oscillation independently of us. And we are very weary of the toil it has thrown upon us; the speculation, inquiry, and self-sustaining energy we have put forth under its compulsion. Moreover, having enlarged our faculties, we want a use for them; having achieved our freedom, we know not what to do with it; having cultivated our wills, consciences, and intellects to the utmost at present possible, they cry out for objects that they do not find. And this is the painful pause— this the suspended animation, seen and felt throughout Christendom— especially throughout Protestant Christendom—and more particularly throughout our own more Protestantized province of the Church. Why is it that the moment we find ourselves in possession of men, whom genius, character, and scholarship fit to lead us in our logical career to new victories and the extension of our faith, they almost uniformly become paralyzed by doubts and scruples, and lose their interest in the progress they might assure? It is simply because the small elevation which gives them command of us, reveals to them the absence of any more road, in the direction we have been going. Not brave enough, or quite clear enough, to announce this, they allow themselves to seem smitten with sudden indifference to their former interests, and leave the rank and file to blunder on and find out the truth for themselves. Of later years this has been our almost constant experience as a body. The moment we have given our faith to our leaders, that moment, without changing their allegiance or opinions, they have lost their own faith in themselves and our cause.

Of course this state of things has been attended with other results. Not a few, less conscious of the unrest, weariness, and dissatisfaction of ultra-protestantism, have pronounced the recoil upon it they began to notice a servile and dangerous retrogradation, and, to resist it, have rushed on, reckless of consequences, into a still bolder self-assertion. Like the new war-rocket, which, having expended its first force, lights with its last ember a fresh fuse that propels another projectile far beyond the place where it falls itself, Protestantism, which has exhausted its own orbit, flings off into space its eccentric particles, henceforth to be contented with a geo-centric, not a heliocentric revolution. Thus the school of Mill and the sec-ularists abroad, and the Emersonian and transcendental school at home, acknowledge only one true movement in humanity—the egoistic—the self-asserting and self-justifying movement—which is Protestantism broken loose from general history, taken out of its place in the providential plan, and made the whole, instead of the part. Toward this position we have of necessity continually tended, and into this many of our bravest and best spirits have gone to dwell, and all of them have been to visit. And now that the ecclesiastical leaders of ultraprotestantism begin to be anxious to turn their forces, not back, but round and up, we may expect to see liter-ary and secular leaders arise who will have none of their scruples, because little of their experience, and who will press on and inspirit the flagging ranks—that for a time may take new courage in the hearing of fresh and cheery voices, and seem to themselves to have great victories before them in the old field. Science, art, and culture will place themselves in the van, which the Church lately held but now deserts—and there are not a few who do not quite say, but hint clearly enough to be understood by the wise, that the Church of the future will be the diffusion of a universal in-telligence, in which natural laws shall take the place of bibles and prayer books, and Science and Art be the high and only priests.

If, however, universal history is to be heeded, if the great common in-stincts of humanity are prophetic, if religion be the earliest and latest, the deepest and the highest interest of man, then we may trust that the sense of want, the yearning for rest, the longing for legitimate authority, the ex-pectation of relief, the general feeling throughout the devouter portion of Protestantism of dissatisfaction with the existing attitude of things, with a secret faith that God or Christ is about to interpose for its relief, indicates the conception—I do not say the birth—of a new religious epoch, to be distinguished as much by faith, as the last has been by doubt—an epoch in which the temple that man has been building and beautifying shall be oc-cupied by its Lord—in which the passive side of humanity shall enjoy its long-neglected rights; and when, instead of seeking God as the solar sys-tem is seeking the star *Aries* in the constellation Hercules, He shall seek us, as the shepherd in the parable, leaving the ninety and nine of the flock, sought the lost lamb and folded it in his arms; and in place of self-assertion, self-abnegation and life in God, shall again become the type of human experience.

Even the intimations of the destructive philosophy of the positivists, which ends in a ritual or worship, and the application of the Hamiltonian metaphysics to orthodoxy, which puts the reason of religion as the mean product of two extremes of absurdity, seem to be lending unwilling testimony to the same yearning for a settled and externalized faith.

Who can believe, or who, intimately acquainted with the inner life of this age, desires to believe, that the nineteenth century, however important in its place, is to be indefinitely continued? Or that the spirit and temper of this inventive, bustling, irreverent, and self-asserting time, is to govern the whole future; a time in which knowingness, curiosity, wit, covetousness, and publicity, external accomplishments, arts, and achievements, have so largely taken the place of the deeper passions and richer experiences of the soul; and in which conjugal love, parental care, filial reverence, domestic quietude, true friendship, spiritual art, poetic imagination, and private peace, seem so lamentably in abeyance. Man's body, tasked by this quick time, is furrowed with the lash, and begs for mercy; his nerves have come to the surface with the unnatural strain; his spirits fagged, or unduly stimulated, send him moping or maudlin to the madhouse, or dig him an early grave. Meanwhile his proud work is to moor the hemispheres side by side with his metallic cable; to decant the oceans with the syphon of his Isthmus canal; or to swallow the continent when he flings toward the Pacific his iron rod. His insolent pleasure is to dance over dread Niagara on the showman's rope, or to hang above it in the slippery clouds, till he dwindles it to a ripple. His architecture, gay with emulative cost, covers cheerless homes; his churches, splendid with sectarian rivalry, shelter unworshipping hearts. His philanthropic assemblies, crowded and frequent, breathe violence and hatred, while they advocate the rights of man, and rebuke the Church in the tones of Mephistopheles. An age, that has to be busy to save itself from knowing its own destitution! to which leisure is a burden and solitude a calamity! What is there that we can desire to see perpetuated in the peculiar spirit—I do not say in the institutions, achievements, or victories—of an age like this? And when this spirit which now animates the highest and most influential classes of society, and produces the self-criticism, the disintegrating individualism, the pride that kills hospitality, and the strain of social emulation which makes elegant fortresses of men's homes; the esoteric want behind the exoteric abundance; when the cold polish, the brilliant surface, the dead enthusiasm of the best and most characteristic products of the nineteenth century, come to strike downwards and to be seen in connection with the inferior culture, the more vulgar tastes, the coarser grain of the masses, as they surely will, we may then perhaps discover the origin of the alarming symptoms of our national life, its vulgar credulity, and as vulgar infidelity, its denial of so many things that are true, and affirmation of so many things that are false; its unspirituality and spiritism; its no faith in the Old Testament, and interest in the Mormon Bible and the Spiritual Telegraph.

Nobody acquainted with that portion of the modern literature of all nations which indicates the inward yearnings of our instant humanity, can fail to acknowledge the omnipresence of a dissatisfied, expectant, and thoroughly bewildered, spirit. The cultivated mind of the rising generation, whether in England or America—that of the young men and women who will help largely to form the next age—is not so much aggressive or progressive as in a painful equipoise which forbids healthful motion—melancholic, sad, astray or afloat. What Lamartine says so well of one of his characters, "Il fut né fatigué," may be said of the most intellectual and spiritual portion of our youth of both sexes. The inherited thought of a Protestant epoch of three centuries' duration, is born tired, in the meditative mind of our generation. As a necessity of this state of things, the Protestant Church has lost its hold of the two ends of society—the cultivated and uncultivated end—of the head, because it is under the dominion of paralyzing ideas, which leave faith a fiction and worship a mockery; of the foot, because it is no longer controlled by that authority which a living and satisfied faith can alone put into the wills and into the actions of the governing classes. The infidelity of our age is not commonly an insolent, self-satisfied, flippant criticism of evidences, or a sour and bitter assault upon Christianity, although we still have that. It is, in the cultivated classes—and with frightful frequency there—a silent, thoughtful, sad consciousness that the soul has no faith, and possesses no religion except the religious sentiment, and knows no God and no Saviour—with a tender reserve toward others, a gentle unwillingness to bring into their own condition those in whom faith still has any existence. And in the uncultivated classes, it is a loss for the time being, in the absorbing interest of life itself, enriched with the emancipated rights and opportunities which this self-asserting epoch has given to the masses—of any sense of a need of religion, with a decay of the affections, instincts, and usages connected with it—a state frightful to consider—not in its immediate, but only in its coming social consequences!

Meanwhile, into the empty crypts and chapels of the human mind have rushed, as by the attraction of a vacuum, the succedaneums and lieutenancies of Worship and Faith. The instructed and thoughtful have attempted to revive the worship of Nature; while demonology and witchcraft have amused the supernatural instincts of the people at large. The microscope and the refracting mirror have become the chief windows of the soul for the educated, whose only spiritual world, it would often seem, now lies in the interstices of the physical laws of the universe; while the people have been bowing down to patent reapers and sewing-machines, the daguerreotype and the stereoscope, trance mediums and homeopathic miracles—and both classes have made hero-worship—whether of a horse-tamer or a chess-conqueror—the unconscious indulgence of their disused and suffering organs of veneration and faith.

It is not strange in a state of things so humiliating, so unsatisfactory, so wearisome for thoughtful spirits as this—so alarming, too, if alarm were not impious as a conclusion, for lovers of their race and their country—that questful inquiries should be made of the past, of philosophy, of experience, of the soul itself, as to the probable issue of this epoch. Nor is it to be at all wondered at, that so many, by either positive or negative consent, should be now acknowledging a longing for a revival of the ages of Faith. Many, already, of the ablest heads and strongest hearts of the time, not chargeable, certainly, with ignorance of science, history, or philosophy, like Newman abroad, and Brownson at home, have gone boldly and bravely back into the Catholic Church, and with them hundreds of the worshipful, tender, and thoughtful young men and women of Protestant Christendom. Without understanding their necessity or their solace, I confess, for one, I value the costly testimony which such a course has given to the worth of the fundamental idea of Catholicism, in a time when puritanical prejudices and terrestrialism combine to confound the superstitious and accidental usages and customs of the Catholic Church, with its essential idea, and so to blind the Protestant world to its own interest in the other and larger half of its integral history.

Protestantism—for I will not say, the Protestant Church—stands, and nobly stands, for human rights—for man as against rulers, kings, institutions, ignorance, want, vice, sloth; stands for morality—which is good usage and wise custom, for citizenship, individuality, faculty, will and knowledge. The Catholic Church stood for revelation, for God condescending, for supernaturalism, for bread from heaven, for the authority, the support, and the benediction of living and divine persons, outside of humanity and above it. As such, independently of its historical identification with Christianity, Romanism had a sacred and indefeasible right in the history of humanity. It represented God coming to man—as Protestantism represents man coming to himself—and then, perchance, and perchance not, going to the Father who comes to meet him. The Church, in every heathen age, has been some rude but potent organization of the idea of God brooding over and descending upon his children; the natural priesthood of the world, having been the spirits, in whom, however crudely, the sense of God overpowered the sense of themselves. What the natural religions of the world thus preluded and typified, the positive religions of history have distinctly articulated and fulfilled. The Christian Church, in its earlier ages, did not embody, nor did it most need to embody, the morality of Christ; for at our time of day, morality is the necessary product of knowledge, which in emancipating the individual, and all individuals, gradually makes order, decency—in short, morality, the only possible condition under which human beings can live together—which is a sufficient account of the tang of worldliness and inadequacy which disflavors the phrase Morality. Morality, though a slow growth, is a sure one, and follows in the wake of education and freedom—matching precisely the political and civil condition of every community.

But the Christian Church, embodied and represented what is no growth of civilization, and what is independent of ages and grades of culture—the doctrine and presence of the Holy Ghost—the descent of God into the world, the gift of himself to his children as the *pleroma*—the only fullness for the infinite emptiness of the human soul. It represented, in short, what alone is entitled to be called religion—the bond and contract between God and man—in which the superior party is God fulfilling his promise, not man observing his obligation. In natures, whose constitutional individuality had been sufficiently secured by a high organization, or by propitious circumstances, the Catholic Church, by the supply of the Holy Spirit which it furnished, and the lively faith it communicated, worked those miracles of saintly character, artistic beauty, and divine poetry, which include, as their afterbirth, even the great ornaments of the age immediately succeeding the Reformation. But it is equally true, that the masses, though immensely and benignantly supported, emancipated and elevated by the earlier ages of the Church, were in the deepest need of the centrifugal movement, which we call Protestantism, when it came—or, rather, when their want of it produced the reaction which was its final cause. For the Church had absorbed the world; the divine had overflowed the shallow channel of humanity, and it needed to be deepened even at the expense of becoming temporarily dry, that it might hold larger measures from the river of God.

The particular, the general, the universal reason for the suspense of faith, we have now successively set forth. It remains only, in conclusion, to look at the form in which we may hope that faith will rally and go on. And this brings us face to face, at last, with what we have been secretly envisaging all the time, the Church question, which is the real question of the earnest, religious thought of the time, and agitates itself and us, under all sorts of disguises. Many, indeed, are striving, with all their might, to prove that there is no such question; that we have got by it; that it is treason to the nineteenth century, to humanity, and to the future, to allow any reality in it; that only priest-craft and quackery give it a seeming importance for their own ends; that the world is going on well enough upon its present tack, and wants only more of what it has already got so much. But these encouraging skeptics cry Peace, peace, when there is no peace. The Church question is a real question in all Protestant countries—most so in Germany, in England, in America;—and it must be met and discussed with a courage which it does not yet find outside of the innermost circles of confidential scholarship, and the private communion of hungering hearts.

Who does not see that the fatal misgiving at the bottom of the mind of Protestantism is this—Have the external institutions of religion any authority but expediency? do they stand for and represent any thing but one portion of the human race educating another portion of the human race, which, in the last analysis, is self-culture? And if they stand only for self-culture, on what other basis do they stand than schools and colleges? None whatever, the logical mind will answer, except that they are *religious* schools and colleges. Make your ordinary schools and colleges, your family education, *religious,* and you may dispense with the Church, which has no basis but expediency, and is founded wholly in man's wit. Accordingly, it is a very common and spreading feeling, that our religious institutions are approaching their natural term of existence. I know, by personal conference with some of the most living minds of Italy and Germany, that *patriotism* is fast getting to be the only religion of the upper classes, and while their ritual is music and revolution, their immortality is to die for fatherland. And why not, if religion means only human development and self-perfection? What furnishes these, is the highest interest of society and man; and if the school does it better than the Church, the school ought to, and will, supersede the Church, as indeed, it already occasionally has done in what are thought to be very advanced neighborhoods of this country. But the Protestant of a less uncompromising kind, may reply, You overlook the fact that Christianity is a positive revelation of truth and duty, and that the Church, having to embody this revelation, has an excuse and a reason, nay, a necessity for existing. But suppose he is asked, Has not this revelation emptied its contents into human reason, into history and civilization, until the Gospel of Christ is so mixed with the moral and spiritual life of society, that philosophy and practical wisdom, nay, that Society itself, is wiser than the Church? What special or exclusive custody of the Gospel given to the world has the Church? and if we have the Gospel, what want we of the Church? I know no answer to this question, if the Gospel mean only or chiefly what it now passes for with most noble spirits, a mere revelation of truth. It is more. It is a gift of life, or communication of power, which is continuous, its force and virtue always residing in its living fountain, making the Church, through which it is given, not a mere reservoir that may be emptied, but a permanent conduit, or channel, through which flows down the eternal river of God. But is the Church, in fact, such a channel, supposing even that the fountain be alive and flowing, that God be really immanent, communicating a force not merely *in* but *to* our souls through His Gospel and by His Son? Is not society itself now, in its total organization, the vehicle through which the consciousness of God, opened by Christ, reveals itself to, and nourishes and makes divine, the life and heart of man? In short, is not that invisible Church, which, without noise of hammer or saw, secretly builds itself up in the spiritual life of humanity, far more real, life-giving, and sustaining, than the visible Church, which the extant religious institutions of Christendom claim to be? The query is plausible, and is proposed by noble men among us. But has it only an affirmative answer? Far be it from me to deny that the Holy Spirit, to an extent seldom appreciated, that God himself, to a degree infinitely beyond any ordinary or possible recognition, that Christ, in these latter ages, in an immeasurable sum, is the secret life of humanity. Were there not a vast deal more of God, and Christ, and the Holy Ghost in the world than the world knows of, or thinks for, we should go to ruin swiftly indeed. But I am persuaded that we have, as social and terrestrial beings living in definite historical relations, a great deal more of obligation to the visible than to the invisible Church. The invisible Church takes due care of itself and of us; the visible Church is committed to our hands. I do not say that the visible is as important as the invisible, or as great in its influence, but only that it is our charge, because, of the two, it alone is within our voluntary reach. Moreover, I am convinced, that, in accordance with the whole analogies of Providence, every radically important relationship of humanity is, and must be, embodied in an external institution; the relation of the exclusive affections in the family, the social relations in society, the political in the state, the religious in the Church.

I am well enough aware that the εκκλεσια of the Scriptures is the collection or congregation of the κλητοι, the called. But it is only an illustration of the common rule governing our humanity in all things, that the collection or calling together of human beings in any one of their radical relationships, or about any one of their essential needs or aspirations, develops at once something which none of the individual parties could have predicted or anticipated, or in himself possessed—a pre-ordained consequent of relationship—a *"tertium quid,"* which is very different from any of the elements of which it is composed. Thus Man is a domestic, a social, a political, an ecclesiastical being; but it is absurd to say that any individual man is this, each one of these things, the family, society, the State, the Church, being impossible to an isolated being, and even inconceivable until it has been experienced as the fruit of a community of life. There is a Church in humanity, as there is a family state, a social state, and a political state—a Church which has always been developed, and has been the principal source of the religious life of humanity. Christianity takes advantage of a previously existent institution, which was not simply Jewish, but human, when she pours her life through the Church. This is the reason why Christ established *his* Church, but not *the* Church; and why so little of the thought and inspiration of our Lord is used to re-construct an institution already organized, through which his spirit was to flow; but that spirit was no less shut up in an institution and an organization than is the family, differing by various shades and usages as that does, but always tending to its pure and holy type of strict monogamy; or than the State is, or than society is.

Would that I could develop here, at a time so forgetful and reckless of the dependence of society on organization, the *doctrine of institutions,* the only instruments, except literature and the blood, by which the riches of ages, the experience and wisdom of humanity, are handed down; institutions the only constant and adequate teachers of the masses, and which are to the average mind all that honor, conscience and intellect are to exceptional men and women. But I forbear.

Christianity, nothing until an institution, seized the Church as the pre-established channel and organ of her influence and transmission, the conduit of her living water, the vehicle of her Holy Spirit; she put her own external marks upon it, as well as her own interior life into it, and has at length made *the* Church to mean HER Church, as THE Bible has come to mean her sacred books. All sacred books predicted the Bible, which has summed them up, and dismissed them from duty; and the Church in the wilderness predicted the Church in Christian civilization which should publish the eternal Word. Thus the Church is neither new nor old, neither fixed nor transitional; it is simply living, and, therefore, like the family and the State, is costumed and uncostumed, is cold, is warm, is recognized, is unrecognized, is Roman, Greek, English, American, but always the Church, the organic, external vehicle of God's Word and the Holy Spirit to aggregate or congregate humanity. The individual can join the Church only in his capacity of a member of the human race. It is his humanity, or oneness with and dependence upon his race, that makes him eligible to Church membership, as it is his relationship to his kind that alone makes the bond of the family, of society, or of the State, and existence in them possible to him.

The common consciousness of God, which is the Gospel, none partake who wilfully cut themselves off from the body of Christ. It is therefore a fact (and anybody may see it who reads the recent letter to his congregation of the gifted heresiarch of this neighborhood, the ultimator of Protestant negations) that hostility to the Church is fatal to the memory of the spirit of Christ once possessed, much more to the attainment of it; that the unction of the Holy one is lost even by those unconscious of their misfortune, in this only possible form of *concision.*

In his individual capacity, as an inorganic, unrelated, independent being, a man has not, and cannot have, the affections, internal experiences and dispositions, or the powers and blessings, which we can, and may, and will receive in his corporate capacity—in either or any of the great departments of his Humanity, the family, the State, the Church. Nor is there any complete and satisfactory, perhaps no real way, to come into this corporate capacity, except through a publicly recognized and legitimate organization, whether domestic, political, or religious. "The powers that be are ordained of God";—the laws governing the family order, are, in each country for the time, divinely empowered, to shield what society did not make and cannot unmake; and the Historical Church for the time being, and the place in which it organizes the Word of God, and institutes the channel of divine grace, is a divine institution, connection with which is the normal, not the only, condition of salvation. I am not to be driven from this ground by arguments drawn from the number and variety of churches, or the profitless character of many of them, or their often imperfect and miserable administration; any more than the unhappy marriages, or the wretched laws applicable to them, should drive me from my reverence for the family, as a divine institution and order. I recognize the fact that in all Christian countries the main channel of the religious life of the people is an external organization. I know that the whole Gospel cannot be taught to individuals as individuals. I believe that the Holy Spirit communicates with Humanity, and not with private persons. God speaks to men, individual men, through their consciences; but the Holy Spirit is God coming into the world through his Word, a living word, but still a word, a spoken, taught, published word, which is neither communicated to individuals, nor from individuals, but from the Church to Humanity. This doctrine does not deny open relations between individual men and their Maker; does not deny spiritual influences to private souls;

but it denies that the Holy Ghost is to be confounded with these private whispers, or that the religious life of the world is mainly due to these independent and inorganic suggestions.

"No prophecy is of any private interpretation." That view of Christianity which makes it the magnificent out-birth of a great private individual, the Galilean peasant, saint, philosopher, and seer; or of the Gospel which makes it a business between one private man, namely, one's-self, and another private man, Jesus Christ; or of religion which, leaving out the bond which is the Church, makes it a matter between a man and his God; or of the Church which establishes it fundamentally in the personal experience and worth of every good man, is a view false to the constitution of humanity, the conditions of man's historic existence and development, a profound psychological, or a wide practical analysis—false to the wants, experiences, instincts, and imaginations of men. It is the cause and consequence, the consequence and cause, of the disintegrating ideas and usages which are now creating the injurious and unsatisfactory aspects of our Christian civilization—and as such, I have now, in conscious infirmity, and with an appalling sense of crudity and blindness, excusable only because the age is crude and groping, attempted to set forth the principal grounds of it.

What, then, have we to do, waiting on God's help, to reanimate the Church, but heartily to recognize the existing religious institutions of Christendom as the chosen channel through which the divine Word is seeking to descend into Humanity and the world? Do you ask whether, upon the theory that the Church contains the power of God, and is a channel of influences independent of human will, we have any ability to increase or diminish its contribution? or whether our recognition of its presence and working can touch its efficacy? I reply, that whatever else we know not, we may safely assume to know this, that no view of God's agency, or Christ's, or the Holy Ghost's, which sets aside human responsibility, or ignores human will, or makes the action of any of them independent of the mental, moral, and spiritual organization of humanity, which they are aiming to bless and save, can be a sound or true view. You might as well attempt to disconnect the freedom of the arm that moves the organ barrel from the previously arranged teeth, and springs, and pipes of the organ itself, or the freedom of the stream from the configuration of the banks that make the river, as disconnect man's freedom and responsibility from God's freedom and help. A revelation comes only to a being made to receive and capable of receiving the Holy Ghost; the Church exists, and is designed for a being fitted to receive spiritual life and salvation through a Church, and his fitness lies in his having faculties and powers corresponding to, not in any degree identical with, the faculties and powers of the Being who makes revelations, sends the Holy Spirit, and animates the Church. The seed has relations to the sun, and it must germinate in the dark, and press up to the surface, before it can receive the direct beams of its God. There are faculties in man that must lay hold on God, as there are powers in God that will lay hold on man; the initiation is to be taken now by one, now by the other—but any theory of the Church, or of the Holy Spirit, which violates, paralyzes, or in any way disparages the activity and responsibility of man's own will in seeking God, is false to human nature and to God.

Meanwhile, the Church, as a divine and specific institution, having the stewardship of the Holy Ghost and the dispensation of the Word of God, is to be maintained and upheld in its external form as a separate and distinct, a precious and indispensable interest of humanity. All the tendencies to merge it in other interests and organizations, to break down the barriers that define its sphere, to extinguish the lineaments of its supernatural origin and superhuman functions, to secularize (I do not say to liberalize) its sacred day, to empty its rites and forms of mystic significance, to rationalize its teachings, are to be resisted. The Church is to be content with its *religious* function and office. It is not the source and vehicle of the general culture of society; it is not the guide and critic of science, and art, and social progress. These precious interests have other protectors and inspirers. Let science and philosophy, the schools and the journals, the critics and the social reformers, fulfil their own high and important tasks. The Church would be blind to her own interests, not to rejoice in, and to bless their exertions, and to pray for their success. But she has her own peculiar and precious work to do, her own sacred department to fill, which cannot be administered with the highest success in commixture or in partnership with other important offices. States of society may arise in which all institutions, organizations, and offices are temporarily confounded, compelled to interchange functions and functionaries;—as, in a fire, or a shipwreck, or a wilderness, age, sex, grade, decorum, order, and usage, are necessarily and usefully forgotten and superseded. But as nobody can desire to return to that semi-barbaric condition in which our American pioneers lived, when one and the same room served as hall, kitchen, parlor, and bed-chamber for the household and its guests—although, no doubt, that compact and versatile style of housekeeping had its charm and its disciplinary influences—so we are not wise nor considerate of the laws and wants of our nature, when we seek to level its great partitions, and to confound the professions and institutions auxiliary to them. It was a great convenience in our early New England life to have what was called a meeting-house, to serve as church, town-hall, concert-room, and exchange, in which, perhaps, a fire-engine shed stood at one corner, a gun-room at another, and a hearse-house at a third; and it may have been economical, at a later era, to occupy the cellars of our city churches for storage of spirits and molasses; but nobody who has considered the law of association can regard such a state of things as one to be cherished, however it might be tolerated.

That alleged superiority to prejudices which would dance in a church, or worship in a theatre, play cards on a Sunday, or end the ball with a benediction, preach and pray in the striped costume of a harlequin, or invite a promiscuous company in the midst of jollity to unite in prayer— is a coarse trampling upon the delicate perceptions of fitness, a rude obliteration of the nicer distinctions of human feeling—which, if carried out, would end in barbarizing humanity. The author of "The Roman Question" wittily complains of the Pontifical rule, that under it "one sole, identical caste possesses the right of administering both sacraments and provinces, of confirming little boys and the judgments of the lower courts, of despatching parting souls and captains' commissions." The transcendental philosophy which generalizes away all diverse concretes into monotonous abstractions, and delights in making the secular and the sacred, the right and the wrong, the grave and the gay, the male and the female, the world and the Church, the human and the divine, the natural and the supernatural, one and the same, pursues the exact reverse of the order of creation, which is a steady multiplication of distinctions, a growth of diversity, an ascent from roots into branches, twigs, flowers, and fruits. The alleged simplification of our modern medico-philosophic theology, is a simplicity like that which might unite and condense family life, by dismissing the servants and burying the children.

Let the Church feel that it has a sphere quite as important as it can fill, in maintaining the worshipful and God-fearing affections—in supplying the purely religious wants of the people. I would have it undertake less, in order to do more; it would exert a larger influence in the end by confining its work to the illumination of the spiritual interior, the communication of the Holy Ghost.

If we imagine this to be a short, a vague, a monotonous work, it is only because we have not considered that the communication of the contents of revelation, the supply of the Holy Spirit, and the publishing of the Word, the conversion, regeneration, and sanctifying of the souls of men, involves the perpetual reproduction of Christ's life, precepts, history, and spirit. I know how degenerate a sense of Christianity the so-called advanced feeling about the Gospel is. The words of the Bible pass for the Word of God, which that Bible is; the words of Jesus, for Jesus himself— the Word that came down from heaven. But God's Word is God's power,

God's Wisdom, God's love made known in the great language of natural and supernatural events. God talks in creation, in history, in revelation. Nations are his alphabet, epochs his syllables, humanity his discourse. The Bible is God's Word, because it is the record of his dealings with nations and ages—the religious and priestly nations and ages. More especially, and in the most pregnant and peculiar sense, Christ is the Word of God; not what he said, but what he was and did and suffered, and thus showed and taught; and his words and promises and precepts are only part and parcel of his life and death, his resurrection, and perpetual epiphany in the Church. Christ must be formed in us, the hope of glory. God speaks peculiarly and savingly to every soul in whom he makes Christ live. And the work of the Church is so to speak to the world in the orotund of great historic incidents; so to preach by emphasizing the commemorative days, and illuminating the holy symbols—and pausing on the successive events which made the doctrines of Christianity—as gradually to thunder into the deaf ear of humanity the saving lesson of the Gospel.

No lecture-room can do this; no preaching-man can do this; no thin, ghostly individualism or meagre congregationalism can do this. It calls for the organic, instituted, ritualized, impersonal, steady, patient work of the Church—which, taking infancy into its arms, shall baptize it, not as a family custom, but a Church sacrament; which shall speak to the growing children by imaginative symbols and holy festivals—and not merely by Sunday-school lessons and strawberry-feasts; which shall confirm them and take them into the more immediate bosom of the Church as they attain adult years, and are about to step beyond the threshold of domestic life; which shall make both marriage and burial rites of the immediate altar—and give back to the communion-service the mystic sanctity which two centuries has been successfully striving to dispel, without gaining by this rationality any thing except the prospect of its extinction. A new Catholic Church—a Church in which the needed but painful experience of Protestantism shall have taught us how to maintain a dignified, symbolic, and mystic church-organization without the aid of the State, or the authority of the Pope—their support being now supplied by the clamorous wants of our starved imaginations and suppressed devotional instincts— this is the demand of the weary, unchurched humanity of our era. How to remove the various obstacles, how to inaugurate the various steps to it— is probably more than any man's wisdom is adequate to direct just now. But to articulate, or even to try to articulate the dumb wants of the religious times, is at least one step to it. It is a cry for help, which God will hear, and will answer by some new word from the Holy Ghost, when humanity is able and willing to bear it.

v THE CHALLENGE OF EMERSON AND TRANSCENDENTALISM

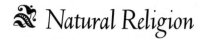 *Natural Religion*

FREDERIC HENRY HEDGE (1805–1890)

When Frederic Henry Hedge rose to deliver the Dudleian Lecture on Natural Religion on May 14, 1851, it was just ninety-six years after President Edward Holyoke had delivered the first lecture in the series. A list of the other speakers who had been similarly honored reads like a roll call of the Standing Order's leadership. One by one they had come to speak in turn on the four subjects stipulated by the lectureship's founder, Chief Justice Paul Dudley (1675–1751). The first of these subjects was to be natural religion, as set forth in the first paragraph of the lecture published here. The second was to be on the evidences of revealed religion; the third was to proclaim the errors of the papacy; and the fourth was to defend the validity of Congregational or Presbyterian ordination. The four taken together, it could be presumed, would present the students of Harvard College with a full and well-rounded defense of the principles of New England's religious heritage. Students would be protected from the inroads of episcopacy and popery; they would gain renewed confidence in those truths set forth in the Holy Scriptures; and they would understand that all their beliefs and moral obligations were firmly rooted in natural theology.

The man who joined the Dudleian company in 1851 was the son of Levi Hedge, a professor of philosophy and ethics at Harvard. He had been tutored by the historian George Bancroft, and then in 1818, he went to Germany in the company of Bancroft and George Ticknor, a trip with profound consequences for his lifetime interests. This visit to Continental seats of learning also had large consequences for American scholarship and education as a whole, for it marked the beginning of a trend that by 1915 had brought ten thousand Americans to enroll in German universities. After four years of study Hedge returned to the United States, entered Harvard, and was graduated from the college in 1825 and the divinity school three years later. Thereafter he served parishes in West Cambridge (Arlington), Massachusetts; Bangor, Maine; and Providence, Rhode Island, before being settled over the First Church in Brookline in 1856. During the following year he was inaugurated as a nonresident professor of ecclesiastical history at the divinity school. He resigned from his parish in 1874 to become professor of German, but for four more years he continued to teach Church history. He was one of the first to study seriously the Lutheran Reformation, and with his knowledge of German, he produced the best known translation of Luther's famous hymn "A Mighty Fortress Is Our God." From this time forward German thought took a more important place among Unitarians. Hedge retired from the university in 1884.

Throughout his career Hedge was prominent in Unitarian affairs. During the late 1830s his importance to the Transcendental Club led to its being referred to as the Hedge Club. After formation of the National Unitarian Conference in 1865, he joined with Bellows, Clarke, and others against the radicals who sought to remove an explicit Christian affirmation from the constitution's preamble. As a prolific author and editor he gave effective voice to his Christian Transcendentalism, his enthusiasm for German thought and letters, and his relatively conservative doctrinal views. His treatise *Reason in Religion* best presents his religious philosophy.

The subject Hedge addressed in 1851 was an especially important one. In natural theology more than anywhere else, the early Unitarians shared the interests and presuppositions of their religious contemporaries. In this and the related fields of Christian evidences, wherein the reliability and credibility of scriptural revelation were examined, the detailed volumes of Archdeacon Paley of the Church of England and of President Mark Hopkins of orthodox Williams College stood side by side with Unitarian formulations of the material. There was much confidence in what Perry Miller later referred to as large and commodious principles of comprehension, upon which lawyers and gentlemen could agree, which quieted all sectarian heats. Natural theology found its place in the curriculum of every New England college and was considered vital to ministerial training.

During the second half of the eighteenth century, before the outbreak of the Unitarian Controversy, it was this lecture on natural religion in the Dudleian series—usually assigned to men of liberal outlook—which was most likely to stir public interest. After the controversy, the place of natural theology and Christian evidences in Unitarian thinking was further enhanced by a new program of annual lectures endowed by John Lowell, Jr., in 1839. John Amory Lowell, who for forty years administered the trust fund, saw to it that the Lowell lecturers more or less reflected the theology of his father's contribution to the controversy, *Are You a Christian or a Calvinist?*. By the mid-nineteenth century, however, the Lockean outlook on natural religion typified by the first century of Dudleian Lectures was showing signs of strain. The intellectual complacency betokened by most of these discourses on reason's religious triumphs provided considerable occasion for Transcendentalist criticism of Boston Unitarianism.

It was fitting, therefore, that two quondam members of the Transcendental Club, William Henry Furness and Hedge, should examine the implications of Emerson's Divinity School Address and introduce a critical spirit into the Dudleian Lecture series. As Perry Miller remarked in his own Dudleian Lecture on the subject in 1953, "The patient student is relieved at last" when the first of these men "gently shakes the venerable structure, and [he] breathes freely . . . when Frederic Henry Hedge demolishes it entirely."[1]

This is not the place, though, to speculate on the validity or even the viability of the traditional arguments of natural theology. It is sufficient to remark that, to the various schools of post-Kantian religious thinkers who dominated the later nineteenth century, the proofs of which Chief Justice Dudley had spoken so confidently seemed irrelevant. To the positivists and utilitarians of the period, as to the logical empiricists of the twentieth century, all of whom recurred admiringly to Hume's *Dialogues on Natural Religion,* the arguments seemed not only irrelevant but illogical and empty. In certain religious traditions this type of natural theology was kept alive, but not in American liberalism, and not in Unitarianism. Hedge's lecture, therefore, is something of a milestone, as he must have realized. The selection that follows is an unabridged transcription of the manuscript, which Hedge deposited in the Harvard University Archives at the time of the lecture. The lecture was published in the *Christian Examiner* 52 (1852): 117–36.

MATTH. XVI, 17: *And Jesus answered and said unto him, Blessed are thou Simon Bar-jona; for flesh and blood hath not revealed it unto thee, but my Father which is in heaven.*

JOHN I, 9: *That was the true light which lighteth every man that cometh into the world.*

ROM. I, 20: *Because that which may be known of God is manifest with them, for God hath shewed it to them.*

The subject of the Dudleian Lecture for this year is Natural Religion. In the words of the Founder it is defined as a Lecture "for the proving, explaining and proper use and improvement of the principles of Natural Religion, as it is commonly called, and understood by Divines and learned men."

The distinction of Natural and Revealed religion is still current in

1. Perry Miller, "The Insecurity of Nature," p. 125.

popular speech, although the antithesis implied in it is less generally admitted and less cordially approved by the thinkers of this century than it was by those of the last. As a philosophic division of the subject of religion, this distinction is not satisfactory, and will not endure the test of a critical analysis.

For if it is intended—and such, I believe, is the common acceptation—if by this distinction it is intended to designate different methods by which religious ideas have been obtained or might be obtained, then the distinction is futile, because it is impossible to ascertain with precision what ideas in this sense are natural to man, and what are not, what might have been attained without the successive dispensations of religion which have hitherto passed upon mankind, and what would have proved unattainable. And not only so, but, if we attempt to define to ourselves what we mean by a natural discovery in religion, as distinct from divine communication, we shall find it impossible to draw a line of demarcation which shall satisfy ourselves and the common judgement of mankind.

I say it is impossible to ascertain with precision what ideas in religion are natural, i.e. discoverable by natural processes, and what are not. We have no data for determining this question. If we assume as a test the conclusions of Christian philosophers who have labored to reproduce, by a dialectic process, or to fix on a basis of pure reason, the primary truths of religion, the value of that test is impaired by the fact that these philosophers were Christian, and, as such, already possessed of those truths which they labored to deduce. It matters little how just the conclusions and irrefragable the logic; they prove nothing as to the native power of the human understanding to discover the truths of religion since the truths to be discovered preexisted in the mind. It is easy to do the sum when the answer is given. You may go to your library in the dark and take the volume which you want from its place on the shelf. But in order to do that, you must have been there before in the light. The question is not whether the conclusions are just, but whether they are spontaneous; not whether the true doctrine has been hit by this process, but whether the groping intellect would ever have seized it without the prevenient grace of a higher illumination. For those who enjoy the light of Christianity to fancy that they really disuse that light while professing to ignore it, is a poor delusion like that of children playing blindfold, and pretending to walk with their eyes covered, while, at every turn, they peep beneath the bandage, and, by surreptitious observations, furnish themselves with a new direction. The truths in these reasonings are always presumed; they are always foreseen. They are not discovered by any light which the process of ratiocination has thrown upon them, but,—as Herschel discovered

Uranus,—by light of their own; our reason being only the speculum in which the truth is mirrored.

Or, shall we seek our proofs of natural discoveries in religion beyond the Christian era? Shall we seek them in the writings of the ancients who have speculated on these subjects? Shall we seek them in Ionic, Eleatic and Italic philosophies, or in Plato, and Cicero, and Seneca? Here, too, the same objection meets us, although in a modified form. Wherever these philosophers have asserted a religious truth, there is reason to suspect the spontaneity of their conclusions. We always find, on investigation, that they had sat down by foreign streams, and filled their earthen vessels with a lore which preexisted before their inquiries. Cicero derived his wisdom from the Academy whose earliest and best voices had taught the same three hundred years before. Plato, whose name denotes a new era of the intellect, and marks the second great monument in the passage from Asia into Europe, was only a lens through which the converging rays of Orphic, Hermaic and Magian wisdom were poured with concentrated power on the western world. Anaxagoras, the first among the Greeks, according to Aristotle, who affirmed that the world was formed and governed by intelligence, had travelled in Egypt and was probably more indebted to the priests of Sais than he was to his own sagacity for that fruitful idea. So, too, Pythagoras, and Zeno, and all the lights of Grecian philosophy, refer us to an elder day. They are only witnesses and media of a light which they transmit from an unknown antiquity with more or less of chromatic error in the passage. We trace that light to the East, we trace it to the banks of the Tigris, of the Ganges, of the Nile, and there its origin is lost in the uncertainty of prehistoric periods. But this is remarkable, that the higher we ascend the historic record, the more theistic and religious the thought and life of man are found to be. All this points, as it seems to me, to a revelation older than history, from which the theologies of India, of Persia and of Egypt, and, after them, the philosophies of Hellas and of Magna Grecia derived whatever of truth they have incorporated in their systems. If the fathers of the Hebrew race, as the Jewish records claim, enjoyed divine illumination, it is not a violent presumption to suppose that other Semitic tribes partook of the same; if less carefully preserved and less generally diffused among the Elamite and Aramean nations than it was in the Abrahamic line. It is fair to presume that the esoteric doctrine of Egypt, as well as the Mithra-worship of Zoroaster were only traditionary fragments of an aboriginal word coeval with civilized man.

And not only is this primal revelation a just inference a posteriori from the history of human thought in relation to the subject; but a priori, also, it is presumable from the very idea of God and the wants of the soul. The presumption, which Paley in his "Evidences," derives in favor of Christianity from the seeming necessity and, therefore, antecedent probability of some revelation to subjects of a moral law, may, with equal justice, be claimed in favor of a revelation prior to Christianity and prior to the Hebrew Law. If such a revelation was necessary two thousand years ago, it was equally necessary four thousand years ago. If it was necessary to the children of Eber, it was equally so to the children of Asshur and of Abram and to those "who divided the isles of the Gentiles." The perception of truths so essential to the well-being of man—God and immortality and a moral law—may reasonably be supposed to have been divinely communicated to infant man as soon as he became sufficiently mature to be the subject of a moral law, if it did not form a part of the original dower of the soul. It may reasonably be supposed that God did not wait the full age of the understanding to make known Himself, but while he left His works to be interpreted by the ordinary, tentative methods of the human understanding; imparted the more necessary knowledge of Himself by a quicker process; interpolating the slow progress of humanity with miraculous intuitions, and kindling, with a breath, the persuasion of Himself which lighteth every man that cometh into the world.

In this view the best voices of the Christian church concur. Cudworth, than whom English theology has no brighter ornament, expressly declares his conviction that those notions of the pagan philosophers which harmonized with Christian truth was the product of revelation. It was a favorite doctrine of the Fathers that all moral teachers and philosophers, who, before the coming of Christ, were truly wise and taught essential truth; partook of the spirit of Christ, enlightened by the same eternal Word not yet made flesh. Origen, Clemens Alexandrinas, Cyril, Lactantius and others bear witness of the strict monotheism which lay behind the polytheism of the Greeks and Romans. And Augustine says that these nations had not so far degenerated as to have lost the idea of one supreme God; thus intimating an earlier period when this idea was more clearly perceived and more fully embraced than it was by the pagans of his day.

But even these testimonies are less explicit and less positive than those of the New Testament writers themselves, who declare, in so many words, this aboriginal revelation. The proem of the fourth gospel is a broad and unequivocal assertion of it. "In the beginning was the Word, and the Word was with God, and God was the Word"; that is, from all eternity God revealed Himself. In this Word "was life, and the life was the light of men." "He came unto his own and his own acknowledged him not. But as many as received him to them gave he power to become the Sons of God." Paul, in the Epistle to the Romans, says "That which may be known of God is manifest to the Gentiles, for God hath showed it unto them. For the invisible things of Him from the creation of the world are clearly seen, being understood by the things that are made, even His eternal power and Godhead. So that they are without excuse, because when they knew God they glorified Him not as God, and changed the glory of the incorruptible God into an image made like to corruptible man."

But setting aside these external evidences of a primal revelation, what do we mean when we speak of a natural origin of religious truth as distinguished from divine communication? Does anything we know of the origin of ideas justify that distinction? Does any experience we have had justify us in affirming that any one of our religious ideas has been generated by the self-action of the mind? We speak of reasoning out truth, as if our reasoning were genetic; as if logic were an inventive process; as if a philosophical truth like God, or freewill, or necessity, were something deposited at the foot of an induction, just as an answer in arithmetic is delivered at the close of the sum. What one of our theological or metaphysical convictions—if we will be candid with ourselves—has been obtained in this way? What one of them has been reasoned out empirically, like an arithmetic problem? It is not thus—it is not by logical methods, by putting major and minor together, that we have been led to these views and beliefs. The only account we can give of them is that they sprung up in our minds, that so it was given us, so it was whispered to us when we turned our thoughts in that direction. It may be we can recall the day and the hour when this or that conviction took possession of the soul. But whence it came we know not, nor how it came, only that it came of itself to the watching mind; and was not elaborated by diligent experiment. Our views of moral and religious truth are not syllogistic conclusions, but impressions, intuitions. They are not calculated, but revealed in us; I know not how better to characterize the manner of their genesis, than by calling them revelations. All personal experiences of religious truth is a revelation made in us of so much truth as we experience, and the real distinction between these subjective experiences and what we call, objectively, a revelation in religion, is not a difference of origin—for the truths of any given revelation must be revealed in us again before we can truly receive them—but the addition, in the one case, of an outward, historic sanction, which is wanting in the other.

All religion, as far as we have any knowledge or can form any plausible conjecture of its origin, in nations or individuals, is revealed. It is not a product of ratiocination, but the gift of Him whose inspiration giveth understanding. What Jesus said of Peter, may be said, with equal justice, of every one who has hold of a religious truth, whether Christian, Turk or Hindoo; "Flesh and blood hath not revealed it to thee, but my Father which is in heaven." And this, too, is worthy of note, that, of all existing historical religions, revelation forms a conspicuous element.

On the other hand, all religion, historical or individual is *natural;* as constituting a natural attribute of man, an essential and indestructible part of human nature. Religion in some form, Christian here, Brahminical there, Magian in one age, and Mohammedan in another, is as much a constitutive element of man's nature as any other manifestation of his being.

What then is meant, or would be meant, by Natural Religion, so called, as distinguished from revealed? What is the origin of the term, and what was intended by those who first employed it? I suppose it was used, originally, to distinguish all other religions from the Christian. The Christian world was said to be in a state of grace, the rest of mankind in a state of nature. Accordingly, the religious faith of the latter was called, natural; and, as Christianity was assumed to be the only revelation, the religion of Christ was, distinctively, called revealed. Then, as certain particulars of the extra Christian religions were seen to coincide with Christian truth, all that part of religion was set down as discoverable by the natural, that is, the uninspired reason, while those particulars of the Christian scheme, which were not observed in other religions, were considered as constituting the specific topics of revelation. Hence the distinction of Natural and Revealed religion, which obtained its greatest prevalence, during the last century. The real distinction, originally intended, was that of Christian and extra Christian religion. The terms, in which this distinction was expressed, are based on a false assumption. Ethnic and Christian would have been the true designation, or, better still, universal and special religion—the term, universal comprehending what is common to all religions, the term, special, as used by Christians, expressing what is peculiar to our own.

By natural religion, then, I mean, universal religion. I mean, those religious ideas which are common to all mankind, or, at least, to all religions of which we have any accurate knowledge.

It follows that in order to determine the elements of Natural Religion the true method is not to interrogate our own consciousness or to test with our understandings what doctrines are capable of being logically legitimated, but to inquire of history and ethnology what doctrines are common to all religions. Whatsoever religious ideas we shall find to have been embraced in all ages, by all nations, that is, by all nations possessing a systematic theology—*quod semper, quod ubique, quod ab omnibus*—there constitute the substance of natural religion.

The adoption of this principle extends the area of natural religion, and brings within its scope some ideas which have not usually been regarded as belonging to that province. The truths heretofore embraced in it are, first, the being of God, with those qualities, natural and moral, which form the essential predicates of Deity, including Creation and Providence; secondly, a moral law, with its correlate notion of moral accountableness, and thirdly, a future life. To these we must add, in the first place, the idea of revelation, an idea common to all religions, either in the form of incarnation, as most nations believe, or of a communication made by divinely accredited prophets, as Judaism and Islamism have received it. "Religion and revelation," it has been said, "are twin thoughts, wherever we find the one, we find the other also." That God should reveal himself lies in the very conception of God, intelligent natures, susceptible of revelation, being supposed. Scarcely will the rudest Fetichism be found to want this organic element in the idea of God.

Worship is another idea of Natural Religion, an idea inseparable from it, and found wherever man is found. Worship, however conceived and rendered, for whatever purpose and in whatever manner performed, as voluntary homage or compulsory tribute for rendering thanks or averting wrath; worship, whether it consist in animal sacrifices, or in sounding of gongs, or swinging of censers, or showing of wafers, or intelligent speech, or meditative silence; worship, of some sort, is universal, and never yet has a people been found to whom it was wanting. "You may travel the world through," says Plutarch, "and find towns and cities without walls, without theatres or places of exercise, but there never was seen, nor shall be seen by man, one city without temples, or without making use of prayers or sacrifices for the obtaining of blessings, and the averting of curses and calamities. Nay, I am of opinion that a city might sooner be built without any ground to stand upon, than a commonweal be constituted altogether void of worship, or, being constituted, be preserved."

I reckon further, as one of the constituents of Natural Religion, the idea of radical Evil inherent in the constitution of things, and perpetually warring against the Good, in nature and in man. Most religions—perhaps all—have personified this principle, and represented the evil that is in the world, as the operation of a conscious and voluntary agent, the malign influence of some demonic Power or Powers, whose being is a contradiction of the Godhead, and whose nature and function it is to contest with divine Love the physical and moral empire of the world. The personification is not, I conceive, a substantive, but only an incidental part of this idea. Its substance consists in the supposition of a negative principle, a contrary power, whose operation is evil, whether it be conceived as an independent, conscious existence, according to the Magian or Manichean theory, the second term in a Dualism coordinate with the act of creation, or only as the reaction of a nature, lapsed from its first estate, and its

primal good. In one form or another, the assertion of an evil principle
runs through every positive religion, and must, therefore, be received as
a fundamental idea of Natural Religion. So fundamental indeed is this
idea, that Kant, who will not be suspected of any undue bias in that direction, maintains the fact of a radical evil in man as a cardinal thesis of his
"Religion within the bounds of Reason." This doctrine, of an evil principle in conflict with the good, supposes the supremacy and final triumph
of the good, an idea which all religions, by various myths of symbols or
prophecies, have sought to express. It is emblemed in the Greek mythology, in the conquest obtained by Jupiter over Typhon. In the doctrine of
the Brahmins, Siva, the destroying god, whose neck is encircled with a
rosary of the skulls of Brahma, that is, with the ruins of successive creations which he has successively dissolved holds his office of destroyer in
subordination to that of reproducer and giver of life. He is not only Siva-
Rudra, the annihilator, but Siva-Vishnu, the regenerator and conserver
of the world.

> So taught of old the Indian seer,
> Destroying Siva, forming Brahm,
> Who wake, by turns, Earth's love and fear,
> Are still the same.

This idea is developed, with the greatest precision, in the Magian religion, of which the distinctive principle is, a dualism of Light and Darkness, or Good + Evil. This dualism, according to the Shasters, had its origin in an elder unity, and will end in unity again. The good will finally
triumph, and the evil will resolve itself into the good, their long hostility
will be reconciled and confounded in light and love.

> Ever wider, ever lighter,
> The holy shafts of Light are cast,
> Ahriman himself, the dark one,
> Will be merged in Light at last.

The recognition of Satanic agency, which pervades the scriptures of the
Old and New Testaments, and the apocalyptic prediction of a time when
Satan shall be bound and rendered powerless constitute the Christian
aspect of this universal belief.

Closely connected with this doctrine is that of redemption, which must
also be regarded as an element of universal religion. The doctrine of redemption supposes an alienation or lapse from God and goodness, and
affirms a restoration by faith and repentance, through the mediation of
some prophet or divine person, providentially appointed, or self-devoted
to that end. In some religions the notion of vicarious expiation comes in

as a form or condition of redemption. Of this we have examples in the Phoenician myth of Jeoud, the son of God, who is sacrificed for the good of his people,—in the Prometheus of the Greek, and the Odin of the Scandinavian mythology. But this notion is not essential to the doctrine. All that is essential to it, is the idea of deliverance from evil, and restoration to God, by mediation.

These, I conceive, are the cardinal doctrines of Natural Religion. Others, that might be enumerated, are subordinate to these, and included in them. These are the primal beliefs of mankind, around which all religious ideas cluster. They are found, with various modifications, in all positive religions of which we have any knowledge, and therefore, according to the principle which I have laid down, are essential constituents of natural religion. For what better criterion can we have of what is natural, than the common consent of mankind. This, and not the deductions of philosophy must be our test and guide in this inquiry. When we ask of the doctrines of natural religion, it is a question of fact and not a question of theory with which we are considering. The question is not what might be believed, or should be believed, but what is believed. It is not what this or that philosopher has demonstrated, or what we ourselves may demonstrate, by strict philosophical methods, but what has obtained the general consent of mankind.

And this general consent of mankind, which determines the doctrines of Natural Religion, furnishes, also, the better part of their proof. It constitutes the main element in the evidences, as it does in the history of religion.

Under this head of evidences, I shall only glance at those which relate to the being of God. The writings, ancient and modern, which bear on this point, which aim to demonstrate the being of God, are striking illustrations of that propensity in man to give account to himself of his convictions, which impels him to seek in demonstration a certitude which preexisted in himself. No conviction of the human mind is stronger than that of the being of God. Of no being or thing, scarcely even of our own being, is the persuasion more absolute. Men differ, infinitely, in their conceptions of God, in the more or less which they comprehend in that conception. The essential attributes of one conception may be wanting to another, but some conception, representing, however imperfectly, the idea of God, is proper to every sane mind, and may be reckoned a necessary and constitutive part or product of the mind. An atheist, in the strict sense of unbelief in any power or law which holds of Deity, is an impossibility. The would-be Atheist, if any such there be, cannot wholly extirpate this idea from his soul. It besets him behind and before. If, in the place of God, he exalts Nature to the authorship and governance of the world, he endows Nature with the attributes of Divinity. If he refers all things to Necessity, he makes a God of Necessity. He may change the name as he pleases; he cannot get rid of the fact. To whatever power or principle he assigns the creation and control of things that power becomes a God to him. Strict atheist there is none, and what passes for atheism, and professes to be atheism, the denial, that is, of a personal, self-conscious, self-determining Deity, is so exceptional a case that we are warranted in affirming all men theists, with whatever distinctness of conception or intensity of faith they may hold that opinion. Every man believes in God, a conscious God, self determined, all determining, a supreme Intelligence and a supreme Will, the centre, source, law, motive, reason, end of all being. It is the strongest of all our convictions. Of all our ideas, that of God is the most necessary, + universal; but it is also the most undefinable and undemonstrable. God is the name we give to our highest conception of power and goodness. It is the ultimate fact, to which, as archetype and ideal, we refer all possible excellence, and to which, as providence and law, we refer the destinies of all creatures, and the moral government of the world. Any precise definition of this idea is impossible and absurd. To define is to limit, to circumscribe, to run the boundary which divides one being from another. We define an object by separating it from all others. But God, who includes all, cannot be thus separated. He who comprehends all limits, is comprehended by none. The nature that explains all, cannot be explained. The thought, which would determine God, is already determined by Him. We can no more define Him, or comprehend Him, than we can go behind our own consciousness, or see behind our own eyes.

As the idea of God is undefinable, so the truth of that idea, the existence of God, is undemonstrable; and all demonstrations of it hitherto attempted, whether by the ontological, kosmological or physico-theological method; or the mathematical, for even that has been pretended, have proved failures. No one of the speculative proofs, which have yet been offered, possesses any logical value. The utmost that can be claimed for them is, that, on the supposition of a God, they help to illustrate the nature of His being, the method of His action, and the character of his government. But the existence of God is always presumed in these reasonings. They add positively nothing to the certitude of that truth. As demonstrations they are valueless, and vanish at the touch of criticism. A little analysis blows them into nothing. The so-called ontological demonstration, *via aseitatis* that is, the attempt to demonstrate the being of God from the idea of God, which became so celebrated in the form which was given to it by Anselm of Canterbury in the 11th century, which, in one form or another, was repeated by Thomas Aquinas, Dun Scotus, and others of the Schoolmen, then revived by Des Cartes, restated by Leibnitz and Spinoza, and even vindicated by Hegel, is nothing more than a logical quibble, + even in the much improved statement of it by Kant, carried no more conviction to the mind than a hundred other scholastic puzzles which turn on a play of words, and which you see, at once, to be absurd and irrefragable. Its whole contribution to Theology consists in developing the idea of self-existence, expressed in the word Jehovah, 3000 years ago.

The teleological argument, or the argument from design, was first started by Socrates, who argued that things which have a manifest use, τα ἐπ' ωφελεία γενομενα, were the work of design, γνωμης, and adduces, among other things, the arrangement of the eye as an illustration of this design. The vein, thus opened, was diligently worked by the ancients, particularly the Stoics. It crops out occasionally in medieval theology; it formed the chief stratum in the religious philosophy of the last century; it was quarried, with particular zeal, by the English mind, and yielded its crowning specimen in Paley's Natural Theology. This argument has the merit of having furnished many excellent and entertaining works in the various provinces of natural philosophy, and, in some cases, perhaps, of deepening the reverent wonder which the contemplation of God in creation excites in every well constituted mind. And, when we have said this, we have conceded, I believe, the uttermost that can be said of its behalf. As a positive proof of the existence of God, it is worthless. It only proves that if there be a God, and that God the maker of the world, he has wrought with consummate skill. But the existence of God is all along presumed. The very word, design, is a begging of the question. What we see in nature is a relation of means and ends. When we call this design or contrivance we commit what in logic is called a subreptio—we assume the very point on which the argument hinges and which requires to be proved. The link which connects the thing observed in this case with the inference drawn from it is not a logical synthesis but a sentiment. No sound mind doubts that there is design in Nature, and no sound mind doubts that there is a God; but moral certitude is one thing and scientific demonstration is another. The imputation of design in any case is a judgement determined by subjective conditions. We see design where we appreciate the use resulting from a given combination, we ignore it where we do not; although, apart from our private feeling of fitness, there is just the same evidence of design in the one case as in the other. That every conceivable triangle, of whatever dimensions, whether it be the constellation, so called, to the left of Andromeda, enclosing incalculable spaces, or whether it be constituted by lines of an inch long in the margin of a text-book, should include precisely 180 degrees no more and no less; that in every product of the number nine, the addition of the digits composing that product should give nine;—these facts have all the substantive proof of design which the theologian finds in the circulation of the blood, or the thoughtful adjustments of the eye, that "cunningest pattern of excelling Nature."

But they do not convey the same impression of design, because they suggest no evident advantage accruing to any sentient subject. Accordingly, we do not call this geometrical or arithmetical law, design, but pronounce it a necessity resulting from the nature of angles and of numbers. And how do we know, the skeptic asks, but "what the whole economy of the universe is conducted by a like necessity, though no human algebra can furnish its key," and that if we could "penetrate into the intimate nature of bodies, we should clearly see why it was absolutely impossible that they could ever admit of any other disposition."

The heart protests against such a supposition and the protest is admissible in the court of the understanding, but admissible only in moral presumption not as a positive proof.

The argument from design has its origin in a law of the mind which demands intelligence as the coordinate of being. Whatever conviction it produces is due to that law, and the statement of that law is the measure of that conviction. Hence the simplest existences are just as convincing as any example in the Bridgewater Treatises. We want God as much for a chaos, as we do for a kosmos; we want Him as much for the first filament of incipient organization, as we do for the finished curiosity of the human hand.

It is related of Napoleon, that conversing one night on a voyage with some philosophers, who were arguing atheistically, he pointed to the stars, and said, "You may talk as much as you please, gentlemen, but who made all that." This expresses the spontaneous judgement of the unsophisticated mind. This is the first impression produced by the contemplation of the outward world, an impression which no labored induction and no analysis of organized structures can add to or improve—intelligence, coordinate with being—the cause of being.

When Vanini was arraigned on the charge of atheism before the Senate of Toulouse, he lifted a straw from the floor, and holding it up to his judges, declared, "This straw compels me to confess that there is a God." It needs nothing more to enforce that confession when we reason from existence to the cause of existence. A straw will suffice for that purpose as well as an animal kingdom. A straw is just as unaccountable without a God as any process of animal life. For once suppose matter to be self-existent, and you may give it what attributes and functions you please.

The first aspect of Nature suggests a God as readily as the most recondite wonders which Science has brought to light. It suggests that Power without which a blade of grass is no more possible than a star, and whose action is as much needed to arrange the petals of the wildflower that blossoms in our path today, as it was in the beginning to unfold the corolla of that celestial flower whose petals are worlds.

He to whom Nature unstudied and undissected is not the immediate presence of God will never reach God by dissection. He who cannot see Him in the living subject will not see Him in the naked paradigm. At this springing and luxuriant season, when the vegetable world, new risen, fills the eye and prospect once more with its gracious presence, and its harvest hopes, amid all this flowering and production, this joyful rushing, and storming into life, in this teeming nature so broad and prodigal and multitudinous and minute, which blooms and flits and waves before our eyes, he who cannot hear, like Adam in Paradise, the voice of the Lord God walking in the garden and the field, will not find Him by following the anatomist along the paths of dusty death.

Besides, though we grant to the argument from design the uttermost that is claimed for it, what does it give us, after all, but the wonderful mechanician, the unfathomable artist, possessing apparently unlimited power, but not, that we can see, unlimited benevolence; a *Deus ex machina,* not the God of religion, not the God who heareth prayer, not the Father of spirits and of mercies. It is not for the solving of physical problems that we want a God. If that were all, some Epicurean theory of a self-existent universe might answer as well. What religion wants and declares, is a Father in Heaven, a moral governor and judge of the rational world. Of this God the natural proofs are our own consciousness, our moral instincts, and the universal consent of mankind, to which I have referred.

The existence of God is given in the moral nature of man. If anything is certain, the moral law is certain—the law which asserts itself in every man as the supreme rule of action. This is a primary fact of our consciousness. But the moral law supposes a God as the necessary condition of the possibility of its fulfillment. This truth was seized upon by Kant, who was the first to appreciate its philosophical significance, and who found in it the highest and only satisfactory proof of a God. And this is one of the great merits of his philosophy, that, while it demolishes dogmatism, and exposes the uncertainty of our cognitions, so far as they depend on the speculative reason, it gives us all the more weight to the practical part of our nature, and recognizes that, as the ultimate ground of all religious certainty. Kant was the first to do this.

He argues that since we are commanded to seek the highest good in obedience to the moral law, and since obedience to the moral law is felt to be the condition of the highest good, and further, since human power

is inadequate to effect that good, we must suppose an almighty moral being, by whom it is effected, as the ruler of the world, that is, morality
leads inevitably to religion.

More concisely we may say, that our moral instincts or better, our
moral experiences imply a God as the objective reality to which they relate, precisely as our sensible experiences imply a material world, to
which they relate. In other words, we have the same evidence for the
being of God that we have for an outward world, that is, our own personal experience. And when to our own experience we add the consent-
ing testimony of every kindred and nation, the great affirmative of history, the eye of all time, we have an amount of evidence than which it is
impossible for me to imagine any more convincing and more irresistible.
This evidence from the universal consent of mankind is pronounced by
Cicero to have the validity of a natural law.

The general consent has no exceptions that are worth regarding. There
have been professed atheists, indeed, and there are atheistical books, and
there are theories, old and recent, of Nature and life, which virtually ex-
plode God from the universe, and a moral government from the order
of things, and make existence a confused jumble of accidents, without law
or aim, but thorough-going, consistent atheism is impossible, or possible
only as a mental disease. ["For if we are not brought to the belief of a God
by reason," says Montaigne, "we are brought to it by force (Eds.)]; atheism being a proposition, not only unnatural and monstrous, but difficult and hard to be digested by the mind of man. There are instances
enough of men who, from vanity, and the pride of broaching uncommon
opinions, and of being reformers of the world, outwardly affect the possession of such opinions. . . . Nevertheless, if you plunge a dagger in
their breast, they will not fail to lift up their hands towards heaven. . . . A
doctrine seriously digested is one thing, and those superficial impressions
are another, which, springing from the depravity of an unsettled mind,
float rashly and at random in the fancy." Perfect theist there is none. Every
man believes in a God. Upon every soul there is laid the consciousness
of some greater than itself. Every man feels himself bosomed and girt
and pierced through by a Power which closes him in on every side and
disposes of him at will. But how great the difference between this dim
consciousness and a genuine faith in God. If by believing in God is
meant merely an impression of Deity, who can look Nature in the face
and say, I believe Him not? If by believing in God is meant a belief
which gives law to the life, who can look into his own heart and say, I
believe? Who believes in God in a sense, in a measure, at all corresponding to the awful import of that idea? Who that really believed in God
could ever knowingly violate His law? What nation, what government,

that really believed in God could ever enact laws which are contrary to His? When we consider what is meant by the proposition, God is, and all that is implied in it with regard to man's nature and destiny, his duty and his calling, the laws which govern us, the retributions which attend us, who can say, I believe. Lord, help our unbelief.

Faith in God, as in all the other truths of religion, is conditioned by the will, and, is in some sort, the product of the will. We conceive very falsely of the mind if we suppose it to be acted on mechanically, by arguments and proofs, and that so much evidence must needs produce so much faith. No evidence can force belief where the mind is predetermined against an opinion, or create an effective faith where the mind is indifferent to it. Faith is not an impression but an act, not passive reception but moral election. We must will to believe if we would come into positive relation with the truth. And here we reach the precise point at which all our speculations, I think, all honest and earnest inquiry on these subjects must land us at last, that is, the necessity of faith to perfect any proof, or to make any opinion true to us. Be the evidence what it may, be the truth what it may, of moral or material import, faith is required as the necessary complement of that evidence, and the realization of that truth. Facts the most certain, or those so esteemed, are not received without faith. And the most inveterate materialist, the most hard-shelled worldling, leads a life of faith in relation to this visible world, and his business and interests in it. It is only because that business and those interests are so pressing, and leave no room for question, that he does not doubt of the visible world, and of every existence but his own. And if faith is wanted for the conduct of worldly affairs, can it be supposed to be unneeded in those of the moral world, and that, if those things be, of which religion testifies, they can have any entrance into us except through faith? We learn from our moral nature—we feel in our consciences, what things should be believed in order to human well-being. We have that shrewd surmise which the Roman, speaking of faith in God, and borrowing a word from Epicurus, called πρόληψις, an anticipation, a forefeeling of the truth, which may be regarded as the finger of God directing attention to the truths of the Spirit, those primary and everlasting truths which one generation declareth to another, and one civilization hands down to the next, which all revelations reveal, and all churches confess.

These are the truths which must be believed to make existence tolerable to any thinking mind. Consider what the world would be without them, and whether, without these, and the belief in these, it is possible to imagine any state of things which is not fraught with despair, in which it would not be better never to have been born. For what is our life—this human existence, into which we have come we know not nor why, if there be no God, and no immortality? It is an island, of small extent, in the midst of a wide, dumb, inexorable deep, which is soon to swallow us up. Why we are here, we know not; we only know that we *are* here, and we make us a home as we can, and store and adorn it as we may. But whenever, in our hurry, we pause to listen, we hear the eternal surf that expects us, and we know that our island is crumbling beneath our feet. Every day the surrounding ocean washes away a part of our territory, encroaching more and more on our mortal life, and we can calculate the time when the whole will be submerged, and the terrible unknown, which encircles it, will carry us away, with its flood, whither we know not, to issues we know not, nor with what conditions, if at all, we shall rise again into conscious life. Against this daily waste and impending doom, human wit, as yet, has devised no remedy, and furnished no solace. Ancient philosophy had two prescriptions, neither of which has been found to answer. The one was the Epicurean, "eat and drink, for tomorrow we die." Of this it was said, truly, that "man is not so constituted, the death of tomorrow spoils the appetite of today." The other was the Stoic resource of lofty indifference, superior to fate, more noble, but no more availing. Nothing will avail here but faith; repose in the thought that God is, with all which that truth comprehends. That God is and reigns, that He has measured our span of life, and that, when our foundation in time is removed from under us, He receives us into His arms, and sends us forth again to renew our race, with new missions, in other spheres. Do we believe this? It must be so, it is the answer of the soul to all serious questioning.

❧ "Antisupernaturalism in the Pulpit"

FREDERIC HENRY HEDGE (1805–1890)

Unitarian history is punctuated by an unusually large number of sermons and addresses which it is not an exaggeration to call "epoch-making." The three most memorable of these are Channing's Baltimore Sermon (1819), Emerson's Divinity School Address (1838), and Parker's South Boston (Hawes Place Church) sermon (1841); hardly less significant are Henry W. Bellows's "Supense of Faith" (1859) and Frederic Henry Hedge's "Antisupernaturalism in the Pulpit" (1864), both of which were delivered to the alumni of the Harvard Divinity School. Channing's words became the platform of early Unitarian denominationalism; Emerson's, the manifesto of Transcendentalism; Parker's, a call for a new, critical, Christian radicalism. The addresses of Bellows and Hedge, on the contrary, were demands for conservatism. One called for a renewal of the Church; the other sought to retard the growth of philosophic naturalism within the Unitarian fold. Delivered, as it was, almost on the eve of the organization of the National Unitarian Conference, Hedge's address took on special and more enduring significance.

Whether the Hedge who attacked anti-supernaturalism in 1864 was more conservative theologically than the Hedge who was an enthusiastic charter member of the Transcendental Club three decades earlier cannot be definitely stated. His life and thought have not received the intensive study justified by his great contribution to American religion and letters. It would appear, however, that it was primarily the intellectual climate that changed. Hedge never allowed Transcendental enthusiasms to sweep him from his Christian moorings, and his well-reasoned philosophical idealism centered his religious life in a realm untouched by Parker's critical attacks. His unusually broad knowledge of Church history, moreover, allowed him to place contested issues in a deeper perspective than most of his contemporaries could. Despite the controversies of his time, therefore, he exhibited a surprising measure of intellectual serenity. It was, nevertheless, the enthusiastic acceptance of the new philosophical views indicated in his Dudleian Lecture coupled with his combative dedication to fairly conservative doctrinal views that makes Hedge such a crucial link between the "Channing Unitarianism" current in his youth and theologians such as Francis Greenwood Peabody and Charles Carroll Everett, who were to become prominent at the century's end.

The intellectual life of this century, so stimulating and so productive in every department of science and the useful arts, has operated with very different effect in the province of religion. Its influence there has been a disturbing and destructive force. I speak of religion as a system of doctrine, of ecclesiastical tradition, of Scriptural authority, not as a principle of spiritual life. Religion as a system of beliefs, intellectually apprehended, has gained nothing with the progress of the time. A pregnant intimation that the speculative intellect is not the source of religious truth.

In the sphere of science the mind has acted with positive and creative energy, extending the domain of knowledge and of use beyond all former precedent. In the sphere of religion its action has been negative or limitary. To the question, What has science gained from modern investigation and experiment? its disciples answer triumphantly with steam-power and photography and electro-magnetism and a hundred significant discoveries. What answer shall we make when asked for positive results in theology? Shall we point to the saints of Utah with their wives? or to Sunday conventicles of "Spiritualists" addressed by preachers in a "trance-state"? For doctrinal discoveries shall we refer to the latest Council of the Church of Rome and the "Bulla Ineffabilis," the grand achievement of Pius IX., at whose instigation the Immaculate Conception of the Mother of Jesus, rejected by the wisdom of the thirteenth century, has been established for the edification of the nineteenth? Or must we not rather confess that the real discoveries, the genuine results, of theological inquiry have been negative,—discoveries of error and limitation,—that the books of the Pentateuch are not the work of Moses and are not historically correct, that the Tripersonality of the Godhead is not taught in the Bible, that the Scriptures of the Old and New Testaments are not infallible in matters of fact?

I do not question the truth of these discoveries; I do not deny their critical value. I do but declare their purport and bearing. I emphasize the fact of this negative tendency in theology.

The question here is not of progress, but a question of continued existence,—a question of life or death. How far will the process of elimination, initiated some hundred years since, extend? Will the criticism which has taken so much, leave anything remaining? Will negation stop short of universal rejection, not only of all Christian, but of all religious ideas and beliefs?

This is the question which perplexes the conservative mind, more impressed with the negative character than edified by the critical gains of recent Biblical investigation. The conservative mind is easily alarmed at any invasion of the sacred domain of faith, well knowing its incompetence to reproduce a perished sanctity or to reinstate a religious idea that has lost its hold of the popular mind.

But let conservatism comfort itself with the thought that nothing in human nature is so indestructible as religion. Its field and aspects may change, but the principle is a fixed star in the human constitution. It may suffer temporary eclipse, but it will beam again, and resume its place of command, and recover its ancient rights. Truth, moreover, has its own divinely appointed and therefore divinely assured destination, which no criticism can countervail, but must eventually serve and promote. "For we can do nothing against the truth but for the truth." To fancy that the future of religion can be seriously compromised by criticism, however radical, is to doubt its divine origin. If its origin is divine, the divine rule is charged with its fortunes, and its future is sure. "If this counsel or this work be of men, it will come to naught, but if it be of God, ye cannot overthrow it." What a sequel and summing up of the history of Christianity would that be, to say that "God sent his Son into the world," "that the world through him might be saved," but the Tübingen School and British "Essays and Reviews" defeated that purpose, and it had to be abandoned?

The cause of traditional belief and the cause of faith are not necessarily identical. There was all the traditional belief of England in the Oxford Declaration, signed by eleven thousand of her clergy, protesting against the recent decision of the Court of Arches; but I think there was less of faith in it than in the writings of the Essayists and Reviewers which provoked it. The committee of three hundred who presented this Declaration to the Archbishop of Canterbury express their fervent joy that so many of the clergy have given their assent to the doctrine, "that the Bible not only contains, but is the Word of God, and that the punishment of the cursed is everlasting"; that thus "they have been enabled to promote the glory of our Lord." Without irreverence, it may be questioned whether our Lord regards with greater complacency the zeal which would limit his truth and mercy in the interest of the letter of Scripture, or the thoughtful inquiry which seeks the truth by aid of the light which lighteth all who come into the world. It is a melancholy, nay, desperate view of human and divine things, which supposes God's truth to be at the mercy of man's caprice. The shallow conservative who fears that the speculative minds of the nineteenth century will undermine Christianity, exhibits as great a want of faith as the shallow antisupernaturalist who fancies that the speculative minds of the first century created it. I can see no difference between the two; the one is as much an unbeliever as the other.

Nevertheless, it must be confessed that the negative spirit in theology has been in our time disproportionately active. I cannot regret the critical labors of even the most radical theologians. I cannot regret the results of those labors, so far as they are warranted by competent learning, by scientific method, by conscientious investigation. I regret no abatement of the letter or canonicity or infallibility of Scripture thus obtained. What I do regret is, that an equal amount of intellectual ability and scientific insight has not been found for the elucidation, and restatement in forms corresponding to the thought and culture of our time, of the spiritual truths represented in other obsolete forms by the Scripture and the Church. I regret the divorce between the intellectual life of the age and its religion. I regret that minds of the first order in this century, with rare exceptions, if engaged in theology at all, have come to it in a negative instead of a positive mood, and have spent their labor on the letter instead of the spirit.

Christianity has nothing to fear from criticism. Nevertheless, it should be understood that, whilst there is a criticism which is quite legitimate, whatever may be destroyed by it, there is also a criticism which is not legitimate,—not because it is destructive, but because it mistakes its method and its objects, and applies its market scale to matters which are incommensurable. The one is a criticism of authors and of books, the other of ideas and beliefs,—a criticism of the letter and a criticism of the spirit. Take an analogy from ancient literature. Suppose you could disprove the genuineness of the Phædon, or of any Greek or Latin work of high repute which treats of the immortality of the soul,—or, admitting their genuineness, suppose you could refute (which would not be difficult) the arguments employed in those writings,—would that settle the question of Immortality? Independently of the Christian revelation and all other revelation, if these were the only books which treat of the subject, would their inadequacy settle the question? The books may be spurious, the reasoning poor, but the doctrine of Immortality is independent of literature and logic. I never read a treatise of the many that undertake to demonstrate the being of God, which did not seem to me very inconclusive,— more apt to raise doubts than to lay them. But the truth of theism is nowise impaired by the weakness of the arguments adduced in its support. So in Christian theology it is one thing to set aside books, to prove them spurious, to point out flaws in the reasoning and testimony of the writers, and quite another thing to reject the ideas or the facts represented and attested by them. Prove if you can that the fourth Gospel is not an Apostolic, but a later production, that its doctrine had been anticipated by an Alexandrian Jew; it would not follow that the doctrine is not true or the writing uninspired. It is truth that makes inspiration, not inspiration truth. Disprove the validity, as testimony admissible in a court of law, of all the statements in the New Testament concerning the resurrection of Christ. The fact itself is not therefore disproved. The fact is beyond the reach of that kind of criticism. We may hold, with Hume, that a miracle is insusceptible of demonstration, and we may see good reason for not believing in this or that particular miracle, in the form in which it is presented in the record. But to treat all miracle as fable, to rule out of the record whatever contradicts the ordinary course of human experience, retaining the rest, or to set aside the whole as unhistorical because of this element in it, is merely wilful, and as unphilosophic in principle as it is contrary to sound criticism.

I am well aware of the difference between historical and abstract truth, and am far from placing the immortality of the soul, or the being of God, on the same ground with the miracles and resurrection of Christ. The analogy touches the one point only of indemonstrableness. I maintain that defective evidence and imperfect demonstration are not conclusive against doctrine or fact.

The truth of the evangelic history rests on different evidence, and carries a different degree of certitude, from that which belongs to the primary truths of religion. But these are no more impregnable than those, if scepticism happens to call them in question. It is prejudice or arbitrary partiality, not logical necessity, that causes denial to stop with the Gospel. Mr. Theodore Parker, whose honest and abounding zeal was early enlisted on the negative side, and with whom impatience of dogmatic authority and ecclesiastical tradition became a controlling principle of thought, could see no exceptional quality in Chirst, but remained to the last a devout theist. His Sermons on Theism have been pronounced the least able of his productions. They suggest the suspicion that unconsciously the stout reformer was held to this belief by the want of a resting-place and base of operations as a controversialist and preacher, rather than by intellectual conviction; that his theism was not a philosophic apperception, but a moral determination, with as much of will and of taking for granted in it as in most men's Christianity.

An English disciple of Mr. Parker, in a recent publication, in which she criticises the theological position of different ecclesiastical parties in England, and in which an uncompromising radicalism is graciously relieved by a deep and tender piety, rejects historical Christianity as obsolete traditionalism, whilst she sweetly invites the religious sentiment of the nation to rally around Theism,—that being, in the estimation of the writer, an inexpugnable fortress, because a universal intuition of the soul. The unsuspecting confidence with which she cherishes this position, the innocent unconsciousness of any possible undermining of this stronghold, the exhortation to Theists to pray as Christians use, the regretful wonder at their neglect so to do, are very touching. Yes! if Theism would but pray and be a religion! If, when the Christ is taken out of it, Christianity would but remain, how "nice" it would be! The cathedral of St. Paul's might then become a church of "Intuitive Morals," and Westminster Abbey a chapel of Pure Reason; as Agrippa's Pantheon became the St. Mary and Martyrs' Church of Christian Rome.

Strange that the fact of a prayerless Theism should not have suggested a doubt whether Theism could ever become a rallying-point of popular religion, or whether the religious sentiment could ever change its relation from that of guardian to that of ward. The religious sentiment embodied in traditional religion has been the guardian of Theism hitherto; and, should popular religion fail, so far from affording protection in its turn, it is doubtful if Theism itself would survive.

The fact is, Theism is also a tradition, and not, as is claimed, a universal intuition of the soul. It is no more a universal intuition than the Holy Ghost is a universal intuition, than miraculous mediation is a universal intuition. It is the intuition of such souls only as happen to come within the range of that particular pencil of light with which Hebrew tradition has streaked the world's history. The larger portion of the human family have always been, and are still, without that illumination and without that idea; and he who fancies that outside of this historic beam he would have had the idea of God which he now has, confounds traditional experience with original intuition.

I will not say that absolutely there is no revelation of God which is not historical. Here and there, in cases of exceptional intelligence or exceptional holiness, individuals have attained to a theism independent of Semitic tradition. For there is a "light which lighteth every man that cometh into the world." But scarcely in one of a hundred million does this light suffice to show the God of the monotheistic religions. The idea of one only God, self-existent, almighty, wise, and good, Creator and Father of all, is a Hebrew tradition. The conceptions which simulate this idea in other faiths will be found, on closer inspection, to have but little affinity with it.

On the whole, the belief in a personal, sole God, so essential to human well-being, is committed to the charge and trust of historical religion. I do not believe it is capable of any social embodiment, of any organized existence, of any existence at all, except as a rare and fitful experience of the private soul, independently of that tutelage. The speculative intellect, uncontrolled by religious faith, unquickened by moral sentiment, the intellect in its own unbiassed action, does not necessarily—I think I may say does not readily—incline to that belief. Science, if I rightly interpret its recent voices, is less and less disposed to adopt it as the best solution of the problem of creation. On the contrary, I suspect that, of those who have lapsed from the faith in historical religion, the majority are atheists. "Our cultivated men," said an eminent and not illiberal German to me some seventeen years since, speaking of the prospects of the nation just before the revolutions of 1848,—"our cultivated men have lost the consciousness of God." The augury which he drew for the future of Germany from that circumstance was not a favorable one.

Whether science in some future development may not to some extent supply the place of popular religious ministrations, is a question I shall not discuss. The thing is conceivable only on condition that science shall have reached the same certainty in matters pertaining to the social and moral well-being of man to which she has arrived in astronomy and chemistry,—that the laws of the soul and of human relations shall be as well understood as the laws of elemental structure and mechanical motion. But whether philosophic Theism or Intuitive Morals can ever supply the place of religion is a question on which I, for one, have no doubt whatsoever. The first and most essential requisite in popular doctrinal ministration, in any preached Gospel, Christian or not Christian, is authority. And authority sufficient for such ministration is derivable only from one of two sources,—a supposed Divine communication from whose record the preacher draws, or, failing that, unquestionable and unquestioned scientific certainty. In concrete terms, the Bible or the mathematics. Personal authority, the authority of the individual preacher for those whom he addresses, is something. When reinforced by character, ability, and long experience, it is much. But that personal authority is based on the supposition of some other, ulterior authority, on which the preacher rests and whose exponent he is. Take away that, and, with all his weight of character, his authority would shrink perceptibly. The authority of a young man just entering the ministry, who shall be understood to speak from no warrant but his private opinion, with only his own talent or his own conceit to back him, cannot be exactly measured, but we are safe in placing it somewhere in the neighborhood of zero.

The Bible or the mathematics as the basis of preaching,—in the long run it must come to that. Either of these represents a valid and intelligible principle; nothing between them does. Either of these stands for authority; nothing between them does. Even now I should say that the graduate of the Scientific School is better qualified to be a preacher of righteousness to his fellow-men than the graduate of the Divinity School, whose three years of theological study have weakened instead of strengthening his faith in the Gospel and all Christian traditions, and have brought him to accept, as his solution of the great historic and miraculous fact of Christianity, the theory thus stated by a recent critic,—that, eighteen hundred years ago, in Galilee and Judæa, on the shores of Tiberias and round about Jordan,—"nothing happened." Hence these wonderful writings, whose inspired breath still perfumes the Church and the closet with the incense of holiness. Hence the tragedies of the Roman amphitheatre. Hence the life of solitude and prayer of countless saints. Hence Peter's "wondrous dome" and Dante's immortal verse, and a winter landing of the Puritans on the outside of the world.

All this the fruit of certain poems which men have styled the Gospels according to St. Matthew, St. Mark, St. Luke, and St. John! Or rather, of the nothing in particular which dictated those poems, and the fabrications they embody and present to us as historical facts,—the only admissible fact being, that, among the teachers who have undertaken to instruct mankind, there was one Jesus whom his followers called the Christ, a pure-minded and benevolent man, who died, as many others have done, a martyr to his well-meant efforts to reform his countrymen.

My quarrel with the antisupernaturalism of the present day is, that it satisfies no spiritual or intellectual want. It is neither one thing nor the other, neither religion nor science; too self-willed for the one, not positive enough for the other. It is any man's opinion of human and divine things, with no definite authority, human or divine, for its warrant.

Let me not be misunderstood: I have no controversy with antisupernaturalism as such, except as one opinion implicitly controverts the opposite opinion. I speak of it only as standing-ground for the preacher who comes before the world as nominally a Christian minister, and assumes the charge of a nominally Christian Church. I say that the preacher who takes that ground betrays the Gospel he is supposed to represent. He places himself in direct antagonism with the radical idea of that Gospel which claims on the face of it superhuman authority. I acknowledge, of course, a code of Christian ethics which may be considered and may be preached independently of this claim, and I am far from denying that an individual whose character and ability are such as to give him weight may do a good work as a preacher of Christian morals, without that faith in Christ which constitutes a Christian believer, in the stricter sense.

But, after all, the moral law alone is mere Judaism over again,—Judaism, without its sanction. Christianity means a great deal more than that. It means participation of the Divine Nature, through faith, and through the communion of the Spirit, of which the Church is supposed to be the repository and the mediator. Of this there is no pretence and no thought in the kind of ministration to which I have referred. Whatever the merit or use of such ministration in any particular case, its meaning is bounded by the speaker's personality; it stands for nothing but his opinion; it surrogates a lectureship and a Sunday lyceum for the Christian Church.

Meanwhile, it owes to that Church its place and opportunity and leave to be. Take away the Christian Church, and how long would the preacher's profession endure? How long would the lecturer on morals and theism find an audience? I mean a stated Sunday audience, a congregation pledged to his support? How long would the Sunday itself survive? Be sure, it is not the itching ear and the fluent tongue, it is not the weekly demand and supply of mortal wit, that created and maintains that sacred custom, and which made it impossible in revolutionary France for a nation to do it away. It has other authors and supports than these: Reverence and Faith and gray Tradition,—already gray when Jesus went into the synagogue at Nazareth on the Sabbath day, "as his custom was." These, and withal a sense of mystery and holiness not yet extinct,—even in curious, questioning New England, God be praised! not quite extinct; the sense of a fathomless and awful background to this every-day world, and a Presence that pervades it, and a righteous God, and the consciousness of sin and the need of pardoning grace; and supplication and sacraments that came not of "art or man's device." All this is in the heart of the Christian Sunday, and this is its warrant and reason for being, without which the Lord's day would straightway subside into the secular week, and the Christian rubric, which now tints the civil calendar as with streaks of a heavenly dawn, would go out in one uniform sanctionless, savorless black. For though the day being given and the temple being given, anti-supernaturalists and secularists, and trance-mediums and all manner of alien voices and ministrations, may find place in its courts; it is not these nor the like of these, for whose sake the temple and the Sunday exist. It is not these that created or can keep them agoing a single year. It is the Christian Church, however disowned, that backs these performers in their several parts, and historical traditional Christianity backs and sustains the Church.

I anticipate the plea that may be urged against the position I here assume. Once yield to tradition, it may be said, and you place yourself at the mercy of tradition; you become a debtor to all the past, you render yourself liable to all the superstitions and irrationalities that have ever worn the pretence of orthodoxy; you sink into a weak Bibliolatry, or you let go your hold of Protestantism, and land in the Church of Rome. I deny that any such conclusion is deducible from my position in theory or is likely to flow from it in fact. I am far enough from counselling a blind and unqualified surrender to tradition or any renunciation of reason in religion. Tradition is one factor, and Reason is another; they are not antagonistic, but complementary the one of the other.

There is, and must be, in all religion an element of faith, a region of the indemonstrable, unaccountable; for this it is which specifically distinguishes religion from science. Its office is communion with that for which reason in its proper and legitimate function does not suffice. There is also in religion a right of reason, as the counterpoise and corrective of faith, which without that corrective tends to boundless superstition and wild disorder. The practical principle here is very obvious. Things which contradict reason are not to be confounded with things which transcend reason. We are bound in wisdom to accept some things which reason alone could never discover and perhaps can never establish, but cannot disprove,—a region of the unaccountable, if you please so to call it, of the preternatural. We are equally bound in wisdom *not* to accept what reason not only does not perceive and cannot legitimate, but emphatically contradicts,—doctrines which outrage reason and the moral sense.

And as to any supposed danger that respect for tradition and resting in faith may lead to Romanism, the facts with us are the other way. Nothing is more notorious than that the converts to Romanism in this country have been mostly recruits from the number of those who had held the most radical and negative views in theology.

The interest of reason and the interest of faith are not contrary, but, rightly understood, essentially one. The office of both is to bring us acquainted with the truth. Faith does this in the way of anticipation, reason in the way of insight. The one is wings to the soul, the other eyes. Faith furnishes the motive power, Reason the method; one the material, the other the form. Without faith the world would have had to this day no idea of God. Without reason, that idea would have been to this day a chimera and a fright, or a barren ecstasy.

If reason in our time is more active than faith, it is because it concerns us more at present to apprehend than to dream, and, so far as may be, to adjust the life of the spirit with the intellectual demands of a scientific age. And if the application of reason to religion by modern critics has operated with disturbing, and, to some extent, with destructive effect, it has operated also with awakening power. I cannot doubt that the critical movement of our time will finally inure in a better understanding and a better use of Christian truth. One good it has already accomplished for those who have followed its course and possessed themselves of its most assured and established results. It has purged traditional Christianity of falsifications and corruptions, and, by clearing its Scriptures of spurious additaments and interpolations and misinterpretations, has brought out the primitive sense and original genius of the Gospel.

After all the pruning and the sifting to which competent and conscientious criticism has subjected the records, enough remains to furnish documentary proof of the reception, in the first century of our era, of the principal facts and ideas which make the substance of the Christian faith.

There is much in these remains which science cannot verify, nor the understanding adjust with known laws and universal experience, but which sound criticism must nevertheless accept, in substance if not in form, as historic truth. This, it seems to me, is the only legitimate ground which a preacher of the Gospel can take in relation to its record.

I believe in a progressive theology, but the method of that progress is a point to be considered. No progress comes of mere negation. It is easy to deny, to thrust aside an improbable statement or unpalatable doctrine. But this does not help us one step forward; it leaves us, theologically, precisely where we were before. If the statement or doctrine be a genuine constituent of Christian tradition, the first step is to understand it, the next to separate the substance from the form, to assimilate and reproduce the one while dismissing the other. For when we talk of progressive theology, we do not mean a progress out of theology by simple denial, but a progress in it. True progress comes by development alone; or rather, progress consists in development. And development supposes, instead of an abrupt renunciation of the old, an unbroken and organic connection with it. Whoever would build permanently must build on the past, he must take the foundation which is given him in the institutions and ideas of the Church, whose offspring he is. He must graft himself on the old stock, and know that he bears not the root, but the root him. It is easy, I say, to deny; a small modicum of talent is required to assail and repudiate existing beliefs. But the true reformer accepts existing beliefs, and unfolds the truth that is in them into new and nobler forms of faith. The most radical reform the world has ever known is Christianity. But radical as it proved in its final operation, Christianity at the start did not break with the past. While protesting against Jewish formalism, and proclaiming a worship in spirit and truth, it respected Jewish ideas; its arguments were drawn from the Jewish law; its ordinances were founded on Jewish rites; its author took upon himself the burden of the prophets and the promised Messiah. He linked his mission with Moses and Elias, and claimed to hold of the ancient sacred stock. He rooted himself in the dear old sanctities of Judaism, and grounded his kingdom on its traditionary hopes. "I am not come to destroy, but to fulfil." Cosmopolite Christianity was but the fulfilment of provincial Judaism. This is the way in which all religious reform must proceed, to obtain a permanent foothold in the world. It is by fulfilment, not by destruction, that we really outgrow the past, that theology outgrows the crude conceptions of an earlier age. Development is God's method in the education of the race. Whatever in religion is destined to endure, must be the offspring of the past. It must be related to the old by natural descent. It must come as Christianity came, by providential agencies springing from the bosom of the Church and working in its name, and not by come-outers acting on the Church from without. All the reformers of the Church hitherto, all who have contributed anything effectual to correct its errors, to enlarge its views, to quicken its zeal,—Luther, Fox, Swedenborg, Wesley, Channing,—have been disciples and preachers of that faith which they have helped to new-mould and reform.

The religious education of the human race cannot deny its lineage. There is a line of Divine communication along which the spiritual progress of mankind has advanced thus far. Whatever of truth and Divine authority is to come, whatever is destined to act with enduring and beneficent effect on the moral and religious condition of the world, will spring from this root and fall in with this line, and whatever appears in opposition to it will finally be absorbed in it, or perish from the world.

One thing more. The prime condition of progress in theology, as in everything else, is conscientious love of truth. This may seem a superfluous caution, as addressed to preachers of the Gospel,—as if one should counsel gentlemen of breeding and honorable rank to abstain from petty larceny. But experience has taught me that love of truth, in the sense I intend, is a very rare quality in preachers of the Gospel. I have known many religious, many devout, many pure livers, many faithful and devoted Christians, but very few whom I could credit with entire intellectual sincerity, few who seemed to me actuated by a sole desire for the truth. Kant has remarked, that, although truthfulness is the least we ask of any reputable character, it is precisely the quality "to which human nature is least inclined." It is rare in all the professions, it is especially rare in theology. Most theologians have some ulterior interest, some theory or creed or prejudice, some cause to which they are unwittingly bound, in the spirit of which they speak, in the spirit of which they investigate or refuse to investigate, and which predetermines all their conclusions. When the committee who presented the Oxford Declaration congratulate themselves on having promoted the glory of God by limiting his saving mercy, they betray a lurking hope of salvation by orthodoxy,—a mean and self-contradictory expectation of purchasing the favor of God by extolling its exclusiveness; much in the same way that the subjects of an Oriental despot seek the favor of their sovereign by magnifying the terror of his name. On the other hand, the radical theologian, who adopts a canon of criticism which eliminates without discrimination whatever in the Gospel record the understanding cannot verify or experience match, commits the absurdity of supposing that the ways of the Infinite must be commensurate with our ways, that the human understanding is a gauge of the possibilities of God.

Give me the theologian whose only aim is to see distinctly and to say what he sees. Criticism is indispensable, but faith is equally so; and the only way in which theology can advance to new and more adequate solution of its problems, is by the joint action of both these factors,—each supplying what the other lacks, both guided and determined by an all-controlling love of truth.

❧ The Personality of Deity

HENRY WARE, JR. (1794–1843)

Much in Ware's sermon on "The Personality of Deity" makes it an important and representative Unitarian pronouncement, but it seemed important at the time because, being delivered less than two months after Emerson's Divinity School Address, it was widely interpreted as a formal reply. This it apparently was not, for it was part of a series Ware was then preaching in the college chapel. However, Ware had been troubled by Emerson's doctrines, and he certainly had them in mind as he composed this sermon. Far more important to religious history than this partly accidental conjunction is the fact that the doctrine here enunciated was as crucial to Unitarian theology as it was repugnant to Emerson and the Transcendentalists. Andrews Norton made this still more clear when on the anniversary of Emerson's address he pointed out to the graduating class the monstrous nature of this "latest form of infidelity."

With regard to theology proper—that is, to the nature of God—the Christian Unitarians stood with their orthodox brethren in upholding the traditional opposition of the Church to all forms of pantheism. Any doctrine that threatened to dissolve the divine personality had to be regarded as heresy lest the Scriptures be reduced to the status of allegory. The doctrines of creation, incarnation, and providence, among others, implied and required a dualistic understanding of the relationship of God to the world. At the same time the Unitarian notion of God's mercy and loving-kindness implied and required a personalistic understanding of God Himself. It was no doubt with these thoughts in mind that Ware formulated the sermon that follows, laying out in logical order the attributes of God. Worth noting, as well, is the existential emphasis in Ware's thought: his assertion that an understanding of God as a person is a prerequisite to a Christian understanding of forgiveness and salvation.

Even if a formal reply to Emerson had been part of the Divinity School strategy, there could have been no better choice than the younger Henry Ware to deliver it. Born in Hingham, Massachusetts while his father was minister of the First Church there, he had been graduated in 1812 from Harvard, where his father was then Hollis Professor of Divinity. Five years later, after teaching for two years at Phillips Exeter Academy and completing his theological studies, he was ordained as minister to the Second Church in Boston, then one of the smallest and least opulent Unitarian societies in the area. His work in this parish, however, established his reputation as the virtual ideal type of Unitarian parish minister, and it was as such that he was called in 1830 to the professorship of pulpit eloquence and pastoral care just established in the Harvard Divinity School. Because Ralph Waldo Emerson had during the preceding year been ordained as Colleague Pastor at Second Church, Ware felt free to accept. He served brilliantly for more than a decade despite precarious health. Great force of character strengthened the impact of his lifetime of preaching, and his numerous publications reached far beyond the church and school where he served. He was, especially within the church, among the most influential Unitarians of his day.

The sermon reprinted here was preceded in the doctrinal series of which it is part by sermons on "The Existence of Deity" and "The Divine Perfections" and followed by two on "The Divine Government—Miracles."

JEREMIAH X, 10: *He is the living God and an everlasting king.*

In treating the doctrine respecting God, the mind is deeply impressed with a sense of its importance in its bearing on human duty and happiness. It is the doctrine of a Creator, the Governor and Father of man. The discussion relates not merely to the laws of the universe and the principles by which its affairs are directed, but to the character and dispositions of the Being, who presides over those laws, and by whose will those affairs are determined. It teaches, not only that there is a wise and holy order to which it is for every man's interest to conform; but that that order is ordained and upheld by an active overruling Intelligence; and that hence virtue is not merely conformity to a rule, but allegiance to a rightful Lawgiver; and happiness not the result merely of obedience to a command, but of affectionate subjection to a Parent.

The importance of this consideration to a true and happy virtue cannot be overestimated. The difference between conformity to a statute and obedience to a father is a difference not to be measured in words, but to be realized in the experience of the soul. It is slightly represented in the difference between the condition of a little child that lives in the presence of a judicious and devoted mother, an object of perpetual affection, and of another that is placed under the charge of a public institution, which knows nothing but a set of rules. Each is alike provided for and governed; but the one enjoys the satisfactions of a trusting and loving heart, while the other, deprived of the natural objects of affection, knows nothing but a life of order and restraint. Take away the Father of the universe, and, though every ordinance remain unchanged, mankind becomes but a company of children in an orphan asylum; clothed, fed, governed, but objects of pity rather than congratulation, because deprived of those resting-places for the affections, without which the soul is not happy.

Our representations of the being and perfections of God are therefore incomplete, until we have taken into consideration the additional view now suggested. The idea of personality must be added to that of natural and moral perfection, in order to the full definition of the Deity. Without this he is but a set of principles or a code of laws. Yet by some philosophers at various times it has been speculatively denied, and by too many in common life it is practically lost sight of. It may be well, then, in connexion with our preceding discussion, to consider a little particularly the doctrine of the Divine Personality; to state what it is; to show the grounds on which it is established; and to survey the evils which must result from a denial of it.

I begin with stating what is meant by the Personality of the Deity.

A *person* is an intelligent, conscious agent; one who thinks, perceives, understands, wills, and acts. What we assert is, that God is such. It is not implied, that any distinct form or shape is necessary to personality. In the case of man, the bodily form is not the person. That form remains after death; but we no longer call it a person, because consciousness and the power of will and of action are gone. The personality resided in them. So also in the case of the Deity; consciousness, and the power of will and of action constitute him a person. Shape, form, or place make no part of the idea.

The evidence of this fact is found in the works of design with which the universe is filled. They imply forethought, plan, wisdom, a designing mind; in other words, an Intelligent Being who devised and executed them. If we suppose, that there is no conscious, intelligent person, we say that there is no plan, no purpose, no design; there is nothing but a set of abstract and unconscious principles. And, strange as it may seem to Christian ears, which have been accustomed to far other expressions of the Divinity, there have been those who maintain this idea; who hold, that the principles which govern the universe constitute the Deity; that power, wisdom, veracity, justice, benevolence, are God: that gravitation, light, electricity, are God. Speculative men have been sometimes fond of this assertion, and in various forms have set up this opposition to the universal sentiment; sometimes with the design of removing the associations of reverence and worship, which make men religious; sometimes under the supposition, that they thereby elevate the mind to a conception of the truth more worthy of its exalted subject. But it will be evident upon a little inquiry, that, in either case, the speculation is inconsistent with just and wholesome doctrine.

1. For, in the first place, one of the most observable and least questionable principles, drawn from our observation of man and nature, is, that the person, the conscious being, is the chief thing, for the sake of which all else is, and subservient to which all principles operate. The person, the conscious, intelligent, active, enjoying, suffering being, is foremost in importance and honor; principles and laws operate for its support, guidance, and well-being; and therefore are secondary. Some of these principles and laws have their origin in the relations which exist amongst intelligent, moral agents; most of them come into action in consequence of the previous existence of those relations. If there were no such agents, there either would be no such principles, or they would have no operation. Thus, for example, veracity, justice, love, are sentiments or obligations which spring up from the relations subsisting between different beings, and can exist only where there are persons. We may say, indeed, that they exist abstractly, in the nature of things; but, if there be no beings to recognise them, no agents to conform to or violate them, they would be as if they were not. They are qualities of being; and like all qualities have no actual existence independent of the substances in which they inhere. They have relation to acts,—voluntary acts of truth, justice, goodness; and acts belong to persons. If there existed no persons in the universe, but only things, there could be neither the act nor the sentiment of justice, goodness, truth; these are qualities of persons, not of things; of actions, not of substances. Suppose the Deity to exist alone in the universe which he has made. Then, from the conscious enjoyment of his own perfections and the exercise of his power in the physical creation, He must dwell in bliss; but, as he has no relations to other conscious existences, he cannot exercise justice, or truth, or love; they lie in the infinite bosom as if they were not; they have only a contingent existence. But the instant he should *create* various tribes, they spring into actual existence; they no longer may be, they are; they rise out of the new relations which are created, and are the expression of sentiments and duties which had not before been possible.

Or make another supposition. Upon the newly created earth one man is placed alone. He knows no other conscious existence but himself. What are truth, justice, charity, to him? They are nothing to him. He cannot have ideas of them. They are sentiments that belong to certain relations between beings, which relations he does not stand in, and knows nothing of. To him, therefore, they do not exist. Now send him companions, and the relations begin, which give those sentiments birth and make their expression possible. He is in society; and those principles, which make the strength and order of society, immediately come into action. The necessities of conscious being call them forth.

Thus what is chiefest in the universe, is conscious, active mind; abstract principles are but the laws of its various relations. . . .

There is another way of considering this point. What is it, that in the whole history and progress of man has proved most interesting to man? What has been the favorite study, the chief subject of contemplation and care? Has it not been men, persons? Have not their character, fortunes, words, deeds, been the chief themes of thought, of conversation, of letters, of arts? Is it not the interest which the soul takes in persons, that is the foundation of society, of its activity, its inventions, its advancement in civilization, its institutions, its laws? . . . We cannot cast this slightest glance upon life, without perceiving the place which belongs to personality; for, take it away, and the whole of that beautiful scene vanishes; sympathy, friendship, love, all social enjoyment, all social life, are annihilated.

Thus the doctrine, which denies personality to God, is in opposition to the general economy of nature, which, as we have seen, sets peculiar honor on persons. In all the other relations of its being, the soul is concerned with nothing so much. Why should it be less so in its highest relation?

2. It also, in the next place, amounts to a virtual denial of God. Indeed, this is the only sense in which it seems possible to make that denial. No one thinks of denying the existence of principles and laws. Gravitation, order, cause and effect, truth, benevolence,—no one denies that these exist; and, if these constitute the Deity, he has not been, and cannot be, denied. The only denial possible is by this exclusion of a personal existence. There can be no atheism but this; and this is atheism. If the material universe rests on the laws of attraction, affinity, heat, motion, still all of them together are no Deity; if the moral universe is founded on the principles of righteousness, truth, love, neither are these the Deity. There must be some Being to put in action these principles, to exercise these attributes. To call the principles and the attributes *God,* is to violate the established use of language, and confound the common apprehensions of mankind. It is in vain to hope by so doing to escape the charge of atheism; there is no other atheism conceivable. There is a personal God, or there is none.

We reason in this case, as in that of a man. Man was made in the image of God. But when we have described so much power, wisdom, goodness, so much beauty, justice, truth, love, we have not described a man; the very essential element is wanting; without adding personality, we may speak of these qualities for ever, and they will not make a man. So, too, we may enlarge them infinitely, but unless we add personality, they will never make up the idea of God.

3. Further: to exclude personality from the idea of God, is, in effect, to destroy the object of worship, and thus to annihilate that essential duty of religion. The sentiment of reverence may, undoubtedly, be felt for a principle, for a code of laws, for an institution of government. But worship, which is the expression of that sentiment, is applicable only to a conscious being; as all the language and customs of men signify. It is praise, thanks, honor, and petition, addressed to one who can hear and reply. If there be no such one,—if the government of the world be at the disposal of unconscious power and self-executing law,—then there can be no such thing as worship.

Let this be seriously considered. What a desolation is wrought in society and in the soul, when the foundation of worship is thus taken away. It is the suppression of a chief instinct; it is the overthrow of a system which has always made an inseparable part of the social order, and in which human character and happiness are intimately concerned. The relation of man, in his weakness and wants, to a kindred spirit infinitely ready to aid him, of the insufficient child of earth to a watchful Father in heaven, is destroyed. There remains no mind higher than my own, which is knowing to my desires; there is no Parent above, to whom my affections can rise and find peace. I am left to myself, and to men as weak as myself. If, following the impulses of my heart and the example of good men, I call on One who cares for me and will bless,—I am driven back, and my heart is chilled by the reply, "The power that is over all sustains and guides, but, having no personality, it cannot appreciate affection, nor give it back in return; be satisfied to reverence and submit." And so the filial spirit is mocked. . . .

We must not consent to the injustice which is thus done to the affections. What an instinct is in them, and how they yearn for something to love and trust, is taught us in all the religious history of the race. From this cause men so multiplied their divinities, that, from amid that great diversity, every variety of human soul might find its want of sympathy supplied. Hence, too, in the Catholic church, the worship of the Virgin; because, in the love for that beautiful and spotless person, was found a gratification that the heart is always seeking. And yet, in the face of this great instinct of humanity, everywhere manifested, Philosophy steps forth, and insists that the soul is to be satisfied with abstractions. As if human nature were any thing, without its affections! as if a man were a man, without his heart! as if to deny and baffle them, were not to pour bitterness into the very fountain of the soul's peace! And this is done, whenever man is made to believe, that the altar at which he kneels is consecrated to a set of principles, and not to a "Living God."

4. In the next place, this notion removes the sense of responsibility,

and so puts in jeopardy the virtue of man, as we have just seen that it trifles with his happiness. The idea of responsibility implies some one, to whom we are responsible, and who has a right to treat us according to our fidelity. We indeed sometimes use the word with a little different application; we say that a man is responsible to his country, to posterity, to the cause of truth; but this is plainly employing the word in a secondary sense; it is not the original, literal signification. We hear it said, also, that a man is responsible to his own conscience; and this is sometimes spoken of as the most solemn responsibility. In one point of view, justly; since it is responsibility to that person, whose disapprobation is nearest to us, and whose awards are of the highest consequence to our peace. We are not, therefore, to speak lightly of the tribunal within the breast. But why is it terrible? Because it is thought to represent and foreshadow the decisions of the higher tribunal of God. Let a man believe that it is ultimate, and he can learn to brave it; and how many accordingly have hardened themselves against it, and persevered in sin, as if it were not! Or let him think that the retributions of guilt are simply the accomplishment of natural laws, which go on mechanically to execute themselves, unattended by any sentiment of approbation or disapprobation, and he can, without great difficulty, defy them. They do not address his moral sensibility. . . . It is idle to talk to men in general of responsibility, without directing them to the Being to whom the account is to be rendered. It is the thought of the Living Lawgiver and Judge, which affects them,—of one whose displeasure they can dread, whose good opinion they can value, whose favor they perceive to be life. And herein is perceived the wisdom of the gospel of Christ, herein is found its efficacy,—that, casting aside all such abstractions, it appeals wholly to the relations of conscious beings, and subdues, and reforms, and blesses, by drawing the human soul to the soul of its Saviour and its God.

5. If now we pass to the declarations of the divine word, we find that the doctrine we are opposing stands in direct contradiction to the whole language and teaching of the Old and the New Testaments. Those volumes speak of God, uniformly and distinctly, as possessed of personal attributes. They so describe his perfections and his government, they so recite his words and his acts, they so assign to him the relations and titles of the Creator, King, Lawgiver, Father,—that no reader could so much as dream that his name is used simply to express the principles and laws of the universe. To fancy it, is to make Scripture unintelligible, and set at naught its express authority. Until language changes its meaning, and all description is falsified, the doctrine of the Divine Impersonality is a direct contradiction of the doctrine of revelation.

6. Further still, it destroys the possibility of a revelation, in any intel-

ligible sense of the word. A revelation is a message, or a direct communication, from the Infinite mind to the human mind. But in order to this, there is required a conscious and individual action on the part of the communicator; and this implies personality. So that this doctrine virtually accuses the Scriptures of imposture, since they purport to contain a revelation from God, which in the nature of things is impossible. Nay, let us see the worst of it;—it accuses the apostles of Christ, and the blessed Saviour himself, of deliberate fraud and imposition; since they and he declared, with the most solemn asseverations, that he was directly sent by God, the Father of mankind, when, if there be no such Being, but only certain principles and laws, he could not have been sent by him. Their language in that case is altogether deceptive. It seems to mean one thing, when it really means something quite the reverse. . . . It takes away all special divinity and authority from the Gospel, reduces it to a level with any other wisdom, and thus robs it of its power over the earth. . . .

By thus tracking this doctrine through its various bearings and observing its tendencies, we come to a clear discernment of its falseness and mischievousness. We see, that it opposes what is taught in nature by all the marks of design which cover the works of creation;—it sets aside the fundamental fact, that conscious, intelligent being, in its various relations, is the chief interest of the universe, for the sake of which every thing else is;—it is a virtual denial of God, and a consequent overthrow of worship and devotion;—it injures happiness by taking from the affections their highest object, and virtue by enfeebling the sense of responsibility;—it contradicts the express lessons of the Bible, excludes the possibility of a revelation in any proper sense of the word, and denies to the Gospel its right to authority and power.

Of course, it will not happen, that all these disastrous consequences will follow from this doctrine in the case of every individual who may receive it. To the pure all things are pure; and some men will dwell for ever in the midst of abstraction and falsehood without being injuriously affected. Express infidelity is not vice, and may exist together with great integrity and purity of life. Atheism is not immorality, and may consist with an unblemished character. But, however it may be with individuals, living in the midst of a believing and worshipping community, it is not to be doubted that a community, unbelieving and godless, would rush to evil unmitigated and hopeless. A philosopher here and there, by his science and skill, might perhaps live without the sun; but, strike it out from the path of all men, and despair and death ensue.

On this subject, then, we are first to look for the truth, and then at the consequences of denying it. And those consequences, we are to remember, may flow as certainly from a practical disregard of it, as from a speculative rejection. It is possible by the mouth to profess God, and in works to deny him. The number of those, who can be misled by the ingenuity of an imaginative mind, is comparatively small; but the world is crowded with those who become aliens from God through the hardening influences of a worldly career, while they fancy themselves to know and acknowledge him as he is. On this account, the views of the present discourse ask the serious regard of all men. For who can doubt, that, among the causes which produce in society so much moral and religious deadness, this is one;—that men satisfy themselves with referring to the laws and principles of nature, and stop short of that Being in whom they reside? How much is this a habit amongst us! We talk of the "laws of our being," and of living by them, and of the consequences of violating them, as we should talk of a machine or of fate. We thus throw out of view the agency and love of the Living God, whose children we are, and claim relationship to inanimate abstractions. According to the common phrase, we stop at second causes. And in so doing, we not only wrong the truth, which is thus denied, but defraud ourselves of that exercise and enjoyment of the thinking, affectionate spirit, in which our highest action and bliss are to be found. This ought not so to be. And, until men come more to realize the presence and the authority of the Living Father, who governs them now, and who will judge them in the end, it is vain to hope for any wider prevalence of elevated piety or of happy devotion to duty.

Unitarianism, Transcendentalism, and the Bible

GEORGE EDWARD ELLIS (1814–1894)

By 1835 the Transcendental movement could no longer be ignored. Emerson had resigned his charge at Second Church, and a new school of religious thought was forming around the standards he, George Ripley, and others had raised. Most of the members of the informal Transcendental Club were ministers. The second Unitarian Controversy had begun. Many men, to be sure, tried to steer a mediating course, but the issues did not lend themselves to moderation, and by a gradual process, admirably documented in Perry Miller's anthology *The Transcendentalists,* theological side-taking became the order of the day. The question of the nature of the Bible was, of course, central to these disputes.

George Edward Ellis was by nature neither a moderate nor a pacificator, and like Andrews Norton he involved himself in controversy against both orthodoxy and Transcendentalism. Son of a Boston merchant, he was graduated from Harvard in 1833 and from the Divinity School in 1836. Four years later, after travel and study abroad, he was ordained minister of the Harvard Unitarian Church in Charlestown, Massachusetts. From 1837 to 1863 he was also nonresident professor of systematic theology in the Harvard Divinity School, but his inflexible temperament made him an unpopular and unsuccessful teacher. He forsook the ministry in 1869 to devote himself to literary and historical pursuits. During the remaining years of his life he made two significant contributions to New England history, *The Puritan Age and Rule in the Colony of the Massachusetts Bay, 1629–1685* and *History of the First Church in Boston.*

During 1855 and 1856 Ellis contributed to the *Christian Examiner,* which he edited from 1849 to 1857, a series of articles reviewing Unitarian conflict with orthodoxy down to his time. Though outwardly an objective historical account, it was actually a comprehensive and systematic vindication of the liberal cause. These articles were consequently answered in the *Puritan Recorder* in another series, running from September 11 to October 23, 1856. Ellis, in turn, devoted thirteen appendices to these criticisms when he published his original essays as a book, *A Half-Century of the Unitarian Controversy.*

Ellis was not entirely successful in his efforts to subordinate the controversial to the historical, but he did produce as clear an exposition of the issues as anyone of his generation could be expected to do. He ranged over all the important matters under dispute and performed a significant service by narrowing down and defining the central problems. It is in connection with the argument from tendency that he most succinctly states the Biblical issue. The constant orthodox charge was that Unitarianism tended toward infidelity. This argument became an increasing irritation and embarrassment to Unitarians as Transcendentalists grew more vocal and more numerous. It could hardly be denied that the new philosophy had prospered in the liberal churches, so Ellis's strategy was to make clear that Unitarians were "Evangelical Christians" and then to emphasize that Transcendentalists were not. Views on Biblical revelation provided the basic instance of divergence.

Another of the expectations which my critic affirms was entertained by the Orthodox was, that *a portion* of the Unitarians would lapse into the infidelity which I have already referred to as the predicted issue of their views for the mass of those who should receive them. The following paragraph is therefore significant.

There was still another result, not only expected, but expressly predicted. It was predicted by Professor Stuart, and others, thirty years ago, that many Unitarians—the young, the adventurous, the men of impulse and progress—would not long remain where they then were. They would drift farther and farther away from the letter of Scripture and the restraints of the Gospel, until they arrived at the very borders of open infidelity. And neither in this have we been disappointed. We have seen it all verified before our eyes; and Mr. Ellis has seen the same. There are ministers around him, calling themselves Unitarians, with whom he would not exchange pulpits more than we should,—with whom, if I mistake not, the more serious part of his brethren have no longer any Christian fellowship.

The implication conveyed in this paragraph is that the form of scepticism known among us by the misused term *Transcendentalism,* was the natural outgrowth of Unitarianism. This charge has often been boldly made, and more often insinuated. It has no just foundation. Plain facts disprove it. The differences between Orthodoxy and Unitarianism arise from questions of interpretation; questions about the meaning of sacred records whose value and authority are admitted by both parties, and which Unitarians have always shown themselves so zealous to maintain, that they have produced works of acknowledged superiority in defence of

revelation and the Scriptures. Transcendentalism, so called, denies a revelation, pronounces its miraculous sanctions to be philosophically impossible and absurd, and subverts the authority of Scripture. The relations
between the three parties—the Orthodox, the Unitarians, and the Transcendentalists—on the subject-matter of revelation may be illustrated by
a reference to the relations of three other parties among us concerning a
political question. We have two large parties divided by a very serious issue touching the organic provisions of the Federal Constitution and the
functions of Congress on slavery, and all the debates and agitations connected with it. Does or does not the Constitution recognize and legitimate
slavery, and implicate all the States in its allowed existence in some of
them, and expose free territory to be overrun by it? Has or has not Congress power to discuss the subject, and legislate upon it? On this issue
our two prominent parties are divided. They make it a question of the interpretation of an instrument, through its own plain or obscure provisions
and through the known views of its authors. Both parties profess to accept and recognize and honor the Constitution. They are willing to receive its fair and decisive meaning, when intelligently expounded, as authoritative, as binding upon them in all their political relations. They will
not go behind the Constitution, nor dispute it, nor resist it. In the mean
while a third party presents itself, which declares that the Constitution is
pro-slavery, that it implicates all our citizens in the iniquity of slavery,
and therefore that it must be denounced and subverted. This third party,
therefore, plants itself outside of the Constitution. The two former parties,
so far as the parallel is designed to illustrate one point of resemblance,
may be regarded as representing the Orthodox and the Unitarians, as divided by questions about the interpretation of records and documents
whose peculiar authority, value, and sanctions they agree in venerating.
Their disputes centre upon and are to be decided by criticism and exposition. The third party, just referred to, represents the Transcendentalists,
who insist that the Bible is committed to an unphilosophical, incredible,
and impossible theory of miracles, and that they must, therefore, reject it
and plant themselves outside of it. Now with what justice can the Orthodox confound Transcendentalists with Unitarians, and condemn the latter
for complicity with the former in a theory of unbelief which comes not
from methods of criticism and exposition, but from philosophical speculation?

As a matter of fact, too, Transcendentalism, so called, and even New
England Transcendentalism, was not the outgrowth of Unitarianism, but
an imported product that had been developed from German Lutheranism.
A few young New England Unitarians have attracted attention to themselves in connection with their adoption of that form of philosophical

scepticism, because of their eminent talents as men of marked endowments. But very many of the undistinguished Orthodox have adopted the same views independently of Unitarianism. It would be an ungracious office to attempt a statistical estimate of the proportionate addition to the ranks of infidelity which has accrued from Unitarianism or Orthodoxy. For myself, I have no doubt on that point. "Secularism," i.e. Atheism, in England numbers millions of adherents. Its leaders came from under the most thorough Orthodox training. Those who compose its ranks were never under the influence of Unitarianism. But Unitarianism is laboring earnestly, and with better promise of success than any other sect has yet realized, to reclaim the Secularists. Professor Stuart's prediction has not been verified among the Unitarians to the extent of its verification among the Orthodox. Justice Story and Dr. Channing both tell us, in their Memoirs, that Unitarianism saved them from the infidelity to which Orthodoxy had exposed them as young men. What saved them has saved thousands. . . .

A Discourse on the Latest Form of Infidelity

ANDREWS NORTON (1786–1852)

When Andrews Norton went to his first (and only) pulpit in Augusta, Massachusetts (now Maine), he lasted but a few weeks. His congregation found his aloofness and nervous pulpit manners too taxing. Norton found the teaching platform more conducive to his manner. In 1813 he was appointed lecturer on the criticism and interpretation of the Scriptures, as well as librarian, at the Harvard Divinity School. In 1819 he became Dexter Professor of Sacred Literature.

Norton, Joseph Buckminster, and Moses Stuart exerted a strong influence in reviving interest in Biblical studies in America. German Biblical criticism had done much to facilitate the rise of liberalism. Buckminster, the most promising of the younger scholars, had died in 1812 at the age of twenty-eight. Moses Stuart at Andover then became the leading scholar of Biblical studies, but Norton had the Harvard position and an audience of eager students. His *Statement of Reasons* made him the acknowledged authority for Unitarian exegesis of Scripture; twenty years later his address before the Alumni Association marked his status as one of the last major representatives of Christian Unitarianism when he sought to respond to Emerson's notable Divinity School Address of the previous year.

When Emerson spoke, in 1838, the Unitarians were outraged. Norton responded immediately in a newspaper article. Evoking Calvin's description of the work of Servetus as a rhapsody, Norton labeled Emerson's address an "incoherent rhapsody." For twenty years Unitarian orthodoxy had stressed the centrality of miracles; now, Emerson destroyed that base, revealing the radicalism of the Transcendentalist position. The Unitarians realized before Emerson's carriage had even returned to Concord that night that his words would have far-reaching consequences, proving to some that Unitarianism was indeed a "half-way house to infidelity." An effective counterattack was necessary, and on July 19, 1839, Andrews Norton spoke from the same pulpit as had Emerson on "The Latest Form of Infidelity."

I address you, Gentlemen, and our friends who are assembled with us, on an occasion of more than common interest; as it is your first meeting since joining together in a society as former pupils of the Theological School in this place. Many of you may look back over a considerable portion of time that has elapsed since your residence here. In thus meeting with those in whose society we have spent some of the earlier years of life, recollections are naturally called up of pleasures that are gone, of ties that have been broken, of hopes that have perished, and of bright imaginations that have faded away. Such recollections produce those serious views of our present existence with which religious sentiment is connected. They make us feel the value of a Christian's faith; of that faith, which, where decay was before written on all most dear to us, stamps immortality instead.

I see among you many, who, I know, will recall our former connexion with the same interest as I do, and whom I am privileged to regard as friends. As for those of you, Gentlemen, to whom I have not stood in the relation of an instructer, we also have an intimate connexion with each other. Your office is to defend, explain, and enforce the truths of Christianity; and with the importance of those truths no one can be more deeply impressed than myself. So far as you are faithful to your duty, the strong sympathy of all good men is with you.

But we meet in a revolutionary and uncertain state of religious opinion, existing throughout what is called the Christian world. Our religion is very imperfectly understood, and received by comparatively a small number with intelligent faith. In proportion as our view is more extended, and we are better acquainted with what is and what has been, we shall become more sensible of the great changes that have long been in preparation, but which of late have been rapidly developed. The present state of things imposes new responsibilities upon all, who know the value of our faith and have ability to maintain it. Let us then employ this occasion in considering some of the characteristics of the times and some of those opinions now prevalent, which are at war with a belief in Christianity.

By a belief in Christianity, we mean the belief that Christianity is a revelation by God of the truths of religion; and that the divine authority of him whom God commissioned to speak to us in his name was attested, in the only mode in which it could be, by miraculous displays of his power. Religious truths are those truths, and those alone, which concern the relations of man to God and eternity. It is only as an immortal being and a creature of God, that man is capable of religion. Now those truths which concern our higher nature, and all that can with reason deeply interest us in our existence, we Christians receive, as we trust, on the testimony of God. He who rejects Christianity must admit them, if he admit them at all, upon some other evidence.

But the fundamental truths of religion taught by Christianity became very early connected with human speculations, to which the same importance was gradually attached, and for the proof of which the same divine authority was claimed. These speculations spread out and consolidated into systems of theology, presenting aspects equally hostile to reason and to our faith; so hostile, that, for many centuries, a true Christian in belief and heart, earnest to communicate to others the blessings of his faith, would have experienced, anywhere in Christendom, a fate similar to that which his Master suffered among the Jews. It would be taking a different subject from what I have proposed, to attempt to explain and trace the causes of this monstrous phenomenon. The false representations of Christianity, that have come down to us from less enlightened times, have ceased to retain their power over far the larger portion of those individuals who form, for good or evil, the character of the age in which they live. But the reaction of the human intellect and heart against their imposition has as yet had but little tendency to procure the reception of more correct notions of Christianity. On the contrary, the inveterate and enormous errors, that have prevailed, have so perverted men's conceptions, have so obscured and perplexed the whole subject, have so stood in the way of all correct knowledge of facts, and all just reasoning; there are so few works in Christian theology not at least colored and tainted by them; and they still present such obstacles at every step to a rational investigation of the truth; that the degree of learning, reflection, judgment, freedom from worldly influences, and independence of thought, necessary to ascertain for one's self the true character of Christianity, is to be expected from but few. The greater number, consequently, confound the systems that have been substituted for it with Christianity itself, and receive them in its stead, or, in rejecting them, reject our faith. The tendency of the age is to the latter result.

This tendency is strengthened by the political action of the times, especially in the Old World. Ancient institutions and traditionary power are there struggling to maintain themselves against the vast amount of new energy that has been brought into action. Long-existing forms of society are giving way. The old prejudices by which they were propped up are decaying. Wise men look with awe at the spectacle; as if they saw in some vast tower, hanging over a populous city, rents opening, and its sides crumbling and inclining. But in the contest between the new and the old, which has spread over Europe, erroneous representations of Christianity are in alliance with established power. They have long been so. The institutions connected with them have long been principal sources of rank and emolument. What passes for Christianity is thus placed in opposition to the demands of the mass of men, and is regarded by them as inimical to their rights; while, on the other hand, those, to whom false Christianity affords aid, repel all examination into the genuineness of its claims.

The commotion of men's minds in the rest of the civilized world, produces a sympathetic action in our own country. We have indeed but little to guard us against the influence of the depraving literature and noxious speculations which flow in among us from Europe. We have not yet any considerable body of intellectual men, devoted to the higher departments of thought, and capable of informing and guiding others in attaining the truth. There is no controlling power of intellect among us.

Christianity, then, has been grossly misrepresented, is very imperfectly understood, and powerful causes are in operation to obstruct all correct knowledge of it, and to withdraw men's thoughts and affections from it. But at the present day there is little of that avowed and zealous infidelity, the infidelity of highly popular authors, acknowledged enemies of our faith, which characterized the latter half of the last century. Their writings, often disfigured by gross immoralities, are now falling into disrepute. But the effects of those writings, and of the deeply seated causes by which they were produced, are still widely diffused. There is now no bitter warfare against Christianity, because such men as then waged it would now consider our religion as but a name, a pretence, the obsolete religion of the state, the superstition of the vulgar. But infidelity has but assumed another form, and in Europe, and especially in Germany, has made its way among a very large portion of nominally Christian theologians. Among them are now to be found those whose writings are most hostile to all that characterizes our faith. Christianity is undermined by them with the pretence of settling its foundations anew. Phantoms are substituted for the realities of revelation.

It is asserted, apparently on good authority, that the celebrated atheist Spinoza composed the work in which his opinions are most fully unfolded, in the Dutch language, and committed it to his friend, the physician Mayer, to translate into Latin; that, where the name *God* now appears, Spinoza had written *Nature;* but that Mayer induced him to substitute the former word for the latter, in order partially to screen himself from the odium to which he might be exposed. Whether this anecdote be true or not, a similar abuse of language appears in many of the works to which I refer. The holiest names are there; a superficial or ignorant reader may be imposed upon by their occurrence; but they are there as words of show, devoid of their essential meaning, and perverted to express some formless and powerless conception. In Germany the theology of which I speak has allied itself with atheism, with pantheism, and with the other irreligious speculations, that have appeared in those metaphysical systems from which the God of Christianity is excluded.

There is no subject of historical inquiry of more interest than the history of opinions; there is none of more immediate concern than the state of opinions; for opinions govern the world. Except in cases of strong temptation, men's evil passions must coincide with or must pervert their opinions, before they can obtain the mastery. It is, therefore, not a light question, what men think of Christianity. It is a question on which, in the judgment of an intelligent believer, the condition of the civilized world depends. With these views we will consider the aspect that infidelity has taken in our times.

The latest form of infidelity is distinguished by assuming the Christian name, while it strikes directly at the root of faith in Christianity, and indirectly of all religion, by denying the miracles attesting the divine mission of Christ. The first writer, so far as I know, who maintained the impossibility of a miracle was Spinoza, whose argument, disengaged from the use of language foreign from his opinions, is simply this, that the laws of nature are the laws by which God is bound, Nature and God being the same, and therefore laws from which Nature or God can never depart. The argument is founded on atheism. The denial of the possibility of miracles must involve the denial of the existence of God; since, if there be a God, in the proper sense of the word, there can be no room for doubt, that he may act in a manner different from that in which he displays his power in the ordinary operations of nature. It deserves notice, however, that in Spinoza's discussion of this subject we find that affectation of religious language, and of religious reverence and concern, which is so striking a characteristic of many of the irreligious speculations of our day, and of which he, perhaps, furnished the prototype; for he has been regarded as a profound teacher, a patriarch of truth, by some of the most noted among the infidel philosophers and theologians of Germany. "I will show from Scripture," he says, "that the decrees and commands of God, and consequently his providence, are nothing but the order of nature."—"If any thing should take place in nature which does not follow from its laws, *that* would necessarily be repugnant to the order which God has established in nature by its universal laws, and, therefore, contrary to nature and its laws; and consequently the belief of such an event would cause universal doubt and lead to atheism." So strong a hold has religion upon the inmost nature of man, that even its enemies, in order to delude their followers, thus assume its aspect and mock its tones.

What has been stated is the great argument of Spinoza, to which every thing in his discussion of the subject refers; but this discussion may appear like the text-book of much that has been written in modern times concerning it. There is one, however, among the writings against the miracles of Christianity, of a different kind, the famous Essay of Hume. None has drawn more attention, or has more served as a groundwork for infidelity. Yet, considering the sagacity of the author, and the celebrity of his work, it is remarkable, that, in his main argument, the whole point to be proved is broadly assumed in the premises. "It is a miracle," he says, "that a dead man should come to life; because that has never been observed, in any age or country. There must, therefore, be a uniform experience against every miraculous event; otherwise the event would not merit that appellation." The conclusion, if conclusion it may be called, is easily made. If a miracle has never been observed in any age or country, if uniform experience shows that no miracle ever occurred, then it follows that all accounts of past miracles are undeserving of credit. But if there be an attempt to stretch this easy conclusion, and to represent it as involving the intrinsic incredibility of a miracle, the argument immediately gives way. "Experience," says Hume, "is our only guide in reasoning concerning matters of fact." Experience is the foundation of such reasoning, but we may draw inferences from our experience. We may conclude from it the existence of a power capable of works which we have never known it to perform; and no one, it may be presumed, who believes that there is a God, will say, that he is convinced by his experience, that God can manifest his power only in conformity to the laws which he has imposed upon nature.

Hume cannot be charged with affecting religion; but in the conclusion of his Essay, he says, in mockery; "I am the better pleased with the method of reasoning here delivered, as I think it may serve to confound those dangerous friends, or disguised enemies, to the Christian religion, who have undertaken to defend it by the principles of human reason. Our most holy religion is founded on *faith*, not on reason; and it is a sure method of exposing it, to put it to such a trial as it is by no means fitted to endure." What Hume said in derision has been virtually repeated, apparently in earnest, by some of the modern disbelievers of miracles, who still choose to profess a belief in Christianity.

To deny that a miracle is capable of proof, or to deny that it may be proved by evidence of the same nature as establishes the truth of other events, is, in effect, as I have said, to deny the existence of God. A miracle can be incapable of proof, only because it is physically or morally impossible; since what is possible may be proved. To deny that the truth of a miracle may be established, involves the denial of creation; for there can be no greater miracle than creation. It equally implies, that no species of being that propagates its kind ever had a commencement; for if there was a first plant that grew without seed, or a first man without parents, or if of any series of events there was a first without such antecedents as the laws of nature require, then there was a miracle. So far is a miracle from being incapable of proof, that you can escape from the necessity of believing innumerable miracles, only by believing that man, and all other animals, and all plants, have existed from eternity upon this earth, without commencement of propagation, there never having been a first of any species. No one, at the present day, will maintain with Lucretius, that they were generated from inanimate matter, by the fermentation of heat and moisture. Nothing can seem more simple or conclusive than the view we have taken; but we may render it more familiar by an appeal to fact. The science of geology has shown us, that man is but a late inhabitant of the earth. The first individuals of our race, then, were not produced as all others have been. They were formed by a miracle, or, in other words, by an act of God's power, exerted in a different manner from that in which it operates according to the established laws of nature. Creation, the most conspicuous, is at the same time the most undeniable, of miracles.

By any one who admits that God exists, in the proper sense of the words, his power to effect a miracle cannot be doubted; and it would be the excess of human presumption and folly to affirm, that it would be inconsistent with his wisdom and goodness ever to exert his power except in those modes of action which he has prescribed to himself in what we call the laws of nature.

On the contrary, a religious philosopher may regard the uniformity of the manifestations of God's power in the course of nature, as solely intended by him to afford a stable ground for calculation and action to his rational creatures; which could not exist, if the antecedents that we call causes, were not, in all ordinary cases, the signs of consequent effects. This uniformity is necessary to enable created beings to be rational agents. The Deity has imposed upon himself no arbitrary and mechanical laws. It is solely, so far as we can perceive, for the sake of his creatures, that he preserves the uniformity of action that exists in his works. Beyond the sphere of their observation, where this cause ceases, we have no ground for the belief of its continuance. There is nothing to warrant the opinion, that the Deity still restrains his power by an adherence to laws, the observance of which his creatures cannot recognise. We have strong reasons for believing that such an apparently causeless uniformity of operation would produce, not good, but evil. We have no ground for supposing, that the operation of the laws of nature, with which we are acquainted, extends beyond the ken of human observation; or that these laws are any thing more than a superficial manifestation of God's power, the mere exterior phenomena of the universe. We have no reason to doubt that the creation may be full of hidden miracles.

But, if the uniformity of the laws of nature, so far as they fall within our cognizance, is ordained by God for the good of his creatures, then, should a case occur in which a great blessing is to be bestowed upon them, the dispensing of which requires that he should act in other modes, no presumption would exist against his so acting. So far as we are able to discern, there would be no reason to doubt that he would so act. A miracle is improbable, when we can perceive no sufficient cause in reference to his creatures, why the Deity should vary his modes of operation; it ceases to be so, when such a cause is assigned. But Christianity claims to reveal facts, a knowledge of which is essential to the moral and spiritual regeneration of men; and to offer, in attestation of the truth of those facts, the only satisfactory proof, the authority of God, evidenced by miraculous displays of his power. The supposed interposition of God corresponds to the weighty purpose which it is represented as effecting. If Christianity profess to teach truths of infinite moment; if we perceive, that such is the character of its teachings, if, indeed, they are true; and if we are satisfied, from the exercise of our own reason and the history of the world, that they relate to facts concerning our relations and destiny, of which we could otherwise obtain no assurance, then this character of our religion removes all presumption against its claims to a miraculous origin.

But incredulity respecting the miracles of Christianity rarely has its source in any process of reasoning. It is commonly produced by the gross misrepresentations which have been made of Christianity. It has also another cause, deeply seated in our nature;—the inaptitude and reluctance of men to extend their view beyond the present and sensible, to raise themselves above the interests, the vexations, the pleasures, innocent or criminal, that lie within the horizon of a year or a week; and to open their minds to those thoughts and feelings, that rush in with the clear apprehension of the fact, that the barrier between the eternal and the finite world has been thrown open. A religious horror may come over us, so that

> "We fain would skulk beneath our wonted covering,
>   Mean as it is."

Man, indeed, in his low estate, loves the supernatural; but it is the supernatural addressed to the imagination, not in all its naked distinctness to the soul; it is the supernatural as belonging to some form of faith more connected with this world than the future; or regarded as the operation of limited beings, presenting a semblance of human nature, on whom man can react in his turn. But let us imagine, if we can, what would be the feelings of an enlightened philosopher, were he to witness an unquestionable miracle, a work breaking through the secondary agency, behind which the Deity ordinarily veils himself, and bringing us into immediate connexion with him. We can hardly conceive of the awe, the almost appalling feeling, with which it would be contemplated by one fully capable of comprehending its character, and alive to all its relations. The miracles of Christianity, when they are brought home to the mind as realities, have somewhat of the same power; dimmed as they are by distance, and clouded over by all the errors that false Christianity has gathered round them. If they be true, if Christianity be true, if its doctrines be certain; it is the most solemn fact we can comprehend, as well as the most joyful. It requires, that our whole character should be conformed to the new relations which it makes known. All things around us change their aspect. Life and death are not what they were. We are walking on the confines of an unknown and eternal world, where none of those earthly passions, that now agitate men so strongly, can find entrance. They bear upon them the mark of their doom, soon to perish. But from the revulsion of feeling, that must take place, when the character of all that surrounds us is thus changed, and the objects of eternity appear before the mind's eye, it is natural that many should shrink, and endeavour to escape from the view, and to forget it amid the familiar things of life; clinging to a vain conception, vain as regards each individual, of an unchanging stability in the order of nature.

Vain, I say, as regards each individual. Whatever we may fancy respecting the unchangeableness of the present order of things, to us it is not permanent. If we are to exist as individuals after death, then we shall soon be called, not to witness, but to be the subjects, of a miracle of unspeakable interest to us. Death will be to us an incontrovertible miracle. For us the present order of things will cease, and the unseen world, from which we may have held back our imagination, our feelings, and our belief, will be around us in all its reality.

If it were not for the abuse of language that has prevailed, it would be idle to say, that, in denying the miracles of Christianity, the truth of Christianity is denied. It has been vaguely alleged, that the internal evidences of our religion are sufficient, and that miraculous proof is not wanted; but this can be said by no one who understands what Christianity is, and what its internal evidences are. On this ground, however, the miracles of Christ were not indeed expressly denied, but were represented by some of the founders of the modern school of German infidelity, as only prodigies, adapted to rouse the attention of a rude people, like the Jews; but not required for the conviction of men of more enlightened minds. By others, the accounts of them in the Gospels have been admitted as in the main true, but explained as only exaggerated and discolored relations of natural events. But now, without taking the trouble to go through this tedious and hopeless process of misinterpretation, there are many who avow their disbelief of all that is miraculous in Christianity, and still affect to call themselves Christians. But Christianity was a revelation from God; and, in being so, it was itself a miracle. Christ was commissioned by God to speak to us in his name; and this is a miracle. No proof of his divine commission could be afforded, but through miraculous displays of God's power. Nothing is left that can be called Christianity, if its miraculous character be denied. Its essence is gone; its evidence is annihilated. Its truths, involving the highest interests of man, the facts which it makes known, and which are implied in its very existence as a divine revelation, rest no longer on the authority of God. All the evidence, if evidence it can be called, which it affords of its doctrines, consists in the real or pretended assertions of an individual, of whom we know very little, except that his history must have been most grossly misrepresented.

It is indeed difficult to conjecture what any one can fancy himself to believe of the history of Christ, who rejects the belief of his divine commission and miraculous powers. What conception can such a one form of his character? His whole history, as recorded in the Gospels, is miraculous. It is vain to attempt to strike out what relates directly or indirectly to his miraculous authority and works, with the expectation that any thing consistent or coherent will remain. It is as if one were to undertake to cut out from a precious agate the figure which nature has inwrought, and to pretend, that, by the removal of this accidental blemish, the stone might be left in its original form. If the accounts of Christ's miracles are mere fictions, then no credit can be due to works so fabulous as the pretended histories of his life. But these supposed miracles, it has been contended, may be explained, consistently with the veracity of the reporters, as natural events, the character of which was mistaken by the beholders. At first glance it is obvious, that such a statement supposes mistakes committed by those beholders, the disciples and apostles of Jesus, hardly consistent with any exercise of intellect; and, at the same time, renders it very difficult to free his character from the suspicion of intentional fraud. A little further consideration may satisfy us, that, if Jesus really performed no miracles, the accounts of his life, that have been handed down from his disciples, give evidence of utter folly, or the grossest deception, or rather of both.

But let us suppose, that the account of some one or more of the miracles of Christ, especially if detached from its connexion, and from all that determines its meaning, admits of being explained as having its origin in some natural event. Take any case one will, however, it must be admitted, that the explanation is not obvious, that it is conjectural; and, in a great majority of cases, it must be allowed, that it is merely possible; and that, to render it deserving of notice, the principle is to be assumed, that whatever is supernatural must be expunged from his history. We will suppose ourselves, then, to have tried this mode of interpretation on one narrative, and to have found it improbable. But, suspending our opinion, let us pass on to another solution of a similar character. A new improbability arises, and after that a new one. These improbabilities consequently multiply upon us in a geometrical ratio, and very soon become altogether overwhelming. Yet I speak not of what may be done, but of what has been done. This process of misinterpretation has been laboriously pursued through the Gospels; and the result has been a mass of monstrous conjectures, and abortive solutions, on which, as we proceed, there falls no glimmering of probability; and which continually shock and grate against all our most cherished sentiments of the inestimable value of Christianity, of admiration and love for its Founder on earth, and of reverence for its divine Author.

The proposition, that the history of Jesus is miraculous throughout, is to be understood in all its comprehensiveness. It is not merely that his history is full of accounts of his miracles; it is, that every thing in his history, what relates to himself and what relates to others, is conformed to this fact, and to the conception of him as speaking with authority from God. This is what constitutes the internal evidence of Christianity, a term, as I have said, often used of late with a very indistinct notion of any meaning attached to it. The consistency in the representations given by the different evangelists of the actions and words of Christ, as a messenger from God to men; their consistency in the representation of a character which it is impossible they should have conceived of, if it had not been exhibited before them, gives us an assurance of their truth, that becomes clearer in proportion as their writings are more studied and better understood; and in connexion with this is the consistency of their whole narrative; the coherence and naturalness with which all the words and actions of others bear upon events and upon a character so marvellous, and imply their existence.

The words of Christ, equally with his miracles, imply his mission from God. They are accordant only with the conception of him as speaking with authority from God. They would be altogether unsuitable to a merely human teacher of religious truth. So considered, if not the language of an impostor, they become the language of the most daring and crazy fanaticism. I speak of the general character of his discourses, a char-

acter of the most striking peculiarity. In ascribing them to one not miraculously commissioned by God, they must be utterly changed and degraded. What is most solemn and sublime must either be rejected as
never having been spoken by him, or its meaning must be thoroughly
perverted; it must be diluted into folly, that it may not be blasphemy.

"I am the good shepherd," said Jesus, "and lay down my life for my
sheep." "For this, the Father loves me; for I lay down my life, to receive
it again. None takes it from me; but I lay it down of my own accord. I
have a commission to lay it down, and I have a commission to receive it
again. This charge I received from my Father." There are but two aspects
under which such words can be regarded, if you suppose it true that they
were uttered by Jesus. You must say, in effect, with the unbelieving Jews
who heard him, "He is possessed by a demon and is mad. Why listen to
him?" Or the view which we take must be essentially that of others who
were present; "Can a demoniac open the eyes of the blind?"

Let us look at another passage. To a Christian it appears of unspeakable grandeur and of infinite moment. It presents before him the Founder
of his religion as contemplating the immeasurable extent of blessings of
which God had made him the minister, as announcing man's immortality amid the sufferings of humanity, on the threshold of the tomb.

"I am the resurrection and the life. He who has faith in me, though
he die, shall live; and he who lives as a believer in me shall never die.
Hast thou faith in this?"

Let us go on to the sepulchre of Lazarus.

"I thank thee, Father, that thou hast heard me; and I know that thou
hearest me always; but I have thus spoken, for the sake of the multitude
who are standing round, that they may believe that thou hast sent me."

We must, then, believe that Jesus Christ was sent by God, commissioned to speak to us in his name; or we cannot reasonably pretend to
know any thing concerning him. We may think it probable, that he was
a reformer of the religion of his nation, who preached for some short
time, principally in Galilee; but, having very soon made himself an
object of general odium, was put to death as a malefactor amid the
execrations of his countrymen, who then strove, though ineffectually, to
suppress his followers. Or, we may fancy him an untaught but enlightened philosopher, whose character, words and deeds, whatever they were,
have been absurdly and fraudulently misrepresented by his disciples. Or,
as the Gospels cannot be regarded as true histories, we may go on to the
conclusion at which infidelity, in its folly and ignorance, arrived within
the memory of some of us, that no such individual existed, and that
Christ is but an allegorical personage. But to whatever conclusion we
may come, if the representation of him in the Gospels be not conformed

to his real character and office, no foundation is left, on which any one can with reason pretend to regard him as an object of veneration, or to consider his teachings, whatever effect they may have had upon the world, as of any importance to himself.

To an infidel, whether he openly profess himself to be so, or whether he call himself a Christian, the history in the Gospels must present an insolvable problem. In the former case, he may turn from it, and say that he is not called upon to solve it; but in the latter, he is, by his profession, bound to do so. He has taken upon himself the task of explaining away the history as it stands, and substituting another in its stead; and of so fabricating the new history, that it may afford him ground for professing admiration and love for the real character of Christ.

The rejection of Christianity, in any proper sense of the word, the denial that God revealed himself by Christ, the denial of the truth of the Gospel history, or, as it is called in the language of the sect, the rejection of *historical* Christianity, is, of course, accompanied by the rejection of all that mass of evidence, which, in the view of a Christian, establishes the truth of his religion. This evidence, it is said, consists only of probabilities. We want certainty. The dwellers in the region of shadows complain, that the solid earth is not stable enough for them to rest on. They have firm footing on the clouds.

To the demand for certainty, let it come from whom it may, I answer, that I know of no absolute certainty, beyond the limit of momentary consciousness, a certainty that vanishes the instant it exists, and is lost in the region of metaphysical doubt. Beyond this limit, absolute certainty, so far as human reason may judge, cannot be the privilege of any finite being. When we talk of certainty, a wise man will remember what he is, and the narrow bounds of his wisdom and of his powers. A few years ago he was not. A few years ago he was an infant in his mother's arms, and could but express his wants, and move himself, and smile and cry. He has been introduced into a boundless universe, boundless to human thought in extent and past duration. An eternity had preceded his existence. Whence came the minute particle of life that he now enjoys? Why is he here? Is he only with other beings like himself, that are continually rising up and sinking in the shoreless ocean of existence; or is there a Creator, Father, and Disposer of all? Is he to continue a conscious being after this life, and undergo new changes; or is death, which he sees everywhere around him, to be the real, as it is the apparent end of what would then seem to be a purposeless and incomprehensible existence? He feels happiness and misery; and would understand how he may avoid the one and secure the other. He is restlessly urged on in pursuit of one object after another; many of them hurtful; most of them such, as the changes of life, or possession itself, or disease, or age, will deprive of their power of gratifying; while, at the same time, if he be unenlightened by revelation, the darkness of the future is rapidly closing round him. What objects should he pursue? How, if that be possible, is happiness to be secured? A creature of a day, just endued with the capacity of thought, at first receiving all his opinions from those who have preceded him, entangled among numberless prejudices, confused by his passions, perceiving, if the eyes of his understanding are opened, that the sphere of his knowledge is hemmed in by an infinity of which he is ignorant, from which unknown region, clouds are often passing over, and darkening what seemed clearest to his view,—such a being cannot pretend to attain, by his unassisted powers, any assurance concerning the unseen and the eternal, the great objects of religion. If men had been capable of comprehending their weakness and ignorance, and of reflecting deeply on their condition here, a universal cry would have risen from their hearts, imploring their God, if there were one, to reveal himself, and to make known to them their destiny. Their wants have been answered by God before they were uttered. Such is the belief of a Christian; and there is no question more worthy of consideration than whether this belief be well founded. It can be determined only by the exercise of that reason which God has given us for our guidance in all that concerns us. There can be no intuition, no direct perception, of the truth of Christianity, no metaphysical certainty. But it would be folly, indeed, to reject the testimony of God concerning all our higher relations and interests, because we can have no assurance, that he has spoken through Christ, except such as the condition of our nature admits of.

It is important for us to understand, that, in all things of practical import, in the exercise of all our affections, in the whole formation of our characters, we are acting, and must act, on probabilities alone. Certainty, in the metaphysical sense of the word, has nothing to do with the concerns of men, as respects this life or the future. We must discuss the subject of religion as we do all other subjects, when men talk with men about matters in which they are in earnest. It would be considered rather as insanity, than folly, were any one to introduce metaphysical skepticism, concerning causality, or identity, or the existence of the external world, or the foundation of human knowledge, into a discussion concerning the affairs of this life, the establishment of a manufactory, for example, or the building of a railroad; or if he should bring it forward to shake our confidence in the facts, of which human testimony and our own experience assure us; or to invalidate the conclusions, so far as they relate to this world, which we found on those facts. But we must use the same faculties, and adopt the same rules, in judging concerning the facts of the world which we have not seen, as concerning those of the world of which we have seen a very little. If it can be shown, according to the common and established principles of reasoning among men, that Christianity is true; if it can be shown, that, to suppose it not true, is to suppose a moral impossibility, we need no further evidence. When we have arrived at this conclusion, our ears will be opened to the accordant voice from the earth and from the skies, which bears testimony to a beneficent Creator. We shall find in the immortality assured to us by Christianity, a solution of the problem of our present life; a solution, which the very existence of that problem confirms. We shall perceive, that all which has been taught us by God's revelation, corresponds with all that our reason, in its highest exercise, had before been striving to establish. Religion will become to us a conviction. And what conviction, I do not say more probable, but what conviction, of any comparative weight, can be opposed to it? We plan for the future; we propose to ourselves some object to be attained within a short period, or during a course of years. But we proceed throughout upon probabilities; upon a probable judgment of its value, of our power to secure it, of the means at our command, and of the accidents by which we may be favored; and, among all these uncertainties, enters one far graver, the uncertainty of life itself. Yet we go on. But, if Christianity be true, there is no doubt about our ability to attain those objects which a religious man proposes to himself; there is no doubt of their inestimable value; and the uncertainty or the shortness of life at once ceases to enter into our calculations.

Of the facts on which religion is founded, we can pretend to no assurance, except that derived from the testimony of God, from the Christian revelation. He who has received this testimony is a Christian; and we may ask now, as was asked by an apostle; "Who is he that overcomes the world, but he who believes that Jesus was the Son of God." Christian faith alone affords such consolation and support as the heart needs amid the deprivations and sufferings of life; it alone gives action and strength to all that is noblest in our nature; it alone furnishes a permanent and effectual motive for growing virtue; it alone enables man to act conformably to his nature and destiny. This is always true. But we may have a deeper sense of the value of our faith, if we look abroad on the present state of the world, and see, all around, the waves heaving and the tempest rising. Everywhere is instability and uncertainty. But from the blind conflict between men exasperated and degraded by injustice and suffering, and men corrupted and hardened by the abuse of power, from the mutual outrages of angry political parties, in which the most unprincipled and violent become the leaders, from the fierce collision of mere earthly passions and cravings, whatever changes may result, no good is to be hoped. All im-

provement in the civilized world, all advance in human happiness, is
identified with the spread of Christian principles, of Christian truth, of
that faith, resting on reason, which connects man with God, makes him
feel, that the good of others is his personal good, assures him of a future
life of retribution, and, by revealing his immortality, calms his passions.

Gentlemen, I have addressed your understandings, not your feelings.
But the subject of Christianity is one which cannot be rightly apprehended without the strongest feeling; not the transient excitement existing for an hour, and then forgotten, but a feeling possessing the whole
heart, and governing our lives. Of the form of infidelity, which we have
been considering, there can be but one opinion among honest men. Great
moral offences in individuals are, indeed, commonly connected with the
peculiar character of their age, and with a prevailing want of moral
sentiment in regard to such offences, in the community in which they are
committed. This may be pleaded in excuse for the individual; but the
essential nature of the offence remains. It is a truth, which few among
us will question, that, for any one to pretend to be a Christian teacher,
who disbelieves the divine origin and authority of Christianity, and would
undermine the belief of others, is treachery towards God and man. If I
were to address such a one, I would implore him by all his remaining
self-respect, by his sense of common honesty, by his regard to the well-
being of his fellow-men, by his fear of God, if he believe that there is a
God, and by the awful realities of the future world, to stop short in his
course; and, if he cannot become a Christian, to cease to be a pretended
Christian teacher, and to assume his proper character.

If we have taken a correct view of the state of opinion throughout the
world, you will perceive, that it is a subject of very serious consideration,
and of individual action, to all of us who have faith in Christianity, and
especially to you, Gentlemen, who have devoted yourselves to the Christian ministry. Every motive, that addresses the better part of our nature,
urges you to be faithful in your office. A sincere moral purpose will
strengthen your judgment and ability; for he who has no other object but
to do right, will not find it difficult to ascertain his duty, and the means
of performing it. He who earnestly desires to serve his fellow-men is so
strongly drawn toward the truth, as the essential means of human happiness, that he is not likely to be turned aside by any dangerous error. Our
Saviour referred to no supernatural illumination when he said; *If any
one will do the will of him who sent me, he shall know concerning my
doctrine, whether it be from God, or whether I speak from myself.* What
you believe and feel, it is the business of your lives, and this is a great

privilege, to make others believe and feel. In the view of the worldly, the sphere of your duties may often appear humble; but you will not on that account break through it to seek for notoriety beyond. Deep and permanent feeling is very quiet and persevering. It cannot fail in its purposes. It cannot but communicate itself in some degree to others, and it is secure of the approbation of God.

☙ Bibliographical Essay

The historical literature on Unitarianism, though voluminous, may well disappoint anyone seeking to interpret the tradition. Study of these works serves mainly to give one a new appreciation for Harnack or Weber or Troeltsch and a deep sense of gratitude for the understanding that Perry Miller has brought to various aspects of New England thought. That the Unitarian movement has not reached the historiographical maturity attained by most American Protestant denominations is one of the clearest facts to emerge.

Whether it is the controversial background of the movement that is accountable or not, often the most important research has been performed or inspired by men outside of the denomination (for example, Miller, Faust, Persons, Burggraaf, Buell, Hutchison, and Stange). Such studies have been rare, however, and one can trace many of the misconceptions and superficialities of modern expositions back to nineteenth-century works written when the issues were being more warmly contested, from the anonymous *An Account of the State of Unitarianism in Boston, in 1812* to Joseph Henry Allen's *Our Liberal Movement in Theology.* The typical present-day evaluation of early Unitarianism is a quickly stated derogation, often echoing the judgments by which Henry Adams converted his lifelong prejudices into a major interpretation of an epoch. Even studies done in the last thirty or forty years are full of inaccuracies. Merle Curti in his prize-winning *The Growth of American Thought* characterizes the movement as a "watered-down Deism."[1] Van Wyck Brooks in *The Flowering of New England* merely postulates Emerson's "pale negation" theory.[2] Vernon L. Parrington reveals a socioeconomic bias even more clearly than does Curti and, consistent with his other value judgments, makes the amused observation that this Unitarianism was "the gospel of Jean Jacques Rousseau," "French liberalism," and "Jacobinical heresy" under a changed name.[3]

Joseph Haroutunian in his *Piety versus Moralism* deals with the more specifically theological issues, but his discussion—which is in fact a running series of notes on individual controversies—fails to deal with the affirmative aspects of Unitarianism. His interpretation is further weakened by his tendency to see liberal theology as merely a transition to

1. Merle E. Curti, *The Growth of American Thought,* p. 531.
2. Van Wyck Brooks, *The Flowering of New England,* p. 12.
3. Vernon L. Parrington, *Main Currents in American Thought,* vol. II, p. 322.

Authors and titles referred to are listed in the Bibliography.

"modern religious ideas" by comparison with which he considers the Reformation to have been a "negligible theological performance."[4] As indicated in the preface and elsewhere, the present writers believe, on the contrary, that the Liberal Faith has a venerable, five-hundred-year tradition that merits a more systematic consideration.

Earlier studies of the movement by Unitarians have tended either to follow the judgment of the earlier Transcendentalist interpretations or to be almost entirely unanalytical. Emerson and Parker perhaps did most to see the pattern, but the urbane condescension of Octavius Brooks Frothingham's numerous books about or peripheral to "literary Unitarianism" established a long-lived pattern of interpretation. Nor could one who deified Parker as enthusiastically as John White Chadwick do justice to earlier Unitarianism. Joseph Henry Allen's works are better, but they often lapse into hagiography despite his own fairly radical point of view. They were written to please all Unitarians. Some of the Channing Hall Lectures collected in *Unitarianism: Its Origin and History* are valuable, but the book as a whole is uncoordinated and uneven, with scant attention to the conservative theology.

Ephraim Emerton's exposition of *Unitarian Thought* makes no effort to be historical, being rather a reasoned statement of the humanistic moralism which he considered to be most representative of denominational thinking of his time.

Minor essays on the movement or its leaders have been written by Joseph Henry Crooker, Thomas R. Slicer, Charles H. Lyttle, William Wallace Fenn, and many others, but none of these have made any interpretations or brought to light any facts not long before presented by the Frothingham-Chadwick group. Slicer groups Thomas Jefferson, Ezra Stiles Gannett, and Emerson as having held the faith of Unitarianism and adds nothing to the understanding of those who were of one mind with, say, Gannett. Lyttle is almost ridiculously encomiastic in the interpretation of Channing with which he introduces his selection of Channing's writings. Fenn, on the other hand, fails to do justice to Henry Ware and other Unitarians when he has them champion revelation as against Channing's stand for reason. Neither Ware nor any Unitarians since then have considered any of their beliefs to be contrary to reason, and the chief arguments among conservatives generally arose from disagreements as to the reasonable meaning of revelation.

George W. Cooke's *Unitarianism in America* is the most adequate chronicle of events. It often becomes a mere catalogue of names, however, and tends to suffuse even the stormiest episodes in a deceptively

[4] Joseph Haroutunian, *Piety versus Moralism,* p. xvi.

irenic afterglow. Earl Morse Wilbur's *Our Unitarian Heritage* is probably the best brief historical account of the entire movement. His two-volume *History of Unitarianism* provides a solid overview of the Unitarian movement throughout the world, although this work is far from thorough and is increasingly dated in parts. Histories of Unitarianism as it spread across the United States written in this century include: Arnold Crompton's *Unitarianism on the Pacific Coast,* Walter Donald Kring's *Liberals Among the Orthodox: Unitarian Beginnings in New York City, 1819–1839,* Elizabeth Geffen's *Philadelphia Unitarianism, 1796–1862,* E. Digby Baltzell's *Puritan Boston and Quaker Philadelphia,* and Charles H. Lyttle's *Freedom Moves West: A History of the Western Unitarian Conference.*

The wide array of reminiscences and biographies by and about Unitarians and their adversaries provides an invaluable avenue by which to understand the movement. No attempt can be made here, however, to evaluate or even to list these many works, even though some of them, for instance, W. H. Channing's biography of William Ellery Channing, have great importance. Such an undertaking would involve bibliographical essays on each figure. Mention should be made, nonetheless, of William Channing Gannett's biography of his father, Ezra Stiles Gannett, which deserves at least as much attention as Frothingham's *Boston Unitarianism.* Daniel T. McColgan's *Joseph Tuckerman: Pioneer in American Social Work* remains a good work, and Walter Donald Kring's *Henry Whitney Bellows* is the first major biography of this important yet neglected figure of the nineteenth century.

Most of the memoirs of the liberal clergymen that have been collected by William B. Sprague, William Ware, and Samuel A. Eliot are extremely uncritical and partisan. Although indispensable repositories of biographical information, they are not of great value to the historian of ideas.

Two Unitarian scholars in the twentieth century have made substantial contributions to interpreting the Liberal Faith. George Huntston Williams, Hollis Professor emeritus of the Harvard Divinity School, has written a number of works which concern Unitarianism, directly and indirectly. His *Radical Reformation* expands our understanding of the Reformation and hence of Christian Unitarianism in its many early forms, especially during the sixteenth century. His short *Rethinking the Unitarian Relationship with Protestantism: An Examination of the Thought of Frederic Henry Hedge, 1805–1890,* had an impact in certain Protestant ecumenical circles before Vatican II. The volume he edited, *The Harvard Divinity School: Its Place in Harvard University and in American Culture,* is an assessment by a group of distinguished younger scholars of the role of the school through its early days of conflict and resolution to 1954. Williams's books and articles are too numerous to list here; however, the student of Christian Unitarianism would do well to consult his works.

C. Conrad Wright, also of the Harvard Divinity School, has served as the major historian of his tradition. His *The Beginnings of Unitarianism in America* still stands as the classic for any student interested in the origins of the liberal movement in America. Wright's other work has called for a reevaluation of Channing and Bellows; and his discovery of the disagreeable effect of the Unitarian minister's preaching in Concord on Emerson has been important. His other books and articles have provided much insight into Congregationalism, Unitarianism, and Transcendentalism. A book he edited called *A Stream of Light: A Sesquicentennial History of American Unitarianism* offers the most readable history of Unitarianism available today, with the exception of Daniel Walker Howe's more concentrated *The Unitarian Conscience: Harvard Moral Philosophy, 1805–1861.*

Many students of nineteenth-century literature will be familiar with such works as Van Wyck Brooks's *The Flowering of New England, 1815–1865* and F. O. Matthiessen's *American Renaissance: Art and Expression in the Age of Emerson and Whitman;* yet neither provides the critical portrait of Unitarianism that the serious student of the American Reformation needs to understand the historical and theological issues involved. Lawrence Buell's *Literary Transcendentalism: Style and Vision in the American Renaissance* offers an excellent treatment of the period, especially of the somewhat difficult and theoretical considerations that differentiate Unitarianism from Transcendentalism. William R. Hutchison has also produced a first-rate study in this regard, *The Transcendentalist Ministers: Church Reform in the New England Renaissance.* Jerry Wayne Brown's *The Rise of Biblical Criticism in America, 1800–1870* is an important study that will enable the modern reader to understand a number of the Biblical issues which concerned nineteenth-century theologians. Ann C. Douglas's *The Feminization of American Culture* should be of great benefit to the reader in understanding the contributions made by women who, having grown up in Unitarian homes, embraced Transcendentalism or retained their Unitarianism—in whatever form. Her study is but a beginning; more work is needed on the role of women in the Liberal Faith.

One must conclude that the clearest understanding of what the early Christian Unitarians believed can be gained from their own words. Thus the student of the movement would do well to consult the primary texts, ranging from pamphlets and books, to periodicals such as the *Christian Examiner,* to such invaluable diaries as that of William Bentley. The

Tracts published by the American Unitarian Association provide their own unique biography of the movement. Most of the leaders wrote a great deal, and many wrote well. The editors of this anthology have attempted to make a selection that is representative of the thinkers who provided intellectual leadership for the movement and that gives a reliable cross section of their thinking. Through a careful consideration of the texts, the reader will grasp the significance of the Christian Unitarians' American Reformation and how it relates to the so-called American Renaissance. At the least, he or she will better comprehend the humor of Ambrose Bierce's definition of a Unitarian in his *Devil's Dictionary* as a person who denies the divinity of a Trinitarian. For Christian Unitarianism involved more than the fatherhood of God, the brotherhood of man, and the neighborhood of Boston, as the preceding pages have sought to reveal. Its adherents struggled hard, even to the point of producing their own scholasticism—Biblical, theological, historical—to be members of the church of Jesus Christ as well as contributors to American culture.

❧ Bibliography
(including section on Unitarian hymns)

Note: Selections marked "•" are sources for documents included in this volume.

Adams, Henry, *The Education of Henry Adams: An Autobiography*, Boston and New York, Houghton Mifflin Co., 1918, 517 pp.

Alexander, James W., *Life of Archibald Alexander, D.D., First Professor in the Theological Seminary at Princeton, New Jersey*, New York, 1854, 700 pp.

• Alger, William Rounseville, *The Christian Theory of Life*, American Unitarian Association. Tracts, 1st series, no. 267, Boston, 1849.

———, *A Critical History of the Doctrine of a Future Life*, Philadelphia, 1861; 10th ed., much augmented, New York, 1878, 914 pp.

———, *The Genius and Posture of America. An Oration Delivered before the Citizens of Boston, July 4, 1857*, Boston, 1857, 60 pp.

———, *History of the Cross of Christ*, Cambridge and Boston, 1851, 90 pp.

———, *The Life of Edwin Forrest, the American Tragedian*, Philadelphia, 1877, 2 vols., 864 pp.

———, *The Poetry of the East*, Boston, 1856, 280 pp.

———, *Prayers Offered in the Massachusetts House of Representatives, During the Session of 1868*, Boston, 1869, 103 pp.

Allen, Joseph Henry, "Historical Sketch of the Unitarian Movement since the Reformation," in *A History of the Unitarians and the Universalists in the United States*, American Church History Series, vol. X, New York, Christian Literature Co., 1894.

———, *Our Liberal Movement in Theology, Chiefly as Shown in Recollections of the History of Unitarianism in New England, Being a Closing Course of Lectures Given in the Harvard Divinity School*, Boston, 1882, 220 pp.

———, *Sequel to "Our Liberal Movement,"* Boston, 1897, 157 pp.

Allen, William, *Memoir of John Codman*, Boston, 1853, 408 pp.

• American Unitarian Association, *First Annual Report of the Executive Committee of the American Unitarian Association*, Boston, Isaac R. Butts and Co., 1826.

———, *The Twenty-eighth Report of the American Unitarian Association*, 1853.

Anonymous, *An Account of the State of Unitarianism in Boston, in 1812*, Boston, 1829, 16 pp.

Baltzell, E. Digby, *Puritan Boston and Quaker Philadelphia*, New York, Free Press, 1979, 585 pp.

Beecher, Lyman, *Works*, vol. 2, *Sermons Delivered on Various Occasions*, Boston, 1852.

Bell, Charles (Sir), *The Hand, Its Mechanism and Vital Endowments as Evincing Design*, London, Pickering, 1833, 288 pp.

Bellows, Henry W., *A Sequel to "The Suspense of Faith" Addressed to His Own Congregation, Sunday, Sept. 25th, 1858, on the Reopening of All Soul's Church, after the Summer Vacation*, New York, 1859.

• ———, *The Suspense of Faith, a Discourse on the State of the Church. An Address to the Alumni of the Divinity School of Harvard University, Cambridge, Mass., Given July 19, 1859,* New York, 1859, 46 pp.

Belsham, Thomas, *Memoirs of the Late Reverend Theophilus Lindsey, M.A., Including a Brief Analysis of His Works, Etc.,* London, 1812, 544 pp.

Bentley, William, *The Diary of William Bentley, D.D., Pastor of the East Church, Salem, Massachusetts,* Salem, Massachusetts, The Essex Institute, 1905–1914, 4 vols.

Bierce, Ambrose, *The Devil's Dictionary,* New York, Dover Publications, 1958, 145 pp.

Blau, Joseph I., ed., *American Philosophic Addresses, 1700–1900,* New York, Columbia University Press, 1946, 762 pp.

Bowen, Francis, *Metaphysics and Ethics, Lowell Lectures on the Application of Metaphysical and Ethical Science to the Evidences of Religion,* Boston, 1849, 465 pp.

Bradford, William, *The History of Plymouth Colony, a Modern English Version by Harold Paget, with an Introduction by George F. Willison,* New York, Van Nostrand, 1948, 428 pp.

Brooks, Van Wyck, *The Flowering of New England, 1815–1865,* New York, E. P. Dutton Co., 1936.

Brown, Jerry Wayne, *The Rise of Biblical Criticism in America, 1800–1870: The New England Scholars,* Middletown, Connecticut, Wesleyan University Press, 1969.

Buell, Lawrence, *Literary Transcendentalism: Style and Vision in the American Renaissance,* Ithaca, New York, Cornell University Press, 1973.

Burggraaf, Winfield, *The Rise and Development of Liberal Theology in America,* New York, Board of Publication and Bible-School Work of the Reformed Church in America, 1928, 211 pp.

Bushnell, Horace, *Christian Nurture,* 1st American ed., New York, 1861, 407 pp.

Butler, Joseph, *The Analogy of Religion, Natural and Revealed, to the Constitution and Course of Nature,* London, 1736, 320 pp.

* "Catechism for Children and Youth." *See* Ministers of the Worcester Association, comps., "Catechism for Children and Youth."

Chadwick, John White, *Old and New Unitarian Belief,* Boston, 1894.

———, *Theodore Parker, Preacher and Reformer,* Boston and New York, Houghton Mifflin Co., 1900, 422 pp.

• Channing, William E., *A Letter to the Rev. Samuel C. Thacher on the Aspersions Contained in a Late Number of the Panoplist, on the Ministers of Boston and the Vicinity,* Boston, 1815, 36 pp.

• ———, "Likeness to God," *The Works of William E. Channing, D.D.,* 6th ed., 3 vols., Boston, 1846, vol. 3, pp. 227–255.

———, *"The Moral Argument against Calvinism"* in *The Works of William E. Channing, D.D.,* 6th ed., 6 vols., Boston, 1846.

———, "The Perfect Life," *Twelve Discourses,* Boston, 1873, 311 pp.

———, *Remarks on the Rev. Dr. Worcester's Letter to Mr. Channing, on the "Review of American Unitarianism"* in a Late Panoplist, Boston, 1815, 39 pp.

———, *Remarks on the Rev. Dr. Worcester's Second Letter to Mr. Channing on American Unitarianism,* Boston, 1815, 48 pp.

• ———, *Unitarian Christianity. A Sermon Delivered at the Ordination of the Rev. Jared Sparks, to the Pastoral Care of the First Independent Church in Baltimore, May 5, 1819,* Baltimore, 1819, 63 pp.

————, *The Works of William E. Channing, D.D.*, 6th ed., 6 vols., Boston.

Channing, William E., and Thacher, Samuel C., *Elements of Religion and Morality in the Form of a Catechism*, Boston, 1813.

Channing, William Henry, *The Life of William Ellery Channing, D.D.*, reprinted, The Regina Press.

Channing Hall Lectures, *Unitarianism: Its Origin and History*, A Course of Sixteen Lectures Delivered in Channing Hall, Boston, 1888–1889, Boston, American Unitarian Association, 1890, 394 pp.

Chauncy, Charles, *Enthusiasm Described and Caution'd Against*, Boston, 1742.

————, *Letter from a Gentleman in Boston, to Mr. George Wishart, One of the Ministers in Edinburgh, Concerning the State of Religion in New-England*, Edinburgh, 1742.

————, *The Mystery Hid from Ages and Generations, Made Manifest by the Gospel-Revelation: or, The Salvation of All Men the Grand Thing Aimed in the Scheme of God*, London, 1784.

• ————, *Seasonable Thoughts on the State of Religion in New-England*, Boston, 1743, Part II, pp. 333–349.

Chillingworth, William, *The Works of William Chillingworth, M.A.*, 10th ed., London, 1742.

Christie, Francis Albert, *The Makers of the Meadville Theological School 1844–1894*, Boston, Beacon Press, 1927, 171 pp.

• Clarke, James F., "The Christian Church," *Orthodoxy: Its Truths and Errors*, Boston, 1866, pp. 391–422.

————, *Ten Great Religions: an Essay in Comparative Theology*, Boston, 1871, 528 pp.

Cooke, George W., *Unitarianism in America, A History of Its Origin and Development*, Boston, American Unitarian Association, 1902, 463 pp.

Crompton, Arnold, *Unitarianism on the Pacific Coast: The First Sixty Years*, Boston, Beacon Press, 1957, 182 pp.

Crooker, Joseph Henry, *The Unitarian Church: Its History and Characteristics*, Boston, n.d. (ca. 1895).

Cross, Barbara M., ed., *The Autobiography of Lyman Beecher*, 2 vols. Cambridge, Mass., Harvard University Press, 1961.

Curti, Merle E., *The Growth of American Thought*, New York and London, Harper and Bros., 1943, 848 pp.

DeWette, Wilhelm Martin Leberecht, *Beitrage zur Einleitung in das Alte Testament*, Halle, Schimmelpfennig und Co., 1806–1807, 2 vols.

Dewey, Orville, *Autobiography and Letters of Orville Dewey, D.D., Edited by his daughter, Mary E. Dewey*, Boston, 1883, 366 pp.

————, *The Old World and the New; or, A Journal of Reflections and Observations Made on a Tour in Europe*, New York, 1836.

• ————, *On the Uses of the Communion*, American Unitarian Association Tracts, 1st series, no. 172, Boston, 1841.

Douglas, Ann C., *The Feminization of American Culture*, New York, Knopf, 1977, 403 pp.

Eaton, Clement, *Freedom of Thought in the Old South*, Durham, North Carolina, Duke University Press, 1940, 343 pp.

Edwards, Jonathan, *Some Thoughts Concerning the Present Revival of Religion in New-England, and the Way in Which It Ought to Be Acknowledged and Promoted, Humbly Offered to the Publick, in a Treatise on that Subject*, Boston, 1742, 378 pp.

Eliot, Charlotte C., *William Greenleaf Eliot; Minister, Educator, Philanthropist,* Boston, Houghton Mifflin Co., 1904.

Eliot, Samuel A., ed., *Heralds of a Liberal Faith,* Boston, American Unitarian Association, 1910, 3 vols.

Eliot, William Greenleaf, *Christian Nurture,* 1st American ed., New York, 1861, 407 pp.

————, *Discourses on the Doctrines of Christianity,* Boston, American Unitarian Association, 1870, 168 pp.

————, *Our Lord Jesus Christ,* American Unitarian Association Tracts, 1st series, nos. 289, 290 (vol. 26, pp. 163–178), Boston, 1853.

• ————, *Regeneration,* American Unitarian Association Tracts, 1st series, no. 294, Boston, 1853.

• Ellis, George Edward, *A Half-Century of the Unitarian Controversy, with Particular Reference to its Origin, its Course and its Prominent Subjects among the Congregationalists of Massachusetts,* Boston, 1857, 511 pp.

————, *A History of the First Church in Boston,* Boston, 1881.

————, *The Puritan Age and Rule in the Colony of the Massachusetts Bay, 1629–1685,* Boston and New York, 1888, 576 pp.

Ely, Ezra Stiles, *A Contrast between Calvinism and Hopkinsianism,* New York, 1811, 280 pp.

Emerson, Ralph Waldo, "Circles," in *Selections from Ralph Waldo Emerson,* edited by Stephen E. Whicher, Boston, Houghton Mifflin, 1960.

————, *Nature,* Boston, 1836, 95 pp.

Emerton, Ephraim, *Unitarian Thought,* New York, Macmillan, 1910.

Faust, Clarence H., "The Background of the Unitarian Opposition to Transcendentalism," *Modern Philology,* vol. 35 (1938), pp. 297–324.

Fenn, William Wallace, "The Revolt against the Standing Order," in *The Religious History of New England,* Lowell Institute Lectures, 1914–1915, Cambridge, Harvard University Press, 1917, 356 pp.

First Annual Report of the Executive Committee of the American Unitarian Association, Boston, 1826, 32 pp.

Foote, Henry W., *James Freeman and King's Chapel, 1782–1787,* Boston, 1873, 29 pp.

Foster, Frank H., *A Genetic History of the New England Theology,* Chicago, University of Chicago Press, 1907, 568 pp.

Frothingham, Octavius Brooks, *Boston Unitarianism, 1820–1850: A Study of the Life and Work of Nathaniel Langdon Frothingham,* New York, G. P. Putnam's Sons, 1890, 272 pp.

————, *Theodore Parker: A Biography,* New York, G. P. Putnam's Sons, 1886, 588 pp.

————, *Transcendentalism in New England, a History,* New York, G. P. Putnam's Sons, 1876, 395 pp.

Fuller, Andrew, *The Calvinistic and Socinian Systems, Examined and Compared, as to Their Moral Tendency,* American edition, Philadelphia, 1796, 325 pp.

Furness, William H., *Discourses,* Philadelphia, 1855, 308 pp.

————, *Nature and Christianity: Dudleian Lecture,* Boston, 1847, 24 pp.

————, *Once More, with Remarks upon the Character of Christ and the Historical Claims of the Four Gospels,* Philadelphia, 1885, 151 pp.

————, *Remarks on the Four Gospels,* Philadelphia, 1836, 340 pp.

————, *Thoughts on the Life and Character of Jesus of Nazareth,* Boston, 1859, 311 pp.

———, *The Veil Partly Lifted and Jesus Becoming Visible*, Boston, 1864, 301 pp.
Gannett, William C., *Ezra Stiles Gannett, Unitarian Minister in Boston, 1824–1871*, Boston, 1875, 572 pp.
• Gay, Ebenezer, *Natural Religion as Distinguish'd from Revealed*, Boston, 1759, 34 pp.
Geffen, Elizabeth, *Philadelphia Unitarianism, 1796–1862*, Philadelphia, University of Pennsylvania Press, 1961.
Godbey, John C., *A Bibliography of Unitarian Universalist History*, Chicago, Meadville/Lombard Theological School, 1982, 101 pp.
Greenwood, F. W. P., *Sermons of Consolation*, Boston, 1842.
Hale, Edward Everett, ed., *On the Elevation of the Poor*, Boston, 1874.
Harnack, A., *History of Dogma*, translated from the 3rd German edition, Dover Publications, New York, 1961.
Haroutunian, Joseph, *Piety versus Moralism: The Passing of the New England Theology*, New York, Henry Holt and Co., 1932, 329 pp.
Hedge, Frederic Henry, "Antisupernaturalism in the Pulpit," *Christian Examiner*, v. 77 (Sept. 1864) pp. 145–159.
• ———, "Natural Religion," *Christian Examiner*, v. 52 (Jan. 1852) pp. 117–136.
———, *Reason in Religion*, Boston, 1865.
Herbert, Edward Herbert (Lord Herbert of Cherbury), *De Veritate*, 1624.
History of the Harvard Church in Charlestown, 1815–1879, Boston, 1879.
Howe, Daniel Walker, *The Unitarian Conscience: Harvard Moral Philosophy, 1805–1861*, Cambridge, Harvard University Press, 1970, 398 pp.
Howe, M. A. DeWolfe, ed., *Journal of the Proceedings of the Society which Conducts the Monthly Anthology and Boston Review, October 3, 1805, to July 2, 1811; with an Introduction by M. A. DeWolfe Howe*, Boston, The Boston Athenaeum, 1910, 344 pp.
Hume, David, *Dialogues Concerning Natural Religion*, 2nd ed., London, 1779, 264 pp.
Hutchison, William R., *The Transcendentalist Ministers: Church Reform in the New England Renaissance*, New Haven, Yale University Press, 1959, 290 pp.
Hymn and Tune Book, for the Church and Home; and Services for Congregational Worship, Boston, 1868, 329 and 215 pp.
The Index, No. 520 (Dec. 11, 1879).
• King's Chapel, *The King's Chapel Liturgy*, 1785.
Kring, Walter Donald, *Henry Whitney Bellows*, Boston, Skinner House Books, 1979.
———, *Liberals among the Orthodox: Unitarian Beginnings in New York City, 1819–1839*, Boston, Beacon Press, 1974, 278 pp.
Livermore, Abiel Abbot, *The Acts of the Apostles: with a Commentary*, Boston, 1844, 330 pp.
• ———, "The Apostle Paul," *The Epistle of Paul to the Romans; with a Commentary and Revised Translation, and Introduction Essay*, Boston, 1854, pp. 42–70.
———, *Discourses*, Boston, 1854.
• "The Epistle of Paul to the Romans," in *The Epistle of Paul to the Romans; with a Commentary and Revised Translation, and Introduction Essay*, Boston, 1854, pp. 74–75.
———, *The Epistle to the Hebrews, the Epistles of James, Peter, John and Jude, and the Revelation of John the Divine, with a Commentary and Essays*, Boston, 1881.

————, *The Epistles of Paul to the Corinthians, Galatians, Ephesians, Phillip-ians, Collossians, Thessalonians, Timothy, Titus and Philemon. With Intro-duction and Commentary,* Boston, 1881, 308 pp.

————, *The Four Gospels: with a Commentary. Volume I. Matthew,* Boston, 1841, 346 pp.

————, *The Four Gospels: with a Commentary. Volume II. Mark, Luke, and John,* Boston, 1842, 358 pp.

• ————, *Reason and Revelation,* American Unitarian Association Tracts, 1st series, no. 136, Boston, 1838.

• Livermore, Leonard Jarvis, *Baptism,* American Unitarian Association Tracts, 4th series, no. 6, Boston, n.d.

Locke, John, *The Reasonableness of Christianity, as Delivered in the Scriptures,* London, 1695, 304 pp.

————, *The Reasonableness of Christianity, with a Discourse of Miracles, and Part of a Third Letter Concerning Toleration,* ed. Ramsey, I. T., Stanford, California, Stanford University Press, 1958.

Lothrop, Thornton Kirkland, *Some Reminiscences of the Life of Samuel Kirk-land Lothrop,* Boston, 1888, 266 pp.

[Lowell, John, Jr.], *Are you a Christian, or a Calvinist. . . . By a Layman,* Bos-ton, 1815, 72 pp.

Lyttle, Charles H. *Freedom Moves West: A History of the Western Unitarian Conference, 1852–1952,* Boston, Beacon Press, 1952, 298 pp.

————, *The Liberal Gospel: as Set Forth in the Writings of William Ellery Channing,* Boston, Beacon Press, 1925, 257 pp.

Matthiessen, Francis O., *American Renaissance: Art and Expression in the Age of Emerson and Whitman,* London and New York, Oxford University Press, 1960, 678 pp.

• Mayhew, Jonathan, "Of the Nature and Principle of Evangelical Obedience," *Sermons,* Boston, 1755, pp. 256–359.

McColgan, Daniel T., *Joseph Tuckerman: Pioneer in American Social Work,* Washington, D.C., Catholic University of America Press, 1940, 450 pp.

McGiffert, Arthur C., *Protestant Thought before Kant,* New York, Charles Scrib-ner and Sons, 1911.

Miller, Perry, "The Insecurity of Nature," in *Nature's Nation,* Cambridge, Har-vard University Press, 1967, pp. 121–133.

————, *The New England Mind From Colony to Province,* Cambridge, Mass., Harvard University Press, 1953.

Miller, Perry, *The New England Mind: from Colony to Province,* Cambridge, Harvard University Press, 1953, 513 pp.

————, *The Transcendentalists,* Cambridge, Mass., Harvard University Press, 1950.

* Ministers of the Worcester Association, comps., "Catechism for Children and Youth" in *A Catechism, in Three Parts,* [*The Worcester Catechism,* Eds.], 5th ed. Boston, Hilliard, Gray, Little, and Wilkins, 1831.

Morse, James King, *Jedidiah Morse: A Champion of New England Orthodoxy,* New York, Columbia University Press, 1939, 180 pp.

Morse, Jedidiah, *Sermon on the National Fast, May 9, 1798,* Boston, 1798.

————, *The True Reasons on Which the Election of a Hollis Professor of Di-vinity in Harvard College Was Opposed at the Board of Overseers, February 14, 1805,* Charlestown, Massachusetts, 1805, 28 pp.

• Norton, Andrews, *A Discourse on the Latest Form of Infidelity; Delivered at the Request of the "Association of the Alumni of the Cambridge Theological School," on the 19th of July, 1839. With Notes,* Cambridge, 1839, 64 pp.

• ———, *A Statement of Reasons for Not Believing the Doctrines of Trinitarians Respecting the Nature of God, and the Person of Christ.* Occasioned by Professor Stuart's Letters to Mr. Channing, Boston, 1819.

Paley, William Gorham, *The Evidences of Christianity,* 1st American edition, New York, 1824.

———, *"Natural Theology" and "Horae Paulinae,"* New York, American Tract Society, n.d.

Palfrey, John Gorham, *The Theory and Uses of Natural Religion; Being the Dudleian Lecture, Read before the University of Cambridge, May 8th, 1839,* Boston, 1839, 76 pp.

Parker, Theodore, *A Discourse of Matters Pertaining to Religion,* Boston, 1842.

———, *A Discourse on the Transient and Permanent in Christianity: Preached at the Ordination of Mr. Charles C. Shackford in the Hawes Place Church in Boston, May 19, 1841,* Boston, 1841, 48 pp.

———, *The Relation of Jesus to His Age and the Ages. A Sermon Preached at the Thursday Lecture, in Boston, December 26, 1844,* Boston, 1845, 18 pp.

———, *The Transient and Permanent in Christianity* (reprint), Boston, Beacon Press, 1948.

———, trans., *A Critical and Historical Introduction to the Canonical Scriptures of the Old Testament,* from the German of Wilhelm Martin Leberecht De-Wette, translated and enlarged by Theodore Parker, Boston, 1843, 2 vols., 517 and 570 pp.

Parrington, Vernon L., *Main Currents in American Thought: An Interpretation of American Literature from the Beginnings to 1920,* 3 vols., New York, Harcourt, Brace, 1927–1930.

• Peabody, Andrew Preston, "The Holy Spirit," *Lectures on Christian Doctrine,* 2nd ed., Boston, 1844, pp. 93–115.

———, *Moral Philosophy, a Series of Lectures,* Boston, 1887, 337 pp.

Persons, Stow, *Free Religion, An American Faith,* New Haven, Yale University Press, 1947, 168 pp.

Proceedings of the Second Church and Parish in Dorchester, Boston, 1812, 124 pp.

Ripley, George, *Letters on the Latest Form of Infidelity, Including a View of the Opinions of Spinoza, Schleiermacher, and DeWette,* Boston, 1840, 3 vols.

Routley, Erik, *Hymns and Human Life,* London, J. Murray, 1952, 346 pp.

• Sears, Edmund H., "Christ the Divine Word," *The Fourth Gospel, the Heart of Christ,* Boston, 1872, pp. 220–225 and 484–490.

Slicer, Thomas R., *The Power and Promise of the Liberal Faith,* Boston, Geo. H. Ellis, 1900, 145 pp.

———, "A Survey of Liberal Religion in the United States," in Fifth International Congress of Free Christianity and Religious Progress, *Proceedings and Papers,* ed. Wendte, Charles W., Berlin-Schöneberg, Protestantischer Schriftenvertrieb, G.m.b.H., 1911, pp. 273–285.

• Sparks, Jared, "The Comparative Moral Tendency of the Leading Doctrines of Calvinism and the Sentiments of Unitarians," *An Inquiry into the Comparative Moral Tendency of Trinitarian and Unitarian Doctrines; in a Series of Letters to the Rev. Dr. Miller, of Princeton,* Boston, 1823, pp. 281–293.

Sprague, William B., ed., *Annals of the American Unitarian Pulpit, or Commemorative Notices of Distinguished American Clergymen of Various De-*

nominations from the Early Settlement of the Country to the Close of the Year Eighteen Hundred Fifty-Five, New York, 9 vols., 1857–1869.

Stange, Douglas C., *Patterns of Antislavery among American Unitarians, 1831–1860*, Rutherford, N.J., Fairleigh Dickinson University Press, 1977, 308 pp.

• Stearns, Oliver, *The Incarnation. A Sermon Preached at the Ordination of Rev. Calvin S. Locke over the Unitarian Church and Society at West Dedham, Wednesday, December 6, 1854, with the Charge, Right Hand of Fellowship, and Address to the People*, Boston, 1855.

Strauss, David Friedrich, *Das Leben Jesu*, Tübingen, 1835–1836, 2 vols.

Stuart, Moses, *Letters to the Rev. Wm. E. Channing, Containing Remarks on His Sermon, Recently Preached and Published at Baltimore*, Andover, 1819, 167 pp.

Tillotson, John, *Works*, London, 1857, 7 vols.

Tracts on the Unitarian Controversy, Boston, 1816.

• Tuckerman, Joseph, *On the Elevation of the Poor*, ed. Edward Everett Hale, Boston, 1874, pp. 84–95.

• ———, *The Principles and Results of the Ministry at Large in Boston*, Boston, 1838, Part II, Letter IV, pp. 286–313.

• Walker, James, "The Day of Judgment," *Sermons Preached in the Chapel of Harvard College*, Boston, 1861, pp. 381–397.

———, *Sermons Preached Chiefly in the College Chapel*, Boston, 1877, 454 pp. Includes volume above.

———, ed., *Essays on the Intellectual Powers of Man, by Thomas Reid, Abridged. With Notes and Illustrations from Sir William Hamilton and Others*, Cambridge, 1850, 462 pp.

———, *The Philosophy of the Active and Moral Powers of Man, by Dugald Stewart, Revised with Omissions and Additions*, Cambridge, 1849, 428 pp.

Ware, Henry, *Answer to Dr. Woods' Reply, in a Second Series of Letters Addressed to Trinitarians and Calvinists*, Cambridge, 1822, 163 pp.

———, *An Inquiry into the Foundation, Evidences and Truths of Religion*, Cambridge, 1842.

• ———, "The Nature of Man," *Letters Addressed to Trinitarians and Calvinists, Occasioned by Dr. Woods' Letters to Unitarians*, Cambridge, 1820, 150 pp.

• ———, "Philosophical Difficulties in the 'Unitarian Controversy,'" *A Postscript to the Second Series of Letters Addressed to Trinitarians and Calvinists, in Reply to the Remarks of Dr. Woods on those Letters*, Cambridge, 1823, pp. 13–15.

• Ware, Henry Jr., "The Personality of Deity," *The Works of Henry Ware, Jr., D.D.*, Boston, 1846–1847, 4 vols., v. 3, pp. 26–39.

• ———, *Sober Thoughts on the State of the Times, Addressed to the Unitarian Community*, American Unitarian Association Tracts, 1st series, no. 99, Boston, 1835, 48 pp.

• Ware, William, *Antiquity and Revival of Unitarian Christianity*, American Unitarian Association Tracts, 1st series, no. 47, Boston, 1831, 28 pp.

———, *Julian: or, Scenes in Judea. By the Author of Letters from Palmyra and Rome*, New York, 1841.

———, *Lectures on the Works and Genius of Washington Allston*, Boston, 1852, 154 pp.

———, *Probus: or, Rome in the Third Century. In Letters of Lucius M. Piso (pseud.) from Rome to Fausta the Daughter of Gracchus, at Palmyra*, New York, 1838.

———, *Zenobia: or, the Fall of Palmyra*, New York, 1838.

————, ed., *American Unitarian Biography: Memoirs of Individuals Who Have Been Distinguished by Their Writings, Characters, and Efforts in the Cause of Liberal Christianity*, Boston and Cambridge, 2 vols., 1850–1851.

Whately, Richard, *Introductory Lectures on Morals and Christian Evidences*, Cambridge, 1857, 330 pp.

Whitehead, Alfred North, *Process and Reality, an Essay in Cosmology*, New York, Macmillan, 1929, 547 pp.

Wilbur, Earl Morse, *A History of Unitarianism. Socinianism and Its Antecedents*, Cambridge, Harvard University Press, 1945, 617 pp.

————, *A History of Unitarianism, in Transylvania, England, and America*, Cambridge, Harvard University Press, 1952, 518 pp.

————, *Our Unitarian Heritage, an Introduction to the History of the Unitarian Movement*, Boston, Beacon Press, 1925, 495 pp.

Williams, George H., *Rethinking the Unitarian Relationship with Protestantism: An Examination of the Thought of Frederic Henry Hedge (1805–1890)*, Boston, Beacon Press, 1949, 42 pp.

————, *The Radical Reformation*, Philadelphia, Westminster Press, 1962.

————, ed., *The Harvard Divinity School: Its Place in Harvard University and in American Culture*, Boston, Beacon Press, 1954, 366 pp.

Woods, Leonard, *Letters to Rev. Nathaniel W. Taylor*, Andover, 1830, 114 pp.

————, *Letters of Unitarianism Occasioned by the Sermon of the Reverend William E. Channing at the Ordination of the Rev. J. Sparks*, Andover, 1820, 160 pp.

————, *Remarks on Dr. Ware's Answer*, Andover, 1822, 63 pp.

————, *A Reply to Dr. Ware's Letters to Trinitarians and Calvinists*, Andover, 1821, 228 pp.

Worcester, Noah, *Letters to the Rev. William E. Channing, Containing Remarks on his Sermon, Recently Preached and Published at Baltimore*, 2nd ed., Andover, 1819, 120 pp.

Worcester Catechism, The. See Ministers of the Worcester Association, comps., "Catechism for Children and Youth."

Wright, Conrad, *The Beginnings of Unitarianism in America*, Boston, Starr King Press, 1955, 305 pp.

————, *The Liberal Christians: Essays on American Unitarian History*, Boston, Beacon Press, 1970, 147 pp.

————, ed., *A Stream of Light: A Sesquicentennial History of American Unitarianism*, Boston, Unitarian Universalist Association, 1975.

Unitarian Hymns

• Adams, John Quincy, "The Death of Children," *The Christian Psalter: A Collection of Psalms and Hymns for Social and Private Worship*, ed. Rev. William Parsons Lunt, for the First Church (Unitarian) in Quincy, Mass., Boston 1841. (1844 edition published by Charles C. Little and James Brown.) The hymn cited here derives from a twenty-stanza poem first published in the *Monthly Anthology and Boston Review*, Jan. 1807.

• Adams, Sarah Flower, "Nearer, My God, to Thee," *Hymns and Anthems*, ed. Rev. W. H. [or W. J.?] Fox, n.p., 1841.

• Follen, Eliza Lee (Cabot), "Remember the Slave," *Hymns, Songs, and Fables for Young People*, Crosby and Nichols, 1831. The original version is slightly different from the one cited in this book. For the latter text, *see* Navias, Eugene B., *Singing Our History.*

Foote, Henry Wilder, "American Hymn Writers and Hymns." Unpublished manuscript prepared for the Hymn Society of America, Cambridge, Mass., 1959.

• Frothingham, Nathaniel L., Communion Hymn ("Remember me, the Saviour said"), *Metrical Pieces, Translated and Original* by Nathaniel L. Frothingham, n.p., 1855. (Also included in Ellis, Rev. Rufus L., *Hymns of the Christian Church,* Little, Brown and Co., Boston, 1869.)

• ———, Communion Hymn (The Son of God gave thanks"), *Metrical Pieces, Translated and Original* by Nathaniel L. Frothingham, n.p., 1855. (Also included in Ellis, Rev. Rufus L., *Hymns of the Christian Church,* Little, Brown and Co., 1869.)

• Hedge, Frederic Henry, "Beneath Thine Hammer, Lord, I Lie," *Hymns for the Church of Christ,* ed. Rev. Frederic Henry Hedge and Rev. Frederic D. Huntington, Crosby, Nichols and Co., Boston, 1853. (The date of composition for this hymn is unknown.

Navias, Eugene B., *Singing Our History,* Unitarian Universalist Association, Boston, 1975.

• Pierpont, Rev. John, Doxology ("All glory to Thy wondrous name"), *Poems* by Rev. John Pierpont, n.p., 1823.

• ———, "O Bow Thine Ear, Eternal One!" *Hymns for the Church of Christ,* ed. Rev. Frederic Henry Hedge and Rev. Frederic D. Huntington, Crosby, Nichols and Co., Boston, 1853. This is probably the first publication of this hymn.

• Sears, Edmund Hamilton, "Calm, On the List'ning Ear." The original poem, longer than the hymn version, was published in the *Boston Observer,* 1834. (A slightly different version of the hymn, attributed to "Anonymous," appears in *The Christian Psalter: A Collection of Psalms and Hymns for Social and Private Worship,* ed. Rev. William Parsons Lunt, for the First Church (Unitarian) in Quincy, Mass., Boston, 1841.

• ———, "It Came Upon the Midnight Clear." The first publication found is in *The Hymn and Tune Book,* American Unitarian Association, Boston, 1882. This version includes a fourth verse, not cited in the present text.

• Ware, Henry, Jr., "Resurrection of Christ," *Christian Disciple,* 1817. (Also included in *Hymns for the Christian Church,* for the use of the First Church in Boston (Unitarian), Little, Brown and Co., Boston, 1869.)

❧ Index

Abbot, Ezra, 68, 231, 350
Abbot, Francis E., 32
Abraham, 17, 329
Acts of the Apostles, The, 7, 195–198,
    254, 284, 285, 288, 296, 297
Adam and Eve:
    fall of, 55, 95, 201, 271
    God revealed to, 54, 247
    innocence of, 56, 382
Adams, John Quincy, 311
Adams, Sarah Flower, 311, 318–319
Alger, William Rounseville, 350–355
Allen, Joseph, 177
American Unitarian Association, 27,
    31, 68, 136, 302, 362
    auxiliary associations of, 168–169,
        170, 173–174
    Circular prepared by, 166, 169–170,
        173
    constitution of, 164, 165, 166
    Executive Committee of, 5, 164–174,
        340, 341
    First Annual Report of, 164–174
    tracts published by, 170–171, 268
American Unitarian Biography
    (Ware), 137
*Analogy of Religion, Natural and Re-
    vealed, To the Constitution and
    Course of Nature, The* (Butler),
    13, 88
Anaxagoras, 405
Andover Theological Institution, 20,
    22, 201
Annals of the American Pulpit
    (Sprague), 22–23
Anonymous Association, 164
Antinominalism, 17, 66
*Antiquity and Revival of Unitarian
    Christianity* (Ware), 136–150
"Anti-supernaturalism in the Pulpit"
    (Hedge), 419–431
Apostle Paul, The (A. Livermore),
    277–291
Apostles, 139, 190, 192
    Acts of, 7, 195–198, 254, 284, 285,
        288, 296, 297

see also Paul the Apostle; Peter the
    Apostle
Apostles' Creed, 4, 151
Are You a Christian or a Calvinist?
    (Lowell), 402
Arianism, 10, 142–144, 221, 237
Aristotle, 7, 34, 405
Arius, 8, 11, 22, 142–144, 149, 311
Arminianism, 17, 22, 45, 61, 268, 323
Arminius, 219
Athanasius, 8, 69, 142, 143, 148, 375
atheists, 56, 324, 325, 331, 411–412,
    425, 436, 439, 444, 448, 449
Aurelian (Ware), 137
Autobiography (Dewey), 257

Backus, Isaac, 251
Bainton, Roland, 301
Bancroft, Aaron, 164, 177
Bancroft, George, 401
baptism, 195, 252–255
    of infants, 254
    as necessary for salvation, 253, 268
    origin of, 233–234
    as outward sign of faith, 252–253,
        254, 255
    as rite, 252–253, 296, 397
    as symbol, 223, 252, 295
Baptism (L. Livermore), 251–255
Baptists, 251
Barnard, Thomas, 23, 85
Bartol, Cyrus A., 31, 257
Baur, Friedrich Christian, 29, 235
Baxter, Richard, 18
Beecher, Lyman, 15
*Beginnings of Unitarianism in
    America, The* (Wright), 136
*Beitrage zur Einleitung in das Alte
    Testament* (DeWette), 29
Bell, Charles, 13
Bellows, Henry Whitney, 41, 293,
    371–397, 402, 419
Belsham, Thomas, 11, 25, 26
    as influence on Unitarianism, 78–80,
        83

"Beneath Thine Hammer, Lord, I Lie" (Hedge), 314–315
Bentley, William, 23, 151
Berkeley, George, 13–14
Biandrata, Giorgio, 10
Bible:
  as allegory, 432, 456–457
  authority of, 94, 425–426, 430, 438–440, 442–443
  as basis of Christianity, 21, 33, 35, 198, 218, 368, 442–444
  as comprehensible work, 92–93, 218–219
  contradictions in, 93–94, 97, 101, 212, 216, 290
  external evidences of, 12–13, 215
  German scientific criticism of, 4, 29, 32, 428–429, 431, 445, 453–454
  human nature as depicted in, 206–209
  interpretation of, 6, 16, 18, 29, 30–33, 58–59, 90–97, 114, 115, 150, 205, 215–218, 231–236, 240, 277–291, 295, 441–445
  language and style of, 72, 93, 103, 177–178, 206–207, 227, 233, 241–245, 280, 283–284, 286–288
  misconceptions about, 74–75, 94–96
  narrative quality of, 177–178
  rational view of, 4, 12–13, 16, 17, 92–97, 215
  as revelation, 33, 37, 65, 94, 97, 236
  teaching of, 178, 183–198, 393
  translation of, 184, 287, 288
  Trinitarianism as unauthorized by, 6, 72, 74–75, 84, 98–99, 102, 138–139, 144, 240–246
  truth of, 35, 58, 93, 96, 212, 218, 420, 421, 422–423, 430, 431, 438–440
  as Word of God, 33, 106, 108, 116, 212, 223, 236, 289, 392, 393, 395, 397, 438
  see also New Testament; Old Testament
Biddle, John, 10–11, 148
Book of Common Prayer, 153
Boston Association of Ministers, 20, 28, 31, 323
Boston Platform (1680), 22
Bowen, Francis, 31, 32, 39–40

Bradford, William, 16
Brattle Street Church, 251
Bridgewater Treatises, The (1833–36), 13, 414
Brook Farm, 28
Brownson, Orestes, 28
Bryant, William Cullen, 256, 257
Buckminster, Joseph, 32, 445
"Bulla Ineffabilis," 420
Bushnell, Horace, 268
Butler, Joseph, 13, 31, 35, 36, 88, 305

"Calm on the List'ning Ear of Night" (Sears), 231, 313–314
Calvin, John:
  heretics persecuted by, 10, 146–147, 149
  Paul's influence on, 282, 283, 289
Calvinism:
  doctrines of, 9, 16, 17, 37, 45, 118, 177, 271–272, 367
  revivalism and, 21, 22, 61, 63–64
  Unitarianism vs., 35, 67–68, 79, 80–81, 82, 145, 146, 333–339, 360, 366
Calvinistic and Socinian Systems Examined and Compared, The (Fuller), 332–333
Cambridge Platform (1648), 251
Cambridge Platonists, 14, 18, 34
Catechism for Children and Youth, 177–198
Catholic Church:
  converts to, 388, 428
  doctrines of, 215, 216, 289, 297, 367, 420
  liturgy of, 100, 140, 141, 153, 222, 258, 420, 437
  Pope as head of, 57, 117, 144, 145, 397, 401
  Protestantism vs., 145, 146, 281, 282, 294, 298, 299, 373, 378, 380–384, 388–389, 396, 397, 427, 437
Cato the Elder, 40
Channing, William Ellery, 76–135
  Baltimore Sermon of, 28, 68, 75, 77, 90–117, 177, 199–200, 332, 350, 419
  beliefs of, 37, 39, 178, 210, 290, 359, 444
  Hopkins' influence on, 22, 37, 76

influence of, 256, 277, 301, 340
Unitarianism defended by, 24, 26, 30, 31, 37–38, 76–89, 164
charity, as virtue, 85, 133, 346–349
Chauncy, Charles, 23, 41, 45, 60–66, 323
Chillingworth, William, 33
Christian Church, The (Clarke), 292–300
Christian Examiner, 137, 301, 371, 403, 441
Christian Fathers, 8, 142, 406
Christian Inquirer, 210, 371
Christianity:
  apologists for, 12–14
  as basis of human progress, 354–355
  as basis of society, 152, 226, 229, 297, 337–338, 390–391, 394, 395–396
  Bible as central to, 21, 33, 35, 198, 218, 368, 442–444
  as Church, 152–153, 254, 283, 292–300, 376, 380–381, 389–397
  as Church of Apostles vs. Church of Christ, 283, 294, 297–298
  as Church of Leaven vs. Church of Mustard-seed, 295–296
  as community, 295, 296–298
  divine origin of, 5, 31, 95, 406–407
  dogmas of, 295–296, 297, 300
  early history of, 137–144, 148–149, 258, 281, 296–298, 389
  evangelical, 4, 41, 60–66, 231, 362, 442
  evidence of, 13, 88, 406, 411–418, 455, 457
  external institution of, 376, 380–381, 389–397
  goodness as central to, 298–300
  ideal of, 298–299
  as invisible vs. visible Church, 294, 295–296, 391
  Jewish influence on, 6, 93, 99, 138, 139, 237, 278, 279, 282, 289, 296, 304–305, 310, 392, 424, 426–427, 429, 453, 456
  necessity of, 293–294
  nominal vs. real, 365–366
  persecution of, 99, 114, 117, 138, 139
  as prophetic religion, 6–7, 409
  rational justifications for, 11–15
  reform of, 22, 29, 35, 67–68, 293–300, 429–430, 443–444
  as salvation, 114, 117, 121, 152, 260, 382–383, 430–431
  social responsibility of, 340–349
  as spiritual system, 132–134
  traditions of, 420, 423, 427–429
  Unitarianism as denomination of, 4–6, 30, 77, 81, 115, 167, 169, 215–216, 217, 218, 333–334, 366–367, 371, 373–374, 419
  unity of, 218–219, 255, 297–298, 364–365
Christian Nurture (Bushnell), 268
Christian Theory of Life, The (Alger), 350–355
Christie, Francis, 221
Christology, 222
Christ the Divine Word (Sears), 231–238
Church of England, 151–152, 367
Cicero, Marcus Tullius, 40, 57, 229, 304, 405, 416
"Circles" (Emerson), 178
Clarke, James Freeman, 28, 40, 41, 267, 268, 292–300, 351, 402
Clarke, Samuel, 10, 15, 151, 153
Codman, John, 24
Collins, Anthony, 11
Common Sense philosophy, 14–15, 31, 32, 33–35, 68, 210, 239, 302
communion, *see* Lord's Supper
Comparative Moral Tendency of the Leading Doctrines of Calvinism and the Sentiments of Unitarians, The (Sparks), 332–339
comprehension, principles of, 402
Congregationalism, 221, 251, 256, 292, 301, 365, 397, 401
  Unitarianism vs., 3–4, 16, 17, 20, 21, 22, 23, 25, 27, 90, 164
conscience:
  awakening of, 113, 129, 133, 269, 285
  as faculty, 14, 111, 212, 384
  guidance by, 111, 122–123, 220, 368
  as inlet of new ideas, 39–40
  as judgment of conduct, 49, 51–52, 302–303
  reason and, 212, 214, 217

conscience: (*Cont.*)
responsibility based on, 111, 112, 438
self-love vs., 132, 273
as voice of duty, 48, 111
as voice of God, 122–123, 225, 302–303, 376, 393
consociation system, 20
Constantine the Great, 143–144, 198
Constantinople, Council of (A.D. 383), 69
contemplative quietism, 39
Contio, Giacomo, 10
conversion, religious, 22, 251, 295, 299, 388, 428
Cotton, John, 4
Cousin, Victor, 32, 34
Covenant of Grace, 17
Critical History of the Doctrine of the Future Life, A (Alger), 350
Curtis, Charles, 256
Curtis, George William, 256
Cyril of Jerusalem, 177

Damasus, Pope, 153
damnation, eternal, 6, 107, 233, 271, 328, 336, 361, 460
Davenport, John, 251
Day of Judgment, 301–310
ancient precedents for, 303–305
Christian doctrine of, 305–310
as dependent on true nature of soul, 308–310
as figurative judgment, 305–306
as self-judgment, 302–303
Day of Judgment, The (Walker), 301–310
"Death of Children, The" (J. Adams), 311–312
Deism, 11–12, 15, 35, 36, 333, 334, 335
DeWette, Wilhelm Martin Leberecht, 29
Dewey, Orville, 256–266, 293, 350
Dial, 28
Dialogues on Natural Religion (Hume), 403
Discourse on Matters Pertaining to Religion, A (Parker), 28
Discourse on the Latest Form of

Infidelity, A (Norton), 28, 432, 445–461
Doddridge, Philip, 15
Dodwell, Henry, 15
Donne, John, 13
"Doxology" (Pierpont), 317
dualism, 17, 35, 409–410
Dudley, Paul, 45, 239, 401, 403
Dunster, Henry, 251

ecclesiology, 292
Edwards, Jonathan, 16, 21, 22, 23, 37, 40, 359
election, doctrine of, 219, 251, 271–272, 289, 336
Elements of Religion and Morality in the Form of a Catechism (Channing and Thacher), 177
Eliot, Charles William, 239
Eliot, T. S., 267
Eliot, William Greenleaf, Jr., 38, 85, 239, 267–276
Ellis, George E., 36
Ellis, Rufus, 231
Emerson, Ralph Waldo:
Divinity School Address of (1838), 3–4, 28, 311, 419, 432, 433, 441, 445
as exponent of Transcendentalism, 4, 27–28, 32, 33, 41, 178, 292
Enneads (Plotinus), 29
Enthusiasm Described and Caution'd Against (Chauncey), 60
Epicureans, 7–8, 325, 351–352, 355, 417, 418
Episcopalians, 151, 216, 373, 401
Epistles:
Gospels vs., 283, 285, 288, 290
see also Paul the Apostle
Ernesti, Johann August, 232
ethics, Christian, 8, 14, 40, 308, 426
Eusebius, 139–140
Evangelical Missionary Society, The, 173
Evangelical Obedience (Mayhew), 323–331
Evarts, Jeremiah, 25–26
Everett, Charles Carroll, 32, 419
Everett, Edward, 200
Evidences of Christianity, The (Paley), 13, 88, 406

Evidences of the Genuineness of the Gospels (Norton), 67
evolution, 221–222

faith:
  affirmation of, 30, 330–331, 416–417, 426
  doubt vs., 385–386, 458
  in early Christianity, 297–298
  evidence as basis of, 216–217, 450
  justification by, 282, 289, 290–291
  maintenance of, 64–65, 218, 459–460
  reason vs., 48, 49–51, 54, 215, 216–217
  suspense of, 371–397
Faith Once Delivered to the Saints, The (Beecher), 15, 170
fanaticism, 95, 96, 128
Farley, Frederick A., 4, 118
fatalism, 352–353
Feathers Petition, 11
Fichte, Johann Gottlieb, 34, 267
First Annual Report of the Executive Committee, 164–174
Follen, Elizabeth Lee Cabot, 311, 317–318
Forrest, Edwin, 350
Fourth Gospel the Heart of Christ, The (Sears), 232
Francis, Converse, 32
Freeman, James, 23, 151, 292
Frothingham, Nathaniel L., 4, 311, 315–316
Frothingham, Octavius Brooks, 19, 68
Fuller, Andrew, 332–333
Fuller, Margaret, 28
Furness, William Henry, 232, 403

Gannett, Ezra Stiles, 25, 38–39
Gay, Ebenezer, 23, 45–59, 323
Gay, Peter, 9
General Repository and Review, 67
"Gloria Patri," 153
God:
  anger of, 51, 206, 271, 337
  attributes of, 5–6, 16, 47, 53–54, 68, 71, 73, 94, 105–106, 115, 119–120, 122, 123, 124, 127, 128, 129, 133, 244, 327, 432
  authority of, 122–123, 454, 455–456
  benevolence of, 35, 51, 75, 105–106, 107, 109, 112–113, 125
  Calvinistic view of, 16, 37
  Christ as Son of, 4–5, 15, 31, 38, 69–75, 81, 100, 102, 121, 126, 142, 181, 183, 219, 227, 289, 326–327
  commandments of, 113, 178, 186–187
  compassion of, 307–308
  as concept in New Testament, 37, 98–99, 102–103, 119, 121, 126
  conscience as voice of, 122–123, 225, 302–303, 376, 393
  conscious existence of, 435–436
  as Creator, 3, 54, 55–56, 120, 123, 124–129, 212, 223, 243, 352, 433
  existence of, 13, 46, 217, 409, 411–418, 422, 423, 424, 428, 435–436, 445–461
  as Father, 37, 69–75, 81, 98, 99, 100, 103, 106, 108, 126, 135, 138, 142, 149, 212, 213, 220, 222, 225, 226, 229, 233–236, 243–247, 288, 326–327, 342, 345, 353, 370, 388, 415, 433, 437, 456
  as First Cause, 100
  forgiveness of, 51, 107, 227
  holiness of, 224–225
  human conception of, 7, 94, 122–123, 393, 406, 411–413, 425, 436
  impersonal vs. personal, 352–355, 424, 433–440
  as infinite, 50, 124, 125
  irresistible influence of, 111–112, 271
  justice of, 105–106, 109–110, 113, 154, 206, 208–209, 272, 308–310, 427
  knowledge of, 48–49, 94, 122–123, 202, 228
  love of, 6, 16, 36, 37, 38, 106, 112, 120, 122
  mercy of, 58, 106, 110, 121, 154, 208, 225, 228, 233, 272, 432
  as Mind, 122, 236–237, 278, 385
  misconceptions about, 106–108
  as moral governor, 134, 324, 325, 415–416, 433, 434
  moral perfection of, 105–108, 112, 123, 201, 202, 208, 359, 415–416, 434

God: *(Cont.)*
    Nature as work of, 54, 55–56, 120,
        123, 124–125, 130, 178–179, 247–
        248, 250, 414–415, 434, 451
    obedience to, 17, 179–181, 205, 323–
        331, 382
    omnipotence of, 17, 74, 105, 119,
        127, 359
    as omniscient, 74, 361
    ontological proof of, 412–413
    perfection of, 47–48, 53, 105–108,
        112, 122, 123, 124, 127, 328, 338,
        434
    as progenitor of kindred beings, 126,
        127–128
    Providence of, 35, 182–183, 223,
        250, 342, 354, 391
    purity of, 113, 121, 127
    relationship between human nature
        and, 47–50, 55, 75, 108, 111–112,
        118–135, 208–209, 246–250, 361,
        381, 389, 438
    soul as concern of, 121, 220, 223–
        224, 245, 246–250, 270, 275, 307,
        383
    as sovereign, 125, 326, 359, 375
    as spiritual energy, 123–125
    as Supreme Being, 104, 105, 119,
        123, 214, 224, 433–440, 446
    teleological proof of, 413–415
    transcendence of, 7, 35
    ubiquity of, 125, 224
    union between Christ and, 81, 103,
        226–227, 230, 236, 237
    unity of, 15, 97–100, 105, 108, 138,
        169, 214, 327
    virtue as dependent on, 7, 52, 86–
        87, 105–106, 121, 122–123, 433–
        434, 437–438
    will of, 7, 48–49, 87, 324
    wisdom of, 18, 50, 52, 87, 96–97,
        106, 120, 123, 124, 127–128
    worship of, 48, 50, 52, 99–100, 108,
        126–127, 128, 129, 153, 154, 182,
        214, 298, 336, 434, 437
Goethe, Johann Wolfgang von, 247
Gospels:
    acceptance of, 253, 279, 425–426
    Epistles vs., 283, 285, 288, 290
    as expression of divine justice, 306,
        307, 309, 346

    precepts of, 62, 149–150, 190–191,
        208, 325, 329–330, 338, 346, 438
    propagation of, 83, 85, 86, 116–117,
        166, 173, 195, 285, 300
    sufficiency of, 390–391
    unity of, 232
    see also Paul the Apostle; Peter the
        Apostle
grace:
    as Christian state, 407–408
    dispensation of, 17, 226, 329–330,
        427
    effectual, 289
    man's dependence on, 16, 36, 223,
        227, 302
    as means of salvation, 53, 223, 230,
        270, 271, 282, 289
    predestined, 36, 271–272, 404
    reason dependent on, 58
Great Awakening, 22, 45, 60–66, 251
Greenwood, Francis William Pitt, 39,
        40, 152
Griffin, Edward Dorr, 24

Hale, Edward Everett, 341
*Half-Century of the Unitarian Contro-
        versy, A* (Ellis), 36, 441
Half-Way Covenant (1662), 22, 251
Hamilton, Alexander, 19
Hamilton, William, 31, 32, 34, 239,
        386
*Hand, Its Mechanism and Vital
        Endowments at Evincing Design,
        The* (Bell), 13
Harnack, Adolf, 9
Hartley, David, 11, 14
Harvard College, as Unitarian institu-
        tion, 19, 20–21, 23–24, 32, 76, 88,
        164, 199, 401
Harvard Divinity School, 20–21, 67,
        177, 277
Hazlitt, William, 151
Hedge, Frederic Henry, 30, 32, 41, 311,
        314–315, 371–372, 401–431
Hedge, Levi, 401
Hegesippus, 139–140
Hepworth, George H., 293, 350, 372
Herbert, Edward, 11–12, 14, 34, 333
heresy:
    in early Christianity, 139–140, 143
    suppression of, 63–65, 66, 115

Unitarianism as, 3–4, 27, 83–84, 87,
216–216, 218, 442–444, 445
Hilliard, Timothy, 199
History of the Cross of Christ (Alger),
350
History of the First Church in Boston
(Ellis), 441
History of Unitarianism (Wilbur),
10
Holley, Horace, 24
Hollis Chair of Divinity, 23–24
Holyoke, Edward, 401
Holy Spirit:
as comforter, 242–243
definition of, 240
in New Testament, 241–245, 296
as part of Trinity, 37, 69–75, 97–98,
142, 240–246
personification of, 242, 244, 246
as sanctifier, 71, 72, 128–129, 207,
219, 222, 240, 242, 243–244, 246–
250, 271, 389, 391, 392–395, 396,
397, 424
as symbolic, 239–250
Holy Spirit, The (Peabody), 239–250
Hooker, Richard, 10
Hopkins, Mark, 402
Hopkins, Samuel, 22, 34, 37, 40, 76
Howard, Simeon, 23, 85
Howe, Daniel Walker, 311
human destiny, 35, 179, 220, 351–355
human nature:
as animalistic, 56
as aware of good and evil, 55, 120,
203, 209, 224, 228, 265, 271–272,
337, 352, 409–410, 451–452
as depicted in Bible, 206–209
as depraved, 5, 16, 17, 36, 106–108,
127, 199–209, 214, 219, 271–272,
288, 289, 333–339, 383
dignity of, 133, 134, 333
as divine, 47–48, 55–56, 118–135,
223, 235
as drawn towards God, 49–50, 120,
131, 381, 438
as essentially good, 5, 15–16, 34,
121, 201–202, 333
as fallible, 95–97, 114, 115, 211–212
free will of, 49, 129, 132, 133, 135,
220, 330, 338, 354, 368–369, 381–
382, 394, 417

as inclined towards sensual pleasures, 56, 57, 224
as infinite, 124–125
innate moral and intellectual powers
of, 32, 35, 49–51, 53, 96–97, 119,
122–123, 204, 223, 302, 414, 415–
416, 430, 451
perfectibility of, 108, 111–112, 113,
118–135
relationship between God's nature
and, 47–50, 55, 75, 108, 111–112,
118–135, 208–209, 246–250, 361,
381, 389, 438
Hume, David, 13–14, 33–34, 403, 423,
450
Huntington, F. D., 293
Huntington, Joshua, 24
Hutchinson, Anne, 251
Hutchison, William R., 293
Hymn, Tune, and Service Book, 252
hymns, Unitarian, 311–319
hypostatic union, 74, 237

idolatry, 100, 114, 235
Incarnation, The (Stearns), 221–230
*Inquiry into the Foundation, Evidences
and Truths of Religion, An*
(Ware), 199
institutions, doctrine of, 392–393
"It Came Upon a Midnight Clear"
(Sears), 231, 311, 313

Jesus Christ:
Atonement of, 6, 29, 36, 38–39, 40–
41, 103–104, 108–111, 219, 295,
296
authority of, 455–456, 457
baptism of, 252
crucifixion of, 104–105, 108–111,
113–114, 193–194, 226, 228, 259,
306
divinity of, 15, 31, 38, 74–75, 78,
95, 100–105, 140–141, 178, 226–
227, 233, 234, 235, 261, 280
dual nature of, 74–75, 100–105,
235–236, 237
earthly mission of, 108–111, 127,
222–223, 225, 229, 449, 455, 456
as example of virtue, 110–111, 113–
114, 116, 130, 234, 260–261, 262–
263, 265, 295

Jesus Christ: (*Cont.*)
    forgiveness of sins accomplished by,
        108–111
    as fulfillment of divine plan, 227–
        229, 236
    God appeased by death of, 109–110
    as historical figure, 4, 29, 265
    human nature of, 74–75, 79, 100–
        105, 110, 140, 141, 178, 226–227,
        232, 234, 237, 261, 375, 425–426
    idolatry of, 235–236
    as immaculate excellence, 260–261
    incarnation of, 104, 221–230, 234,
        235, 328, 409, 420
    as judge, 233, 237–238, 306, 309–
        310, 327, 368, 370
    life of, 190–198, 262–263, 265, 288,
        396, 454–455
    as light of world, 228–229
    as light to Gentiles, 58
    as Logos, 140, 141, 225–226, 228,
        230, 232–238, 406
    love and mercy of, 104, 113–114,
        115, 127
    mediation of, 108–111, 114, 118,
        126, 135, 153, 226, 229, 325, 328,
        330–331, 411
    as Messiah, 31, 71, 79, 108–111,
        192, 195, 219, 222–227, 236, 237,
        243, 244, 252, 253, 255, 265–266,
        309, 327, 329, 410–411
    miracles of, 192, 219, 229, 235, 423,
        449–457
    parables of, 295–296
    as part of Trinity, 69–75, 97–98, 237
    pre-existence of, 38, 237–238
    as prophet, 141, 234, 295
    remembrance of, 258, 259–260, 262,
        263, 264
    resurrection of, 114, 194, 223, 229,
        235, 296, 328, 422–423
    Second Coming of, 53, 63, 183, 233,
        263
    as Son of God, 4–5, 15, 31, 38, 69–
        75, 81, 100, 102, 121, 126, 142,
        181, 183, 219, 227, 289, 326–327
    as subordinate being, 4–5, 70–71,
        102, 138, 375
    sufferings of, 7, 102–103, 104, 108–
        111, 113–114, 181, 226, 228–229,
        262, 263

    teachings of, 40, 84, 115–116, 133,
        138, 149, 153, 182–183, 212–213,
        229, 232, 253, 255, 263, 290, 295–
        296, 460–461
    two minds of, 101–102, 104
    unified nature of, 100–105, 108
    union between God and, 81, 103,
        226–227, 230, 236, 237
    veneration of, 3, 108, 113–115, 235–
        236, 258, 297, 457
John the Apostle, 197–198
    Gospel of, 120, 140, 190, 231–238,
        242, 297
    Paul compared to, 278, 280, 281, 287
John the Baptist, 191–192, 252
Jouffroy, Théodore, 34
Judaism:
    as influence on Christianity, 6, 93,
        99, 138, 139, 237, 278, 279, 282,
        289, 296, 304–305, 310, 392, 424,
        426–427, 429, 453, 456
    as prophetic religion, 6, 409
    traditions of, 252–254, 328–329, 405
Judas Iscariot, 193, 258
Julian the Apostate, 8

Kant, Immanuel, 32, 33–34, 410, 413,
    415, 430
Kay, James, 171
King James Bible, 287, 288
King's Chapel, 23, 25, 151–152
King's Chapel Liturgy, The, 151–163,
    200, 257
Kirkland, John Thornton, 24, 90
Knickerbocker Magazine, 137
Koran, 306

Lardner, Nathaniel, 15, 148
Latest Form of Infidelity, The (Nor-
    ton), 67
Lathrop, Joseph, 24
Leben Jesu, Das (Strauss), 29
Lectures on Christian Doctrine
    (Peabody), 239, 240
Letter from a Gentleman in Boston
    (Chauncey), 60
*Letters Addressed to Trinitarians and
    Calvinists* (Ware), 200
Letters to Unitarians (Woods), 200
*Letter to the Rev. Samuel C. Thacher,
    A* (Channing), 76–89

Leverett, John, 23
Likeness to God (Channing), 118–135
Lindsey, Theophilus, 11, 25, 26, 151, 153
Livermore, Abiel Abbot, 210–220, 277–291
Livermore, Leonard Jarvis, 251–255, 293
Locke, John, 10, 12, 14, 34, 148, 210, 213, 308
Longfellow, Henry Wadsworth, 221
Lord's Prayer, 155
Lord's Supper, 257–266
  hymns for, 315–316
  as means of salvation, 260, 265–266, 268
  origin of, 258, 296
  as profession of Christianity, 258–259
  as remembrance of Christ, 258, 259–260, 262, 263, 264
  as sacrament, 3, 193, 257, 298, 299, 397
  as symbol, 295
Lothrop, Samuel Kirkland, 29–30
Lowell, John, Jr., 402
Luther, Martin, 9, 66, 90–91, 149
  hymns composed by, 311, 401–402
  Paul's influence on, 277, 282, 283, 290
Lutheranism:
  doctrines of, 9, 64, 66, 144, 146, 177, 367, 443–444
  in Reformation, 401–402

McColgan, Daniel T., 340
Mansel, Henry L., 32
Mary, Virgin, 100, 140, 141, 222, 420, 437
Mather, Cotton, 22
Mayhew, Jonathan, 23, 45, 323–331
meditation, religious, 260–265, 280
"Mighty Fortress Is Our God, A" (Luther and Hedge), 311, 401–402
Miller, Perry, 18, 61, 402, 403, 441
Miller, Samuel, 332, 333
Milton, John, 10, 148, 213, 378
ministers:
  controversy avoided by, 81, 82–83, 88, 116
  duties of, 61–66, 83, 85, 91, 116–117, 118, 128, 430, 460–461
  as examples of morality, 116–117, 130–135, 425–426, 427
  preaching by, 116, 131–134, 229–230, 300, 334–335, 379, 397
  proselytizing by, 82–83
  training of, 19–20, 88, 164, 402
  vows of, 62
missionaries, 171–172, 298–299, 362, 373–374, 376
monism, 9, 17
Monthly Anthology, 25
Monthly Religious Magazine, 231
morality:
  commitment to, 40, 115, 346, 423
  as force, 124, 129
  laws of, 325–326, 406, 409, 415–416
  metaphysics vs., 359–361
  ministers as examples of, 116–117, 130–135, 425–426, 427
  nature of, 49–50, 106, 212
  perfection of, 118
  perversion of, 107–108, 440
  responsibility and, 273–274
Mormons, 420
Morning Prayer, 152, 154–163
Morse, Jedidiah, 24, 25–26, 301
  Unitarianism attacked by, 76–89
Mystery Hid from Ages and Generations, The (Chauncy), 61
mysticism, 6, 9, 39, 95, 113, 120, 215

National Unitarian Conference (1865), 27, 31, 41, 165, 292, 371, 402, 419
natural laws, 325–326, 388, 416, 440, 449, 453
Natural Religion (Hedge), 401–418
Natural Religion as Distinguished from Revealed (Gay), 45–59
"Nature" (Emerson), 28
Nature of Man, The (Ware, Sr.), 199–209
"Nearer, My God, to Thee" (S. Adams), 311, 318–319
New Light Divinity, 21, 22
New Testament:
  Christ as depicted in, 102–103, 110–111

New Testament: (*Cont.*)
  God as concept in, 37, 98–99, 102–103, 119, 121, 126
  Holy Spirit as depicted in, 241–245, 296
  human nature in, 207–209
  language of, 241–245, 303, 306, 308–309, 346
  sin as defined by, 40, 207–208
  soul as described in, 244–245
  teaching of, 137–138, 183, 189, 190–198
  see also Epistles; Gospels
Newton, Isaac, 10, 12, 148, 213
Nice, Council of (A.D. 325), 69, 142, 143, 220
Nicene Creed, 4, 151, 375
Nicodemus, 207, 253
Norton, Andrews, 137, 164
  Biblical criticism of, 32, 277
  Transcendentalism attacked by, 27, 28, 432, 445–461
  Unitarianism defended by, 30, 31, 67–75, 200, 231
Noyes, George, 32, 277

"O, Bow Thine Ear, Eternal One" (Pierpont), 311, 316–317
"Objections to Unitarian Christianity Considered," 170
Ochino, Bernardino, 10
Old Testament:
  God as depicted in, 37, 310
  interpretation of, 40, 304–305, 438
  teaching of, 183–189
Old World and the New, The (Dewey), 256
On the Elevation of the Poor (Tuckerman), 346–349
On the Uses of Communion (Dewey), 256–266
Osgood, Samuel, 293, 350
Oxford Declaration, 421, 430

Paley, William, 12–13, 15, 31, 35, 88, 200, 351, 402, 406, 413
Palfrey, John Gorham, 32, 90, 239
Panoplist, 25, 76, 77, 78
pantheism, 432, 448
Parker, Isaac, 26

Parker, Theodore, 350
  Biblical criticism of, 29, 31–32
  unorthodox views of, 4, 19, 28, 29–30, 31, 41, 277, 419, 423
Paul the Apostle:
  as Apostle to Gentiles, 278, 279, 281, 283
  as compared to other apostles, 7, 278, 280, 281–282, 285, 296
  conversion of, 195–196, 279, 280
  epistolary style of, 280, 281, 283–285, 286–287, 288
  as forerunner of Protestantism, 281, 282
  imprisonment of, 139
  influence of, 17, 277, 281, 282, 283, 289, 290
  interpretation of, 277–291
  obscurity of, 286–287
  personality of, 280, 281, 282, 284
  teachings of, 8, 13, 46–47, 84, 94, 196–197, 207, 219, 224, 229, 244, 253, 277–291, 297, 305, 306, 326, 353, 406–407
pauperism, 342–343, 347, 348
Peabody, Andrew Preston, 4–5, 36, 38, 239–250
Peabody, Ephraim, 39
Peabody, Francis Greenwood, 419
Pearson, Eliphalet, 23, 24
Pentecost, 71, 72, 93, 141, 296
Perfect Life, The (Channing), 39
"Personality of the Deity, The" (Ware, Jr.), 432–440
Peter the Apostle:
  life of, 193, 196, 407–408
  Paul compared to, 278, 280, 281, 282, 296
  teachings of, 196, 278, 297, 309, 330
Phaedrus (Plato), 39
"Philosophical Difficulties in the 'Unitarian Controversy'" (Ware, Sr.), 359–361
philosophy:
  Common Sense, 14–15, 31, 32, 33–35, 68, 210, 239, 302
  empiricist, 13–14, 31, 33–34, 403, 423, 450
  German Romantic, 29, 30–33, 68, 235, 239, 277, 302
  Hegelian, 235

of historical progress, 15–16, 35–36, 301, 354–355
Kantian, 32, 33–34, 410, 413, 415, 430
Lockean, 10, 12, 14, 34, 148, 210, 213, 308, 402
medieval, 6, 9, 144, 148–149
Neo-Platonic, 7, 10, 29, 33
Platonic, 7, 10, 14, 34, 39, 141, 405
rationalist, 11–15
religious, 6, 33, 115, 404–405
secularization of, 8–9, 11
sensationalist, 12, 13–14, 302
Pierpont, John, 311, 316–317
pietistic movement, 22
piety:
　as non-denominational, 79, 82–83, 299, 364–365
　reason vs., 113, 378
　Unitarian conception of, 39, 105, 112, 115, 124
Pilgrims, 16–18
Pius IX, Pope, 420
Plato, 7, 34, 39, 141, 405
Plotinus, 7, 18, 29
Plutarch, 409
political economy, 344, 346, 348
"popery," 57, 117, 144, 145, 397, 401
positivists, 386, 403
prayer, 250, 265, 271
predestination, 6, 17, 107–108, 351
Presbyterians, 10, 21, 90, 335, 336, 401
Price, Richard, 15
Priestley, Joseph, 11, 14
Prince, John, 23
Princeton Review, 30, 67
Principles and Results of the Ministry at Large in Boston, The (Tuckerman), 341–346
progress:
　as philosophy of history, 15–16, 35–36, 301, 354–355
　in theology, 19–20, 429–431
"Progress and Present State of the Unitarian Churches in America" (Belsham), 25
Protestantism, 96, 117, 198
　Catholicism vs., 145, 146, 281, 282, 294, 298, 299, 373, 378, 380–384, 388–389, 396, 397, 427, 437
　Paul as forerunner of, 281, 282

secular tendencies in, 373, 376–381, 395
Unitarianism as leading edge of, 362–370, 373
in unreligious age, 379–381, 385–389, 390
see also individual denominations
punishment:
　on Day of Judgment, 301–310
　as eternal damnation, 6, 107, 233, 271, 328, 336, 361, 460
　future, 13, 219, 307, 308, 460
　of sin, 107, 109–110, 111, 180–181, 182
Puritan Recorder, 441
Puritans, Unitarianism influenced by, 6, 16–18, 19, 21, 41, 257, 364

Quakers, 254
Quarterly Review, 28

Racovian Catechism, 9–10, 11, 145
reason:
　conscience and, 212, 214, 217
　education as cultivation of, 55, 211
　emotion vs., 95–96, 132, 134, 202, 203, 213, 265, 273
　faith vs., 48, 49–51, 54, 215, 216–217
　as fallible, 211–212
　as gift of God, 58, 211, 324
　perversion of, 95, 211–212
　piety vs., 113, 378
　revelation vs., 17–18, 74–75, 92–97, 122, 123, 210–220, 390, 407, 459
Reasonableness of Christianity, The (Locke), 12, 210
Reason and Revelation (A. Livermore), 210–220
Reason in Religion (Hedge), 30, 402
Reformation:
　in England, 10–11
　as influence on Unitarianism, 6, 9, 10–11, 17, 144–148
　as interpretation of Bible, 217–218, 368
　Lutheranism in, 401–402
　origins of, 66, 198, 363, 389
　sacraments excluded by, 258
regeneration, 17, 39, 40, 225, 267–276
　doctrine of, 269, 271–272

regeneration (*Cont.*)
  necessity of, 334, 452
  outward signs of, 269, 275–276
  as radical change, 273–274
  in revivals, 268, 269–270
Regeneration (Eliot), 267–276
Reid Thomas, 31, 34, 302
religion:
  as adoration of God, 126–127, 128, 129
  anti-supernaturalism in, 419–431, 452–453, 455
  common life blended with, 128–129, 131
  comparative, 4, 277, 292, 407–410
  duties of, 51, 55, 58
  experience of, 224, 250, 264, 274, 279
  history of, 31, 424–425, 437
  natural vs. revealed, 12, 15, 45–59, 128, 129, 382–383, 389, 401–418
  pagan worship vs., 54, 57, 94, 105, 304, 324, 352, 354–355
  personal, 294, 366, 393–394
  philosophy of, 6, 33, 115, 404–405
  practice of, 49, 260
  prophetic, 6–7, 409
  as "reasonable service," 213, 215
  revelation as guide for, 57–58, 390–391, 424, 446–447, 454, 457–458
  rituals of, 178, 257, 258, 328–329, 397
  science vs., 131–132, 378–379, 381 420, 424–425, 427–428
  sects in, 63–64, 65, 81, 94, 115, 363, 375, 377, 380
  separation of government and, 116–117
  survival of, 379–381
  teaching of, 19–20, 132, 177–198, 215, 430
  truth of, 118–119, 126–127, 129, 260, 294–295, 447, 459, 460
  universal, 408–409
"Remember the Slave" (Follen), 311, 317–318
Republic (Plato), 303–304
"Resurrection of Christ" (Ware, Jr.), 311, 312–313
revelation:
  as guide for religion, 57–58, 390–391, 424, 446–447, 454, 457–458

  in history of world, 56–57, 228
  impersonality of God vs., 438–439
  necessity of, 35, 55, 457–458
  reason vs., 17–18, 74–75, 92–97, 122, 123, 210–220, 390, 407, 459
"Revelation of Jesus to His Age and the Ages, The" (Parker), 4
revivals, religious, opposition to, 21–22, 23, 60–66, 268, 269–270
Reynolds, Grindall, 221
Ripley, George, 28, 441
Routley, Eric, 311
Royce, Josiah, 32

sacraments, 178, 257, 258, 397
  see also baptism; Lord's Supper
Sargent, John T., 28
Satan, 17, 62, 64, 121
Saybrook Platform (1708), 251
Schleiermacher, Friedrich, 268
Scottish Realists, 14–15, 31, 32, 33–35, 68, 210, 239, 302
Scriptures, *see* Bible
Sears, Edmund Hamilton, 221, 231–238, 311, 313–314, 372
Seasonable Thoughts on the State of Religion in New-England (Chauncy), 60–66
Sequel to "The Suspense of Faith," A (Bellows), 372
Sermon on the Mount, 232, 233, 289, 309–310
Servetus, Michael, 10, 146–147, 149
"Sewall's Sermon on Human Depravity," 170
Shackford, Charles C., 28
Sherlock, William, 200
Sidney, Algernon, 10
sin:
  in children, 204–206, 273
  debt of, 109, 133
  forgiveness of, 51, 107, 108–111, 154–155, 181, 225, 270–271, 354
  God's hatred of, 122–123, 228
  malignity of, 133
  as natural state, 51, 52–53, 55, 121–122, 202, 207, 225, 271, 273
  original, 118, 201, 203, 252, 271–272
  punishment of, 107, 109–110, 111, 180–181, 182
  remission of, 108–111, 222

repentance of, 40, 154, 338
responsibility for, 36
universality of, 207, 208, 337
Sober Thoughts on the State of the Times (Ware, Jr.), 362–370
social work, 340–349
Society for the Promotion of Christian Knowledge, Piety and Charity, The, 173
Socinians, 11, 25–26, 33
Socinus, Laelius, 9, 11, 144, 145, 221
Socrates, 40, 413
Some Thoughts Concerning the Present Revival of Religion in New-England (Edwards), 60
soul:
  as aided by Holy Spirit, 128–129
  as arbiter of belief, 219–220
  birth of, 223–224, 274
  body vs., 272–273, 274, 275
  as concern of God, 121, 220, 223–224, 245, 246–250, 270, 275, 307, 383
  debasement of, 133
  as described in New Testament, 244–245
  final judgment of, 301–310
  immortality of, 35, 114, 126, 181, 212, 219, 225, 305, 307, 352, 353, 406, 418, 422, 423, 453, 457, 459, 460
  infinite nature of, 124–125, 132, 248
  moral sense of, 123, 213, 219–220, 272–273
  perfection of, 128, 274, 275–276
  struggles of, 133, 265, 274–275
Sources of Consolation in Human Life (Alger), 350
Sozzini, Faustus, 9–10, 144
Sparks, Jared, 26, 90, 332–339
Spencer, Herbert, 221–222
Spinoza, Baruch, 448–449
Sprague, William B., 22–23
Statement of Reasons for Not Believing the Doctrines of Trinitarians, A (Norton), 67–75, 200, 445
Stearns, Oliver, 221–230
Stebbins, Rufus P., 221
Stewart, Dugald, 14, 31, 302
Stoics, 7–8, 413, 418

Stowe, Harriet Beecher, 19
Strauss, David Friedrich, 29
Stuart, Moses, 3, 27, 68, 75, 91, 200, 256, 444, 445
Sunday Schools, 177, 178, 397
Suspense of Faith, The (Bellows), 371–397, 419
Swedenborg, Emanuel, 282

Tappan, David, 23, 199
Taylor, Nathaniel W., 200
Ten Commandments, 178, 186–187
Ten Great Religions (Clarke), 292
Thacher, Samuel C., 76–89, 177, 340
Thayer, Nathaniel, 177, 332
theism, 324–328, 412, 416, 422–425
theocracy, 304
theology:
  anthropocentric vs. theocentric, 359–361
  controversies in, 362–363, 366, 402, 447–448
  in Germany, 448–449
  liberal, 132, 292–293
  modern, 287, 288, 290, 366, 447
  natural, 32, 35, 49, 95, 351, 402, 403, 419
  oriental, 352–353
  progressive, 19–20, 429–431
  radical, 421–422, 428, 429, 430
Theophylact, 140–141
Thirty-nine Articles, 151–152
Ticknor, George, 401
Tillotson, John, 12
Toleration Act (1689), 10
Transcendental Club, 30, 292, 302, 402–403, 419, 441
Transcendentalism:
  Emerson as exponent of, 4, 27–28, 32, 33, 41, 178, 292
  as Hellenic revival, 28–29
  Norton's attack on, 27, 28, 432, 445–461
  as reform movement, 22, 29, 35, 67–68, 293, 443–444
  Unitarianism vs., 4, 5, 27–33, 34, 67–68, 239, 292, 302, 371, 385, 396, 442 461
Transcendentalist Ministers, The (Hutchison), 293
Transcendentalists, The (Miller), 441

"Transient and Permanent in Christianity, The" (Parker), 28
Translation of the Gospels (Norton), 67
transubstantiation, 96, 144
Trinitarianism:
   ancient doctrine of, 69–70, 139–144, 282, 289
   arguments against, 67–75, 215, 216, 219, 246–247
   Christ as part of, 69–75, 97–98, 237
   devotion impaired by, 99–100, 221, 296
   historical opposition to, 9, 10–11, 15
   Holy Spirit as part of, 37, 69–75, 97–98, 142, 240–246
   modal or nominal, 71, 73, 221
   modification of, 70–71
   practical influence of, 99–100
   as unauthorized by Scripture, 6, 72, 74–75, 84, 98–99, 102, 138–139, 144, 240–246
   Unitarianism vs., 78–80, 83–84, 97–100, 332, 375, 420
Trinity:
   covenant of, 241
   as distinct persons, 69, 71–73, 97–98, 99–100, 215, 237
   and duality of Christ's nature, 74–75, 100–105
   as equal divinities, 71, 72–73, 84, 100
True Reasons (Morse), 24
Tuckerman, Joseph, 340–349
Tyscovicious, 145–146

Unitarian Christianity (Channing), 90–117
Unitarian Conscience, The (Howe), 311
Unitarianism:
   Belsham's influence on, 78–80, 83
   Calvinism vs., 35, 67–68, 79, 80–81, 82, 145, 146, 333–339, 360, 366
   as Christian denomination, 4–6, 30, 77, 81, 115, 167, 169, 215–216, 217, 218, 333–334, 366–367, 371, 373–374, 419
   churches formed by, 26–27, 167–168, 172, 257

   before Civil War, 32, 41, 67, 152
   as community, 362–370
   confessional position of, 5, 20, 30–32, 154, 155, 372
   Congregationalism vs., 3–4, 16, 17, 20, 21, 22, 23, 25, 27, 90, 164
   conservative vs. liberal, 21–22, 30–31, 77, 91, 106–107, 177, 199–200, 210, 231, 268, 300, 302, 365–366, 402, 419, 420–421, 442–443
   controversy about, 11, 16, 22–27, 37, 76–89, 91, 177, 332, 359–377, 402, 441–442
   defense of, 24, 26, 30, 31, 37–38, 67–89, 164, 200, 231
   definition of, 4–6, 37–38, 78, 81
   doctrines of, 18–41, 83–84, 88, 92, 97–116, 137, 333–339, 374–375
   as early Christian belief, 137–144, 148–149
   in England, 10–15
   Enlightenment ideas and, 6, 8, 14–15, 16–17
   as evangelical religion, 4, 231, 362, 442
   founding of, 164–174
   Hellenic influence on, 6, 7–8, 10, 14, 33, 34, 41
   as heresy, 3–4, 27, 83–84, 87, 215–216, 218, 442–444, 445
   history of, 6, 22–27, 136–150
   intellectual background of, 6–16
   Judaic precedent for, 138, 139
   as leading edge of Protestantism, 362–370, 373
   as Liberal Faith, 3, 4, 6, 9, 11, 15–16, 18–25, 33, 67, 79, 90, 118, 136, 210, 268, 292–293, 350, 378
   liturgy of, 151–163
   in Middle and Western states, 31, 166–167, 168, 172, 210
   misinterpretation of, 78–80, 91, 446–448, 452, 454, 455
   mystic strain in, 39, 120
   in New England, 3–4, 10, 15, 16–18, 19, 21, 26, 41
   opposition to, 22–27, 76–89, 142–147, 333–336
   ostracism of, 78, 83–85
   Platonic tradition and, 7, 10, 14, 34
   in Poland, 9–10, 145, 146, 149

public opinion of, 369–370
Puritan background of, 6, 16–18, 19, 21, 41, 257, 364
rationalism in, 6, 9, 14–16, 17–18, 22, 33–34, 41, 210, 215–216, 311, 335–336, 376, 377–378, 420–431
Reformation as influence on, 6, 9, 10–11, 17, 144–148
as religion of New Testament, 137–138
as religion of upper class, 19, 86
Renaissance as influence on, 6, 8–10, 15, 35, 118
righteousness of, 85–88
Standing Order of, 77, 90, 164, 251, 401
supposed deception practiced by, 78, 80–83
Transcendentalism vs., 4, 5, 27–33, 34, 67–68, 239, 292, 302, 371, 385, 396, 442–461
Trinitarianism vs., 78–80, 83–84, 97–100, 332, 375, 420
"Unitarianism, Transcendentalism and The Bible" (Ellis), 441–444
Unitarian Miscellany, 332
"Unitarian's Answer," 170

virtue:
as benevolence, 114–115, 130, 345–346
charity as, 85, 133, 346–349
Christ as example of, 110–111, 113–114, 116, 130, 234, 260–261, 262–263, 265, 295
as dependent on God, 7, 52, 86–87, 105–106, 121, 122–123, 433–434, 437–438
inculcation of, 131–132

nature of, 111–116, 128, 203
trials of, 86–87, 249, 345
vice compared to, 203, 303, 307, 325, 347
zeal for truth as, 113, 114–115

Walker, James, 5, 31, 32, 301–310
Ware, Henry, Jr., 27, 28, 311, 312–313, 362–370, 432–440
Ware, Henry, Sr., 24, 76, 90, 136, 199–209, 333, 359–361
Ware, William, 136–150
Watts, Isaac, 81, 148
Weber, Max, 351
Webster, Daniel, 19
Weiss, John, 32
Western Conference of Unitarians, 31, 210, 267, 268
Western Messenger, 268, 292
Westminster Catechisms, 177, 201, 220
Whately, Richard, 13
Whitehead, Alfred North, 7
Wilberforce, William, 27
Wilbur, Earl Morse, 10
Willard, Joseph, 23, 85
Williams, Roger, 251
Winthrop, John, 4
Woods, Leonard, 91, 199–200, 201, 202, 333
Worcester, Samuel, 25–26
Worcester Catechism, 177–198
Works and Genius of Washington Allston, The (Ware), 137
Wright, Conrad, 136

Zeno, 40, 405
Zenobia; or, the Fall of Palmyra (Ware), 137

About the Editors

Sydney E. Ahlstrom, a distinguished church historian and winner of a National Book Award for his 1972 book, *A Religious History of the American People,* was, until his death in 1984, Samuel Knight Professor of American History and Modern Religious History at Yale University. He was a graduate of Gustavus Adolphus College (B.A., 1941) and of the University of Minnesota (M.A., 1946) and received his Ph.D. at Harvard University in 1952. He joined the Yale faculty in 1954 and was for several years chairman of its American Studies program. He was the author of, among other books, *The Harvard Divinity School* (with G. H. Williams, ed.) and *Theology in America.*

Jonathan S. Carey is a degree candidate in moral theology at Green College, Oxford. A graduate of Boston College (B.A.), Princeton Theological Seminary (M.Div.), and Yale Divinity School (S.T.M.), he has been minister of the First Congregational Society, Unitarian, Jamaica Plain, and the Eliot Church (Federated), South Natick, Massachusetts.